THE OFFICIAL®
PRICE GUIDE TO
MEMORABILIA OF
ELVIS PRESLEY
& THE BEATLES

THE OFFICIAL® PRICE GUIDE TO MEMORABILIA OF ELVIS PRESLEY & THE BEATLES

FIRST EDITION

Jerry Osborne, Perry Cox, and Joe Lindsay

House of Collectibles
New York, New York 10022

Cover art: Beatles and Elvis props courtesy of Strider Records, New York, NY.

© 1988 by Jerry Osborne

All rights reserved under International and
Pan-American Copyright Conventions.

Published by: The House of Collectibles
201 East 50th Street
New York, New York 10022

Distributed by Ballantine Books, a division of Random House, Inc., New York
and simultaneously in Canada by Random House of Canada Limited, Toronto.

Manufactured in the United States of America

ISBN: 0-876-37080-6

10 9 8 7 6 5 4 3 2 1

Contents

Preface

The Hero (or Heroine), scholars tell us, is a person who, through the sum of his efforts, transforms the world around him. The Hero provides us with a moral compass point, influencing how we think, how we feel, how we believe. The Hero serves as a benchmark for our own lives—for some a model to live by, for others a means of marking the milestones of their lives. In the case of true heroism, it is impossible to imagine what life would be like if the Hero had not existed.

What would the world be like today if there had not been Elvis Presley and the Beatles—not just in terms of music but in our style, in our very ways of thinking?

It is in this sense—in the classical meaning of the word—that Elvis Presley and the Beatles are "Heroes." In the days of ancient Greece, religions evolved around such characters. Stories about them were told—passed down from one generation to the next. A collection of priests and priestesses developed rites and rituals to celebrate the Hero, and events in the Hero's life were marked on the calendar as days of social celebration and commemoration. Shrines were built as memorials of thanks and gratitude for their existence.

In our own way, we have done much the same thing with Elvis and the Beatles.

Consider the matter of stories. Who cannot remember the very first time he or she saw them on national television? Who does not remember seeing them for the first time in concert? Who does not remember the circumstances in which one first heard their songs—late at night, hiding under the covers with the transistor at the ear, turning the dial in search of some far-off station that might be playing their latest song? Or standing in line to see their movies—the joy and excitement of seeing the movie not once or twice but over and over again. What first was the excitement of discovery later became the confidence of knowledge, and we could tell what was going to happen next. Far from being dragged out by the notion, we took comfort in it in much the same way that we take comfort in having old friends—we know them because we like them and like them because we know them. This was the golden era of the 45, when a strong single could hit the top of the charts and stay there forever, without sounding tired, without becoming *boring*.

Finally, who does not recall the time and the place one first heard that Elvis had died or that John Lennon had been shot? These are measures of their impact on our personal lives, the milestones they represent for each and every one of us. But there is, on a larger scale, the social memory that reinforces our individual beliefs and recollections—the books and magazines, the films and the documentaries. Then there are the shrines to which so many of us make a kind of pilgrimage to pay homage to these people. For Elvis fans, it is primarily Graceland, Elvis' home in Memphis, or Tupelo, where he was born. For Beatles fans, it is any of a number of places—their family homes in Liverpool or London, the recording studio on Abbey Road where they worked, the Dakota apartment building in New York where Lennon was shot, or Strawberry Fields, located right across from the Dakota in Central Park.

We differ from the ancient Greeks in that they would have turned this into the stuff of religion, whereas in modern America we license rights to reproduce the image. A far cry perhaps from our Western heritage but not as far as one might think. As odd it may sound, we are really doing the same thing the ancient Greeks did. In the strange assortment of objects and memorabilia—from records to bubble gum cards, plastic guitars to dolls—we commemorate these performers and celebrate what they mean to us.

So we tell the stories and remember—not merely the recollections of long-lost youth but the fantasies these heroes inspired. For us, the writers of this book, Elvis and the Beatles provided the direction markers that led us to where we are today. Our editor tells us he became involved with music because John Lennon looked so hip playing his guitar in the "You're Gonna Lose That Girl" sequence in *Help!* Twenty years later he's still playing.

These are the essential ingredients of the stories that make Elvis and the Beatles so important, not only to every one of us on a personal level but to us all as a nation. They were—and are—powerful charismatic figures. These are the ingredients of the stories we have passed on to our children, who in turn are keeping the memory of these performers alive for future generations by discovering Elvis and the Beatles for themselves.

Acknowledgments

The single most important element in putting together a price guide of this kind is the many people to whom we have turned for information—be it about prices, little-known items, or just plain facts. We've all received the most wonderful help from dealers and collectors living throughout the continent—indeed, the *world*—and to all these good folks, we extend our deepest gratitude: Kathleen Abbott; Bob Alaniz; Carol Alaniz; Patsy Andersen; Ace Anderson; Steve Anderson; Gordy Arlin; Mike Babuin; J. L. Baley; Mike Baute; Jim and Lucy Bis Photography; Joyce Blankenship; Wade Blythe; Jacque Bosbury; Jackson Braider; Jim Britton; Denise Brown; Kip Brown; Pat Brown; Kenneth Bub; Barbara Burbes; Darla Burcham; Bud Buschardt; Debbi Buttram; Michael Cain; Pat Carr; Bob Cattaneo; Christopher Chatman; Dennis Chiesa; Phil Ciula; Ernie Clark; Teresa Clifford; Maria Columbus; Jesse Cox; Edyth Cox; Rick Cox; Rosalind Cranor; Frank Daniels; Lloyd Davis; Joan Deary; Steve Derda; Jack Dey; George De Young; Jerry Dodson; Fred Dougherty; John Ebner; Judy Ebner; Marty Eck; Dick Egger; Eddie Fadal; Tom Fairchild; Mike Fields; Larry Finn; David Fisher; Ake Flodin; D.J. Fontana; Eddie Forcier; Janie Forcier; Michael Fox; Arnie Ganem; Claude Gantt; Jean-Marc Gargiulo; Larry Garland; David Gasbarro; Steve Goddard; Donald Goodyear; Eugene Green; Thomas Grosh; Gary Guthrie; Jean Haffner; Eddie Hammer; Lin and Kelly Hammerschmidt; John Hansman; Michael Harris; Chris Hartlaub; Gary Hein; Jeff Henry; Cal Hicks; Greg Hillabrand; Paul Hochsprung; David Hoffman; Tom Howe; Pauline Hubbard; Bill Jackson; Linda Jacobs; Mark James; Jon E. Johnson; Linda Jones; Paula Jones; Jim Kaysinger; Gary Keltner; David Kent; Thomas Komorowski; Casey Korenek; Adam Kuligowski; Bob Lafollette; Gladys Lambert; Steve Lambroukes; Darwin Lamm; Douglas Leftwich; Lenz Photography; Eric Levake; Jeff Leve; Paul Lichter; Holly Lindsay; Sylvia Martinez; Tammera Massey; Mike McCance; Pete McClellan; Janelle McComb; Mitch McGeary; James McNally; Nick Mele; Karen Miller; Maynard and Maynette Miller; Mike Miller; Robert Miller; Charles Moore; Todd Morgan; Roy Morlen; Kim Murrie; Rory and Gina Musil; Charlie Neu; Lee O'Donnell; Jim Olson; Vincent Oppedisano; Gareth Pawlowski; Victor Pearlin; Alice Peters; Dave Petrelle; Carla Peyton; Walter Piotrowski; Steve Polwort; Danny Prisco; Lew Rainbolt; Rick Rann; Robert Raingruber; Helmut Rauch; Don Rawlins; Record Exchange; Record Research; Tom Salva; John Sanidad; David Sarver; Alice Schlichte; Harvey Seremko; John Singleton; Shelby Singleton; Barbara Smith; Gary Smith; Laura Serra; Walter Smith; Cass Solomon; Jennifer Spurlock; Carlo Stevan; Howell Q. Strye; John Teftellar; Lou Telloni; Steve Templeton; The Jordanaires; Mike Thomas; Peter A. Toner; Michael Tufariello; Travis Tyler; Todd Van Sidert; Very English and Rolling Stone; Sybil Vessels; Don Vogel; Bob Walker; Craig Warren; Peter Weber; Tom Wenzel; Boogers Werner; Lonnie West; Lynn Wille; Art Williams; Rory Williams; Terry Wilson; Vic Wright; Cliff Yamasaki; Roger Ybanez; Ted Young.

Introduction

By Jerry Osborne

Elvis Presley and the Beatles are the greatest one-two musical punch since Thomas Edison cranked up his first recorded disc player. Both artists were responsible for adding words to the English language that ended in "mania." Together, their images have emblazoned more products, publications, and assorted doo-dads than all other recording artists in history combined. Their consolidated record sales are surely approaching the billions.

Who would have thought or could possibly have known that all those bubble gum cards, plastic guitars, lunch boxes, and key chains on dime store toy shelves would end up on the refined auction blocks at Christie's and Sotheby's? That this wide a range of novelty items and gadgets was licensed is striking testimony to the impact that the King and Fab Four had on our lives. That most of these items sold in such quantities says even more. But the telling thing is the growing market for both recorded and non-recorded materials. A dozen years after Elvis died and two decades since the Beatles broke up, the enthusiasm for their work continues unabated—refreshed even, as a new generation of fans comes to know and love their music.

In this guide we have gathered a vast and strange assortment of information about Elvis and the Beatles. Here, for the first time anywhere, is a complete reckoning of their official American record releases—the singles, the EPs, and the albums, the first releases and the subsequent reissues, as well as the many compilations and syndicated radio shows that have featured their material. Also included here for the first time in any book are the various—and already numerous—compact disc releases.

Collecting the wealth of data we've included here into a single, easy-to-carry, volume is clearly an idea whose time has come. Adding to that storehouse of information the necessary documentation to price the key Elvis and Beatles (non-recorded) memorabilia was the coup de grâce. Finally, in one handy guide, there's a myriad of valuable data for all Elvis and Beatles collectibles.

With both acts, their fame first came from recordings, followed by personal appearances and films. A cyclic pattern developed as the films and concerts promoted the songs, with new songs boosting new films and concerts. The formula was in place. The magic potion was ready for consumption by teens worldwide.

Each ingredient in the elixir (records, concerts, films) established a new market that was in place, waiting for the merchandise waterfall. Printing presses worked around the clock, churning out special cards and packaging materials that could instantly turn a plain dinner plate or T-shirt into an "official" Elvis plate or "souvenir" Beatles shirt.

The majority of the collectibles in this edition first saw the light of day in the 1950s or 1960s. The presses have long since stopped, but the market for these artifacts is stronger than ever. In fact, the need for this guide stems from the vibrant and flourishing position enjoyed by the hobby of collecting Elvis and the Beatles.

The introductory material informs the reader of the ground rules of collecting Elvis and Beatles records and the memorabilia dedicated to them. Along with the general guidelines that provide the foundation for collecting—the ever-important matters of condition, trading, and value—we also look into some of the curious places passionate collecting can lead the enthusiast. For record fans, there is the little-known realm of acetates and test pressings. But along with these by-products of the recording process, we also examine certain special areas of collecting—the exclusive domain of the gold record and the autograph.

From there, the book divides into separate sections on Elvis and the Beatles. The two parts begin with the memorabilia—from the ticket stubs to the plastic guitars, the framed photos to the films. For dealers, this guide marks the first time that many of these objects have been catalogued and priced. For the people who have never thrown away anything in their lives, this will provide happy justification for being pack rats. And for those who are interested in getting a sense of the extraordinary range of stuff out there, this guide is a very good place to start.

But the preponderance of both halves of this book is devoted to records. Elvis and the Beatles represent the most documented recording artists of the modern age, and we have gone to tremendous lengths to be sure that this is not *just* another discography of their work. Along with a complete catalog of their American releases, we have researched areas of special interest to the fan. For hardcore Elvis collectors, there is an update on the material that has yet to appear in true stereo, while Beatle fans will be amazed at the number of tunes "in the can" that have never appeared on the market.

Given the scope of this project, there have no doubt been some oversights on our parts. Throughout the book, names and addresses are provided for your queries and comments. We encourage you to write or call. We have tried our very best to get this right the first time around, but when we hear from you, we know we can make a good thing even better.

COLLECTING AUTOGRAPHS

Wouldn't it be terrific if we could simply say: an item featuring Elvis Presley's signature or all of the Beatles' signatures is worth $1,500, while the solo autographs range anywhere from $200 to $300 for John Lennon's and $100 to $200 for those of Paul, George or Ringo. Well, although we can say that, autograph collecting is not that facile. It's not simply that the value depends a great deal on the item itself; rather, the value placed on the signed item depends on a kind of chemistry between the item and the signature.

Consider the example of a baking pan signed by John Lennon and Yoko Ono at a party in 1969. Of course, given the fact that John and Yoko signed it, it isn't really a baking pan anymore. That is to say, nothing has been baked in this pan since 1969—one would hope not, in any event. It was signed during a party at the Lennons' Ascot house and given to a guest as a memento of the occasion. Unlike many pieces of paper bearing the autograph of a famous individual, it hasn't been folded or creased, and obviously some care has been taken with the piece since the signatures haven't blurred or faded. It's almost as good as new, only better.

How does one put a value on it? If it were for sale—which it isn't—the value would depend on how much the buyer accepts the concept underlying John and Yoko's signing a *baking pan.* One might take it as one of the spontaneous pieces of art they were creating around that time—the films, for example, or the bed-ins. Clearly, it is worth much more than the standard $200 to $300 for a Lennon signature.

Similarly, the value of autographs given by Elvis can vary widely. Of paramount importance is the intrinsic value of the item bearing the autograph. A Sun record signed by Elvis in 1955 will be far more valuable than a napkin signed in 1975. If *you* put your name on one of your Elvis or Beatles albums, you will diminish the value. But a valid autograph from the artist(s) themselves will never devalue a collectible.

In the main, documents or letters are considerably more valuable when the subject is recognized or important. For example, the Beatles' songs are extremely well known, but the handwritten lyrics are very hard to come by. Generally, the older the song in the Beatles catalog, the heftier the value. Lyrics collected from the *Let It Be* sessions in London were estimated at a recent sale to be worth between $2,000 and $2,500. "Get Back," typed with annotations by John, went for three times the estimated value. (This was also noteworthy for the expurgated verse: "We don't dig no Pakistanis/Taking other people's jobs." At that time, England was experiencing a rash of racist sentiment.)

The value of the autographed object also may be enhanced by the signer's elaborations. An original mono copy of the British *Please Please Me* LP signed by Paul, George, and Ringo only once features a manic Lennon signing it *seven* times. A $500 to $600 estimate fell some $1,200 below the final bid. Similarly, little drawings and doo-dads will affect the value. A good governing rule in collecting or buying autographs is to remember that items of significance command higher values.

Authenticating the originality of signatures is of key importance when attempting to purchase any type of autograph. Unfortunately, there are too many cases in which high prices have been paid for fraudulent items. The best way to avoid being ripped off is to have the item examined by a professional who specializes in authenticating signatures and handwriting. These specialists are referred to as scripophilists; they have access to verified original examples of many famous autographs and have been highly trained to detect any imitations. These services can usually be sourced through various legal and detective agencies.

Other good practices include dealing with reputable collectors or dealers, who will gladly grant you reasonable time to authenticate an item *before* you make the transaction. Getting a little history and the origin of the item is also a good idea.

COLLECTING ELVIS AND BEATLES (GROUP AND SOLO) U.S. GOLD AND PLATINUM RECORD AWARDS
By Douglas Leftwich and Christopher Chatman

Because of their rarity, gold and platinum records awarded to Elvis Presley and the Beatles are extremely difficult to obtain. They can also be very expensive. Ultimately though, it is their rarity that makes their acquisition a major triumph for any collector.

Some History

Gold records officially came into existence in 1958, when the RIAA (Record Industry Association of America) decided to recognize the sales of $1,000,000 worth of long-playing records or one million units in singles sales, by designating such records "gold." Previously, a haphazard system of awarding gold records existed in which sales numbers did not need to be certified by any official body. Consequently, the status of gold records is often questionable. Also, it should be noted that even after 1958 many record companies were not members of the RIAA, thus not eligible for official certification. (Vee Jay, Tollie, and Swan were among these companies, and although some of the Beatles' releases on these labels qualified for official gold record status, only "token" awards could be issued: Buyer beware! These are not as valuable as the real thing. See "In-House" Awards below.)

The RIAA's standards remained unchanged until 1975, when inflation forced a change in sales requirements. Instead of the $1,000,000 in sales required for LPs, it was now necessary for 500,000 units (a "unit" being either a record or tape) to be sold for gold-record status. Singles, however, retained their original requirement for gold designation.

In 1976 the RIAA introduced the platinum record award. In order to achieve platinum status an LP would require one million units sold, with singles having to sell two million units. Under the rules set by the RIAA, albums and singles released prior to January 1, 1976, could not be considered for platinum.

Very few of these RIAA-certified gold and platinum record awards ever become available. During the heydays of Elvis and the Beatles, a very small number of certified record awards were handed out. These were distributed, of course, to the performers, their producers, their managers, and a small circle of record company executives. During these early years, as few as fourteen Beatles gold record awards were issued per record, whereas today as many as one hundred or more are handed out for a certified gold or platinum record. Very few original gold and platinum record awards, presented to Elvis or on his behalf, are in private collections. This kind of rarity consequently causes any Elvis or Beatles gold or platinum record award to bring a premium price. Indeed, at recent Sotheby's auctions, winning bids for such awards have been in the tens of thousands of dollars.

A considerable amount of expertise and care is required to enter this area of collecting safely. As we will see later, bootleggers have become proficient at manufacturing credible facsimiles of gold and platinum record awards. Even experts are sometimes unable to distinguish the authentic from the counterfeit.

Pre-1975 RIAA-Certified Gold Album Awards

An RIAA-certified record award constructed before 1975 appears as a framed, gold-plated metal record consisting of a thin wood frame detailed on inner corners in gold trim; a white, off-white, or light gray cloth-mat backing; a reduced photograph facsimile of the album cover located on the bottom left corner; an engraved metal identification plate with wording and RIAA logo located to the right of the photograph; and a Plexiglas (thermo-plastic) front surface. Using *Meet the Beatles* as an example, the identification plate reads:

PRESENTED TO
THE BEATLES
TO COMMEMORATE THE SALE OF MORE THAN
ONE MILLION DOLLARS WORTH OF THE
CAPITOL RECORDS
LONG-PLAYING RECORD ALBUM
"MEET THE BEATLES"

On all awards presented through 1974, the wording and RIAA logo are engraved into the metal and highlighted in glossy black enamel.

Some pre-1975 Elvis, Beatles, and solo Beatles LPs on RCA Victor, Capitol and Apple have recently been "recertified" gold. This means that these particular LPs have sold over 500,000 copies since 1974. These awards presented after 1974 are in the post-1974 styles (see below). They are less valuable than the original award styles.

Post-1974 RIAA-Certified Gold and Platinum LP Awards

When the RIAA revised its requirements for gold record certification and determined requirements for platinum award status, the visual designs for RIAA certified awards changed as well. Before 1975 most RIAA-certified gold awards were made at the New York Frame and Picture Company. Since that time many other companies have been authorized to construct RIAA-certified record awards.

The most common style of post-1974 RIAA gold record awards is a gold-plated record set in a black, textured cardboard with a reduced photograph facsimile of the album cover and a gold-plated (for gold records) identification plate with lettering and RIAA logo located to the right of the photograph. The whole thing is covered with Plexiglas and enclosed in a gold-colored wooden frame. Using *Rock & Roll Music* as an example, the identification plate reads:

PRESENTED TO
THE BEATLES
TO COMMEMORATE THE SALE OF MORE THAN
500,000 COPIES OF THE
CAPITOL RECORDS
LONG-PLAYING RECORD ALBUM
"ROCK & ROLL MUSIC"
(RIAA LOGO)

The RIAA logo is located to the right of the wording. On this particular style of award, the "presented to" information and RIAA logo is silk-screened in black ink, while the artist(s) name(s), the title of the LP, and the record company name are engraved in the metal.

In recent years, instead of the RIAA logo, RIAA-certified awards will sometimes have the words "Certified by the Record Industry Association of America" underneath the other wording on the identification plate. Currently, RIAA LP record awards have a gold- or silver-plated cassette (depending on the status of the award) mounted above the identification plate. In addition, the wording mentions cassette as well as album sales, and the engraved RIAA logo has been replaced with an RIAA holographic image.

RIAA-Certified Gold 45 Awards

The design of an RIAA-certified gold 45 award has remained similar to its LP counterpart in appearance during the entire history of RIAA certification. The design for an RIAA award is different only in the following ways: there is no reduced photograph facsimile of the LP cover, the identification plate is centered under the gold-plated 45 and the award itself is somewhat smaller.

RIAA-Certified Platinum Awards

Since 1976 RIAA platinum LP and 45 record awards have been designed identically to gold RIAA record awards, except for a silver-painted frame and silver-plated record and identification plate. Also, the wording on the identification plate will read "more than one million copies." A platinum 45 will read "more than two million copies."

"In House" or "Token" Gold and Platinum Awards

"In House" or "Token" gold and platinum awards resemble RIAA certified awards in most ways, except they do not have the RIAA logo. In place of the RIAA logo there will be the insignia of the record company that released the record.

Often, a record company will give awards to as many as one hundred people and organizations that had a direct or indirect role in the promotion and sales of a given record. This is now done as a kind of customary "thank you" to radio stations and some major record chains. The record company is required to pay a fee for every record award carrying the RIAA logo. In order to reduce the cost to the record company, many of these "thank you" awards are made without the RIAA logo. Some of these awards are simply a framed gold or platinum record with no identification plate. These awards are valued less than RIAA record awards.

Counterfeit Awards

Because of the high prices realized in auctions for authentic RIAA-certified Elvis and Beatles gold and platinum record awards, counterfeiting has become a major problem. Furthermore, replicas of gold-award Elvis singles and albums are plentiful. Fortunately, they are easily recognizable as reproductions.

If possible, it is important to locate the original source of any award you may be interested in purchasing. Many honest dealers will provide a letter of authenticity along with the award. It is always best to deal with someone who has a reputation for honesty and who offers a money-back guarantee, especially when your investment may be a great deal of money.

Here are some telltale signs to watch for:

1. Stenciling or writing an RIAA logo on identification plate on awards presumably made before 1975. All information on the identification plate should be machine-engraved.

2. Gold- or silver-plated vinyl records on pre-1975 awards. Before 1975, all discs on RIAA record awards were made of metal, *not* metal-coated vinyl discs.

3. In the case of the Beatles, awards for records presented to individuals for Capitol or Apple records. (These are *extremely* rare.)

4. Obviously poor construction.

5. It should be noted that the discs used in the construction of these awards are seldom a copy of the actual record earning the award. Using any disc is and has been common practice in the construction of legitimate, authorized awards.

If, after checking all of these signs, you still don't feel right about the award, don't buy it. Listen to your intuition and follow your gut reaction.

A Final Word

As discouraging as all this may sound to the Elvis or Beatles record collector who would "love to have just one" of their gold, silver, or platinum record awards but can't afford the seemingly exorbitant prices bid at the auction houses, take heart. Some awards have been offered for sale by collectors and even by original recipients of the awards through estate sales, newspaper classified ads, record collector periodicals and record swap meets, to name a few sources. Although still quite expensive by most standards, they are usually offered for sale far below the winning bids at the major auction houses.

Elvis in Silver, Gold, and Platinum

Given the history of the precious metal record award, it has been very difficult to document which of Elvis' releases, *by RIAA standards and procedures,* have actually been awarded silver, gold, or platinum records. For example, since the concept of the gold record was not developed until 1958, all of Elvis' early recordings were disqualified from the gold record list, though practically all of them—with the exception of the Sun recordings—would have undoubtedly made the grade. (Collectors, beware! What this means is that anyone selling a "1957" gold record for "Jailhouse Rock," say, is not offering a genuine article.)

A photograph of an "in-house" gold record for the *Promised Land* LP is included in our color section. And given RCA's re-issue policy (see the chronology of Elvis' releases, pages 86–102) his sales on a per-release basis could not have been as strong as they once had been. There was obviously a strong and loyal market, but it did not have the volatility, the *craving* of an audience that was obliged, as was the case with the Beatles, to wait months anticipating the next release.

Still, there were many gold records, but no one at this point has done the research necessary to bridge this important gap in Elvis' recording history.

The Beatles in Silver, Gold, and Platinum

The Beatles' first American gold records were awarded for their debut Capitol LP, *Meet the Beatles,* and single, "I Want to Hold Your Hand." These were awarded simultaneously on February 3, 1964. As would be the case with most of their Capitol and Apple offerings, their next two Capitol releases, *The Beatles' Second Album* and *Can't Buy Me Love,* actually shipped gold, meaning that advance orders of both were well above the RIAA certification requirements before they even left the factory!

From *Meet the Beatles* through *Magical Mystery Tour,* there were no individuals named on RIAA-certified record awards. All recipients, even including the individual Beatles, were issued awards using the group name "The Beatles." (For example, regardless of whether an RIAA gold record award was given to John Lennon or Brian Epstein or the president of Capitol records, all three gold records will say "presented to the Beatles.")

RIAA record awards for Beatles releases on the Apple label through *The Beatles 1967–1970* were shown as presented to either the Beatles or Capitol. Later Beatles releases on the Capitol label, such as *Rock & Roll Music, Love Songs* and *The Beatles Live at the Hollywood Bowl,* were likewise presented either to the Beatles or Capitol. Starting in the 1980s, RIAA-certified awards for albums such as *Reel Music* and *20 Greatest Hits* were awarded to individual Beatles members as well as other people directly involved with the success of the album. Unlike RIAA record awards given for albums that the Beatles produced as a group, solo Beatles awards (such as John Lennon's *Imagine* LP) on all labels were presented to people individually as well as the associated record companies.

Only two Beatles LPs have gone platinum: the 1976 repackage *Rock & Roll Music* and the concurrently released *The Beatles at the Hollywood Bowl*. None of Capitol's post-1976 Beatles singles have gone gold or platinum.

The following is a list of RIAA certified Beatles and solo-Beatles gold and platinum record awards:

Beatles Albums

Meet the Beatles

The Beatles' Second Album

Something New

The Beatles' Story

Beatles '65

The Early Beatles

Beatles VI

Help!

Rubber Soul

Yesterday and Today

Revolver

Sgt. Pepper's Lonely Hearts Club Band

Magical Mystery Tour

The Beatles

Yellow Submarine

Abbey Road

Hey Jude

Let It Be

The Beatles 1962–1966

The Beatles 1967–1970

Rock & Roll Music

The Beatles at the Hollywood Bowl*

Love Songs

Reel Music

20 Greatest Hits

Beatles Singles

I Want to Hold Your Hand

Can't Buy Me Love

A Hard Day's Night

I Feel Fine

Eight Days a Week

Help!

Yesterday

We Can Work It Out

Nowhere Man

Paperback Writer

Yellow Submarine

Penny Lane

*Indicates certified platinum.

All You Need Is Love

Hello Goodbye

Lady Madonna

Hey Jude

Get Back

The Ballad of John and Yoko

Come Together

Let It Be

Paul McCartney Albums

McCartney

Ram

Wild Life

Red Rose Speedway

Band on the Run

Wings at the Speed of Sound*

Wings Over America*

London Town*

Wings Greatest*

Back to the Egg*

McCartney II

Tug of War*

Pipes of Peace*

Give My Regards to Broad Street

Paul McCartney Singles

Uncle Albert/Admiral Halsey

My Love

Live and Let Die

Band on the Run

Listen to What the Man Said

Silly Love Songs

Let 'Em In

Goodnight Tonight

Coming Up (Live at Glasgow)

Ebony and Ivory (with Stevie Wonder)

John Lennon Albums

The Plastic Ono Band/Live Peace In Toronto

John Lennon/Plastic Ono Band

Imagine

Mind Games

Walls and Bridges

Double Fantasy*

Milk and Honey

John Lennon Singles

Instant Karma (We All Shine On)

(Just Like) Starting Over

Woman

*Indicates certified platinum.

George Harrison Albums

All Things Must Pass
The Concert for Bangladesh
Living in the Material World
Dark Horse
Extra Texture (Read All about It)
The Best of George Harrison
Thirty-Three & ⅓
George Harrison

George Harrison Singles

My Sweet Lord

Ringo Starr Albums

Ringo
Good Night Vienna

Ringo Starr Singles

It Don't Come Easy
Photograph
You're Sixteen

TEST PRESSINGS AND ACETATES: A CLOSER LOOK

In recent years, we have received a great deal of encouragement to evaluate the wide variety of Elvis and Beatles test pressings available.

As a rule, there are a few test pressings made for every record. Any given single or album can, in fact, have several different test pressings made during its production; "A" side only, "B" side only, both sides, alternate mixes, unsweetened (prior to the adding of background vocals and/or orchestration) takes, and so on.

Then, too, when an artist changes record companies and retains their prior material, every LP and single is subject to re-mastering and to the whole production process again. Of course, this means new test pressings as well.

Frequently, record companies will subcontract a percentage of the total press run to one or more different manufacturers. This can result in varied test pressing labelings and vinyl characteristics.

In general, test pressings are used to sample or "test" the quality of a particular recording after being pressed on disc. However, in some cases, the pressing will be unacceptable for any of a number of reasons. Therefore, it may not be hard to find test pressings with noticeable differences from the final commercial product, including alternate takes and mixes, longer or shorter versions, different flip sides, etc. Because of their irregularity, the values on the test pressings with alternate takes are usually much higher than those containing commercially available tracks.

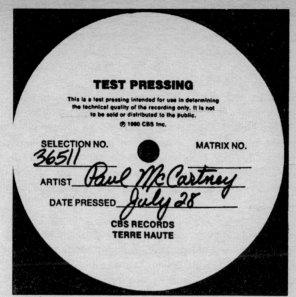

TEST PRESSING

This is a test pressing intended for use in determining
the technical quality of the recording only. It is not
to be sold or distributed to the public.

℗ 1980 CBS Inc.

SELECTION NO.   MATRIX NO.

3651 1

ARTIST *Paul McCartney*

DATE PRESSED *July 28*

CBS RECORDS
TERRE HAUTE

Paul McCartney test pressing, CBS plant, Terre Haute, Indiana, 1980.

It is possible to find test pressings of songs that have remained unreleased to the public and, consequently, are quite desirable and valuable. Prices on unique items such as these are usually decided between buyer and seller.

Due to the nature and function of test pressings, flaws such as writing, typing, stickers or stampings on the labels do not affect the value nearly as much as on conventional records. In the case of most test pressings, titles and information are written on them to identify the recorded material, though the value for clean label pressings is customarily 5% to 10% higher.

Unfortunately, counterfeit test pressings have also surfaced. The best way to determine if a pressing is a legitimate copy is to compare the characteristics between a known legitimate copy and the item in question.

Test pressings generally have the same vinyl characteristics as their promo or stock counterparts. Look for identifying symbols and stampings in the trail-off area of the disc. Remember, many records are produced by the different manufacturers, and symbols and distinctive characteristics can vary.

Acetates

Due to the limited nature of their use, acetates are generally quite obscure. As a rule, they are usually more difficult to obtain than test pressings and promotional records. Acetates can be found in seven-, ten- and twelve-inch formats, as well as 33, 45 and 78 rpm speeds.

The materials, equipment and process used in producing acetates makes them quite expensive in terms of unit production costs, a factor which keeps their quantities limited. The acetic acid and cellulose composition used in the manufacturing of acetates is very soft and not designed for repeated play. The metal core that is sandwiched between the lacquer surfaces makes the disc fairly heavy when compared to a conventional record. These factors make the playing surface of the acetate quite fragile and subject to rapid wear and scratching.

Unlike test pressings, acetates are less likely to be distributed to radio stations and media people for advance airplay and review. Labeling is usually limited to company name or logo, with blanks for title and reference information. For the most part, acetates find their way into the hands of collectors the same way most manufacturing by-products do, channeling through

Elvis acetate, for single "I Gotta Know."

friends and relatives in the industry. Since the acetate is pressed at the early stages of production, changes are often made before the final version of the record is completed. Because of this, it is not uncommon to find acetates with altered, expanded or reduced selections. Differences in mixing alternate takes with different running times also occur. Items such as these are valued higher than standard versions.

In some cases, "working titles" can be found printed on the label when the final title is still undecided (i.e., "Black Star"—"Flaming Star").

Although a somewhat limited specialization, acetate collecting is definitely becoming more popular. When buying an acetate, learn as much about the source as possible. If the dealer or collector is reputable, the chances are good that it is authentic.

PRICING AND GRADING MEMORABILIA: CONDITION IS *EVERYTHING*

The following pages are devoted to the matter of determining *value.* As a potential Elvis or Beatles collector (if you are not one already), the items listed in this guide are inherently valuable to you. But if you are new to the world of collecting as a whole, you will soon learn a maxim that collectors live by: In the marketplace, condition is *everything.* Dealers base the fair price of an item, be it a record or a piece of memorabilia, on its condition. The rarest record cover, the most singular piece of memorabilia—either one of these will be greatly devalued if damaged, altered, or mutilated. That's the reason why there is such variation in the pricing of objects in fair, good, and near-mint condition.

What you will find is that even if you have an item, your "job" as a collector will be to keep it in the best possible condition. Collecting is not merely accumulating vast amounts of things; it has much to do with upgrading the quality of the collection. This is one of the great sources of satisfaction in the world of collecting. If there is something that you must absolutely have, buy it by all means. But always keep your eyes open to upgrade it.

The values listed here represent an *average,* based on the monitoring of both sales reports and auction results over the past fourteen years. As always, prices can vary from place to place and time to time and are certainly subject to the laws of supply and demand.

Since there is such variation in the kinds of Elvis and Beatles memorabilia available, grading guidelines have been customized for the different sections. However, the same general classifications in grading apply to all collectibles, whether they are records or nonrecord memorabilia.

How the Record Prices Are Determined

Record values featured in this guide were derived and averaged from a number of sources:

- The most important is a proven review program, to which many of the world's most active dealers and collectors regularly contribute additional listings and corrections to existing data. Price changes, in either direction, are often brought to our attention by these reviewers.

- As is the case with most types of collectibles, record prices can vary drastically from one region of the country to another. Having reviewers and annotators in every state, as well as around the world, enables us to present a realistic average of the highest and lowest current asking prices for an identically graded item.

- Other sources include: set sale lists, auction results, record convention trading, conversations with private collectors and retailers around the country, and many hours on the telephone with our key advisors.

An important thing to note here is that while the prices cited were accurate at press time, the market can change drastically. At any time there may be a major bulk discovery or a quantity dump—both can affect availability, scarcity, and demand.

Record Grading and the Price Range

The pricing shown in this edition represents the price range for *near-mint* condition copies of the records listed. So, while the range we offer is for near-mint records, it also allows for the countless variables that affect record pricing, of which condition is only one.

The standardized system of record grading endorsed by the House of Collectibles and used by sellers and buyers worldwide is as follows:

MINT: A mint item must be perfect—nothing less will do. Even brand new purchases can easily be flawed in some manner and not qualify as mint. To allow for tiny blemishes, the highest grade used in our record series is near-mint. An absolutely pristine mint item may carry a slight premium above the near-mint range shown in this guide.

NEAR MINT: This is generally the highest quality record in which record collectors deal. Neither the records nor the covers will be flawed except with the lightest scuff (even the scuffing a record might undergo as it is being put into the sleeve at the factory may affect its playability, thereby turning a mint into a near-mint item). Naturally, because this tends to be the highest grade available, both the record and the cover must be without scratches, handwriting (such as a previous owner's name on the label or the jacket), or similar flaws.

VERY GOOD: Records in very good condition should have a minimum of visible or audible imperfections, which should not detract much from your enjoyment of owning it.

GOOD: Practically speaking, the grade of "good" means that the item is good enough to fill a gap in your collection until a better copy comes along. Good-condition merchandise will show definite signs of wear and tear, indicating that no protective care was given the record. Even so, records in good condition should play all the way through without skipping.

There are other, lesser scales of quality ("fair" and "poor"), but these apply to recordings that are generally unplayable and so are not even considered here.

Naturally, most older records are going to be in something less than near-mint condition. It is very important to realize, then, that the price range listed for "near-mint" in this guide is really a starting point in record appraising. Be honest about the actual condition. Apply the same standards to the records you trade or sell as you would to the records you buy. The following formula is a good rule of thumb in determining the value of lesser-quality records:

- For VERY GOOD condition, figure the price to be 50% to 70% of the near-mint price.
- For GOOD condition, figure about 10% to 20% of the near-mint price.

Remember, though, all of the price guides in the world—no matter how authoritative—won't change the fact that true value is nothing more than what one person is willing to accept and another is willing to pay. In the end, it's always a matter of *scarcity and demand.* A recording—or anything else, for that matter—can be fifty or one hundred years old, but if no one wants it, the actual value will be minimal. Just because something is old does not necessarily mean that it is valuable. On the other hand, a recent release, perhaps just weeks old, can have exceptionally high value if it has already become scarce and is by an artist who is very much in demand. Old or new, the point here is that someone has to want it!

PROMOTIONAL ISSUES

When identifying a "promotional issue," we are usually describing a record with a special promotional label or sleeve (marked "Not for Sale," "Dee Jay Copy," etc.) and not a "designate promo." Designate promos are identical to commercial releases, except that they have been rubber- or mechanically stamped, stickered, written on by hand, or in some way altered to accommodate their use for promotional purposes.

In some instances, though, the promo can have a different mix—for example, the trumpet tag at the end of "*Penny Lane*" (currently found on the American *Rarities* album) was originally available only on the promo record.

FOREIGN RELEASES

This guide, by design, lists only U.S. releases. There is, however, an occasional exception. A handful of records that were widely distributed in the United States or sold via widespread U.S. advertising, even though manufactured outside this country, are included.

Releases from Canada, Europe, and elsewhere certainly have collector value for fans in those countries as well as for many U.S. collectors. Unfortunately, the tremendous volume of material and the variations in pricing make it impossible to consider documenting many foreign releases.

BOOTLEG AND COUNTERFEIT RECORDS

Bootleg and counterfeit records are not intended to be listed in this guide.

For the record, a bootleg recording is one illegally manufactured, usually containing material that has not previously appeared in a legitimate form. With the serious collector in mind, a bootlegger often will package previously issued tracks that have achieved some degree of value or scarcity. If the material is easily and legally available, the bootlegger would have nothing to gain.

A counterfeit record is one manufactured as close as possible in sound and appearance to the source disc from which it was taken. Not all counterfeits were created to fool an unsuspecting buyer, but some were. Many were designated in some way—usually a slight marking or variance—so as to distinguish them from the original. Such a fake record will only fill the gap in a collection until the real thing comes along.

With both bootleg and counterfeit records, the appropriate and deserving recipients of royalties are, of course, denied remuneration for their works.

Since most valuable Elvis and Beatles records have been counterfeited, it is always a good idea to consult with an expert when there is any doubt. The trained eye can usually spot a fake.

This does not mean that *unauthorized* releases do not appear in this guide. There are many legitimate releases that are unauthorized by one entity or another. But these are not necessarily bootlegs or counterfeits; unauthorized does not mean illegal.

WHAT TO EXPECT WHEN SELLING YOUR RECORDS TO A DEALER

As nearly everyone in the hobby knows, there is a notable difference between the prices reported in this guide and the prices that one can expect a dealer to pay when buying records for resale.

Unless a dealer is buying for a personal collection and without thoughts of resale, he or she is simply not in a position to pay full price. Dealers work on a percentage basis, largely determined by the total dollar investment, quality, and quantity of material offered, as well as the general financial condition and inventory of the dealer at the time.

Another very important consideration is the length of time it will take the dealer to recover at least the amount of the original investment. The quicker the demand for the stock and the better the condition, the quicker the return and therefore the greater the percentage that can be paid. Our experience has shown that, day in and day out, most dealers will pay from 25 to 50% of "guide" prices. And that's assuming they are planning to resell at guide prices. If they traditionally sell below guide, that will be reflected in what they can pay for stock.

If you have records to sell, it would be wise to check with several shops. In doing so, you'll begin to get a good idea of the value of your collection to a dealer.

Consult the Buyer-Seller Directory at the back of this guide (page 430) for the names of many dealers who not only might be interested in buying but from whom many collectible records are available for purchase.

HOW TO USE THIS GUIDE

As this guide represents the work of several different writers, we have attempted to standardize the presentation of the contents in the two halves. In both the Elvis and the Beatles memorabilia sections, for example, the entries are alphabetized according to the type of item. "Thermos" will come before "Tie," which will come before "Tiki Mug." Where possible, we have ganged items together—books, for instance, and movies. If you are looking for posters or lobby cards for *Help!* or *Double Trouble,* then, look under "Movie Memorabilia." We have also provided cross-references where possible.

The record sections are broken down by format—Singles, EPs, and LPs— and are listed in alphabetical order by title. In the case of the Beatles, we have taken this one step further and provided separate sections for Pete Best, Harrison, Lennon, McCartney, and Starr. Thus, under "Singles," we list first the Beatles' releases, then those by Best, Harrison, *et al.*

We have also included many of the "Various Artists Compilations" in which these performers have been featured, because these represent the artists' work on *record*. A good portion of these were radio shows and never generally available to the public, but they do come up in sales from time to time.

The style of the listing depends on the format. Singles will appear this way:

TITLE (A side)/title (B side)
    Label and Catalog Number   Release Date   Price Range
    Note:

Notes may explain label variations used for reissues, describe specific elements affecting value, itemize the extras and bonus items important to the complete package, or highlight some feature of the release.

In the few instances where a record contains music by *both* Elvis and the Beatles, different values may be shown for the same recording in each of the sections of this guide. This is because such price differences exist in the two separate marketplaces.

One important point to remember: The price range shown in this guide, for both records and nonrecorded memorabilia, is for *near-mint* condition. You must adjust values downward for items in lesser condition.

PART 1
ELVIS PRESLEY

Elvis Aron Presley, 1935–1977

What was it that hooked us on Elvis? Hindsight tells us how much he changed the music world—the curious way in which he crossed the boundaries that had existed between the staid world of white popular music and the raw power of rhythm 'n' blues. One indication we had of this was the way he was once shown on television in 1957 only from the waist up. When the tube was geared to family entertainment, the way the man moved on stage was a bit—well—*much*. Even his voice sometimes threw us: Was he black or white? It's hard to believe this all happened more than thirty years ago—his greatest tracks sound so real and fresh.

Elvis was certainly wild when compared with the likes of Perry Como, Johnny Ray, or Tony Bennett. Even Bill Haley, whose "Rock Around the Clock" was setting teenagers on fire, was tame stuff next to the boy from Memphis. But Elvis was really a mass of contradictions. The same character who made women swoon always spoke softly, even respectfully. He called his elders "sir" and "ma'am"—then his smile at the girl would always have just a *hint* of danger.

He was born in Tupelo, Mississippi, on January 8, 1935, one of a pair of identical twins; brother Jesse Garon was stillborn. Located near the Mississippi Delta, Tupelo was a powerful place in the tradition of black American music. For every note of country and western music that passed through the airwaves, the land itself provided fertile ground for the blues; the plaintive call of Hank Williams and the earthy passion of Robert Johnson. And like his contemporaries Jerry Lee Lewis and Little Richard, Elvis was absorbed with the power of the spirituals.

All this was apparent in the performer at a very young age. In September 1945, a ten-year-old Elvis entered the talent contest at the Mississippi-Alabama Fair and Dairy Show held in Tupelo. Singing "Old Shep," he won second prize, good for $5 cash and free admission on all of the rides. Later, when his family had moved to Memphis and he was a senior in high school, Elvis was the only performer to get an encore in the school talent show.

Elvis' first visit to a recording studio was in August 1953. Eighteen years old, and just out of high school, he went to Sam Philips' Memphis Recording Service and sang "My Happiness" and "That's When Your Heartaches Begin." The original demo acetate containing these two songs was kept by a high school chum of Presley's, Edwin Leek, and there's every reason to believe commercial release of these historic tracks will be forthcoming.

The *Humes Herald* yearbook of 1953 reminds its readers to go "out to the 'Silver Horse,' on Onion Avenue to hear the singing hillbillies of the road. Elvis Presley, Albert Teague, Doris Wilburn, and Mary Ann Propst are doing a bit of picking and singing out that-a-way."

On January 4, 1954, Elvis, now working as a truck driver, returned to Memphis Recording Service and recorded "Casual Love" and "I'll Never Stand In Your Way." Like the tracks recorded in 1953, these were personal, not professional, recordings, and they aren't available in any form.

He would be back at Memphis Recording Service very soon.

Sam Philips was the owner, producer, A & R man, president, and probably janitor of Sun Records. He operated out of Memphis Recording Service and was always looking for new talent. Not white music exactly but not black music either—more of a combination of the two. Marion Keisker, Sam's receptionist, told him about the young truck driver who came by every now and then, who didn't sound black, didn't sound white—in fact, didn't sound like *anybody*.

In July 1954, Philips brought Elvis back to the Sun studios, this time to record professionally. Five songs were recorded, two of them—"That's All Right/Blue Moon of Kentucky" (one sounding "black," the other "white")— making up his first commercial record release.

It was with his third Sun release ("Baby Let's Play House," July 1955) that Elvis broke into *Billboard's* "Best Selling Country & Western Hits" chart. Not a monster hit but enough to draw the attention of RCA Victor, and in November 1955 RCA Victor purchased the Presley contract from Sun for $35,000. Elvis himself got a $5,000 bonus in the deal. The local boy had made good.

Elvis' real break-out year was 1956. On January 10, 1956, Elvis made his first trip to New York to record for his new label, and two weeks later hit the national scene. First there was his appearance (January 28) on CBS-TV's Jackie Gleason/Dorsey Brothers "Stage Show," then the Top Ten charts, then the movies. On August 22 Elvis found himself in Hollywood, standing before the cameras in *Love Me Tender*. Thirty-two other films were to come.

In November 1956, just as the film was reaching the local neighborhood moviehouses, the first contracts for Elvis Presley merchandise were signed.

The notable thing about the products licensed by Elvis Presley Enterprises is the fact that while they were intended primarily for the teenage market, they were directed at boys as well as girls. It was a reflection of how a heartthrob could appeal to both genders. The direct target was, of course, girls. A quick scan of the memorabilia listings reveals the anklets, the lipstick, the charm bracelets, the framed and signed portrait ("Love Me Tender, Sincerely Elvis Presley"), the diary, the doll, the handbag. But for the boys, there were the bolo ties, the cuff links, the dog tags, the belts, the jeans.

Somehow, the earrings, properly licensed and authorized, would bring the girl closer to the object of her adoration, as if to wear his earrings one was somehow wearing *him*. For the boys, it was a matter of seeming more Elvis-like—a stand-in, an understudy. Of course there was admiration for his work, and boys took on Elvis' mannerisms and gestures in the way they spoke, how they walked. Then there were the accouterments to make the imitation more lifelike. The jeans, the shirts, the tie, the cuff links—totems and sacrifices to the being who drove the girls to tears and screams.

We loved the early Elvis in our various ways. He had real style and charisma. An idol for the girls and a hero for the boys, Elvis set the standards that all others had to live by and shoot for. He pushed the limits of what our parents could or would take.

But dangerous as he was, Elvis was never threatening. On December 20, 1957, when Milton Bowers, chairman of the Memphis draft board, personally delivered to Elvis a "Greeting" from Uncle Sam, the idol of millions did as he was ordered, and on March 24, 1958, Elvis reported for basic training processing at Fort Chaffee, Arkansas.

It is difficult to imagine what Elvis would have become had he used his influence to avoid the draft. Whatever the case, he gave up personal appearances and devoted his efforts almost exclusively to making movies and records. The magazines and memorabilia show this. All the rage at the end of the '50s, Elvis' face only occasionally graces the covers of the screen and music magazines after 1961. The odd token appears here and there—a "Follow That Dream" bracelet, a few "G.I. Blues" items, 1961 benefit concert—but in the main, right up to December 3, 1968, when he returned with the remarkable "Singer Presents Elvis" on NBC, Elvis was mostly a face on the silver screen, larger than life and just as far away as the moon.

In August 1969, Elvis finally returned to the concert stage in Las Vegas, headlining at the International Hotel. By then, however, his audience was older, more respectable, and the youth—so often the targets of the pop commemoratives blitz—were on their way to Woodstock. What material there is from the third period in his career generally comes in the form of promotional items for his records and his stage appearances. There were two movies, but these were filmed concerts, not stories built around songs.

Eight years later Elvis died at Graceland. Hundreds of thousands of people pass through the mansion's gates every year to celebrate his work, to remember the man. They come from all over the world—Europe and the Far East, Australia and the southern continents, as well as from the United States and Canada—to see the place where Elvis lived and died.

Elvis Presley Memorabilia, 1955–1977

This chapter documents and prices thousands of manufactured articles that bear the name and/or likeness of Elvis Presley. As the time frame indicates, this compilation is strictly limited to items produced during his lifetime. To attempt a similar post-August 1977 guidebook would require even more pages than in this entire volume. Furthermore, many recent "collectibles" are widely thought of as riffraff, or contrived. There are some wonderful, respectful Elvis souvenirs from this period, but they are few and far between.

Any itemization of nonrecord Presley memorabilia begins with Elvis Presley Enterprises merchandise. Within months of Elvis' meteoric rise to fame in early 1956, licenses to manufacture virtually everything under the sun were issued to dozens of avaricious applicants. A glance at this chapter will astound many readers, seeing, perhaps for the first time, the vast assortment of trinkets, doo-dads, and novelties licensed by Elvis Presley Enterprises.

However, E. P. Enterprises was not the only source of legitimate collectibles. Some of the most desirable items listed here were produced by or for companies promoting his records and films.

RCA VICTOR

RCA Victor developed hundreds of promotional items aimed at furthering interest and sales in Elvis' recordings. While all materials pertaining to actual phonograph record releases, such as bonus photos, are listed in the Records chapters, there are plenty of RCA-created items in this segment.

MOVIE MEMORABILIA

The thirty-three films starring Elvis Presley generated a plethora of advertising and promotional merchandise. The release of each film meant an avalanche of assorted audio and visual goodies, all of which are fancied by Elvis fans.

PUBLICATIONS

Elvis has been the subject of hundreds of publications. Books and magazines have analyzed every conceivable shred of fact and fiction about the man, his professional as well as personal life.

Not surprisingly, most of the Elvis publications were spewed forth after his death, thus eliminating them from this edition.

Included in the category of publications is sheet music. As a rule, the sheet music and lyrics for Elvis' hit singles would be available from the song's publisher. However, there were some unanticipated booklets of sheet music for Elvis songs that could hardly be considered Presley standards. The following is a mere sampling of curious songs for which sheet music was marketed:

A Dog's Life

Animal Instinct

Catchin' On Fast

El Toro

Golden Coins

Have a Happy

I'll Take Love

Ito Eats

Petunia, the Gardener's Daughter

Smorgasbord

Who Needs Money

Yoga Is As Yoga Does

About the only ilk of Elvis memorabilia not dealt with in this edition are printed items that defy accurate description in a text-only format. Included in this maverick cluster are Las Vegas/Tahoe signs and trappings, photographs, concert paraphernalia, and postcards. Documenting and sorting collectibles from these categories requires many, many individual comparative illustrations. Fortunately, a comprehensive reference guide exists that assiduously does just that: *Elvis Collectibles* (Overmountain Press, Johnson City, Tennessee).

Some noteworthy environs of Elvis memorabilia collecting that we don't attempt to appraise in detail are autographs, awards, and personal items once owned by or given as gifts by Presley (see "Collecting Autographs," pages 3–4, on the blessings and pitfalls of autograph collecting). We also avoid the troublesome issue of Elvis' gold records, because of their scarcity (see the article on collecting gold and platinum records, pages 4–12, for identification information).

But if there is one facet of Elvis memorabilia collecting that resists inclusion in a price guide, it is the personal items owned or given by Elvis. Presley's unrestrained spending and generosity is legendary. A piece of jewelry, for example, given by Elvis is no longer an everyday accessory. The gold and craftsmanship making up one of Elvis' "TCB" ("Taking Care of Business") or "TLC" ("Tender Loving Care") necklaces might be estimated at $150 to $200. Regardless, I've seen offers of $15,000 *turned down* for an original TCB given by Elvis. Its sentimental value to the lucky owner far exceeded the cash offered.

Items owned by Elvis are of immense interest to collectors. Nothing is considered too preposterous or absurd. No Elvis-owned object is insignificant. If it once belonged to the King, there's no telling what someone might pay to become its new owner. A car worth about $10,000 if previously owned by you or me, for example, can sell for $90,000 if it belonged to Presley. A $150 wrist watch made for Elvis fetched a whopping $12,000 in a recent sale. Of course, authentication is crucial when contemplating such an investment.

There are numerous other examples, but you get the idea. You also understand why it is so difficult to include such trinkets in a price guide of this kind. A cookie jar may be a cookie jar, but as auction watchers pointed out after the Andy Warhol sale in April 1988, it is impossible to anticipate just how much a cookie jar will command when a celebrity is associated with it. The same holds true for Elvis memorabilia. Pondering the prices of peculiar Presley paraphernalia is not the purpose of this guide, though a few are spotlighted in our color photo section.

Exceptions established, ahead you'll find an alphabetical listing of nonrecord memorabilia produced between 1955 and August 1977. Unless the object is a movie collectible or a publication, look first for the most obvious heading. If it's not there, a cross-reference should point you in the right direction. Movie memorabilia and publications are alphabetically listed in their respective sections.

One important point to remember: The price range shown in this guide, for both records and nonrecorded memorabilia, is for *near-mint* condition. You must adjust values downward for items in lesser condition.

NONRECORD MEMORABILIA

Anklets (Elvis Presley Enterprises), 1956
Two pairs attached to card **150–250**
Card/package by itself **25–50**
Note: The anklets by themselves are not identified as an Elvis item, thus
the significance of the card.
Ashtray (Elvis Presley Enterprises; has an autographed photo of
Elvis in the glass), 1956 . . . .   **100–200**
Autograph book (Elvis Presley Enterprises), 1956 . . . .   **250–350**
Bags: see Handbags, Plastic bags, Souvenir opening night pack-
age
Balloon (California Toytime), 1962
Balloon with cardboard base **15–30**
Balloon by itself **10–20**
Bear: see Teddy bear
Belt (Elvis Presley Enterprises), 1956
Leather belt **250–350**
Plastic belt **225–325**
Belt buckle (Elvis Presley Enterprises), 1956 . . . .   **100–200**
Billfold (Elvis Presley Enterprises), 1956 . . . .   **250–350**
Binder (Elvis Presley Enterprises, zipper model, reads "Love Me
Tender"), 1956 . . . .   **400–450**
Board game: see Game
Bobby sox: see Sox
Bolo tie (Elvis Presley Enterprises), 1956 . . . .   **150–225**
Bookends (Elvis Presley Enterprises), 1956
Both bookends **450–600**
Single bookend **225–300**

Books (Even though thousands of magazines devoted space to Elvis during
his lifetime, very few books devoted exclusively to Elvis were published. Most
originated in Europe. After Elvis' death, an avalanche of Elvis books
was published, flowing from virtually every country on earth. For books
containing sheet music/lyrics, see Song folios, Magazines, and Books sheet
music.)

Elvis by Jerry Hopkins, 1971 (hardbound)
With dust jacket **15–20**
Without dust jacket **10–15**
Films and Career of Elvis Presley by Steven and Boris Zmijewsky,
1976 . . . .   **15–20**
Meet Elvis Presley by Favius Friedman, 1971 (paperback) **15–25**

Operation Elvis by Alan Levy, 1960 (hardbound)

With dust jacket	**35–50**
Without dust jacket	**15–30**

Bracelet (Elvis Presley Enterprises; reads "Follow That Dream"), 1962 .... **20–40**

Bracelet (identification) (Elvis Presley Enterprises; reads "Love Me Tender"), 1962 .... **20–40**

Browser Box (RCA Victor), 1956 .... **100–200**

Reads "Now . . . Everything Elvis Presley Has Recorded . . . available here on RCA Victor Single Recordings." Pictures the same photo of Elvis singing to the hound dog, as was used on the picture sleeve for "Hound Dog"/"Don't Be Cruel."

Bubble gum card (Topps), 1957

Individual "Hit Stars" card **20–30**

Bubble gum card counter display (Elvis Presley Enterprises; 24-count box of 5-cent packages), 1956

Display box, full, with 24 packages of gum and cards	**800–1200**
Display box by itself	**300–600**

Bubble gum card wrapper (Elvis Presley Enterprises), 1956

With 5-cent retail price	**50–75**
With 1-cent retail price	**25–50**

Bubble gum cards (Elvis Presley Enterprises, full color) 1956

Unopened package of 1-cent gum and card	**50–100**
Unopened package of 5-cent gum and card	**75–125**
Any individual card	**8–15**

Bubble gum wrapper (Topps), 1957

"Hit Stars" series card **20–30**

Buckle: see Belt buckle

Carrying case (Elvis Presley Enterprises), 1956 .... **400–500**

Ceramic tile (Elvis Presley Enterprises; 6-inch-square tile, reads "Best Wishes, Elvis Presley"), 1956 .... **100–200**

Charm bracelet (Elvis Presley Enterprises), 1956

Bracelet attached to card	**100–200**
Bracelet by itself	**75–100**

Chewing gum card: see Bubble gum card

Coaster (Elvis Presley Enterprises; has an autographed photo of Elvis in the glass), 1956 .... **100–200**

Coin purse/key chain (pictures Elvis in striped shirt) **100–200**

Concert Placards

The most collectible Elvis concert placards are those from the pre-Army years. Before Presleymania, in early 1956, Elvis was often booked on tours with other performers—usually country and western acts.

1954–1956: Elvis listed, but not headlined	**200–300**
1956–1958: The Elvis Presley Show	**150–250**
1960–1961: The Elvis Presley Show	**100–200**

1969–1977: Elvis In Concert **25–75**
   (One exception in this grouping is a placard reading "Elvis—Extra
   Special Show by popular demand. Sunday Morning, Sept. 2nd AT
   3:00 A.M.—Make your reservations NOW." There were only fifty
   of these placards made, for placement throughout the Las Vegas
   Hilton, to promote an unexpectedly announced show. It may have
   been the only 3:00 A.M. show in Elvis' career. Value: 100–200.)

Counter merchandiser: see Browser box
Crew hat: see Hat
Cuff links (Elvis Presley Enterprises; read "Elvis"), 1958
   Cuff links in original box **200–400**
   Cuff links by themselves **150–200**
Diary (one year) (Elvis Presley Enterprises), 1956 . . . .   **350–450**

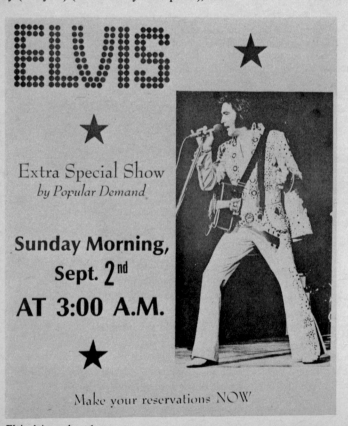

Elvis doing a *late* show.

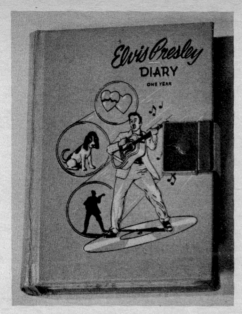

Elvis diary—complete with lock to protect your deepest secrets.

Dog: see Hound dog

Dog tag (Elvis Presley Enterprises; reads "I'm An Elvis Fan"),
  1962 . . . .   **20–40**

Dog tag (Elvis Presley Enterprises; reads "Presley, Elvis—
  53310761"), 1962 . . . .   **20–40**

Dog tag anklet (Elvis Presley Enterprises), 1958
  Anklet attached to card **25–50**
  Anklet by itself **15–30**

Dog tag bracelet (boy's) (Elvis Presley Enterprises), 1958
  Bracelet attached to card **20–35**
  Bracelet by itself **15–25**

Dog tag bracelet (girl's) (Elvis Presley Enterprises), 1958
  Bracelet attached to card **20–30**
  Bracelet by itself **15–20**

Dog tag key chain (Elvis Presley Enterprises), 1958
  Key chain attached to card **75–100**
  Key chain by itself **20–40**

Dog tag necklace (Elvis Presley Enterprises), 1958
  Necklace attached to card **75–100**
  (Card reads "Authentic" and has a $1 price.)

Necklace attached to card **25–50**
(Card does not read "Authentic" nor have the $1 price.)
Necklace by itself **15–30**
Dog tag sweater holder (Elvis Presley Enterprises), 1958
   Holder attached to card **150–200**
   Holder by itself **100–150**
Doll (Elvis Presley Enterprises, 18-inch), 1957
   With all clothing, in original box **1500–2000**
   With all clothing, without original box **1000–1500**
Drinking glass: see Glass
Earrings (Elvis Presley Enterprises; picture Elvis), 1956
   Earrings attached to card **200–300**
   Earrings by themselves **100–200**
Eau de parfum: see Perfume
Elvis NBC-TV Special electric display (Promotional store display,
   has same cover as RCA LPM-4088, but made into a self-
   standing unit with an electric light behind the cover), 1968   **100–200**
Fan Club Membership Package (1956)
   One "Personal Note to you From EP" with "Elvis Presley, National
     Headquarters, Madison, Tenn" at bottom of page **100–150**
   One "Elvis Presley Complimentary Fan Club Membership Card" . **40–50**
   One "Elvis Presley National Fan Club—I Like Elvis And His RCA
     Records" pin-on button **75–100**
   Complete package (letter, card and button) **225–325**
Framed portrait (Elvis Presley Enterprises; reads "Love Me Ten-
   der, Sincerely Elvis Presley"), 1956 .... **250–300**
G.I. Blues LP special electric display (Promotional store display,
   has same cover slick as RCA LPM/LSP-2256, made into a
   self-standing unit with an electric light behind the cover),
   1960 .... **200–300**
Game (board) (Elvis Presley Enterprises; reads "The Elvis Presley
   Game—A Party Game for the Young at Heart"), 1956 . **750–1000**
Glass (drinking) (Elvis Presley Enterprises), 1956 .... **150–225**
Gloves: see Mittens
Guitar (Elvis Presley Enterprises—Emenee), 1956–1957
   Guitar with carrying case **1000–1800**
   Guitar by itself **750–1200**
   Song book "For Emenee Guitar Including Elvis Presley Song Hits" **25–50**
Gum cards: see Bubble gum cards
Handbag (clutch) (Elvis Presley Enterprises), 1956 .... **300–400**
Handkerchief (Elvis Presley Enterprises), 1956 .... **250–325**
Hats (Elvis Presley Enterprises—Magnet), 1956
   With manufacturer's tag **75–150**

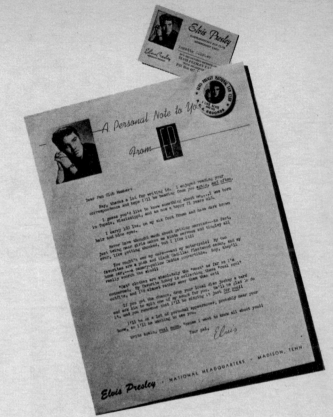

Elvis fan club package.

Three portraits of the King.

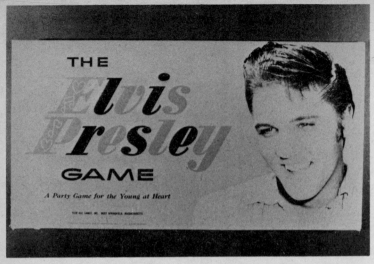

Game box for the young at heart.

Game board—among the true/false questions in this exciting game: "Elvis is afraid to go up in a plane."

Glasses, 1956.

Handkerchiefs—for some, only Elvis could take the tears away.

Without special tag **50–125**

Tag by itself **20–25**

Paper army hat that served as *G.I. Blues* theater ticket; also promoted
both the *G.I. Blues* film and soundtrack LP, 1960

Hat/ticket with box office stub **40–60**

Hat/ticket without box office stub **25–50**

Styrofoam "straw" hat with "Elvis Summer Festival" (Nevada hotels)
band **15–20**

Hawaiian lei: see Lei

Hot plate holder: see Ceramic tile

Hound dog

(Elvis Presley Enterprises; 10-inch dog, with "Hound Dog" hat), 1956 **200–300**

Small (approximately 8–9-inches, "Elvis Summer Festival" dog with
ribbon), 1972 . . . . **35–45**

Large (approximately 12–15-inches, "Elvis Summer Festival" dog with
ribbon), 1972 . . . . **40–60**

Identification bracelet: see Bracelet

Invitations: see Opening night invitations

Iron-on emblem: see Patch

Jeans (Elvis Presley Enterprises—Blue Ridge), 1956

With "Elvis Presley Jeans" tag **100–150**

Without tag **75–125**

Tag by itself **20–30**

Juke box title strips: see Title strips

Key chain (flasher) (Elvis Presley Enterprises—Pictorial Prod.),
1956 . . . . **15–25**

Stuffed toy hound dog, 1972.

Key chain/coin purse: see Coin purse/key chain

Lei (Pictures Elvis on one side, promotes the *Blue Hawaii* LP on
the reverse), 1966 . . . . **75–100**

Lipstick (Elvis Presley Enterprises—Teen-ager Lipstick Corp.),
1956

    Tube of lipstick attached to card **700–800**

    Tube of lipstick by itself **250–300**

Locket (Elvis Presley Enterprises; heart shape, reads "Elvis Presley"), 1957 . . . . **25–50**

Magazines (July 1955–August 16, 1977)

    Amazing Elvis Presley, 1956 . . . . **50–75**

    Best Songs, June 1956 . . . . **25–50**

    Circus Pinups #3: The Elvis Years, August 1975 . . . . **10–20**

    Complete TV, February 1957 . . . . **15–25**

    Confidential (any issue with Elvis' picture on the cover), 1957 . . . **15–25**

    Cool: "Special Issue on Elvis Presley," 1957 . . . . **40–60**

    Country Music, November 1975 . . . . **8–12**

    Country Song Roundup, July 1955 (Pictures Hank Snow on cover, but
has headline reading "Elvis Presley—Folk Music Fireball." Elvis'
picture appears with story, on page 14. Significant in that front
cover mention on any nationally distributed magazine was unusual
in mid-1955. Was this the first? We know of none earlier.) . . . **40–60**

    Country Song Roundup (any issue with Elvis' picture on the cover),
1956–1960 . . . . **20–35**

    Dig (any issue with Elvis' picture on the cover), 1956–1958 . . . . **40–60**

    Elvis and Jimmy (Dean), 1956 . . . . **75–100**

    Elvis & Tom (Jones), 1969 . . . . **15–25**

Lipstick and card, from the
Teen-ager Lipstick Corp. It's
"excitingly alive."

Elvis Answers Back, 1956
 With cardboard 78rpm record attached to front cover **300–325**
 With record removed from cover **150–200**
Elvis: His Loves & Marriage, 1957 . . . . **50–75**
Elvis in the Army, 1959 . . . . **50–75**
Elvis: 1971 Presley Album, 1971 . . . . **10–20**
Elvis 1974 Calendar **10–15**
Elvis Photo Album ("125 Photos Never Before Published"), 1956 . **50–75**
Elvis Presley ("More Than 100 Pictures," "Complete Life Story," etc.),
 1956 . . . . **50–75**
Elvis Presley: Hero or Heel, 1956 . . . . **100–125**
Elvis Presley in Hollywood, 1956 . . . . **50–80**
Elvis Presley Song Hits, 1965 . . . . **20–30**
Elvis Presley Speaks!, 1956 . . . . **50–75**
Elvis: The Hollywood Years, 1976 . . . . **10–15**
Elvis: The Intimate Story, 1957 . . . . **50–75**
Elvis the King Returns, 1960 . . . . **25–50**
Elvis: The Trials and Triumphs of the Legendary King of Rock & Roll,
 1976 . . . . **10–15**
Elvis vs. the Beatles, 1965 . . . . **50–75**
Elvis Yearbook, 1960 . . . . **25–50**
Elvis Years: see *Circus*
Elvis Yesterday . . . Today, 1975 . . . . **10–20**
Filmland, 1957 . . . . **20–35**
Folk and Country Songs (any issue with Elvis' picture on the cover),
 1956–1959 . . . . **15–25**
Hep Cats (any issue with Elvis' picture on the cover), 1956–1958 . **50–75**
Hit Parader (any issue with Elvis' picture on the cover), 1956–1972 **12–25**
Hollywood Rebels, 1957 . . . . **20–30**
I Love You #60: Here Comes Elvis, 1966 . . . . **30–60**
Life (story and photos, no cover photo), April 30, 1956 . . . . . . **20–30**
Life (story and photos, no cover photo), August 27, 1956 . . . . . **20–30**
Life (story and photos, no cover photo), March 25, 1957 . . . . . . **20–30**
Look (story and photos, no cover photo), August 7, 1956 . . . . . **20–30**
Look (story only, no cover photo), November 13, 1956 . . . . **20–30**
Look (cover photo), May 4, 1971 . . . . **15–25**
Look (no cover photo, May 11, 1971, part 2 of story) **8–15**
Lowdown, 1956 . . . . **25–40**
Magazine supplements for newspapers (any issue with Elvis' picture on
 the cover), as published by many local newspapers or inserted in
 their papers.
 1956–1959 . . . . **20–40**
 1960–1969 . . . . **15–30**
 1970–1977 . . . . **10–20**
Modern Screen (any issue with Elvis' picture on the cover), 1956–1957 **20–30**
Modern Teen, 1960 . . . . **20–30**
Motion Picture, 1957–1958 . . . . **15–25**

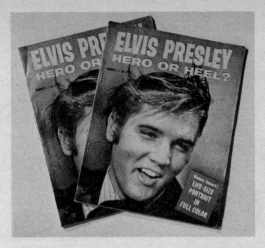

Hero or Heel?

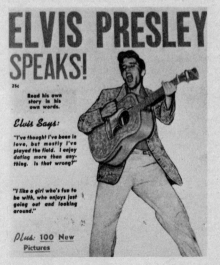

Elvis Presley Speaks!

Look cover.

Movie Album, 1965	**15–20**
Movie & TV Show, 1960	**20–30**
Movie Digest (any issue with Elvis' picture on the cover), 1972	**5–10**
Movie Dream Guys, 1960	**20–25**
Movie Life (any issue with Elvis' picture on the cover), 1957–1960	**20–30**
Movie Life Year Book, 1958	**20–25**
Movie Mirror, 1959	**15–20**
Movie Stars Parade, 1957	**20–30**
Movie Stars TV Close-ups (any issue with Elvis' picture on the cover), 1960	**20–25**
Movie Stars TV Close-ups Parade, 1958	**20–35**
Movie TV Album, 1957	**20–30**
Movie TV Record Stardom, 1960	**20–30**
Movie TV Secrets (any issue with Elvis' picture on the cover), 1959–1960	**15–20**
Movie Teen: Special Elvis Issue, 1961	**20–40**
Movie Teen Illustrated, 1959	**15–25**
Movie World (any issue with Elvis' picture on the cover), 1959–1960	**20–25**
Movieland (any issue with Elvis' picture on the cover), 1957	**20–30**
Movieland and TV Time (any issue with Elvis' picture on the cover), 1959–1961	**15–25**
Official Elvis Presley Album, 1956	**50–75**
People, January 13, 1975	**5–10**
Personalities, 1957	**40–60**
Photoplay (any issue with Elvis' picture on the cover),	
1957–1959	**15–25**
1960–1976	**5–15**
Popular Screen, 1960	**15–25**
Popular TV Movie and Record Stars, 1960	**15–25**

Various magazines featuring Elvis on the cover.

Record Time—TV Movies, 1960 . . . .   **15–20**
Record Whirl, 1956 . . . .   **25–50**
Rock and Roll Roundup, 1957 . . . .   **40–60**
Rock and Roll Songs (any issue with Elvis' picture on the cover),
1956–1958 . . . .   **12–25**
Rock & Roll Stars #1: The Real Elvis Presley Story, 1956 . . . . .   **40–60**
Rock & Roll Stars #2: Elvis Answers 10 Important Teenage Questions,
1957 . . . .   **25–50**
Rock & Roll Stars #3: Elvis in the Army?, 1958 . . . .   **25–50**
Rock 'n' Roll Battlers, 1956 . . . .   **40–60**
Rock 'n' Roll Jamboree, 1956 . . . .   **40–60**
Rock 'n' Roll Rivals, 1957 . . . .   **40–60**
Rolling Stone (any issue with Elvis' picture on the cover), 1969–1972   **5–10**
Screen Parade, 1958 . . . .   **20–30**
Screen Stars, 1959 . . . .   **20–30**
Silver Screen, 1960 . . . .   **20–30**
Sixteen (any issue with Elvis' picture on the cover) **20–40**
Song Hits Magazine (any issue with Elvis' picture on the cover), 1956–
1963 . . . .   **15–25**
Songs and Stars, 1965 . . . .   **10–20**
Songs That Will Live Forever, 1956 . . . .   **20–35**
Souvenir Photo Album, 1956 . . . .   **75–100**
(Reads "Elvis Presley, 'Mr. Dynamite' Nation's Only Atomic Pow-
ered Singer.")
Stardom, 1960 . . . .   **20–30**
Starlife TV & Movies Direct from Hollywood, 1959 . . . .   **20–30**
Story of Life **5–10**
Suppressed Annual, 1956 . . . .   **25–50**
TV and Movie Screen (any issue with Elvis' picture on the cover),
1956–1962 . . . .   **12–25**
TV and Screen Life (1960) **15–20**
TV Film Stars (any issue with Elvis' picture on the cover), 1960 . .   **15–25**
TV Guide
Elvis on cover, September 8–14, 1956 . . . .   **100–150**
Elvis not on cover, September 22–28, 1956 . . . .   **50–100**
Elvis not on cover, September 29–October 5, 1956 . . . .   **50–100**
Elvis and Frank Sinatra on cover, May 7–13, 1960 . . . .   **50–75**
Elvis not on cover (seven-page story on the making of the NBC-TV
special), November 30, 1968 . . . .   **10–15**
Elvis not on cover (piece on "Elvis, Aloha from Hawaii via Satel-
lite"), March 31, 1973 . . . .   **5–10**
Elvis and others on cover, November 10–16, 1973 . . . .   **8–15**
TV Headliner (any issue with Elvis' picture on the cover), 1957 . .   **20–25**
TV Movie Fan, 1956 . . . .   **20–30**
TV-Movie Men, 1959 . . . .   **20–25**
TV Picture Life (any issue with Elvis' picture on the cover), 1959–1960   **15–30**
TV Picture Life, 1960 . . . .   **15–20**

Samples of *TV* and *Movie Screen*.

TV Radio Mirror, 1960 . . . .   **10–20**
TV Record Superstars, 1970 . . . .   **15–20**
TV Screen Diary (any issue with Elvis' picture on the cover), 1961   **25–50**
  Note: This was issue No. 1. We're not sure if this magazine, a *TV Guide* clone, published another issue.
TV Star Parade (any issue with Elvis' picture on the cover), 1958–
  1960 . . . .   **15–20**
TV magazine supplements for newspapers (any issue with Elvis' picture on the cover), as inserted in city newspapers in virtually any city:
  1956–1959 . . . .   **12–25**
  1960–1969 . . . .   **10–20**
  1970–1977 . . . .   **5–10**
TV World, December 1956 . . . .   **20–30**
Teen Life, 1957 . . . .   **50–75**
Teen Screen, 1961 . . . .   **15–20**
Teenage Rock and Roll Review, October 1956 . . . .   **40–60**
Teenage Rock and Roll Review, December 1956 . . . .   **40–60**
Tommy Sands vs. Belafonte and Elvis, 1957 . . . .   **50–75**
Top Secret, 1960 . . . .   **15–25**
Young Lovers #18: The Real Elvis Presley Complete Life Story,
  1957 . . . .   **150–175**
Zoo World, September 13, 1973 . . . .   **3–5**
Medallion (Elvis Presley Enterprises; reads "I Want You, I Need You, I Love You—Don't Be Cruel—Hound Dog—Heartbreak Hotel"), 1956 . . . .   **100–200**
Menus (Las Vegas and Lake Tahoe)
  1969 . . . .   **50–100**
  1970 . . . .   **30–50**
  1971–1976 . . . .   **15–30**
Menu/photo album: see Photo album/opening night menu
Mittens (Elvis Presley Enterprises—Nolan), 1956
  Pair of mittens **150–250**
  One mitten **50–100**

Movies: Listed here are the most commonly traded collectibles from the film studios, used in the promotion and exploitation of Elvis' movies. This list does not include Elvis Presley Enterprises items that just happen to mention a film title. Such articles are listed elsewhere in this guide.

Films appear in alphabetical order. Some unfamiliar terms may appear in this section, all of which are explained here: A *one-sheet* is a colorful 27- × 41-inch paper poster, usually displayed by theaters in a glass case outside the building or in the lobby. This was the most commonly circulated movie poster, as every theater used one-sheets, even if they didn't display the larger sheets. Usually, theaters in bigger cities ordered more merchandising paraphernalia than rural and small-town theaters. For those reasons, the one-sheet is the only movie poster size listed in this edition.

To gauge the value of larger sheets, use the following formula:

Three-sheet (41 × 81 inch) = 25 to 50% increase over one-sheet
Six-sheet (81 × 81 inch) = double the value of the one-sheet
24-sheet (108 × 162 inch) = four or five times the value of the one-sheet.

Similar to one-sheets in appearance, but different in size are the following:

Stills are simply studio 8 × 10 inch photo prints showing scenes from the film. Stills for Elvis films are most often in black and white, but there are some exceptions.

Lobby card (11 × 14 inch)—Usually issued in sets of eight, each picturing a different scene from the film. These differ from stills not only in size but in production. Lobby cards are printed (in full color), whereas stills are developed prints, usually black and white.

Window card (14 × 22 inch)
Insert card (14 × 36 inch)
Lobby photo (22 × 28 inch)

All sizes are approximate. There may be slight variations in size from one film to another.

Blue Hawaii, 1961
Insert card	**25–40**
Lobby card	**10–20**
Lobby photo	**25–40**
Mug (Tiki) (Reads "Hal Wallis Production, Elvis Presley, 'Blue Hawaii' A Paramount Picture, T.O.A. Convention 1961, New Orleans, La"), 1961	**100–200**
One-sheet	**50–60**
Still	**5–15**
Window card	**25–40**

Change of Habit, 1969
Insert card	**10–15**
Lobby card	**5–10**
Lobby photo	**10–20**
One-sheet	**20–35**
Still	**4–8**
Window card	**10–15**

Charro, 1969
Insert card	**10–20**
Lobby card	**5–10**
Lobby photo	**15–20**
One-sheet	**20–35**
Still	**4–8**
Window card	**10–20**

Clambake, 1967
Insert card	**10–20**
Lobby card	**5–10**
Lobby photo	**15–20**
One-sheet	**25–35**
Still	**4–8**
Window card	**10–20**

Double Trouble, 1967
Insert card	**10–20**

Blue Hawaii, lobby cards.

Blue Hawaii, lobby cards.

Promotional tiki mug for *Blue Hawaii.*

Charro, lobby cards.

Clambake, lobby cards.

Easy Come, Easy Go, lobby cards.

Lobby card	**5–10**
Lobby photo	**15–20**
One-sheet	**25–35**
Still	**4–8**
Window card	**10–20**

Easy Come, Easy Go,
1967

Insert card	**10–20**
Lobby card	**5–10**
Lobby photo	**15–20**
One-sheet	**25–35**
Still	**4–8**
Window card	**10–20**

Elvis on Tour, 1972

Insert card	**15–25**
Lobby card	**10–20**
Lobby photo	**25–50**
One-sheet	**40–60**
Still	**4–8**
Window card	**15–25**

Follow That Dream,
1962

Insert card	**30–50**
Lobby card	**10–15**
Lobby photo	**25–40**
One-sheet	**50–75**
Still	**5–10**
Window card	**25–40**

Flaming Star, 1960

Insert card	**30–50**
Lobby card	**15–20**
Lobby photo	**30–50**
One-sheet	**50–75**
Still	**5–10**
Window card	**30–50**

Frankie and Johnny,
1966

Insert card	**15–20**
Lobby card	**8–12**
Lobby photo	**15–20**
One-sheet	**25–40**

Still	**5–10**
Window card	**15–20**

Fun in Acapulco, 1963

Insert card	**15–25**
Lobby card	**8–15**
Lobby photo	**20–25**
One-sheet	**30–50**
Still	**5–10**
Window card	**15–25**

*Fun in Acapulco/Girls!
Girls! Girls!,* (double bill
re-release), 1966

Insert card	**15–20**
Lobby card	**8–12**
Lobby photo	**15–20**
One-sheet	**25–40**
Still	**5–10**
Window card	**15–20**

G.I. Blues, 1960

Insert card	**30–50**
Lobby card	**15–20**
Lobby photo	**30–50**
Mug (glass; reads "Hal Wallis' G.I. Blues," with signatures of Elvis Presley and Juliet Prowse)	**50–75**
One-sheet	**50–75**
Still	**8–15**
Window card	**30–50**

Girl! Girls! Girls!, 1962

Insert card	**20–30**
Lobby card	**10–15**
Lobby photo	**20–30**
One-sheet	**30–50**
Still	**5–10**
Window card	**20–30**

Girl Happy, 1965

Insert card	**15–20**
Lobby card	**8–12**

Elvis on Tour, lobby cards.

Follow That Dream, lobby cards.

Follow That Dream, one sheet.

Flaming Star, lobby cards.

Frankie and Johnny, lobby cards.

Fun in Acapulco, lobby cards.

G.I. Blues, lobby cards.

Girls! Girls! Girls!, lobby cards.

Girls! Girls! Girls!, one sheet.

Lobby photo **15–20**
One-sheet **25–40**
Still **5–10**
Window card **15–20**

Harum Scarum, 1965
Insert card **15–20**
Lobby card **8–12**
Lobby photo **15–20**
One-sheet **25–40**
Still **5–10**
Window card **15–20**

It Happened at the World's Fair, 1963
Insert card **15–25**
Lobby card **10–15**
Lobby photo **20–30**
One-sheet **30–50**
Still **5–10**
Window card **15–25**

Jailhouse Rock, 1957
Insert card **75–100**
Lobby card **20–25**
Lobby photo **50–100**
One-sheet **150–225**
Still **8–15**
Window card **50–100**

Kid Galahad, 1962
Insert card **25–35**
Lobby card **10–15**
Lobby photo **25–30**
One-sheet **40–60**
Still **5–10**
Window card **25–35**

King Creole, 1958
Insert card **60–100**
Lobby card **20–25**
Lobby photo **60–100**
One-sheet **100–150**
Still **8–15**
Window card **60–100**

King Creole (second run, while Elvis was in Germany), 1959
Insert card **40–60**
Lobby card **15–20**
Lobby photo **40–60**
One-sheet **50–80**
Still **8–15**
Window card **60–80**

Kissin' Cousins, 1964
Button (reads "I'm A Kissin' Cousin") . . **40–50**
Insert card **15–20**
Lobby card **8–12**
Lobby photo **15–20**
One-sheet **25–40**
Still **5–10**
Window card **15–20**

Live a Little, Love a Little, 1968
Insert card **10–20**
Lobby card **5–10**
Lobby photo **15–20**
One-sheet **20–35**
Still **4–8**
Window card **10–20**

Love Me Tender, 1956
Insert card **75–125**
Lobby card **25–30**
Lobby photo **75–150**
One-sheet **150–250**
Still **8–15**
Theater Pictorial (magazine) **175–225**
Window card **75–150**

Loving You, 1957
Insert card **50–80**
Lobby card **20–25**
Lobby photo **60–80**
One-sheet **100–150**
Still **8–15**
Window card **60–80**

Girl Happy, lobby cards.

Harum Scarum, lobby cards.

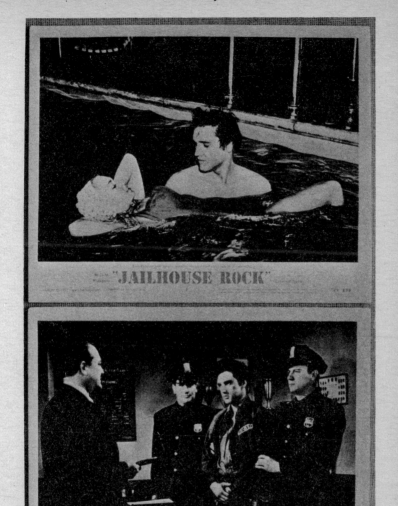

Jailhouse Rock, lobby cards.

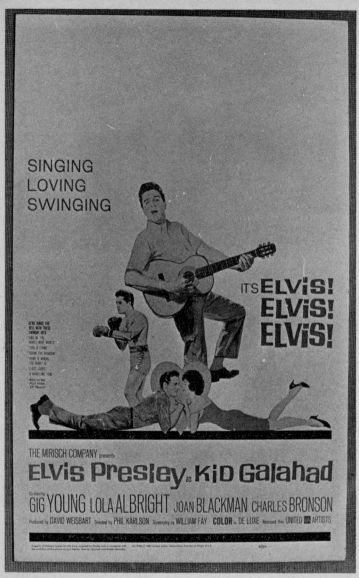

Kid Galahad, one sheet.

Kid Galahad, lobby cards.

King Creole, lobby cards.

Kissin' Cousins, lobby cards.

Love Me Tender, lobby cards.

Paradise Hawaiian
Style, 1966

Insert card	**10–20**
Lobby card	**5–10**
Lobby photo	**15–20**
One-sheet	**25–40**
Still	**5–10**
Window card	**10–20**

Roustabout, 1964

Insert card	**15–20**
Lobby card	**8–12**
Lobby photo	**15–20**
One-sheet	**30–50**
Still	**5–10**
Window card	**15–20**

Speedway, 1968

Insert card	**10–20**
Lobby card	**5–10**
Lobby photo	**15–20**
One-sheet	**25–35**
Still	**4–8**
Window card	**10–20**

Spinout, 1966

Insert card	**10–20**
Lobby card	**5–10**
Lobby photo	**15–20**
One-sheet	**25–35**
Still	**5–10**
Window card	**10–20**

Stay Away Joe, 1968

Insert card	**10–20**
Lobby card	**5–10**
Lobby photo	**15–20**
One-sheet	**25–35**
Still	**4–8**
Window card	**10–20**

That's the Way It Is,
1970

Insert card	**15–20**
Lobby card	**10–20**
Lobby photo	**10–20**
One-sheet	**25–40**

Still	**4–8**
Window card	**15–20**

Tickle Me, 1965

Insert card	**15–20**
Lobby card	**8–12**
Lobby photo	**15–20**
One-sheet	**25–40**
Pen (with feather on one end; reads "Elvis Presley in Tickle Me"), 1965	**10–20**
Press pack (with feathers inside; reads "Elvis At His Best in Tickle Me," and lists song titles in the film), 1965	**40–50**
Still	**5–10**
Window card	**15–20**

Trouble with Girls,
1969

Insert card	**10–15**
Lobby card	**5–10**
Lobby photo	**10–20**
One-sheet	**20–35**
Still	**4–8**
Window card	**10–15**

Viva Las Vegas, 1964

Insert card	**25–35**
Lobby card	**10–20**
Lobby photo	**35–45**
One-sheet	**50–80**
Still	**5–12**
Window card	**25–35**

Wild in the Country,
1961

Insert card	**25–40**
Lobby card	**10–20**
Lobby photo	**25–40**
One-sheet	**50–60**
Still	**5–10**
Window card	**25–40**

Loving You, lobby cards.

Paradise Hawaiian Style, lobby cards.

Roustabout, lobby cards.

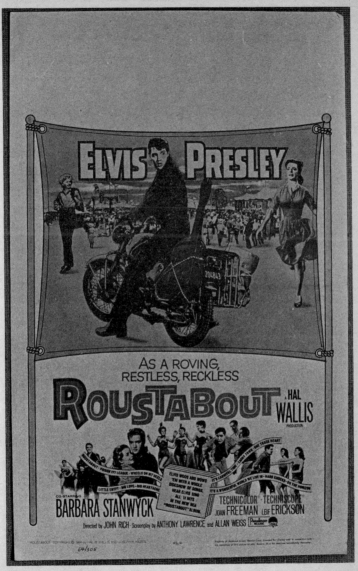

Roustabout, lobby cards.

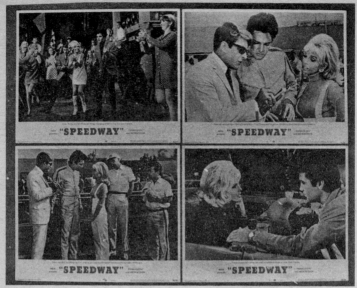

Speedway, lobby cards.

Spinout, lobby cards.

Stay Away Joe, lobby cards.

That's the Way It Is, stills.

Tickle Me, lobby cards.

The Trouble with Girls, stills.

Viva Las Vegas, stills.

Wild in the Country, lobby cards.

Necklace (Elvis Presley Enterprises; heart shaped with engraving
    of Elvis), 1956

    Necklace attached to card **150–250**
    Necklace by itself **125–175**

Necklace (Elvis Presley Enterprises; reads "Follow That
    Dream"), 1962 . . . . **20–40**

Notebook: see Binder

Opening night invitations (Las Vegas and Lake Tahoe) (opening
    night invitations to these engagements were sent to the press
    and assorted VIPs. Most were printed on paper, though
    some were more elaborate. Most invited guests also received
    a personal letter from the publicity director of the hotel.)

    Printed (paper) invitation **5–15**
    Felt, 3-foot, banner invitation, for January 26, 1972 . . . . **40–60**

Overnight case: see Carrying case

Paint set (prenumbered, oil colors) (Elvis Presley Enterprises),
    1956 . . . . **450–550**

Pajamas (Elvis Presley Enterprises; pictures Elvis singing, lists the
    songs: "Heartbreak Hotel," "Don't Be Cruel," "Hound
    Dog," and "I Want You, I Need You") **175–275**

Pants: see Jeans

"Love Me Tender" necklace,
by Alabaster.

Patches (Elvis Presley Enterprises; heart shaped, reads "My Heart
  Belongs To Elvis Presley" or "I Love Elvis Presley" or
  "Elvis Presley Is A Doll"), 1956

Display card with patches attached	**50–100**
Individual patch	**20–30**
Tour patches/ribbons, 1970–1977	**20–30**

Pencil (Elvis Presley Enterprises—Union Pencil Co.), 1956

Complete box of "one dozen packs" of "Elvis Presley Pencils"	**1500–2500**
Box by itself	**75–125**
Wrapped 12-pack of pencils	**150–200**
Individual pencil	**10–15**

Pencil sharpener (Elvis Presley Enterprises), 1956 .... **100–175**

Perfume (Elvis Presley Enterprises; reads "Elvis Presley's 'Teddy
  Bear.'" Has a 1957 picture of Elvis on label. "Elvis Presley
  Enterprises, Inc." is on two lines. "Eau de Parfum"), 1957 **100–200**

Elvis' own pencils, to go with
Elvis' binder.

Elvis Presley's "Teddy Bear" eau de parfum, 1957.

Perfume (Elvis Presley Enterprises; reads "Elvis Presley's 'Teddy Bear.' " Has a 1965 picture of Elvis on label. "Elvis Presley Enterprises, Inc." is on one line. "Eau De Parfum"), 1965   **25–50**

Phonograph (Elvis Presley Enterprises; portable "Autograph" model), 1956

   Manual record change player **450–550**

   Automatic record change model **550–700**

   Printed instructions telling "How to Use and Enjoy Your RCA Victor Portable Phonograph" **50–100**

Photo album (Elvis Presley Enterprises), 1956 . . . .   **250–350**

Photo albums (souvenir tour and concert)

   "In Person—Elvis Presley, Country Music's Mr. Rhythm," 1956   .   **200–300**

   "Elvis Presley—Mr. Dynamite," 1956 . . . .   **200–300**

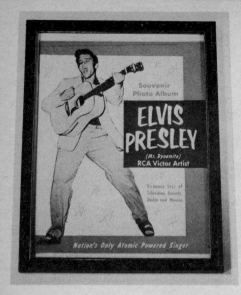

Photo album featuring "The nation's only atomic powered singer."

"Souvenir Photo Album—Elvis Presley" (Has "Love Me Tender" photos on back cover and on inside back cover page. Inside front cover has Elvis' "Vital Statistics"), 1956 . . . . **100–200**

"Elvis Presley Photo Folio" (Features "Jailhouse Rock" photos), 1957   **100–150**

Photo albums from 1970–1977 . . . .   **15–35**

Photo album/opening night menu (Las Vegas Hilton), 1975 . .   **25–50**

Pillow (Elvis Presley Enterprises), 1956 . . . .   **200–300**

Pin (Elvis Presley Enterprises; framed picture of Elvis, attached to a guitar), 1956

Pin attached to card **250–350**

Pin by itself **150–250**

Pin (flasher) (Elvis Presley Enterprises—Vari-Vue), 1956 . . . .   **15–25**

Pin (flasher) (Elvis Presley Enterprises—Pictorial Productions), 1956 . . . .   **15–25**

Plastic bags (Nevada hotels, complimentary, LP-size bags), 1970– 1972 . . . .   **15–20**

Plate (Elvis Presley Enterprises, 12-inch platter/plate), 1956 . .   **200–275**

Pocket watch (with 1964 photo of Elvis wearing a jacket and playing the guitar; back of watch has a polished finish), 1964   **75–150**

Pocket watch (with 1964 photo of Elvis wearing a jacket and playing the guitar; back of watch has a knurled finish) .   **25–35**

Polo shirt: see Shirt

The changing face of Elvis Presley in a 1956 flasher pin, by Pictorial Productions.

Portrait: see Framed portrait

Pumps: see Shoes

Purse (clutch) (Elvis Presley Enterprises. With three pictures of
    Elvis and his guitar. Lists three song titles: "Heartbreak
    Hotel," "Hound Dog" and "I Want You, I Need You"),
    1956 . . . .   **300–400**

Purse: see Handbag

Record case (Elvis Presley Enterprises), 1956 . . . .   **350–450**

Record player: see Phonograph

Ribbons (tour): see Patches

Ring (adjustable) (Elvis Presley Enterprises, with color picture of
    Elvis), 1956

12-count counter display, with 12 rings **1200–2000**

Individual ring **75–125**

Display card without rings **300–500**

Ring (flasher), 1957 . . . .   **25–50**

Scarves (Elvis Presley Enterprises; two drawings of Elvis and
    guitar and one of him posing. Lists songs: "I Want You, I
    Love You," "Love Me Tender," "Don't Be Cruel" and
    "You're Nothing But A Hound Dog." Pictures records and
    a dog. Reads "Best wishes, Elvis Presley"), 1956 . . . .   **250–350**

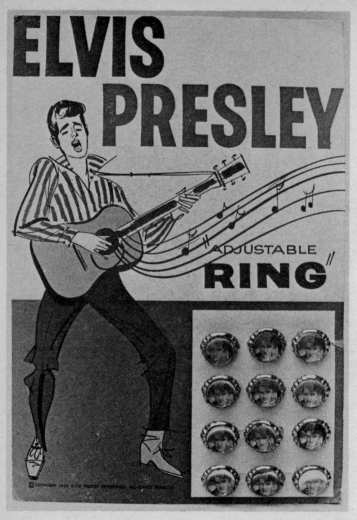

A full center display card of the King's own adjustable rings.

Goes with any outfit—a 1956 Elvis scarf.

International Hotel/RCA "Summer Festival," 28-inch, scarf	**100–200**
Concert souvenir autographed scarves, with or without Hilton logo	**20–30**
Scrap book (Elvis Presley Enterprises), 1956	**250–350**

Sheet music (Elvis)

1956–1959	**20–40**
1960–1977 (with picture of Elvis)	**10–20**
1960–1977 (with no picture of Elvis)	**8–12**

Sheet music (other)

"Elvis Presley For President" was an attention-getting release by Lou Monte (RCA Victor 6704). The sheet music for this song pictured Elvis on the cover	**50–75**
Shirt (Elvis Presley Enterprises—Blue Ridge; green and white striped shirt), 1956	**100–125**
Shirt (Elvis Presley Enterprises; pictures Elvis singing. Lists the songs: "Heartbreak Hotel," "Don't Be Cruel," "Hound Dog" and "I Want You, I Need You"), 1956	**150–250**
Shirt (RCA Records; reads "For The Heart/Elvis"), 1976 . . .	**20–40**

Shoes (pumps) (Elvis Presley Enterprises—Faith Shoe Co.), 1956

Pair of pumps with box	**400–600**
One pump	**100–150**

And for the guys, this 1956 T-shirt.

Pumps by themselves	300–500
Box by itself	100–125
Shoes (sneakers) (Elvis Presley Enterprises), 1956	
Pair of sneakers with box	400–600
One sneaker	100–150
Sneakers by themselves	300–500
Box by itself	100–125
Side Burns Machine Label, 1956	50–60

The only piece of the Elvis Side Burns Machine known to exist today
is the label from the front of the machine. A complete vending
machine would be valued at several hundred dollars, but we know
of none.

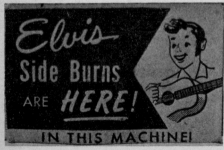

An idea that didn't quite
catch—Elvis side burns.

Skirt (Elvis Presley Enterprises—Little Jean Togs), 1956 . . . .   **400–600**
Sneakers: see Shoes
Song book for Emenee guitar: see Guitar
Song folios, magazines and books (sheet music)

    Elvis Presley Album of Juke Box Favorites (Hill & Range), 1956 . .   **25–50**
    Love Me Tender Song Folio with Pictures (Hill & Range), 1956 . .   **20–40**
    Songs Recorded by Elvis Presley, 1968 . . . .   **20–30**
    Songs Recorded by Elvis Presley, Vol. 2, 1968 . . . .   **20–30**
    We Call on Him—A Collection of Gospel Songs Recorded by Elvis
    Presley (Gladys Music—Hill & Range), 1968 . . . .   **20–40**

Souvenir menu: see Menus
Souvenir opening night package (Las Vegas Hilton), 1975 (very
    similar to *Special souvenir package*)

    Specially printed paper bag with the following items: 1975 photo
    album/menu, color tour photo, Summer Festival 1975 Hilton post-
    card, Elvis and Santa Claus Christmas postcard, and a 1976 pocket
    calendar **75–125**
    Paper bag by itself **40–60**

Souvenir photo album/folio: see Photo albums
Sox (bobby sox) (Elvis Presley Enterprises), 1956

    Two pair attached to card **150–250**
    Card/package by itself **25–50**
    The sox by themselves are not identified as an Elvis item. Also see
    Anklets

Special souvenir package (Las Vegas Hilton), 1975 (very similar
    to *Souvenir opening night package*)

    Specially printed paper bag with the following items: 1975 photo
    album/menu, color tour photo, Summer Festival 1975 Hilton post-
    card, Elvis and Santa Claus Christmas postcard, and a 1976 pocket
    calendar **50–100**
    Paper bag by itself **25–50**

Statuette (bronze) (Elvis Presley Enterprises; 8-inch figure), 1956   **500–600**
Stretch anklets: see Anklets
T-shirt: see Shirt
Tag (for shirt or jeans) (Elvis Presley Enterprises), 1956 . . . .   **30–40**
    Pictures Elvis and his guitar.
Teddy bears (Elvis Presley Enterprises; 24-inch bear with "Elvis
    Presley" and "Teddy Bear" ribbons), 1957 . . . .   **200–300**
    International Hotel bear, pink and white with pin-on metal badge,
    1971 . . . .   **30–50**
Throw pillow: see Pillow
Tickets (Standard paper tickets for admission to Elvis concerts,
    filmings, press conferences, and other such personal appear-
    ances. Prices are for complete ticket, not stub or portion.)

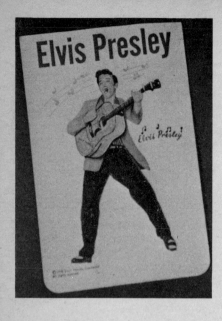

The tag makes all the
difference between old jeans
and the real thing.

1955–1960	**50–75**
1961–1968	**25–50**
1969–1977	**15–25**

Ticket stubs (Standard ticket stubs for admission to Elvis concerts,
filmings, press conferences, and other such personal appearances. Prices are for stubs or portions that clearly identify
the event.)

1955–1960	**20–30**
1961–1968	**15–25**
1969–1977	**8–15**

Tie: see Bolo tie

Tiki mug: see Movies, *Blue Hawaii*

Tile: see Ceramic tile

Title strips (Available to jukebox operators; factory-printed with
titles of both sides of disc on each strip. Strips were usually
made on sheets of 10 strips. Price is for full sheets only.)

Releases from 1955–1959	**10–20**
Releases from 1960–1969	**8–15**
Releases from 1970–1979	**5–10**
Releases from 1980–present	**3–6**

Victrola: see Phonograph

Wallet, coin purse and key chain (Elvis Presley Enterprises), 1956   **350–425**
  With two drawings and one photo of Elvis. Reads "Elvis Presley—
  Rock 'n' Roll."

Wallet (clutch) (Elvis Presley Enterprises; folding, with two coin
  compartments; also known as a "French Purse"), 1956 .   **250–350**

Wallet (money) (Elvis Presley Enterprises), 1956 . . . .   **250–350**

Wallet (for photos) (Elvis Presley Enterprises), 1956 . . . . . .   **250–350**

A key chain, coin purse, and a wallet—all in one convenient package.

Elvis on Record

The following features will be of special interest to Elvis collectors: There's a chronological listing of all of Elvis' standard catalog releases, from 1954–1988; a thorough review of RCA's Dynaflex discs will set the record straight in a previously confusing area; our continuing series of Labels and Changes is brought up to date; and we must report that the "lost single" is still lost. Finally, a 1988 update of our in-depth analysis of unissued, true stereo Elvis tracks appears.

ELVIS' MAJOR RELEASES THROUGH THE YEARS
(Release date, title, format(s), label and catalog number)

7/54, That's All Right/Moon of Kentucky (78) (45), Sun 209

9/54, Good Rockin' Tonight/I Don't Care If the Sun Don't Shine (78) (45), Sun 210

1/55, You're a Heartbreaker/Milkcow Blues Boogie (78) (45), Sun 215

4/55, Baby Let's Play House/I'm Left, You're Right, She's Gone (78) (45), Sun 217

9/55, Mystery Train/I Forgot to Remember to Forget, (78) (45), Sun 223

11/55, Mystery Train/I Forgot to Remember to Forget, (78) RCA Victor 20-6357

11/55, Mystery Train/I Forgot to Remember to Forget, (45) RCA Victor 47-6357

11/55, That's All Right/Blue Moon of Kentucky (78), RCA Victor 20-6380

11/55, That's All Right/Blue Moon of Kentucky (45), RCA Victor 47-6380

11/55, Good Rockin' Tonight/I Don't Care If the Sun Don't Shine (78), RCA Victor 20-6381

11/55, Good Rockin' Tonight/I Don't Care If the Sun Don't Shine (45), RCA Victor 47-6381

11/55, You're a Heartbreaker/Milkcow Blues Boogie (78), RCA Victor 20-6382

11/55, You're a Heartbreaker/Milkcow Blues Boogie (45), RCA Victor 47-6382

11/55, Baby Let's Play House/I'm Left, You're Right, She's Gone (78), RCA Victor 20-6383

11/55, Baby Let's Play House/I'm Left, You're Right, She's Gone (45), RCA Victor 47-6383

1/56, Heartbreak Hotel/I Was the One (78), RCA Victor 20-6420

1/56, Heartbreak Hotel/I Was the One (45), RCA Victor 47-6420

3/56, *Elvis Presley* (EP), RCA Victor EPA-747

3/56, *Elvis Presley* (EP), RCA Victor EPB-1254

3/56, *Elvis Presley* (LP), RCA Victor LPM-1254

4/56, *Heartbreak Hotel* (EP), RCA Victor EPA-821

5/56, I Want You, I Need You, I Love You/My Baby Left Me (78), RCA Victor 20-6540

5/56, I Want You, I Need You, I Love You/My Baby Left Me (45), RCA Victor 47-6540

7/56, Don't Be Cruel/Hound Dog (78), RCA Victor 20-6604

7/56, Don't Be Cruel/Hound Dog (45), RCA Victor 47-6604

9/56, Blue Suede Shoes/Tutti Frutti (78), RCA Victor 20-6636

9/56, Blue Suede Shoes/Tutti Frutti (45), RCA Victor 47-6636

9/56, I Got a Woman/I'm Counting on You (78), RCA Victor 20-6637

9/56, I Got a Woman/I'm Counting on You (45), RCA Victor 47-6637

9/56, I'll Never Let You Go (Little Darlin')/I'm Gonna Sit Right Down and Cry over You (78), RCA Victor 20-6638

9/56, I'll Never Let You Go (Little Darlin')/I'm Gonna Sit Right Down and Cry over You (45), RCA Victor 47-6638

9/56, Tryin' to Get to You/I Love You Because (78), RCA Victor 20-6639

9/56, Tryin' to Get to You/I Love You Because (45), RCA Victor 47-6639

9/56, Blue Moon/Just Because (78), RCA Victor 20-6640

9/56, Blue Moon/Just Because (45), RCA Victor 47-6640

9/56, Money Honey/One-Sided Love Affair (78), RCA Victor 20-6641

9/56, Money Honey/One-Sided Love Affair (45), RCA Victor 47-6641

9/56, Lawdy Miss Clawdy/Shake, Rattle and Roll (78), RCA Victor 20-6642

9/56, Lawdy Miss Clawdy/Shake, Rattle and Roll (45), RCA Victor 47-6642

9/56, *Elvis Presley* (EP), RCA Victor EPA-830

9/56, *The Real Elvis* (EP), RCA Victor EPA-940

10/56, Love Me Tender/Anyway You Want Me (That's How I Will Be) (78), RCA Victor 20-6643

10/56, Love Me Tender/Anyway You Want Me (That's How I Will Be) (45), RCA Victor 47-6643

10/56, *Anyway You Want Me* (EP), RCA Victor EPA-965

11/56, *Elvis* (LP), RCA Victor LPM-1382

11/56, *Love Me Tender* (EP), RCA Victor EPA-4006

11/56, *Elvis (Vol. 1)* (EP), RCA Victor EPA-992

11/56, *Elvis (Vol. 2)* (EP), RCA Victor EPA-993

11/56, *Strictly Elvis (Vol. 3)* (EP), RCA Victor EPA-994

1/57, Too Much/Playing for Keeps (78), RCA Victor 20-6800

1/57, Too Much/Playing for Keeps (45), RCA Victor 47-6800

3/57, All Shook Up/That's When Your Heartaches Begin (78), RCA Victor
    20-6870

3/57, All Shook Up/That's When Your Heartaches Begin (45), RCA Victor
    47-6870

3/57, *Just for You* (EP), RCA Victor EPA-4041

3/57, *Peace in the Valley* (EP), RCA Victor EPA-4054

6/57, (Let Me Be Your) Teddy Bear/Loving You (78), RCA Victor 20-7000

6/57, (Let Me Be Your) Teddy Bear/Loving You (45), RCA Victor 47-7000

7/57, *Loving You* (LP), RCA Victor LPM-1515

7/57, *Loving You (Vol. 1)* (EP), RCA Victor EPA 1-1515

7/57, *Loving You (Vol. 2)* (EP), RCA Victor EPA 2-1515

9/57, Jailhouse Rock/Treat Me Nice (78), RCA Victor 20-7035

9/57, Jailhouse Rock/Treat Me Nice (45), RCA Victor 47-7035

10/57, *Jailhouse Rock* (EP), RCA Victor EPA-4114

11/57, *Elvis' Christmas Album* (LP), RCA Victor LOC-1035

11/57, *Elvis Sings Christmas Songs* (EP), RCA Victor EPA-4108

1/58, Don't/I Beg of You (78), RCA Victor 20-7150

1/58, Don't/I Beg of You (45), RCA Victor 47-7150

4/58, *Elvis' Golden Records* (LP), RCA Victor LPM-1707

4/58, Wear My Ring Around Your Neck/Doncha Think It's Time (78),
    RCA Victor 20-7240

4/58, Wear My Ring Around Your Neck/Doncha Think It's Time (45),
    RCA Victor 47-7240

6/58, Hard Headed Woman/Don't Ask Me Why (78), RCA Victor 20-7280

6/58, Hard Headed Woman/Don't Ask Me Why (45), RCA Victor 47-7280

8/58, *King Creole* (LP), RCA Victor LPM-1884

8/58, *King Creole (Vol. 1)* (EP), RCA Victor EPA-4319

8/58, *King Creole (Vol. 2)* (EP), RCA Victor EPA-4321

10/58, *Elvis Sails* (EP), RCA Victor EPA-4325

10/58, One Night/I Got Stung (78), RCA Victor 20-7410

10/58, One Night/I Got Stung (45), RCA Victor 47-7410

11/58, *Elvis' Christmas Album* (LP), RCA Victor LPM-1951

11/58, *Christmas with Elvis* (EP), RCA Victor EPA-4340

3/59, *For LP Fans Only* (LP), RCA Victor LPM-1990

3/59, Mystery Train/I Forgot to Remember to Forget (Gold Standard) (45), RCA Victor 447-0600

3/59, That's All Right/Blue Moon of Kentucky (Gold Standard) (45), RCA Victor 447-4601

3/59, Good Rockin' Tonight/I Don't Care If the Sun Don't Shine (Gold Standard) (45), RCA Victor 447-0602

3/59, You're a Heartbreaker/Milkcow Blues Boogie (Gold Standard) (45), RCA Victor 447-0603

3/59, Baby Let's Play House/I'm Left, You're Right, She's Gone (Gold Standard) (45), RCA Victor 447-0604

3/59, Heartbreak Hotel/I Was the One (Gold Standard) (45), RCA Victor 447-0605

3/59, I Want You, I Need You, I Love You/My Baby Left Me (Gold Standard) (45), RCA Victor 447-0607

3/59, Don't Be Cruel/Hound Dog (Gold Standard) (45), RCA Victor 447-0608

3/59, Blue Suede Shoes/Tutti Frutti (Gold Standard) (45), RCA Victor 447-0609

3/59, I Got a Woman/I'm Counting on You (Gold Standard) (45), RCA Victor 447-0610

3/59, I'll Never Let You Go (Little Darlin')/I'm Gonne Sit Right Down and Cry (Over You) (Gold Standard) (45), RCA Victor 447-0611

3/59, Tryin' to Get to You/I Love You Because (Gold Standard) (45), RCA Victor 447-0612

3/59, Blue Moon/Just Because (Gold Standard) (45), RCA Victor 447-0613

3/59, Money Honey/One-Sided Love Affair (Gold Standard) (45), RCA Victor 447-0614

3/59, Lawdy Miss Clawdy/Shake, Rattle and Roll (Gold Standard) (45), RCA Victor 447-0615

3/59, Love Me Tender/Anyway You Want Me (That's How I'll Be) (Gold Standard) (45), RCA Victor 447-0616

3/59, Too Much/Playing for Keeps (Gold Standard) (45), RCA Victor 447-0617

3/59, All Shook Up/That's When Your Heartaches Begin (Gold Standard) (45), RCA Victor 447-0618

3/59, (Now and Then There's) A Fool Such As I/I Need Your Love Tonight (45), RCA Victor 47-7506

4/59, *A Touch of Gold (Vol. 1)* (Gold Standard) (EP), RCA Victor EPA-5088

7/59, A Big Hunk O' Love/My Wish Came True (45), RCA Victor 47-7600

9/59, *A Date with Elvis* (LP), RCA Victor LPM-2011

9/59, *A Touch of Gold (Vol. 2)* (Gold Standard) (EP), RCA Victor EPA-5088

11/59, *The Real Elvis* (Gold Standard) (EP), RCA Victor EPA-5120

11/59, *Peace in the Valley* (Gold Standard) (EP), RCA Victor EPA-5121

11/59, *King Creole* (Gold Standard) (EP), RCA Victor EPA-5122

12/59, *Elvis' Gold Records, Vol. 2 (50,000,000 Elvis Fans Can't Be Wrong)* (LP), RCA Victor LPM-2075

1/60, *A Touch of Gold, Vol. 3* (EP), RCA Victor EPA-5141

4/60, Stuck on You/Fame and Fortune (45), RCA Victor 47-7740

4/60, Stuck on You/Fame and Fortune (Living Stereo) (45), RCA Victor 61-7740

4/60, *Elvis Is Back!* (LP), RCA Victor LPM/LSP-2231

7/60, It's Now or Never/A Mess of Blues (45), RCA Victor 47-7777

7/60, It's Now or Never/A Mess of Blues (Living Stereo) (45), RCA Victor 61-7777

10/60, *G.I. Blues* (LP), RCA Victor LPM/LSP-2256

11/60, Are You Lonesome Tonight/I Gotta Know (45), RCA Victor 47-7810

11/60, Are You Lonesome Tonight/I Gotta Know (Living Stereo) (45), RCA Victor 61-7810

12/60, *His Hand in Mine* (LP), RCA Victor LPM/LSP 2328

1/61, *Elvis by Request (Flaming Star)* (EP), RCA Victor LPC-128

2/61, Surrender/Lonely Man (45), RCA Victor 47-7850

2/61, Surrender/Lonely Man (Living Stereo) (45), RCA Victor 47-7850

2/61, Surrender/Lonely Man (Compact 33 Single), RCA Victor 37-7850

2/61, Surrender/Lonely Man (Stereo Compact 33 Single), RCA Victor 68-7850

5/61, I Feel So Bad/Wild in the Country (45), RCA Victor 47-7880

5/61, I Feel So Bad/Wild in the Country (Compact 33 Single), RCA Victor 37-7880

6/61, *Something for Everybody* (LP), RCA Victor LPM/LSP 2370

8/61, (Marie's the Name) His Latest Flame/Little Sister (45), RCA Victor 47-7908

8/61, (Marie's the Name) His Latest Flame/Little Sister (Compact 33 Single), RCA Victor 37-7908

10/61, *Blue Hawaii* (LP), RCA Victor LPM/LSP-2426

12/61, Can't Help Falling in Love/Rock-a-Hula Baby (45), RCA Victor 47-7968

12/61, Can't Help Falling in Love/Rock-a-Hula Baby (Compact 33 Single), RCA Victor 37-7968

The following Gold Standard singles were issued in 1961, but exact month of release is unknown.

Jailhouse Rock/Treat Me Nice (Gold Standard) (45), RCA Victor 447-0619

(Let Me Be Your) Teddy Bear/Loving You (Gold Standard) (45), RCA Victor 447-0620

Don't/I Beg of You (Gold Standard) (45), RCA Victor 447-0621

Wear My Ring Around Your Neck/Doncha Think It's Time (Gold Standard) (45), RCA Victor 447-0622

Hard Headed Woman/Don't Ask Me Why (Gold Standard) (45), RCA Victor 447-0623

One Night/I Got Stung (Gold Standard) (45), RCA Victor 447-0624

(Now and Then There's) A Fool Such As I/I Need Your Love Tonight (Gold Standard) (45), RCA Victor 447-0625

2/62, A Big Hunk O' Love/My Wish Came True (Gold Standard) (45), RCA Victor 447-0626

2/62, Stuck on You/Fame and Fortune (Gold Standard) (45), RCA Victor 447-0627

2/62, It's Now or Never/A Mess of Blues (Gold Standard) (45), RCA Victor 447-0628

2/62, Are You Lonesome Tonight/I Gotta Know (Gold Standard) (45), RCA Victor 447-0629

2/62, Surrender/Lonely Man (Gold Standard) (45), RCA Victor 447-0630

2/62, I Feel So Bad/Wild in the Country (Gold Standard) (45), RCA Victor 447-0631

2/62, *Elvis Presley* (Electronically Reprocessed Stereo) (LP), RCA Victor LSP-1254(e)

2/62, *Elvis* (Electronically Reprocessed Stereo) (LP), RCA Victor LSP-1382(e)

2/62, *Loving You* (Electronically Reprocessed Stereo) (LP), RCA Victor LSP-1515(e)

2/62, *Elvis' Golden Records* (Electronically Reprocessed Stereo) (LP), RCA Victor LSP-1707(e)

2/62, *King Creole* (Electronically Reprocessed Stereo) (LP), RCA Victor LSP-1884(e)

2/62, *Elvis' Gold Records, Vol. 2 (50,000,000 Elvis Fans Can't Be Wrong)* (Electronically Reprocessed Stereo) (LP), RCA Victor LSP-2075(e)

3/62, Good Luck Charm/Anything That's Part of You (45), RCA Victor 47-7992

3/62, Good Luck Charm/Anything That's Part of You (Compact 33 Single), RCA Victor 37-7992

5/62, *Follow That Dream* (EP), RCA Victor EPA-4368

6/62, *Pot Luck* (LP), RCA Victor LPM/LSP-2523

7/62, She's Not You/Just Tell Her Jim Said Hello (45), RCA Victor 47-8041

9/62, *Kid Galahad* (EP), RCA Victor EPA-4371

10/62, Return to Sender/Where Do You Come From (45), RCA Victor 47-8100

11/62, *Girls! Girls! Girls!* (LP), RCA Victor LPM/LSP-2621

11/62, (Marie's the Name) His Latest Flame/Little Sister (Gold Standard) (45), RCA Victor 447-0634

11/62, Can't Help Falling in Love/Rock-a-Hula Baby (Gold Standard) (45), RCA Victor 447-0635

11/62, Good Luck Charm/Anything That's Part of You (Gold Standard) (45), RCA Victor 447-0636

2/63, One Broken Heart for Sale/They Remind Me Too Much of You (45), RCA Victor 47-8134

4/63, *It Happened at the World's Fair* (LP), RCA Victor LPM/LSP-2697

6/63, (You're the) Devil in Disguise/Please Don't Drag That String Along (45), RCA Victor 47-8188

6/63, She's Not You/Just Tell Her Jim Said Hello (Gold Standard) (45), RCA Victor 447-0637

6/63, Return to Sender/Where Do You Come From (Gold Standard) (45), RCA Victor 447-0638

9/63, *Elvis' Gold Records, Vol. 3* (LP), RCA Victor LPM/LSP-2765

10/63, Bossa Nova Baby/Witchcraft (45), RCA Victor 47-8243

1/64, Kissin' Cousins/It Hurts Me (45), RCA Victor 47-8307

3/64, *Kissin' Cousins* (LP), RCA Victor LPM/LSP-2894

4/64, Kiss Me Quick/Suspicion (Gold Standard) (45), RCA Victor 447-0639

4/64, Viva Las Vegas/What'd I Say (45), RCA Victor 47-8360

6/64, *Viva Las Vegas* (EP), RCA Victor EPA-4382

7/64, Such a Night/Never Ending (45), RCA Victor 47-8400

8/64, One Broken Heart for Sale/They Remind Me Too Much of You (Gold Standard) (45), RCA Victor 447-0640

8/64, (You're the) Devil in Disguise/Please Don't Drag That String Along (Gold Standard) (45), RCA Victor 447-0641

8/64, Bossa Nova Baby/Witchcraft (Gold Standard) (45), RCA Victor 447-0642

9/64, Ain't That Lovin' You Baby/Ask Me (45), RCA Victor 47-8440

10/64, *Roustabout* (LP), RCA Victor LPM/LSP-2999

11/64, Roustabout/One Track Heart (45), RCA Victor SP 45-139

11/64, Blue Christmas/Wooden Heart (Gold Standard) (45), RCA Victor 447-0720

11/64, *Elvis' Christmas Album* (Electronically Reprocessed Stereo) (LP), RCA Victor LSP-1951(e)

1/65, *For LP Fans Only* (Electronically Reprocessed Stereo) (LP), RCA Victor LSP-1990(e)

1/65, *A Date with Elvis* (Electronically Reprocessed Stereo) (LP), RCA Victor LSP-2011(e)

2/65, Do the Clam/You'll Be Gone (45), RCA Victor 47-8500

4/65, Crying in the Chapel/I Believe in the Man in the Sky (Gold Standard) (45), RCA Victor 447-0643

4/65, *Girl Happy* (LP), RCA Victor LPM/LSP-3338

5/65, Kissin' Cousins/It Hurts Me (Gold Standard) (45), RCA Victor 447-0644

5/65, Such a Night/Never Ending (Gold Standard) (45), RCA Victor 447-0645

5/65, Viva Las Vegas/What'd I Say (Gold Standard) (45), RCA Victor 447-0646

5/65, *Elvis Sails* (Gold Standard) (EP), RCA Victor EPA-5157

6/65, (Such an) Easy Question/It Feels So Right (45), RCA Victor 47-8585

6/65, *Tickle Me* (LP), RCA Victor LPM/LSP-4383

7/65, *Elvis for Everyone* (LP), RCA Victor LPM/LSP-3450

8/65, I'm Yours/(It's a) Long Lonely Highway (45), RCA Victor 47-8657

10/65, Puppet on a String/Wooden Heart (Gold Standard) (45), RCA Victor 447-0650

10/65, *Harum Scarum* (LP), RCA Victor LPM/LSP-3468

11/65, Blue Christmas/Santa Claus Is Back in Town (Gold Standard) (45), RCA Victor 447-0647

11/65, Do the Clam/You'll Be Gone (Gold Standard) (45), RCA Victor 447-0648

11/65, Ain't That Loving You Baby/Ask Me (Gold Standard) (45), RCA Victor 447-0649

1/66, Tell Me Why/Blue River (45), RCA Victor 47-8740

2/66, Joshua Fit the Battle/Known Only to Him (Gold Standard) (45), RCA Victor 447-0651

2/66, Milky White Way/Swing Down Sweet Chariot (Gold Standard) (45), RCA Victor 447-0652

3/66, Frankie and Johnny/Please Don't Stop Loving Me (45), RCA Victor 47-8780

4/66, *Frankie and Johnny* (LP), RCA Victor LPM/LSP-3553

6/66, *Paradise Hawaiian Style* (LP), RCA Victor LPM/LSP-3643

6/66, Love Letters/Come What May (45), RCA Victor 47-8870

9/66, Spinout/All That I Am (45), RCA Victor 47-8941

10/66, *Spinout* (LP), RCA Victor LPM/LSP-3702

11/66, (Such an) Easy Question/It Feels So Right (Gold Standard) (45), RCA Victor 447-0653

11/66, I'm Yours/(It's a) Long Lonely Highway (Gold Standard) (45), RCA Victor 447-0654

11/66, If Everyday Was Like Christmas/How Would You Like To Be (45), RCA Victor 47-8950

1/67, Indescribably Blue/Fools Fall in Love (45), RCA Victor 47-9056

2/67, *Easy Come, Easy Go* (EP), RCA Victor EPA-4387

3/67, *How Great Thou Art (as Sung by Elvis)* (LP), RCA Victor LPM/LSP-3758

4/67, How Great Thou Art/So High (45), RCA Victor SP 45-162

5/67, Long Legged Girl (with the Short Dress On)/That's Someone You Never Forget (45), RCA Victor 47-9115

6/67, *Double Trouble* (LP), RCA Victor LPM/LSP-3787

8/67, Judy/There's Always Me (45), RCA Victor 47-9287

9/67, Big Boss Man/You Don't Know Me (45), RCA Victor 47-9341

11/67, *Clambake* (LP), RCA Victor LPM/LSP-3893

1/68, Guitar Man/High Heel Sneakers (45), RCA Victor 47-9425

2/68, Tell Me Why/Blue River (Gold Standard) (45), RCA Victor 447-0655

2/68, Frankie and Johnny/Please Don't Stop Loving Me (Gold Standard) (45), RCA Victor 447-0656

2/68, Love Letters/Come What May (Gold Standard) (45), RCA Victor 447-0657

2/68, Spinout/All That I Am (Gold Standard) (45), RCA Victor 447-0658

2/68, *Elvis' Gold Records, Vol. 4* (LP), RCA Victor LPM/LSP-3921

3/68, U.S. Male/Stay Away (45), RCA Victor 47-9465

4/68, You'll Never Walk Alone/We Call on Him (45), RCA Victor 47-9600

6/68, Your Time Hasn't Come Yet Baby/Let Yourself Go (45), RCA Victor 47-9547

6/68, *Speedway* (LP), RCA Victor LPM/LSP-3989

9/68, A Little Less Conversation/Almost in Love (45), RCA Victor 47-9610

11/68, If I Can Dream/Edge of Reality (45), RCA Victor 47-9670

12/68, *Elvis* (NBC TV Special) (LP), RCA Victor LPM-4088

3/69, Memories/Charro (45), RCA Victor 47-9731

4/69, How Great Thou Art/His Hand in Mine (45), RCA Victor 47-0130

4/69, *Elvis Sings Flaming Star* (LP), RCA/Camden CAS-2304

4/69, In the Ghetto/Any Day Now (45), RCA Victor 47-9731

5/69, *From Elvis in Memphis* (LP), RCA Victor LSP-4155

6/69, Clean Up Your Own Back Yard/The Fair Is Moving On (45), RCA Victor 47-9747

9/69, Suspicious Minds/You'll Think of Me (45), RCA Victor 47-9764

11/69, *From Memphis to Vegas/From Vegas to Memphis* (LP), RCA Victor LSP-6020

11/69, Don't Cry Daddy/Rubberneckin' (45), RCA Victor 47-9768

2/70, Kentucky Rain/My Little Friend (45), RCA Victor 47-791

4/70, *Let's Be Friends* (LP), RCA/Camden CAS-2408

5/70, The Wonder of You/Mama Liked the Roses (45), RCA Victor 47-9835

6/70, *On Stage—February, 1970* (LP), RCA Victor LSP-4362

7/70, I've Lost You/The Next Step Is Love (45), RCA Victor 47-9873

8/70, *Worldwide 50 Gold Award Hits, Vol. 1* (LP), RCA Victor LPM-6401

10/70, You Don't Have to Say You Love Me/Patch It Up (45), RCA Victor 47-9916

11/70, *Elvis in Person at the International Hotel, Las Vegas, Nevada* (LP), RCA Victor LSP-4428

11/70, *Elvis Back in Memphis* (LP), RCA Victor LSP-4429

11/70, *Elvis' Christmas Album* (LP), RCA/Camden CAL-2428

11/70, *Almost in Love* (LP), RCA/Camden CAS-2440

12/70, I Really Don't Want to Know/There Goes My Everything (45), RCA Victor 47-9960

12/70, *Elvis—That's the Way It Is* (LP), RCA Victor LSP-4445

12/70, You'll Never Walk Alone/We Call on Him (Gold Standard) (45), RCA Victor 447-0665

12/70, Your Time Hasn't Come Yet Baby/Let Yourself Go (Gold Standard) (45), RCA Victor 447-0666

12/70, A Little Less Conversation/Almost in Love (Gold Standard) (45), RCA Victor 447-0667

12/70, If I Can Dream/Edge of Reality (Gold Standard) (45), RCA Victor 447-0668

12/70, Memories/Charro (Gold Standard) (45), RCA Victor 447-0669

12/70, How Great Thou Art/His Hand in Mine (Gold Standard) (45), RCA Victor 447-0670

12/70, In the Ghetto/Any Day Now (Gold Standard) (45), RCA Victor 447-0671

12/70, Clean Up Your Own Back Yard/The Fair Is Moving On (Gold Standard) (45), RCA Victor 447-0672

12/70, Suspicious Minds/You'll Think of Me (Gold Standard) (45), RCA Victor 447-0673

The following Gold Standard singles were issued in 1970, but exact month of release is unknown.

Indescribably Blue/Fools Fall in Love (Gold Standard) (45), RCA Victor 447-0659

Long Legged Girl (with the Short Dress On)/That's Someone You Never Forget (Gold Standard) (45), RCA Victor 447-0660

Judy/There's Always Me (Gold Standard) (45), RCA Victor 447-0661

Big Boss Man/You Don't Know Me (Gold Standard) (45), RCA Victor 447-0662

Guitar Man/High Heel Sneakers (Gold Standard) (45), RCA Victor 447-0663

U.S. Male/Stay Away (Gold Standard) (45), RCA Victor 447-0664

1/71, *Elvis Country* (LP), RCA Victor LSP-4460

2/71, Rags to Riches/Where Did They Go Lord (45), RCA Victor 47-9980

3/71, *You'll Never Walk Alone* (LP), RCA/Camden CALX-2472

5/71, Life/Only Believe (45), RCA Victor 47-4530

5/71, *Love Letters from Elvis* (LP), RCA Victor LSP-4530

7/71, I'm Leavin'/Heart of Rome (45), RCA Victor 47-9998

8/71, *Worldwide Gold Award Hits, Volume 2* (LP), RCA Victor LPM-6402

8/71, Kentucky Rain/My Little Friend (Gold Standard) (45), RCA Victor 447-0675

8/71, The Wonder of You/Mama Liked the Roses (Gold Standard) (45), RCA Victor 447-0676

8/71, I've Lost You/The Next Step Is Love (Gold Standard) (45), RCA Victor 447-0677

9/71, *C'mon Everybody* (LP), RCA/Camden CAL-2518

9/71, It's Only Love/The Sound of Your Cry (45), RCA Victor 48-1017

10/71, *I Got Lucky* (LP), RCA/Camden CAL-2533

10/71, *Elvis Sings the Wonderful World of Christmas* (LP), RCA Victor LSP-4579

12/71, Merry Christmas Baby/O Come All Ye Faithful (45), RCA Victor 74-0572

1/72, Until It's Time for You to Go/We Can Make the Morning (45), RCA Victor 74-0619

2/72, *Elvis Now* (LP), RCA Victor LSP-4671

2/72, You Don't Have to Say You Love Me/Patch It Up (Gold Standard) (45), RCA Victor 447-0678

2/72, I Really Don't Want to Know/There Goes My Everything (Gold Standard) (45), RCA Victor 447-0679

2/72, Rags to Riches/Where Did They Go Lord (Gold Standard) (45), RCA Victor 447-0680

3/72, He Touched Me/Bosom of Abraham (45), RCA Victor 74-0651

4/72, *He Touched Me* (LP), RCA Victor LSP-4690

4/72, An American Trilogy/The First Time Ever I Saw Your Face (45), RCA Victor 74-0672

5/72, If Everyday Was Like Christmas/How Would You Like to Be (Gold Standard) (45), RCA Victor 447-0681

5/72, Life/Only Believe (Gold Standard) (45), RCA Victor 447-0682

5/72, I'm Leavin'/Heart of Rome (Gold Standard) (45), RCA Victor 447-0683

5/72, It's Only Love/The Sound of Your Cry (Gold Standard) (45), RCA Victor 447-0683

6/72, *Elvis Sings Hits from His Movies, Vol. 1* (LP), RCA/Camden CAS-2567

6/72, *Elvis as Recorded at Madison Square Garden* (LP), RCA Victor LSP-4776

8/72, Burning Love/It's a Matter of Time (45), RCA Victor 74-0679

11/72, *Burning Love and Hits from His Movies, Vol. 2* (LP), RCA/Camden CAS-2595

11/72, Separate Ways/Always on My Mind (45), RCA Victor 74-0815

1/73, *Separate Ways* (LP), RCA/Cadmen CAS-2611

2/73, *Aloha from Hawaii via Satellite* (LP), RCA Victor VPSX-6089

3/73, *Almost in Love* (LP), RCA/Camden CAS-2440

4/73, Steamroller Blues/Fool (45), RCA Victor 74-0910

5/73, An American Trilogy/Until It's Time for You to Go (Gold Standard) (45), RCA Victor 447-0685

7/73, *Elvis (Including "Fool")* (LP), RCA Victor APL1-0283

9/73, Raised on Rock/For Ol' Times Sake (45), RCA Victor APBO-0088

11/73, *Raised on Rock/For Ol' Times Sake* (LP), RCA Victor APL1-0388

1/74, I've Got a Thing About You Baby/Take Good Care of Her (45), RCA Victor APBO-0196

1/74, *Elvis: A Legendary Performer (Vol. 1)* (LP), RCA Victor CPL1-0341

3/74, *Good Times* (LP), RCA Victor CPL1-0475

5/74, If You Talk in Your Sleep/Help Me (45), RCA Victor APBO-0280

6/74, *Elvis Recorded Live on Stage in Memphis* (LP), RCA Victor CPL1-0606

6/74, *Elvis Recorded Live on Stage in Memphis* (quad) (LP), RCA Victor APD1-0606

10/74, Promised Land/It's Midnight (45), RCA Victor PB-10074

1/75, My Boy/Thinking About You (45), RCA Victor PB-10191

1/75, *Promised Land* (LP), RCA Victor APL1-0873

3/75, Steamroller Blues/Fool (Gold Standard) (45), RCA Victor GB-10156

3/75, If You Talk in Your Sleep/Raised on Rock (Gold Standard) (45), RCA Victor GB-10157

4/75, T-R-O-U-B-L-E/Mr. Songman (45), RCA Victor PB-10278

5/75, *Elvis Today* (LP), RCA Victor APL1-1039

6/75, *Pure Gold* (LP), RCA Victor ANL1-0971(e)

10/75, Bringing It Back/Pieces of My Life (45), RCA Victor PB-10401

12/75, *Elvis Sings Flaming Star* (LP), Pickwick/Camden CAS-2304

12/75, *Let's Be Friends* (LP), Pickwick/Camden CAS-2408

12/75, *Almost in Love* (LP), Pickwick/Camden CAS-2440

12/75, *Elvis' Christmas Album* (LP), Pickwick/Camden CAS-2448

12/75, *You'll Never Walk Alone* (LP), Pickwick/Camden CAS-2472

12/75, *C'mon Everybody* (LP), Pickwick/Camden CAS-2518

12/75, *I Got Lucky* (LP), Pickwick/Camden CAS-2553

12/75, *Elvis Sings Hits from His Movies, Vol. 1* (LP), Pickwick/Camden CAS-2567

12/75, *Burning Love and Hits from His Movies, Vol. 2* (LP), Pickwick/Camden CAS-2595

12/75, *Separate Ways* (LP), Pickwick/Camden CAS-2611

12/75, *Double Dynamite* (LP), Pickwick/Camden DL2-5001

1/76, *Elvis in Hollywood* (LP), RCA Victor DPL2-0168

1/76, *Elvis: A Legendary Performer, Vol. 2* (LP), RCA Victor CPL1-1349

2/76, I've Got a Thing About You Baby/Take Good Care of Her (Gold Standard) (45), RCA Victor GB-10485

2/76, Separate Ways/Always on My Mind (Gold Standard) (45), RCA Victor GB-10486

2/76, T-R-O-U-B-L-E/Mr. Songman (Gold Standard) (45), RCA Victor GB-10487

2/76, Promised Land/It's Midnight (Gold Standard) (45), RCA Victor GB-10488

2/76, My Boy/Thinking About You (Gold Standard) (45), RCA Victor GB-10489

3/76, *The Sun Sessions* (LP), RCA Victor APM1-1675

3/76, *His Hand in Mine* (LP), RCA Victor ANL1-1319

3/76, Hurt/For the Heart (45), RCA Victor PB-10601

5/76, *From Elvis Presley Boulevard, Memphis, Tennessee* (LP), RCA Victor APL1-1506

8/76, *Elvis—A Collectors Edition* (LP), RCA Victor TB-1

12/76, Moody Blue/She Thinks I Still Care (45), RCA Victor PB-10857

3/77, *Welcome to My World* (LP), RCA Victor APL1-2274

7/77, Way Down/Pledging My Love (45), RCA Victor PB-10998

9/77, *Harum Scarum* (LP), RCA Victor APL1-2558

9/77, *Frankie and Johnny* (LP), RCA Victor APL1-2559

9/77, *Spinout* (LP), RCA Victor APL1-2560

9/77, *Double Trouble* (LP), RCA Victor APL1-2561

9/77, *Clambake* (LP), RCA Victor APL1-2562

9/77, *It Happened at the World's Fair* (LP), RCA Victor APL1-2563

10/77, *Elvis in Concert* (LP), RCA Victor APL2-2587

10/77, *15 Golden Records/30 Golden Hits* (45), RCA Victor PP-11301

11/77, My Way/America the Beautiful (45), RCA Victor PB-11165

11/77, *Good Times* (LP), RCA Victor CPL1-0475

11/77, *Elvis Recorded Live on Stage in Memphis* (LP), RCA Victor CPL1-0606

12/77, *20 Golden Hits in Full Color Sleeves* (45), RCA Victor PP-11340

3/78, Softly, As I Leave You/Unchained Melody (45), RCA Victor PB-11212

4/78, *He Walks Beside Me* (LP), RCA Victor AFL1-2772

6/78, *Mahalo from Elvis* (LP), Pickwick/Camden ACL-7064

7/78, *Elvis Sings for Children and Grownups Too!* (LP), RCA Victor CPL1-2901

8/78, (Let Me Be Your) Teddy Bear/Puppet on a String (45), RCA Victor PB-11320

8/78, Moody Blue/For the Heart (Gold Standard) (45), RCA Victor GB-11326

9/78, *Worldwide Gold Award Hits, Parts 3 and 4* (LP), RCA Victor R-214657

9/78, *From Elvis with Love* (LP), RCA Victor R-234340

9/78, *Elvis—Legendary Concert Performances* (LP), RCA Victor R-244047

9/78, *Country Memories* (LP), RCA Victor R-244069

9/78, *Memories of Elvis* (LP), RCA Victor DML5-0347

9/78, *The Greatest Show on Earth* (LP), RCA Victor DML1-0348

9/78, *Elvis Commemorative Album* (LP), RCA Victor DPL2-0056(e)

12/78, *Elvis: A Legendary Performer, Vol. 3* (LP), RCA Victor CPL1-3082

2/79, *Our Memories of Elvis* (LP), RCA Victor AQL1-3279

5/79, Are You Sincere/Solitaire (45), RCA Victor PB-11533

5/79, Way Down/My Way (Gold Standard) (45), RCA Victor GB-11504

8/79, There's a Honky Tonk Angel (Who Will Take Me Back In)/I Got a Feelin' in My Body (45), RCA Victor PB-11679

8/79, *Our Memories of Elvis (More of the Pure Elvis Sound)* (LP), RCA Victor AQL1-3449

8/79, *Pure Elvis* (LP), RCA Victor DJL1-3455

10/79, *The Legendary Recordings of Elvis Presley* (LP), RCA Victor DML6-0412

3/80, *Elvis Country Classics* (LP), RCA Victor R-233299(e)

4/80, *This Is Elvis* (LP), RCA Victor CPL2-4031

5/80, Are You Sincere/Unchained Melody (Gold Standard) (45), RCA Victor GB-11988

5/80, *Blue Hawaii* (Best Buy series) (LP), RCA Victor AYL1-3732

5/80, *Spinout* (Best Buy series) (LP), RCA Victor AYL1-3684

7/80, *Elvis Aron Presley* (LP), RCA Victor CPL8-3699

10/80, *The Legendary Magic of Elvis Presley* (LP), RCA Victor DVL1-0461

11/80, *Pure Gold* (Best Buy series) (LP), RCA Victor AYL1-3732

11/80, *King Creole* (Best Buy series) (LP), RCA Victor AYL1-3733

11/80, *G.I. Blues* (Best Buy series) (LP), RCA Victor AYL1-3735

1/81, Guitar Man/Faded Love (45), RCA Victor PB-12158

2/81, *Elvis in Person at the International Hotel, Las Vegas, Nevada* (Best Buy series) (LP), RCA Victor AYL1-3892

2/81, *The Sun Sessions* (Best Buy series) (LP), RCA Victor AYM1-3893

2/81, *Elvis (NBC TV Special)* (Best Buy series) (LP), RCA Victor AYM1-3894

4/81, Lovin' Arms/You Asked Me To (45), RCA Victor PB-12205

5/81, *His Hand in Mine* (Best Buy series) (LP), AYM1-3935

5/81, *Elvis Country* (Best Buy series) (LP), AYM1-3936

9/81, *Elvis—That's the Way It Is* (Best Buy series) (LP), RCA Victor AYM1-4114

9/81, *Kissin' Cousins* (Best Buy series) (LP), RCA Victor AYM1-4115

9/81, *Something for Everybody* (Best Buy series) (LP), RCA Victor AYM1-4116

11/81, *Elvis—Greatest Hits, Vol. 1* (LP), RCA Victor AHL1-2347

2/82, *Elvis for Everyone* (Best Buy series) (LP), RCA Victor AYM1-4332

2/82, You'll Never Walk Alone/There Goes My Everything (45), RCA Victor PB-13058

4/82, *Double Dynamite* (LP), RCA/Pair PDL2-1010

8/82, *Memories of Christmas* (LP), RCA Victor CPL1-4395

11/82, The Elvis Medley/Always on My Mind (45), RCA Victor PB-13351

11/82, *The Elvis Medley* (LP), RCA Victor AHL1-4530

1/83, Suspicious Minds/You'll Think of Me (Gold Standard) (45), RCA Victor GB-13275

4/83, I Was the One/Wear My Ring Around Your Neck (45), RCA Victor PB-13500

5/83, *I Was the One* (LP), RCA Victor AHL1-4678

6/83, Little Sister/Paralyzed (45), RCA Victor PB-13547

11/83, *A Country Christmas, Vol. 2* (LP), RCA Victor AYL1-4809

11/83, *Elvis: A Legendary Performer (Vol. 4)* (LP), RCA Victor CPL1-4848

11/83, *Remembering Elvis* (LP), RCA/Pair PDL2-1037

1/84, *Elvis—HBO Special* (LP), RCA Victor DVM1-0704

2/84, *Elvis' Gold Records, Vol. 5* (LP), RCA Victor AFL1-4941

5/84, *The Beginning Years* (LP), Louisiana Hayride LH-3061

6/84, *The Elvis Presley Collection* (LP), RCA Victor DML3-0632

8/84, Baby Let's Play House/Hound Dog (45), RCA Victor PB-13875

8/84, *Elvis' Golden Records* (LP), RCA Victor AFM1-5196

8/84, *Elvis' Gold Records, Vol. 2 (50,000,000 Elvis Fans Can't Be Wrong)* (LP), RCA Victor AFM1-5197

8/84, *Elvis Presley* (LP), RCA Victor AFM1-5198

8/84, *Elvis* (LP), RCA Victor AFM1-5199

8/84, *A Golden Celebration* (LP), RCA Victor CPM6-5172

10/84, *The Savage Young Elvis* (cassette), RCA Victor DPK1-0679

11/84, *Elvis Country* (LP), RCA Victor DPL1-0647

11/84, *Rocker* (LP), RCA Victor AFM1-5182 (LP)

12/84, *Elvis' Greatest Hits—Golden Singles, Vol. 1* (45), RCA Victor PB-13897

12/84, *Elvis' Greatest Hits—Golden Singles, Vol. 2* (45), RCA Victor PB-13898

12/84, Blue Suede Shoes/Promised Land (45), RCA Victor PB-13929

1/85, *Elvis: 50 Years—50 Hits* (LP), RCA Victor SVL3-0710

4/85, *Reconsider Baby* (LP), RCA Victor AFL1-5418

6/85, Always on My Mind/My Boy (45), RCA Victor PB-14090

6/85, *Always on My Mind* (LP), RCA Victor AFL1-5430

7/85, *Rock and Roll—The Early Days* (LP), RCA Victor AFM1-5463

7/85, *Elvis' Christmas Album* (LP), RCA Victor AFM1-5486

12/85, Merry Christmas Baby/Santa Claus Is Back in Town (45), RCA Victor PB-14237

4/86, *Elvis—Return of the Rocker* (LP), RCA Victor 5600-1-R

4/86, *Elvis: His Songs of Faith and Inspiration* (LP), RCA Victor DVL2-0728

8/86, *Elvis: The Legend Lives On* (LP), RCA Victor RBA-191/A

The following were issued in 1986, but exact month is not known.

You're a Heartbreaker/Milkcow Blues Boogie (45), Collectables 4501

Baby, Let's Play House/I'm Left, You're Right, She's Gone (45), Collectables 4502

I Got a Woman/I'm Counting on You (45), Collectables 4503

I'll Never Let You Go (Little Darlin')/I'm Gonna Sit Right Down and Cry (Over You) (45), Collectables 4504

Tryin' to Get to You/I Love You Because (45), Collectables 4505

Money Honey/One-Sided Love Affair (45), Collectables 4506

Too Much/Playing for Keeps (45), Collectables 4507

A Big Hunk O' Love/My Wish Came True (45), Collectables 4508

Stuck on You/Fame and Fortune (45), Collectables 4509

I Feel So Bad/Wild in the Country (45), Collectables 4510

She's Not You/Jailhouse Rock (45), Collectables 4511

One Broken Heart for Sale/Devil in Disguise (45), Collectables 4512

Bossa Nova Baby/Such a Night (45), Collectables 4513

Love Me/Flaming Star (45), Collectables 4514

Follow That Dream/When My Blue Moon Turns to Gold Again (45), Collectables 4515

Frankie and Johnny/Love Letters (45), Collectables 4516

U.S. Male/Until It's Time for You to Go (45), Collectables 4517

Old Shep/You'll Never Walk Alone (45), Collectables 4518

Poor Boy/An American Trilogy (45), Collectables 4519

How Great Thou Art/His Hand in Mine (45), Collectables 4520

Big Boss Man/Paralyzed (45), Collectables 4521

Fools Fall in Love/Blue Suede Shoes (45), Collectables 4522

7/87, *The Memphis Record* (LP), RCA Victor 6221-1-R

7/87, *Elvis Talks!* (LP), RCA Victor 6313-1-R

7/87, *The Number One Hits* (LP), RCA Victor 6382-1-R

7/87, *The Top Ten Hits* (LP), RCA Victor 6383-1-R

7/87, *The Complete Sun Sessions* (LP), RCA Victor 6414-1-R

8/87, *Elvis Presley: Great Hits of 1956-57* (LP), RCA Victor RBA-072/D

1/88, *Essential Elvis* (LP), RCA Victor 6738-1-R

1/88, *Good Rockin' Tonight* (LP), RCA Victor SVL2-0824

5/88, *Elvis, Scotty & Bill: 1954–1955, The Beginning* (LP), Marvenco 101

6/88, *Elvis, The Alternate Aloha* (LP), RCA 6985-1-R

7/88, *Elvis Aron Presley "Forever"* (LP), Pair PDL2-1185

8/88, *Elvis (With Ray Green Backstage)* (LP), Creative Radio Network CRN-E1

DYNAFLEX: THE REAL STORY

There has been a great deal of confusion as to how Dynaflex fits into the story of the RCA orange label. According to RCA, Dynaflex discs were both *dyna*mic and *flex*ible. Well, they certainly were flexible, at least in the beginning. For the official explanation of Dynaflex, see the back cover of any RCA or Camden LP issued between March 1971 and February 1972 (except *C'mon Everybody*).

The date of March 1971 may surprise Elvis discographers who thought *Love Letters* (May 1971) was the first Dynaflex Elvis album. That distinction must go, in fact, to *Worldwide 50 Gold Award Hits, Volume 1,* an August 1970 release, which was the first standard Elvis catalog orange RCA flexi press, though not yet named Dynaflex. The theory that *all* orange label LPs before *Love Letters* were first pressed on rigid, then later (1972–1975) on Dynaflex, is absolutely untrue. RCA was using the flexible discs for several months before they actually identified the process on covers and later on labels as Dynaflex.

The first Elvis LP bearing the Dynaflex identification was *You'll Never Walk Alone,* issued two months before *Love Letters.* The back cover of *You'll Never Walk Alone* was the first to carry the pitch about Dynaflex.

From *Love Letters* through *Promised Land* (January 1975) most Elvis LPs had the Dynaflex name at the bottom of the record label. Among the exceptions were the quad releases, labeled "QuadraDisc," of which there were three during that time: *Aloha from Hawaii via Satellite, Elvis Recorded Live on Stage in Memphis,* and *Promised Land. Elvis—A Legendary Performer,* with its custom label, is another exception.

From *You'll Never Walk Alone* to *Promised Land,* the degree of Dynaflex flexibility varied considerably. Some were paper-thin and could be rolled up like cigarette paper. Other Dynaflex issues were flexible, but not as flimsy. Among the more rigid were *Elvis As Recorded at Madison Square Garden, Elvis (Including 'Fool'),* and *Elvis* (Brookville LP).

Advance promotional copies of *Worldwide 50 Gold Award Hits, Volume 1, Elvis in Person at the International Hotel, Las Vegas, Nevada, Elvis Back in Memphis, Elvis—That's the Way It Is,* and *Elvis Country* were all on the flexible discs.

We have verified this not only by researching several of the foremost Elvis collections, but by reviewing other 1970 RCA LPs as well. We were especially careful to check the collections of dee jays who received promo copies during the summer of 1970. RCA was making widespread use of the flexible format by mid-1970, on albums by nearly everyone on the label: from Perry Como to Charley Pride. The August 1970 release of *Perry Como in Person at the International Hotel, Las Vegas, Nevada,* was issued only on the flexible discs, for example.

From the standpoint of evaluating records, to devalue these obvious first pressings to any extent would be foolish indeed. There was no special promotional pressing of any LP from this period; they were simply commercial copies identified as promos with adhesive stickers, and so on.

There is no doubt the four orange label LPs issued before August 1970 were first produced on rigid vinyl. They were *Elvis (NBC-TV Special), From Elvis in Memphis, From Memphis to Vegas/From Vegas to Memphis,* and *On Stage—February 1970.* Only these four have a "first pressing" premium allowed for rigid vinyl copies.

Promised Land was the last standard catalog Presley LP to actually mention Dynaflex, but RCA was still using the name as late as 1976. Tan label RCA Record Club issues of *Aloha from Hawaii via Satellite* have Dynaflex

Photo courtesy of Jim Reid.

on the label, placing it among the last Elvis LPs (standard catalog or otherwise) to be so designated. However, many subsequent albums were pressed in an almost-Dynaflex fashion. Even the 1984 "Digitally Remastered Quality Pressings On Heavy Virgin Vinyl" series of reissues were more pliant than the LPs manufactured before 1971. At least the quality of vinyl used on these remastered LPs was superior to predecessors.

THE LOST SINGLE IS STILL LOST!

In 1980 when we first published *Presleyana,* we brought nine Elvis songs to the attention of RCA—nine tracks that originally appeared on RCA singles but had never been included in an LP collection. Within a year all but one, "Come What May," was available on an RCA LP. We then brought this oversight to their attention, hoping that it would soon be rectified. No such luck.

To everyone's surprise, "Come What May" is still unavailable on LP. With all of the special album packages and collector's issues that have been released, one cannot help but wonder how they can overlook this important track. *When* RCA finally gets around to including "Come What May" on an LP, perhaps they will go the extra mile and present it in true stereo.

STEREO UPDATE

Fortunately, many of the post-army Elvis songs that had not previously appeared in true stereo have been released in that form during the past eight years.

Since then, we have made a thorough search of all of Elvis' recordings, looking for every post-army recording that has yet to appear in true stereo in the United States. Some of these tunes have been released in stereo in Europe, though a few others were probably recorded only in monaural:

A Whistling Tune. All six songs on the *Kid Galahad* EP appear to have been recorded in monaural only. None of them have turned up in stereo *anywhere.*

America (the Beautiful). Both this tune and "Softly As I Leave You" were probably recorded on cassette and only in monaural.

Baby What You Want Me to Do. From the live arena show recorded for the '68 TV special. Probably recorded only in monaural.

Britches. Recorded August 8, 1960, along with "Summer Kisses, Winter Tears," "Flaming Star," and "Cane and a High Starched Collar." Only

"Flaming Star" has been issued in stereo from this session, leaving it up in the air as to whether the other three were recorded in stereo. It certainly seems likely that they would have been.

Cane and a High Starched Collar. See comment for "Britches."

Come What May. Never heard in stereo because it's never been on a U.S. LP. Definitely recorded in stereo, from the May 1966 sessions.

Dark Moon. Recorded in monaural.

Earth Angel. Recorded in monaural.

Easy Come, Easy Go. All six songs contained on the original EP have been issued in stereo, most notably on the *Easy Come, Easy Go* LP, released in New Zealand in 1967. None have been released in stereo in the U.S.

Follow That Dream. The original EP version of this tune has never appeared in stereo, though it most certainly was recorded in stereo since an alternate take appeared in stereo on "Elvis Aron Presley."

Fools Fall in Love. Recorded immediately after "Come What May," in May 1966. These were the only two tracks from those sessions that have not been issued in stereo.

Forget Me Never. Neither this song nor "In My Way," from the October 1960 session have appeared in stereo. From this same session, "Lonely Man" and "I Slipped, I Stumbled, I Fell" have been issued in stereo. Because both "In My Way" and "Forget Me Never" are just Elvis and a guitar, it's possible they were done only in monaural.

He's Only a Prayer Away. Recorded in monaural.

Home Is Where the Heart Is. See comment for "A Whistling Tune."

I Got Lucky. See comment for "A Whistling Tune."

I Need Somebody to Lean On. All of the songs from the *Viva Las Vegas* EP have been issued in both England and New Zealand, and perhaps elsewhere, in stereo. So far, U.S. buyers have been denied these fine stereo recordings.

If Everyday Was Like Christmas. The release of an alternate take of this song in stereo, on *Memories Of Christmas,* leaves no doubt about the stereo existence of the original single version. We just haven't heard it yet.

If You Think I Don't Need You. See comment for "I Need Somebody To Lean On."

I'll Take Love. See comment for "Easy Come, Easy Go."

I'm Beginning to Forget You. Recorded in monaural.

I'm Not the Marrying Kind. This song and "What A Wonderful Life," from the *Follow That Dream* EP, have never been heard in stereo. Surely they were recorded in stereo since "Follow That Dream" and "Angel" have been issued in stereo.

In My Way. See comment for "Forget Me Never."

I've Lost You. Everything from the June 1970 sessions, except "I've Lost You" and "Patch It Up" has been issued in stereo. A live recording, in stereo, of these two tracks can be heard on *Elvis—That's The Way It Is*, but so far the studio versions have appeared only in monaural.

King of the Whole Wide World. See comment for "A Whistling Tune."

Let's Forget about the Stars. The *Let's Be Friends* LP states that this song was recorded only in monaural. If so, it would be the only track from the *Change of Habit* session that wasn't recorded in stereo.

Mama. The *Let's Be Friends* LP states that this song was recorded only in monaural. If so, it and "Plantation Rock" would be the only tracks from the *Girls! Girls! Girls!* session that wasn't recorded in stereo.

Patch It Up. See comment for "I've Lost You."

Riding the Rainbow. See comment for "A Whistling Tune."

Sing You Children. See comment for "Easy Come, Easy Go."

Softly, As I Leave You. See comment for "America the Beautiful."

Sound Advice. As with the other songs recorded for *Follow That Dream*, this probably exists in stereo.

Stay Away. The *Almost In Love* LP states that this song was recorded only in monaural. If so, it would be the only track from the *Stay Away Joe* session that wasn't recorded in stereo.

Summer Kisses, Winter Tears. See comment for "Britches."

The Love Machine. See comment for "Easy Come, Easy Go."

This Is Living. See comment for "A Whistling Tune."

Tiger Man. The only version known to exist, except for the "Mystery Train"/"Tiger Man" medley, is from the live recordings made for the '68 special, which were probably recorded only in monaural.

Today, Tomorrow and Forever. See comment for "I Need Somebody To Lean On."

Viva Las Vegas. Even though this track wasn't on the EP of the same title, it has been available overseas in stereo since 1967, along with the other *Viva Las Vegas* tunes.

What a Wonderful Life. See comment for "I'm Not The Marrying Kind."

Wild in the Country. The stereo alternate take on *Elvis Aron Presley* confirms that the original single version was recorded in stereo.

Yoga Is As Yoga Does. See comment for "Easy Come, Easy Go."

There you have 44 post-army Elvis recordings that have never been made available to U.S. fans in true stereo. Of these, many were definitely recorded in stereo and probably could be released at any time.

Singles

All of Elvis' U.S. singles, commercial and promotional, are listed alphabetically in this chapter.

When a 78rpm single was issued on a particular title, it is listed before the 45 version. Generally, all releases of a given single are listed in chronological order.

Picture sleeves are listed separately, as they are often bought and sold separately.

Remember, most used records will fall somewhere below the Near-Mint price range. Keep the spread in mind when evaluating your records. Refer to our section on Record Grading for more information on this.

Finally, if you look up a particular Elvis title and do not find it listed, check the flip side of the disc. A complete listing of flip sides can be found on page 141.

LISTINGS

A BIG HUNK O' LOVE/My Wish Came True
RCA Victor 47-7600 . . . . *7/59*   **10–15**
Black label, dog on top.

RCA Victor 47-7600 . . . . *7/59*   **25–35**
Picture sleeve.

RCA Victor 447-0626 . . . *2/62*   **10–12**
Gold Standard; black label, dog on top.

RCA Victor 447-0626 . . . . *65*   **4–8**
Gold Standard; black label, dog on side.

RCA Victor 447-0626 . . . . *68*   **8–10**
Gold Standard; orange label.

RCA Victor 447-0626 . . . . *70*   **3–5**
Gold Standard; red label.

Collectables 4508 . . . . *86*   **1–3**

A FOOL SUCH AS I/I Need Your Love Tonight
RCA Victor 47-7506 . . . . *3/59*   **10–15**
Black label, dog on top.

RCA Victor 47-7506 . . . . *3/59*   **150–200**
Picture sleeve; with promotion of *Elvis Sails* EP on back of sleeve.

RCA Victor 47-7506 . . . . *4/59*   **25–35**
Picture sleeve; with listing of Elvis EPs and Gold Standard singles on back.

RCA Victor 447-0625 . . . . *61*   **10–12**
Gold Standard; black label, dog on top.

RCA Victor 447-0625 . . . . *65*   **4–8**
Gold Standard; black label, dog on side.

RCA Victor 447-0625 . . . . *68*   **8–10**
Orange label.

RCA Victor 447–0625 . . . . *70*   **3–5**
Gold Standard; red label.

RCA Victor 447-0625 . . . . *77*   **2–3**
Black label, dog near top.
Note: Listed here and shown on the picture sleeves as "A Fool Such as I," even though the

record label gives the full title as "(Now and Then There's) A Fool Such As I."

A LITTLE LESS CONVERSATION/Almost in Love

RCA Victor 47-9610 . . . . *9/68*   **5–8**
Black label, dog on side.

RCA Victor 47-9610 . . . . *9/68*   **10–15**
Picture sleeve.

RCA Victor 47-9610 . . . . *9/68*   **10–15**
Yellow label, promotional issue only.

RCA Victor 447-0667 . . *12/70*   **3–5**
Gold Standard; red label.

AIN'T THAT LOVING YOU BABY/Ask Me

RCA Victor 47-8440 . . . . *9/64*   **8–10**
Black label, dog on top.

RCA Victor 47-8440 . . . . *9/64*   **15–20**
Picture sleeve; reads "Coming Soon! Roustabout LP Album."

RCA Victor 47-8440 . . . *10/64*   **15–20**
Picture sleeve; reads "Ask For Roustabout LP Album."

RCA Victor 47-8440 . . . . *9/64*   **20–25**
White label, promotional issue only.

RCA Victor 447-0649 . . *11/65*   **4–8**
Gold Standard; black label, dog on side.

RCA Victor 447-0649 . . . . *70*   **3–5**
Gold Standard; red label.

ALL SHOOK UP/(Let Me Be Your) Teddy Bear

RCA Victor PB-13888 . . *12/84*   **1–3**
Gold vinyl. Originally included as one of the singles in the boxed set *Elvis' Greatest Hits— Golden Singles, Vol. 1.*

RCA Victor PB-13888 . . *12/84*   **1–3**
Picture sleeve.

ALL SHOOK UP/That's When Your Heartaches Begin

RCA Victor 20-6870 . . . . *3/57*   **50–75**
Black label 78rpm.

RCA Victor 20-6870 . . . . *3/57*   **175–200**
White label 78rpm, promotional issue only.

RCA Victor 47-6870 . . . . *3/57*   **25–35**
Black label, dog on top, with horizontal silver line.

RCA Victor 47-6870 . . . . *3/57*   **15–25**
Black label, dog on top, without horizontal silver line.

RCA Victor 47-6870 . . . . *3/57*   **40–60**
Picture sleeve.

RCA Victor 447-0618 . . . *3/59*   **10–12**
Gold Standard; black label, dog on top.

RCA Victor 447-0618 . . . *7/64*   **50–75**
Picture sleeve; Special Gold Standard sleeve.

RCA Victor 447-0618 . . . *7/64*   **40–50**
Gold Standard; white label, promotional issue only.

RCA Victor 447-0618 . . . . *65*   **4–8**
Gold Standard; black label, dog on side.

RCA Victor 447-0618 . . . . *70*   **3–5**
Gold Standard; red label.

RCA Victor 447-0618 . . . . *77*   **2–3**
Gold Standard; black label, dog near top.

RCA Victor PB-11099 . . *10/77*   **2–3**
Originally included as one of the singles in the boxed sets *15 Golden Hits—30 Golden Hits* and *20 Golden Hits in Full Color Sleeves.*

RCA Victor PB-11099 . . *10/77*   **2–3**
Picture sleeve.

ALWAYS ON MY MIND/My Boy

RCA Victor PB-14090 . . . *6/85*   **5–8**
Purple vinyl, gold "Elvis 50th Anniversary" label.

RCA Victor PB-14090 . . . *6/85*   **5–10**
Picture sleeve.

RCA Victor PB-14090 . . . *6/85*   **5–8**
Promotional issue, purple vinyl, gold "Elvis 50th Anniversary" label, "Not For Sale" on right side.

AMAZING WORLD OF SHORT WAVE LISTENING, The (Side One)/The Amazing World Of Short Wave Listening (Side Two)

Hallicrafters N2MW-4434 . *6/57*   **50–60**
Note: Narrated by Alex Dreier, this promotional record demonstrated the advantages of getting involved in the hobby of short wave radio. Contains an excerpt of a French radio station playing "Loving You."

AN AMERICAN TRILOGY/The First Time Ever I Saw Your Face

RCA Victor 74-0672 . . . . *4/72*   **10–12**
Orange label.

RCA Victor 74-0672 . . . . *4/72*   **10–12**
Picture sleeve. *Note:* Sleeve reads "From Elvis' 'Standing Room Only' Album," which was never released. The "live" LP that summer turned out to be *Elvis As Recorded at Madison Square Garden.* The single version of "An American Trilogy" was recorded in Las Vegas, although another version of the song, recorded in New York, appeared on the *Madison Square Garden* LP.

RCA Victor 74-0672 . . . . *4/72*   **12–20**
Yellow label, promotional issue only.

RCA Victor 447-0685 . . . *5/73*   **3–5**
Gold Standard; red label.

RCA Victor 447-0685 . . . . *77*   **2–3**
Gold Standard; black label, dog near top.

ARE YOU LONESOME TONIGHT/Can't Help Falling in Love

RCA Victor PB-13895 . . *12/84*   **1–3**
Gold vinyl. Originally included as one of the singles in the boxed set *Elvis' Greatest Hits— Golden Singles, Vol. 2.*

RCA Victor PB-13895 . . *12/84*   **1–3**
Picture sleeve.

ARE YOU LONESOME TONIGHT/I Gotta Know

RCA Victor 47-7810 . . . *11/60*   **8–12**
Black label, dog on top.

RCA Victor 47-7810 . . . *11/60*   **15–25**
Picture sleeve.

RCA Victor 61-7810 . . . *11/60*   **275–300**
Living Stereo.

RCA Victor 447-0629 . . . *2/62*   **10–12**
Gold Standard; black label, dog on top.

RCA Victor 447-0629 . . . . *65*   **4–8**
Gold Standard; black label, dog on side.

RCA Victor 447-0629 . . . . *68*   **8–10**
Gold Standard; orange label.

RCA Victor 447-0629 . . . . *70*   **3–5**
Gold Standard; red label.

RCA Victor 447-0629 . . . . *77*   **2–3**
Gold Standard; black label, dog near top.
Note: Shown on many reissues as "Are You Lonesome Tonight."

RCA Victor PB-11104 . . *10/77*   **2–3**
Originally included as one of the singles in the boxed sets *15 Golden Hits—30 Golden Hits* and *20 Golden Hits In Full Color Sleeves.*

RCA Victor PB-11104 . . *10/77*   **2–3**
Picture sleeve.

ARE YOU SINCERE/Solitaire

RCA Victor PB-11533 . . . *5/79*   **3–5**
Black label, dog near top.

RCA Victor PB-11533 . . . *5/79*   **5–10**
Picture sleeve.

RCA Victor JB-11533 . . . *5/79*   **6–10**
Light yellow label, promotional issue only.

ARE YOU SINCERE/Unchained Melody

RCA Victor GB-11988 . . . *5/80*   **2–3**
Gold Standard; black label, dog near top.

BABY LET'S PLAY HOUSE/Hound Dog

RCA Victor PB-13875 . . . *8/84*   **20–40**
Gold vinyl, gold "Elvis 50th Anniversary" label, live recordings from September 26, 1956.

RCA Victor PB-13875 . . . *8/84*   **20–40**
Picture sleeve.

RCA Victor PB-13875 . . . *8/84*   **150–175**
Promotional issue, gold vinyl, gold "Elvis 50th Anniversary" label with "Not For Sale" at top.

BABY LET'S PLAY HOUSE/I'm Left, You're Right, She's Gone

Sun 217 . . . . *4/55*   **200–250**
78rpm.

Sun 217 . . . . *4/55*   **350–400**

RCA Victor 20-6383 . . . *11/55*   **75–100**
Black label, 78rpm.

RCA Victor 47-6383 . . . *11/55*   **40–60**
Black label, dog on top, with horizontal silver line.

"BABY LET'S PLAY HOUSE/Hound Dog," on gold vinyl with picture sleeve.

RCA Victor 47-6383 . . . *11/55* 25–35
Black label, dog on top, without horizontal silver line.

RCA Victor 447-0604 . . . *3/59* 10–12
Gold Standard; black label, dog on top.

RCA Victor 447-0604 . . . . *65* 4–8
Gold Standard; black label, dog on side.
Note: Bootleg picture sleeves exist for both the Sun and RCA original 45s.

Collectables 4502 . . . . *86* 1–3

BIG BOSS MAN/Paralyzed
Collectables 4521 . . . . *86* 1–3

BIG BOSS MAN/You Don't Know Me
RCA Victor 47-9341 . . . . *9/67* 5–8
Black label, dog on side.

RCA Victor 47-9341 . . . . *9/67* 15–20
Picture sleeve.

RCA Victor 47-9341 . . . . *9/67* 20–25
White label, promotional issue only.

RCA Victor 447-0662 . . . . *70* 8–10
Gold Standard; red label.

BLUE CHRISTMAS/Blue Christmas
RCA Victor H07W-0808. *11/57* 1000–1200
White label, promotional issue only.

BLUE CHRISTMAS/Santa Claus Is Back in Town
RCA Victor 447-0647 . . *11/65* 5–8
Gold Standard; black label, dog on side.

RCA Victor 447-0647 . . *11/65* 20–25
Picture sleeve; reads "Gold Standard Series" in upper left corner.

RCA Victor 447-0647 . . *11/65* 25–30
Gold Standard; white label, promotional issue only.

RCA Victor 447-0647 . . . . *70* 3–5
Gold Standard; red label.

RCA Victor 447-0647 . . *11/77* 2–3
Gold Standard; black label, dog near top.

RCA Victor 447-0647 . . *11/77* 8–10
Picture sleeve; does not mention "Gold Standard Series."

BLUE CHRISTMAS/Wooden Heart
RCA Victor 447-0720 . . *11/64* 10–15
Gold Standard; black label, dog on top.

RCA Victor 447-0720 . . *11/64* 30–40
Picture sleeve; special Gold Standard sleeve.

RCA Victor 447-0720 . . *11/64* 25–30
Gold Standard; white label, promotional issue only.

"BLUE CHRISTMAS/Blue Christmas," an early promo 45.

Note: Despite a higher Gold Standard catalog number, this single was released one year before 447-0647.

BLUE MOON/Just Because
RCA Victor 20-6640 . . . . *9/56* 60–75
Black label, 78rpm.

RCA Victor 47-6640 . . . . *9/56* 40–50
Black label, dog on top, with silver horizontal line.

RCA Victor 47-6640 . . . . *9/56* 20–30
Black label, dog on top, without silver horizontal line.

RCA Victor 447-0613 . . . *3/59* 10–12
Gold Standard; black label, dog on top.

RCA Victor 447-0613 . . . . *65* 4–8
Gold Standard; black label, dog on side.

RCA Victor 447-0613 . . . . *68* 8–10
Gold Standard; orange label.

RCA Victor 447-0613 . . . . *70* 3–5
Gold Standard; red label.

RCA Victor 447-0613 . . . . *77*   **2–3**
Gold Standard; black label, dog near top.

BLUE SUEDE SHOES/Promised Land

RCA Victor PB-13929 . . *12/84*   **8-12**
Blue vinyl, gold "Elvis 50th Anniversary" label, with "Blue Suede Shoes" shown as stereo, "Promised Land" as mono.

RCA Victor PB-13929 . . *12/84*   **5–8**
Blue vinyl, gold "Elvis 50th Anniversary" label, with "Blue Suede Shoes" shown as mono, "Promised Land" as stereo.

RCA Victor PB-13929 . . *12/84*   **5–10**
Picture sleeve.

RCA Victor PB-13929 . . *12/84*   **10–20**
Promotional issue, blue vinyl, gold "Elvis 50th Anniversary" label, with "Not For Sale" at top.

BLUE SUEDE SHOES/Tutti Frutti

RCA Victor 20-6636 . . . . *9/56*   **60–75**
Black label, 78rpm.

RCA Victor 47-6636 . . . . *9/56*   **40–50**
Black label, dog on top, with horizontal silver line.

RCA Victor 47-6636 . . . . *9/56*   **20–30**
Black label, dog on top, without horizontal silver line.
Note: Bootleg picture sleeves for RCA 47-6636 exist.

RCA Victor 447-0609 . . . *3/59*   **10–12**
Gold Standard; black label, dog on top.

RCA Victor 447-0609 . . . . *65*   **4–8**
Gold Standard; black label, dog on side.

RCA Victor 447-0609 . . . . *70*   **3–5**
Gold Standard; red label.

RCA Victor 447-0609 . . . . *77*   **2–3**
Gold Standard; black label, dog near top.

RCA Victor PB-11107 . . *10/77*   **2–3**
Originally included as one of the singles in the boxed sets *15 Golden Hits—30 Golden Hits* and *20 Golden Hits In Full Color Sleeves.*

RCA Victor PB-11107 . . *10/77*   **2–3**
Picture sleeve.

RCA Victor PB-13885 . . *12/84*   **1–3**
Gold vinyl, originally included as one of the singles in the boxed set *Elvis' Greatest Hits—Golden Singles, Vol. 1.*

RCA Victor PB-13885 . . *12/84*   **1–3**
Picture sleeve.

BOSSA NOVA BABY/Such A Night

Collectables 4513 . . . . . . *86*   **1–3**

BOSSA NOVA BABY/Witchcraft

RCA Victor 47-8243 . . . *10/63*   **6–10**
Black label, dog on top.

RCA Victor 47-8243 . . . *10/63*   **15–20**
Picture sleeve; reads "Coming Soon! 'Fun In Acapulco' LP Album" across bottom.

RCA Victor 47-8243 . . . *12/63*   **15–20**
Picture sleeve; reads "Ask For 'Fun In Acapulco' LP Album."

RCA Victor 47-8243 . . . . *1/64*   **15–20**
Picture sleeve; omits the announcement of the forthcoming *Fun in Acapulco* LP.

RCA Victor 447-0642 . . . *8/64*   **20–25**
Gold Standard; black label, dog on top.

RCA Victor 447-0642 . . . . *65*   **4–8**
Gold Standard; black label, dog on side.

RCA Victor 447-0642 . . . . *68*   **3–5**
Gold Standard; red label.

BRINGING IT BACK/Pieces of My Life

RCA Victor PB-10401 . . *10/75*   **45–55**
Orange label.
Note: This was the last single release on the orange label.

RCA Victor PB-10401 . . *10/75*   **3–5**
Tan label.

RCA Victor PB-10401 . . *10/75*   **8–12**
Picture sleeve.

RCA Victor JA-10401 . . *10/75*   **8–10**
Light yellow label, promotional issue only.

BURNING LOVE/It's a Matter of Time

RCA Victor 74-0769 . . . . *8/72*   **75–100**
Gray label.

RCA Victor 74-0769 . . . . *8/72*   **3–5**
Orange label.

RCA Victor 74-0769 . . . . *8/72*   **8–12**
Picture sleeve.

RCA Victor 74-0769 . . . . *8/72*   **8–10**
Yellow label, promotional issue only.

BURNING LOVE/Steamroller Blues

RCA Victor GB-10156. . . *3/75*   **3–5**
Gold Standard; red label.

RCA Victor GB-10156. . . . *77*   **2–3**
Gold Standard; black label, dog near top.

CAN'T HELP FALLING IN LOVE/Rock-a-Hula Baby

RCA Victor 47-7968 . . . *12/61*   **8–10**
Black label, dog on top.

RCA Victor 47-7968 . . . *12/61*   **15–20**
Picture sleeve.

RCA Victor 37-7968 . . . *12/61* 600–750
Compact 33 single.

RCA Victor 37-7968 . . . *12/61* 600–750
Picture sleeve; compact 33 picture sleeve.

RCA Victor 447-0635 . . *11/62* 8–10
Gold Standard; black label, dog on top.

RCA Victor 447-0635 . . . . *65* 4–8
Gold Standard; black label, dog on side.

RCA Victor 447-0635 . . . . *68* 8–10
Gold Standard; orange label.

RCA Victor 447-0635 . . . . *70* 3–5
Gold Standard; red label.

RCA Victor 447-0635 . . . . *77* 2–3
Gold Standard; black label, dog near top.

RCA Victor PB-11102 . . *10/77* 2–3
Originally included as one of the singles in the
boxed sets *15 Golden Hits—30 Golden Hits* and
20 Golden Hits In Full Color Sleeves.

RCA Victor PB-11102 . . *10/77* 2–3
Picture sleeve.

CLEAN UP YOUR OWN BACK YARD/The Fair Is Moving On

RCA Victor 47-9747 . . . . *6/69* 3–5
Orange label.

RCA Victor 47-9747 . . . . *6/69* 10–15
Picture sleeve.

RCA Victor 47-9747 . . . . *6/69* 10–15
Yellow label, promotional issue only.

RCA Victor 447-0672 . . *12/70* 3–5
Gold Standard; red label.

COUNTRY SIDE—ELVIS, The Country Music's Radio Magazine

Creative Radio *5/82* 50–100
Demo disc, issued to radio stations only.

CRYING IN THE CHAPEL/I Believe in the Man in the Sky

RCA Victor 447-0643 . . . *4/65* 5–8
Gold Standard; black label, dog on side.

RCA Victor 447-0643 . . . *4/65* 15–20
Picture sleeve; special Gold Standard sleeve.

RCA Victor 447-0643 . . . *4/65* 15–20
Gold Standard; white label, promotional issue
only.

RCA Victor 447-0643 . . . . *70* 3–5
Gold Standard; red label.

RCA Victor 447-0643 . . . . *77* 2–3
Gold Standard; black label, dog near top.

RCA Victor PB-11113 . . *10/77* 2–3
Originally included as one of the singles in the
boxed set *15 Golden Hits—30 Golden Hits.*

RCA Victor PB-11113 . . *10/77* 2–3
Picture sleeve.

(YOU'RE THE) DEVIL IN DISGUISE/Please Don't Drag That String Along

RCA Victor 47-8188 . . . . *6/63* 50–100
Black label, dog on top. For copies incorrectly
showing the flip side title as "Please Don't Drag
That String ALONG."

(YOU'RE THE) DEVIL IN DISGUISE/Please Don't Drag That String Around

RCA Victor 47-8188 . . . . *6/63* 6–10
Black label, dog on top.

RCA Victor 47-8188 . . . . *6/63* 15–20
Picture sleeve.

RCA Victor 447-0641 . . . *8/64* 20–25
Gold Standard; black label, dog on top.

RCA Victor 447-0641 . . . . *65* 4–8
Gold Standard; black label, dog on side.

RCA Victor 447-0641 . . . . *70* 3–5
Red label.

DO THE CLAM/You'll Be Gone

RCA Victor 47-8500 . . . . *2/65* 6–10
Black label, dog on side.

RCA Victor 47-8500 . . . . *2/65* 15–20
Picture sleeve.

RCA Victor 47-8500 . . . . *2/65* 20–25
White label, promotional issue only.

RCA Victor 447-0648 . . *11/65* 4–8
Gold Standard; black label, dog on side.

RCA Victor 447-0648 . . . . *70* 3–5
Gold Standard; red label.

Note: This Gold Standard single and the one
issued next, 447-0649 ("Ain't That Loving You
Baby"/"Ask Me"), were the only Elvis singles
originally issued with the dog on top.

DON'T/I Beg of You

RCA Victor 20-7150 . . . . *1/58* 60–75
Black label, 78rpm.

RCA Victor 47-7150 . . . . *1/58* 12–15
Black label, dog on top.

RCA Victor 47-7150 . . . . *1/58* 40–50
Picture sleeve.

RCA Victor 447-0621 . . . . *61* 8–10
Gold Standard; black label, dog on top.

RCA Victor 447-0621 . . . . *65* 4–8
Gold Standard; black label, dog on side.

RCA Victor 447-0621 . . . . *68* 8–10
Gold Standard; orange label.

RCA Victor 447-0621 . . . . *70* 3–5
Gold Standard; red label.

RCA Victor 447-0621 . . . . *77* 2–3
Gold Standard; black label, dog near top.

DON'T/Wear My Ring Around Your Neck

RCA Victor SP-45-76 . . . *1/60*   **500–550**
Black label, dog on top, promotional issue only.

RCA Victor SP-45-76 . . . *1/60*   **900–1200**
Picture sleeve.

DON'T BE CRUEL/Hound Dog

RCA Victor 20-6604 . . . . *7/56*   **60–75**
Black label, 78rpm.

RCA Victor 20-6604 . . . . *7/56*   **175–200**
White label, 78rpm, promotional issue only.

RCA Victor 47-6604 . . . . *7/56*   **25–30**
Black label, dog on top, with horizontal silver line.

RCA Victor 47-6604 . . . . *7/56*   **15–25**
Black label, dog on top, without horizontal silver line.

"DON'T/Wear My Ring Around Your Neck," promo sleeve announcing "50,000,000 ELVIS FANS CAN'T BE WRONG" to DJ's U.S.A.

RCA Victor 47-6604 . . . . *7/56*   **60–75**
Picture sleeve. Front side of sleeve has "Don't Be Cruel" on top of "Hound Dog!"

RCA Victor 47-6604 . . . . *7/56*   **50–60**
Picture sleeve. Front side of sleeve has "Hound Dog!" on top of "Don't Be Cruel."

RCA Victor 447-0608 . . . *3/59*   **10–12**
Gold Standard; black label, dog on top.

RCA Victor 447-0608 . . . *7/64*   **50–75**
Picture sleeve; special Gold Standard sleeve.

RCA Victor 447-0608 . . . *7/64*   **40–50**
Gold Standard; white label, promotional issue only.

RCA Victor 447-0608 . . . . *65*   **4–8**
Gold Standard; black label, dog on side.

RCA Victor 447-0608 . . . . *68*   **8–10**
Gold Standard; orange label.

RCA Victor 447-0608 . . . . *70*   **3–5**
Gold Standard; red label.

RCA Victor 447-0608 . . . . *77*   **2–3**
Gold Standard; black label, dog near top.

RCA Victor PB-11099 . . *10/77*   **2–3**
Originally included as one of the singles in the boxed sets *15 Golden Hits—30 Golden Hits* and *20 Golden Hits In Full Color Sleeves.*

RCA Victor PB-11099 . . *10/77*   **2–3**
Picture sleeve.

RCA Victor PB-13886 . . *12/84*   **1–3**
Gold vinyl, originally included as one of the singles in the boxed set *Elvis' Greatest Hits— Golden Singles, Vol. 1.*

RCA Victor PB-13886 . . *12/84*   **1–3**
Picture sleeve.

DON'T CRY DADDY/Rubberneckin'

RCA Victor 47-9768 . . . *11/69*   **3–5**
Orange label.

RCA Victor 47-9768 . . . *11/69*   **8–12**
Picture sleeve.

RCA Victor 47-9768 . . . *11/69*   **10–15**
Yellow label, promotional issue only.

RCA Victor 447-0674 . . *12/70*   **3–5**
Gold Standard; red label.

RCA Victor 447-0674 . . . . *77*   **2–3**
Gold Standard; black label, dog near top.

(SUCH AN) EASY QUESTION/It Feels So Right

RCA Victor 47-8585 . . . . *5/65*   **5–8**
Black label, dog on side.

RCA Victor 47-8585 . . . . *5/65*   **15–20**
Picture sleeve; sleeve reads "Coming Soon! Special 'Tickle Me' EP."

RCA Victor 47-8585 . . . . *6/65*   **15–20**
Picture sleeve; sleeve reads "Ask For Special
'Tickle Me' EP."

RCA Victor 47-8585 . . . . *6/65*   **20–25**
White label, promotional issue only.

RCA Victor 447-0653 . . *11/66*   **4–8**
Gold Standard; black label, dog on side.

RCA Victor 447-0653 . . . . *70*   **3–5**
Gold Standard; red label.

Elvis' Greatest Hits—Golden Singles,
Vol. 1
RCA Victor PB-13897 . . *12/84*   **10–15**
Package of five gold vinyl singles in color
sleeves, individually numbered PB-13885
through PB-13890.

Elvis' Greatest Hits—Golden Singles,
Vol. 2
RCA Victor PB-13898 . . *12/84*   **10–15**
Package of five gold vinyl singles in color
sleeves, individually numbered PB-13891
through PB-13896.

ELVIS HOUR, The/Gary Owens'
Supertracks
Creative Radio *1/86*   **20–30**
Demo disc for radio stations, offering a sample
of each of the two syndicated programs availa-
ble from Creative Radio.

ELVIS MEDLEY, The/Always on My
Mind
RCA Victor PB-13351 . . *11/82*   **3–5**
Black label, dog near top.

RCA Victor PB-13351 . . *11/82*   **5–10**
Picture sleeve.

Collectables 4564 . . . . . . *87*   **1–3**

ELVIS MEDLEY, The (Long
Version)/The Elvis Medley (Short
Version)
RCA Victor JB-13351 . . *11/82*   **6–10**
Light yellow label, promotional issue only.

RCA Victor JB-13351 . . *11/82*   **200–225**
Gold vinyl, gold label, promotional issue only.

ELVIS: SIX HOUR
SPECIAL/Listen!
Eva-Tone 1037710A&BX   *11/77*   **15–20**
A 33 plastic soundsheet used by the Chicago
Radio Syndicate to promote their six-hour Elvis
broadcast. This promotional item also con-
tained a similar plug for "Jamboree U.S.A."
The flip side, "Listen," was simply another pro-
motional message.

ELVIS LIVE (Side One)/Elvis Live
(Side Two)
Eva-Tone 1037710A&BX . *4/78*   **35–40**
A 33 plastic soundsheet containing Elvis' 1961
Memphis press conference. This soundsheet
originally came bound in the magazine *Collec-*
tor's Issue. This price is for the magazine and
soundsheet still intact.

Eva-Tone 1037710A&BX . *4/78*   **15–20**
Price for soundsheet only.

ELVIS PRESLEY SHOW
Royal *4/56*   **100–200**
78rpm, one-sided disc, issued to radio stations
to promote Elvis' concert appearances, contains
an excerpt of "Heartbreak Hotel."

ELVIS PRESLEY "SPEAKS—IN
PERSON!"/Directions for Playing
This Disc
Rainbow Records *11/56*   **300–325**
A 78rpm cardboard disc with Elvis speaking to
his fans, originally attached to the cover of the
Elvis Answers Back! magazine. This price is for
the magazine and disc still intact.

Rainbow Records *11/56*   **100–125**
Price for cardboard disc only.

ELVIS PRESLEY "THE TRUTH
ABOUT ME"
Rainbow Records *11/56*   **300–325**
A 78rpm cardboard disc with Elvis speaking to
his fans, originally attached to the cover of the
Elvis Answers Back! magazine. This price is for
magazine and disc still intact. Both the disc and
the magazine came in two variations. Besides
the difference in titles between this disc and
"Elvis Presley Speaks—In Person," the label
colors are two different shades of blue. The
magazine came in both red and green lettering,
with no particular combination of disc and
magazine used.

Rainbow Records *11/56*   **100–125**
Price for cardboard disc only.

ELVIS SPEAKS!! "THE TRUTH
ABOUT ME"
Lynchburg Audio 1401-1L *12/56*   **125–150**
This 45rpm soundsheet version of "The Truth
about Me" was made available by *Teen Parade*
magazine for their readers.

Eva-Tone EL-38713T   **30–40**

ELVIS 10TH ANNIVERSARY/The
Elvis Hour
Creative Radio *5/87*   **15–20**

Demonstration discs offering samples of Creative Radio's *Elvis 10th Anniversary* syndicated show.

Demo disc for radio stations, offering a sample of each of the two syndicated programs available from Creative Radio.

ELVIS—THE 50TH BIRTHDAY RADIO SPECIAL/The Day the Music Died

Creative Radio *11/84*   **20–30**
Demo disc for radio stations, offering a sample of each of the two syndicated programs available from Creative Radio. First pressings have the date "1-8-85" etched in the vinyl trail-off and a smaller size print on the labels.

Creative Radio *1/87*   **10–20**
Second pressings. These don't have the date etched in the vinyl trail-off, and they have larger print on the labels.

15 GOLDEN RECORDS/30 Golden Hits

RCA Victor PP-11301 . . *10/77*   **45–55**
A package of 15 singles, each with its own picture sleeve. Price is for complete set.
Note: Specially printed browser boxes, containing six of the 15-record packages were made available to record stores. Value of the complete box with six sets would be no less than six times the value of one set.

FOLLOW THAT DREAM/When My Blue Moon Turns to Gold Again

Collectables 4515 . . . . *86*   **1–3**

FOOL/Steamroller Blues

RCA Victor 74-0910 . . . . *4/73*   **3–6**
Orange label.

RCA Victor 74-0910 . . . . *4/73*   **8–12**
Picture sleeve.

RCA Victor 74-0910 . . . . *4/73*   **8–10**
Light yellow label, promotional issue only.
Note: "Fool" has yet to appear on a Gold Standard single. "Steamroller Blues" was the flip side of "Burning Love" on Gold Standard.

FOOLS FALL IN LOVE/Blue Suede Shoes

Collectables 4522 . . . . *86*   **1–3**

FRANKIE AND JOHNNY/Love Letters

Collectables 4516 . . . . *86*   **1–3**

FRANKIE AND JOHNNY/Please Don't Stop Loving Me

RCA Victor 47-8780 . . . . *3/66*   **5–10**
Black label, dog on side.

RCA Victor 47-8780 . . . . *3/66*   **15–20**
Picture sleeve.

RCA Victor 47-8780 . . . . *3/66*   **20–25**
White label, promotional issue only.

RCA Victor 47-0656 . . . . *2/68*   **4–8**
Gold Standard; black label, dog on side.

RCA Victor 47-0656 . . . . . *70*   **3–5**
Gold Standard; red label.

RCA Victor 47-0656 . . . . . *77*   **2–3**
Gold Standard; black label, dog near top.

GOOD LUCK CHARM/Anything That's Part of You

RCA Victor 47-7992 . . . . *3/62*   **8–10**
Black label, dog on top.

RCA Victor 47-7992 . . . . *3/62*   **15–20**
Picture sleeve; with titles in blue and pink letters.

RCA Victor 47-7992 . . . . *3/62*   **15–20**
Picture sleeve; with titles in rust and lavender letters.

RCA Victor 37-7992 . . . . *3/62* **1000–1200**
Compact 33 single.

RCA Victor 37-7992 . . . . *3/62* **1200–1500**
Picture sleeve; Compact 33 picture sleeve.

RCA Victor 447-0636 . . *11/62*   **8–10**
Gold Standard; black label, dog on top.

RCA Victor 447-0636 . . *65–66*   **4–8**
Gold Standard; black label, dog on side.

RCA Victor 447-0636 . . *68–69*   **8–10**
Gold Standard; orange label.

RCA Victor 447-0636 . . *70–74*   **3–5**
Gold Standard; red label.

RCA Victor 447-0636 . . . . *77*   **2–3**
Gold Standard; black label, dog near top.

GOOD ROCKIN' TONIGHT/I Don't Care If the Sun Don't Shine

Sun 210 . . . . *9/54* **200–275**
78rpm.

Sun 210 . . . . *9/54* **375–400**

RCA Victor 20-6381 . . . *11/55* **75–100**
Black label, 78rpm.

RCA Victor 47-6381 . . . *11/55* **40–60**
Black label, dog on top, with horizontal silver line.

RCA Victor 47-6381 . . . *11/55* **25–35**
Black label, dog on top, without horizontal silver line.

RCA Victor 447-0602 . . . *3/59* **10–12**
Gold Standard; black label, dog on top.

RCA Victor 447-0602 . . . *7/64* **50–75**
Picture sleeve, special Gold Standard sleeve.

RCA Victor 447-0602 . . . *7/64* **40–50**
Gold Standard; white label, promotional issue only.

RCA Victor 447-0602 . . . . *65*   **4–8**
Gold Standard; black label, dog on side.

GRACELAND TOUR, The/Blank

Record Digest 25794 . . . . *2/79*   **4–6**
Red plastic soundsheet, all-Elvis novelty break-in, offered as a bonus to buyers of the book *Our Best To You.* Narration by Jerry Osborne.

RCA Victor 447-0602 . . . . *70*   **3–5**
Gold Standard; red label.

Note: Bootleg picture sleeves exist for both the RCA and Sun original 45s.

GUITAR MAN/Faded Love

RCA Victor PB-12158 . . . *1/81*   **3–5**
Black label, dog near top.

RCA Victor PB-12158 . . . *1/81*   **5–10**
Picture sleeve.

GUITAR MAN (Stereo)/Guitar Man (Mono)

RCA Victor JH-12158 . . . *1/81*   **6–10**
Light yellow label, promotional issue only.

RCA Victor JH-12158 . . . *1/81* **225–250**
Red vinyl, mustard label, promotional issue only.

Note: Both of these tracks, from the *Guitar Man* LP, offer completely reworked backings and instrumentations than that found on the initial release (see immediately below).

GUITAR MAN/High Heel Sneakers

RCA Victor 47-9425 . . . . *1/68*   **5–8**
Black label, dog on side.

RCA Victor 47-9425 . . . . *1/68* **10–20**
Picture sleeve; reads "Coming Soon, Elvis' Gold Records, Volume 4."

RCA Victor 47-9425 . . . . *2/68* **10–20**
Picture sleeve; reads "Ask for Elvis' Gold Records, Volume 4."

RCA Victor 47-9425 . . . . *1/68* **15–20**
Yellow label, promotional issue only.

RCA Victor 447-0663 . . . . *70*   **3–5**
Gold Standard; red label.

RCA Victor 447-0663 . . . . *77*   **2–3**
Gold Standard; black label, dog near top.

Note: Some copies of this release show "High Heel Sneakers" as "Hi-Heel Sneakers."

HARD HEADED WOMAN/Don't Ask Me Why

RCA Victor 20-7280 . . . . *6/58* **75–100**
Black label, 78rpm.

RCA Victor 47-7280 . . . . *6/58* **10–15**
Black label, dog on top.

RCA Victor 47-7280 . . . . *6/58* **35–45**
Picture sleeve.

RCA Victor 447-0623 . . . . *61* **10–12**
Gold Standard; black label, dog on top.

RCA Victor 447-0623 . . . . *65* **4–8**
Gold Standard; black label, dog on side.

RCA Victor 447-0623 . . . . *68* **8–10**
Gold Standard; orange label.

RCA Victor 447-0623 . . . . *70* **3–5**
Gold Standard; red label.

RCA Victor 447-0623 . . . . *77* **2–3**
Gold Standard; black label, dog near top.

HE TOUCHED ME/Bosom of Abraham

RCA Victor 74-0651 . . . . *3/72* **3–5**
Orange label.

RCA Victor 74-0651 . . . . *3/72* **40–50**
Picture sleeve.

RCA Victor 74-0651 . . . . *3/72* **45-55**
Yellow label, promotional issue only.

Note: An error in production resulted in some copies of the commercial release of this record to be pressed at approximately 35rpm on the "He Touched Me" side only. Collectors have placed an $80–$100 value on this oddity for near-mint copies.

HEARTBREAK HOTEL/I Was the One

RCA Victor 20-6420 . . . . *1/56* **60–75**
Black label, 78rpm.

RCA Victor 20-6420 . . . . *1/56* **175–200**
White label, 78rpm, promotional issue only.

RCA Victor 47-6420 . . . . *1/56* **25–30**
Black label, dog on top, with horizontal silver line.

RCA Victor 47-6420 . . . . *1/56* **15–25**
Black label, dog on top, without horizontal silver line.

RCA Victor 447-0605 . . . *3/59* **10–12**
Gold Standard; black label, dog on top.

RCA Victor 447-0605 . . . *7/64* **50–75**
Picture sleeve, special Gold Standard sleeve.

RCA Victor 447-0605 . . . *7/64* **40–50**
Gold Standard; white label, promotional issue only.

RCA Victor 447-0605 . . . . *65* **4–8**
Gold Standard; black label, dog on side.

RCA Victor 447-0605 . . . . *68* **8–10**
Gold Standard; orange label.

RCA Victor 447-0605 . . . . *70* **3–5**
Gold Standard; red label.

RCA Victor 447-0605 . . . . *77* **2–3**
Gold Standard; black label, dog near top.

RCA Victor PB-11105 . . *10/77* **2–3**
Originally included as one of the singles in the boxed sets *15 Golden Hits—30 Golden Hits* and *20 Golden Hits In Full Color Sleeves.*

RCA Victor PB-11105 . . *10/77* **2–3**
Picture sleeve.

Note: Bootleg picture sleeves exist for the original RCA 45 of this release. Also, "I Was the One" was reissued in 1983, backed with "Wear My Ring Around Your Neck."

HEARTBREAK HOTEL/Jailhouse Rock

RCA Victor PB-13892 . . *12/84* **1–3**
Gold vinyl, originally included as one of the singles in the boxed set *Elvis' Greatest Hits—Golden Singles, Vol. 2*

RCA Victor PB-13892 . . *12/84* **1–3**
Picture sleeve.

(Marie's The Name) HIS LATEST FLAME/Little Sister

RCA Victor 47-7908 . . . . *8/61* **8–10**
Black label, dog on top.

RCA Victor 47-7908 . . . . *8/61* **15–25**
Picture sleeve.

RCA Victor 37-7908 . . . . *8/61* **450–500**
Compact 33 single.

RCA Victor 37-7908 . . . . *8/61* **450–500**
Picture sleeve; Compact 33 picture sleeve.

RCA Victor 447-0634 . . . *11/62* **8–10**
Gold Standard; black label, dog on top.

RCA Victor 447-0634 . . . . *65* **4–8**
Gold Standard; black label, dog on side.

RCA Victor 447-0634 . . . . *70* **3–5**
Gold Standard; red label.

RCA Victor 447-0634 . . . . *77* **2–3**
Gold Standard; black label, dog near top.

RCA Victor PB-13894 . . *12/84* **1–3**
Gold vinyl, originally included as one of the singles in the boxed set *Elvis' Greatest Hits—Golden Singles, Vol. 2.*

RCA Victor PB-13894 . . *12/84* **1–3**
Picture sleeve.

HOW GREAT THOU ART/His Hand in Mine

RCA Victor 74-0130 . . . . *4/69* **15–20**
Orange label.

RCA Victor 74-0130 . . . . *4/69*   **75–100**
Picture sleeve.

RCA Victor 74-0130 . . . . *4/69*   **25–30**
Yellow label, promotional issue only.

RCA Victor 447-0670 . . *12/70*   **3–5**
Gold Standard; red label.

Collectables 4520 . . . . *86*   **1–3**

HOW GREAT THOU ART/So High
RCA Victor SP-45-162. . . *4/67*   **125–150**
White label, promotional issue only.

RCA Victor SP-45-162. . . *4/67*   **100–125**
Picture sleeve.

HURT/For the Heart
RCA Victor PB-10601 . . . *3/76*   **3–5**
Tan label.

RCA Victor PB-10601 . . . *7/76*   **90–100**
Black label, dog near top.
Second pressings of this release became the first
Elvis single pressed with the newer RCA black
label, with the dog just to the right of the top.

RCA Victor PB-10601 . . . *3/76*   **8–10**
Picture sleeve.

RCA Victor JB-10601 . . . *3/76*   **8–10**
Light yellow label, promotional issue only.
Note: For the Gold Standard release of "For
The Heart," see "Moody Blue."

I FEEL SO BAD/Wild in the Country
RCA Victor 47-7880 . . . . *5/61*   **8–10**
Black label, dog on top.

RCA Victor 47-7880 . . . . *5/61*   **15–25**
Picture sleeve.

RCA Victor 37-7880 . . . . *5/61*   **300–400**
Compact 33 single.

RCA Victor 37-7880 . . . . *5/61*   **300–400**
Picture sleeve; Compact 33 single.

RCA Victor 447-0631 . . . *2/62*   **8–12**
Gold Standard; black label, dog on top.

RCA Victor 447-0631 . . . . *65*   **4–8**
Gold Standard; black label, dog on side.

RCA Victor 447-0631 . . . . *70*   **3–5**
Gold Standard; red label.

Collectables 4510 . . . . *86*   **1–3**

I GOT A WOMAN/I'm Counting on You
RCA Victor 20-6637 . . . . *9/56*   **60–75**
Black label, 78rpm.

RCA Victor 47-6637 . . . . *9/56*   **40–50**
Black label, dog on top, with horizontal silver
line.

RCA Victor 47-6637 . . . . *9/56*   **20–30**
Black label, dog on top, without horizontal silver line.

RCA Victor 447-0610 . . . *3/59*   **10–12**
Gold Standard; black label, dog on top.
Note: Bootleg picture sleeves exist for the origi-
nal RCA 45 of this release.

Collectables 4503 . . . . *86*   **1–3**

I REALLY DON'T WANT TO KNOW/There Goes My Everything
RCA Victor 47-9960 . . . *12/70*   **3–5**
Orange label.

RCA Victor 47-9960 . . . *12/70*   **8–12**
Picture sleeve; reads "Coming Soon—New
Album."

RCA Victor 47-9960 . . . . *1/71*   **8–12**
Picture sleeve; reads "Now Available—New
Album."

RCA Victor 47-9960 . . . *12/70*   **10–15**
Yellow label, promotional issue only.

RCA Victor 447-0679 . . . *2/72*   **3–5**
Gold Standard; red label.

RCA Victor 447-0679 . . . . *77*   **2–3**
Gold Standard; black label, dog near top.

I WANT YOU, I NEED YOU, I LOVE YOU/Love Me
RCA Victor PB-13887 . . *12/84*   **1–3**
Gold vinyl, originally included as one of the
singles in the boxed set *Elvis' Greatest Hits—
Golden Singles, Vol. 1.*

RCA Victor PB-13887 . . *12/84*   **1–3**
Picture sleeve.

I WANT YOU, I NEED YOU, I LOVE YOU/My Baby Left Me
RCA Victor 20-6540 . . . . *5/56*   **60–75**
Black label, 78rpm.

RCA Victor 20-6540 . . . . *5/56*   **175–200**
White label 78rpm, promotional issue only.

RCA Victor 47-6540 . . . . *5/56*   **25–30**
Black label, dog on top, with horizontal silver
line.

RCA Victor 47-6540 . . . . *5/56*   **15–25**
Black label, dog on top, without horizontal silver line.

RCA Victor 47-6540 . . . . *5/56*   **350–400**
Picture sleeve; special "This Is His Life" sleeve.
Note: Though not numbered as such, this was
the first picture sleeve of any type issued with
an Elvis record. Also, bootleg sleeves exist for
this release but are completely different from
the above mentioned sleeve.

Special—and quite unusual—picture sleeve for "I Want You, I Need You, I Love You." Was Elvis' life *really* like that?

I WAS THE ONE/Wear My Ring Around Your Neck
RCA Victor PB-13500 . . . *4/83* **3–5**
Black label, dog on top.

RCA Victor PB-13500 . . . *4/83* **5–10**
Picture sleeve.

RCA Victor JB-13500 . . . *4/83* **6–10**
Light yellow with black print, promotional issue only.

RCA Victor JB-13500 . . . *4/83* **200–225**
Gold vinyl; yellow with red print, promotional issue only.
Note: These two selections, from the *I Was the One* LP, have some additional instrumentation added to the original masters.

I'LL NEVER LET YOU GO (LITTLE DARLIN')/I'm Gonna Sit Right Down and Cry (over You)
RCA Victor 20-6638 . . . . *9/56* **60–75**
Black label, 78rpm.

RCA Victor 47-6638 . . . . *9/56* **40–50**
Black label, dog on top, with horizontal silver line.

RCA Victor 47-6638 . . . . *9/56* **20–30**
Black label, dog on top, without horizontal silver line.

RCA Victor 447-0611 . . . *3/59* **10–12**
Gold Standard; black label, dog on top.
Note: Bootleg picture sleeves exist for the original RCA 45 of this release.

Collectables 4504 . . . . *86* **1–3**

I'M LEAVIN'/Heart of Rome
RCA Victor 47-9998 . . . . *7/71* **3–5**
Orange label.

RCA Victor 47-9998 . . . . *7/71* **8–15**
Picture sleeve.

RCA Victor 47-9998 . . . . *7/71* **10–15**
Yellow label, promotional issue only.

RCA Victor 447-0683 . . . *5/72* **3–5**
Gold Standard; red label.

I'M YOURS/(It's a) Long Lonely Highway
RCA Victor 47-8657 . . . . *8/65* **5–8**
Black label, dog on side.

RCA Victor 47-8657 . . . . *8/65* **15–20**
Picture sleeve.

RCA Victor 47-8657 . . . . *8/65* **20–25**
White label, promotional issue only.

RCA Victor 447-0654 . . *11/66* **4–8**
Gold Standard; black label, dog on side.

RCA Victor 447-0654 . . . . *70* **3–5**
Gold Standard; red label.

I'VE GOT A THING ABOUT YOU BABY/Take Good Care of Her

RCA Victor APBO-0196. . *1/74* **3–5**
Orange label.

RCA Victor APBO-0196. . *1/74* **8–12**
Picture sleeve.

RCA Victor DJBO-0196. . *1/74* **8–10**
Light yellow label, promotional issue only.

RCA Victor GB-10485. . . *2/76* **3–5**
Gold Standard; red label.

RCA Victor GB-10485. . *77–78* **2–3**
Gold Standard; black label, dog near top.

I'VE LOST YOU/The Next Step Is Love

RCA Victor 47-9873 . . . . *7/70* **3–5**
Orange label.

RCA Victor 47-9873 . . . . *7/70* **8–12**
Picture sleeve.

RCA Victor 47-9873 . . . . *7/70* **10–15**
Yellow label, promotional issue only.

RCA Victor 447-0677 . . . *8/71* **3–5**
Gold Standard; red label.

IF EVERYDAY WAS LIKE CHRISTMAS/How Would You Like to Be

RCA Victor 47-8950 . . . *11/66* **5–8**
Black label, dog on side.

RCA Victor 47-8950 . . . *11/66* **15–20**
Picture sleeve.

RCA Victor 47-8950 . . . *11/66* **20–35**
White label, promotional issue only.

RCA Victor 447-0681 . . . *5/72* **3–5**
Gold Standard; red label.

RCA Victor 447-0681 . . . . *77* **2–3**
Gold Standard; black label, dog near top.

IF I CAN DREAM/Edge of Reality

RCA Victor 47-9670 . . . *11/68* **3–5**
Orange label.

RCA Victor 47-9670 . . . *11/68* **10–15**
Picture sleeve; reads "As Featured On His NBC-TV Special."

RCA Victor 47-9670 . . . . *1/69* **10–15**
Picture sleeve; sleeve makes no mention of TV special.

RCA Victor 47-9670 . . . *11/68* **10–15**
Yellow label, promotional issue only.

RCA Victor 447-0668 . . *12/70* **3–5**
Gold Standard; red label.

RCA Victor 447-0668 . . . . *77* **2–3**
Gold Standard; black label, dog near top.

IF YOU TALK IN YOUR SLEEP/Help Me

RCA Victor APBO-0280. . *5/74* **3–5**
Orange label.

RCA Victor APBO-0280. . *5/74* **8–12**
Picture sleeve.

RCA Victor DJBO-0280. . *5/74* **8–10**
Light yellow label, promotional issue only.

IF YOU TALK IN YOUR SLEEP/Raised on Rock

RCA Victor GB-10157. . . *3/75* **1**
Gold Standard; red label.

IMPOSSIBLE DREAM, The/An American Trilogy

RCA Victor JH-13302 . . . *8/82* **75–100**
Gold label, commemorative giveaway record distributed to visitors to Elvis' birthplace in Tupelo, Mississippi, in August 1982.

RCA Victor JH-13302 . . . *8/82* **75–100**
Special commemorative sleeve.

IN THE GHETTO/Any Day Now

RCA Victor 47-9741 . . . . *4/69* **3–5**
Orange label.

RCA Victor 47-9741 . . . . *4/69* **10–15**
Picture sleeve; reads "Coming Soon—'From Elvis In Memphis' LP Album."

RCA Victor 47-9741 . . . . *5/69* **10–15**
Picture sleeve; reads "Ask For—'From Elvis In Memphis' LP Album."

RCA Victor 47-9741 . . . . *4/69* **10–15**
Yellow label, promotional issue only.

RCA Victor 447-0671 . . *12/70* **3–5**
Gold Standard; red label.

RCA Victor 447-0671 . . . . *77* **2–3**
Gold Standard; black label, dog near top.

RCA Victor PB-11100 . . *10/77* **2–3**
Originally included as one of the singles in the boxed sets *15 Golden Hits—30 Golden Hits* and *20 Golden Hits In Full Color Sleeves.*

RCA Victor PB-11100 . . *10/77* **2–3**
Picture sleeve.

IN THE GHETTO/If I Can Dream

RCA Victor PB-13890 . . *12/84* **1–3**
Gold vinyl; originally included as one of the singles in the boxed set *Elvis' Greatest Hits— Golden Singles, Vol. 1.*

RCA Victor PB-13890 . . *12/84*   **1–3**
Picture sleeve.

INDESCRIBABLY BLUE/Fools Fall in Love
RCA 47-9056 . . . . *1/67*   **5–8**
Black label, dog on side.

RCA Victor 47-9056 . . . . *1/67*   **15–20**
Picture sleeve.

RCA Victor 47-9056 . . . . *1/67*   **20–25**
White label, promotional issue only.

RCA Victor 447-0659 . . . . *70*   **10–15**
Gold Standard; red label.

IT'S NOW OR NEVER/A Mess of Blues
RCA Victor 47-7777 . . . . *7/60*   **8–12**
Black label, dog on top.

RCA Victor 47-7777 . . . . *7/60*   **15–25**
Picture sleeve.

RCA Victor 61-7777 . . . . *7/60*   **250–300**
Living Stereo.

RCA Victor 447-0628 . . . *2/62*   **8–10**
Gold Standard; black label, dog on top.

RCA Victor 447-0628 . . . . *65*   **4–8**
Gold Standard; black label, dog on side.

RCA Victor 447-0628 . . . . *68*   **8–10**
Gold Standard; orange label.

RCA Victor 447-0628 . . . . *70*   **3–5**
Gold Standard; red label.

RCA Victor 447-0628 . . . . *77*   **2–3**
Gold Standard; black label, dog near top.

RCA Victor PB-11101 . . *10/77*   **2–3**
Originally included as one of the singles in the boxed set *15 Golden Hits—30 Golden Hits.*

RCA Victor PB-11101 . . *10/77*   **2–3**
Picture sleeve.
Note: Reportedly, some copies of 47-7777 were pressed without the piano track. Collectors may place a value of $250–$300 on this oddity for near-mint copies.

IT'S NOW OR NEVER/I Walk the Line (by Jaye P. Morgan)
U.S.A.F. Pgm. #125/6 . . *2/61*   **300–325**
A public service 5-minute radio show, part of the U.S. Air Force's "Music in the Air" series, contains an edited version of "It's Now or Never."
Note: This record was shipped in a special box which identified the two records included by program number. Add $25–$35 to the value for the box.

IT'S NOW OR NEVER/Surrender
RCA Victor PB-13889 . . *12/84*   **1–3**
Gold vinyl, originally included as one of the singles in the boxed set *Elvis' Greatest Hits— Golden Singles, Vol. 1.*

RCA Victor PB-13889 . . *12/84*   **1–3**
Picture sleeve.

IT'S ONLY LOVE/The Sound of Your Cry
RCA Victor 48-1017 . . . . *9/71*   **3–5**
Orange label.

RCA Victor 48-1017 . . . . *9/71*   **8–12**
Picture sleeve.

Two five-minute radio shows, part of the U.S. Air Force's "Music in the Air" series, containing edited versions of "It's Now or Never" and "Surrender."

RCA Victor 48-1017 . . . .   *9/71*   **10–15**
Yellow label, promotional issue only.

RCA Victor 447-0684 . . . *5/72*   **3–5**
Gold Standard; red label.

JAILHOUSE ROCK/Treat Me Nice

RCA Victor 20-7035 . . . .   *9/57*   **50–75**
Black label, 78rpm.

RCA Victor 20-7035 . . . .   *9/57*   **175–200**
White label, 78rpm, promotional issue only.

RCA Victor 47-7035 . . . .   *9/57*   **35–40**
Black label, dog on top, with horizontal silver line.
Note: This was the last Elvis single pressed that used the horizontal silver line.

RCA Victor 47-7035 . . . .   *9/57*   **15–20**
Black label, dog on top, without horizontal silver line.

RCA Victor 47-7035 . . . .   *9/57*   **40–60**
Picture sleeve.

RCA Victor 47-7035 . . . *10/57*   **300–400**
MGM sleeve; special press preview theater ticket wrapped around the standard picture sleeve and record; promotional issue only.

RCA Victor 447-0619 . . . .   *61*   **8–10**
Gold Standard; black label, dog on top.

RCA Victor 447-0619 . . . .   *65*   **4–8**
Gold Standard; black label, dog on side.

RCA Victor 447-0619 . . . .   *68*   **8–10**
Gold Standard; orange label.

RCA Victor 447-0619 . . . .   *70*   **3–5**
Gold Standard; red label.

RCA Victor 447-0619 . . . .   *77*   **2–3**
Gold Standard; black label, dog near top.

RCA Victor PB-11101 . . *10/77*   **2–3**
Originally included as one of the singles in the boxed set *15 Golden Hits—30 Golden Hits.*

RCA Victor PB-11101 . . *10/77*   **2–3**
Picture sleeve.

Special press preview theater tickets were wrapped around the standard picture sleeve by MGM for the *Jailhouse Rock* film.

Special Easter Programming Kit, containing both 1966 Easter singles, a special mailer sleeve, and an Easter card from the King himself.

JOSHUA FIT THE BATTLE/Known Only to Him

RCA Victor 447-0651 . . . *3/66*   **10–12**
Black label, dog on side.

RCA Victor 447-0651 . . . *3/66*   **50–75**
Picture sleeve; special Gold Standard sleeve.

RCA Victor 447-0651 . . . *3/66*   **30–40**
Gold Standard; white label, promotional issue only.

RCA Victor 447-0651 . . . . *70*   **3–5**
Gold Standard; red label.

RCA Victor 447-0651 . . . *4/66*   **450–550**
"Special Easter Programming Kit," picture sleeve mailer, contained both 1966 Easter singles, "Joshua Fit the Battle" and "Milky White Way" in their sleeves and an Easter card from Elvis; price is for complete kit.

RCA Victor 447-0651 . . . *4/66*   **300–400**
"Special Easter Programming Kit." This price is for the sleeve-mailer by itself.

JOY OF CHRISTMAS, THE/The Joy of Christmas Promos

Creative Radio (SP) *9/86*   **20–30**
This edition, programmed for adult contemporary formats, was issued to radio stations only.

Creative Radio (SP) *9/86*   **20–30**
This edition, programmed for country music formats, was issued to radio stations only.

JUDY/There's Always Me

RCA Victor 47-9287 . . . . *8/67*   **5–8**
Black label, dog on side.

RCA Victor 47-9287 . . . . *8/67*   **15–20**
Picture sleeve.

RCA Victor 47-9287 . . . . *8/67*   **20–25**
White label, promotional issue only.

RCA Victor 447-0661 . . . . *70*   **10–15**
Gold Standard; red label.

KENTUCKY RAIN/My Little Friend

RCA Victor 47-9791 . . . . *2/70*   **3–5**
Orange label.

RCA Victor 47-9791 . . . . *2/70*   **8–12**
Picture sleeve.

RCA Victor 47-9791 . . . . *2/70*   **10–15**
Yellow label, promotional issue only.

RCA Victor 447-0675 . . . *8/71*   **3–5**
Gold Standard; red label.

KING IS DEAD LONG LIVE THE KING, The (Elvis Presley Is Still the King!)/Blank

Eva-Tone 52578X. *5/78*   **90–100**
Yellow plastic soundsheet sampler, made for Universal Sounds Unlimited to promote a taped Elvis radio special.

KING OF THE WHOLE WIDE WORLD/Home Is Where the Heart Is

RCA Victor SP-45-118. . . *5/62*   **175–225**
Black label, dog on top, promotional issue only.

RCA Victor SP-45-118. . . *5/62*   **150–200**
Picture sleeve.

KISS ME QUICK/Suspicion

RCA Victor 447-0639 . . . *4/64*   **8–10**
Gold Standard; black label, dog on top.

RCA Victor 447-0639 . . . *4/64*   **20–25**
Picture sleeve; special Gold Standard sleeve.

RCA Victor 447-0639 . . . *4/64*   **20–25**
Gold Standard; white label, promotional issue only.

RCA Victor 447-0639 . . . . *68*   **8–10**
Gold Standard; orange label.

RCA Victor 447-0639 . . . . *70*   **3–5**
Gold Standard; red label.

RCA Victor 447-0639 . . . . *77*   **2–3**
Gold Standard; black label, dog near top.

KISSIN' COUSINS/It Hurts Me

RCA Victor 47-8307 . . . . *1/64*   **6–10**
Black label, dog on top.

RCA Victor 47-8307 . . . . *1/64*   **15–20**
Picture sleeve.

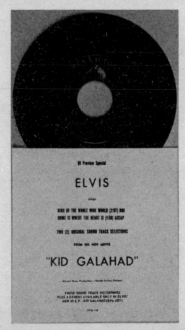

Special promo release and sleeve for two songs from *Kid Galahad*.

RCA Victor 47-8307 . . . . *1/64*   **8–10**
Black label, dog on top.
RCA Victor 447-0644 . . . *5/65*   **4–8**
Gold Standard; black label, dog on side.
RCA Victor 447-0644 . . . . *70*   **3–5**
Gold Standard; red label.
RCA Victor 447-0644 . . . . *77*   **2–3**
Gold Standard; black label, dog near top.

LAWDY, MISS CLAWDY/Shake, Rattle and Roll
RCA Victor 20-6642 . . . . *9/56*   **60–75**
Black label, 78rpm.
RCA Victor 47-6642 . . . . *9/56*   **125–175**
Black label, no dog on label.
RCA Victor 47-6642 . . . . *9/56*   **40–50**
Black label, dog on top, with horizontal silver line.
RCA Victor 47-6642 . . . . *9/56*   **20–30**
Black label, dog on top, without horizontal silver line.
RCA Victor 447-0615 . . . *3/59*   **10–12**
Gold Standard; black label, dog on top.
RCA Victor 447-0615 . . . . *65*   **4–8**
Gold Standard; black label, dog on side.
RCA Victor 447-0615 . . . . *68*   **8–10**
Gold Standard; orange label.
RCA Victor 447-0615 . . . . *70*   **3–5**
Gold Standard; red label.
RCA Victor 447-0615 . . . . *77*   **2–3**
Gold Standard; black label, dog near top.

LET ME BE THERE (Stereo)/Let Me Be There (Mono)
RCA Victor JH-10951 . . . *6/74*   **100–125**
Light yellow label, promotional issue only, distributed by Al Gallico Publishing to radio stations only.

LIFE/I Don't Know How to Love Him (by Helen Reddy)
What's It All About
TRAV PGM #78/77 . . . . *77*   **45–55**
A public-service religious program, also contains interviews with Hugh Jarrett of the Jordanaires and with Helen Reddy.

LIFE/Only Believe
RCA Victor 47-9985 . . . . *5/71*   **3–5**
Orange label.
RCA Victor 47-9985 . . . . *5/71*   **20–30**
Picture sleeve.
RCA Victor 47-9985 . . . . *5/71*   **10–15**
Yellow label, promotional issue only.

RCA Victor 447-0682 . . . *5/72*   **3–5**
Gold Standard; red label.

LITTLE SISTER/Paralyzed
RCA Victor PB-13547 . . . *6/83*   **3–5**
Black label, dog near top.
RCA Victor PB-13547 . . . *6/83*   **5–10**
Picture sleeve.
RCA Victor JB-13547 . . . *6/83*   **6–10**
Light yellow label, promotional issue only.
RCA Victor JB-13547 . . . *6/83*   **175–200**
Blue vinyl.

LITTLE SISTER/Rip It Up
RCA Victor EP-0517 . . . . *6/83*   **100–125**
12-inch single, promotional issue only.
Note: This was the first 12-inch Elvis single ever. To date, there have been no commercial 12-inch Elvis singles in the United States, though several have been produced in Europe.

LONG LEGGED GIRL (WITH THE SHORT DRESS ON)/That's Someone You Never Forget
RCA Victor 47-9115 . . . . *5/67*   **5–8**
Black label, dog on side.
RCA Victor 47-9115 . . . . *5/67*
Picture sleeve; reads "Coming Soon—'Double Trouble' LP Album."
RCA Victor 47-9115 . . . . *6/67*   **15–20**
Picture sleeve; reads "Ask For—'Double Trouble' LP Album."
RCA Victor 47-9115 . . . . *5/67*   **20–25**
White label, promotional issue only.
RCA Victor 447-0660 . . . . *70*   **25–35**
Gold Standard; red label.

LOVE LETTERS/Come What May
RCA Victor 47-8870 . . . . *6/66*   **5–8**
Black label, dog on side.
RCA Victor 47-8870 . . . . *6/66*   **20–25**
White label, promotional issue only.
RCA Victor 47-8870 . . . . *6/66*   **15–20**
Picture sleeve; reads "Coming Soon—'Paradise Hawaiian Style.'"
RCA Victor 47-8870 . . . . *7/66*   **15–20**
Picture sleeve; reads "Ask For—'Paradise Hawaiian Style.'"
RCA Victor 447-0657 . . . *2/68*   **4–8**
Gold Standard; black label, dog on side.
RCA Victor 447-0657 . . . . *70*   **3–5**
Gold Standard; red label.

LOVE ME/Flaming Star
Collectables 4514 . . . . *86*   **1–3**

This was the first, and so far only, 12-inch Elvis single in the United States.

LOVE ME TENDER/Any Way You Want Me (That's How I Will Be)
RCA Victor 20-6643 . . . *10/56*   **50–75**
Black label, 78rpm.

RCA Victor 20-6643 . . . *10/56*   **175–200**
White label, 78rpm, promotional issue only.

RCA Victor 47-6643 . . . *10/56*   **25–30**
Black label, dog on top, with horizontal silver line.

RCA Victor 47-6643 . . . *10/56*   **15–20**
Black label, dog on top, without horizontal silver line.

RCA Victor 47-6643 . . . *10/56*   **100–150**
Picture sleeve; black and white sleeve.

RCA Victor 47-6643 . . . *10/56*   **60–75**
Picture sleeve; black and green color sleeve.

RCA Victor 47-6643 . . . *10/56*   **35–45**
Picture sleeve; black and dark pink color sleeve.

RCA Victor 47-6643 . . . *10/56*   **30–35**
Picture sleeve; black and light pink color sleeve.

RCA Victor 447-0616 . . . *3/59*   **10–12**
Gold Standard; black label, dog on top.

RCA Victor 447-0616 . . . . *65*   **4–8**
Gold Standard; black label, dog on side.

RCA Victor 447-0616 . . . . *68*   **8–10**
Gold Standard; orange label.

RCA Victor 447-0616 . . . . *70*   **3–5**
Gold Standard; red label.

RCA Victor 447-0616 . . . . *77*   **2–3**
Gold Standard; black label, dog near top.

RCA Victor PB-11108 . . *10/77*   **2–3**
Originally included as one of the singles in the boxed sets *15 Golden Hits—30 Golden Hits* and *20 Golden Hits In Full Color Sleeves*.

RCA Victor PB-11108 . . *10/77*   **2–3**
Picture sleeve.

LOVE ME TENDER/Loving You
RCA Victor PB-13893 . . *12/84*   **1–3**
Gold vinyl, originally included as one of the singles in the boxed set *Elvis' Greatest Hits—Golden Singles, Vol. 2*.

RCA Victor PB-13893 . . *12/84*   **1–3**
Picture sleeve.

LOVIN' ARMS/You Asked Me To
RCA Victor PB-12205 . . . *4/81*   **3–6**
Black label, dog near top.

RCA Victor JB-12205 . . . *4/81*   **6–10**
Light yellow label, promotional issue only.

RCA Victor JB-12205 . . . *4/81*   **250–275**
Yellow label, green vinyl; promotional issue only.

Note: It is also noteworthy that with PB-12205, for the first time since 1956, RCA did not issue a picture sleeve of some sort with a standard catalog Elvis release.

Marie's the Name HIS LATEST FLAME: see HIS LATEST FLAME

MEMORIES/Charro
RCA Victor 47-9731 . . . . *3/69*   **3–5**
Orange label.

RCA Victor 47-9731 . . . . *3/69*   **10–15**
Picture sleeve.

RCA Victor 47-9731 . . . . *3/69* **10–15**
Yellow label, promotional issue only.

RCA Victor 447-0669 . . *12/70* **3–5**
Gold Standard; red label.

RCA Victor 447-0669 . . . . *77* **2–3**
Gold Standard; black label, dog near top.

MEMORIES OF ELVIS/The Elvis Hour
Creative Radio *7/87* **15–20**
Demo disc for radio stations, offering a sample of each of the two syndicated programs available from Creative Radio.

MERRY CHRISTMAS BABY/O Come, All Ye Faithful
RCA Victor 74-0572 . . . *12/71* **12–15**
Orange label.

RCA Victor 74-0572 . . . *12/71* **20–30**
Picture sleeve.

RCA Victor 74-0572 . . . *12/71* **12–15**
Yellow label, promotional issue only.

MERRY CHRISTMAS BABY/Santa Claus Is Back in Town
RCA Victor PB-14237 . . *12/85* **5–8**
Black vinyl, gold "Elvis 50th Anniversary" label.

RCA Victor PB-14237 . . *12/85* **10–15**
Green vinyl, gold "Elvis 50th Anniversary" label.

RCA Victor PB-14237 . . *12/85* **8–12**
Picture sleeve.

MILKY WHITE WAY/Swing Down Sweet Chariot
RCA Victor 447-0652 . . . *3/66* **10–12**
Gold Standard; black label, dog on side.

RCA Victor 447-0652 . . . *3/66* **50–75**
Picture sleeve; special Gold Standard sleeve.

RCA Victor 447-0652 . . . *3/66* **30–40**
White label, promotional issue only.

RCA Victor 447-0652 . . . . *70* **3–5**
Red label.
Note: see *JOSHUA FIT THE BATTLE/Known Only to Him* for listing of the "Special Easter Programming Kit."

MONEY HONEY/One-Sided Love Affair
RCA Victor 20-6641 . . . . *9/56* **60–75**
Black label 78rpm

RCA Victor 47-6641 . . . . *9/56* **40–50**
Black label, dog on top, with horizontal silver line.

RCA Victor 47-6641 . . . . *9/56* **20–30**
Black label, dog on top, without horizontal silver line.

RCA Victor 447-0614 . . . *3/59* **10–12**
Gold Standard; black label, dog on top.

RCA Victor 447-0614 . . *65–66* **4–8**
Gold Standard; black label, dog on side.
Note: Bootleg picture sleeves exist for the original RCA 45 of this release.

Collectables 4506 . . . . . . *86* **1–3**

MOODY BLUE/For The Heart
RCA Victor GB-11326. . . *8/78* **2–3**
Gold Standard; black label, dog near top.

MOODY BLUE/She Thinks I Still Care
RCA Victor PB-10857 . . *12/76* **3–5**
Black label, dog near top.

RCA Victor PB-10857 . . *12/76* **6–10**
Picture sleeve.

RCA Victor JB-10857 . . *12/76* **6–10**
Light yellow label, promotional issue only.

RCA Victor JB-10857 . . . *5/77* **900–1000**
Colored vinyl, experimental production singles done in red, white, gold, blue, and green; price is for any of the five colors.

MY BOY/Loving Arms
RCA Victor 2458 EX *74* **200–300**
Pressed in the U.S. but never sold in the states. Manufactured for export to Europe. Price includes a single-sheet insert that reads "Elvis Presley My Boy."

MY BOY (Stereo)/My Boy (Mono)
RCA Victor JH-10191 . . . *1/75* **8–10**
Light yellow label, promotional issue only.

MY BOY/Thinking About You
RCA Victor PB-10191 . . . *1/75* **3–5**
Orange label.

RCA Victor PB-10191 . . . *1/75* **8–10**
Tan label.

RCA Victor PB-10191 . . . *1/75* **8–10**
Picture sleeve.

RCA Victor GB-10489. . . *2/76* **3–5**
Gold Standard; red label.

MY WAY/America
RCA Victor PB-11165 . . *11/77* **3–5**
Black label, dog near top.

RCA Victor PB-11165 . . *11/77* **6–10**
Picture sleeve.

RCA Victor JH-11165 . . *11/77* **6–10**
Light yellow label, promotional issue only.

MY WAY/America the Beautiful
RCA Victor PB-11165 . . *11/77* **15–20**
Black label, dog near top, with the full "America The Beautiful" title.

RCA Victor PB-11165 . . *11/77* **15–25**
Picture sleeve; with the full "America the Beautiful" title.

RCA Victor PB-11165 . . *11/77*   **15–20**
Black label, dog near top. This issue carries the full title, but can be distinguished from the previous two by its lack of vocal and production credits on the left side of the label. This issue is also stamped 13S in the vinyl trail-off instead of 12S.
Note: See *"Way Down"* for Gold Standard issue of "My Way."

MYSTERY TRAIN/I Forgot to Remember to Forget

Sun 223 . . . . *9/55*   **200–275**
78rpm.

Sun 223 . . . . *9/55*   **250–300**

RCA Victor 20-6357 . . . *11/55*   **75–100**
Black label, 78rpm.

RCA Victor 47-6357 . . . . *1/55*   **40–60**
Black label, dog on top, with horizontal silver line.

RCA Victor 47-6357 . . . *11/55*   **25–35**
Black label, dog on top, without horizontal silver line.

RCA Victor 47-6357 . . . *11/55*   **140–160**
White label, promotional issue only.
Note: This single was both the first standard catalog RCA Elvis release and later the first Gold Standard Elvis single. We should also point out that there were foreign issues of "Dealer Prevues" other than "Mystery Train." This was, however, the only U.S. white-label dealer's prevue ever released on 45rpm single.

RCA Victor 447-0600 . . . *3/59*   **10–12**
Gold Standard; black label, dog on top.

RCA Victor 447-0600 . . . . *65*   **4–8**
Gold Standard; black label, dog on side.

RCA Victor 447-0600 . . . . *70*   **3–5**
Gold Standard; red label.

RCA Victor 447-0600 . . . . *77*   **2–3**
Gold Standard; black label, dog near top.

OLD SHEP/Blank groove

RCA Victor CR-15. . . . *12/56*   **600–650**
White label, one-sided disc, promotional issue only.
Note: Counterfeits exist for this release but can easily be identified. The matrix numbers in the vinyl trail-off are stamped in the vinyl on the originals rather than etched by hand.

OLD SHEP/You'll Never Walk Alone

Collectables 4518 . . . . . . *86*   **1–3**

ONE BROKEN HEART FOR SALE/Devil in Disguise

Collectables 4512 . . . . . . *86*   **1–3**

ONE BROKEN HEART FOR SALE/They Remind Me Too Much of You

RCA Victor 47-8134 . . . . *2/63*   **8–10**
Black label, dog on top.

RCA Victor 47-8134 . . . . *2/63*   **15–20**
Picture sleeve.

RCA Victor 447-0640 . . . *8/64*   **20–25**
Gold Standard; black label, dog on top.

RCA Victor 447-0640 . . . . *65*   **4–8**
Gold Standard; black label, dog on side.

RCA Victor 447-0640 . . . . *70*   **3–5**
Gold Standard; red label.

ONE NIGHT/I Got Stung

RCA Victor 20-7410 . . . *10/58*   **250–350**
Black label, 78rpm. "One Night"/"I Got Stung" was the last Elvis 78rpm issued in the United States.

RCA Victor 47-7410 . . . *10/58*   **10–15**
Black label, dog on top.

RCA Victor 47-7410 . . . *10/58*   **35–45**
Picture sleeve.

RCA Victor 447-0624 . . . . *61*   **8–10**
Gold Standard; black label, dog on top.

RCA Victor 447-0624 . . . . *65*   **4–8**
Gold Standard; black label, dog on side.

RCA Victor 447-0624 . . . . *68*   **8–10**
Gold Standard; orange label.

RCA Victor 447-0624 . . . . *70*   **3–5**
Gold Standard; red label.

RCA Victor 447-0624 . . . . *77*   **2–3**
Gold Standard; black label, dog near top.

RCA Victor PB11112 . . *10/77*   **2–3**
Originally included as one of the singles in the boxed set *15 Golden Hits—30 Golden Hits.*

RCA Victor PB-11112 . . *10/77*   **2–3**
Picture sleeve.

POOR BOY/An American Trilogy

Collectables 4519 . . . . *86*   **1–3**

PROMISED LAND/It's Midnight

RCA Victor PB-10074 . . *10/74*   **3–5**
Orange label.

RCA Victor PB-10074 . . *10/74*   **20–25**
Gray label.

RCA Victor PB-10074 . . *10/74*   **8–12**
Tan label.

RCA Victor PB-10074 . . *10/74*   **8–10**
Picture sleeve.

RCA Victor JA-10074 . . *10/74*   **8–10**
Light yellow label, promotional issue only.

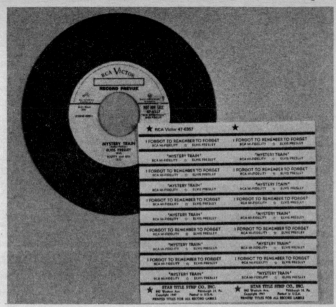

The only U.S. white-label dealer's prevue ever released on a 45rpm single.

Farewell to a format—RCA takes advantage of the last Elvis 78rpm issued in the United States to extoll the virtues of the 45 on the sleeve.

RCA Victor GB-10488. . . *2/76*   **3–5**
Gold Standard; red label.

PUPPET ON A STRING/Wooden Heart

RCA Victor 447-0650 . . *10/65*   **5–8**
Gold Standard; black label, dog on side.

RCA Victor 447-0650 . . *10/65*   **20–25**
Picture sleeve; special Gold Standard sleeve.

RCA Victor 447-0650 . . *10/65*   **20–25**
Gold Standard; white label, promotional issue only.

RCA Victor 447-0650 . . . . *70*   **3–5**
Gold Standard; red label.

RCA Victor 447-0650 . . . . *77*   **2–3**
Gold Standard; black label, dog near top.

RAGS TO RICHES/Where Did They Go Lord

RCA Victor 47-9980 . . . . *2/71*   **3–5**
Orange label.

RCA Victor 47-9980 . . . . *2/71*   **8–15**
Picture sleeve.

RCA Victor 47-9980 . . . . *2/71*   **10–15**
Yellow label, promotional issue only.

RCA Victor 447-0680 . . . *2/72*   **3–5**
Gold Standard; red label.

RAISED ON ROCK/For Ol' Times Sake

RCA Victor APBO-0088. . *9/73*   **4–6**
Orange label.

RCA Victor APBO-0088. . *9/73*   **8–12**
Picture sleeve.

RCA Victor DJAO-0088. . *9/73*   **8–10**
Light yellow label, promotional issue only.
Note: "Raised on Rock" appeared on a Gold Standard single backed with "If You Talk In Your Sleep." See that listing for more information.

RETURN TO SENDER/Where Do You Come From

RCA Victor 47-8100 . . . *10/62*   **8–10**
Black label, dog on top.

RCA Victor 47-8100 . . . *10/62*   **15–20**
Picture sleeve.

RCA Victor 447-0638 . . . *6/63*   **6–10**
Gold Standard; black label, dog on top.

RCA Victor 447-0638 . . . . *65*   **4–8**
Gold Standard; black label, dog on side.

RCA Victor 447-0638 . . . . *68*   **8–10**
Gold Standard; orange label.

RCA Victor 447-0638 . . . . *70*
Gold Standard; red label.

RCA Victor 447-0638 . . . . *77*   **2–3**
Gold Standard; black label, dog near top.

RCA Victor PB-11111 . . *10/77*   **2–3**
Originally included as one of the singles in the boxed sets *15 Golden Hits—30 Golden Hits* and *20 Golden Hits In Full Color Sleeves.*

RCA Victor PB-11111 . . *10/77*   **2–3**
Picture sleeve.

ROUSTABOUT/One Track Heart

RCA Victor SP-45-139. . *11/64*   **175–200**
White label, promotional issue only.

ROUSTABOUT THEATRE LOBBY SPOT (Coming Soon)/Roustabout Theatre Lobby Spot (Now Playing)

Paramount Pictures SP-2414
. . . . *11/64* **1000–1500**
Promotional issue to theaters for lobby play during the run of the *Roustabout* film, contains an alternate take of "Roustabout" not available elsewhere.

SEPARATE WAYS/Always on My Mind

RCA Victor 74-0815 . . . *11/72*   **3–5**
Orange label.

RCA Victor 74-0815 . . . *11/72*   **8–12**
Picture sleeve.

RCA Victor 74-0815 . . . *11/72*   **8–10**
Yellow label, promotional issue only.

RCA Victor GB-10486. . . *2/76*   **3–5**
Gold Standard; red label.

RCA Victor GB-10486. . . . *77*   **2–3**
Gold Standard; black label, dog near top.

SHE'S NOT YOU/Jailhouse Rock

Collectables 4511 . . . . *86*   **1–3**

SHE'S NOT YOU/Just Tell Her Jim Said Hello

RCA Victor 47-8041 . . . . *7/62*   **8–10**
Black label, dog on top.

RCA Victor 47-8041 . . . . *7/62*   **15–20**
Picture sleeve.

RCA Victor 447-0637 . . . *6/63*   **8–10**
Gold Standard; black label, dog on top.

RCA Victor 447-0637 . . . . *65*   **4–8**
Gold Standard; black label, dog on side.

RCA Victor 447-0637 . . . . *68*   **8–10**
Gold Standard; orange label.

RCA Victor 447-0637 . . . . *70*   **3–5**
Gold Standard; red label.

As part of the promotion for the film, Paramount theaters played this record in the lobby. This contains an alternate of "Roustabout" not available anywhere else.

SOFTLY, AS I LEAVE
YOU/Unchained Melody
RCA Victor PB-11212 . . . *3/78*   **3–5**
Black label, dog near top.

RCA Victor PB-11212 . . . *3/78*   **5–10**
Picture sleeve.

RCA Victor JH-11212 . . . *3/78*   **6–10**
Light yellow label, promotional issue only.
Note: See *"Are You Sincere"* for Gold Standard issue of "Unchained Melody."

SPECIAL EASTER
PROGRAMMING KIT: see *JOSHUA*
FIT THE BATTLE/Known Only to
Him

SPINOUT/All That I Am
RCA Victor 47-8941 . . . . *9/66*   **5–8**
Black label, dog on side.

RCA Victor 47-8941 . . . . *9/66*   **15–20**
Picture sleeve; reads " 'Watch For Elvis' 'Spinout' LP."

RCA Victor 47-8941 . . . *10/66*   **15–20**
Picture sleeve; reads "Ask For Elvis' 'Spinout' LP."

RCA Victor 47-8941 . . . . *9/66*   **20–25**
White label, promotional issue only.

RCA Victor 447-0658 . . . *2/68*   **4–8**
Gold Standard; black label, dog on side.

RCA Victor 447-0658 . . . . *70*   **3–5**
Gold Standard; red label.

STUCK ON YOU/Fame and Fortune
RCA Victor 47-7740 . . . . *4/60*   **8–10**
Black label, dog on top.

RCA Victor 47-7740 . . . . *4/60*   **15–25**
Picture sleeve; special die-cut sleeve displaying the record label.

RCA Victor 61-7740 . . . . *4/60*   **175–225**
Living Stereo.

RCA Victor 447-0627 . . . *2/62*   **8–10**
Gold Standard; black label, dog on top.

RCA Victor 447-0627 . . . . *65*   **4–8**
Gold Standard; black label, dog on side.

RCA Victor 447-0627 . . . . *68*   **8–10**
Gold Standard; orange label.

RCA Victor 447-0627 . . . . *70*   **3–5**
Gold Standard; red label.

Collectables 4509 . . . . *86*   **1–3**

All four Elvis singles, issued in 1960–1961, included in RCA's "Living Stereo" series.

A rare promotional copy (white label) of "Such a Night," along with standard issue single and picture sleeve.

SUCH A NIGHT/Never Ending

RCA Victor 47-8400 . . . . *7/64*   **6–10**
Black label, dog on top.

RCA Victor 47-8400 . . . . *7/64*   **15–20**
Picture sleeve.

RCA Victor 47-8400 . . . . *7/64*   **500–525**
White label, promotional issue only.

RCA Victor 447-0645 . . . *5/65*   **25–35**
Gold Standard; black label, dog on top.

RCA Victor 447-0645 . . . *5/65*   **4–8**
Gold Standard; black label, dog on side.

RCA Victor 447-0645 . . . . *70*   **3–5**
Gold Standard; red label.

SURRENDER/Lonely Man

RCA Victor 47-7850 . . . . *2/61*   **8–10**
Black label, dog on top.

RCA Victor 47-7850 . . . . *2/61*   **15–20**
Picture sleeve.

RCA Victor 61-7850 . . . . *2/61*   **225–275**
Living Stereo.

RCA Victor 37-7850 . . . . *2/61*   **250–300**
Compact 33 single.

RCA Victor 37-7850 . . . . *2/61*   **250–300**
Picture sleeve; Compact 33 picture sleeve.

RCA Victor 68-7850 . . . . *2/61*   **900–1100**
Living Stereo 33; stereo Compact 33 single.
Note: The stereo Compact 33 single, 68-7850, was the only one of its kind ever issued with Elvis.

RCA Victor 447-0630 . . . *2/62*   **20–25**
Gold Standard; black label, dog on top.

RCA Victor 447-0630 . . . . *65*   **4–8**
Gold Standard; black label, dog on side.

RCA Victor 447-0630 . . . . *68*   **8–10**
Gold Standard; orange label.

RCA Victor 447-0630 . . . . *70*   **3–5**
Gold Standard; red label.

RCA Victor 447-0630 . . . . *77*   **2–3**
Gold Standard; black label, dog near top.

SURRENDER/Out of a Clear Blue Sky (by Lawrence Welk)

U.S.A.F. Pgm. #159/60. . *3/61*   **300–325**
A public-service five-minute radio show, part of the U.S. Air Force's "Music in the Air" series.
Note: This record was shipped in a special box that identified the two records included by program number. Add $25–$35 to the value for the box.

SUSPICIOUS MINDS/Burning Love

RCA Victor PB-13896 . . *12/84*   **1–3**
Gold vinyl, originally included as one of the singles in the boxed set *Elvis' Greatest Hits— Golden Singles, Vol. 2.*

RCA Victor PB-13896 . . *12/84*   **1–3**
Picture sleeve.

SUSPICIOUS MINDS/You'll Think of Me

RCA Victor 47-9764 . . . . *9/69*   **3–5**
Orange label.

RCA Victor 47-9764 . . . . *9/69*   **8–12**
Picture sleeve.

RCA Victor 47-9764 . . . . *9/69*   **10–15**
Yellow label, promotional issue only.

RCA Victor 447-0673 . . *12/70*   **3–5**
Gold Standard; red label.

RCA Victor PB-11103 . . *10/77*   **2–3**
Originally included as one of the singles in the boxed set *15 Golden Hits—30 Golden Hits.*

RCA Victor PB-11103 . . *10/77*   **2–3**
Picture sleeve.

RCA Victor GB-13275 . . . *1/83*   **2–3**
Gold Standard; black label, dog near top.

(LET ME BE YOUR) TEDDY BEAR/Loving You

RCA Victor 20-7000 . . . . *6/57*   **50–75**
Black label, 78rpm.

RCA Victor 20-7000 . . . . *6/57*   **175–200**
White label, 78rpm, promotional issue only.

RCA Victor 47-7000 . . . . *6/57*   **25–30**
Black label, dog on top, with horizontal silver line.

RCA Victor 47-7000 . . . . *6/57*   **15–20**
Black label, dog on top, without horizontal silver line.

RCA Victor 47-7000 . . . . *6/57*   **20–25**
Black label, dog on top, does not have parentheses around "Let Me Be Your."

RCA Victor 47-7000 . . . . *6/57*   **40–60**
Picture sleeve.

RCA Victor 47-0620 . . . . . *61*   **8–10**
Gold Standard; black label, dog on top.

RCA Victor 447-0620 . . . . *65*   **4–8**
Gold Standard; black label, dog on side.

RCA Victor 447-0620 . . . . *68*   **8–10**
Gold Standard; orange label.

RCA Victor 447-0620 . . . . *70*   **3–5**
Gold Standard; red label.

RCA Victor 447-0620 . . . . *77*   **2–3**
Gold Standard; black label, dog near top.

Five different Elvis releases were included in RCA's Compact 33 Singles series. All five sleeves and six discs ("Surrender" was issued in both monaural and stereo) are pictured here.

The complete collection of RCA's Elvis Gold Standard series picture sleeves.

RCA Victor PB-11109 . .   *10/77*   **2–3**
Originally included as one of the singles in the boxed sets *15 Golden Hits—30 Golden Hits* and *20 Golden Hits In Full Color Sleeves.*

RCA Victor PB-11109 . .   *10/77*   **2–3**
Picture sleeve.

(LET ME BE YOUR) TEDDY BEAR/Puppet on a String

RCA Victor PB-11320 . . .   *8/78*   **3–5**
Black label, dog near top.

RCA Victor PB-11320 . . .   *8/78*   **5–10**
Picture sleeve.

RCA Victor JH-11320 . . .   *8/78*   **6–10**
Light yellow label, promotional issue only.

TELL ME WHY/Blue River

RCA Victor 47-8740 . . .   *12/65*   **5–10**
Black label, dog on side.

RCA Victor 47-8740 . . .   *12/65*   **15–20**
Picture sleeve.

RCA Victor 47-8740 . . .   *12/65*   **20–25**
White label, promotional issue only.

RCA Victor 447-0655 . . .   *2/68*   **4–8**
Gold Standard; black label, dog on side.

RCA Victor 447-0655 . . . .   *70*   **3–5**
Gold Standard; red label.

THAT'S ALL RIGHT/Blue Moon of Kentucky

Sun 209 . . . .   *7/54*   **200–300**
78rpm.

Sun 209 . . . .   *7/54*   **375–400**

RCA Victor 20-6380 . . .   *11/55*   **75–100**
Black label, 78rpm.

RCA Victor 47-6380 . . .   *11/55*   **40–60**
Black label, dog on top, with horizontal silver line.

RCA Victor 47-6380 . . .   *11/55*   **25–35**
Black label, dog on top, without horizontal silver line.

RCA Victor 447-0601 . . .   *3/59*   **10–12**
Gold Standard; black label, dog on top.

RCA Victor 447-0601 . . .   *7/64*   **50–75**
Picture sleeve; special Gold Standard sleeve.

RCA Victor 447-0601 . . .   *7/64*   **40–50**
Gold Standard; white label, promotional issue only.

RCA Victor 447-0601 . . . .   *65*   **4–8**
Gold Standard; black label, dog on side.

RCA Victor 447-0601 . . . .   *70*   **3–5**
Gold Standard; red label.

RCA Victor 447-0601 . . . .   *77*   **2–3**
Gold Standard; black label, dog near top.
Note: Bootleg picture sleeves exist for the original 45 of this release.

RCA Victor PB-13891 . .   *12/84*   **1–3**
Gold vinyl, originally included as one of the singles in the boxed set *Elvis' Greatest Hits—Golden Singles, Vol. 2.*

RCA Victor PB-13891 . .   *12/84*   **1–3**
Picture sleeve.

THERE'S A HONKY TONK ANGEL (WHO WILL TAKE ME BACK IN)/I Got a Feelin' in My Body

RCA Victor PB-11679 . . .   *8/79*   **12–15**
Black label, dog near top, with production *and* backing credits shown on left side of label.
Note: Since the tracks used on this single were *without* the vocal and string accompaniment credited, this was printed in error.

RCA Victor PB-11679 . . .   *8/79*   **3–5**
Black label, dog near top, with production credits only.

RCA Victor PB-11679 . . .   *8/79*   **5–10**
Picture sleeve.

RCA Victor JB-11679 . . .   *8/79*   **6–10**
Light yellow label, promotional issue only.

THOMPSON VOCAL ELIMINATOR/Thompson Analog Delay

Eva-Tone 12-27785 . . . .   *12/78*   **15–20**
An 8-inch soundsheet used as a promotional item for LT Sound's Thompson Vocal Eliminator, contains a portion of "You Don't Have to Say You Love Me."

TOO MUCH/Playing for Keeps

RCA Victor 20-6800 . . . .   *1/57*   **50–75**
Black label, 78rpm.

RCA Victor 20-6800 . . . .   *1/57*   **175–200**
White label, 78rpm, promotional issue only.

RCA Victor 47-6800 . . . .   *1/57*   **100–125**
Black label, no dog on label.

RCA Victor 47-6800 . . . .   *1/57*   **25–30**
Black label, dog on top, with horizontal silver line.

RCA Victor 47-6800 . . . .   *1/57*   **15–20**
Black label, dog on top, without horizontal silver line.

RCA Victor 47-6800 . . . .   *1/57*   **40–60**
Picture sleeve.

RCA Victor 447-0617 . . .   *3/59*   **10–12**
Gold Standard; black label, dog on top.

RCA Victor 447-0617 . . . . *65*   **4–8**
Gold Standard; black label, dog on side.

RCA Victor 447-0617 . . . . *68*   **8–10**
Gold Standard; orange label.

RCA Victor 447-0617 . . . . *70*   **3–5**
Gold Standard; red label.

Collectables 4507 . . . . *86*   **1–3**

TREAT ME NICE/Nellie Was a Lady
Laurel 41 623 . . . . *10/57* **2000–2500**
Sleeve only. Pictures Elvis, but shows artist as
Vince Everett. This black-and-white "sleeve"
was made as a prop for the film *Jailhouse Rock*.
The printed sheet had no reverse side and was
applied to a randomly selected EP. In the case
of the only known (at this time) sleeve to have
survived, the EP was *Charlie Mariano*, Impe-

rial 125. Other sleeves were probably attached
to various EPs, or perhaps plain pieces of cardboard. Since there was never an actual Laurel
record made, the overall construction of the
sleeve was moot.

T-R-O-U-B-L-E/Mr. Songman
RCA Victor PB-10278 . . . *4/75*   **3–5**
Orange label.

RCA Victor PB-10278 . . . *4/75*   **20–25**
Gray label.

RCA Victor PB-10278 . . . *4/75*   **8–10**
Tan label.

RCA Victor PB-10278 . . . *4/75*   **8–10**
Picture sleeve.

RCA Victor GS-10487 . . . *2/76*   **3–5**
Red label.

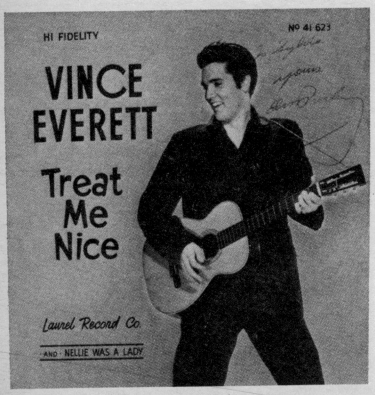

A mock-up cover used as a prop in *Jailhouse Rock*.

T-R-O-U-B-L-E (Stereo)/T-r-o-u-b-l-e (Mono)

RCA Victor JH-10278 . . . *4/75*   **8–10**
Light yellow label, promotional issue only.

TRYIN' TO GET TO YOU/I Love You Because

RCA Victor 20-6639 . . . . *9/56*   **60–75**
Black label, 78rpm.

RCA Victor 47-6639 . . . . *9/56*   **40–50**
Black label, dog on top, with horizontal silver line.

RCA Victor 47-6639 . . . . *9/56*   **20–30**
Black label, dog on top, without horizontal silver line.

RCA Victor 447-0612 . . . *3/59*   **10–12**
Gold Standard; black label, dog on top.

Collectables 4505 . . . . . . *86*   **1–3**

20 GOLDEN HITS IN FULL COLOR SLEEVES

RCA Victor PP-11340 . . *12/77*   **65–75**
A package of 10 singles, each with its own picture sleeve; price is for complete set.
Note: Also see *15 GOLDEN RECORDS/30 Golden Hits.*

U.S. MALE/Stay Away

RCA Victor 47-9465 . . . . *3/68*   **5–8**
Black label, dog on side.

RCA Victor 47-9465 . . . . *3/68*   **10–20**
Picture sleeve.

RCA Victor 47-9465 . . . . *3/68*   **15–20**
Yellow label, promotional issue only.

RCA Victor 447-0664 . . . . *70*   **3–5**
Gold Standard; red label.

U.S. MALE/Until It's Time for You to Go

Collectables 4517 . . . . *86*   **1–3**

UNTIL IT'S TIME FOR YOU TO GO/We Can Make the Morning

RCA Victor 74-0619 . . . . *1/72*   **3–5**
Orange label.

RCA Victor 74-0619 . . . . *1/72*   **8–12**
Picture sleeve.

RCA Victor 74-0619 . . . . *1/72*   **10–12**
Yellow label, promotional issue only.
Note: On Gold Standard, "Until It's Time for You to Go" was coupled with "An American Trilogy." See that listing for more information.

VIVA LAS VEGAS/What'd I Say

RCA Victor 447-0646 . . . *5/65*   **25–35**
Gold Standard; black label, dog on top.

RCA Victor 47-8360 . . . . *4/64*   **6–10**
Black label, dog on top.

RCA Victor 47-8360 . . . . *4/64*   **15–20**
Picture sleeve.

RCA Victor 47-8360 . . . . *4/64*   **20–25**
White label, promotional issue only.

RCA Victor 447-0646 . . . *5/65*   **4–8**
Gold Standard; black label, dog on side.

RCA Victor 447-0646 . . . . *68*   **8–10**
Gold Standard; orange label.

RCA Victor 447-0646 . . . . *70*   **3–5**
Gold Standard; red label.

RCA Victor 447-0646 . . . . *77*   **2–3**
Gold Standard; black label, dog near top.

WAY DOWN/My Way

RCA Victor GB-11504 . . . *5/79*   **2–3**
Black label, dog near top.

WAY DOWN/Pledging My Love

RCA Victor PB-10998 . . . *7/77*   **3–5**
Black label, dog near top.

RCA Victor PB-10998 . . . *7/77*   **6–10**
Picture sleeve.

RCA Victor JB-10998 . . . *7/77*   **125–175**
White label, promotional issue only.

RCA Victor JB-10998 . . . *7/77*   **6–10**
Light yellow label, promotional issue only.

WEAR MY RING AROUND YOUR NECK/Doncha' Think It's Time

RCA Victor 20-7240 . . . . *4/58*   **60–75**
Black label, 78rpm.

RCA Victor 47-7240 . . . . *4/58*   **10–15**
Black label, dog on top.

RCA Victor 47-7240 . . . . *4/58*   **40–50**
Picture sleeve.

RCA Victor 447-0622 . . . . *61*   **8–10**
Gold Standard; black label, dog on top.

RCA Victor 447-0622 . . . . *65*   **4–8**
Gold Standard; black label, dog on side.

RCA Victor 447-0622 . . . . *68*   **8–10**
Gold Standard; orange label.

RCA Victor 447-0622 . . . . *70*   **3–5**
Gold Standard; red label.

RCA Victor 447-0622 . . . . *77*   **2–3**
Gold Standard; black label, dog near top.
Note: "Wear My Ring Around Your Neck" was issued on a special promotional 45, backed with "Don't." See that listing for more information. Also see *I Was The One* for an additional listing.

WHAT'S IT ALL ABOUT?

MA-1840 (Pgm 555/6). . *12/80* **70–75**
A summary of Elvis' life story, hosted by Bill Huey, with excerpts of Elvis' songs and interviews.
MA-3025 (Pgm 644/4). . . . *82* **50–60**
Note: Discs in this series are provided as religious programming for radio stations.

WONDER OF YOU, The/Mama Liked the Roses

RCA Victor 47-9835 . . . . *5/70* **3–5**
Orange label.

RCA Victor 47-9835 . . . . *5/70* **8–12**
Picture sleeve.

RCA Victor 47-9835 . . . . *5/70* **10–15**
Yellow label, promotional issue only.

RCA Victor 447-0676 . . . *8/71* **3–5**
Gold Standard; red label.

RCA Victor 447-0676 . . . . *77* **2–3**
Gold Standard; black label, dog near top.

YOU DON'T HAVE TO SAY YOU LOVE ME/Patch It Up

RCA Victor 47-9916 . . . *10/70* **3–5**
Orange label.

RCA Victor 47-9916 . . . *10/70* **8–12**
Picture sleeve.

RCA Victor 47-9916 . . . *10/70* **10–15**
Yellow label, promotional issue only.

RCA Victor 447-0678 . . . *2/72* **3–5**
Gold Standard; red label.

RCA Victor 447-0678 . . . . *77* **2–3**
Gold Standard; black label, dog near top.

YOU'LL NEVER WALK ALONE/There Goes My Everything

RCA Victor PB-13058 . . . *2/82* **3–5**
Black label, dog near top.

RCA Victor PB-13058 . . . *2/82* **5–10**
Picture sleeve.

RCA Victor JB-13058 . . . *2/82* **6–10**
Light yellow label, promotional issue only.

YOU'LL NEVER WALK ALONE/We Call On Him

RCA Victor 47-9600 . . . . *4/68* **5–10**
Black label, dog on side.

RCA Victor 47-9600 . . . . *4/68* **35–45**
Picture sleeve.

Bill Huey's condensation of Elvis' life in song and interviews.

RCA Victor 47-9600 . . . . *4/68*   **15–20**
Yellow label, promotional issue only.

RCA Victor 447-0665 . . *12/70*   **3–5**
Gold Standard; red label.

RCA Victor 447-0665 . . . . *77*   **2–4**
Black label, dog near top.

YOUR TIME HASN'T COME YET BABY/Let Yourself Go

RCA Victor 47-9547 . . . . *6/68*   **5–8**
Black label, dog on side.

RCA Victor 47-9547 . . . . *6/68*   **10–20**
Picture sleeve; reads "Coming Soon—'Speedway' LP."

RCA Victor 47-9547 . . . . *7/68*   **10–20**
Picture sleeve; reads "Ask For—'Speedway' LP."

RCA Victor 47-9547 . . . . *6/68*   **15–20**
Yellow label, promotional issue only.

RCA Victor 447-0666 . . *12/70*   **3–5**
Gold Standard; red label.

YOU'RE A HEARTBREAKER/Milkcow Blues Boogie

Sun 215 . . . . *1/55*   **200–300**
78rpm.

Sun 215 . . . . *1/55*   **375–425**

RCA Victor 20-6382 . . . *11/55*   **75–100**
Black label, 78rpm.

RCA Victor 47-6382 . . . *11/55*   **40–60**
Black label, dog on top, with horizontal silver line.

RCA Victor 47-6382 . . . *11/55*   **25–35**
Black label, dog on top, without horizontal silver line.

RCA Victor 447-0603 . . . *3/59*   **10–12**
Gold Standard; black label, dog on top.

RCA Victor 447-0603 . . . . *65*   **4–8**
Gold Standard; black label, dog on side.

RCA Victor 447-0603 . . . . *70*   **3–5**
Gold Standard; red label.

Collectables 4501 . . . . *86*   **1–3**

ALPHABETICAL LISTING OF FLIP SIDES

When you can think of only one side of an Elvis disc, and when that one tune happens to be listed as a flip side in our pricing section, this handy listing will give you the "A" side. Then simply look up that title.

TO LOCATE:/LOOK FOR:

A Mess of Blues/**It's Now Or Never**

All That I Am/**Spinout**

Almost in Love/**A Little Less Conversation**

Always on My Mind/**Separate Ways**

Always on My Mind/**The Elvis Medley**

America/**My Way**

Any Day Now/**In the Ghetto**

Any Way You Want Me/**Love Me Tender**

Anything That's Part of You/**Good Luck Charm**

Ask Me/**Ain't That Loving You Baby**

Blue Moon of Kentucky/**That's All Right**

Blue River/**Tell Me Why**

Bosom of Abraham/**He Touched Me**

Charro/**Memories**

Come What May/**Love Letters**

Doncha' Think It's Time/**Wear My Ring Around Your Neck**

Don't Ask Me Why/**Hard Headed Woman**

Edge of Reality/**If I Can Dream**

Faded Love/**Guitar Man**

Fame and Fortune/**Stuck on You**

Fools Fall in Love/**Indescribably Blue**

For Ol' Times Sake/**Raised on Rock**

For the Heart/**Hurt**

For the Heart/**Moody Blue**

Heart of Rome/**I'm Leavin'**

Help Me/**If You Talk in Your Sleep**

High Heel Sneakers/**Guitar Man**

His Hand in Mine/**How Great Thou Art**

Home Is Where the Heart Is/**King Of the Whole Wide World**

Hound Dog/**Don't Be Cruel**

Hound Dog (live)/**Baby, Let's Play House**

How Would You Like to Be/**If Everyday Was Like Christmas**

I Beg of You/**Don't**

I Believe in the Man in the Sky/**Crying in the Chapel**

I Don't Care If the Sun Don't Shine/**Good Rockin' Tonight**

I Forgot to Remember to Forget/**Mystery Train**

I Got a Feelin' in My Body/**There's a Honky Tonk Angel (Who'll Take Me Back In)**

I Got Stung/**One Night**

I Gotta Know/**Are You Lonesome Tonight**

I Love You Because/**Tryin' To Get To You**

I Need Your Love Tonight/**A Fool Such As I**

I'm Counting on You/**I Got a Woman**

I'm Gonna Sit Right Down and Cry/**I'll Never Let You Go**

I'm Left, You're Right, She's Gone/**Baby Let's Play House**

It Feels So Right/**Easy Question**

It Hurts Me/**Kissin' Cousins**

It's a Matter of Time/**Burning Love**

It's Midnight/**Promised Land**

Just Because/**Blue Moon**

Just Tell Her Jim Said Hello/**She's Not You**

Known Only to Him/**Joshua Fit The Battle**

Let Yourself Go/**Your Time Hasn't Come Yet Baby**

Little Sister/**His Latest Flame**

Lonely Man/**Surrender**

Long Lonely Highway/**I'm Yours**

Loving You/**Teddy Bear**

Mama Liked the Roses/**The Wonder Of You**

Milkcow Blues Boogie/**You're A Heartbreaker**

Mr. Songman/**T-R-O-U-B-L-E**

My Baby Left Me/**I Want You, I Need You, I Love You**

My Boy/**Always On My Mind**

My Little Friend/**Kentucky Rain**

My Wish Came True/**A Big Hunk O' Love**

Never Ending/**Such A Night**

O Come, All Ye Faithful/**Merry Christmas Baby**

One Sided Love Affair/**Money Honey**

Only Believe/**Life**

Paralyzed/**Little Sister**

Patch It Up/**You Don't Have To Say You Love Me**

Pieces of My Life/**Bringing It Back**

Playing for Keeps/**Too Much**

Please Don't Drag That String Around/**Devil In Disguise**

Please Don't Stop Loving Me/**Frankie And Johnny**

Pledging My Love/**Way Down**

Promised Land/**Blue Suede Shoes**

Puppet on a String/**Teddy Bear**

Rip It Up/**Little Sister**

Rock-A-Hula Baby/**Can't Help Falling In Love**

Rubberneckin'/**Don't Cry Daddy**

Santa Claus Is Back in Town/**Blue Christmas**

Santa Claus Is Back in Town/**Merry Christmas Baby**

Shake, Rattle and Roll/**Lawdy Miss Clawdy**

She Thinks I Still Care/**Moody Blue**

So High/**How Great Thou Art**

Solitaire/**Are You Sincere**

Stay Away/**U.S. Male**

Steamroller Blues/**Fool**

Suspicion/**Kiss Me Quick**

Swing Down Sweet Chariot/**Milky White Way**

Take Good Care of Her/**I've Got A Thing About You Baby**

That's Someone You Never Forget/**Long Legged Girl (With The Short Dress On)**

That's When Your Heartaches Begin/**All Shook Up**

The Fair Is Moving On/**Clean Up Your Own Backyard**

The First Time Ever I Saw Your Face/**An American Trilogy**

The Next Step Is Love/**I've Lost You**

The Sound of Your Cry/**It's Only Love**

There Goes My Everything/**I Really Don't Want To Know**

There Goes My Everything/**You'll Never Walk Alone**

There's Always Me/**Judy**

They Remind Me Too Much of You/**One Broken Heart For Sale**

Thinking About You/**My Boy**

Treat Me Nice/**Jailhouse Rock**

Tutti Frutti/**Blue Suede Shoes**

Unchained Melody/**Softly, As I Leave You**

We Call on Him/**You'll Never Walk Alone**

We Can Make the Morning/**Until It's Time For You To Go**

What'd I Say/**Viva Las Vegas**

Where Did They Go Lord/**Rags To Riches**

Where Do You Come From/**Return To Sender**

Wild in the Country/**I Feel So Bad**

Witchcraft/**Bossa Nova Baby**

Wooden Heart/**Blue Christmas**

Wooden Heart/**Puppet On A String**

You Asked Me To/**Lovin' Arms**

You Don't Know Me/**Big Boss Man**

You'll Be Gone/**Do The Clam**

You'll Think of Me/**Suspicious Minds**

EPs

All of Elvis' U.S. extended plays (EPs), commercial and promotional, are listed alphabetically in this chapter. With untitled EPs, they will be found by looking for their catalog number (prefix and number) in its normal alphabetical position. SPA-7-61, for example, will be found in the "S" section.

Various artists EPs, cross-referenced by title here, will be found in the Various-Artists Compilations section.

Unless listed separately, all EP covers and jackets are included in the price range. It is assumed that the cover condition is very close to the disc condition; however, an adjustment may be necessary in cases where there is a variance.

LISTINGS

A TOUCH OF GOLD
RCA Victor EPA-5088. . . *4/59*   **75–85**
Black label, dog on top.

RCA Victor EPA-5088. . . *4/59*   **250–350**
Maroon label.

RCA Victor EPA-5088. . . . *65*   **25–35**
Black label, dog on side.

RCA Victor EPA-5088. . . . *68*   **20–35**
Orange label.
Note: All issues of this EP are Gold Standard series.

Side 1
   Hard Headed Woman
   Good Rockin' Tonight
Side 2
   Don't
   I Beg of You

A TOUCH OF GOLD VOLUME II
RCA Victor EPA-5101. . . *9/59*   **75–85**
Black label, dog on top.

RCA Victor EPA-5101. . . *9/59*   **250–350**
Maroon label.

RCA Victor EPA-5101. . . . *65*   **25–35**
Black label, dog on side.

RCA Victor EPA-5101. . . . *68*   **20–35**
Orange Label.
Note: All issues of this EP are Gold Standard series.

Side 1
   Wear My Ring Around Your Neck
   Treat Me Nice
Side 2
   One Night
   That's All Right

A TOUCH OF GOLD VOLUME 3
RCA Victor EPA-5141. . . *1/60*   **75–85**
Black label, dog on top.

RCA Victor EPA-5141. . . *1/60*   **250–350**
Maroon label.

RCA Victor EPA-5141. . . . *65*   **25–35**
Black label, dog on side.

RCA Victor EPA-5141. . . . *68*   **20–35**
Orange label.
Note: All issues of this EP are Gold Standard series. Some copies of the *Touch Of Gold* series EPs contained an insert thanking buyers of RCA records, which could add $10–$20 to the value.

Side 1
  All Shook Up
  Don't Ask Me Why
Side 2
  Too Much
  Blue Moon of Kentucky

ALOHA FROM HAWAII VIA SATELLITE

RCA Victor DTF0-2006 . . *2/73*   60–75
This was the only stereo Elvis EP, and was made available for stereo juke boxes. Included in the shrink wrap was a sheet of ten juke box title strips.

Side 1
  Something
  You Gave Me a Mountain
  I Can't Stop Loving You
Side 2
  My Way
  What Now My Love
  I'm So Lonesome I Could Cry

ANY WAY YOU WANT ME

RCA Victor EPA-965 . . *10/56*   70–90
Black label, dog on top, with horizontal silver line.

RCA Victor EPA-965 . . *10/56*   55–75
Black label, dog on top, without horizontal silver line.

RCA Victor EPA-965 . . *10/56*   150–200
Black label, no dog on label.

RCA Victor EPA-965 . . . . *65*   30–40
Black label, dog on side.

RCA Victor EPA-965 . . . . *68*   20–35
Orange label.
Note: Original issues of this EP have a black and white title strip across the top of the jacket.

Side 1
  Anyway You Want Me
  I'm Left, You're Right, She's Gone
Side 2
  I Don't Care If the Sun Don't Shine
  Mystery Train

CHRISTMAS WITH ELVIS

RCA Victor EPA-4340 . . *11/58*   75–95
Black label, dog on top.

RCA Victor EPA-4340 . . *65-66*   30–40
Black label, dog on side.

RCA Victor EPA-4340 . . *68-69*   20–35
Orange label.

Side 1
  White Christmas
  Here Comes Santa Claus

Side 2
  Oh Little Town of Bethlehem
  Silent Night

DEALER'S PREVIEW: see SDS-7-2 and SDS-57-39 in Various-Artists Compilations section.

DJ7 (LOVE ME TENDER)

RCA Victor DJ-7 (47-6643)*10/56*   125–150
White label, promotional issue only, not issued with cover.

Side 1 **(Elvis)**
  Love Me Tender
  Anyway You Want Me (That's How I Will Be)
Side 2 **(Jean Chapel)**
  Welcome to the Club
  I Won't Be Rockin' Tonight

DJ-56 (TOO MUCH)

RCA Victor DJ-56 (47-6800)*1/57*   125–150
White label, promotional issue only, not issued with cover.

Side 1 **(Elvis)**
  Too Much
  Playing For Keeps
Side 2 **(Dinah Shore)**
  Chantes-Chantez
  Honkytonk Heart

EASY COME, EASY GO

RCA Victor EPA-4387. . . *2/67*   40–50
Black label, dog on side.

RCA Victor EPA-4387. . . *2/67*   75–100
White label, promotional issue only.

RCA Victor EPA-4387. . . . *68*   20–35
Orange label.

Side 1
  Easy Come, Easy Go
  The Love Machine
  Yoga Is As Yoga Does
Side 2
  You Gotta Shop
  Sing You Children
  I'll Take Love

ELVIS (Volume 1)

RCA Victor EPA-992 . . *11/56*   70–90
Black label, dog on top, with horizontal silver line.

RCA Victor EPA-992 . . *11/56*   55–75
Black label, dog on top, without horizontal silver line.

RCA Victor EPA-992 . . *11/56*   150–200
Black label, no dog on label.

RCA Victor EPA-992 . . . . *65*   30–40
Black label, dog on side.

RCA Victor EPA-992 . . . . *68* **20–35**
Orange label.
Note: Original issues of this EP have a black and white title strip across the top of the jacket.

Side 1
 Rip It Up
 Love Me
Side 2
 When My Blue Moon Turns to Gold Again
 Paralyzed

ELVIS (Volume 2)

RCA Victor EPA-993 . . *11/56* **70–90**
Black label, dog on top, with horizontal silver line.

RCA Victor EPA-993 . . *11/56* **55–75**
Black label, dog on top, without horizontal silver line.

RCA Victor EPA-993 . . *11/56* **150–200**
Black label, no dog on label.

RCA Victor EPA-993 . . . . *65* **30–40**
Black label, dog on side.

RCA Victor EPA-993 . . . . *68* **20–35**
Orange label.
Note: Original issues of this EP have a black and white title strip across the top of the jacket.

Side 1
 So Glad You're Mine
 Old Shep
Side 2
 Reddy Teddy
 Anyplace Is Paradise

ELVIS (Volume 3): see *STRICTLY ELVIS.*

ELVIS/JAYE P. MORGAN (2 EP)

RCA Victor EPA-992/689 *12/56* **1000–1500**
Double pocket two-EP set. Promotional sampler used to encourage retail stores to establish themselves in the music/record business. The idea of the Elvis/Jaye P. Morgan coupling was to point out that the Elvis EP, EPA-992, sold 1,000 times better than the Morgan EP, EPA-689, and that record and phonograph sales were on the rise.

ELVIS BY REQUEST (FLAMING STAR)

RCA Victor LPC-128 . . . *1/61* **50–75**
Compact 33 double.

Side 1
 Flaming Star
 Summer Kisses, Winter Tears
Side 2
 Are You Lonesome Tonight
 It's Now or Never

ELVIS PRESLEY

RCA Victor EPA-747 . . . *3/56* **70–90**
Black label, dog on top, with horizontal silver line.

RCA Victor EPA-747 . . . *3/56* **55–75**
Black label, dog on top, without horizontal silver line.

RCA Victor EPA-747 . . . *3/56* **150–200**
Black label, no dog on label.

RCA Victor EPA-747 . . . . *65* **30–40**
Black label, dog on side.

RCA Victor EPA-747 . . . . *68* **20–35**
Orange label.

RCA Victor EPA-747 . . . *3/56* **500–525**
Special sleeve. This temporary paper sleeve was used until the standard EP jackets were available. A typed letter of explanation was included in shipments to retailers.
Note: There are at least four variations of the commercial cover for this EP. The differences are strictly in the layout and choice of other RCA products promoted on the back cover. Original issues of this EP have a black and white title strip across the top of the jacket. As with the other EPs that have this note, the title strip may be either black with white letters or white with black letters.

Side 1
 Blue Suede Shoes
 Tutti Frutti
Side 2
 I Got a Woman
 Just Because

ELVIS PRESLEY

RCA Victor EPA-830 . . . *9/56* **70–90**
Black label, dog on top, with horizontal silver line.

RCA Victor EPA-830 . . . *9/56* **55–75**
Black label, dog on top, without horizontal silver line.

RCA Victor EPA-830 . . . *9/56* **150–200**
Black label, no dog on label.

RCA Victor EPA-830 . . . . *65* **30–40**
Black label, dog on side.

RCA Victor EPA-830 . . . . *68* **20–35**
Orange label.
Note: Original issues of this EP have black and white title strips across the top of the jacket.

Side 1
 Shake, Rattle and Roll
 I Love You Because
Side 2
 Blue Moon
 Lawdy, Miss Clawdy

Eagerly anticipating the eager anticipation of Elvis' restless fans, RCA could not wait for the intended packaging, so they shipped his first EP in this temporary sleeve.

ELVIS PRESLEY (2 EP)

RCA Victor EPB-1254. . . *4/56*   **350–400**
Black label, no dog on label.

RCA Victor EPB-1254. . . *4/56*   **300–350**
Black label, dog on top, with horizontal silver line.

RCA Victor EPB-1254. . . *4/56*   **275–325**
Black label, dog on top, without horizontal silver line.

Note: There are at least three variations of the back cover for this EP. There are two different layouts of other RCA products and one with a picture of Elvis. There is also a variation in the playing order on some copies, with Record One containing Sides 1 and 2, in some pressings, and Sides 1 and 4 in others (with Record Two containing the remaining two sides in each case). Counterfeit copies of this EP exist, but can easily be identified by their hand-etched matrix numbers. Originals have those numbers mechanically stamped in the vinyl.

ELVIS PRESLEY (2 EP)

RCA Victor SPD-22 . . . *10/56*   **600–650**
Black label, dog on top, this version was given as a bonus to buyers of a $32.95 Victrola.

Side 1
  Blue Suede Shoes
  I'm Counting on You
Side 2
  I Got a Woman
  One-Sided Love Affair

Side 3
  Tutti Frutti
  Tryin' to Get to You
Side 4
  I'm Gonna Sit Right Down and Cry
  I'll Never Let You Go

ELVIS PRESLEY (3 EP)

RCA Victor SPD-23 . . . *10/56* **2000–2500**
Black label, dog on top; this triple pocket EP was given as a bonus to buyers of a $47.95 Victrola. Price includes six-page brochure, "How To Use And Enjoy Your RCA Victor Elvis Presley Autograph, Automatic 45 'Victrola' Portable Phonograph," which represents $40–$60 of the value.

Side 1
  Blue Suede Shoes
  I'm Counting on You
Side 2
  I Got a Woman
  One-Sided Love Affair
Side 3
  I'm Gonna Sit Right Down and Cry
  I'll Never Let You Go
Side 4
  Tutti Frutti
  Tryin' to Get to You
Side 5
  Don't Be Cruel
  I Want You, I Need You, I Love You
Side 6
  Hound Dog
  My Baby Left Me

ELVIS REMEMBERED/Frank Sinatra-Nat King Cole

Creative Radio Shows *79*   **40–45**
Promotional sales demonstration disc, for a three-hour Elvis special. See the LP section for more information. Side two is a sales demo for other Creative Radio shows, featuring Frank Sinatra and Nat King Cole.

ELVIS SAILS

RCA Victor EPA-4325. . *10/58*   **70–90**
Black label, dog on top, cover has a 1959 calendar on back of jacket.

RCA Victor EPA-5157. . . *5/65*   **30–40**
Gold Standard; black label, dog on side.

RCA Victor EPA-5157. . . . *68*   **20–35**
Orange label.

Side 1
  Press Interviews with Elvis Presley
Side 2
  Elvis Presley's Newsreel Interview
  Pat Hernon Interviews Elvis in the Library of
    the U.S.S. Randall at Sailing

ELVIS SINGS CHRISTMAS SONGS

RCA Victor EPA-4108. . *11/57*   **55–75**
Black label, dog on top.

RCA Victor EPA-4108. . . . *65*   **30–40**
Black label, dog on side.

RCA Victor EPA-4108. . . . *68*   **20–35**
Orange label.

Side 1
  Santa Bring My Baby Back
  Blue Christmas
Side 2
  Santa Claus Is Back in Town
  I'll Be Home for Christmas

FLAMING STAR: see *ELVIS BY REQUEST.*

FOLLOW THAT DREAM

RCA Victor EPA-4368. . . *5/62*   **45–60**
Black label, dog on top.

RCA Victor EPA-4368. . . *5/62*   **100–150**
Special sleeve; paper, for coin operator/DJ prevue.

RCA Victor EPA-4368. . . . *65*   **30–40**
Black label, dog on side.

RCA Victor EPA-4368. . . . *68*   **20–35**
Orange label.

Side 1
  Follow That Dream
  Angel

Side 2
  What a Wonderful Life
  I'm Not the Marrying Kind

GREAT COUNTRY/WESTERN HITS (10 EP): see Various-Artists Compilations section.

HEARTBREAK HOTEL

RCA Victor EPA-821 . . . *4/56*   **70–90**
Black label, dog on top, with horizontal silver line.

RCA Victor EPA-821 . . . *4/56*   **55–75**
Black label, dog on top, without horizontal silver line.

RCA Victor EPA-821 . . . *4/56*   **150–200**
Black label, no dog on label.

RCA Victor EPA-821 . . . . *65*   **30–40**
Black label, dog on side.

RCA Victor EPA-821 . . . . *68*   **20–35**
Orange label.

Note: Original issues of this EP have a black and white title strip across the top of the jacket.

Side 1
  Heartbreak Hotel
  I Was the One
Side 2
  Money Honey
  I Forgot to Remember to Forget

JAILHOUSE ROCK

RCA Victor EPA-4114. . *10/57*   **55–75**
Black label, dog on top.

RCA Victor EPA-4114. . . . *65*   **25–35**
Black label, dog on side.

RCA Victor EPA-4114. . . . *68*   **20–35**
Orange label.

Side 1
  Jailhouse Rock
  Young and Beautiful
Side 2
  I Want to Be Free
  Don't Leave Me Now
  Baby I Don't Care

JUST FOR YOU (ELVIS PRESLEY)

RCA Victor EPA-4041. . . *3/57*   **70–90**
Black label, dog on top, with horizontal silver line.

RCA Victor EPA-4041. . . *3/57*   **55–75**
Black label, dog on top, without horizontal silver line.

RCA Victor EPA-4041. . . *3/57*   **150–200**
Black label, no dog on label.

RCA Victor EPA-4041. . . . *65*   **30–40**
Black label, dog on side.

RCA Victor EPA-4041. . . . *68*   **20–35**
Orange label.

Side 1
 I Need You So
 Have I Told You Lately That I Love You
Side 2
 Blueberry Hill
 Is It So Strange

KID GALAHAD
RCA Victor EPS-4371 . . . *9/62*   **45–60**
Black label, dog on top.

RCA Victor EPA-4371. . . . *65*   **25–35**
Black label, dog on side.

RCA Victor EPA-4371. . . . *68*   **20–35**
Orange label.

Side 1
 King of the Whole Wide World
 This Is Living
 Riding the Rainbow
Side 2
 Home Is Where the Heart Is
 I Got Lucky
 A Whistling Tune

KING CREOLE
RCA Victor EPA-4319. . . *8/58*   **55–70**
Black label, dog on top.

RCA Victor EPA-5122. . *11/59*   **50–60**
Gold Standard; black label, dog on top.

RCA Victor EPA-5122. . *11/59*   **300–400**
Gold Standard; maroon label.

RCA Victor EPA-5122. . . . *65*   **30–40**
Gold Standard; black label, dog on side.

RCA Victor EPA-5122. . . . *68*   **20–35**
Gold Standard; orange label.

Side 1
 King Creole
 New Orleans
Side 2
 As Long As I Have You
 Lover Doll

KING CREOLE, VOL. 2
RCA Victor EPA-4321. . . *8/58*   **55–70**
Black label, dog on top.

RCA Victor EPA-4321. . . . *65*   **30–40**
Black label, dog on side.

RCA Victor EPA-4321. . . . *68*   **20–35**
Orange label.

Side 1
 Trouble
 Young Dreams
Side 2
 Crawfish
 Dixieland Rock

LOVE ME TENDER
RCA Victor EPA-4006. . *11/56*   **55–75**
Black label, dog on top.

RCA Victor EPA-4006. . *11/56*   **150–200**
Black label, no dog on label.

RCA Victor EPA-4006. . . . *65*   **30–40**
Black label, dog on side.

RCA Victor EPA-4006. . . . *68*   **20–35**
Orange label.
Note: Original issues of this EP have a black and white title strip across the top of the jacket.

Side 1
 Love Me Tender
 Let Me
Side 2
 Poor Boy
 We're Gonna Move

LOVING YOU, VOL. I
RCA Victor EPA 1-1515 . *7/57*   **70–90**
Black label, dog on top, with horizontal silver line.

RCA Victor EPA 1-1515 . *7/57*   **55–75**
Black label, dog on top, without horizontal silver line.

RCA Victor EPA 1-1515 *65-66*   **30–40**
Black label, dog on side.

RCA Victor EPA 1-1515 *68-69*   **20–35**
Orange label.

Side 1
 Loving You
 Party
Side 2
 Teddy Bear
 True Love

LOVING YOU, VOL. II
RCA Victor EPA 2-1515 . *7/57*   **70–90**
Black label, dog on top, with horizontal silver line.

RCA Victor EPA 2-1515 . *7/57*   **55–75**
Black label, dog on top, without horizontal silver line.

RCA Victor EPA 2-1515 *65-66*   **30–40**
Black label, dog on side.

RCA Victor EPA 2-1515 *68-69*   **20–35**
Orange label.

Side 1
 Lonesome Cowboy
 Hot Dog
Side 2
 Mean Woman Blues
 Got a Lot o' Livin' to Do

PEACE IN THE VALLEY

RCA Victor EPA-4054. . . *3/57* **70–90**
Black label, dog on top, with horizontal silver line.

RCA Victor EPA-4054. . . *3/57* **55–75**
Black label, dog on top, without horizontal silver line.

RCA Victor EPA-5121. . *11/59* **50–60**
Gold Standard; black label, dog on top.

RCA Victor EPA-5121. . *11/59* **300–400**
Gold Standard; maroon label.

RCA Victor EPA-5121. . *65-66* **30–40**
Gold Standard; black label, dog on side.

RCA Victor EPA-5121. . *68-69* **20–35**
Gold Standard; orange label.

Note: Original issues of this EP have a black and white title strip across the top of the jacket.

Side 1
  Peace in the Valley
  It Is No Secret
Side 2
  I Believe
  Take My Hand, Precious Lord

PERFECT FOR PARTIES HIGHLIGHT ALBUM (EP): see Various-Artists Compilations section.

POP TRANSCRIBED 30 SEC. SPOT with VAUGHN MONROE: see Various-Artists Compilations section.

RCA FAMILY RECORD CENTER (EP): see Various-Artists Compilations section.

SAVE-ON-RECORDS (EP): see Various-Artists Compilations section.

SDS-7-2 (EPs): see Various-Artists Compilations section.

SDS-57-39 (EPs): see Various-Artists Compilations section.

SPA 7-27 (EPs): see Various-Artists Compilations section.

SPA 7-61 (EXTENDED PLAY SAMPLER): see Various-Artists Compilations section.

SPD-15 (EP): see Various-Artists Compilations section.

SPD-19 (EP): see Various-Artists Compilations section.

STRICTLY ELVIS (ELVIS VOL. 3)

RCA Victor EPA-994 . . *11/56* **70–90**
Black label, dog on top, with horizontal silver line.

RCA Victor EPA-994 . . *11/56* **55–75**
Black label, dog on top, without horizontal silver line.

RCA Victor EPA-994 . . *11/56* **150–200**
Black label, no dog on label.

RCA Victor EPA-994 . . . . *65* **30–40**
Black label, dog on side.

RCA Victor EPA-994 . . . . *68* **20–35**
Orange label.

Note: Original issues of this EP have a black and white title strip across the top of the jacket.

Side 1
  Long Tall Sally
  First in Line
Side 2
  How Do You Think I Feel
  How's the World Treating You

T.V. GUIDE PRESENTS ELVIS PRESLEY

RCA Victor GB-MW-8705 *9/56* **950–1000**
Blue label, promotional issue only. This one-sided disc contained Elvis' responses to questions that any dee jay could ask, giving the impression that an actual interview was being done.

RCA Victor GB-MW-8705 *9/56* **200–250**
Explanatory insert. This gray card explained a bit about the interview.

RCA Victor GB-MW-8705 *9/56* **125–150**
Suggested continuity. This pink insert contained the suggested script for conducting the interview. Some copies have been discovered, of the complete set, with *two* copies of this pink insert. This could have been an error since there would be no reason for sending two copies of the script. Also, reproductions exist of this insert, but reportedly are identified as such.

Note: Counterfeit copies exist of the *T.V. Guide* disc, but are easily identified. Originals have locked grooves (needle has to be lifted from disc to pass to next track) and have the matrix number machine stamped in the vinyl trail-off. Counterfeits do not have locked grooves and have the matrix number hand etched in the vinyl.

THE ELVIS PRESLEY STORY

Eva-Tone 726771XS *7/77* **8–10**
Candlelite music sampler soundsheet.

THE MOST TALKED-ABOUT NEW PERSONALITY IN THE LAST TEN YEARS OF RECORDED MUSIC (12 Great New Sides From His New Albums!!!) (2 EP)

RCA Victor EPB-1254. . . *3/56* **1000–1200**
Black label, dog on top, this single pocket EP has the records separated, in some cases anyway, by a copy of "Dee-Jay Digest," with news for radio announcers, promotional issue only.

RCA Victor EPB-1254. . . *3/56* **400–450**
Price for discs without the sleeve.

Side 1
  Blue Suede Shoes
  I'm Counting on You
  I Got a Woman
Side 2
  One-Sided Love Affair
  I Love You Because
  Just Because
Side 3
  Tutti Frutti
  Tryin' to Get to You
  I'm Gonna Sit Right Down and Cry
Side 4
  I'll Never Let You Go
  Blue Moon
  Money Honey

THE REAL ELVIS

RCA Victor EPA-940 . . . *9/56* **70–90**
Black label, dog on top, with horizontal silver line.

RCA Victor EPA-940 . . . *9/56* **55–75**
Black label, dog on top, without horizontal silver line.

RCA Victor EPA-940 . . . *9/56* **150–200**
Black label, no dog on label.

RCA Victor EPA-5120. . *11/59* **50–60**
Gold Standard; black label, dog on top.

RCA Victor EPA-5120. . *11/59* **300–400**
Gold Standard; maroon label.

RCA Victor EPA-5120. . . . *65* **30–40**
Gold Standard; black label, dog on side.

RCA Victor EPA-5120. . . . *68* **20–35**
Gold Standard; orange label.

Side 1
  Don't Be Cruel
  I Want You, I Need You, I Love You

Side 2
  Hound Dog
  My Baby Left Me

THE SOUND OF LEADERSHIP: See Various-Artists Compilations section.

TICKLE ME

RCA Victor EPA-4383. . . *6/65* **40–50**
Black label, dog on side, cover reads "Coming Soon! Special Elvis Anniversary LP Album."

RCA Victor EPA-4383. . . *7/65* **40–50**
Black label, dog on side, cover reads "Ask For Special Elvis Anniversary LP Album."

RCA Victor EPA-4383. . . . *65* **40–50**
Black label, dog on side, cover makes no mention of the LP.

RCA Victor EPA-4383. . *68-69* **20–35**
Orange label.

Side 1
  I Feel That I've Known You Forever
  Slowly But Surely
Side 2
  Night Rider
  Dirty, Dirty Feeling

TUPPERWARE'S HIT PARADE (EP): see Various-Artists Compilations section.

VIVA LAS VEGAS

RCA Victor EPA-4382. . . *6/64* **50–60**
Black label, dog on top.

RCA Victor EPA-4382. . . . *65* **30–40**
Black label, dog on side.

RCA Victor EPA-4382. . . . *68* **20–35**
Orange label.

Side 1
  If You Think I Don't Need You
  I Need Somebody to Lean On
Side 2
  C'mon Everybody
  Today, Tomorrow and Forever

WOHO FEATURING RCA VICTOR: see PRO-12 in Various-Artists Compilations section.

LPs

All of Elvis's U.S. long-play albums (LPs), commercial and promotional, are listed alphabetically in this chapter. Generally, the listings under each entry are chronologically ordered.

Unless listed separately, all LP covers or jackets are included in the price range. It is assumed that the cover condition is very close to the disc condition; however, some adjustment in value may be warranted in cases where there is a significant variance.

The contents of each LP, if known, follow the listing. Slight variations in titles may occur since they were copied directly from each individual LP. Following the label name on each listing, you'll find the Stereo Designation. This key, along with the additional stereo information contained in many footnotes, will reveal the amount of true stereo, if any, on each LP. See "Stereo Update" (page 105) for more information.

LPs featuring various artists, while cross-referenced in this section, will be found detailed in the Various-Artists Compilations section.

LISTINGS

A DATE WITH ELVIS: see *DATE WITH ELVIS, A.*

A JOURNEY INTO YESTERDAY: see Various-Artists Compilations section.

A LEGENDARY PERFORMER: see *ELVIS: A LEGENDARY PERFORMER.*

AGE OF ROCK, THE: see Various-Artists Compilations section.

ALL-TIME CHRISTMAS FAVORITES: see Various-Artists Compilations section.

ALL-STAR ROCK (VOL. II): see *ROCK, ROCK, ROCK (ALL-STAR*

ROCK, VOL. II) **in Various-Artists Compilations section.**

ALL-TIME GREATS: see Various-Artists Compilations section.

ALMOST IN LOVE
RCA/Camden (ST) CAS-2440
. . . . *11/70* **25–30**
Blue label. First pressings contained the song "Stay Away, Joe." Camden and Pickwick reissues replaced this track with "Stay Away."

Side 1
  Almost in Love
  Long Legged Girl
  Edge of Reality
  My Little Friend
  A Little Less Conversation

Side 2
Rubberneckin'
Clean Up Your Own Backyard
U.S. Male
Charro
Stay Away, Joe

RCA/Camden (SP) CAS-2440
. . . . *3/73*   **15–18**
Blue label. Contains "Stay Away" instead of
"Stay Away, Joe."

Pickwick/Camden (SP) CAS-2440
. . . . *12/75*   **8–10**

Side 1
Almost in Love
Long Legged Girl
Edge of Reality
My Little Friend
A Little Less Conversation

Side 2
Rubberneckin'
Clean Up Your Own Backyard
U.S. Male
Charro
Stay Away

ALOHA FROM HAWAII VIA SATELLITE (2 LP)

RCA Victor (Q) VPSX-6089 *2/73*   **75–90**
Red/Orange label. First pressing covers didn't
show the song titles but used a gold sticker to
list the LP contents. Also applied was a gold
"QuadraDisc" sticker, since the cover indicated
it was a stereo, rather than quad, release.

RCA Victor (Q) VPSX-6089 *2/73*   **200–250**
With white stickers applied to front cover listing LP contents and times. Promotional issue
only.

RCA Victor (Q) VPSX-6089 *2/73*   **1000–1500**
With special "Chicken of the Sea Sneak Preview" sticker on front cover. These copies were
distributed within the Van Camps, or Chicken
of the Sea, organization. Promotional issue
only.

RCA Victor (ST) R-213736 . *73*   **45–55**
RCA Record Club. Orange label. Note that the
RCA Record Club issue of this LP was in
stereo, not quad.

RCA Victor VPSX-6089 . . . *74*   **25–30**
With Quadradisc/RCA logo in lower right corner of front cover. Titles are printed on back
cover. Orange label.

RCA Victor (Q) CPD2-2642 *75*   **15–20**
Orange label.

RCA Victor VPSX-6089 . . . *76*   **25–30**
Tan label.

RCA Victor (ST) R-213736 . *76*   **18–20**
RCA Record Club.
Tan label. All issues of this LP were packaged
with special photo inner-sleeves to hold the records.

RCA Victor (Q) CPD2-2642 *77*   **10–12**
Black label, dog near top.

As one of the major sponsors of the *Aloha from Hawaii* TV special, Chicken of the
Sea made a catch of an unusual kind—this rare and highly desirable promo of the
LP from the TV show.

Side 1
  Introduction: Also Sprach Zarathustra
  See See Rider
  Burning Love
  Something
  You Gave Me a Mountain
  Steamroller Blues
Side 2
  My Way
  Love Me
  Johnny B. Goode
  It's Over
  Blue Suede Shoes
  I'm So Lonesome I Could Cry
  I Can't Stop Loving You
  Hound Dog
Side 3
  What Now My Love
  Fever
  Welcome to My World
  Suspicious Minds
  Introductions By Elvis
Side 4
  I'll Remember You
  Medley: Long Tall Sally/Whole Lot-ta Shakin' Goin' On
  An American Trilogy
  A Big Hunk O' Love
  Can't Help Falling in Love

ALWAYS ON MY MIND
RCA Victor (ST) AFL1-5430
. . . . *6/85*   **5–8**
Purple vinyl.

Side A
  Separate Ways
  Don't Cry Daddy
  My Boy
  Solitaire
  Bigger They Are, Harder The Fall
  Hurt
Side B
  Pieces of My Life
  I Miss You
  It's Midnight
  I've Lost You
  You Gave Me a Mountain
  Unchained Melody
  Always on My Mind

AMERICAN CHRISTMAS: see
Various-Artists Compilations section.

AMERICAN TOP 40: see
Various-Artists Compilations section.

APRIL POP SAMPLERS: see
Various-Artists Compilations section.

AUGUST 1979 SAMPLER: see
Various-Artists Compilations section.

AVON VALENTINE FAVORITES:
see Various-Artists Compilations section.

BACK IN MEMPHIS, ELVIS
RCA Victor (ST) LSP-4429
. . . . *11/70*   **15–20**
Orange label.
RCA Victor (ST) LSP-4429 . *76*   **10–15**
Tan label.
RCA Victor (ST) AFL1-4429 *77*   **8–10**
Black label, dog near top.
Note: This LP was previously issued as one-half of the two-LP set *From Memphis to Vegas/From Vegas to Memphis,* LSP-6020.

Side 1
  Inherit the Wind
  This Is the Story
  Stranger in My Own Home Town
  A Little Bit of Green
  And the Grass Won't Pay No Mind
Side 2
  Do You Know Who I Am
  From a Jack to a King
  The Fair Is Moving On
  You'll Think of Me
  Without Love

BEGINNING YEARS, THE
Louisiana Hayride (M) LH-3061
. . . . *2/84*   **300–350**
White label advance pressing from RCA, Indianapolis, where this LP was manufactured.
Louisiana Hayride (M) LH-3061
. . . . *5/84*   **10–15**
Price includes 20-page "D. J. Fontana Remembers Elvis' booklet, a four-sheet copy of Elvis' Hayride contract and a 10″ × 10″ "Presleyana" flyer, all of which represent about $5–$8 of the value.
Note: Selections from this LP were also issued on The Music Works 3601 and 3602.

BEST OF (series): see Various-Artists Compilations section.

BILLBOARD'S 1975 YEARBOOK:
see Various-Artists Compilations section.

BIRTHDAY TRIBUTE TO ELVIS
Creative Radio (SP), no number given *1/88*   **25–50**
Issued to radio stations only. Not issued with special cover. Price includes one-page script.

Syndicated radio shows are often distributed on LPs, as was the case with Creative Radio's *Birthday Tribute to Elvis.*

Side 1
  Elvis Medley
  That's All Right
  Heartbreak Hotel
  All Shook Up
  Teddy Bear
  Blue Suede Shoes
Side 2
  Love Me Tender
  Jailhouse Rock
  Suspicious Minds
  Hound Dog
  My Way
  Don't Be Cruel
  I'll Remember You

**BLUE CHRISTMAS: see
Various-Artists Compilations section.**

BLUE HAWAII
RCA Victor (M) LPM-2426
. . . . *10/61*   **75–90**
Black label, with the words "Long Play" at the bottom of the label.

RCA Victor (ST) LSP-2426 *10/61*   **90–100**
Black label, with the words "Living Stereo" at the bottom. Some copies of the 1961 mono and

stereo issues carried a red sticker on the cover noting the inclusion of "Rock-a-Hula Baby" and "Can't Help Falling in Love."
RCA Victor (M) LPM-2426
. . . . *11/63*   **40–50**
Black label, with the word "Mono" at the bottom.

RCA Victor (M) LPM-2426. *64*   **25–30**
Black label, with the word "Monaural" at the bottom.

RCA Victor (ST) LSP-2426 . *64*   **25–30**
Black label, with the RCA logo in white at the top of the label and the word "Stereo" at the bottom.

RCA Victor (ST) LSP-2426 . *68*   **10–20**
Orange label.

RCA Victor (ST) LSP-2426 . *76*   **10–15**
Tan label.

RCA Victor (ST) AFL1-2426
. . . . *9/77*   **8–10**
Black label, dog near top.

RCA Victor (ST) AYL1-3683
. . . . *5/80*   **5–8**
Black label, dog near top. Issued as part of RCA's "Best Buy" series.

Side 1
Blue Hawaii
Almost Always True
Aloha Oe
No More
Can't Help Falling in Love
Rock-a-Hula Baby
Moonlight Swim
Side 2
Ku-u-i-po
Ito Eats
Slicin' Sand
Hawaiian Sunset
Beach Boy Blues
Island of Love
Hawaiian Wedding Song

BRIGHTEST STARS OF CHRISTMAS: see Various-Artists Compilations section.

BURNING LOVE (AND HITS FROM HIS MOVIES VOL. 2)
RCA/Camden (ST) CAS2595
. . . . *11/72*   **20–30**
Blue Label.
Pickwick/Camden (ST) 2595
. . . . *12/75*   **8–10**
Note: 1972 original issues were packed with a bonus 8″ × 10″ color photo, which is included in the above price range. Deduct $8–$15 if this photo is missing.

Side 1
Burning Love
Tender Feeling
Am I Ready
Tonight Is So Right for Love
Guadalajara
Side 2
It's a Matter of Time
No More
Santa Lucia
We'll Be Together
I Love Only One Girl

CANADIAN TRIBUTE, A
RCA Victor (SP) KKL1-7065 *78*   **10–12**
Gold vinyl.
Note: Originally manufactured and distributed in Canada, this LP was picked up and distributed by RCA in the United States. It is only the U.S. issue that is priced here. U.S. copies are so noted on the back cover, at bottom-center. U.S. issues also have a "Gold Album" sticker on the front of the jacket. This LP was issued with a special photo inner-sleeve.

Side 1
Intro—Jailhouse Rock

Intro—Teddy Bear
Loving You
Until It's Time for You to Go
Early Morning Rain
Vancouver Press Conference (1957)
Side 2
I'm Movin' On
Snowbird
For Lovin' Me
Put Your Hand in the Hand
Little Darlin'
My Way

CHRISTMAS PROGRAMMING FROM RCA: see *RCA 12-INCH SAMPLERS* in Various-Artists Compilations section.

CHRISTMAS WITH ELVIS
Creative Radio (SP), no number
given. *12/87*   **50–100**
Issued to radio stations only. Not issued with special cover. Price includes one-page script.

Side 1
The Wonderful World of Christmas
I'll Be Home for Christmas
O Come All Ye Faithful
Santa Claus Is Back in Town
Rockin' Around the Christmas Tree (Brenda Lee)
Santa Bring My Baby Back to Me
Silver Bells
White Christmas
Sleigh Ride (Salsoul Orchestra)
If I Get Home on Christmas Day
Side 2
Here Comes Santa Claus
Holly Leaves and Christmas Trees
On a Snowy Christmas Night
It Won't Seem Like Christmas
Blue Christmas
If I Can Dream
Winter Wonderland
Silent Night

CHRONOLOGY OF AMERICAN MUSIC, A: see Various-Artists Compilations section.

CLAMBAKE
RCA Victor (M) LPM-3893
. . . . *11/67*   **150–200**
Black label, with the word "Monaural" at the bottom.

RCA Victor (ST) LSP-3893 *11/67*   **60–70**
Black label, with the RCA logo in white at the top of the label and the word "Stereo" at the bottom.

Along with providing the music in an easy-to-use format, syndicated programs are often packaged with scripts to assist their presentation on the air.

RCA Victor (ST) AFL1-2565
. . . . *9/77*   **8–10**
Black label, dog near top.
Note: 1967 original issues were packaged with a bonus 12″ × 12″ color photo of Elvis and Priscilla, which is included in the above price range. Deduct $25–$30 if this photo is missing.

Side 1
  Guitar Man
  Clambake
  Who Needs Money
  A House That Has Everything
  Confidence
  Hey, Hey, Hey
Side 2
  You Don't Know Me
  The Girl I Never Loved
  How Can You Lose What You Never Had
  Big Boss Man
  Singing Tree
  Just Call Me Lonesome

C'MON EVERYBODY
RCA/Camden (M) CAL-2518
. . . . *9/71*   **15–18**
Blue Label.

Pickwick/Camden (M) CAS-2518
. . . . *12/75*   **8–10**
Despite the CAS prefix, the Pickwick LP is still monaural.

Side 1
  C'Mon Everybody
  Angel
  Easy Come, Easy Go
  A Whistling Tune
  Follow That Dream
Side 2
  King of the Whole Wide World
  I'll Take Love
  Today, Tomorrow and Forever
  I'm Not the Marrying Kind
  This Is Living

COLLECTORS EDITION, A (5 LP)
RCA Victor (SP) TB-1. . . . *76*   **75–100**
This three-LP, five-disc, boxed set contained these previously released albums: *Elvis in Hollywood, Elvis Forever* and *Elvis,* the two-LP set issued in the United States as DPL2-0056e.
Note: Manufactured in Canada but offered for sale in the United States through TV mail-order ads. Packaged with a 20-page color booklet,

which is included in the above price range. Deduct $10 if this booklet is missing.

COMPLETE SUN SESSIONS, THE (2 LP)

RCA Victor (M) 6414-1-R. *7/87* **10–15**
Includes a bonus color 15″ × 22″ poster and "Elvis Talks" LP flyer.

COUNTRY CLASSICS (2 LP)

RCA Victor (SP) R-233299e. *80* **20–25**
RCA Record Club.

Side 1
Faded Love
Guitar Man
Blue Moon of Kentucky
Crying in the Chapel
Tomorrow Night
Side 2
I'm Coming Home
(Now and Then There's) A Fool Such As I
From a Jack to a King
I Really Don't Want to Know
That's All Right
Side 3
Have I Told You Lately That I Love You
Tomorrow Never Comes
It's a Sin
He Touched Me
I Love You Because
Side 4
I'm Left, You're Right, She's Gone
Just Call Me Lonesome
(There'll Be) Peace in the Valley (for Me)
There Goes My Everything

COUNTRY MEMORIES (2 LP)

RCA Victor (SP) R-244069 . *78* **20–25**
RCA Record Club
Black label, dog near top.

Side A
I'll Hold You in My Heart
Welcome to My World
It Keeps Right On A-Hurtin'
Release Me
Make the World Go Away
Side B
Snowbird
Early Morning Rain
I'm So Lonesome I Could Cry
Funny How Time Slips Away
I'm Moving On
Side C
Help Me Make It Through the Night
You Don't Know Me
How Great Thou Art
I Washed My Hands in Muddy Water
I Forgot to Remember to Forget

Side D
Your Cheatin' Heart
Baby, Let's Play House
Whole Lot-ta Shakin' Goin' On
Gentle on My Mind
For the Good Times

COUNTRY MUSIC

Time-Life (SP) STW-106. . . *81* **35–45**
One of a series of 20 LPs by country music performers. These albums were generally sold in supermarkets.

Side 1
Blue Moon of Kentucky
Old Shep
When My Blue Moon Turns to Gold Again
Are You Lonesome Tonight?
Your Cheatin' Heart
Side 2
Wooden Heart
Suspicious Minds
Little Cabin Home on the Hill
U.S. Male

COUNTRY MUSIC IN THE MODERN ERA (1940s–1970s): see Various-Artists Compilations section.

COUNTRY SIDE—ELVIS, THE (3 LP)

Creative Radio (SP) *8/82* **250–300**
Issued to radio stations only. Not issued with special cover. Price includes script.

COUNTRY SUPER SOUNDS: see Various-Artists Compilations section.

COUNTRY & WESTERN CLASSICS: see Various-Artists Compilations section.

CURRENT AUDIO MAGAZINE: see Various-Artists Compilations section.

DATE WITH ELVIS, A

RCA Victor (M) LPM-2011 *9/59* **150–175**
Black label, with the words "Long Play" at the bottom of the label. With gatefold cover and 1960 calendar on the back. Song titles were on a red sticker on front cover.

RCA Victor (M) LPM-2011 *9/59* **300–400**
Black label, with the words "Long Play" at the bottom of the label. Same as above, but with a foil wraparound banner announcing this LP as one of 24 Alcoa Wrap "New Golden Age of Sound Albums."

RCA Victor (M) LPM-2011 *1/65* **45–55**
Black label, with the word "Mono" at the bottom. Standard cover.

RCA Victor (M) LPM-2011 *1/65*   **25–30**
Black label, with the word "Monaural" at the
bottom.

RCA Victor (SE) LSP-2011(e)
. . . . *1/65*   **25–30**
Black label, with the RCA logo in white at the
top of the label and the word "Stereo" at the
bottom.

RCA Victor (SE) LSP-2011(e) *68*   **10–20**
Orange label.

RCA Victor (SE) LSP-2011(e) *76*   **10–15**
Tan label.

RCA Victor (SE) AFL1-2011(e)
. . . . *77*   **8–10**
Black label, dog near top.
Note: All songs on the stereo issue of this LP are
electronically enhanced to simulate stereo.

Side 1
  Blue Moon of Kentucky
  Young and Beautiful
  (You're So Square) Baby I Don't Care
  Milkcow Blues Boogie
  Baby Let's Play House
Side 2
  Good Rockin' Tonight
  Is It So Strange
  We're Gonna Move
  I Want to Be Free
  I Forgot to Remember to Forget

DECEMBER '63 POP SAMPLER:
see *RCA 12-INCH SAMPLERS* in
Various-Artists Compilations section.

DINER (soundtrack): see
Various-Artists Compilations section.

DOUBLE DYNAMITE (2 LP)
Pickwick/Camden (SP) DL2-5001
. . . . *12/75*   **25–30**
Side 1
  Burning Love
  I'll Be There
  Fools Fall in Love
  Follow That Dream
  You'll Never Walk Alone
Side 2
  Flaming Star
  Yellow Rose of Texas/The Eyes of Texas
  Old Shep
  Mama
Side 3
  Rubberneckin'
  U.S. Male
  Frankie and Johnny
  If You Think I Don't Need You
  Easy Come, Easy Go

Side 4
  Separate Ways
  Peace in the Valley
  Big Boss Man
  It's a Matter of Time

DOUBLE DYNAMITE (2 LP)
RCA/Pair (SP) PDL2-1010 . *82*   **20–25**
Black label, dog near top. RCA Special Prod-
ucts. Repackage, omits "You'll Never Walk
Alone" and "If You Think I Don't Need You."

Side 1
  Burning Love
  I'll Be There
  Fools Fall in Love
  Follow That Dream
Side 2
  Flaming Star
  Yellow Rose of Texas/The Eyes of Texas
  Old Shep
  Mama
Side 3
  Rubberneckin'
  U.S. Male
  Frankie and Johnny
  Easy Come, Easy Go
Side 4
  Separate Ways
  Peace in the Valley
  Big Boss Man
  It's a Matter of Time

DOUBLE TROUBLE
RCA Victor (M) LPM-3787 *6/67*   **40–50**
Black label, with the word "Monaural" at the
bottom. Front cover announces the inclusion of
a bonus photo inside LP.

RCA Victor (M) LPM-3787 . *68*   **30–40**
Black label, with the word "Monaural" at the
bottom. Bonus photo mention is replaced by the
words "Trouble Double."

RCA Victor (ST) LSP-3787 *6/67*   **40–50**
Black label, with the RCA logo in white at the
top of the label and the word "Stereo" at the
bottom. Front cover announces the inclusion of
a bonus photo inside LP.

RCA Victor (ST) LSP-3787 . *68*   **30–40**
Black label, with the RCA logo in white at the
top of the label and the word "Stereo" at the
bottom. Bonus photo mention is replaced by the
words "Trouble Double."

RCA Victor (ST) LSP-3787 . *68*   **10–20**
Orange label.

RCA Victor (ST) LSP-3787 . *76*   **10–15**
Tan label.

RCA Victor (ST) AFL1-2564
.... *9/77* **8–10**
Black label, dog near top.
Note: 1967 original issues were packaged with a bonus 7″ × 9″ color photo, which is included in the above price range. Deduct $5 if this photo is missing.

Side 1
Double Trouble
Baby If You'll Give Me All Your Love
Could I Fall in Love
Long Legged Girl
City by Night
Old MacDonald
Side 2
I Love Only One Girl
There Is So Much World to See
It Won't Be Long
Never Ending
What Now, What Next, Where to

EARTH NEWS (FOR THE WEEK AUGUST 29, 1977)

Earth News (M) EN8-22-77 *8/77* **300–350**
This LP, sent to subscribing radio stations, contained 14 five-minute programs, 12 devoted to Elvis news, music, and interviews. Contains excerpts of the following Elvis songs: "Blue Suede Shoes" (1956 live TV appearance), "Don't Be Cruel" (1956 live TV appearance), "Heartbreak Hotel" (1956 live TV appearance), and "Hound Dog."
Note: This LP was shipped with a letter expressing the need to air this series the week of August 22nd, even though the label indicates August 29th.

Side 1
1956 Elvis Interview
Blue Suede Shoes (from the Dorsey Bros. TV Show)
1956 Elvis Interview
Don't Be Cruel (from Ed Sullivan Show)
Heartbreak Hotel (from Dorsey Bros. TV Show)
1956 Elvis Interview
Jay Thompson's Elvis Interview
Elvis Sails Interview
Dick Clark/Elvis Phone Call
The Truth About Me
Side 2
1956 Elvis Interview
1961 Elvis Interview
Red West Interview
The Truth About Me
Hound Dog
Willie Mae Thornton Interview
The Truth About Me

In the Ghetto
Steve Bender Interview
Medley: Hey Mr. Presley/I Dreamed I Was Elvis/My Baby's Crazy About Elvis/Elvis Presley For President

ELVIS

RCA Victor (M) LPM-1382
.... *11/56* **100–125**
Black label, with the words "Long Play" at the bottom of the label. Original covers for this issue have the RCA catalog number under the RCA logo in the upper right corner.

RCA Victor (M) LPM-1382
.... *11/56* **200–225**
Black label, with the words "Long Play" at the bottom of the label. The label on this issue shows the sequence of titles as "Band" 1 through 6 on each side of the LP.

RCA Victor (M) LPM-1382
.... *11/56* **750–1000**
Black label, with the words "Long Play" at the bottom of the label. Original covers for this issue have the RCA catalog number under the RCA logo, in the upper right corner. This is the unique pressing of *Elvis* that contained an alternate version of "Old Shep." The pressing of this LP with the alternate take has a "17S" following the matrix in the vinyl trail-off, but only by playing the song can you determine for certain if it's the alternate take.

RCA Victor (M) LPM-1382
.... *11/63* **45–55**
Black label, with the word "Mono" at the bottom. Covers for this issue have the RCA catalog number on the left side of the front cover.

RCA Victor (M) LPM-1382. *64* **25–30**
Black label, with the word "Monaural" at the bottom. Covers for this issue have the RCA catalog number on the left side of the front cover.

RCA Victor (SE) LSP-1382(e)
.... *2/62* **75–85**
Black label, with the RCA logo in silver at the top of the label and the word "Stereo" at the bottom. Covers for this issue have the RCA catalog number on the left side of the front cover.

RCA Victor (SE) LSP-1382(e) *64* **25–30**
Black label, with the RCA logo in white at the top of the label and the word "Stereo" at the bottom. Covers for this issue have the RCA catalog number on the left side of the front cover.

RCA Victor (SE) LSP-1382(e) *68* **10–20**
Orange label.

RCA Victor (SE) LSP-1382(e) *76*   **10–15**
Tan label.

RCA Victor (SE) AFL1-1382(e)
. . . . *77*   **8–10**
Black label, dog near top.
Note: All songs on the stereo issue of this LP are electronically enhanced to simulate stereo.

RCA Victor (M) AFM1-5199
. . . . *8/84*   **5–8**
Digitally remastered quality mono pressing. Price includes gold banner: "The Definitive Rock Classic."

Side 1
  Rip It Up
  Love Me
  When My Blue Moon Turns to Gold Again
  Long Tall Sally
  First in Line
  Paralyzed
Side 2
  So Glad You're Mine
  Old Shep
  Reddy Teddy
  Anyplace Is Paradise
  How's the World Treating You
  How Do You Think I Feel

ELVIS (2 LP)
RCA Victor (SP) DLP2-0056(e)
. . . . *8/73*   **40–50**
Mustard-color label. Marketed through Brookville Records as a mail-order offer. Cover reads "Brookville Records" in upper right corner.

RCA Victor (SP) DLP2-0056(e)
. . . . *9/73*   **20–25**
Blue label. Cover does not mention Brookville Records. This LP set was repackaged and reissued in 1978, titled *Elvis Commemorative Album.*

Side 1
  Hound Dog
  I Want You, I Need You, I Love You
  All Shook Up
  Don't
  I Beg of You
Side 2
  A Big Hunk O' Love
  Love Me
  Stuck on You
  Good Luck Charm
  Return to Sender
Side 3
  Don't Be Cruel
  Loving You
  Jailhouse Rock

  Can't Help Falling in Love
  I Got Stung
Side 4
  Teddy Bear
  Love Me Tender
  Hard Headed Woman
  It's Now or Never
  Surrender

ELVIS (INCLUDING "FOOL")
RCA Victor (ST) APL1-0283
. . . . *7/73*   **50–60**
Orange label.

Side 1
  Fool
  Where Do I Go from Here
  Love Me, Love the Life I Lead
  It's Still Here
  It's Impossible
Side 2
  For Lovin' Me
  Padre
  I'll Take You Home Again Kathleen
  I Will Be True
  Don't Think Twice, It's All Right

ELVIS (NBC-TV SPECIAL)
RCA Victor (SP) LPM-4088
. . . . *12/68*   **15–20**
Orange label, rigid disc.

RCA Victor (SP) LPM-3643   *71*   **10–15**
Orange label, flexible disc.

RCA Victor (SP) LPM-3643   *76*   **10–15**
Tan label.

RCA Victor (SP) AFM1-4088   *77*   **8–10**
Black label, dog near top.

RCA Victor (SP) AYM1-3894
. . . . *2/81*   **5–10**
Black label, dog near top. Issued as part of RCA's "Best Buy" series.
Note: "If I Can Dream" on this issue was not the version that was used in the actual NBC-TV Special broadcast. The actual version has never been released by RCA, although it has appeared on bootleg albums. Despite the monaural (LPM) prefix, there are several stereo tracks on this LP.

Side 1
  Trouble/Guitar Man
  Lawdy Miss Clawdy/Baby What Do You
    Want Me to Do
  Medley: Heartbreak Hotel/Hound Dog/One
    Night/All Shook Up/Can't Help Falling
    in Love/Jailhouse Rock/Love Me Tender
Side 2
  Where Could I Go But to the Lord/Up
    Above My Head/Saved

Blue Christmas
Memories
Medley: Nothingville/Big Boss Man/Guitar
Man/Little Egypt/Trouble/Guitar Man
If I Can Dream

ELVIS (SPEAKS TO YOU) (2 LP)
Green Valley (SP) GV-2001/2003
. . . . *4/78* **25–30**
Double pocket set, one LP being exactly the
same disc previously issued as *Elvis Exclusive
Live Press Conference.*

ELVIS—A CANADIAN TRIBUTE:
see CANADIAN TRIBUTE, A.

ELVIS—A COLLECTORS EDITION:
see COLLECTORS EDITION, A

ELVIS—A LEGENDARY
PERFORMER: see LEGENDARY
PERFORMER, A

ELVIS: A THREE HOUR SPECIAL
(3 LP)
Drake-Chenault (SP) *8/77* **300–350**
Price includes three pages of cue sheets. Issued
to radio stations only.

ELVIS: ALOHA FROM HAWAII
VIA SATELLITE: see *ALOHA FROM
HAWAII VIA SATELLITE*

ELVIS ARON PRESLEY (8 LP)
RCA Victor (SP) CPL8-3699
. . . . *7/80* **80–100**
Limited-edition boxed set, with each of the
eight discs in its own color sleeve.
Note: Issued as a 25th anniversary (with RCA
Victor) set, using custom labels.

RCA Victor (SP) NS (Box Num-
ber) *7/80* **450–500**
Reviewer Series. Promotional issue only. This
was the complimentary copy of the complete
box set. No other letter prefix was used with the
limited-edition numbers on these issues. Each
LP in this set had its own title and differing
stereo content; therefore, we will list each separately:

An Early Live Performance (M) CPL8-3699-1
Side A
 Heartbreak Hotel
 Long Tall Sally
 Blue Suede Shoes
 Money Honey
Side B
 An Elvis Monolog

An Early Live Performance (M) CPL8-3699-2
Side A
 Heartbreak Hotel
 All Shook Up
 (Now and Then There's) A Fool Such As I
 I Got a Woman
 Love Me
 Introductions
 Such a Night
 Reconsider Baby
Side B
 I Need Your Love Tonight
 That's All Right
 Don't Be Cruel
 One Night
 Are You Lonesome Tonight
 It's Now or Never
 Swing Down Sweet Chariot
 Hound Dog

Collectors' Gold from the Movie Years (SP)
CPL8-3699-3
All tracks are stereo except "Can't Help Falling
in Love." "Follow That Dream" and "Wild in
the Country" appeared for the first time in
stereo on this LP, although the original EP and
single versions have yet to be released in stereo.

Side A
 They Remind Me Too Much of You
 Tonight Is So Right for Love
 Follow That Dream
 Wild in the Country
 Datin'
Side B
 Shoppin' Around
 Can't Help Falling in Love
 A Dog's Life
 I'm Falling in Love Tonight
 Thanks to the Rolling Sea

The TV Specials (SP) CPL8-3699-4
Side A
 Jailhouse Rock
 Suspicious Minds
 Lawdy Miss Clawdy
 Baby What You Want Me to Do
 Blue Christmas
Side B
 You Gave Me a Mountain
 Welcome to My World
 Tryin' to Get to You
 I'll Remember You
 My Way

The Las Vegas Years (SP) CPL8-3699-5
Side A
 Polk Salad Annie
 You've Lost That Lovin' Feelin'

Sweet Caroline
Kentucky Rain
Are You Lonesome Tonight
Side B
My Babe
In the Ghetto
An American Trilogy
Little Sister/Get Back
Yesterday

Lost Singles (SP) CPL8-3699-6
"Unchained Melody," "America the Beautiful," and "Softly, As I Leave You" are monaural on this LP. For the first time, true stereo
versions of "I'm Leavin," "The First Time Ever
I Saw Your Face," "Hi-Heel Sneakers," "Rags
to Riches" and "It's Only Love" became available. This LP also offered seven songs for the first
time on LP, the exceptions being "Fool" and
"Unchained Melody," although this version
was not the same take as appeared on *Moody
Blue.*

Side A
I'm Leavin'
The First Time Ever I Saw Your Face
Hi-Heel Sneakers
Softly, As I Leave You
Side B
Unchained Melody
Fool
Rags to Riches
It's Only Love
America the Beautiful

*Elvis at the Piano (S)/The Concert
Years—Part 1* (M) CPL8-3699-7
Since three of the four songs on Side A are just
Elvis and his piano, the stereo is not much of a
factor. On "Beyond the Reef" it is much more
enjoyable. Side B is a monaural live concert.

Side A
It's Still Here
I'll Take You Home Again Kathleen
Beyond the Reef
I Will Be True
Side B
Also Sprach Zarathustra
See See Rider
I Got a Woman/Amen
Love Me
If You Love Me (Let Me Know)
Love Me Tender
All Shook Up
(Let Me Be Your) Teddy Bear/Don't Be
  Cruel

The Concert Years—Concluded (M) CPL8-
3699-8
Side A
Hound Dog
The Wonder of You
Burning Love
Dialog/Introductions/Johnny B. Goode
Introductions/Long Live Rock And Roll
T-R-O-U-B-L-E
Why Me Lord
Side B
How Great Thou Art
Let Me Be There
An American Trilogy
Funny How Time Slips Away
Little Darlin'
Mystery Train/Tiger Man
Can't Help Falling In Love
Note: What is labeled as "Long Live Rock And
Roll" is nothing more than a few lines from
Chuck Berry's "School Day." Also included in
this set was a 20-page booklet, which is included
in the above price range. Deduct $5 if this book-
let is missing. The booklet was also packaged
with the cassette and eight-track editions. As an
additional challenge to the Presley collector,
there was a series of limited-edition numbers for
each letter prefix used in the spelling of *Elvis
Aron Presley,* a total of 11 different box sets to
assemble. The letters necessary to complete the
set of commercial issues are: E-L-V-I-S-A-R-O-
N-P-Y. The other letters in the name are simply
duplicates. Since I personally know the diffi-
culty of obtaining a copy of each letter of the
eleven, I would have to estimate that a complete
set, should one ever be offered for sale, would
be worth considerably more than 11 times the
value of a single set. It should also be noted that
the same letters and limited edition numbers
were used in the cassette and eight-track box
sets. See those listings for more information.

ELVIS ARON PRESLEY
RCA Victor (SP) CPK8-3699
. . . . 7/80   **80–100**
Cassette tape edition. Four double cassettes,
eight color Elvis pictures, and the 20-page
booklet make up this set. The eight pictures are
the same as used in the LP edition on the inner-
sleeves.

RCA Victor (SP) CPS8-3699 7/80   **100–125**
Eight-track tape edition. Four double eight-
tracks, plus the photos and booklet shown
above for the cassette edition, make up this set.

ELVIS ARON PRESLEY *(Excerpts from the 8-record Set)*

RCA Victor (SP) DJL1-3729 *7/80*   **100–125**
Distributed to retail record locations, designed for in-store play. Promotional issue only.

Side A
  Also Sprach Zarathustra
  See See Rider
  Heartbreak Hotel
  Long Tall Sally
  Introduction/Heartbreak Hotel
  Hi-Heel Sneakers
  In the Ghetto
  My Babe
  Welcome to My World
  Beyond the Reef
  Baby What You Want Me to Do
  Tonight Is So Right for Love
  Thanks to the Rolling Sea
  Datin'
  All Shook Up
  (Let Me Be Your) Teddy Bear/Don't Be
    Cruel
  Swing Down Sweet Chariot
  How Great Thou Art
  America the Beautiful
Side B
  Polk Salad Annie
  You've Lost That Lovin' Feelin'
  Little Darlin'
  Hound Dog
  I'll Take You Home Again Kathleen
  Shoppin' Around
  Yesterday
  Blue Suede Shoes
  Reconsider Baby
  Are You Lonesome Tonight
  An American Trilogy
  Love Me Tender
  Burning Love
  T-R-O-U-B-L-E
  Unchained Melody
  Why Me Lord
  Can't Help Falling in Love
  My Way

Note: On both the eight-LP box set and the above in-store sampler, the song "Tonight Is So Right for Love" is listed as appearing on the LP. This song does not appear on this set anywhere. The song that is used is "Tonight Is All Right for Love." Also, on the above sampler the excerpt from "Thanks to the Rolling Sea" is not listed on either the cover or label. It is listed in its proper place above.

ELVIS ARON PRESLEY *(Selections from the 8-record Set)*

RCA Victor (SP) DJL1-3781
. . . . *7/80*   **100–125**
Issued to radio stations, this LP contained 12 *complete* tracks whereas the above DJL1-3729 offered 37 selected excerpts. Promotional issue only.

Side A
  Long Tall Sally
  An Elvis Monolog
  Heartbreak Hotel
  All Shook Up
  Datin'
  Lawdy Miss Clawdy/Baby What You Want
    Me to Do
Side B
  Are You Lonesome Tonight
  Hi-Heel Sneakers
  Beyond the Reef
  (Let Me Be Your) Teddy Bear/Don't Be
    Cruel
  How Great Thou Art
  Little Darlin'

ELVIS AS RECORDED AT MADISON SQUARE GARDEN

RCA Victor (ST) LSP-4776 *6/72*   **15–18**
Orange label.

RCA Victor (ST) SPS-33-571-1
(LSP-4776) *6/72*   **250–300**
White label, double LP with double-pocket jacket. Promotional issue only.
Note: This two-LP set contains the same material as the single disc commercial version but was banded for dee jay convenience. The cover was plain white, with the titles and contents information applied on two white stickers.
RCA Victor (ST) LSP-4776 . *77*   **8–10**
Black label, dog near top.

Side 1
  Introduction: Also Sprach Zarathustra
  That's All Right
  Proud Mary
  Never Been to Spain
  You Don't Have to Say You Love Me
  You've Lost That Lovin' Feelin'
  Polk Salad Annie
  Love Me
  All Shook Up
  Heartbreak Hotel
  Medley: Teddy Bear/Don't Be Cruel
  Love Me Tender
Side 2
  The Impossible Dream
  Introductions by Elvis

Hound Dog
Suspicious Minds
For the Good Times
American Trilogy
Funny How Time Slips Away
I Can't Stop Loving You
Can't Help Falling in Love
Closing Riff

ELVIS BACK IN MEMPHIS: see BACK IN MEMPHIS, ELVIS.

ELVIS' CHRISTMAS ALBUM
RCA Victor (M) LOC-1035
. . . . *11/57*   **475–525**
Black label, with the words "Long Play" at the bottom of the label. First issued with gatefold cover and 10 pages of color photos bound in. Price here is for copies of this LP that still have the gold foil Christmas gift sticker attached to the plastic LP bag. Issued with either gold or silver printing on spine.

RCA Victor (M) LOC-1035
. . . . *11/57*   **250–300**
Same as above but without the gold foil Christmas gift sticker.

RCA Victor (M) LPM-1951
. . . . *11/58*   **90–100**
Black label, with the words "Long Play" at the bottom of the label. Repackage of the LOC-1035 LP in a standard jacket, which, of course, also eliminated the color photos that were part of the original issue. Original covers for this issue have the RCA catalog number under the RCA logo, in the upper right corner.

RCA Victor (M) LPM-1951
. . . . *11/63*   **45–55**
Black label, with the word "Mono" at the bottom. Covers for this issue have the RCA catalog number on the left side of the front cover.

RCA Victor (M) LPM-1951
. . . . *11/64*   **25–30**
Black label, with the word "Monaural" at the bottom. Covers for this issue have the RCA catalog number on the left side of the front cover.

RCA Victor (SE) LSP-1951(e)
. . . . *11/64*   **25–30**
Black label, with the RCA logo in white at the top of the label and the word "Stereo" at the bottom. Covers for this issue have the RCA catalog number on the left side of the front cover.

RCA Victor (SE) LSP-1951(e)
. . . . *11/68*   **20–25**
Orange label.

RCA Victor (M) AFM1-5486
. . . . *7/85*   **5–8**
Green vinyl. July release date is correct! Copies were on sale in August at the Memphis convention in 1985.

RCA Victor (M) AFM1-5486
. . . . *12/85*   **25–50**
Black vinyl. Thus far, all black vinyl copies discovered were packaged with stickers reading "pressed on green vinyl."

Side 1
  Santa Claus Is Back in Town
  White Christmas
  Here Comes Santa Claus
  I'll Be Home for Christmas
  Blue Christmas
  Santa Bring My Baby Back
Side 2
  Oh Little Town of Bethlehem
  Silent Night
  Peace in the Valley
  I Believe
  Take My Hand, Precious Lord
  It Is No Secret

ELVIS' CHRISTMAS ALBUM
RCA/Camden (M) CAL-2428
. . . . *11/70*   **15–18**
Blue label. This repackage added "If Everyday Was Like Christmas" and "Mama Liked the Roses" while eliminating the four sacred, non-Christmas songs from the earlier issues.

Pickwick/Camden (SE) CAS-2428
. . . . *12/75*   **8–10**
Issued with two different back cover designs. *Note:* In November 1978 Pickwick issued a specially wrapped package of seven LPs, including this one. After the holidays, they replaced the Christmas LP with *Frankie and Johnny.* See "Pickwick Pack" for more information on this set. All songs on the reprocessed stereo issue of this LP are electronically enhanced to simulate stereo.

Side 1
  Blue Christmas
  Silent Night
  White Christmas
  Santa Claus Is Back in Town
  I'll Be Home for Christmas
Side 2
  If Every Day Was Like Christmas
  Here Comes Santa Claus
  Oh Little Town of Bethlehem
  Santa Bring My Baby Back
  Mama Liked the Roses

ELVIS COMMEMORATIVE ALBUM (2 LP)

RCA Victor (SP) DPL2-0056(e)

. . . . *78*   **75–80**

Gold vinyl. A "Limited-Edition" repackage of the 1973 *Elvis* two-LP set that was marketed originally by Brookville. This LP was sold through TV mail-order offers. Also included in the package was a "Registered Certificate of Ownership."

ELVIS COUNTRY

RCA Victor (SP) DPL1-0647 *84*   **15–20**

RCA Special Products issue, for ERA Records, ERA number BU-3930.

Side 1

Are You Lonesome Tonight
Suspicion
Your Cheatin' Heart
Blue Moon of Kentucky
Don't
I Forgot to Remember to Forget
Help Me Make It Through the Night

Side 2

Kentucky Rain
I Really Don't Want to Know
Hurt
There's a Honky Tonk Angel (Who Will Take Me Back In)
Always on My Mind
Green, Green Grass of Home

ELVIS COUNTRY ("I'M 10,000 YEARS OLD")

RCA Victor (ST) LSP-4460 *1/71*   **20–25**

Orange label.

Note: 1971 originals were issued with a 5″ × 7″ color photo, which is included in the above price range. Deduct $5–$10 if this photo is missing.

RCA Victor (ST) LSP-4460 .   *76*   **10–15**

Tan label.

RCA Victor (ST) AFL1-4460   *77*   **8–10**

Black label, dog near top.

RCA Victor (ST) AYM1-3956

. . . . *5/81*   **5–8**

Black label, dog near top. Issued as part of RCA's "Best Buy" series.

Side 1

Snowbird
Tomorrow Never Comes
Little Cabin on the Hill
Whole Lot-ta Shakin' Goin' On
Funny How Time Slips Away
I Really Don't Want to Know

Side 2

There Goes My Everything
It's Your Baby, You Rock It
The Fool
Faded Love
I Washed My Hands in Muddy Water
Make the World Go Away

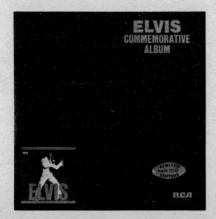

The phrase "limited edition" conjures up notions of scarcity, while the "registered certificate of ownership" that accompanied every copy of this album sold enhanced the sense of exclusivity that many collectors crave. As the price range shows, it worked!

ELVIS COUNTRY CLASSICS: see COUNTRY CLASSICS.

ELVIS EXCLUSIVE LIVE PRESS CONFERENCE (MEMPHIS, TENNESSEE—FEBRUARY 1961)—see EXCLUSIVE LIVE PRESS CONFERENCE.

ELVIS FOR EVERYONE

RCA Victor (M) LPM-3450 *7/65*   **35–45**
Black label, with the word "Monaural" at the bottom.

RCA Victor (SP) LSP-3450 *7/65*   **35–45**
Black label, with the RCA logo in white at the top of the label and the word "Stereo" at the bottom.

RCA Victor (SP) LSP-3450 .   *68*   **10–20**
Orange label.

RCA Victor (ST) LSP-3450 .   *76*   **10–15**
Tan label.

RCA Victor (SP) AFL1-3450   *77*   **8–10**
Black label, dog near top.

RCA Victor (SP) AYL1-4232
. . . . *2/82*   **5–8**
Black label, dog near top. Issued as part of RCA's "Best Buy" series.

Side 1
  Your Cheatin' Heart
  Summer Kisses, Winter Tears
  Finders Keepers, Losers Weepers
  In My Way
  Tomorrow Night
  Memphis, Tennessee
Side 2
  For the Millionth and the Last Time
  Forget Me Never
  Sound Advice
  Santa Lucia
  I Met Her Today
  When It Rains It Really Pours
Note: Only "Finders Keepers, Losers Weepers," "For the Millionth and the Last Time," "I Met Her Today," "Memphis" and "Santa Lucia" are in stereo on this LP.

ELVIS FOREVER (2 LP)

RCA Victor (SP) KSL2-7031 *74*   **25–35**
Mustard-color label. Manufactured in Canada but offered to U.S. buyers through a TV mail-order campaign.

Side 1
  Treat Me Nice
  I Need Your Love Tonight
  That's When Your Heartaches Begin
  G.I. Blues

  Blue Hawaii
  Easy Come, Easy Go
Side 2
  Suspicion
  Puppet on a String
  Heartbreak Hotel
  One Night
  Memories
  Blue Suede Shoes

Side 3
  Are You Lonesome Tonight
  Hi-Heel Sneakers
  Old Shep
  Rip It Up
  Such a Night
  A Fool Such As I
Side 4
  Tutti Frutti
  In the Ghetto
  Wear My Ring Around Your Neck
  Wooden Heart
  Crying in the Chapel
  Don't Cry Daddy

ELVIS' GOLDEN RECORDS

RCA Victor (M) LPM-1707 *4/58*   **100–125**
Black label, with the words "Long Play" at the bottom of the label. LP title is printed in light blue letters across the top, and contents are *not* shown on front cover. Original covers for this issue have the RCA catalog number under the RCA logo, in the upper right corner.
Note: Some copies of 1958 issues of this LP contained an insert that made a "Fabulous Offer!" For 25 cents one could obtain a 12-page 8" × 10" Elvis photo booklet. A coupon, for ordering the booklet, was attached to the insert.

RCA Victor (M) LPM-1707
. . . . *11/63*   **45–55**
Black label, with the word "Mono" at the bottom. LP title is in white lettering. Song titles are listed on front cover. Covers for this issue have the RCA catalog number on the left side of the front cover.

RCA Victor (M) LPM-1707
. . . . *64–65*   **25–30**
Black label, with the word "Monaural" at the bottom. Covers for this issue have the RCA catalog number on the left side of the front cover.

RCA Victor (SE) LSP-1707(e)
. . . . *2/62*   **75–85**
Black label, with the RCA logo in silver at the top of the label and the word "Stereo" at the bottom.

RCA Victor (SE) LSP-1707(e) *64*   **25–30**
Black label, with the RCA logo in white at the
top of the label and the word "Stereo" at the
bottom.

RCA Victor (SE) LSP-1707(e)
. . . . *68–69*   **10–20**
Orange label.

RCA Victor (SE) LSP-1707(e) *76*   **10–15**
Tan label.

RCA Victor (SE) AFL1-1707(e)
. . . . *77*   **8–10**
Black label, dog near top.

RCA Victor (SE) AQL1-1707(e)
. . . . *79*   **5–10**
Black label, dog near top.
Note: All songs on the stereo issue of this LP
were electronically enhanced to simulate stereo.

RCA Victor (M) AFM1-5196
. . . . *8/84*   **5–8**
Digitally remastered quality mono pressing.
Price includes gold banner: "The Definitive
Rock Classic."

Side 1
   Hound Dog
   Loving You
   All Shook Up
   Heartbreak Hotel
   Jailhouse Rock
   Love Me
   Too Much
Side 2
   Don't Be Cruel
   That's When Your Heartaches Begin
   Teddy Bear
   Love Me Tender
   Treat Me Nice
   Anyway You Want Me
   I Want You, I Need You, I Love You

ELVIS' GOLD RECORDS, VOL. 2 (50,000,000 ELVIS FANS CAN'T BE WRONG)

RCA Victor (M) LPM-2075
. . . . *12/59*   **100–125**
Black label, with the words "Long Play" at the
bottom of the label. Original covers for this
issue have the RCA catalog number under the
RCA logo, in the upper right corner.

RCA Victor (M) LPM-2075
. . . . *11/63*   **45–55**
Black label, with the word "Mono" at the bottom. Covers for this issue have the RCA catalog
number on the left side of the front cover.

RCA Victor (M) LPM-2075
. . . . *64–65*   **25–30**
Black label, with the word "Monaural" at the
bottom. Covers for this issue have the RCA
catalog number on the left side of the front
cover.

RCA Victor (SE) LSP-2075(e)
. . . . *2/62*   **75–85**
Black label, with the RCA logo in silver at the
top of the label and the word "Stereo" at the
bottom.

RCA Victor (SE) LSP-2075(e) *64*   **25–30**
Black label, with the RCA logo in white at the
top of the label and the word "Stereo" at the
bottom.

RCA Victor (SE) LSP-2075(e)
. . . . *68–69*   **10–20**
Orange label.

RCA Victor (SE) LSP-2075(e) *76*   **10–15**
Tan label.

RCA Victor (SE) AFL1-2075(e)
. . . . *77*   **8–10**
Black label, dog near top.

RCA Victor (M) AFM1-5197
. . . . *8/84*   **5–8**
Digitally remastered quality mono pressing.
Price includes gold banner: "The Definitive
Rock Classic."
Note: There was never an RCA release of this
LP with a black cover. Some copies show the
title on the label as *Elvis' Gold Records, Vol. 2,*
dropping the subtitle "50,000,000 Elvis Fans
Can't Be Wrong."

Side 1
   I Need Your Love Tonight
   Don't
   Wear My Ring Around Your Neck
   My Wish Came True
   I Got Stung
Side 2
   One Night
   A Big Hunk O' Love
   I Beg of You
   A Fool Such As I
   Doncha' Think It's Time

ELVIS' GOLDEN RECORDS—VOLUME 3

RCA Victor (M) LPM-2765 *9/63*   **90–100**
Black label, with the word "Mono" at the bottom.

RCA Victor (M) LPM-2765 . *64*   **25–30**
Black label, with the word "Monaural" at the
bottom.

RCA Victor (ST) LSP-2765 *9/63* **90–100**
Black label, with the RCA logo in silver at the top of the label and the word "Stereo" at the bottom.

RCA Victor (ST) LSP-2765 . *64* **25–30**
Black label, with the RCA logo in white at the top of the label and the word "Stereo" at the bottom.

RCA Victor (ST) LSP-2765 . *68* **10–20**
Orange label.

RCA Victor (ST) LSP-2765 . *76* **10–15**
Tan label.

RCA Victor (ST) AFL1-2765 *77* **8–10**
Black label, dog near top.

Note: 1963 original issues were packaged with a bonus 8″ × 10″ photo booklet, which is included in the above price range. Deduct $30 if this photo booklet is missing.

Side 1
　It's Now or Never
　Stuck on You
　Fame and Fortune
　I Gotta Know
　Surrender
　I Feel So Bad
Side 2
　Are You Lonesome Tonight
　His Latest Flame
　Little Sister
　Good Luck Charm
　Anything That's Part of You
　She's Not You

ELVIS' GOLD RECORDS—VOLUME 4
RCA Victor (M) LPM-3921 *2/68* **450–500**
Black label, with the word "Monaural" at the bottom.

RCA Victor (SP) LSP-3921 *2/68* **35–45**
Black label, with the RCA logo in white at the top of the label and the word "Stereo" at the bottom. All songs except "Ain't That Loving You Baby," which was recorded in monaural in 1958, are in stereo on this LP.

RCA Victor (SP) LSP-3921 . *68* **10–20**
Orange label.

RCA Victor (SP) LSP-3921 . *76* **10–15**
Tan label.

RCA Victor (SP) AFL1-3921 *77* **8–10**
Black label, dog near top.

Side 1
　Love Letters
　Witchcraft
　It Hurts Me

What'd I Say
Please Don't Drag That String Around
Indescribably Blue
Side 2
　Devil In Disguise
　Lonely Man
　A Mess of Blues
　Ask Me
　Ain't That Loving You Baby
　Just Tell Her Jim Said Hello

ELVIS' GOLD RECORDS—VOLUME 5
RCA Victor (ST) AFL1-4941
. . . . *2/84* **5–8**
Note: The hit single versions of "Kentucky Rain" and "If I Can Dream" appeared for the first time in stereo on this LP.

Side 1
　Suspicious Minds
　Kentucky Rain
　In the Ghetto
　Clean Up Your Own Backyard
　If I Can Dream
Side 2
　Burning Love
　If You Talk in Your Sleep
　For the Heart
　Moody Blue
　Way Down

ELVIS—HBO SPECIAL
RCA Victor (SP) DVM1-0704
. . . . *1/84* **25–35**
Special Products issue for HBO cable TV subscribers. Price includes a 24″ × 36″ bonus poster, which represents $4–$8 of the value.
Note: This material was first issued as *Elvis (NBC TV Special)*, LPM-4088.

ELVIS: HIS FIRST AND ONLY PRESS CONFERENCE: see *CURRENT AUDIO MAGAZINE* in Various-Artists Compilations section.

ELVIS! HIS GREATEST HITS (8 LP)
RCA/Custom (SP) RD4A-010 *79* **400–450**
Reader's Digest commemorative album, white box. This deluxe boxed set was prepared by *Reader's Digest*, intended to be offered to readers. The idea was scrapped even though a small quantity of sets was manufactured. Although not announced as such, this LP did contain a previously unavailable alternate take of "Your Cheatin' Heart."

Record 1
Side 1
Heartbreak Hotel
Don't Be Cruel (to a Heart That's True)
I Want You, I Need You, I Love You
Blue Suede Shoes
Anyway You Want Me (That's How I Will Be)
Hound Dog
Side 2
Love Me Tender
Too Much
Love Me
I Was the One
Playing for Keeps
(Let Me Be Your) Teddy Bear

Record 2
Side 1
All Shook Up
Loving You
Treat Me Nice
Blue Christmas
That's When Your Heartaches Begin
Jailhouse Rock
Side 2
Don't
I Beg of You
Wear My Ring Around Your Neck
One Night
King Creole
Hard Headed Woman

Record 3
Side 1
I Got Stung
A Fool Such As I
I Need Your Love Tonight
My Wish Came True
Doncha' Think It's Time
A Big Hunk of Love
Side 2
Are You Lonesome Tonight
Stuck on You
I Gotta Know
Fame and Fortune
A Mess of Blues
It's Now or Never

Record 4
Side 1
Can't Help Falling in Love
Surrender
Little Sister
Flaming Star
I Feel So Bad
His Latest Flame

Side 2
Return to Sender
Good Luck Charm
Follow That Dream
Wooden Heart
She's Not You
Rock-a-Hula Baby

Record 5
Side 1
Blue Hawaii
You're the Devil in Disguise
One Broken Heart for Sale
Bossa Nova Baby
Such a Night
King Of The Whole Wide World
Side 2
Kissin' Cousins
Ask Me
Ain't That Loving You Baby
Viva Las Vegas
Kiss Me Quick
What'd I Say

Record 6
Side 1
Suspicious Minds
In the Ghetto
(Such an) Easy Question
Don't Cry Daddy
If I Can Dream
Puppet on a String
Side 2
You Don't Have to Say You Love Me
Burning Love
The Wonder of You
Steamroller Blues
Kentucky Rain
My Way

Record 7
Side 1
Mystery Train
I'm Left, You're Right, She's Gone
I Forgot to Remember to Forget
Baby, Let's Play House
That's All Right
You're a Heartbreaker
Side 2
Your Cheatin' Heart
I Really Don't Want to Know
When My Blue Moon Turns to Gold Again
There Goes My Everything
Have I Told You Lately That I Love You
I Can't Stop Loving You

Record 8
Side 1
How Great Thou Art
Somebody Bigger Than You and I

In the Garden
It Is No Secret (What God Can Do)
His Hand in Mine
Take My Hand, Precious Lord
Side 2
Crying in the Chapel
(There'll Be) Peace in the Valley (for Me)
Put Your Hand in the Hand
Where Did They Go Lord
I Believe
You'll Never Walk Alone

ELVIS! HIS GREATEST HITS (7 LP)

RCA/Custom (SP) RD4A-010
. . . . *8/83*   **40–60**
Reader's Digest Commemorative Album, yellow box.
Note: Contains one less album than the 1979 edition.

ELVIS HOUR, THE

Creative Radio (SP) 1-52. *86–88*   **10–20**
Price is for any of the weekly discs in this series, issued without special covers, to radio stations only. Includes script pages.

ELVIS IN CONCERT (2 LP)

RCA Victor (ST) APL2-2587
. . . . *10/77*   **15–20**
Special blue "Elvis" label.
Note: Included in this LP was a color flyer that listed other Elvis albums, which is included in the above price range. Deduct $2 if this flyer is missing.

RCA Victor (st) CPL2-2587. *82*   **12–15**

Side A
Elvis' Fans Comments/Opening Riff
Also Sprach Zarathustra/Opening Riff
See See Rider
That's All Right
Are You Lonesome Tonight
Medley: Teddy Bear/Don't Be Cruel
Elvis' Fans Comments
You Gave Me a Mountain
Jailhouse Rock
Side B
Elvis' Fans Comments
How Great Thou Art
Elvis' Fans Comments
I Really Don't Want to Know
Elvis Introduces His Father
Closing Riff
Special Message from Elvis' Father, Vernon Presley
Side C
Medley: I Got a Woman/Amen
Elvis Talks

Love Me
I You Love Me (Let Me Know)
Medley: O Sole Mio (Sherril Nielsen Solo)/
   It's Now or Never
Trying to Get to You
Side D
Hawaiian Wedding Song
Fairytale
Little Sister
Early Morning Rain
What'd I Say
Johnny B. Goode
And I Love You So

ELVIS IN HOLLYWOOD (2 LP)

RCA Victor (SP) DPL2-0618
. . . . *1/76*   **35–45**
RCA's blue Special Products label. Offered by Brookville Marketing through TV mail order.
Note: Original issues were packaged with a 20-page bonus photo booklet, which is included in the above price range. Deduct $10 if this booklet is missing.

Side A
Jailhouse Rock
Rock-a-Hula Baby
G.I. Blues
Kissin' Cousins
Wild in the Country
Side B
King Creole
Blue Hawaii
Fun in Acapulco
Follow That Dream
Girls! Girls! Girls!
Side C
Viva Las Vegas
Bossa Nova Baby
Flaming Star
Girl Happy
Frankie and Johnny
Side D
Roustabout
Spinout
Double Trouble
Charro
They Remind Me Too Much of You

ELVIS IN PERSON AT THE INTERNATIONAL HOTEL, LAS VEGAS, NEVADA

RCA Victor (ST) LSP-4428
. . . . *11/70*   **15–18**
Orange label.

RCA Victor (ST) LSP-4428 . *76*   **10–15**
Tan label.

RCA Victor (ST) AFL1-4428 *77* **8–10**
Black label, dog near top.

RCA Victor (ST) AYL1-3892
. . . . *2/81* **5–8**
Black label, dog near top. Issued as part of
RCA's "Best Buy" series.
Note: This LP was previously issued as one-half
of the 2-LP set *From Memphis to Vegas/From
Vegas to Memphis.*

Side 1
 Blue Suede Shoes
 Johnny B. Goode
 All Shook Up
 Are You Lonesome Tonight
 Hound Dog
 I Can't Stop Loving You
 My Babe
Side 2
 Medley: Mystery Train/Tiger Man
 Words
 In the Ghetto
 Suspicious Minds
 Can't Help Falling in Love

ELVIS IN THE GREATEST SHOW ON EARTH: see *THE GREATEST SHOW ON EARTH*

ELVIS IS BACK

RCA Victor (M) LPM-2231 *4/60* **100–125**
Black label, with the words "Long Play" at the
bottom of the label. Song titles may be printed
on a yellow sticker that was attached to the
front cover. Regardless, titles are not printed on
cover itself.

RCA Victor (M) LPM-2231
. . . . *11/63* **45–55**
Black label, with the word "Mono" at the bottom. With song titles printed on front cover.

RCA Victor (M) LPM-2231 . *64* **25–30**
Black label, with the word "Monaural" on the
bottom.

RCA Victor (ST) LSP-2231 *4/60* **125–150**
Black label, with the words "Living Stereo" at
the bottom. Song titles may be printed on a
yellow sticker that was attached to the front
cover. Regardless, titles are not printed on
cover itself.

RCA Victor (ST) LSP-2231 . *64* **25–30**
Black label, with the RCA logo in white at the
top of the label and the word "Stereo" at the
bottom. With song titles printed on front cover.

RCA Victor (ST) LSP-2231 . *68* **10–20**
Orange label.

RCA Victor (ST) LSP-2231 . *76* **10–15**
Tan label.

RCA Victor (ST) AFL1-2231 *77* **8–10**
Black label, dog near top.
Note: Issued with a gatefold cover. This was the
first Elvis album to contain true stereo recordings.

Side 1
 Make Me Know It
 The Girl of My Best Friend
 I Will Be Home Again
 Dirty, Dirty Feeling
 Thrill of Your Love

Perhaps because of a designer's
oversight, the song titles on
the original issues of this
album had to be listed on a
yellow sticker attached to the
front.

Side 2
Soldier Boy
Such a Night
It Feels So Right
The Girl Next Door
Like a Baby
Reconsider, Baby

ELVIS—LEGENDARY CONCERT PERFORMANCES (2 LP)

RCA Victor (ST) R-244047 .   *78*   **20–25**
RCA Record Club. Black label, dog near top.

ELVIS LOVE SONGS

K-TEL (SP) NU9900 . . . . *81*   **15–20**

Side 1
Suspicious Minds
She's Not You
The Wonder of You
Love Letters
Wooden Heart
I Want You, I Need You, I Love You
Memories
Kentucky Rain
Side 2
Love Me Tender
It's Now or Never
Are You Lonesome Tonight?
You Don't Have to Say You Love Me
I Just Can't Help Believin'
Can't Help Falling in Love
Surrender
Loving You (shown as "Lovin' You")

ELVIS MEDLEY, THE

RCA Victor (SP) AHL1-4530
. . . . *11/82*   **8–10**
Black label, dog near top.

Side A
The Elvis Medley (Jailhouse Rock—Teddy
   Bear—Don't Be Cruel—Burning Love—
   Suspicious Minds)
Jailhouse Rock
(Let Me Be Your) Teddy Bear
Hound Dog
Don't Be Cruel (To a Heart That's True)
Side B
Burning Love
Suspicious Minds
Always on My Mind
Heartbreak Hotel
Hard Headed Woman

ELVIS MEMORIES (3 LP)

ABC Radio (SP) ASP-1003
. . . . *12/78*   **425–500**
A three-LP boxed set, sent by ABC Radio to
subscribing stations airing the "Elvis Memories" three hour special, originally broadcast
January 7, 1979.
Note: Included in this set was a 16-page "Program Operation Instructions" booklet and four
pages of "Commercial/Final Program Instructions." Deduct $50 if these inserts are missing.

Side 1
Memories
Elvis Memories (Jingle/Logo)
That's All Right
Good Rockin' Tonight

K-Tel, one of the more
aggressive re-issue companies,
used this sultry shot from
Elvis' comeback period to
promote their package.

Another radio show, this one elaborately presented by ABC Radio to its subscribing stations at the end of 1978. Along with a script, booklet, and program instructions, this three-hour show also included a reel tape featuring on-the-air promotional spots.

Mystery Train
I Want You, I Need You, I Love You
Heartbreak Hotel
Side 2
   Burning Love
   Rip It Up
   Follow That Dream
   Loving You
   Love Me Tender
   Hound Dog
   Don't Be Cruel
   Way Down
   Moody Blue
   Devil in Disguise
   Suspicion
Side 3
   Elvis Memories (Jingle/Logo)
   His Latest Flame
   All Shook Up
   Teddy Bear

Jailhouse Rock
It's Now or Never
Elvis Memories (Jingle/Logo)
I Got Stung
One Night
Wear My Ring Around Your Neck
Stuck on You
Side 4
   Elvis Memories (Jingle/Logo)
   My Wish Came True
   Good Luck Charm
   And the Grass Won't Pay No Mind
   Fame and Fortune
   Kentucky Rain
   In the Ghetto
Side 5
   Viva Las Vegas
   Don't Cry Daddy
   Separate Ways
   You Don't Have to Say You Love Me

Elvis Memories (Jingle/Logo)
Blue Christmas
Are You Lonesome Tonight
Can't Help Falling in Love
Side 6
Elvis Memories (Jingle/Logo)
My Way
How Great Thou Art
Crying in the Chapel
If I Can Dream
The Wonder of You
Memories
Also see: *MICHELOB PRESENTS HIGH-LIGHTS OF ELVIS MEMORIES.*

ELVIS MEMORIES (Reel Tape)
ABC Radio *12/78*   **40–50**
A 7" reel tape with "Promotional Ad Spots for Elvis Memories." Sent to radio stations for advance promotion of their upcoming airing of "Elvis Memories."

ELVIS—MEMORIES OF CHRISTMAS: see *MEMORIES OF CHRISTMAS.*

ELVIS NOW
RCA Victor (ST) LSP-4671 *2/72*   **15–20**
Orange label.
RCA Victor (ST) LSP-4671 *2/72*   **50–60**
With white sticker on front cover with titles and times. Promotional issue only.
RCA Victor (ST) LSP-4671 . *76*   **10–15**
Tan label.
RCA Victor (ST) AFL1-4671 *77*   **8–10**
Black label, dog near top.

Side 1
Help Me Make It Through the Night
Miracle of the Rosary
Hey Jude
Put Your Hand in the Hand
Until It's Time for You to Go
Side 2
We Can Make the Morning
Early Morning Rain
Sylvia
Fools Rush In
I Was Born About Ten Thousand Years Ago

ELVIS PRESLEY
RCA Victor (M) LPM-1254 *3/56*   **100–125**
Black label, with the words "Long Play" at the bottom of the label. Original covers for this issue have the RCA catalog number under the RCA logo, in the upper right corner.
RCA Victor (M) LPM-1254
. . . . *11/63*   **45–55**

Black label, with the word "Mono" at the bottom. Covers for this issue have the RCA catalog number on the left side of the front cover.
RCA Victor (M) LPM-1254. *64*   **25–30**
Black label, with the word "Monaural" at the bottom. Covers for this issue have the RCA catalog number on the left side of the front cover.
RCA Victor (SE) LSP-1254(e)
. . . . *2/62*   **75–85**
Black label, with the RCA logo in silver at the top of the label and the word "Stereo" at the bottom.
RCA Victor (SE) LSP-1254(e) *64*   **25–30**
Black label, with the RCA logo in white at the top of the label and the word "Stereo" at the bottom.
RCA Victor (SE) LSP-1254(e) *68*   **10–20**
Orange label.
RCA Victor (SE) LSP-1254(e) *76*   **10–15**
Tan label.
RCA Victor (SE) AFL1-1254(e)
. . . . *77*   **8–10**
Black label, dog near top.
Note: All songs on the stereo issue of this LP are electronically enhanced to simulate stereo.
RCA Victor (M) AFM1-5198
. . . . *8/84*   **5–8**
Digitally remastered quality mono pressing. Price includes gold banner: "The Definitive Rock Classic."

Side 1
Blue Suede Shoes
I'm Counting on You
I Got a Woman
One-Sided Love Affair
I Love You Because
Just Because
Side 2
Tutti Frutti
Tryin' to Get to You
I'm Gonna Sit Right Down and Cry
I'll Never Let You Go
Blue Moon
Money Honey

ELVIS PRESLEY: 1954–1961 (2 LP)
Time-Life (SP) STL-106 . . *9/86*   **15–18**
One of the "Rock 'N' Roll Era" series of box sets available from Time-Life by mail order. The other LPs in this series did not feature Elvis. Includes fold-open brochure.

Side 1
That's All Right
Heartbreak Hotel

Technology generally moves us forward, but in the age of digital remastering, we are also getting to hear once again the original mono mixes. When something sounds this good, who needs "enhanced stereo"?

Hound Dog
Love Me Tender
Don't Be Cruel
All Shook Up
Side 2
I Want You, I Need You, I Love
    You
Jailhouse Rock
Love Me
(Let Me Be Your) Teddy Bear
Too Much
Side 3
Hard Headed Woman
One Night
Wear My Ring Around Your
    Neck
A Fool Such As I
Don't
A Big Hunk O' Love
Side 4
It's Now or Never
Stuck on You
Are You Lonesome Tonight?

Little Sister
Can't Help Falling in Love

**ELVIS PRESLEY INTERVIEW
RECORD—AN AUDIO
SELF-PORTRAIT**
RCA Victor (M) DJM1-0835
. . . . *10/84*   **75–100**
Promotional issue only.

Side A
The 1956 Interviews:
Elvis Presley—Excerpt from a *TV Guide* Interview 1956; Colonel Tom Parker—Excerpt from a *TV Guide* Interview 1956
Vernon and Gladys Presley—Tupelo, Mississippi, September 26, 1956
Elvis Presley—Tupelo, Mississippi, September 26, 1956
Side B
The 1960–61 Interview
Image Change Since Discharge from the Army—By Accident or Design?
Elvis Talks About His Mother

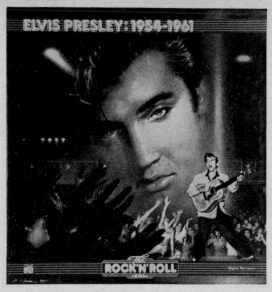

Time-Life Productions have presented fine repackages of Elvis' work as parts of various ongoing series.

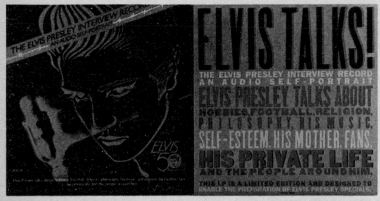

The Elvis interviews available on the promotional only *Elvis Presley Interview Record* were commercially issued, via mail order, on *Elvis Talks*.

How Does Elvis View Himself?
Does He Enjoy His Work?
How Does He Relax?
Does He Have Any Time to Read? If So, What Does He Read?
Does He Like Himself?
Does He Like to Work?
If He Were Starting Out Again (in 1961) Would He Do Anything Differently? Does He Have Any Specific Goals for the Future?
Does He Think He Has Changed Much As a Person? How Does He View the Criticism That Has Been Leveled at Some of the People Surrounding Him?
If He Were a Father and Could Only Give His Child One Piece of Advice, What Would That Be?

ELVIS PRESLEY COLLECTION, THE (3 LP)

RCA Victor (SP) DML3-0632 *84* **50–60**
Special Products boxed set, produced for Candlelite Music. A mail-order offer. Price includes 12-page booklet, which represents $10–$15 of the value.

Side A
Don't Be Cruel
Loving You
Trouble
I Was the One
When My Blue Moon Turns to Gold Again
Side B
Are You Lonesome Tonight
Hard Headed Woman
Don't
Little Sister

Side C
One Night
A Big Hunk O' Love
(Marie's the Name) His Latest Flame
I Got Stung
I Want You, I Need You, I Love You
Side D
Jailhouse Rock
The Wonder of You
Too Much
Love Me

Side E
All Shook Up
Heartbreak Hotel
Crying in the Chapel
(Let Me Be Your) Teddy Bear
Can't Help Falling in Love
Side F
Hound Dog
Love Me Tender

Return to Sender
It's Now or Never

ELVIS PRESLEY STORY, THE (1975) (13 LP)

Watermark (SP) EPS 1A-13B *75* **800–900**
A complete 13-hour radio program. The 1975 issue had the title in pink letters and had the 1975 copyright date on the label.
Note: Packaged with the LP set was a special programmer's "Manual of Operations," which is included in the above price range. Deduct $100 if this manual is missing.

Side 1
Introduction: Medley of Elvis Hits
Old Shep
Jesus Knows What I Need *(Comparison of versions by the Statesmen Quartet and by Elvis)*
Side 2
That's All Right (Arthur Crudup)
Hound Dog (Willie Mae Thornton)
Early Fifties Medley: Harbor Lights (Sammy Kaye)/Rag Mop (Ames Bros.)/Tennessee Waltz (Patti Page)/Cry of the Wild Goose (Frankie Lane)/You Belong to Me (Jo Stafford)/My Heart Cries for You (Guy Mitchell)/Come-On-A My House (Rosemary Clooney)/Cry (Johnny Ray)
Working on the Building *(Comparison of versions by the Blackwood Brothers and by Elvis)*
Side 3
That's All Right
Blue Moon of Kentucky
Good Rockin' Tonight
You're a Heartbreaker
Just Because
Side 4
Milkcow Blues Boogie
The Truth About Me
Baby Let's Play House
I'm Left, You're Right, She's Gone
Blue Moon
I Forgot to Remember to Forget
Mystery Train
Side 5
Heartbreak Hotel
I Was the One
Heartbreak Hotel (Stan Freberg)
Medley: Reddy Teddy/Blueberry Hill/ Money Honey/Rip It Up/I Got a Woman/Lawdy Miss Clawdy/Long Tall Sally/Shake, Rattle and Roll/Tutti Fruitti
Blue Suede Shoes
I Want You, I Need You, I Love You

Side 6
Hound Dog
Don't Be Cruel
Love Me
Love Me Tender
One-Sided Love Affair
Too Much
Side 7
All Shook Up
Loving You
Teddy Bear
Got a Lot of Living to Do
Peace in the Valley
Side 8
Medley of Songs about Elvis
Party
Jailhouse Rock
Baby I Don't Care
Oh Little Town of Bethlehem
Blue Christmas
Don't
Side 9
King Creole
Dear 53310761 (The Thirteens)
Wear My Ring Around Your Neck
Hard Headed Woman
If We Never Meet Again
Elvis Sails Interview
Side 10
Trouble
I Got Stung
A Fool Such As I
My Wish Came True
A Big Hunk O' Love
I Will Be Home Again
Side 11
I'm Hanging Up My Rifle (Bill [Bobby Bare]
   Parsons)
Dirty, Dirty Feeling
Stuck on You
It's Now or Never
Fever
G.I. Blues
Side 12
Wooden Heart
Flaming Star
Are You Lonesome Tonight
I Slipped, I Stumbled, I Fell
His Hand in Mine
Surrender
I'm Coming Home
Side 13
Medley of Elvis' Film Songs
Blue Hawaii
I Feel So Bad
Can't Help Falling in Love

Good Luck Charm
Return to Sender
Side 14
One Broken Heart for Sale
Medley: Elvis' Film Songs
Bossa Nova Baby
Happy Ending
Memphis, Tennessee
Fun in Acapulco
Side 15
Devil in Disguise
Santa Lucia
What'd I Say
Crying in the Chapel
Ain't That Loving You Baby
Your Cheatin' Heart
Side 16
Little Egypt
Medley of Silly Elvis Film Songs
Down by the Riverside/When the Saints Go
   Marching In
Puppet on a String
Do the Clam
When It Rains It Really Pours
Side 17
Old MacDonald
Long Lonely Highway
Down in the Alley
Tomorrow Is a Long Time
Paradise Hawaiian Style
Side 18
If Everyday Was Like Christmas
There Ain't Nothing Like a Song
He's Your Uncle, Not Your Dad
Big Boss Man
How Great Thou Art
Side 19
Guitar Man
U.S. Male
A Little Less Conversation
Memories
Yellow Rose of Texas/The Eyes of Texas
If I Can Dream
Side 20
"Songs from NBC-TV Special"
Only the Strong Survive
Gentle on My Mind
In the Ghetto
Side 21
"Songs from *Elvis Live at the International
   Hotel, Las Vegas, Nevada* LP"
Don't Cry Daddy
Kentucky Rain
Side 22
"Songs from *On Stage* LP"
You've Lost That Lovin' Feeling

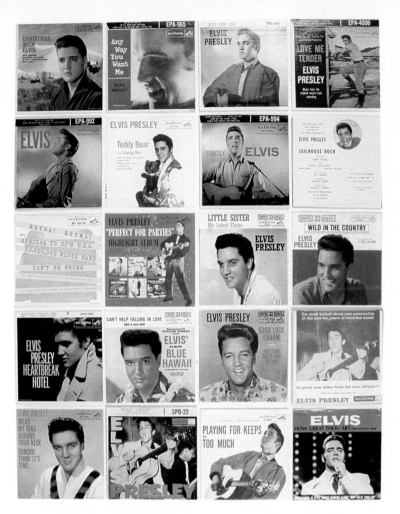

The complete collection of RCA's Elvis Gold Standard
Series picture sleeves.

One of a dozen Mathey-Tissot wristwatches that Elvis had made for his immediate staff and friends. With the name "Elvis Presley" circling the bezel, these command prices upward of $15,000.

Elvis designed the TCB (Taking Care of Business) lightning bolt as his personal logo; Beverly Hills jeweler Schwartz & Ableser transformed the sketch into pure gold. For the ladies, Schwartz & Ableser made the TLC (Tender Loving Care) necklaces. Frequently copied following Elvis's death, originals vary widely in price—from $1,000 to as high as $10,000.

A 1956 Elvis Presley Enterprises carrying, or overnight, case. Inside tray is also pictured. Valued at $400 to $500.

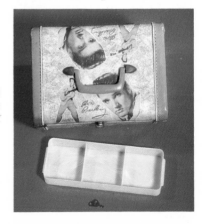

The RCA Autographed Model Victrola. Pictured is the automatic changer. The triple EP (left) was a bonus to buyers of this player; the double EP (right) for buyers of the manual Victrola. Total value of items pictured—$3,000 to $3,500.

An RCA "In House" Gold Record (for 500,000 copies sold) for the *Promised Land* LP, released January 1975.

The official Elvis Presley hat, or crew hat, originally sold for $1.25. Today, its value is $75 to $150.

On this 1955 Louisiana Hayride show, Elvis was just another country singer on the bill—his name is no larger than that of the unrenowned Debbie Day. Valued at $200 to $300.

This Hawaiian lei, picturing Elvis with lei and ukelele, was backed with a plug for his *Blue Hawaii* LP.

The tie-in with Elvis's army stint and the film, *G.I. Blues,* made an Elvis army hat a natural promotional item. One side announced the album, the other, the film. Valued at $40 to $60.

The Beatles "nodder" dolls. Hand-painted ceramic figures, these effigies of the beloved moptops go for upward of $400 for the set.

It is doubtful that the Beatles themselves ever wore them on the stage, but these tie-tacks — one for each Beatle, valued originally at 59 cents — now go for $18 to $20.

The Beatles tea tray, Wentworth, England. Transfer on metal. A cool $40 to $50.

Among the most collectible of the Beatles' apparel is this sweatshirt from 1964. Valued at $70 to $80.

What Merchandisers Hath Wrought: The panoply of Beatles memorabilia. Those in "the know" estimated that the Beatles, during their first visit to the United States, grossed $2 million in licensing alone. By 1970, this figure had grown to ten times that amount.

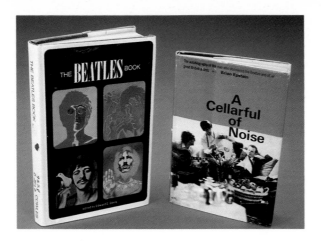

The Beatles have proven to be among the most durable subjects in the world of publishing. Left, E. E. Davis's *The Beatles Book,* published by Cowles in 1968. Valued at $25 to $35. Right, Brian Epstein's *Cellarful of Noise,* his memoir of the group's rise to fame, published by Doubleday and Co. in 1964. Valued at $35 to $45.

These 3-inch tall Beatle-like figures were hand-painted and adorned many a fan's dresser top and window sill. With the original box, they can go for $35.

Above Left: For the full story on this infamous cover, please see the section on The Beatles' LPs. This "new, improved" stereo version of the original cover alone can fetch as much as $3,000.

Above Right: Misadventures in marketing are the source of some of the finest collectibles. When Vee Jay's first version of this LP failed in the marketplace, they simply repackaged and tried again, using the portrait cover shown here. The original LP is valued between $70 and $80, but the one depicted here can bring in $1,300 or more on a good day.

The Stereo Compact 33 did not prove to be a viable product in the marketplace; indeed, Capitol intended this version of *Meet the Beatles* only for use in jukeboxes. With the miniature album cover and title strips, this is valued at $300 to $325.

The Wonder of You
The Next Step Is Love
Side 23
Patch It Up
Bridge over Troubled Water
Rags to Riches
There Goes My Everything
Whole Lot-ta Shakin' Goin' On
I'm Leavin'
Side 24
Help Me Make It Through the Night
American Trilogy
Don't Think Twice
Also Sprach Zarathustra/See See Rider
Hound Dog
Burning Love
It's a Matter of Time
Side 25
Separate Ways
My Way
I'm So Lonesome I Could Cry
Raised on Rock
Talk About the Good Times
Steamroller Blues
Side 26
Medley of Elvis Hits
I've Got a Thing About You Baby
Help Me
Promised Land

ELVIS PRESLEY STORY, THE (1977) (13 LP)

Watermark (SP) EPA-1A-13B 77   700–800
This revised edition was issued shortly after
Elvis' death. These LPs have the title in blue
letters, and have the 1977 copyright date on the
label.
Note: Packaged with the LP set was a special
programmer's "Manual of Operations," which
is included in the above price range. Deduct
$100 if this manual is missing. A 12-hour ver-
sion of this program aired in 1970 but was produced only on reel tapes. The contents of the
1977 edition are exactly the same as those for
the 1975 edition, with the exception of Side 26.

Side 26
Medley of Elvis Hits
I've Got a Thing About You Baby
Medley of Elvis' Hits Through 1977

ELVIS PRESLEY SUN COLLECTION: see *SUN COLLECTION*

ELVIS RECORDED LIVE ON STAGE IN MEMPHIS

RCA Victor (ST) CPL1-0606
. . . . *6/74*   **15–20**
Orange label.

RCA Victor (ST) DJL1-0606
. . . . *6/74*   **250–275**
This "banded" edition was distributed to radio
stations so that dee jays could easily select a
certain track for air play. Promotional issue
only.

RCA Victor (Q) APD1-0606
. . . . *6/74*   **120–130**
Quadradisc. Orange label. Reportedly, the quad
version of this LP contains some dialogue by
Elvis that can only be heard when played on a
quad system.

RCA Victor (ST) CPL1-0606 76   **10–15**
Tan label.

RCA Victor (ST) AFL1-0606 77   **8–10**
Black label, dog near top.

RCA Victor (ST) AQL1-4776 79   **8–10**
Black label, dog near top.

Side A
See See Rider
I Got a Woman
Love Me
Tryin' to Get to You
Medley: Long Tall Sally/Whole Lot-ta Shak-
in' Goin' On/Your Mama Don't Dance/
Flip, Flop and Fly
Jailhouse Rock/Hound Dog
Why Me
How Great Thou Art
Side B
Medley: Blueberry Hill/I Can't Stop Loving
You
Help Me
American Trilogy
Let Me Be There
My Baby Left Me
Lawdy Miss Clawdy
Can't Help Falling in Love
Closing Vamp

ELVIS REMEMBERED (3 LP)

Creative Radio Shows (M) 1A–3B
. . . . *78*   **275–300**
A three-hour radio program from Creative
Radio Shows, featuring songs and interviews.
Not issued with any special box or cover.
Note: Includes script and cue sheets, plus an
insert explaining that the discs must be returned
after airing and another insert promoting their
other syndicated shows. This packet is included

in the above price range. Deduct $25–$30 if these materials are missing.

Side 1
Heartbreak Hotel
Medley: Your Cheatin' Heart/When the Saints Go Marching In/Won't You Wear My Ring Around Your Neck
Medley: Hound Dog/King Creole/Don't Be Cruel/Teddy Bear/Blue Suede Shoes/Reconsider, Baby/Hard Headed Woman/Loving You
All Shook Up
That's All Right
I Really Don't Want to Know
Hound Dog
Make the World Go Away
Side 2
Jailhouse Rock
I Forgot to Remember to Forget
Money Honey
Are You Sincere
You Gave Me a Mountain
Such a Night
Fame and Fortune
Side 3
Medley: I Got Stung/A Big Hunk O' Love/One Broken Heart for Sale/Return to Sender/Surrender/Down by the Riverside
How Great Thou Art
Treat Me Nice
I Can't Stop Loving You/I Got a Woman/Amen
I Want You, I Need You, I Love You
Side 4
In the Ghetto
It's Now or Never
I Beg of You
She Wears My Ring
Wear My Ring Around Your Neck
Where Did They Go Lord
Side 5
Love Me Tender
I Can Help
A Fool Such As I
Crying in the Chapel
If I Can Dream
Suspicious Minds
Side 6
See See Rider
Hurt
There Goes My Everything
Green, Green Grass of Home
There's a Honky-Tonk Angel (Who'll Take Me Back In)
Memories
My Way

Note: Also see *Elvis Remembered* in the EP section of this book.

ELVIS SINGS COUNTRY FAVORITES
RCA Victor (SP) RDA-242/D
.... *84*   20–30
Offered as a bonus LP by *Reader's Digest* with the purchase of their boxed set, *The Great Country Entertainers.*

Side 1
Make the World Go Away
I'm Movin' On
Are You Lonesome Tonight?
Faded Love
Your Cheatin' Heart
Gentle on My Mind
Side 2
Release Me
Welcome to My World
I Can't Stop Loving You
Funny How Time Slips Away
I'm So Lonesome I Could Cry
You Gave Me a Mountain

ELVIS SINGS FLAMING STAR
RCA/Camden (SP) CAS-2304
.... *4/69*   15–18
Blue label. "Tiger Man" is monaural on this LP. All other tracks are in stereo.
Pickwick/Camden (SP) CAS-2304
.... *12/75*   8–10
This LP is a repackage of *Singer Presents Elvis Singing Flaming Star and Others.*

Side 1
Flaming Star
Wonderful World
Night Life
All I Needed Was the Rain
Too Much Monkey Business
Side 2
Yellow Rose of Texas/The Eyes of Texas
She's a Machine
Do the Vega
Tiger Man

ELVIS SINGS FOR CHILDREN AND GROWNUPS TOO!
RCA Victor (SP) CPL1-2901
.... *7/78*   8–10
Black label, dog near top. This LP contained the first appearance of "Angel" in stereo. Also, though not announced as such, "Big Boots" is an alternate take on this LP.
Note: This LP, issued with gatefold cover, had an Elvis "Special Memories" greeting card attached to the back cover, which is included in the above price range. Deduct $3–$5 if this card

is missing. Although common in the industry, this was the first time an Elvis LP came with the song lyrics printed on it.

Side A
   Teddy Bear
   Wooden Heart
   Five Sleepyheads
   Puppet on a String
   Angel
   Old MacDonald
Side B
   How Would You Like to Be
   Cotton Candy Land
   Old Shep
   Big Boots
   Have a Happy

ELVIS SINGS HITS FROM HIS MOVIES VOLUME ONE
RCA/Camden (ST) CAS-2567

. . . . *6/72* **15–18**
Blue label.
Pickwick/Camden (ST) CAS-2567
. . . . *12/75* **8–10**

Side 1
   Down by the Riverside/When the Saints Go Marching In
   They Remind Me Too Much of You
   Confidence
   Frankie and Johnny
   Guitar Man
Side 2
   Long Legged Girl
   You Don't Know Me
   How Would You Like to Be
   Big Boss Man
   Old MacDonald

ELVIS SINGS INSPIRATIONAL FAVORITES
RCA Victor (SP) RDA-181/D

. . . . *83* **15–20**
Special Products issue. A *Reader's Digest* mail-order bonus LP for buyers of the 1983 edition of *Elvis! His Greatest Hits*, RCA Victor RD4A-010. Price includes ·24-page *Reader's Digest* Music catalog.

Side 1
   How Great Thou Art
   Somebody Bigger Than You and I
   In the Garden
   It Is No Secret (What God Can Do)
   His Hand in Mine
   Take My Hand, Precious Lord
Side 2
   Crying in the Chapel
   (There'll Be) Peace in the Valley (for Me)

   Put Your Hand in the Hand
   Where Did They Go, Lord
   I Believe
   You'll Never Walk Alone

ELVIS SINGS THE WONDERFUL WORLD OF CHRISTMAS
RCA Victor (ST) LSP-4579

. . . . *10/71* **20–25**
Orange label.
RCA Victor (ST) LSP-4579 . *76* **10–15**
Tan label.
RCA Victor (ST) ANL1-1936 *77* **5–10**
Black label, dog near top.
Note: Originally issued with a bonus 5″ × 7″ Elvis postcard, which is included in the above price range. Deduct $5–$10 if this postcard is missing. There was also a red sticker on the shrink wrap announcing the autographed card.

Side 1
   O Come, All Ye Faithful
   The First Noel
   On a Snowy Christmas Night
   Winter Wonderland
   The Wonderful World of Christmas
   It Won't Seem Like Christmas (Without You)
Side 2
   I'll Be Home on Christmas Day
   If I Get Home on Christmas Day
   Holly Leaves and Christmas Trees
   Merry Christmas Baby
   Silver Bells

ELVIS STORY, THE (5 LP)
RCA Victor (SP) DML5-0263

. . . . *7/77* **30–40**
Black label, dog near top. RCA Special Products, made for Candlelite Music and offered through mail order.

Side 1
   It's Now or Never
   Treat Me Nice
   For the Good Times
   I Got Stung
   Ask Me
   Return to Sender
Side 2
   The Wonder of You
   Hound Dog
   Make the World Go Away
   His Latest Flame
   Loving You

Side 3
   One Night
   You Don't Know Me
   Blue Christmas
   Good Luck Charm

Blue Suede Shoes
Surrender
Side 4
In the Ghetto
Too Much
Help Me Make It Through the Night
I Was the One
Love Me
Little Sister

Side 5
Can't Help Falling in Love
Trouble
Memories
Wear My Ring Around Your Neck
Blue Hawaii
Burning Love
Side 6
Love Me Tender
Stuck on You
Funny How Time Slips Away
All Shook Up
Puppet on a String
Jailhouse Rock

Side 7
Heartbreak Hotel
I Just Can't Help Believin'
I Beg of You
Don't Cry Daddy
Hard Headed Woman
Are You Lonesome Tonight
Side 8
Teddy Bear
Hawaiian Wedding Song
A Big Hunk O' Love
I'm Yours
A Fool Such As I
Don't

Side 9
I Want You, I Need You, I Love You
Kissin' Cousins
I Can't Stop Loving You
Devil in Disguise
Suspicion
Don't Be Cruel
Side 10
She's Not You
From a Jack to a King
I Need Your Love Tonight
Wooden Heart
Have I Told You Lately That I Love You
You Don't Have to Say You Love Me
Also see *ELVIS—HIS SONGS OF INSPIRA-
TION*

ELVIS TALKS!
RCA Victor (M) 6313-1-R. 7/87   **10–15**
Mail-order LP offer.

Note: The contents for this album are the same
as those found on *Elvis Presley Interview Record,* DJM1-0835.

ELVIS TAPES: see *THE ELVIS TAPES.*

ELVIS 10TH ANNIVERSARY (6 LP)
Creative Radio (SP) 1A-6B *8/87*   **200–300**
Price includes eight pages of programming instructions and cues. Deduct $25–$30 if these
pages are missing. Packaged in a specially
printed box. Issued to radio stations only.

Record 1
Elvis Medley
Love Me
All Shook Up
A Big Hunk of Love
That's Alright
Teddy Bear
Blue Suede Shoes
I Just Can't Help Believing
I Was the One
Rip It Up
Don't
(Marie's the Name) His Latest Flame
Loving You
My Baby Left Me
Wonder of You
Record 2
Elvis Medley
Hound Dog
Welcome to My World
Devil in Disguise
Wear My Ring Around Your Neck
Trying to Get to You
Mean Woman Blues
Now and Then
Tomorrow Never Comes
What Now My Love
Whole Lotta Shaking Goin' On
American Trilogy
G.I. Blues
Frankfort Special
Record 3
Elvis Medley
Heartbreak Hotel
Easy Come, Easy Go
Gotta Lot-ta Living to Do
If You Talk in Your Sleep
Old Shep
Patch It Up
Steamroller Blues
Burning Love
Memories
In the Ghetto
Don't Cry Daddy
Too Much

All Shook Up
Don't Be Cruel
Record 4
That's Alright (live)
Didja Ever
Good Luck Charm
Johnny B. Goode
For the Heart
Hurt
How Great Thou Art
Green, Green Grass of Home
Polk Salad Annie
I'll Remember You
Hard Headed Woman
Love Me Tender
I Want You, I Need You, I Love You
Lawdy Miss Clawdy
Record 5
You Gave Me a Mountain
Shake, Rattle and Roll
I Can't Stop Loving You
Impossible Dream
Let It Be Me
Jailhouse Rock
Treat Me Nice
Moody Blue
Little Darlin'
Are You Lonesome Tonight
Young and Beautiful
Follow That Dream
Fame and Fortune
Return to Sender
Little Sister
Can't Help Falling in Love
Record 6
See See Rider
Baby What You Want Me to Do
Blue Suede Shoes
If I Can Dream
Unchained Melody
Trying to Get to You
Suspicious Minds
It's Now or Never
Way Down
Kentucky Rain
What Now My Love
You'll Never Walk Alone
My Way

ELVIS—THAT'S THE WAY IT IS
RCA Victor (ST) LSP-4445
. . . . *12/70*   **15–18**
Orange label.
RCA Victor (ST) LSP-4445 . *76*   **10–15**
Tan label.
RCA Victor (ST) AFL1-4445 *77*   **8–10**
Black label, dog near top.

RCA Victor (ST) AYL1-4114
. . . . *9/81*   **5–8**
Black label, dog near top. Issued as part of
RCA's "Best Buy" series.

Side 1
I Just Can't Help Believin'
Twenty Days and Twenty Nights
How the Web Was Woven
Patch It Up
Mary in the Morning
You Don't Have to Say You Love Me
Side 2
You've Lost That Lovin' Feelin'
I've Lost You
Just Pretend
Stranger in the Crowd
The Next Step Is Love
Bridge over Troubled Water

ELVIS: THE KING SPEAKS (FEBRUARY 1961, MEMPHIS, TENNESSEE)
The Great Northwest Music Com-
pany (M) GNW-4006 . . *12/77*   **8–10**
This LP offers a slightly different presentation
of the same press conference that was previously issued as *Elvis Exclusive Live Press Conference (Memphis, Tennessee—February 1961)*.

ELVIS, THE LEGEND LIVES ON (7 LP)
RCA Victor (SP) RBA-191/A
. . . . *8/86*   **40–45**
A boxed set sold mail order by *Reader's Digest*.
Price includes 12-page booklet.

Record 1
Side 1
Medley: Also Sprach Zarathustra/That's All
    Right
Medley: Mystery Train/Tiger Man
Medley: (Let Me Be Your) Teddy Bear/
    Don't Be Cruel (to a Heart That's True)
Medley: Long Tall Sally/Whole Lot-ta Sha-
    kin' Goin' On
Little Darlin'
Johnny B. Goode
Side 2
See See Rider
Fever
A Big Hunk O' Love
Jailhouse Rock
Love Me
All Shook Up

Record 2
Side 1
I Just Can't Help Believin'
You Don't Have to Say You Love Me

Little Sister
You've Lost That Lovin' Feelin'
In the Ghetto
Suspicious Minds
Side 2
What Now My Love
Are You Lonesome Tonight?
Medley: I Got a Woman/Amen
Medley: O Sole Mio/It's Now or Never
Unchained Melody
Let It Be Me

Record 3
Side 1
Burning Love
Steamroller Blues
It's Impossible
An American Trilogy
Let Me Be There
Bridge over Troubled Water
Side 2
Kentucky Rain
Don't Cry Daddy
Fairytale
You Gave Me a Mountain
My Way
The Impossible Dream

Record 4
Side 1
Good Rockin' Tonight
Tryin' to Get to You
Medley: Shake, Rattle and Roll/Flip, Flop
  and Fly
Heartbreak Hotel
Hound Dog
Don't Be Cruel (To a Heart That's True)
Side 2
Rip It Up
Money Honey
Blue Moon
One-Sided Love Affair
Got a Lot o' Livin' to Do
Reddy Teddy

Record 5
Side 1
Blue Suede Shoes
Medley: Lawdy Miss Clawdy/Baby, What
  You Want Me to Do
Medley: Heartbreak Hotel/Hound Dog/All
  Shook Up
Love Me Tender
Blue Christmas
One Night
Side 2
Release Me (and Let Me Love Again)
Help Me Make It Through the Night
Always on My Mind

I'm So Lonesome I Could Cry
I Can't Stop Loving You
Green, Green Grass of Home

Record 6
Side 1
Welcome to My World
And I Love You So
Mary in the Morning
Can't Help Falling in Love
Love Letters
Until It's Time for You to Go
Side 2
Hurt
Separate Ways
Indescribably Blue
Fool
I've Lost You
For the Good Times

Record 7
Side 1
Promised Land
U.S. Male
I'm Leavin'
Early Mornin' Rain
Moody Blue
Way Down
Side 2
The Elvis Medley: Jailhouse Rock/(Let Me
  Be Your) Teddy Bear/Hound Dog/Don't
  Be Cruel (to a Heart That's True)/Burning
  Love/Suspicious Minds
Loving Arms
Funny How Time Slips Away
Yesterday
Memories
Life

ELVIS: THE OTHER SIDES: see
WORLDWIDE GOLD AWARD HITS
VOL. 2—THE OTHER SIDES

ELVIS TODAY
RCA Victor (ST) APL1-1039
. . . . 5/75   **15–18**
Orange label.
RCA Victor (Q) APD1-1039
. . . . 5/75   **100–125**
Quadradisc. Orange label.
RCA Victor (ST) APL1-1039 76   **10–15**
Tan label.
RCA Victor (ST) AFL1-1039 77   **8–10**
Black label, dog near top.
RCA Victor (Q) APD1-1039 77   **40–50**
Quadradisc. Black label, dog near top.

Side A
  T-R-O-U-B-L-E
  And I Love You So
  Susan When She Tried
  Woman Without Love
  Shake a Hand
Side B
  Pieces of My Life
  Fairytale
  I Can Help
  Bringing It Back
  Green Grass of Home

EPIC OF THE 70s: see
Various-Artists Compilations section.

ESSENTIAL ELVIS
RCA Victor (M) 6738-1-R. *1/88*   **5-10**

EXCLUSIVE LIVE PRESS
CONFERENCE (MEMPHIS,
TENNESSEE—FEBRUARY 1961)
Green Valley (M) GV-2001 *10/77*   **30-50**
Green label. First-pressing covers are soft stock,
as is often used on import LPs, and have a black
1½ " bar on the back cover that does *not* wrap
around the spine. First issue labels do not have
the catalog number on either the label or jacket.

Green Valley (M) GV-2001 *12/77*   **12-15**
Second-issue covers were standard stock, with
the black bar wrapping from the back cover
around onto the spine. Also, some copies contained a script for this interview.
Note: The material on this LP was repacked
and included as one disc in the *Elvis (Speaks to
You)* two-LP set. It was issued later as *Elvis the
King Speaks.*

E-Z COUNTRY PROGRAMMING:
see Various Artists Compilations
section.

FELTON JARVIS TALKS ABOUT
ELVIS
RCA Victor (M) FJ-1981 . *1/81*   **150-200**
Red label. Contains an open-end interview with
Felton Jarvis, with most of the discussion devoted to Elvis' *Guitar Man* LP. Includes script.
Promotional issue only.
Note: Along with this LP, selected radio stations received an "Elvis" belt buckle with the
contents of *Guitar Man* engraved on it. Offically
part of the promotional package, this buckle is
included in the above price range. Deduct
$25-$40 if it is missing.

50TH ANNIVERSARY (6 LP)
Creative Radio (SP) 1A-6B *8/85*   **300-350**
Price includes seven pages of programming in-
structions and cues. Deduct $25-$30 if these

pages are missing. Packaged in a plain, un-
printed, box. Issued to radio stations only.

50 YEARS—50 HITS (3 LP)
RCA Victor (SP) SVL3-0710 *1/85*   **20-25**
Offered by TV mail order and through the RCA
Record Club.

Side A
  Heartbreak Hotel
  Don't Be Cruel
  I Want You, I Need You, I Love You
  Too Much
  Viva Las Vegas
  Hound Dog
  Old Shep
Side B
  The Wonder of You
  Loving You
  Kissin' Cousins
  Suspicion
  All Shook Up
  Love Me Tender
  What'd I Say
  Don't
Side C
  One Broken Heart for Sale
  Danny Boy
  (Let Me Be Your) Teddy Bear
  Good Luck Charm
  Suspicious Minds
  Treat Me Nice
  Return to Sender
  If I Can Dream
Side D
  A Big Hunk O' Love
  One Night
  Such a Night
  Love Me
  Don't Cry Daddy
  Wear My Ring Around Your Neck
  It's Now or Never
  My Wish Came True
Side E
  I Got Stung
  (Now and Then There's) A Fool Such As I
  Blue Hawaii
  Kentucky Rain
  Can't Help Falling in Love
  Stuck on You
  (Such an) Easy Question
  Hard Headed Woman
  I Beg of You
Side F
  You Don't Have to Say You Love Me
  Crying in the Chapel
  She's Not You
  Puppet on a String

Two of the Elvis LPs in RCA's ill-fated Quadradisc format. All quadraphonic albums are now scarce.

As part of its effort to promote the "pure Elvis" sound, RCA prepared this open-ended interview with producer Felton Jarvis. Along with the script, a belt buckle listing the *Guitar Man* song titles was included in the package.

Moody Blue
Surrender
In the Ghetto
Memories

**50,000,000 ELVIS FANS CAN'T BE
WRONG: see *ELVIS' GOLD
RECORDS—VOLUME 2***

**50,000,000 ELVIS FANS WEREN'T
WRONG**
Eva-Tone 831942 . . . . . . *8/83*   **5–10**
Promotional red vinyl soundsheet, given as a
bonus to early buyers of Jerry Osborne's *Presleyana*, second edition. Features Elvis talking
and Elvis tribute cut-ins.

FIRST LIVE RECORDINGS, THE
Music Works (M) PB-3601 *2/84*   **8–10**

Side A
  Introduction with Elvis Presley and Horace
    Logan
  I Wanna Play House with You
  Maybelline
  Tweedle Dee
Side B
  That's All Right
  Recollections by Frank Page
  Hound Dog

FOR LP FANS ONLY
RCA Victor (M) LPM-1990 *3/59*   **100–125**
Black label, with the words "Long Play" at the
bottom of the label. Original covers for this
issue have the RCA catalog number under the
RCA logo, in the upper right corner.

RCA Victor (M) LPM-1990
. . . . *11/63*   **45–55**
Black label, with the word "Mono" at the bottom. Covers for this issue have the RCA catalog
number on the left side of the front cover.
Note: Some copies of this LP have the same
picture on the back cover as on the front. We're
not certain whether this was unintentional on
the part of RCA or whether they wanted to
replace the picture of Elvis in his U.S. Army
clothes with another. A premium may be placed
on these copies.

RCA Victor (M) LPM-1990
. . . . *1/65*   **25–50**
Black label, with the word "Monaural" at the
bottom. Covers for this issue have the RCA
catalog number on the left side of the front
cover.

RCA Victor (SE) LSP-1990(e)
. . . . *1/65*   **25–30**
Black label, with the RCA logo in white at the
top of the label and the word "Stereo" at the
bottom.

RCA Victor (SE) LSP-1990(e) *68*   **10–20**
Orange label.

RCA Victor (SE) LSP-1990(e) *76*   **10–15**
Tan label.

Side 1
  That's All Right
  Lawdy Miss Clawdy
  Mystery Train
  Playing for Keeps
  Poor Boy

The contents of *Elvis—The Beginning Years* were divided into two separate LPs by
The Music Works.

Side 2
My Baby Left Me
I Was the One
Shake, Rattle and Roll
I'm Left, You're Right, She's Gone
You're a Heartbreaker

14 #1 COUNTRY HITS: see Various-Artists Compilations section.

FRANKIE AND JOHNNY

RCA Victor (M) LPM-3553 *4/66*   **65-75**
Black label, dog on top with the word "Monaural" on the bottom.

RCA Victor (ST) LSP-3553 *4/66*   **65-75**
Black label, with the RCA logo in white at the top of the label and the word "Stereo" at the bottom.

RCA Victor (ST) APL1-2559
. . . . *9/77*   **8-10**
Black label, dog near top.
Note: 1966 original issues were packaged with a bonus 12″ × 12″ color print, which is included in the above price range. Deduct $25-$30 if this print is missing.

Side 1
Frankie and Johnny
Come Along
Petunia, the Gardener's Daughter
Chesay
What Every Woman Lives For
Look Out, Broadway
Side 2
Beginner's Luck
Down by the Riverside/When the Saints Go Marching In
Shout It Out
Hard Luck
Please Don't Stop Loving Me
Everybody Come Aboard

FRANKIE AND JOHNNY

Pickwick/Camden (ST) ACL-7007
. . . . *76*   **10-12**
In 1979, Pickwick issued a pack of seven Elvis LPs. The specially wrapped pack of LPs was originally issued in November 1978 including *Elvis' Christmas Album,* which was replaced with *Frankie and Johnny* after the Holiday season. See *Pickwick Pack* for more information.

Side 1
Frankie and Johnny
Come Along
What Every Woman Lives For
Hard Luck
Please Don't Stop Loving Me

Side 2
Down by the Riverside/When the Saints Go Marching In
Petunia, the Gardener's Daughter
Beginner's Luck
Shout It Out

FRANTIC FIFTIES: see *THE FRANTIC FIFTIES.*

FROM ELVIS IN MEMPHIS

RCA Victor (ST) LSP-4155 *6/69*   **30-45**
Orange label. Rigid disc.

RCA Victor (ST) LSP-4155 .   *71* ' **10-15**
Orange label. Flexible disc.
Note: 1969 originals were issued with an 8″ × 10″ color photo, which is included in the above price range. Deduct $15-$20 if this photo is missing.

RCA Victor (ST) LSP-4155 .   *76*   **10-15**
Tan label.

RCA Victor (ST) AFL1-4155 *77*   **8-10**
Black label, dog near top.

RCA Victor (ST) MFSL1-059 *82*   **15-25**
Half-speed master. This is the only Elvis LP issued by Mobile Fidelity Sound Lab. Taken from original stereo master tapes, MFSL albums are produced at half-speed using special plating and High-Definition Super Vinyl, for maximum reproduction.

Side 1
Wearin' That Loved On Look
Only the Strong Survive
I'll Hold You in My Arms (Till I Can Hold You in My Heart)
Long Black Limousine
It Keeps Right On A-hurtin'
I'm Moving On
Side 2
Power of My Love
Gentle On My Mind
After Loving You
True Love Travels on A Gravel Road
Any Day Now
In the Ghetto

FROM ELVIS PRESLEY BOULEVARD, MEMPHIS, TENNESSEE

RCA Victor (ST) APL1-1506
. . . . *5/76*   **12-15**
Tan label.

RCA Victor (ST) AFL1-1506 *77*   **8-10**
Black label, dog near top.
Note: This is one of only two Elvis LPs to have been issued originally on the tan label. The other was *The Sun Sessions.*

Side A
  Hurt
  Never Again
  Blue Eyes Crying in the Rain
  Danny Boy
  The Last Farewell
Side B
  For the Heart
  Bigger They Are, Harder They Fall
  Solitaire
  Love Coming Down
  I'll Never Fall in Love Again

FROM ELVIS WITH LOVE (2 LP)

RCA Victor (SP) R-234340 . *78*   **20–25**
RCA Record Club; black label, dog near top.

Side A
  Love Me Tender
  Can't Help Falling in Love
  The Next Step Is Love
  I Need Your Love Tonight
  I Can't Stop Loving You
Side B
  I Want You, I Need You, I Love You
  I Love You Because
  Love Letters
  A Thing Called Love
  A Big Hunk O' Love

Side C
  Love Me
  Without Love
  Faded Love (alternate version)
  Loving You
  You've Lost That Lovin' Feelin'
Side D
  Have I Told You Lately That I Love You
  You Don't Have to Say You Love Me
  True Love
  Ain't That Loving You Baby
  Please Don't Stop Loving Me

FROM MEMPHIS TO VEGAS/FROM VEGAS TO MEMPHIS (2 LP)

RCA Victor (ST) LSP-6020 *11/69*   **30–40**
Orange label. First pressing, incorrectly shows
writers of "Words" as Tommy Boyce and
Bobby Hart. Also shows writer of "Suspicious
Minds" as Frances Zambon.

RCA Victor (ST) LSP-6020 *12/69*   **20–30**
Orange label. Rigid disc. Correctly shows writ-
ers of "Words" as Barry, Robin and Maurice
Gibb, and writer of "Suspicious Minds" as
Mark James.

RCA Victor (ST) LSP-6020 . *71*   **15–20**
Orange label. Flexible disc.

RCA Victor (ST) LSP-6020 . *76*   **15–20**
Tan label.

RCA Victor (ST) LSP-6020 . *77*   **10–15**
Black label, dog near top.
Note: This was the first time an Elvis release
contained more than one disc. Packaged with
original issues were two 8″ × 10″ black and
white photos, which are included in the above
price range. Deduct $8–$10 when either of
these photos is missing.

Side 1
  Blue Suede Shoes
  Johnny B. Goode
  All Shook Up
  Are You Lonesome Tonight
  Hound Dog
  I Can't Stop Loving You
  My Babe
Side 2
  Medley: Mystery Train/Tiger Man
  Words
  In the Ghetto
  Suspicious Minds
  Can't Help Falling in Love

Side 3
  Inherit the Wind
  This Is My Story
  Stranger in My Own Home Town
  A Little Bit of Green
  And The Grass Won't Pay No Mind
Side 4
  Do You Know Who I Am
  From a Jack to a King
  The Fair Is Moving On
  You'll Think of Me
  Without Love (There Is Nothing)

FUN IN ACAPULCO

RCA Victor (M) LPM-2756
. . . . *12/63*   **60–70**
Black label, with the word "Mono" at the bottom.

RCA Victor (M) LPM-2756 . *64*   **25–30**
Black label, with the word "Monaural" at the
bottom.

RCA Victor (ST) LSP-2756
. . . . *12/63*   **60–70**
Black label, with the RCA logo in silver at the
top of the label and the word "Stereo" at the
bottom.

RCA Victor (ST) LSP-2756 . *64*   **25–30**
Black label, with the RCA logo in white at the
top of the label and the word "Stereo" at the
bottom.

RCA Victor (ST) LSP-2756 . *68*   **10–20**
Orange label.

RCA Victor (ST) LSP-2756 .   *76*   **10–15**
Tan label.

RCA Victor (ST) AFL1-2756   *77*   **8–10**
Black label, dog near top.

Side 1
   Fun in Acapulco
   Vino, Dinero Y Amor
   Mexico
   El Toro
   Marguerita
   The Lady Was a Bullfighter
   No Room to Rhumba in a Sports Car
Side 2
   I Think I'm Gonna Like It Here
   Bossa Nova Baby
   You Can't Say No in Acapulco
   Guadalajara
   Love Me Tonight
   Slowly But Surely

G.I. BLUES
RCA Victor (M) LPM-2256
. . . .   *10/60*   **100–125**
Black label, with the words "Long Play" at the
bottom of the label.

RCA Victor (M) LPM-2256
. . . .   *11/63*   **45-55**
Black label, with the words "Mono" at the bottom.

RCA Victor (M) LPM-2256
. . . .   *64-65*   **25-30**
Black label, with the word "Monaural" at the
bottom.

RCA Victor (ST) LSP-2256
. . . .   *10/60*   **100–125**
Black label, with the words "Living Stereo" at
the bottom.

RCA Victor (ST) LSP-2256 .   *64*   **25-30**
Black label, with the RCA logo in white at the
top of the label and the word "Stereo" at the
bottom.

RCA Victor (ST) LSP-2256 .   *68*   **10-20**
Orange label.

RCA Victor (ST) LSP-2256 .   *76*   **10-15**
Tan label.

RCA Victor (ST) AFL1-2256 .   *7*   **8-10**
Black label, dog near top.

RCA Victor (ST) AYL1-3735
. . . .   *11/80*   **5-10**
Note: This LP was originally issued with a special "Elvis Is Back" inner-sleeve, which is included in the 1960 price range. Deduct $15–$25
if this sleeve is missing. Also, 1960 issues came
with a sticker on the front wrap noting that the
LP featured "Wooden Heart."

Side 1
   Tonight Is So Right for Love
   What's She Really Like
   Frankfort Special
   Wooden Heart
   G.I. Blues
Side 2
   Pocket Full of Rainbows
   Shoppin' Around
   Big Boots
   Didja' Ever
   Blue Suede Shoes
   Doin' the Best I Can

GIRL HAPPY
RCA Victor (M) LPM-3338   *4/65*   **35–45**
Black label, with the word "Monaural" at the
bottom.

RCA Victor (ST) LSP-3338   *4/65*   **35–45**
Black label, with the RCA logo in white at the
top of the label and the word "Stereo" at the
bottom.

RCA Victor (ST) LSP-3338 .   *68*   **10–20**
Orange label.

RCA Victor (ST) LSP-3338 .   *76*   **10–15**
Tan label.

RCA Victor (ST) AFL1-3338   *77*   **8–10**
Black label, dog near top.

Side 1
   Girl Happy
   Spring Fever
   Fort Lauderdale Chamber of Commerce
   Startin' Tonight
   Wolf Call
   Do Not Disturb
Side 2
   Cross My Heart and Hope to Die
   The Meanest Girl in Town
   Do The Clam
   Puppet on a String
   I've Got to Find My Baby
   You'll Be Gone

GIRLS! GIRLS! GIRLS!
RCA Victor (M) LPM-2621
. . . .   *11/62*   **100–125**
Black label, with the words "Long Play" at the
bottom of the label.

RCA Victor (M) LPM-2621
. . . .   *11/63*   **40–50**
Black label, with the word "Mono" at the bottom.

RCA Victor (M) LPM-2621 .   *64*   **25–30**
Black label, with the word "Monaural" at the
bottom.

RCA Victor (ST) LSP-2621
· · · · · · · · · · · · · · · *11/62* **115–135**
Black label, with the words "Living Stereo" at
the bottom.

RCA Victor (ST) LSP-2621 . *64* **25–30**
Black label, with the RCA logo in white at the
top of the label and the word "Stereo" at the
bottom.

RCA Victor (ST) LSP-2621 . *68* **10–20**
Orange label.

RCA Victor (ST) LSP-2621 . *76* **10–15**
Tan label.

RCA Victor (ST) AFL1-2621 *77* **8–10**
Black label, dog near top.

Note: 1962 originals were issued with an 11″ ×
11″ 1963 calendar, which is included in the
above price range. Deduct $25–$35 if this calendar is missing.

Side 1
  Girls! Girls! Girls!
  I Don't Want to Be Tied
  Where Do You Come From
  I Don't Want To
  We'll Be Together
  A Boy Like Me, A Girl Like You
  Earth Boy
Side 2
  Return to Sender
  Because of Love
  Thanks to the Rolling Sea
  Song of the Shrimp
  The Walls Have Ears
  We're Coming in Loaded

GOLDEN CELEBRATION, A (3 LP)
Westwood One · · · · · · *11/84* **200–250**
Boxed set. Price includes instructions and cue
sheets, which represent $5–$10 of the value.
Issued to radio stations only.

Side 1
  All Shook Up
  That's All Right, Mama
  Good Rockin' Tonight
  I Got a Woman
  Maybelline
  Heartbreak Hotel
Side 2
  Money Honey
  Hound Dog
  Too Much
  Long Tall Sally
  I Was the One
  Baby, Let's Play House
Side 3
  Blue Moon of Kentucky
  Tutti Frutti

  Swing Down Sweet Chariot
  Love Me Tender
  Jailhouse Rock
  Can't Help Falling in Love
Side 4
  Don't
  Big Hunk O' Love
  Earth Angel
  Stuck on You
  It's Now or Never
  Such a Night
  Get Back
Side 5
  Heartbreak Hotel
  Shake, Rattle and Roll
  Hard-headed Woman
  Blue Suede Shoes
  Tiger Man
  Lawdy Miss Clawdy
  Baby What You Want Me to Do
  Love Me
  Tryin' To Get To You
Side 6
  Mystery Train Medley
  In the Ghetto
  Are You Lonesome Tonight
  Burnin' Love
  Don't Be Cruel
  Little Sister
  If I Can Dream

GOLDEN CELEBRATION, A
(Cassette)
RCA Victor (M) No Number
Given · · · · · · · · · · · *9/84* **15–20**
Special "Advance Cassette" promotional only
sampler of the boxed set.

Side 1
  The Sun Sessions—Outtakes: Blue Moon of
    Kentucky
  The Dorsey Bros. Stage Show: Shake, Rattle
    and Roll/Flip, Flop and Fly/I Gotta
    Woman
  The Milton Berle Show: Hound Dog/Dia-
    logue
  The Steve Allen Show: I Want You, I Need
    You, I Love You
  The Mississippi-Alabama Fair and Dairy
    Show: Blue Suede Shoes
Side 2
  The Ed Sullivan Show: Peace in the Valley
  Elvis at Home: The Fool
  Collector's Treasures: Dark Moon
  Elvis in Burbank: Tiger Man
  Tryin' to Get to You

GOLDEN CELEBRATION, A (6 LP)
RCA Victor (M) CPM6-5172
. . . . *10/84* **40-50**
A boxed set. Price includes custom inner-
sleeves and envelope containing an 8" × 10"
Elvis photo and a 50th Anniversary flyer, all of
which represents $5–$10 of the value.

Side 1
"The Sun Sessions—Outtakes, Memphis
    Tennessee, 1954 and 1955"
Harbor Lights
That's All Right
Blue Moon of Kentucky
I Don't Care If the Sun Don't Shine
I'm Left, You're Right, She's Gone (My
    Baby's Gone)
I'll Never Let You Go (Little Darlin')
When It Rains, It Really Pours

Side 2
"The Dorsey Brothers Stage Show, New
    York, 1956"
Shake, Rattle and Roll/Flip, Flop and Fly
I Got a Woman
Baby, Let's Play House
Tutti Frutti
Blue Suede Shoes
Heartbreak Hotel

Side 3
"The Dorsey Brothers Stage Show, New
    York, 1956"
Tutti Frutti
I Was the One
Blue Suede Shoes
Heartbreak Hotel
Money Honey
Heartbreak Hotel

Side 4
"The Milton Berle Show, California, 1956"
Heartbreak Hotel
Blue Suede Shoes/Dialogue/Blue Suede
    Shoes (reprise)
Hound Dog/Dialogue
I Want You, I Need You, I Love You
The Steve Allen Show, New York, 1956
Dialogue/I Want You, I Need You, I Love
    You
Introduction/Hound Dog

Side 5
"The Mississippi-Alabama Fair and Dairy
    Show, Tupelo, Mississippi, September 26,
    1956"
Heartbreak Hotel
Long Tall Sally
Introductions and Presentations/I Was the
    One
I Want You, I Need You, I Love You
I Got a Woman

Side 6
"The Mississippi-Alabama Fair and Dairy
    Show, Tupelo, Mississippi, September 26,
    1956"
Don't Be Cruel
Reddy Teddy
Love Me Tender
Hound Dog
Vernon and Gladys Presley
Nick Adams
A Fan
Elvis

Side 7
"The Mississippi-Alabama Fair and Dairy
    Show, Tupelo, Mississippi, September 26,
    1956"
Love Me Tender
I Was the One
I Got a Woman
Don't Be Cruel
Blue Suede Shoes
Baby, Let's Play House
Hound Dog/Announcements

Side 8
"The Ed Sullivan Show, California and New
    York, 1956"
Don't Be Cruel
Love Me Tender
Reddy Teddy
Hound Dog
Don't Be Cruel
Love Me Tender
Love Me
Hound Dog

Side 9
"The Ed Sullivan Show, New York, January
    6, 1957"
Hound Dog
Love Me Tender
Heartbreak Hotel
Don't Be Cruel
Too Much
When My Blue Moon Turns to Gold Again
Peace in the Valley

Side 10
"Elvis at Home, Germany, 1958–60"
Danny Boy
Soldier Boy
The Fool
Earth Angel
He's Only a Prayer Away

Side 11
"Collector's Treasures, Discovered at Grace-
    land"
Excerpt from an Interview for *TV Guide*
My Heart Cries for You
Dark Moon

Write to Me from Naples
Suppose
Side 12
"Elvis, Burbank, California, June 27, 1968"
Blue Suede Shoes
Tiger Man
That's All Right
Lawdy Miss Clawdy
Baby What You Want Me to Do/Monologue
Love Me
Are You Lonesome Tonight?
Baby What You Want Me to Do (reprise)
Monologue/Blue Christmas/Monologue
One Night
Tryin' to Get to You

GOOD ROCKIN' TONIGHT
RCA Victor SVL2-0824 . . *1/88*   **15–20**
A TV mail-order double album.

Side A
Good Rockin' Tonight
Jailhouse Rock
Blue Suede Shoes
Little Sister
Tryin' to Get to You
Lawdy Miss Clawdy
Heartbreak Hotel
That's All Right
Side B
Hound Dog
Tutti Frutti
Hard Headed Woman
I Got a Woman
Baby, Let's Play House
I Feel So Bad
Mean Woman Blues
I Got Stung
Side C
One Night
It Feels So Right
I Want You with Me
Too Much
Money Honey
Rip It Up
Down in the Alley
Side D
Mystery Train
Teddy Bear
A Big Hunk O' Love
So Glad You're Mine
Like a Baby
I Was the One
Soldier Boy

GOOD TIMES
RCA Victor (ST CPL1-0475 *3/74*   **15–20**
Orange label.

RCA victor (ST) AFL1-0475   *77*   **8–10**
Black label, dog near top.

Side A
Take Good Care of Her
Loving Arms
I Got a Feelin' in My Body
If That Isn't Love
She Wears My Ring
Side B
I've Got a Thing About You Baby
My Boy
Spanish Eyes
Talk About the Good Times
Good Time Charlie's Got the Blues

GREAT HITS OF 1956–57
RCA Victor (M) RBA-072/D *87*   **10–20**
Offered as a bonus LP by *Reader's Digest* with
the purchase of a boxed record set, one that
contains no Elvis tracks.

Side 1
Hound Dog
Don't Be Cruel
Love Me Tender
I Want You, I Need You, I Love You
Heartbreak Hotel
Playing for Keeps
Side 2
Blue Suede Shoes
I Was the One
Love Me
(Let Me Be Your) Teddy Bear
Any Way You Want Me (That's How I Will
  Be)
Too Much

GREATEST HITS VOLUME ONE
RCA Victor (ST) AHL1-2347
. . . . *11/81*   **10–15**
Black label, dog near top. With embossed letters on front cover.

RCA Victor (ST) AHL1-2347 *83*   **5–8**
Black label, dog near top. Without embossed
lettering on cover.
Note: This LP marked the first availability in
true stereo of "The Sound of Your Cry" and of
the single version of "Suspicious Minds." It was
also the first time "The Sound of Your Cry"
appeared on any U.S. Elvis LP.

Side A
The Wonder of You
A Big Hunk O' Love (unreleased live)
There Goes My Everything
Suspicious Minds
What'd I Say (unreleased live)

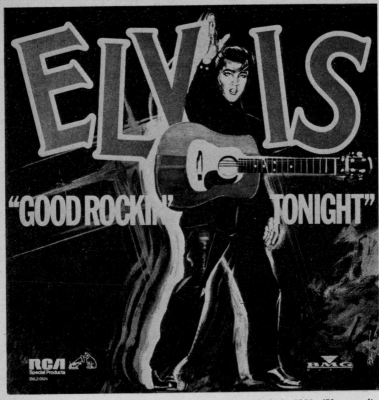

A special mail-order LP produced by RCA for BMG Music in 1988. *(Photo credit: Ace Anderson and Wayne S. Young)*

Side B
  Don't Cry Daddy (unreleased live)
  The Sound of Your Cry
  Burning Love
  You'll Never Walk Alone

GREATEST MOMENTS IN MUSIC
RCA Victor (SP) DML1-0413 *80*   **10–15**
Black label, dog near top. This LP was included as a bonus with Candlelite Music's shipment of *The Legendary Recordings of Elvis Presley,* a six-LP box set. All "live" recordings are in stereo and all studio tracks in monaural on this LP.

Side A
  True Love
  Sweet Caroline
  Harbor Lights
  Rags to Riches
  Let It Be Me
Side B
  Your Cheating Heart
  Yesterday
  Blueberry Hill
  Words
  Bridge over Troubled Water

GREATEST SHOW ON EARTH, THE

RCA Victor (ST) DML1-0348 *78*   **10–12**
Black label, dog near top. RCA Special Products made for Candlelite Music and offered as a bonus to their mail-order customers ordering the 5-LP *Memories of Elvis* set.
Note: Title shown on the label as *Elvis In The Greatest Show On Earth.*

Side A
  I'll Remember You
  Without Love
  Gentle on My Mind
  It's Impossible
  What Now My Love
Side B
  Until It's Time for You to Go
  Early Morning Rain
  Something
  The First Time Ever I saw Your Face
  The Impossible Dream
Also see *MEMORIES OF ELVIS.*

GUITAR MAN

RCA Victor (ST) AAL1-3917
. . . . *1/81*   **8–12**
Black label, dog near top.
Note: Packaged with a color flyer advertising the film *This Is Elvis,* which is included in the above price range. Deduct $4–$6 if this flyer is missing. All tracks on this LP feature Elvis' original vocals with updated instrumentation.

Side A
  Guitar Man
  After Loving You
  Too Much Monkey Business
  Just Call Me Lonesome
  Lovin' Arms
Side B
  You Asked Me To
  Clean Up Your Own Backyard
  She Thinks I Still Care
  Faded Love
  I'm Movin' On
Also see *FELTON JARVIS TALKS ABOUT ELVIS.*

HAPPY HOLIDAYS: see

Various-Artists Compilations section.

HARUM SCARUM

RCA Victor (M) LPM-3468
. . . . *10/65*   **65–75**
Black label, with the word "Monaural" at the bottom.

RCA Victor (ST) LSP-3468
. . . . *10/65*   **65–75**

Black label, with the RCA logo in white at the top of the label and the word "Stereo" at the bottom.

RCA Victor (ST) AFL1-2558
. . . . *9/77*   **8–10**
Black label, dog near top.

RCA Victor (ST) AYL1-3734
. . . . *11/80*   **5–10**
Note: 1965 original issues were packaged with a 12″ × 12″ color photo, which is included in the above price range. Deduct $25–$30 if this photo is missing.

Side 1
  Harem Holiday
  My Desert Serenade
  Go East, Young Man
  Mirage
  Kismet
  Shake That Tambourine
Side 2
  Hey Little Girl
  Golden Coins
  So Close, Yet So Far
  Animal Instinct
  Wisdom of the Ages

HAVING FUN WITH ELVIS ON STAGE

Boxcar (M), no number given
. . . . *8/74*   **100–125**
This LP was sold at Elvis' personal appearances only.

RCA Victor (M) CPM1-0818
. . . . *10/74*   **15–20**
Orange label.

RCA Victor (M) CPM1-0818 *76*   **10–15**
Tan label.

RCA Victor (M) AFM1-0818 *77*   **8–10**
Black label, dog near top.

HE TOUCHED ME

RCA Victor (ST) LSP-4960 *4/72*   **15–20**
Orange label.

RCA Victor (ST) LSP-4690 *4/72*   **50–60**
Orange label. With contents and programming information on a white sticker. Promotional issue only.

RCA Victor (ST) LSP-4690 . *76*   **10–15**
Tan label.

RCA Victor (ST) AFL1-4690 *77*   **8–10**
Black label, dog near top.

Side 1
  He Touched Me
  I've Got Confidence
  Amazing Grace
  Seeing Is Believing

He Is My Everything
Bosom of Abraham
Side 2
An Evening Prayer
Lead Me, Guide Me
There Is No God But God
A Thing Called Love
I, John
Reach Out to Jesus

HE WALKS BESIDE ME
RCA Victor (ST) AFL1-2772
. . . . *4/78*   **8–10**
Black label, dog near top. "If I Can Dream"
appeared for the first time in stereo on this LP,
although the original single (NBC-TV special)
version has never been released in stereo. Also,
"Miracle of the Rosary" is an alternate mix on
this LP, differing from the version on *Elvis Now*.
Note: Originally issued with a 20-page bonus
mini-photo booklet, which is included in the
above price range. Deduct $3–$5 if this booklet
is missing.

Side A
He Is My Everything
Miracle of the Rosary
Where Did They Go Lord
Somebody Bigger Than You and I
An Evening Prayer
The Impossible Dream (unreleased version)
Side B
If I Can Dream (unreleased version)
Padre
Known Only to Him
Who Am I
How Great Thou Art

HELLO CAROL!: see Various-Artists Compilations section.

HILLBILLY CAT, THE
Music Works (M) PB-3602   *7/84*   **8–10**
Side A
Introduction of Louisiana Hayride with
    Frank Page
Elvis Presley with Horace Logan
That's All Right Momma
Elvis talks about his musical style with Horace Logan
Blue Moon of Kentucky
Side B
Recollections by Frank Page of Elvis Presley
    and Colonel Tom Parker
Good Rockin' Tonight
I Got a Woman

HIS HAND IN MINE
RCA Victor (M) LPM-2328
. . . . *12/60*   **75–90**
Black label, with the words "Long Play" at the
bottom of the label.
RCA Victor (M) LPM-2328
. . . . *11/63*   **40–50**
Black label, with the word "Mono" at the bottom.
RCA Victor (M) LPM-2328
. . . . *64–65*   **25–30**
Black label, with the word "Monaural" at the
bottom.
RCA Victor (ST) LSP-2328
. . . . *12/60*   **90–100**
Black label, with the words "Living Stereo" at
the bottom.
RCA Victor (ST) LSP-2328 .   *64*   **25–30**
Black label, with the RCA logo in white at the
top of the label and the word "Stereo" at the
bottom.
RCA Victor (ST) LSP-2328
. . . . *68–69*   **10–20**
Orange label.
RCA Victor (ST) ANL1-1319
. . . . *3/76*   **10–15**
Orange label. This was the last Elvis LP to be
issued on the RCA orange label.
RCA Victor (ST) LSP-2328 .   *76*   **10–15**
Tan label.
RCA Victor (ST) AYM1-3935
. . . . *5/81*   **5–10**
Black label, dog near top. Issued as part of
RCA's "Best Buy" series.

Side 1
His Hand in Mine
I'm Gonna Walk Dem Golden Stairs
In My Father's House
Milky White Way
Known Only to Him
I Believe in the Man in the Sky
Side 2
Joshua Fit the Battle
Jesus Knows What I Need
Swing Down Sweet Chariot
Mansion Over the Hilltop
If We Never Meet Again
Working on the Building

HIS SONGS OF FAITH AND INSPIRATION (2 LP)
RCA Victor (SP) DVL2-0728
. . . . *4/86*   **15–18**
A mail-order offer.

Record 1
Side A
How Great Thou Art
Stand by Me
Joshua Fit the Battle
So High
In My Father's House (Are Many Mansions)
He Touched Me
I've Got Confidence
It Is No Secret (What God Can Do)
He Is My Everything
Side B
Working on the Building
In the Garden
We Call on Him
His Hand in Mine
By and By
Farther Along
Known Only to Him
I Believe in the Man in the Sky
You'll Never Walk Alone *(from "Carousel")*

Record 2
Side C
An Evening Prayer
Mansion Over the Hilltop
Milky White Way
Reach Out to Jesus
Who Am I?
Take My Hand, Precious Lord
Gonna Walk Dem Golden Stairs
If the Lord Wasn't Walking by My Side
(There'll Be) Peace in the Valley
Side D
Crying in the Chapel
Where No One Stands Alone
He Knows Just What I Need
Bosom of Abraham
Where Could I Go But to the Lord
Without Him
Swing Down Sweet Chariot
Amazing Grace
If We Never Meet Again

HIS SONGS OF INSPIRATION
RCA Victor (SP) DML1-0264 *77*   **10–15**
Black label, dog near top. Offered by Candlelite
Music as a bonus to customers ordering *The
Elvis Presley Story.*

Side A
Crying in the Chapel
Put Your Hand in the Hand
I Believe
How Great Thou Art
If I Can Dream
Side B
Peace in the Valley
Amazing Grace

An American Trilogy
Follow That Dream
You'll Never Walk Alone

HISTORY OF COUNTRY MUSIC—HANK WILLIAMS/ELVIS PRESLEY
Sunrise Media (M) SM-3011.   *81*   **10–15**
One side of this LP is devoted to each artist.
Side 1 is by Hank Williams, Side 2 by Elvis.

Side 1
I Can't Help It (If I'm Still in Love with You)
Half As Much
Honky Tonk Blues
Why Don't You Love Me
Side 2
Heartbreak Hotel
(Let Me Be Your) Teddy Bear
Love Me Tender
Jailhouse Rock

HOW GREAT THOU ART (As Sung by ELVIS)
RCA Victor (M) LPM-3758 *3/67*   **40–50**
Black label, reads "Mono Dynagroove" at the
bottom. This was the only commercial Elvis
release to be so labeled.

RCA Victor (ST) LSP-3758 *3/67*   **35–45**
Black label, with the RCA logo in white at the
top of the label and the word "Stereo" at the
bottom.

RCA Victor (ST) LSP-3758
. . . . *68–69*   **10–20**
Orange label.

RCA Victor (ST) LSP-3758 .   *76*   **10–15**
Tan label.

RCA Victor (ST AFL1-3758   *77*   **8–10**
Black label, dog near top.

Side 1
How Great Thou Art
In the Garden
Somebody Bigger Than You and I
Farther Along
Stand By Me
Without Him
Side 2
So High
Where Could I Go But to the Lord
By and By
If The Lord Wasn't Walking by My Side
Run On
Where No One Stands Alone
Crying in the Chapel

I GOT LUCKY
RCA/Camden (M) CAL-2533
. . . . *10/71*   **15–18**
Blue label.

Pickwick/Camden (M) CAS-2533
. . . . *12/75*
Note: Despite the stereo Pickwick prefix, all songs on this LP are monaural. Thus far, none of these tunes exist in true stereo in the United States.

Side 1
I Got Lucky
What a Wonderful Life
I Need Somebody to Lean On
Yoga Is As Yoga Does
Ridin' the Rainbow

Side 2
Fools Fall in Love
The Love Machine
Home Is Where the Heart Is
You Gotta Stop
If You Think I Don't Need You

I WAS THE ONE
RCA Victor (M) AHL1-4678
. . . . *5/83*   **8–10**
Special "Elvis" pink label. This LP is a collection of older Elvis songs with a slight vocal backing or instrumentation enhancement.
Note: The first truly custom Elvis LP label appeared with the release of *I Was the One.*

Side A
My Baby Left Me
(You're So Square) Baby I Don't Care
Little Sister
Don't
Wear My Ring Around Your Neck
Paralyzed

Side B
Baby, Let's Play House
I Was the One
Rip It Up
Young and Beautiful
Reddy Teddy

IN THE BEGINNING: see Various-Artists Compilations section.

INTERNATIONAL HOTEL, LAS VEGAS, NEVADA, PRESENTS ELVIS—AUGUST 1969 (Boxed set)
RCA Victor (SP), no number given
. . . . *8/69*   **900–1000**

A specially prepared complimentary boxed set, given away at the International Hotel during Elvis' opening engagement there.
Note: This box contained the following:

One copy of the *Elvis (NBC-TV Special)* LP

One copy of the *From Elvis In Memphis* LP

A nine-page letter from RCA and the Colonel

An Elvis record and tape catalog

An Elvis 1969 pocket calendar

Two 8" × 10" black and white Elvis photos

One 8" × 10" color Elvis photo

The price range given is for the complete set. Most of the value is in the box itself, especially since the records are standard commercial copies.

INTERNATIONAL HOTEL, LAS VEGAS, NEVADA, PRESENTS ELVIS—1970 (Boxed set)
RCA Victor (SP), no number given
. . . . *2/70*   **900–1000**
A second specially prepared complimentary box set, given away at the International Hotel during Elvis' 1970 appearance there.
Note: This box contained the following:

One copy of the double LP *From Memphis To Vegas/From Vegas to Memphis*

A single of "Kentucky Rain"/"My Little Friend" with picture sleeve

One 8" × 10" black and white Elvis photo

An Elvis 1970 pocket calendar

An Elvis record and tape catalog

A souvenir photo album

An International Hotel menu

An introductory note from Elvis and the Colonel

The price range given is for a complete set. Most of the value is in the box itself, especially since the records are standard commercial copies.

INTERVIEWS WITH ELVIS
Starday (M) SD-995 . . . . . *78*   **30–50**
Reissue of the Canadian interviews previously heard on *The Elvis Tapes.*

IT HAPPENED AT THE WORLD'S FAIR
RCA Victor (M) LPM-2697 *4/63*   **125–150**
Black label, with the words "Long Play" at the bottom of the label.

RCA Victor (M) LPM-2697
. . . . *11/63*   **40–50**
Black label, with the word "Mono" at the bottom.

RCA Victor (M) LPM-2697.   *64*   **25–30**
Black label, with the word "Monaural" at the bottom.

RCA Victor (ST) LSP-2697 *4/63*   **135–160**
Black label, with the words "Living Stereo" at the bottom.

RCA Victor (ST) LSP-2697 .   *64*   **25–30**
Black label, with the RCA logo in white at the top of the label and the word "Stereo" at the bottom.

RCA Victor (ST) APL1-2568
. . . . *9/77*   **8–10**
Black label, dog near top.

Note: 1963 originals were issued with an 8″ × 10″ color photo, which is included in the above price range. Deduct $40–$50 if this photo is missing.

Side 1
  Beyond the Bend
  Relax
  Take Me to the Fair
  They Remind Me Too Much of You
  One Broken Heart for Sale
Side 2
  I'm Falling in Love Tonight
  Cotton Candy Land
  A World of Our Own
  How Would You Like to Be
  Happy Ending

JOY OF CHRISTMAS, THE: see Various-Artists Compilations section.

JUST LET ME HEAR SOME OF THAT ROCK 'N' ROLL MUSIC: see Various-Artists compilations section.

KING CREOLE

RCA Victor (M) LPM-1884 *8/58*   **200–225**
Black label, with the words "Long Play" at the bottom of the label. Original covers for this issue have the RCA catalog number under the RCA logo, in the upper right corner.

Note: 1958 originals were packaged with an 8″ × 10″ black and white photo of Elvis in his Army uniform, which is included in the above price range. Deduct $75–$100 if this photo is missing.

RCA Victor (M) LPM-1884
. . . . *11/63*   **45–55**

Black label, with the word "Mono" at the bottom. Covers for this issue have the RCA catalog number on the left side of the front cover.

RCA Victor (M) LPM-1884.   *64*   **25–30**
Black label, with the word "Monaural" at the bottom. Covers for this issue have the RCA catalog number on the left side of the front cover.

RCA Victor (SE) LSP-1884(e)
. . . . *2/62*   **75–85**
Black label, with the RCA logo in silver at the top of the label and the word "Stereo" at the bottom.

RCA Victor (SE) LSP-1884(e) *64*   **25–30**
Black label, with the RCA logo in white at the top of the label and the word "Stereo" at the bottom.

RCA Victor (SE) LSP-1884(e) *68*   **10–20**
Orange label.

RCA Victor (SE) LSP-1884(e) *76*   **10–15**
Tan label.

RCA Victor (SE) AFL1-1884(e)
. . . . *77*   **8–10**
Black label, dog near top.

RCA Victor (SE) AYL1-3733
. . . . *11/80*   **5–10**
Black label, dog near top. Issued as part of RCA's "Best Buy" series.

Note: All songs on the stereo issue of this LP are electronically enhanced to simulate stereo.

Side 1
  King Creole
  As Long As I Have You
  Hard Headed Woman
  Trouble
  Dixieland Rock
Side 2
  Don't Ask Me Why
  Lover Doll
  Crawfish
  Young Dreams
  New Orleans

KING'S GOLD, THE

Media Entertainment (S). . . *85*   **50–75**
Three reel-to-reel tapes, issued only to radio stations. Price includes cue sheets, which represent $4–$6 of the value. Not known to exist on disc.

KISSIN' COUSINS

RCA Victor (M) LPM-2894 *3/64*   **100–150**
Black label, with the word "Mono" at the bottom. Without film cast photo in lower right corner of cover.

RCA Victor (M) LPM-2894 *3/64*   **60–70**
Black label, with the word "Mono" at the bottom. With film cast photo in lower right corner of cover.

RCA Victor (M) LPM-2894. *64*   **25–30**
Black label, with the word "Monaural" at the bottom.

RCA Victor (ST) LSP-2894 *3/64* **100–150**
Black label, with the RCA logo in silver at the top of the label and the word "Stereo" at the bottom. Without film cast photo in lower right corner of the cover.

RCA Victor (ST) LSP-2894 *3/64*   **60–70**
Black label, with the RCA logo in silver at the top of the label and the word "Stereo" at the bottom. With film cast photo in lower right corner of cover.

RCA Victor (ST) LSP-2894. *64*   **25–30**
Black label, with the RCA logo in white at the top of the label and the word "Stereo" at the bottom.

RCA Victor (ST) LSP-2894. *68*   **10–20**
Orange label.

RCA Victor (ST) LSP-2894. *76*   **10–15**
Tan label.

RCA Victor (ST) AFL1-2894 *77*   **8–10**
Black label, dog near top.

RCA Victor (ST) AYM1-4115
. . . . *9/81*   **5–10**
Black label, dog near top. Issued as part of RCA's "Best Buy" series.

Side 1
Kissin' Cousins (No. 2)
Smokey Mountain Boy
There's Gold in the Mountains
One Boy, Two Little Girls
Catchin' On Fast
Tender Feeling
Side 2
Anyone (Could Fall in Love with You)
Barefoot Ballad
Kissin' Cousins
Echoes of Love
(It's a) Long Lonely Highway

LE DISQUE D'OR

RCA Victor (SP) 6886 807. *77*   **10–12**
This LP was imported from France and distributed throughout the United States.

Side 1
C'mon Everybody
A Whistling Tune
I'll Be There (If You Want Me)
I Love Only One Girl

Easy Come, Easy Go
Santa Lucia
Side 2
Tonight Is So Right for Love
Guadalajara
Angel
A Little Less Conversation
Follow That Dream
Long Legged Girl

LEGEND LIVES ON: see *THE LEGEND LIVES ON.*

LEGEND OF A KING: see *THE LEGEND OF A KING.*

LEGENDARY MAGIC OF ELVIS PRESLEY, THE

RCA Victor (SP) DVL1-0461 *80*   **10–15**
Black label, dog near top. RCA Special Products, made for Candlelite Music and offered through mail order.

Side A
The Wonder of You
Baby, I Don't Care
My Wish Came True
Suspicious Minds
I Want You, I Need You, I Love You
Little Sister
It's Now or Never
Too Much
Are You Lonesome Tonight?
Side B
Burning Love
A Fool Such As I
Hard Headed Woman
In the Ghetto
When My Blue Moon Turns to Gold Again
Don't Cry Daddy
Jailhouse Rock
His Latest Flame
One Night

LEGENDARY PERFORMER, A—ELVIS (Volume 1)

RCA Victor (M) CPL1-0341
. . . . *1/74*   **20–25**
Packaged with the bonus booklet "The Early Years," which is included in the above price range. Deduct $5 if this booklet is missing. Also, this LP was issued with a specially printed inner-sleeve.

RCA Victor (M) CPL1-0341 *83*   **5–8**
Reissued without die-cut cover, special inner-sleeve, and bonus booklet. During the transition some copies with the newer cover *do* include the special inner-sleeve.

RCA Victor (M) CPL1-0341

. . . . *1/78* **800-1000**
Experimental Elvis picture disc, using the contents of CPL1-0341, though not actually numbered, and the photos of several other Elvis albums for the picture on the disc. This was the very first Elvis picture disc ever produced, although less than a dozen copies were done.

Side 1
    That's All Right
    I Love You Because (unreleased version)
    Heartbreak Hotel
    Don't Be Cruel
    Love Me (unreleased live version)
    Trying to Get to You (unreleased live version)
Side 2
    Love Me Tender
    Peace in the Valley
    A Fool Such As I
    Tonight's All Right for Love (unreleased in English speaking countries)
    Are You Lonesome Tonight (unreleased live version)
    Can't Help Falling in Love

LEGENDARY PERFORMER, A—ELVIS (Volume 2)
RCA Victor (SP) CPL1-1349

. . . . *1/76* **20-25**
Packaged with the bonus booklet "The Early Years . . . Continued," which is included in the above price range. Deduct $5 if this booklet is missing. Issued with a specially printed inner-sleeve.

RCA Victor (SP) CPL1-1349

. . . . *1/76* **45-55**
Unintentionally pressed without the false starts and outtakes on "Such a Night" and "Cane and a High Starched Collar."

RCA Victor (SP) CPL1-1349 *83* **5-8**
Reissued without die-cut cover, special inner-sleeve and bonus booklet. During the transition, some copies with the newer cover *do* include the special inner-sleeve.
Note: The previously unreleased "Blue Hawaii" on this LP is true stereo. "Cane and a High Starched Collar," appearing for the first time on record, is monaural on this LP. The "Such a Night" outtakes are in stereo.

Side 1
    Harbor Lights
    Jay Thompson Interviews Elvis (1956)
    I Want You, I Need You, I Love You (unreleased alternate take)
    Blue Suede Shoes (unreleased live version)

    Blue Christmas
    Jailhouse Rock
    It's Now or Never
Side 2
    Cane and a High Starched Collar
    Presentation of Awards to Elvis
    Blue Hawaii (unreleased version)
    Such a Night
    Baby What Do You Want Me to Do (unreleased live version)
    How Great Thou Art
    If I Can Dream

LEGENDARY PERFORMER, A—ELVIS (Volume 3)
RCA Victor (SP) CPL1-3078

. . . . *12/78* **15-20**
Picture disc. Packaged with the booklet "Yesterdays," which is included in the above price range. Deduct $5 if this booklet is missing.

RCA Victor (SP) CPL1-3082

. . . . *12/78* **8-12**
Packaged with the bonus booklet "Yesterdays," which is included in the above price range. Deduct $5 if this booklet is missing. Issued with a specially printed inner-sleeve. The previously unreleased versions of "Fame and Fortune," "Frankfort Special," "Guadalajara," "It Hurts Me," "Let Yourself Go," and "Let It Be Me" are all in stereo. "Britches," appearing for the first time on record, is monaural on this LP.

Side 1
    Hound Dog
    1956 (*TV Guide* Interview)
    Danny
    Fame and Fortune (unreleased alternate version)
    Frankfort Special (unreleased alternate version)
    Britches
    Crying in the Chapel
Side 2
    Surrender
    Guadalajara (unreleased alternate version)
    It Hurts Me (unreleased version)
    Let Yourself Go (unreleased version)
    In the Ghetto
    Let It Be Me (unreleased live version)

LEGENDARY PERFORMER, A—ELVIS (Volume 4)
RCA Victor (SP) CPL1-4848

. . . . *11/83* **8-10**
Price includes a 12-page "Memories of the King" booklet.

Side A
When It Rains, It Really Pours
Interview
One Night
I'm Beginning to Forget You
Mona Lisa
Wooden Heart
Plantation Rock

Side B
The Lady Loves Me
Swing Down Sweet Chariot
That's All Right
Are You Lonesome Tonight?
Reconsider Baby
I'll Remember You

LEGENDARY RECORDINGS OF ELVIS PRESLEY, THE (6 LP)

RCA Victor (SP) DML6-0412 *79*   **30–40**
Black label, dog near top. RCA Special Products, made for Candlelite Music and offered through mail order in a special box set with custom inner sleeves.

Record 1
Side A
Take My Hand, Precious Lord
Where Could I Go (But to the Lord)
In the Garden
It Is No Secret
Stand By Me

Side B
Mama Liked the Roses
Padre
All That I Am
I'm Leavin'
Forget Me Never (shown as "Forgive Me Never")

Record 2
Side A
Frankie and Johnny
Down by the Riverside/When the Saints Go Marching In
Girl Happy
Do the Clam
G.I. Blues

Side B
See See Rider/Also Sprach Zarathustra
Johnny B. Goode
Lawdy Miss Clawdy/Baby What You Want Me to Do
Whole Lotta Shakin' Goin' On/Long Tall Sally
It's Over

Record 3
Side A
Snowbird
I Love You Because

Just Because
Release Me
Mystery Train

Side B
Blue Moon of Kentucky
It Keeps Right on A-Hurtin'
I Don't Care If the Sun Don't Shine
I'm Movin' On
Baby, Let's Play House

Record 4
Side A
Shake, Rattle and Roll
I Slipped I Stumbled, I Fell
Tutti Frutti
Ain't That Lovin' You Baby
Rip It Up

Side B
Party
Tiger Man
Paralyzed
Hi-Heel Sneakers
I Got a Woman

Record 5
Side A
Any Day Now
How's the World Treating You
Only the Strong Survive
Just for Old Times Sake
You've Lost That Lovin' Feelin'

Side B
They Remind Me Too Much of You
Lonely Blue Boy (Danny)
Indescribably Blue
It Feels So Right
Tell Me Why

Record 6
Side A
Fools Rush In
Please Don't Stop Loving Me
Proud Mary
Never Been to Spain
Don't Think Twice, It's All Right

Side B
Fools Fall in Love
Walk a Mile in My Shoes
Blue Moon
Witchcraft
Runaway

LET'S BE FRIENDS

RCA/Camden (SP) CAS-2408
. . . . *4/70*   **15–18**
Blue label. "Mama" is monaural on this LP, which states that it was recorded only in mono.

Pickwick/Camden (SP) CAS-2408
. . . . *12/75*   **8–10**

Note: A gold vinyl copy of this LP was recently offered for auction, with a $500 minimum bid. This was an experimental copy made for some reason. There was no colored vinyl commercial or promotional edition of this issue. Also, a series of standard catalog RCA Elvis LPs recently came out of their Indianapolis plant, on colored vinyl. These were also experimental items, which were sold for approximately $1,000 each.

LIGHTNING STRIKES TWICE—ELVIS PRESLEY/THE SILVER BEATLES
United Distributors (M) UDL-2382 . . . . *81*   **25–50**
Promotional issue only. One side of this LP is devoted to each artist. Side 1 is by the Silver Beatles, from their Decca auditions; Side 2 is by Elvis.

Side 1
September in the Rain
Besame Mucho
Shiek of Araby
To Know You
Hello Little Girl
Side 2
Baby Let's Play House
I've Got a Woman
That's All Right
Blue Moon of Kentucky
Tweedle Dee

LOUISIANA HAYRIDE
Louisiana Hayride (M) NR-8454
. . . . *76*   **550–650**
Light yellow label.
Louisiana Hayride (M) NR-8454
. . . . *76*   **300–325**
Gold label.
Note: This disc contains one complete Louisiana Hayride radio program, which included Elvis' "Tweedle Dee." The original issues, with the light yellow label, will have the label filled in, indicating that it is Program 836 and that the featured artist is Bobby G. Rice. The gold label issues appear to have never been used for air play.

In all probability, the gold label issues were never distributed outside the Hayride until the entire quantity was offered in 1981. Even though produced in larger quantity, the older yellow label issues were mostly destroyed by subscribing stations, making them rarer than the gold version.

LOVE LETTERS FROM ELVIS
RCA Victor (ST) LSP-4530 *5/71*   **25–40**
Orange label. With "Love Letters From" on one line, above "Elvis."

RCA Victor (ST) LSP-4530 *5/71*   **20–35**
Orange label. "Love Letters" on the top line, "From" on the second line, and "Elvis" on the third.
Note: We're getting conflicting opinions about which of these "Love Letters" covers is the rarer. The first issue, with the three words on one line, theoretically should be rarer. It was quickly replaced with the three-line version, which has the letters RE (Reissue) in the lower left corner. However, quantities of the first version have turned up to offset the difference in value. For now, we've put them in a closer range than ultimately may exist. Additional input is encouraged.
RCA Victor (ST) LSP-4530 . *76*   **10–15**
Tan label.
RCA Victor (ST) AFL1-4530 *77*   **8–10**
Black label, dog near top.

Side 1
Love Letters
When I'm Over You
If I Were You
Got My Mojo Working
Heart of Rome
Side 2
Only Believe
This Is Our Dance
Cindy Cindy
I'll Never Know
It Ain't No Big Thing
Life

LOVING YOU
RCA Victor (M) LPM-1515 *7/57*   **100–125**
Black label, with the words "Long Play" at the bottom of the label. Original covers for this issue have the RCA catalog number under the RCA logo, in the upper right corner.
RCA Victor (M) LPM-1515
. . . . *11/63*   **45–55**
Black label, with the word "Mono" at the bottom. Covers for this issue have the RCA catalog number on the left side of the front cover.
RCA Victor (M) LPM-1515. *64*   **25–30**
Black label, with the word "Monaural" at the bottom. Covers for this issue have the RCA catalog number on the left side of the front cover.

RCA Victor (SE) LSP-1515(e)
. . . . 2/62   **75–85**
Black label, with the RCA logo in silver at the top of the label and the word "Stereo" at the bottom.

RCA Victor (SE) LSP-1515(e) *64*   **25–30**
Black label, with the RCA logo in white at the top of the label and the word "Stereo" at the bottom.

RCA Victor (SE) LSP-1515(e) *68*   **10–20**
Orange label.

RCA Victor (SE) LSP-1515(e) *76*   **10–15**
Tan label.

RCA Victor (SE) AFL1-1515(e)
. . . . *77*   **8–10**
Black label, dog near top.
Note: All songs on the stereo issue of this LP are electronically enhanced to simulate stereo.

Side 1
　Mean Woman Blues
　Teddy Bear
　Loving You
　Got a Lot O' Livin' to Do
　Lonesome Cowboy
　Hot Dog
　Party
Side 2
　Blueberry Hill
　True Love
　Don't Leave Me Now
　Have I Told You Lately That I Love You
　I Need You So

MCA MUSIC (4 LP)
MCA, no number given (S)   **40–60**
Contains excerpts of 200 songs by various artists, including five Elvis songs. Promotional issue only.

MAHALO FROM ELVIS
Pickwick/Camden (ST) ACL-7064
. . . . *78*   **15–20**
Note: "Blue Hawaii," "Early Morning Rain," "Hawaiian Wedding Song," and "Ku-u-i-po" were newly recorded in 1973 for the "Aloha from Hawaii Via Satellite" TV special, and were included in that show but were not on the RCA soundtrack LP of the show. "No More" was recorded at the same time as the other four songs on this side but *not* included in the TV special.

Side 1
　Blue Hawaii
　Early Morning Rain
　Hawaiian Wedding Song
　Ku-u-i-po
　No More

Side 2
　Relax
　Baby If You'll Give Me All Your Love
　One Broken Heart for Sale
　So Close, Yet So Far (from Paradise)
　Happy Ending

(1957) MARCH OF DIMES GALAXY OF STARS: see Various-Artists Compilations section.

MEMORIES OF CHRISTMAS
RCA Victor (SP) CPL1-4395
. . . . 8/82   **8–10**
Black label, dog near top.
Note: This LP marked the first appearance of "If Everyday Was Like Christmas" in true stereo, even though this is an alternate take. The original single version of the song has not been released in stereo yet. The "Christmas Message From Elvis" was originally on the *Elvis Presley—Special Christmas Program* disc and reel tape. Packaged with this LP was a 7" × 9" 1982–83 calendar, which is included in the above price range. Deduct $2–$3 if this calendar is missing.

Side 1
　O Come, All Ye Faithful (unreleased version)
　Silver Bells
　I'll Be Home on Christmas Day (unreleased version)
　Blue Christmas
　Santa Clause Is Back in Town
Side 2
　Merry Christmas Baby (unreleased complete studio performance)
　If Everyday Was Like Christmas
　Christmas Message from Elvis/Silent Night

MEMORIES OF ELVIS (5 LP)
RCA Victor (SP) DPL5-0347 *78*   **35–45**
Black label, dog near top. RCA Special Products, made for Candlelite Music and offered through mail order.
Note: Packaged with a 16-page booklet, "Musical History's Finest Hour," and a Bonus Portrait Print, which is included in the above price range. Deduct $10 if these materials are missing.

Side 1
　One Broken Heart for Sale
　Young and Beautiful
　A Mess of Blues
　The Next Step Is Love
　I Gotta Know
　Love Letters

This budget LP features additional material from the *Aloha from Hawaii* LP.

Side 2
   When My Blue Moon Turns to Gold Again
   If Everyday Was Like Christmas
   Steamroller Blues
   Anyway You Want Me
   (Such An) Easy Question
   That's When Your Heartaches Begin
Side 3
   Kentucky Rain
   Money Honey
   My Way
   Girls! Girls! Girls!
   Lonely Man
   U.S. Male
Side 4
   My Wish Came True
   Kiss Me Quick
   As Long As I Have You
   Bossa Nova Baby
   I Forgot to Remember to Forget
   Such a Night
Side 5
   I Really Don't Want to Know
   Doncha' Think It's Time
   His Hand in Mine

   That's All Right
   Nothingville Medley
   Baby, I Don't Care
Side 6
   Playing for Keeps
   King of the Whole Wide World
   Don't Ask Me Why
   Flaming Star
   I'm Left, You're Right, She's Gone
   What'd I Say
Side 7
   There Goes My Everything
   Patch It Up
   Reconsider Baby
   Good Rockin' Tonight
   You Gave Me a Mountain
   Rock-a-Hula Baby
Side 8
   Mean Woman Blues
   It Hurts Me
   Fever
   I Want to Be Free
   Viva Las Vegas
   Old Shep

Side 9
Anything That's Part of You
My Baby Left Me
Wild in the Country
Memphis, Tennessee
Don't Leave Me Now
I Feel So Bad
Side 10
Separate Ways
Polk Salad Annie
Fame and Fortune
Trying to Get to You
I've Lost You
King Creole
Note: Also see: *THE GREATEST SHOW ON EARTH.*

MEMORIES OF ELVIS (3 LP)
Creative Radio (SP) 1A-3B *10/87*   **100–150**
Price includes three pages of programming instructions and cues. Deduct $10–$15 if these pages are missing. Issued to radio stations only.

Record 1
Elvis Medley
I Want You, I Need You, I Love You
Love Me Tender
Blue Suede Shoes
Harbor Lights
That's All Right
I Can't Stop Loving You
An American Trilogy
It's Now or Never
Are You Lonesome Tonight
What'd I Say
Heartbreak Hotel
Wear My Ring Around Your Neck
Record 2
The Wonder of You
All Shook Up
Lawdy Miss Clawdy
Kentucky Rain
Too Much
I'll Remember You
Rock Medley
Treat Me Nice
Can't Help Falling in Love
Hound Dog
Steamroller Blues
Don't Cry Daddy
Return to Sender
In the Ghetto
If I Can Dream
Record 3
Love Me
Elvis Medley
(Now and Then There's) A Fool Such As I
Good Luck Charm

There Goes My Everything
Devil in Disguise
A Big Hunk O' Love
Suspicious Minds
Follow That Dream
I've Got a Woman
Impossible Dream
His Latest Flame
You Gave Me a Mountain
Don't Be Cruel
Memories

MEMPHIS RECORD, THE (2 LP)
RCA Victor (ST) 6621-1-R *7/87*   **10–15**
Includes a bonus color 15″ × 22″ poster and "Elvis Talks" LP flyer.
Note: The single versions of "Don't Cry Daddy" and "Mama Liked The Roses" appear for the first time in stereo on this LP.

Side A
Stranger in My Own Home Town
Power of My Love
Only the Strong Survive
Any Day Now
Suspicious Minds
Side B
Long Black Limousine
Wearin' That Loved On Look
I'll Hold You in My Heart
After Loving You
Rubberneckin'
I'm Movin' On
Side C
Gentle on My Mind
True Love Travels on a Gravel Road
It Keeps Right on A-Hurtin'
You'll Think of Me
Mama Liked the Roses
Don't Cry Daddy
Side D
In the Ghetto
The Fair Is Moving On
Inherit the Wind
Kentucky Rain
Without Love
Who Am I?

MICHELOB PRESENTS HIGHLIGHTS OF ELVIS MEMORIES
ABC (SP) OCC810. . . . *12/78* **100–150**
Contains highlights from the three-hour "Elvis Memories," as broadcast by the ABC radio affiliates. This sampler was distributed within the Michelob organization only.

Side 1
  Memories
  Heartbreak Hotel
  Love Me Tender
  Hound Dog
  Don't Be Cruel
  Jailhouse Rock
  It's Now or Never
Side 2
  Viva Las Vegas
  Separate Ways
  You Don't Have to Say You Love Me
  Are You Lonesome Tonight
  Can't Help Falling in Love
  If I Can Dream
Note: Also see *ELVIS MEMORIES.*

MOODY BLUE

RCA Victor (ST) AFL1-2428
. . . . 6/77 **1000–1200**
White vinyl. Black label, dog near top. Only a
half-dozen or so copies were done on white
vinyl and were originally distributed within the
RCA organization.

RCA Victor (ST) AFL1-2428
. . . . 7/77   **10–12**
Blue vinyl. Black label, dog near top.

RCA Victor (ST) AFL1-2428
. . . . 8/77   **125–150**
Black vinyl. First copies of the second pressing
were on black vinyl. Almost immediately after
production began on this run, Elvis died. RCA
then switched back to blue vinyl, making a U.S.
black vinyl pressing scarce.

RCA Victor (ST) AQL1-2428
. . . . 8/77   **8–10**
Black label, dog near top.

Side A
  Unchained Melody
  If You Love Me (Let Me Know)
  Little Darlin'
  He'll Have to Go
  Let Me Be There
Side B
  Way Down
  Pledging My Love
  Moody Blue
  She Thinks I Still Care
  It's Easy for You

MOVIE SPOTS AND PROMOTIONALS (Various)

Most of Elvis' films had specially produced
radio spots that were supplied to stations on 7",

10", and 12" discs. These discs usually contained an assortment of 10-, 30-, and 60-second
announcements for the film. Many of these featured excerpts of Elvis' songs from that particular film. Although prices will vary, usually with
higher values attached to the older releases,
these discs will usually fall into the $150–$300
range for near-mint copies.

MUSIC YOU CAN'T FORGET: see Various-Artists Compilations section.

NUMBER ONE HITS, THE

RCA Victor (SP) 6382-1-R *7/87*   **8–10**
Includes a bonus color 15" × 22" poster and
"Elvis Talks" LP flyer.

Side A
  Heartbreak Hotel
  I Want You, I Need You, I Love You
  Hound Dog
  Don't Be Cruel
  Love Me Tender
  Too Much
  All Shook Up
  Teddy Bear
  Jailhouse Rock
Side B
  Don't
  Hard Headed Woman
  A Big Hunk O' Love
  Stuck on You
  It's Now or Never
  Are You Lonesome Tonight?
  Surrender
  Good Luck Charm
  Suspicious Minds

OCTOBER CHRISTMAS SAMPLER: see *RCA 12-INCH SAMPLERS;* Various-Artists Compilations section.

OFFICIAL GRAMMY AWARD ARCHIVE COLLECTION, THE: see Various-Artists Compilations section.

OLD & HEAVY GOLD: see Various-Artists Compilations section.

ON STAGE—FEBRUARY 1970

RCA Victor (ST) LSP-4362 *6/70*   **15–18**
Orange label. Rigid disc.

RCA Victor (ST LSP-4362 . *71*   **10–15**
Orange label. Flexible disc.

RCA Victor (ST) LSP-4362 . *76*   **10–15**
Tan label.

RCA Victor (ST) AFL1-4362 *77*   **10–12**
Black label, dog near top. Jumpsuit photo on back cover.

RCA Victor (ST) AQL1-4362
. . . . *2/83*   **5–10**
Black label, dog near top. Shirt photo on back cover.

Note: As with many other Elvis LPs, RCA simply used a white sticker with the newer "AFL" prefix to cover the older "LSP" prefix. After all of the "LSP" copies were sold, covers were manufactured with the "AFL" catalog number printed on them. Copies of *On Stage—February 1970* with the sticker are the same as "LSP" issues. Also, we have received sketchy information about a promo sampler, SPS-33-507, containing what is possibly an alternate version of "Runaway." Regardless of whether the track is an alternate, we would like to know about this disc—if it contains Elvis' voice and if it's a U.S. issue.

Side 1
See See Rider
Release Me
Sweet Caroline
Runaway
The Wonder of You
Side 2
Polk Salad Annie
Yesterday
Proud Mary
Walk a Mile in My Shoes
Let It Be Me (Je t'appartiens)

ON THE RECORD—EVENTS OF 1977

Cardmon (M) TC-1572. . . *1/78*   **50–75**
United Press International's recap of 1977's top news stories. Contains brief excerpts of "All Shook Up" (a concert version) and "Hound Dog."

ORIGINAL ELVIS PRESLEY MEDLEY, THE

Disconet 309 . . . . *80*   **25–50**
Promotional issue only. One side of this LP is by a group called Fear.

OUR MEMORIES OF ELVIS

RCA Victor (ST) AQL1-3279
. . . . *2/79*   **8–10**
Black label, dog on top.
Note: This LP was the first of two volumes containing the "pure Elvis" sound.

Side A
Are You Sincere (unreleased version)
It's Midnight
My Boy
Girl of Mine
Take Good Care of Her
I'll Never Fall in Love Again
Side B
Your Love's Been a Long Time Coming
Spanish Eyes
Never Again
She Thinks I Still Care
Solitaire

OUR MEMORIES OF ELVIS—VOL. 2 (MORE OF THE PURE ELVIS SOUND)

RCA Victor AQL1-3448. . *8/79*   **8–10**
Black label, dog near top.

Side A
I Got A Feelin' in My Body
Green Green Grass of Home
For the Heart
She Wears My Ring
I Can Help
Side B
Way Down
There's a Honky Tonk Angel (Who'll Take Me Back In)
Find Out What's Happening
Thinking About You
Don't Think Twice, It's All Right (unreleased complete studio jam session)
Also see: PURE ELVIS

PARADISE HAWAIIAN STYLE

RCA Victor (M) LPM-3643 *6/66*   **35–45**
Black label, with the word "Monaural" at the bottom.

RCA Victor (ST) LSP-3643 *6/66*   **35–45**
Black label, with the RCA logo in white at the top of the label and the word "Stereo" at the bottom.

RCA Victor (ST) LSP-3643 . *68*   **10–20**
Orange label.

RCA Victor (ST) LSP-3643 . *76*   **10–15**
Tan label.

RCA Victor (ST) AFL1-3643 *77*   **8–10**
Black label, dog near top.

Side 1
Paradise Hawaiian Style
Queenie Wahine's Papaya
Scratch My Back (I'll Scratch Yours)
Drums of the Islands
Datin'

Side 2
  A Dog's Life
  A House of Sand
  Stop Where You Are
  This Is My Heaven
  Sand Castles

PERSONALLY ELVIS (2 LP)

Silhouette Music (M) 10001/2 *79*   **20–25**
A double pocket two-LP set, containing five
different Elvis interviews.
Note: Packaged with this LP is an Elvis silhouette transfer, which is included in the above
price range. Deduct $2 if this transfer is miss-
ing.

PICKWICK PACK (7 LP)

Pickwick/Camden (SP) . *11/78*   **50–60**
A specially wrapped package of these Pickwick
LPs: *Elvis' Christmas Album, I Got Lucky, Sep-
arate Ways, Mahalo From Elvis, Burning Love
(and Hits From His Movies), You'll Never Walk
Alone,* and *Elvis Sings Hits From His Movies,
Vol. 1.*

Pickwick/Camden (SP) . . *2/79*   **50–60**
Reissue of the above package, with *Elvis' Christmas Album* being replaced with *Frankie and
Johnny.*
Note: The special LP packs, which had all seven
albums shrink-wrapped inside the overall wrapping, was actually untitled. It is known in fan-
dom as the *Pickwick Pack.* These issues were
the last Elvis releases by Pickwick.

PLAYBOY MUSIC HALL OF FAME WINNERS: see Various-Artists Compilations section.

POT LUCK

RCA Victor (M) LPM-2523 *6/62*   **75–90**
Black label, with the words "Long Play" at the
bottom of the label.

RCA Victor (M) LPM-2523
. . . . *11/63*   **40–50**
Black label, with the word "Mono" at the bottom.

RCA Victor (M) LPM-2523 . *64*   **25–30**
Black label, with the word "Monaural" at the
bottom.

RCA Victor (ST) LSP-2523 *6/62*   **90–100**
Black label, with the words "Living Stereo" at
the bottom.

RCA Victor (ST) LSP-2523 . *64*   **25–30**
Black label, with the RCA logo in white at the
top of the label and the word "Stereo" at the
bottom.

RCA Victor (ST) LSP-2523 . *68*   **10–20**
Orange label.

RCA Victor (ST) LSP-2523 . *76*   **10–15**
Tan label.

RCA Victor (ST) AFL1-2523 *77*   **8–10**
Black label, dog near top.

Side 1
  Kiss Me Quick
  Just for Old Times Sake
  Gonna Get Back Home Somehow
  (Such an) Easy Question
  Steppin' Out of Line
  I'm Yours
Side 2
  Something Blue
  Suspicion
  I Feel That I've Known You Forever
  Night Rider
  Fountain of Love
  That's Someone You Never Forget

PROMISED LAND

RCA Victor (ST) APL1-0873
. . . . *1/75*   **15–18**
Orange label.

RCA Victor (Q) APD1-0873
. . . . *1/75*   **100–125**
Quadradisc. Orange label.

RCA Victor (ST) APL1-0873 *76*   **10–15**
Tan label.

RCA Victor (ST) AFL1-0873 *77*   **8–10**
Black label, dog near top.

RCA Victor (Q) APD1-0873 *77*   **40–50**
Quadradisc. Black label, dog near top.

Side A
  Promised Land
  There's a Honky Tonk Angel (Who'll Take
    Me Back In)
  Help Me
  Mr. Songman
  Love Song of the Year
Side B
  It's Midnight
  Your Love's Been a Long Time Coming
  If You Talk in Your Sleep
  Thinking About You
  You Asked Me To

PURE ELVIS

RCA Victor (ST) DJL1-3455
. . . . *8/79*   **275–325**
White label. Promotional issue only.
Note: This unusual LP contained four songs on
one side, exactly as originally issued, and the
same four songs on the other side in the "pure
Elvis" style. This album was a promotional
piece for the *Our Memories of Elvis—Volume 2.*

A demonstration of the "pure Elvis" sound, something which was a far cry from what had been originally issued on record.

Side 1
 I Got a Feelin' in My Body
 For the Heart
 She Wears My Ring
 Find Out What's Happening
Side 2
 I Got a Feelin' in My Body
 For the Heart
 She Wears My Ring
 Find Out What's Happening

PURE GOLD
RCA Victor (SP) ANL1-0971(e)
. . . . *6/75*   **15–18**
Orange label.
RCA Victor (SP) ANL1-0971(e)
. . . . *76*   **10–15**
Yellow label.
RCA Victor (SP) ANL1-0971(e)
. . . . *77*   **8–10**
Black label, dog near top.
RCA Victor (SP) AYL1-3732
. . . . *11/80*   **5–10**
Black label, dog near top.

Note: The (e) on the end of the catalog number usually indicates that the LP is reprocessed (electronic) stereo. In this case, this is not completely true since there are three true stereo tracks on this LP.

Side A
 Kentucky Rain
 Fever
 It's Impossible
 Jailhouse Rock
 Don't Be Cruel
Side B
 I Got a Woman
 All Shook Up
 Loving You
 In the Ghetto
 Love Me Tender

QSP PRESENTS A GIFT OF MUSIC: see Various-Artists Compilations section.

RCA RADIO VICTROLA DIVISION SPOTS
RCA Victor (M) 0401 . . *10/56*   **600–800**

One-sided disc, containing four 50-second radio commercials for RCA's Victrolas, as well as for the SPD-22 and SPD-23 EPs that were offered as a bonus. Elvis is the announcer on all of the spots, which include excerpts of some of his songs. Issued only to radio stations running the spots.

RCA 12-INCH SAMPLERS: see Various-Artists Compilations section.

RAISED ON ROCK/FOR OL' TIMES SAKE
RCA Victor (ST) APL1-0388
. . . . *11/73*   **15–20**
Orange label.

RCA Victor (ST) APL1-0388 *77*   **8–10**
Black label, dog near top.

Side A
　Raised on Rock
　Are You Sincere
　Find Out What's Happening
　I Miss You
　Girl of Mine
Side B
　For Ol' Times Sake
　If You Don't Come Back
　Just a Little Bit
　Sweet Angeline
　Three Corn Patches

RECONSIDER BABY
RCA Victor (SP) AFL1-5418
. . . . *4/85*   **5–8**
Blue vinyl.

Side A
　Reconsider Baby
　Tomorrow Night
　So Glad You're Mine
　One Night
　When It Rains, It Really Pours
　My Baby Left Me
　Ain't That Loving You Baby
Side B
　I Feel So Bad
　Down in the Alley
　Hi-Heel Sneakers
　Stranger in My Own Home Town
　Merry Christmas Baby

REFLECTIONS OF ELVIS (3 LP)
Diamond P. Productions (S) *8/77*   **450–500**
Price includes cue sheets. Promotional issue only.

REMEMBERING ELVIS (2 LP)
RCA/Pair (SP) PDL2-1037 . *83*   **20–25**

Record 1
Side 1
　Blue Moon of Kentucky
　Young and Beautiful
　Milkcow Blues Boogie
　Baby Let's Play House
Side 2
　Good Rockin' Tonight
　We're Gonna Move
　I Want to Be Free
　I Forgot to Remember to Forget

Record 2
Side 1
　Kiss Me Quick
　Just for Old Times Sake
　Gonna Get Back Home Somehow
　(Such an) Easy Question
Side 2
　Suspicion
　I Feel That I've Known You Forever
　Night Rider
　Fountain of Love

RETURN OF THE ROCKER
RCA Victor (SP) 5600-1-R *4/86*   **5–8**

Side A
　King of the Whole Wide World
　(Marie's the Name) His Latest Flame
　Little Sister
　A Mess of Blues
　Like a Baby
　I Want You With Me
Side B
　Stuck on You
　Return to Sender
　Make Me Know It
　Witchcraft
　I'm Comin' Home
　Follow That Dream

ROBERT W. SARNOFF—25 YEARS OF RCA LEADERSHIP: See Various-Artists Compilations section.

ROCK 'N' ROLL FOREVER
RCA Victor (M) DM1-0437. *81*   **10–15**
Black label, dog near top. Although the label reads "Stereo," these songs are in true monaural, not reprocessed stereo.
Note: This RCA Special Products LP was offered by Candlelite Music as a bonus to its customers.

Side A
　One Night
　Teddy Bear

Love Me Tender
Don't Be Cruel
I Want You, I Need You, I Love You
Side B
Jailhouse Rock
Heartbreak Hotel
Blue Suede Shoes
Hound Dog
All Shook Up

ROCK AND ROLL ROOTS: see Various-Artists Compilations section.

ROCK ROCK ROCK: see Various-Artists Compilations section.

ROCK, ROLL & REMEMBER: see Various-Artists Compilations section.

ROCK, ROLL & REMEMBER, 1982 (4 LP)

Clark Productions (SP). . . . *82*   **250–300**
Contains 48 songs by Elvis. Price includes four programming sheets. Issued to radio stations only. Also see *ROCK, ROLL & REMEMBER* in Various-Artists Compilations section.

ROCKER

RCA Victor (M) AFM1-5182
. . . . *11/84*   **5–8**
Side A
Jailhouse Rock
Blue Suede Shoes
Tutti Frutti
Lawdy Miss Clawdy
I Got a Woman
Money Honey
Side B
Ready Teddy
Rip It Up
Shake, Rattle and Roll
Long Tall Sally
(You're So Square) Baby I Don't Care
Hound Dog

ROUSTABOUT

RCA Victor (M) LPM-2999
. . . . *10/64*   **60–70**
Black label, with the word "Mono" at the bottom.

RCA Victor (M) LPM-2999
. . . . *64–65*   **25–30**
Black label, with the word "Monaural" at the bottom.

RCA Victor (ST) LSP-2999
. . . . *10/64* **550–750**
Black label, with the RCA logo in silver at the top of the label and the word "Stereo" at the bottom.

RCA Victor (ST) LSP-2999
. . . . *11/64*   **25–30**
Black label, with the RCA logo in white at the top of the label and the word "Stereo" at the bottom.

RCA Victor (ST) LSP-2999
. . . . *68–69*   **10–20**
Orange label.

RCA Victor (ST) LSP-2999 . *76*   **10–15**
Tan label.

RCA Victor (ST) AFL1-2999 *77*   **8–10**
Black label, dog near top.

Side 1
Roustabout
Little Egypt
Poison Ivy League
Hard Knocks
It's a Wonderful World
Big Love, Big Heartache
Side 2
One Track Heart
It's Carnival Time
Carny Town
There's a Brand New Day on the Horizon
Wheels on My Heels

SAVAGE YOUNG ELVIS, THE (Cassette)

RCA Victor DPK1-0679. . . *84*   **5–8**
Cassette tape of a package that was never available on LP. Price is for tape still attached to 12″ × 12″ photo card.

SEPARATE WAYS

RCA/Camden (SP) CAS-2611
. . . . *1/73*   **15–18**
Blue label.

Pickwick/Camden (SP) CAS-2611
. . . . *12/75*   **8–10**
Note: 1973 originals were packaged with a 3″ × 5″ Elvis greeting card, which is included in the above price range. Deduct $5–$10 if this card is missing.

Side 1
Separate Ways
Sentimental Me
In My Way
I Met Her Today
What Now, What Next, Where To
Side 2
Always on My Mind
I Slipped, I Stumbled, I Fell
Is It So Strange
Forget Me Never
Old Shep

SHELBY SINGLETON MUSIC, INC. (AND AFFILIATES) PRESENTS SONGS FOR THE SEVENTIES: see Various-Artists Compilations section.

SINGER PRESENTS ELVIS SINGING FLAMING STAR & OTHERS
RCA Victor (SP) PRS-279 *11/68*   **70-80**
Mustard-color label. "Tiger Man" is monaural on this LP. All other tracks are stereo.

Side 1
  Flaming Star
  Wonderful World
  Night Life
  All I Needed Was the Rain
  Too Much Monkey Business
Side 2
  Yellow Rose of Texas/The Eyes of Texas
  She's a Machine
  Do the Vega
  Tiger Man

60 YEARS OF COUNTRY MUSIC: see Various-Artists Compilations section.

SOCIAL SECURITY PRESENTS DONNA FARGO: see Various-Artists Compilations section.

(DICK CLARK'S) SOLID GOLD: see Various-Artists Compilations section.

SOLID GOLD COUNTRY: see Various-Artists Compilations section.

SOLID GOLD SCRAPBOOK Starring Dick Bartley: see Various-Artists Compilations section.

SOMETHING FOR EVERYBODY
RCA Victor (M) LPM-2370
. . . . *6/61*   **75-90**
Black label, with the words "Long Play" at the bottom of the label. Back cover pictures a scene from "Wild in the Country," and two Compact 33 Singles.

RCA Victor (M) LPM-2370
. . . . *11/63*   **40-50**
Black label, with the word "Mono" at the bottom. Back cover pictures something other than "Wild in the Country" scene and Compact 33 Singles.

RCA Victor (M) LPM-2370. *64*   **25-30**
Black label, with the word "Monaural" at the bottom. Back cover pictures something other

than "Wild in the Country" scene and Compact 33 Singles.

RCA Victor (ST) LSP-2370 *7/61*   **90-100**
Black label, with the words "Living Stereo" at the bottom. Back cover pictures a scene from "Wild in the Country," and two Compact 33 Singles.

RCA Victor (ST) LSP-2370 .   *64*   **25-30**
Black label, with the RCA logo in white at the top of the label and the word "Stereo" at the bottom. Back cover pictures something other than "Wild in the Country" scene and Compact 33 Singles.

RCA Victor (ST) LSP-2370 .   *68*   **10-20**
Orange label. Back cover pictures something other than "Wild in the Country" scene and Compact 33 Singles.

RCA Victor (ST) LSP-2370 .   *76*   **10-15**
Tan label. Back cover pictures something other than "Wild in the Country" scene and Compact 33 Singles.

RCA Victor (ST) AFL1-2370 *77*   **8-10**
Black label, dog near top.

RCA Victor (ST) AYM1-4116
. . . . *9/81*   **5-10**
Black label, dog near top. Issued as part of RCA's "Best Buy" series.

Side 1
  There's Always Me
  Give Me the Right
  It's a Sin
  Sentimental Me
  Starting Today
  Gently
Side 2
  I'm Comin' Home
  In Your Arms
  Put the Blame on Me
  Judy
  I Want You with Me
  I Slipped, I Stumbled, I Fell

SONGS FOR THE SEVENTIES: see SHELBY SINGLETON MUSIC, INC. (AND AFFILIATES) PRESENTS SONGS FOR THE SEVENTIES in Various-Artists Compilations section.

SOUND IDEAS: see Various-Artists Compilations section.

SOUND OF '77: see Various-Artists Compilations section.

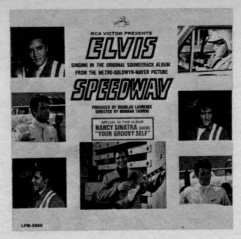

A rare mono record in an era when stereo was the rule.

**SOUNDS OF SOLID GOLD: see
UNITED STATES ARMED
SERVICES PROGRAM.**

**SPECIAL PALM SUNDAY
PROGRAMMING: see ELVIS
PRESLEY—SPECIAL PALM
SUNDAY PROGRAMMING**

SPEEDWAY
RCA Victor (M) LPM-3839 *6/68*   **800–900**
Black label, with the word "Monaural" at the
bottom.

RCA Victor (ST) LSP-3989 *6/68*   **40–50**
Black label, with the RCA logo in white at the
top of the label and the word "Stereo" at the
bottom.

RCA Victor (ST) LSP-3989
. . . . *68–69*   **10–20**
Orange label.

RCA Victor (ST) LSP-3989 .   *76*   **10–15**
Tan label.

RCA Victor (ST) AFL1-3989   *77*   **8–10**
Black label, dog near top.
Note: 1968 originals were issued with an 8″ ×
10″ color photo, which is included in the above
price range. Deduct $15–$25 if this photo is
missing. This was the last black label RCA
Elvis LP release of the sixties. The next release,
Elvis (NBC-TV Special), began several years of
orange label issues. This is the only standard

catalog Elvis release to contain a solo track by
another artist (Nancy Sinatra).

Side 1
  Speedway
  There Ain't Nothing Like a Song (duet with
    Nancy Sinatra)
  Your Time Hasn't Come Yet, Baby
  Who Are You (Who Am I)
  He's Your Uncle, Not Your Dad
  Let Yourself Go
Side 2
  Your Groovy Self (Nancy Sinatra solo)
  Five Sleepy Heads
  Western Union
  Mine
  Goin' Home
  Suppose

**SPECIAL CHRISTMAS
PROGRAMMING**
RCA Victor (M) UNRM-5697
. . . . *11/67*   **800–1000**
Contains the same material as is heard on the
reel tape, EPC-1. Promotional issue only.
Note: A 10-inch bootleg issue of this material,
on red vinyl, exists. There was never a legitimate release of this program on a 10-inch LP.

  Here Comes Santa Claus
  Blue Christmas
  O Little Town of Bethlehem
  Silent Night

I'll Be Home for Christmas
I Believe
If Everyday Was Like Christmas
How Great Thou Art
His Hand in Mine
Special Elvis Christmas Message
I'll Be Home for Christmas

SPECIAL CHRISTMAS PROGRAMMING (Reel Tape)

RCA Victor (M) EPC-1 . *11/67* **300–325**
A full-track, 7½ ips reel tape provided to radio stations for the December 3, 1967, airing of the Elvis Christmas Special. Promotional issue only.

Note: Originally issued with a color script and programming information insert. Deduct $25 if this insert is missing. Also included in this package was a promo copy, with sleeve, of "If Everyday Was Like Christmas." See this listing and deduct appropriately if this single is missing. This tape was also sent in a special mailer.

Here Comes Santa Claus
Blue Christmas
O Little Town of Bethlehem
Silent Night
I'll Be Home for Christmas
I Believe
If Everyday Was Like Christmas
How Great Thou Art
His Hand in Mine
Special Elvis Christmas Message
I'll Be Home for Christmas

SPECIAL PALM SUNDAY PROGRAMMING

RCA Victor (M) SP-33-461 *4/67* **500–600**
White label. A complete 30-minute radio program. Promotional issue only.

Note: A script and programming information packet was sent along with this disc and is included in the above price range. Deduct $125 if these sheets are missing. Also, this LP has been counterfeited, but originals can easily be identified by the stamped matrix numbers in the vinyl trail-off. Fakes have those numbers hand etched.

Side 1
How Great Thou Art
In the Garden
Somebody Bigger Than You and I
Stand by Me
Side 2
Without Him
Where Could I Go But to the Lord
Where No One Stands Alone

Crying in the Chapel
How Great Thou Art (excerpt)

SPINOUT

RCA Victor (M) LPM-3702
. . . . *10/66* **65–75**
Black label, with the word "Monaural" at the bottom.

RCA Victor (ST) LSP-3702
. . . . *10/66* **65–75**
Black label, with the RCA logo in white at the top of the label and the word "Stereo" at the bottom.

RCA Victor (ST) APL1-2560
. . . . *9/77* **8–10**
Black label, dog near top.

RCA Victor (ST) AYL1-3684
. . . . *5/80* **5–10**
Black label, dog near top.

Note: 1966 originals were packaged with a bonus 12" × 12" color photo, which is included in the above price range. Deduct $25–$30 if this photo is missing.

Side 1
Stop, Look and Listen
Adam and Evil
All That I Am
Never Say Yes
Am I Ready
Beach Shack
Side 2
Spinout
Smorgasbord
I'll Be Back
Tomorrow Is a Long Time
Down in the Alley
I'll Remember You

SUN COLLECTION, THE

RCA Victor (M) HY-1001. *8/75* **20–25**
Green label English import, widely distributed in the United States. Does not say "Starcall" on the label.

RCA Victor (M) HY-1001 *10/75* **15–20**
Green label, with "Starcall" on the label.

Note: The back cover for the first version listed above has ads for other albums in the Starcall series. The back cover for the issue with Starcall on the label has discographical and session information on it.

Side A
That's All Right
Blue Moon of Kentucky
I Don't Care If the Sun Don't Shine
Good Rockin' Tonight
Milkcow Blues Boogie
You're a Heartbreaker

I'm Left, You're Right, She's Gone
Baby Let's Play House
Side B
  Mystery Train
  I Forgot to Remember to Forget
  I'll Never Let You Go
  Tryin' to Get to You
  I Love You Because *(standard version)*
  Blue Moon
  Just Because
  I Love You Because *(newly discovered track)*

SUN SESSIONS, THE
RCA Victor (M) APM1-1675
. . . . *3/76*   **12–15**
Tan label. This was the U.S. version of *The Sun Collection.*

RCA Victor (M) AFM1-1675 *77*   **8–10**
Black label, dog near top.

RCA Victor (ST) AYM1-3893
. . . . *2/81*   **5–8**
Note: This was the first of only two Elvis LPs, in the standard catalog, to be issued originally on the tan label. The other was *From Elvis Presley Boulevard, Memphis, Tennessee.*

Side A
  That's All Right
  Blue Moon of Kentucky
  I Don't Care If the Sun Don't Shine
  Good Rockin' Tonight
  Milkcow Blues Boogie
  You're a Heartbreaker
  I'm Left, You're Right, She's Gone
  Baby, Let's Play House
Side B
  Mystery Train
  I Forgot to Remember to Forget
  I'll Never Leave You
  Tryin' to Get to You
  I Love You Because *(standard version)*
  Blue Moon
  Just Because
  I Love You Because *(newly discovered track)*

SUN STORY, THE: see
Various-Artists Compilations section.

SUN YEARS (INTERVIEWS AND
MEMORIES): see *THE SUN YEARS*
(INTERVIEWS AND MEMORIES).

SUPER SONGS: see Various-Artists
Compilations section.

THAT'S THE WAY IT IS: see
ELVIS—THAT'S THE WAY IT IS.

THE AGE OF ROCK: see
Various-Artists Compilations section.

THE BRIGHTEST STARS OF
CHRISTMAS: see Various-Artists
Compilations section.

THE ELVIS PRESLEY STORY: see
ELVIS PRESLEY STORY, THE.

THE ELVIS STORY: see *ELVIS*
STORY, THE.

THE ELVIS PRESLEY SUN
COLLECTION: see *SUN*
COLLECTION, THE.

THE ELVIS TAPES
Great Northwest Music Company
(M) GNW-4005. . . . . . *10/77*   **10–15**

THE FIRST YEAR
Golden Editions Limited (M)
GEL-101 . . . . *79*   **15–25**
Print in upper corners on front cover is in gold. Label is white. Includes a 12-page booklet and one-page copy of a 1954 Elvis/Scotty Moore contract, which represents $5–$8 of the value. *Note:* Most of the material on this LP was previously issued on *The First Years,* HALW 00001.

Golden Editions Limited (M)
KING-1 . . . . *6/79*   **10–20**
Print in upper corners on front cover is in white. Label is black. Includes 12-page booklet and one-page copy of a 1954 Elvis/Scotty Moore contract, which represents $5–$8 of the value.

Side 1
  Biff Collie Interview
  There's Good Rockin' Tonight
  Baby, Let's Play House
  Blue Moon of Kentucky
  I've Got a Woman
  That's All Right Little Mama
  Elvis Interview (with Bob Hoffer)
Side 2
  Scotty Moore Tells the Story of the First
  Year

THE FIRST YEARS
HALW Inc. (M) HALW-00001
. . . . *12/78*   **60–75**
This "Special Limited Edition" had a serial number stamped in the upper right corner of the cover. Also, Side 2 is titled "Elvis Presley Live."

HALW (M) 0001. . . . . . . *78*   **35–45**
Without serial number stamped on front cover. This LP was repackaged in 1979 on Golden Editions 1.

Note: This LP incorrectly states that the live recordings are from a concert at Cook's Hoedown Club in Houston, Texas. The concert was actually at the Eagle's Hall in Houston.

Side 1
  Scotty Moore Talks About Elvis
Side 2
  Good Rockin' Tonight
  Baby Let's Play House
  Blue Moon of Kentucky
  I Got a Woman
  That's All Right

THE FRANTIC FIFTIES: see Various-Artists Compilations section.

THE GREATEST SHOW ON EARTH: see *GREATEST SHOW ON EARTH, THE.*

THE LEGEND OF A KING
Associated Broadcasters (M) AB1-1001 . . . . *8/80* **125–150**
Special white label demonstration disc, with highlights from the three-hour radio program.
Note: Packaged with this LP was an insert with information on obtaining the picture disc from Associated Broadcasters, which is included in the above price range.

Associated Broadcasters (M) 1001
. . . . *80* **25–30**
Picture disc. First pressings were numbered from 3000 through 6000. Number appears under "Side One" on the disc itself. Cover is standard, die-cut, picture disc cover. Several spelling errors on back cover, including "idle"

for idol and "Jordinaires" instead of Jordanaires.

Associated Broadcasters (M) 1001
. . . . *80* **20–25**
Picture disc. Second pressings were numbered from 6001 through 9000. Most of the spelling errors were corrected on this cover.

Associated Broadcasters (M) 1001
. . . . *80* **15–20**
Picture disc. Third pressings were numbered from 00001 through 02999 and 09001 through 15000. Cover errors have all been corrected.

Associated Broadcasters (M) 1001
. . . . *84* **10–12**
Picture disc. Fourth pressings were also numbered from 3000 through 6000, but were packaged in a clear plastic sleeve instead of a conventional cover.

Associated Broadcasters (M) 1001
. . . . *85* **8–10**
Picture disc. Discs are not numbered. Packaged in a plastic sleeve.

Associated Broadcasters (SP) 1A-3E *85* **200–250**
A three-hour, three-LP set. Not boxed. Price includes six pages of cue sheets. Available to radio stations only.

Associated Broadcasting (SP) 1A-3E *85* **300–350**
Same as above but packaged in a specially printed box.

Associated broadcasters (SP) 1A-3E *86* **300–350**

To get the one, you had to have the other. Included with the demonstration disc was an order form one could use to get the picture disc.

Three-LP boxed set, same as above except time on segment 1-B is increased from 14:25 to 15:15 in order to include a Johnny Bernero interview.

Side 1
Rhythm and Blues collage
Old Shep
Sweet Sweet Spirit
That's All Right
Blue Moon of Kentucky/That's All Right (reprise)
Good Rockin' Tonight (reprise)
My Baby's Gone
I'm Left, You're Right, She's Gone
Baby Let's Play House
Mystery Train
Side 2
Heartbreak Hotel
Hound Dog
Don't Be Cruel
Love Me Tender
Loving You
Teddy Bear
Got a Lot of Living to Do
Jailhouse Rock
King Creole
G.I. Blues
Flaming Star
Blue Hawaii
Girls! Girls! Girls!
Trouble
Lawdy Miss Clawdy
You Gave Me a Mountain

Side 3
All Shook Up
Peace in the Valley
Wear My Ring Around Your Neck
A Fool Such As I
My Wish Came True
It's Now or Never
Side 4
Are You Lonesome Tonight?
Surrender
Can't Help Falling in Love
Blue Hawaii
Soundtrack song collage
Return to Sender
Little Sister
If I Can Dream
Suspicious Minds
Side 5
Johnny B. Goode
Separate Ways
Welcome to My World
Moody Blue
Way Down

How Great Thou Art
My Way
Side 6
Memories
Beyond the Reef
Hound Dog
Guitar Man (original version)
Guitar Man (1980 version)
Danny Boy
Write to Me from Naples
American Trilogy

THE LEGENDARY MAGIC OF ELVIS PRESLEY: see *LEGENDARY MAGIC OF ELVIS PRESLEY, THE.*

THE LEGENDARY RECORDINGS OF ELVIS PRESLEY: see *LEGENDARY RECORDINGS OF ELVIS PRESLEY, THE.*

THE SUN COLLECTION: see *SUN COLLECTION, THE.*

THE SUN SESSIONS: see *SUN SESSIONS, THE.*

THE SUN STORY: see Various-Artists Compilations section.

THE SUN YEARS (INTERVIEWS & MEMORIES)
Sun (M) 1001 . . . . *9/77*   **75–80**
Light yellow label, 1950's style with "Memphis, Tennessee" at the bottom. Light yellow cover with light brown printing.

Sun (M) 1001 . . . . *9/77*   **10–15**
Yellow label, with "Nashville, U.S.A." at the bottom. Yellow cover with dark brown printing.

Sun (M) 1001 . . . . *9/77*   **20–25**
Yellow label, with "Nashville, U.S.A." at the bottom. White cover with brown printing.

THE WORLD IN SOUND—1977: see *WORLD IN SOUND* **in Various-Artists Compilations section.**

30 YEARS OF NO. 1 COUNTRY HITS: see Various-Artists Compilations section.

THIS IS ELVIS (2 LP)
RCA victor (SP) CPL2-4031
. . . . *4/80*   **10–15**
Black label, dog near top. Double-pocket jacket, with special inner-sleeves.

Note: Though not announced as such, "Memories" is an alternate take on this LP. It is also the only time this song has been issued in true stereo.

Side A
  (Marie's The Name) His Latest Flame
  Moody Blue
  That's All Right
  Shake, Rattle and Roll/Flip, Flop and Fly *(unreleased, from the Dorsey TV show)*
  Heartbreak Hotel *(unreleased, from the Dorsey TV show)*
  Hound Dog *(unreleased, from the Milton Berle Show)*
  Excerpt from Hy Gardner interview *(unreleased)*
  My Baby Left Me
Side B
  Merry Christmas Baby
  Mean Woman Blues *(unreleased)*
  Don't Be Cruel *(unreleased, from the Ed Sullivan Show)*
  (Let Me Be Your) Teddy Bear
  Jailhouse Rock
  Army Swearing In *(unreleased)*
  G.I. Blues
  Excerpt from Departure for Germany Press Conference ("Elvis Sails")
  Excerpt from Home from Germany Press Conference *(unreleased)*
Side C
  Too Much Monkey Business *(unreleased)*
  Love Me Tender
  I Got a Thing About You Baby
  I Need Your Love Tonight
  Blue Suede Shoes *(unreleased)*
  Viva Las Vegas
  Suspicious Minds/Excerpt from JC's Award to Elvis *(unreleased)*
  Promised Land
Side D
  Excerpt from Madison Square Garden Press Conference *(unreleased)*
  Always on My Mind *(unreleased)*
  Are You Lonesome Tonight?
  My Way
  An American Trilogy *(unreleased)*
  Memories

TIME-LIFE TREASURY OF CHRISTMAS, THE: see **Various-Artists Compilations section.**

TO ELVIS: LOVE STILL BURNING
Fotoplay (SP) FSP-1001 . . *5/78* **40–50**
Special collector's preview copy. This advance issue, before jackets were ready, consisted of a disc and a printed 11″ × 11″ insert. Both were in a plastic bag.

Fotoplay (SP) FSP-1001 . . *5/78* **20–25**
LP does not have "Side One" and "Side Two" printed on the disc. Cover is white with black printing.

Fotoplay (SP) FSP-1001 . . *6/78* **15–20**
White cover. LP has "Side One" and "Side Two" printed on the disc.

Fotoplay (SP) FSP-1001 . . *8/78* **10–12**
Black cover with white printing. LP has "Side One" and "Side Two" printed on the disc.
Note: This LP contains 11 Elvis tribute songs. An Elvis portrait appears on both sides of the disc, which is why it's listed here and not in the Various-Artists Compilations section.

Side 1
  I Remember Elvis Presley (Danny Mirror)
  What Will We Do Without You (Bobby Fisher)
  Goodbye King of Rock & Roll (Leon Everette)
  Dark Cloud over Memphis (Johnny Tillison)
  Candy Bars for Elvis (Barry Tiffin)
  Goodbye Elvis (Jim Whittington)
Side 2
  The Day the Beat Stopped (Ral Donner)
  Just a Country Boy (Frankie Allen)
  Elvis, the Man from Tupelo (George Pickard)
  For Every Star That Rises (Michael Morgan)
  The Passing of a King (Tony Copeland)
"Candy Bars for Elvis" and "Just a Country Boy" are monaural on this LP.

TODAY: see *ELVIS TODAY.*

TOP TEN HITS, THE (2 LP)
RCA Victor (SP) 6383-1-R *7/87* **10–15**
Includes a bonus color 15″ × 22″ poster and "Elvis Talks" LP flyer.

Side A
  Heartbreak Hotel
  I Want You, I Need You, I Love You
  Hound Dog
  Don't Be Cruel
  Love Me Tender
  Love Me
  Too Much
  All Shook Up
  Teddy Bear
  Jailhouse Rock

Side B
Don't
I Beg of You
Wear My Ring Around Your Neck
Hard Headed Woman
One Night
I Got Stung
A Fool Such As I
I Need Your Love Tonight
Big Hunk O' Love

Side C
Stuck on You
It's Now or Never
Are You Lonesome Tonight?
Surrender
I Feel So Bad
Little Sister
His Latest Flame
Can't Help Falling in Love
Good Luck Charm
She's Not You

Side D
Return to Sender
Devil in Disguise
Bossa Nova Baby
Crying in the Chapel
In the Ghetto
Suspicious Minds
Don't Cry Daddy
The Wonder of You
Burning Love

**TRANSCRIBED RADIO
INTERVIEW WITH JERRY
LEIBER AND MIKE STOLLER
FOR JAILHOUSE ROCK**
MGM Air-View (M) MGM-12-
232. . . . . *10/57*   **300–350**
With commentary by Dick Simmons. This red
vinyl transcription contains an interview with
"Jailhouse Rock" songwriters Jerry Leiber and
Mike Stoller. It does not feature Elvis at all.
Note: Issued with an interview transcript,
which is included in the above price range. De-
duct $50–$60 if this transcript is missing. The
second side of this disc contains the same interview, without the announcer, for open-end
broadcast.

TRIBUTE TO ELVIS, A
Country Sessions U.S.A. (S) 126
. . . . *83*   **225–250**
Price includes cue sheets. Promotional issue
only.

TRIBUTE TO DORSEY, VOLUME 1
RCA Victor (M) LPM-1432 *4/57*   **15–25**
An album by Tommy Dorsey and His Orchestra. Of interest to Elvis collectors because of a
picture of Elvis and the Dorsey Brothers,
Tommy and Jimmy, on the back cover. The
photo was taken when Elvis appeared on their
TV show, the same one pictured on the inner
sleeve for Side 3 in *Elvis—a Golden Celebration.*
A photo of Elvis on the LP of another artist is
rare, and this was the first time it was done.

**25 YEARS IN LOWERY COUNTRY:
see Various-Artists Compilations
section.**

**UNITED STATES ARMED FORCES
PROGRAMS**
Hundreds of radio programming discs have
been issued by the various branches of the service. These specially produced LPs may be
made for public service broadcasting and contain an assortment of tunes by various artists.
Any of these that contains Elvis' music could
fall into the $10–$20 range for near-mint copies,
depending on the year of release and amount of
packaging. Complete box sets, such as the U.S.
Marine Corps *Sound of Solid Gold* series, can
bring around $40–$60. Other kinds of Armed
Forces LPs are those specially made for airing
on Armed Forces Radio Network stations.
These discs usually contain the same songs as
the commercially released version of the LP.
Several of these were produced using Elvis albums, and these should fall into the $50–$100
range for near-mint copies. It should also be
noted that Armed Forces discs can be found as
16-inch LPs, in addition to standard 12-inch
LPs.

VALENTINE GIFT FOR YOU, A
RCA Victor (SP) AFL1-5353
. . . . *2/85*   **8–10**
Red vinyl.
RCA Victor AFL1-5353 . . *8/85*   **5–8**
Black vinyl.

Side A
Are You Lonesome Tonight?
I Need Somebody to Lean On
Young and Beautiful
Playing for Keeps
Tell Me Why
Give Me the Right
It Feels So Right

Side B
I Was the One
Fever

Tomorrow Is a Long Time
Love Letters
Fame and Fortune
Can't Help Falling in Love

WRCA PLAYS THE HITS FOR YOUR CUSTOMERS: see Various-Artists Compilations section.

WELCOME TO MY WORLD
RCA Victor (SP) APL1-2274
. . . . 3/77   **10–15**
Black label, dog near top.

RCA Victor (SP) AFL1-2274   77   **8–10**
Black label, dog near top.

RCA Victor (SP) AQL1-2274   77   **5–10**
Black label, dog near top.
Note: This was the first Elvis LP to be issued on the newer black label, with the dog near the top.

Side A
Welcome to My World
Help Me Make It Through the Night
Release Me (and Let Me Love Again)
I Really Don't Want to Know
For the Good Times
Side B
Make the World Go Away
Gentle on My Mind
I'm So Lonesome I Could Cry
Your Cheatin' Heart
I Can't Stop Loving You *(unreleased live version)*

WHITE CHRISTMAS, VOLS. 1 AND 2: see Various-Artists Compilations section.

WORLD OF ELVIS PRESLEY, THE
World of Elvis Presley 1-30   4/83   **50–75**
A one-hour weekly radio show, on discs numbered Program 1 through Program 30. The show began in April and ceased operation after 30 programs. Each disc was accompanied by a cue sheet, included in the price. Value shown is for any one of the discs.

WORLDWIDE 50 GOLD AWARD HITS, VOL. 1 (4 LP)
RCA Victor (M) LPM-6401   8/70   **60–75**
Orange label. Four-LP box set.

RCA Victor (M) LPM-6401.   76   **30–40**
Tan label.

RCA Victor (M) LPM-6401.   77   **20–25**
Black label, dog near top.
Note: Originally packaged with a 20-page, color, bonus photo booklet, which is included in the above price range. Deduct $10–$20 if this booklet is missing. Black label issues omitted this booklet.

Side 1
Heartbreak Hotel
I Was the One
I Want You, I Need You, I Love You
Don't Be Cruel
Hound Dog
Love Me Tender

These two box sets resemble the LP package, except that they contained double eight-track and cassette versions of the set.

Side 2
Anyway You Want Me
Too Much
Playing for Keeps
All Shook Up
That's When Your Heartaches Begin
Loving You
Side 3
Teddy Bear
Jailhouse Rock
Treat Me Nice
I Beg of You
Don't
Wear My Ring Around Your Neck
Hard Headed Woman
Side 4
I Got Stung
A Fool Such As I
A Big Hunk O' Love
Stuck on You
A Mess of Blues
It's Now or Never
Side 5
I Gotta Know
Are You Lonesome Tonight
Surrender
I Feel So Bad
Little Sister
Can't Help Falling in Love
Side 6
Rock-a-Hula Baby
Anything That's Part of You
Good Luck Charm
She's Not You
Return to Sender
Where Do You Come From
One Broken Heart for Sale
Side 7
Devil in Disguise
Bossa Nova Baby
Kissin' Cousins
Viva Las Vegas
Ain't That Loving You Baby
Wooden Heart
Side 8
Crying in the Chapel
If I Can Dream
In the Ghetto
Suspicious Minds
Don't Cry Daddy
Kentucky Rain
Excerpts from "Elvis Sails"

WORLDWIDE 50 GOLD AWARD HITS, VOL. 2—ELVIS, THE OTHER SIDES
RCA Victor (M) LPM-6402 *8/71*   **60–75**
Orange label. Four-LP box set.

RCA Victor (M) LPM-6402. *76*   **30–40**
Tan label.
RCA Victor (M) LPM-6402. *77*   **25–35**
Black label, dog near top.
Note: Originally packaged with special envelope, supposedly containing a piece of Elvis' wardrobe, and a folded color portrait print of Elvis, which are included in the above price range. Deduct $10–$20 if these materials are missing. Black label issues omitted these materials.

Side 1
Puppet on a String
Witchcraft
Trouble
Poor Boy
I Want To Be Free
Doncha' Think It's Time
Young Dreams
Side 2
The Next Step Is Love
You Don't Have to Say You Love Me
Paralyzed
My Wish Came True
When My Blue Moon Turns to Gold Again
Lonesome Cowboy
Side 3
My Baby Left Me
It Hurts Me
I Need Your Love Tonight
Tell Me Why
Please Don't Drag That String Around
Young and Beautiful
Side 4
Hot Dog
New Orleans
We're Gonna Move
Crawfish
King Creole
I Believe in the Man in the Sky
Dixieland Rock
Side 5
The Wonder of You
They Remind Me Too Much of You
Mean Woman Blues
Lonely Man
Any Day Now
Don't Ask Me Why
Side 6
His Latest Flame
I Really Don't Want to Know
Baby I Don't Care
I've Lost You
Let Me
Love Me

Side 7
Got a Lot O' Livin to Do
Fame and Fortune
Rip It Up
There Goes My Everything
Lover Doll
One Night
Side 8
Just Tell Her Jim Said Hello
Ask Me
Patch It Up
As Long As I Have You
You'll Think of Me
Wild in the Country

WORLDWIDE GOLD AWARD HITS, PARTS 1 & 2 (2 LP)

RCA Victor (M) R-213690 . *74* . **75–100**
RCA Record Club. Orange label.

RCA Victor (M) R-213690 . *76* **25–30**
RCA Record Club. Tan label.

RCA Victor (M) R-213690 . *77* **12–15**
RCA Record Club. Black label, dog near top.

Side 1
Heartbreak Hotel
I Was the One
I Want You, I Need You, I Love You
Don't Be Cruel
Hound Dog
Love Me Tender
Side 2
Anyway You Want Me
Too Much
Playing for Keeps
All Shook Up
That's When Your Heartaches Begin
Loving You
Side 3
Teddy Bear
Jailhouse Rock
Treat Me Nice
I Beg of You
Don't
Wear My Ring Around Your Neck
Hard Headed Woman
Side 4
I Got Stung
A Fool Such As I
A Big Hunk O' Love
Stuck on You
A Mess of Blues
It's Now or Never

WORLDWIDE GOLD AWARD HITS, PARTS 3 & 4 (2 LP)

RCA Victor (M) R-214657 . *78* **12–15**
RCA Record Club. Black label, dog near top.

Side 1
I Gotta Know
Are You Lonesome Tonight
Surrender
I Feel So Bad
Little Sister
Can't Help Falling in Love
Side 2
Rock-a-Hula Baby
Anything That's Part of You
Good Luck Charm
She's Not You
Return to Sender
Where Do You Come From
One Broken Heart for Sale
Side 3
Devil in Disguise
Bossa Nova Baby
Kissin' Cousins
Viva Las Vegas
Ain't That Loving You Baby
Wooden Heart
Side 4
Crying in the Chapel
If I Can Dream
In the Ghetto
Suspicious Minds
Don't Cry Daddy
Kentucky Rain
Excerpts from "Elvis Sails"

YOU'LL NEVER WALK ALONE

RCA/Camden (SP) CALX-2472
. . . . *3/71* **15–18**
Blue label.

Pickwick/Camden (SP) CAS-2472
. . . . *12/75* **8–10**
Note: Even though the label identifies this as a mono LP, "You'll Never Walk Alone," "Who Am I," "Let Us Pray" and "We Call On Him" are true stereo.

Side 1
You'll Never Walk Alone
Who Am I
Let Us Pray
Peace in the Valley
We Call on Him
Side 2
I Believe
It Is No Secret
Sing You Children
Take My Hand Precious Lord

Various Artists Compilations

One of the more complicated areas of Elvis record collecting is the realm of various artists compilations. From in-store samplers to syndicated radio programs to TV mail-order records and music to accompany Tupperware parties, Elvis' recordings have popped up in all kinds of places. For the purposes of this guide, we have divided these various artists compilations first by format (EP, LP), then alphabetically by title. Ideally, we would list every artist and track listed in these recordings, but space is limited. With rare exception, you will find the reference to the Elvis track and its location in the set under each listing.

EPs

GREAT COUNTRY/WESTERN HITS (10 EP)
RCA Victor SPD-26 . . . *11/56* **900–1000**
A 10-EP boxed set, packaged with special RCA paper inserts. There was also a plain cardboard slip cover for the entire box. The set devotes one EP to Elvis. "Milkcow Blues Boogie" is listed on the label as "Milkcow Boogie Blues."
RCA Victor SPD-26 (599-9141)
. . . . *11/56* **200–250**

Elvis contents:
Side 6
  Blue Moon of Kentucky
  Love Me Tender
Side 15
  Mystery Train
  Milkcow Boogie Blues

PERFECT FOR PARTIES HIGHLIGHT ALBUM (EP)
RCA Victor SPA-7-37 . . *11/56* **75–90**
Black label, dog on top. With horizontal silver line. Promotional issue only.

RCA Victor SPA-7-37 . . *11/56* **75–90**
Black label, dog on top. Without horizontal silver line.

RCA Victor SPA-7-37 . . *11/56* **90–100**
Picture sleeve. Special paper sleeve. Listed separately since the disc often is offered for sale without the sleeve.
Note: Features Elvis' spoken instructions to all tracks as well as his song "Love Me." Counterfeit copies exist of this EP, but they are on a white label and can easily be identified.

Elvis contents:
Side 1
  Love Me (Track 1)

POP TRANSCRIBED 30-SECOND SPOT WITH VAUGHN MONROE
RCA Victor J8OW-3736/7 *4/58* **400–500**
Promotional issue only. Announcer, Vaughn Monroe, gives sales pitch and features excerpts from four new RCA albums, including *Elvis' Golden Records,* slightly mistitled on the EP.

Elvis may not have recorded all the tracks on this EP, but he is featured everywhere, as he personally introduces all the songs.

Elvis contents:
Side A
  Elvis Golden Record Album (Elvis Presley)

PRO-12
RCA Victor PRO-12 . . . *12/56*   **750–800**
White label. Promotional issue only.

RCA Victor PRO-12 . . . *12/56*   **750–800**
Special sleeve. Specially printed sleeve for radio station WOHO, Toledo, Ohio. We have yet to learn of RCA preparing this same sleeve for any other radio station.

Elvis contents:
Side 1
  Old Shep (Track 1)

RCA FAMILY RECORD CENTER (33)
RCA Victor PR-121 . . . . *2/62* **1000–1200**

White label. In-store promotional issue with an announcer playing the latest RCA releases and promoting the artists

Elvis contents:
Side 1
  Good Luck Charm (Track 1)

SAVE-ON-RECORDS (BULLETIN FOR JUNE)
RCA Victor SPA-7-27 . . . *6/56*   **200–225**
Special issue to "coupon book" record buyers, sampling the latest RCA product. "I'm Gonna Sit Right Down and Cry (over You)," shown as "Gonna Sit Right Down and Cry." Price for disc only.

RCA Victor SPA-7-27 . . . *6/56*   **500–525**
Picture sleeve.

Record companies work hard to get people to hear their releases. (A) One way is to create special promotional packages with local radio stations. (B) Another is to produce in-store promotional records that people will hear as they buy records. (C) Another is to offer a terrific deal by mail. Various artists compilations like these are among the most highly prized Elvis record collectibles.

Elvis contents:
Side 1
  Gonna Sit Right Down And Cry (Track 3)

SDS-7-2 (DEALER'S PREVUE)

RCA Victor SDS-7-2. . . . *6/57* 700–750
White label, promotional issue only. Sent to record dealers in a special picture envelope.

RCA Victor SDS-7-2. . . . *6/57* 350–400
Mailing envelope with "Elvis Presley at His Greatest" banner and Elvis photo.

Elvis contents:
Side 1
  Loving You (Track 1)
  Teddy Bear (Track 2)

SDS-57-39 (DEALER'S PREVUE)

RCA Victor SDS 57–39 . *10/57* 600–650
White label, promotional issue only.

RCA Victor SDS-57-39 . *10/57* 350–400
Mailing envelope for this EP.

Elvis contents:
Side 1
  Jailhouse Rock (Track 3)
  Treat Me Nice (Track 4)

SPA 7-27: see SAVE-ON-RECORDS (BULLETIN FOR JUNE).

SPA 7-61 (EXTENDED PLAY SAMPLER)

RCA Victor SPA-7-61 . . *10/57* 1000–1200
Black label, dog on top. This EP offered a sampling of RCA's latest EP issues. From EPA-4114 the Elvis track here is "Jailhouse Rock."

SPD-15 (10 EP)

RCA Victor SPD-15 . . . . *1/56* 2500–3500
Black labels. Only one of the 10 EPs in this set is by Elvis. Despite widespread publicity given this item, there have been no discoveries of a box or package for these discs. Since no sales have taken place, the estimated value range is

based on offers as well as the sales of the similar, but more common, SPD-19. Price is for complete package, which probably includes paper inserts, etc.

RCA Victor SPD-15 (Elvis disc 9089, black label). *1/56* 750–900
Price is for the Elvis EP from SPD-15, by itself.

RCA Victor SPD-15 . . . . *1/56* 2500–3500
Gray labels, for jukebox operators. Price is for complete package, which probably includes paper inserts, title strips, etc.

RCA Victor SPD-15 (Elvis disc 9089, gray label) *1/56* 600–700
Price is for the Elvis EP from SPD-15 by itself.

SPD-19: see THE SOUND OF LEADERSHIP.

THE SOUND OF LEADERSHIP (SOUVENIR OF THE MIAMI MEETING, JUNE 1956) (8 EP)

RCA Victor SPD-19 . . . . *6/56* 1800–2200
An eight-EP gray label boxed set, packaged with "The Sound of Leadership" paper insert, set contains 32 RCA million-sellers and was prepared as a souvenir for company distributors attending the June 1956 Miami meeting.

RCA Victor SPD-19 . . . . *6/56* 750–800
Price for the Elvis disc by itself.

Elvis contents:
Side 16
  Heartbreak Hotel (1956)
  (Elvis Presley)

TUPPERWARE'S HIT PARADE (33)

Tupperware THP-11973 . . *1/73* 50–75
Special EP, containing segments of 11 hits by various artists, including "All Shook Up." Distributed to Tupperware sales representatives.

WOHO FEATURING RCA VICTOR: see PRO-12.

LPs

A CHRONOLOGY OF AMERICAN MUSIC: see CHRONOLOGY OF AMERICAN MUSIC, A.

AGE OF ROCK: see THE AGE OF ROCK.

ALL-STAR ROCK (VOL. II): see ROCK, ROCK, ROCK (ALL-STAR ROCK, VOL. II).

ALL-TIME CHRISTMAS FAVORITES (5 LP)

Collector's Edition (SP) CE-505
. . . . *11/78* 250–275
Note: One side of one LP in this box set is by Elvis, and features:

  O Come All Ye Faithful (shown as "Come All Ye Faithful")
  The First Noel (shown as "Noel")

Elvis' many Christmas recordings have become a standard part of our holiday listening.

If I Get Home on Christmas Day (shown as "I'll Be Home for Christmas")
Silver Bells
Winter Wonderland (shown as "Walking in a Winter Wonderland")
The label name is shown on the box as "Collector's Edition" and on the labels as "Collector's Addition." The Elvis songs are true stereo.

ALL TIME GREATS, VOL. 1
Promo (S)   20–30
A various-artists collection, containing one Elvis track.

ALL TIME GREATS, VOL. 3
Promo (S)   20–30
A various-artists collection, containing one Elvis track.

AMERICAN CHRISTMAS, AN (12 LP)
Otis Conner Productions (SP)
. . . . *12/84*   150–200
Boxed set from the archives of *The Saturday Evening Post.* Issued only to radio stations. Includes 14 pages of script and cue sheets.

Elvis contents:
Hour 1
    Blue Christmas (Side 2, Segment 5)
Hour 3
    Silent Night (Side 2, Segment 4)
Hour 7
    Santa Claus Is Back in Town (Side 2, Segment 4)
Hour 10
    Silver Bells (Side 2, Segment 4)
Hour 12
    Merry Christmas Baby (Side 1, Segment 1)

AMERICAN TOP 40
Any of the *American Top 40* boxed sets containing an Elvis track should fall into the $30–$60 range.

AVON VALENTINE FAVORITES
RCA Victor (ST) DPL1-0751
. . . . *1/86*   10–15
Available only from Avon representatives as a bonus item. Packaged in a specially printed cardboard mailer that is included in the price.

Two various artists albums were offered by Avon: first a collection of Christmas songs; next, a group of "love" songs for Valentine's Day.

Elvis contents:
Side 2
  Can't Help Falling in Love (Track 3)
BEST OF CHRISTMAS, THE
RCA Victor (ST) CPL1-7013
. . . . *11/85*   **8–10**
Elvis contents:
Side B
  Silver Bells (Track 3)
BEST OF COUNTRY SESSIONS
Country Sessions U.S.A. (S) 122
. . . . *83*   **75–100**
Contains various country artists, including two tracks by Elvis. Price includes cue sheets. Promotional issue only.

BEST OF THE '50s
RCA Victor (SP) AEL1-5800
. . . . *6/86*   **10–15**
Includes a return mail card, part of an RCA/Nashville customer survey.
Elvis contents:
Side B
  Love Me Tender (Track 5)
BEST OF THE '60s
RCA Victor (ST) AEL1-5802
. . . . *6/86*   **10–15**
Includes a return mail card, part of an RCA/Nashville customer survey.
Elvis contents:
Side A
  Crying in the Chapel (Track 5)

BEST OF THE '70s
RCA Victor (ST) AEL1-5837
. . . . *6/86*   **10–15**
Includes a return mail card, part of an RCA/Nashville customer survey.

Elvis contents:
Side A
  Burning Love (Track 2)

BEST OF THE '50s, '60s AND '70s
RCA Victor (SP) AEL1-5838
. . . . *6/86*   **10–15**
Includes a return mail card, part of an RCA/Nashville customer survey.

Elvis contents:
Side B
  Love Me Tender (Track 2)

**BILLBOARD'S 1975 YEARBOOK
(5 LP)**
Billboard Publications (SP) no number given *12/79*   **175–200**
This boxed five-LP set reviewed the news events and music of 1979. Contains the Elvis song "Hound Dog." Includes script. Promotional issue only.
Note: also see *SOUND OF '77.*

BLUE CHRISTMAS
Welk Music Group (SP) WM-3002
. . . . *10/84*   **50–75**
Promotional issue only.

Note: A novel idea for an album—sixteen artists singing the same song.

Elvis contents:
Side 1
  Blue Christmas (Track 1)

BRIGHTEST STARS OF CHRISTMAS: see *THE BRIGHTEST STARS OF CHRISTMAS.*

CHRISTMAS COLLECTION, A (10 LP)
Snowflake (SP) *12/85*   **75–100**
Ten assorted Christmas LPs packaged in a special slipcover.

Elvis contents:
Elvis' Christmas Album (Pickwick CAS-2428)
Side 1
  Blue Christmas
  Silent Night
  White Christmas
  Santa Claus Is Back in Town
  I'll Be Home for Christmas
Side 2
  If Everyday Was Like Christmas
  Here Comes Santa Claus
  O Little Town of Bethlehem
  Santa, Bring My Baby Back
  Mama Liked the Roses

CHRISTMAS TREASURY FROM AVON, A
RCA Victor (SP) DPL1-0716
. . . . *11/85*   **8–12**
Available only from Avon representatives as a Christmas bonus item. Packaged in a specially printed cardboard mailer that is included in the price.

Elvis contents:
  Silver Bells

CHRONOLOGY OF AMERICAN MUSIC, A (ALL THE NUMBER ONE SONGS) (21 LPs)
More Music Productions (M)
MM-333-72 . . . . *12/72*   **500–600**
Note: In all probability this massive LP set was issued with a programming script of some type.

  This special 10½-hour radio program featured 325 number-one hits, in order, beginning with "Rock Around the Clock," from July 9, 1955, and ending with "Me And Mrs. Jones," the last number-one hit of 1972. There are 16 Elvis tunes featured.

Elvis contents:
Side 2
  Heartbreak Hotel (Track 1)
  I Want You, I Need You, I Love You/My Baby Left Me (Track 4)
  Don't Be Cruel (Track 6)
  Hound Dog (Track 7)
  Love Me Tender (Track 9)
Side 3
  All Shook Up (Track 3)
  (Let Me Be Your) Teddy Bear/Loving You (Track 5)
Side 4
  Jailhouse Rock (Track 6)
Side 5
  Don't/I Beg of You (Track 1)
  Hard Headed Woman (Track 7)
Side 7
  A Big Hunk O' Love (Track 7)
Side 8
  Stuck on You (Track 9)
Side 9
  It's Now or Never (Track 6)
Side 10
  Are You Lonesome Tonight? (Track 5)
Side 11
  Surrender (Track 1)
Side 13
  Good Luck Charm (Track 5)
Side 31
  Suspicious Minds (Track 7)

COUNTRY CHRISTMAS
RCA Victor (ST) AYL1-4809
. . . . *11/83*   **8–10**

Elvis contents:
Side B
  Silver Bells (Track 2)

COUNTRY CROSSROADS
Country Crossroads (S) 32–83 *83*   **75–100**
A Southern Baptist Radio-TV issue. Contains one track by Elvis.

COUNTRY GOLD
RCA Victor (ST) DPL1-0561 *82*   **20–25**
RCA Special Products LP.

Elvis contents:
Side B
  Are You Lonesome Tonight? (Track 5)

COUNTRY MUSIC IN THE MODERN ERA (1940s–1970s)
New World Records (SP) NW-207
. . . . *77*   **40–60**

A novel idea for an album—sixteen artists performing the very same song.

There may be twelve days of Christmas, but where does the song mention ten Christmas records?

Red label. With fold-open cover and bound-in six-page booklet. Made available to libraries stocking records.

Elvis contents:
Side 1
  Mystery Train (Track 9)

COUNTRY SUPER SOUNDS (1956)
Omega Sales Inc., number unknown *56*   **35–40**
One LP of a 16-volume various-artists set contains at least one Elvis track.

COUNTRY SUPER SOUNDS (1957)
Omega Sales Inc., number unknown *57*   **35–40**
One LP of a 16-volume various-artists set contains at least one Elvis track.

COUNTRY SUPER SOUNDS (1958)
Omega Sales Inc., number unknown *58*   **35–40**
One LP of a 16-volume various-artists set contains at least one Elvis track.

COUNTRY & WESTERN CLASSICS (1955)
Economic Consultants Inc., number unknown *56*   **35–40**
One LP of a various-artists series.

COUNTRY & WESTERN CLASSICS (1957)
Economic Consultants Inc., number unknown *57*   **35–40**
One LP a various-artists series.

COUNTRY & WESTERN CLASSICS (1958)
Economic Consultants Inc, number unknown *58*   **35–40**
One LP of a various-artists series.

CURRENT AUDIO MAGAZINE—ELVIS: HIS FIRST AND ONLY PRESS CONFERENCE
Current Audio Magazine (SP) CM-Vol. 1 . . . . *8/72*   **35–45**
With fold-open cover and eight-page insert. Contains a segment of Elvis' 1972 New York press conference plus features on other personalities.

Elvis contents:
Side 2
  Elvis Presley

DECEMBER '63 POP SAMPLER:
see *RCA 12-INCH SAMPLERS.*

DINER (2 LP)
Elektra (SP) E1-60107E . . . *82*   **8–12**
Original soundtrack LP. This was the first release of a non-Elvis soundtrack LP to contain an Elvis track.

Elvis contents:
Side 4
  Don't Be Cruel (Track 4)

EPIC OF THE 70s (6 LP)
Century 21 Productions (SP) 1A-6B *76*   **150–200**
A six-hour radio program, highlighting the songs of the '70s, along with interviews with most of the artists featured. Contains "Burning Love" as well as a few words from Elvis.
Note: This set was issued to radio stations that arranged to broadcast the program in their market. In all probability, a script and programming information was issued with this set.

Elvis contents:
Side 4B
  Elvis Interview (Track 2)
  Burning Love (Track 3)

E-Z COUNTRY PROGRAMMING (NO. 2)
RCA Victor (M) G70L-0108/9
. . . . *11/55*   **250–275**
A 10-inch sampler of RCA's country & western catalog. Promotional issue only.

Elvis contents:
Side 1
  Mystery Train (Track 3)
Side 2
  I Forgot to Remember to Forget (Track 1)

E-Z COUNTRY PROGRAMMING (NO. 3)
RCA Victor (M) G80L-0199/200
. . . . *2/56*   **250–275**
A 10-inch sampler of RCA's country & western catalog. Promotional issue only.

Elvis contents:
Side 1
  Heartbreak Hotel (Track 1)
Side 2
  I Was the One (Track 6)

E-Z POP PROGRAMMING (NO. 5)
RCA Victor (M) F70P-9681/2
. . . . *11/55*   **250–275**
A 12-inch sampler of RCA's pop catalog. Promotional issue only.

Elvis contents:
Side 1
  I Forgot to Remember to Forget (Track 7)

Side 2
  Mystery Train (Track 5)

E-Z POP PROGRAMMING (NO. 6)
RCA Victor (M) G70L-0197/8
. . . . *2/56* **250–275**
A 10-inch sampler of RCA's pop catalog. Promotional issue only.

Elvis contents:
Side 2
  I Was the One (Track 5)

14 #1 COUNTRY HITS
RCA Victor (ST) AHL1-7004 *85*   **10–12**

Side A
  Guitar Man (Track 5)

FRANTIC FIFTIES, THE (AS BROADCAST IN "THE WORLD TODAY," DECEMBER 28 & 29, 1959)
Mutual Broadcast System (M)
RW-4082-L80P *12/59* **175–200**
Issued to radio stations only. Contains an excerpt of "Hound Dog."

GOLDEN YEARS OF COUNTRY, THE (25 LP)
Drake-Chenault (SP) no number
given. *80* **250–300**
One LP for each year, 1955–1979. Includes eight songs by Elvis. Price includes 55-page operations manual, which represents $25–$50 of the value. Issued to radio stations only.

Elvis contents:
1955—Side 2
  I Forgot to Remember to Forget (Segment D)
1956—Side 1
  Heartbreak Hotel (Segment B)
  I Want You, I Need You, I Love You (Segment B)
1956—Side 2
  Don't Be Cruel (Segment F)
1957—Side 1
  Jailhouse Rock (Segment C)
1958—Side 2
  I Beg of You (Segment D)
1974—Side 2
  Take Good Care of Her (Segment E)
1977—Side 1
  Way Down (Segment C)

GRAMMY AWARDS: see OFFICIAL GRAMMY AWARD ARCHIVE COLLECTION, THE.

HAPPY HOLIDAYS, VOL. 18
RCA Victor (SP) DPL1-0608 *83*   **8–10**
Sold only at True Value Hardware Stores.

Elvis contents:
Side A
  If Everyday Was Like Christmas (Track 5)

HAPPY HOLIDAYS, VOL. 20
RCA Victor (SP) DPL1-0713 *85*   **8–10**
Sold only at True Value Hardware Stores.

Elvis contents:
Side A
  Blue Christmas (Track 5)

HAPPY HOLIDAYS, VOL. 21
RCA Victor (SP) DPL1-0739 *86*   **8–10**
Sold only at True Value Hardware Stores.

Elvis contents:
Side A
  Silver Bells (Track 5)

HELLO CAROL! (SOCIAL SECURITY PRESENTS MUSIC YOU CAN'T FORGET)
Social Security (M) 157–169 . *74*   **20–30**
Contains a series of 15-minute shows hosted by Carol Channing. Issued to radio stations as public service programming. The Elvis segment contains: "Spanish Eyes," "That's All Right," "Love Me Tender" and "Don't Be Cruel."

IN THE BEGINNING
ATV (M) VM1 . . . . *80*   **50–75**
A various artists collection, containing "Lawdy Miss Clawdy."

JOURNEY INTO YESTERDAY, A (1956)
Economic Consultants Inc., number unknown.   **40–45**
One LP of a various-artists series contains at least one Elvis track.

JOURNEY INTO YESTERDAY, A (1969)
Economic Consultants Inc., number unknown.   **40–45**
One LP of a various-artists series contains at least one Elvis track.

JOY OF CHRISTMAS, THE (18 LP)
Creative Radio (SP)   **150–250**
This edition programmed for adult contemporary formats. Price includes 18 pages of programming instructions and cues. Deduct $15–$25 if these pages are missing. Issued to radio stations only.

Elvis contents:
Hour 2
  Silver Bells
Hour 3
  Blue Christmas
Hour 6
  Blue Christmas
Hour 8
  If Everyday Was Like Christmas
Hour 11
  O Come All Ye Faithful
Hour 14
  Blue Christmas
Hour 16
  Oh Little Town of Bethlehem
Hour 17
  Silver Bells

JOY OF CHRISTMAS, THE (18 LP)

Creative Radio (SP)   150–250
This edition programmed for country music
formats. Price includes 18 pages of programming instructions and cues. Deduct $15–$25 if
these pages are missing. Issued to radio stations
only.

Elvis contents:
Hour 7
  Here Comes Santa Claus (Segment A)
Hour 9
  Blue Christmas (Segment D)
  I'll Be Home on Christmas Eve (Segment D)
Hour 10
  Oh Come All Ye Faithful (Segment D)
Hour 11
  Holly Leaves & Christmas Trees (Track E)

JUST LET ME HEAR SOME OF THAT ROCK 'N' ROLL MUSIC (2 LP)

The Goodman Group (M) GG-
PRO-1 . . . . *79*   **60–100**
A two-LP set containing excerpts of 100 songs,
including three by Elvis. Promotional issue
only.

Elvis contents:
Record 1, Side A
  Big Boss Man (Track 3)
Record 2, Side A
  Promised Land (Track 2)
  Reconsider Baby (Track 3)

(1957) MARCH OF DIMES GALAXY OF STARS (DISCS FOR DIMES)

GM-8M-0653/4 . . . . . *12/56* **1400–1600**
A 16-inch transcription, containing spoken
statements by Elvis and other personalities.

Note: Included with this disc were 16 pages of
dee jay announcements, which are included in
the above price range. Deduct $25 if these pages
are missing.
Side 1
  Elvis Presley (Track 8)

(1957) MARCH OF DIMES GALAXY OF STARS (DISC JOCKEY INTERVIEWS)

GM-8M-0657/8 . . . . . . *12/56* **1400–1600**
A 16-inch transcription, containing open-end
interviews and songs by Elvis and others. Contains "Love Me Tender."
Note: Included with this disc was a cover letter
and interview script for each track on the disc.
By far, the most important of these is the Elvis
script, which is included in the above price
range. Deduct $90–$100 if this script is missing.

Side 1
  Love Me Tender (Track 2)
Note: In addition to the songs, each of the six
entertainers provides an open-end interview. A
guideline script was provided with the disc.

MISCELLANEOUS SYNDICATED RADIO SHOWS

There have been quite a number of syndicated
radio shows, such as "Wolfman Jack," "Robert
W. Morgan," "Ralph Emery," "Country
Countdown" and others, that were issued to
subscribing radio stations on disc. Some of these
featured Elvis's music and may be of interest to
his fans. Generally speaking, these types of LPs
would fall into the $10–$20 range for near-mint
copies. Although there are too many to list individually, a few, such as "American Top 40" and
"Rock and Roll Roots" are listed separately in
this edition because the information was easily
available.

MUSIC YOU CAN'T FORGET

GSS (M) CC-167   25–35
Designated as show #167 in the series. Sponsored by the Social Security Administration and
hosted by Carol Channing, this radio program
featured various artists. Included were "Love
Me Tender," "Spanish Eyes," "That's All
Right," and "Don't Be Cruel" by Elvis.

OFFICIAL GRAMMY AWARD ARCHIVE COLLECTION, THE (4 LP)

RCA Victor (SP) GMY-016 . *84*   **60–100**
One disc from one of the four-LP boxed sets in
a series of 17 sets, available by mail order from
the Franklin Mint Record Society. The individual disc has Peggy Lee on one side and Elvis on
the other. This set features eight different art-

ists, each heard on one full side of a disc. Besides Elvis and Peggy Lee, this box includes Frank Sinatra, Judy Garland, Billie Holiday, Tony Bennett, Lena Horn and Nat "King" Cole. Issued on red vinyl. Contains a 16-page booklet.

Side B
    Blue Suede Shoes
    Are You Lonesome To-night
    Rock-a-Hula Baby
    Wooden Heart
    Blue Hawaii
    Can't Help Falling in Love

OCTOBER CHRISTMAS SAMPLER: see *RCA 12-INCH SAMPLERS*.

OLD & HEAVY GOLD (1956)
Economic Consultants Inc., number unknown; contains at least one Elvis track.   35–40

OLD & HEAVY GOLD (1957)
Economic Consultants Inc., number unknown; contains at least one Elvis track.   35–40

OLD & HEAVY GOLD (1958)
Economic Consultants Inc., number unknown; contains at least one Elvis track.   35–40

OLD & HEAVY GOLD (1960)
Economic Consultants Inc., number unknown; contains at least one Elvis track.   35–40

OLD & HEAVY GOLD (1961)
Economic Consultants Inc., number unknown; contains at least one Elvis track.   35–40

OLD & HEAVY GOLD (1962)
Economic Consultants Inc., number unknown; contains at least one Elvis track.   35–40
Note: These LPs were part of a series of mail-order oldies albums, each of which featured various artists.

PLAYBOY MUSIC HALL OF FAME WINNERS, THE (3 LP)
Playboy 7473 (S) 78   **50–75**
Contains 26 songs by 18 different artists. Issued in a triple pocket gatefold cover. Strangely, the Elvis track is the film soundtrack version of "Long Lonely Highway," but is shown on label as "Movin' Down the Line." Offered by mail-order only, from *Playboy* magazine.

QSP PRESENTS A GIFT OF MUSIC
RCA Victor (SP) QSP1-0034 *84*   **50–75**
QSP is a direct sales subsidiary of *Reader's Digest.* This LP was a company promotional sampler, which contains 12 songs by 12 artists, including Elvis.

Elvis contents:
Side B
    Love Me Tender (Track 3)

RCA 12-INCH SAMPLERS:
Note: Even though these RCA Samplers feature various artists, they still rank as some of the most valuable Elvis collectibles. Often, there is only one, two or three known copies.

SP-33-4 (untitled)
RCA Victor (M) SP-33-4 . *7/56* **1000–1500**
Black label, with the words Long Play at the bottom of the label.

Elvis contents:
Side 2
    Don't Be Cruel (Track 5)

SP-33-10P (untitled)
RCA Victor SP-33-10P. . . *8/58* **900–1000**
Black label, with the words "Long Play" at the bottom of the label.

Elvis contents:
Side 2
    King Creole (Track 6)

SPS-33-27 (AUGUST 1959 SAMPLER)
RCA Victor (SP) SPS-33-27 *8/59* **700–900**
Black label, with the words "Living Stereo" at the bottom.
Note: All songs, except for "Blue Moon of Kentucky," are true stereo on this sampler.

Elvis contents:
Side 2
    Blue Moon of Kentucky (Track 2)

SPS-33-54 (OCTOBER CHRISTMAS SAMPLER 59-40-41)
RCA Victor (SP) SPS-33-54
. . . . *10/59* **600–700**
Black label, with the words "Living Stereo" at the bottom.
Note: All songs, except for "Blue Christmas" and "Have Yourself a Merry Little Christmas" (by Gisele MacKenzie), are in true stereo.

Elvis contents:
Side 1
    Blue Christmas (Track 1)

SP-33-66 (CHRISTMAS PROGRAMMING FROM RCA VICTOR)

RCA Victor (M) SP-33-66 *11/59* **500–550**
Black label, with the words "Long Play" at the bottom of the label. Contains "I'll Be Home For Christmas."

Elvis contents:

Side 2
  I'll Be Home For Christmas (Track 2)
RCA Victor (M) SP-33-66 *11/59* **550–600**
Special paper sleeve that pictures RCA Christmas releases, from which these tracks are sampled, including *Elvis' Christmas Album.*, LPM-1951.
Note: Several of these tracks appeared on the previously issued SPS 33–54.

SP-33-59-7 (FEBRUARY SAMPLER)

RCA Victor (M) SP-33-59-7
. . . . *2/59* **600–700**
Has RCA Victor black label on Side 1 and RCA Camden label on Side 2, thus sampling tunes from LPs on both labels. Promotional issue only.
Note: Despite having a higher catalog number, this sampler was issued eight months before SP-33-54.

Elvis contents:

Side 1 (RCA Victor)
  That's All Right (Track 4)

SPS 33-96 (OCTOBER 1960 POPULAR STEREO SAMPLER)

RCA Victor (ST) SPS 33–96
. . . . *10/60* **500–600**
Black label, with the words "Living Stereo" at the bottom.

Elvis contents:
Side 1
  Tonight Is So Right for Love (Track 6)

SPS 33-141 (OCTOBER '61 POP SAMPLER)

RCA Victor (ST) SPS 33–141
. . . . *10/61* **500–600**
Black label, *no dog,* with the words "Living Stereo" at the bottom.

Elvis contents:
Side 2
  Blue Hawaii (Track 1)

SPS 33-191 (title unknown)

RCA Victor (S) SPS 33-191 . *62* **500–600**
Reportedly contains "I Don't Want to Be Tied" and "Where Do You Come From."

SPS 33-219 (OCTOBER '63 POP SAMPLER)

RCA Victor (S) SPS 33-219
. . . . *10/63* **500–600**
Black label, Stereo Dyna-Groove.

Elvis contents:
Side 2
  Are You Lonesome Tonight? (Track 6)

SPS 33-247 (DECEMBER '63 POP SAMPLER)

Black label, *no dog,* with the word "Stereo" at the bottom. All songs, except Eddie Fisher's "Anytime," are in stereo.

Elvis contents:
Side 2
  Fun in Acapulco (Track 1)

SPS 33-272 (APRIL '64 POP SAMPLER)

RCA Victor (SP) SPS 33-272
. . . . *4/64* **500–600**
Side 1 has the Stereo Dynagroove black dogless label, but Side 2 has the black dogless label, with the word "Stereo" at the bottom. Since I've not seen another copy of this sampler, I can't determine if they all had a different label on each side, or if it's just my copy. All songs except for Carlos Montoya's "Saeta," are true stereo.

Elvis contents:
Side 2
  Kissin' Cousins (Track 6)

SPS 33-331 (APRIL '65 POP SAMPLER)

RCA Victor (SP) SPS 33-331
. . . . *4/65* **500–600**
Black dogless Stereo Dynagroove label. All songs, except Juan Serrano's "Chapines," are true stereo.

Elvis contents:
Side 2
  The Meanest Girl in Town (Track 2)

SPS 33-347 (AUGUST '65 POP SAMPLER)

RCA Victor (SP) SPS-33-347
. . . . *8/65* **500–600**
Black dogless Stereo Dynagroove label, but without the special print and underscore of "Dynagroove."
Note: All songs, except "Your Cheatin' Heart," are in true stereo.

Elvis contents:
Side 2
  Your Cheatin' Heart (Track 6)

SPS 33-403 (APRIL '66 POP SAMPLER)

RCA Victor (ST) SPS 33-403

. . . . *4/66*   **500–600**

Black dogless Stereo Dynagroove label, but without the special print and underscore of "Dynagroove."

Elvis contents:
Side 2
    Frankie and Johnny (Track 5)

RADIO'S MILLION PERFORMANCE SONGS

CBS Songs (SP) SNGS-101 . *84*   **25–50**

Promotional issue only.

Elvis contents:
Side 1
    Don't Be Cruel (Track 2)

REBIRTH OF BEALE STREET

Beale Street (SP), no number given

. . . . *83*   **200–250**

A collection of songs from 1923 to 1983 by Memphis recording artists. A limited-edition, numbered promotional LP from the City of Memphis. Price includes an eight-page photo booklet, which represents $20–$25 of the value.

Elvis contents:
Side B
    Mystery Train (Track 3)
    That's All Right (Track 4)

ROBERT W. SARNOFF—25 YEARS OF RCA LEADERSHIP

RCA Victor (S) RWS-0001 . *73*   **600–800**

Elvis contents:
Side 1, Band 2
    Hound Dog (Track 6)
    Don't Be Cruel (Track 7)
    Heartbreak Hotel (Track 8)
    In The Ghetto (Track 9)

ROCK AND ROLL ROOTS

During the short run of this syndicated radio show, quite a number of their weekly disc packages featured Elvis's music. Any of those could be expected to fall into the $10–$20 range for near-mint copies.

ROCK AND ROLL—THE EARLY DAYS

RCA Victor (M) AFM1-5463

. . . . *7/85*   **5–8**

Includes insert, offering the "Rock and Roll—The Early Days" videocassette.

Elvis contents:
Side B
    That's All Right (Track 1)

ROCK ROCK ROCK (ALL STAR ROCK—VOLUME 11)

Original Sound Recordings (SP)
OSR-11 . . . . *2/72*   **45–55**

Orange label.

Original Sound Recordings (SP)
OSR-11 . . . . *2/72*   **35–45**

This version is titled *All Star Rock, Vol. 11,* instead of *Rock Rock Rock.* Otherwise, they're the same LP.

Elvis contents:
Side 1
    Until It's Time for You to Go (Track 6)

ROCK, ROLL & REMEMBER (6 LP)

Dick Clark Productions (SP) DPE-
402. . . . . *77*   **225–250**

A three-hour radio special, based on the book of the same title, featuring various artists and interviews. Contains two Elvis songs as well as an Elvis telephone interview by Dick Clark.

Note: Issued with a six-page script and programming packet. See also *ROCK, ROLL & REMEMBER* in the Elvis LP section.

Elvis contents:
Side 1A
    I Want You, I Need You, I Love You (Track 6)
Side 5A
    Wear My Ring Around Your Neck (Track 2)

SHELBY SINGLETON MUSIC, INC. (AND AFFILIATES) PRESENTS SONGS FOR THE SEVENTIES (2 LP)

Shelby Singleton Music (M) #1
. . . . *12/69*   **300–325**

White label. Promotional issue only. A collection of songs published by Shelby Singleton Music, Inc. and Affiliates.

Note: This double-pocket promo set was sent to select radio stations along with a 66-page song and lyrics book, which is included in the above price range. Deduct $50–$60 if this book is missing.

Elvis contents:

Record 1
Side 1
    Such a Night (Track 10)

60 YEARS OF COUNTRY MUSIC (2 LP)

RCA Victor (SP) CPL1-4351
. . . . *6/82*

Black label, dog near top.

Elvis contents:
Side C
Heartbreak Hotel (Track 2)

SOCIAL SECURITY PRESENTS DONNA FARGO (2 LP)

Dept. of Health, Education and
Welfare (M) DHEW-77-10762
. . . . *1/77*   **20–25**
This double-pocket set contains a dozen five-
minute radio programs to be broadcast as a
public service. One of these shows features
"Moody Blue."
Note: Since this series ran for several years, it is
possible that there are others that contain an
Elvis track. If so, their value would be the same
as this one.

(DICK CLARK'S) SOLID GOLD

A weekly syndicated radio show containing
various artists. Any of these discs that feature
an Elvis song would fall into the $10–$15 range
for near-mint copies.

SOLID GOLD COUNTRY (5 LP)

United Stations (SP) (April 8–12,
1985). *4/85*   **20–40**
One LP in this set, dated April 10, 1985, is
devoted to Elvis. Price includes six pages of
script and information and a "Proof of Broadcasting" reply card. By itself, the Elvis LP is
worth $15–$25.

Side 1
Stuck on You
G.I. Blues
Jerry Reed (interview)
Jailhouse Rock
Don't
Wear My Ring Around Your Neck
Hard Headed Woman
One Night
A Fool Such As I
I Need Your Love Tonight
Gordon Stoker, The Jordanaires
(interview)
Big Hunk O' Love
Side 2
All Shook Up
King Creole
I Was the One
I Beg of You
I Forgot to Remember to Forget
Treat Me Nice
I Got Stung

SOLID GOLD SCRAPBOOK

Starring Dick Bartley
United Stations (SP)   **15–30**

A syndicated oldies radio program, usually
boxed in sets of five one-hour shows. Many contain Elvis, some feature Elvis "profiles." Price
is for any in the series with Elvis music. Issued
only to radio stations.

SONGS FOR THE SEVENTIES: see *SHELBY SINGLETON MUSIC, INC. (AND AFFILIATES) PRESENTS SONGS FOR THE SEVENTIES.*

SOUND IDEAS (6 LP)

Welk Music Group. *86*   **50–75**
A six-LP set containing excerpts, including two
of Elvis' songs. Promotional issue only.

SOUND OF '77 (5 LP)

Billboard Publications (SP) *12/77*   **175–200**
This boxed special program looked back at
1977's music and news. Along with "Moody
Blue," this contains a medley of "That's All
Right," "Baby, Let's Play House," "Mystery
Train," "I Forgot to Remember to Forget,"
"Just Because," "Heartbreak Hotel," and "My
Way."
Note: Packaged with special script and pro-
gramming information, which is included in the
above price.

Elvis contents:
Side 7
Moody Blue (Track 1)
Side 10
Medley of Elvis' Hits (Track 1)
Also see: *BILLBOARD'S 1979 YEARBOOK.*

SUN STORY, THE (2 LP)

Rhino (M) RNDA-71103 . *1/86*   **8–12**
Price includes four-page booklet.

Elvis contents:
Side 1
Good Rockin' Tonight (Track 1)
Side 3
That's All Right (Track 7)

SUPER SONGS (3 LP)

Mutual (S)   **50–75**
A three-LP broadcast set for radio stations.
Contains one Elvis track.

THE AGE OF ROCK

EMR Enterprises (M) EMR RH-8
. . . . *69*   **100–125**
Issued to radio stations to promote the book
The Age of Rock, by Jonathan Eisen. Contains
"Tutti Frutti," "Love Me Tender," and "Blue
Suede Shoes."

THE BRIGHTEST STARS OF CHRISTMAS

RCA Victor (SP) DLP1-0086

. . . . *11/74*   **35–45**

Blue Special Products label. Manufactured especially for the J. C. Penney Company and sold only in their stores.

Elvis contents:
Side 1
  Here Comes Santa Claus (Track 2)

30 YEARS OF NO. 1 COUNTRY HITS (7 LP)

RCA Victor (SP) RBA-215/A

. . . . *86*   **40–45**

A boxed set containing 84 songs, including 3 by Elvis. Sold mail-order by *Reader's Digest.* Price includes 12-page booklet.

Elvis contents:
Record 2
Side 1
  I Forgot to Remember to Forget (Track 6)
Side 2
  (Let Me Be Your) Teddy Bear

Record 7
Side 1
  Moody Blue (Track 6)

TIME-LIFE TREASURY OF CHRISTMAS, THE (3 LP)

Time-Life (SP) STL-107 . *10/86*   **15–18**

Boxed set available from Time-Life by mail order.

Elvis contents:
Side 2
  Here Comes Santa Claus (Track 4)
Side 4
  If Every Day Was Like Christmas (Track 2)

TIME-LIFE TREASURY OF CHRISTMAS, VOLUME 2, THE (3 LP)

Time-Life (SP) STL-108 . *10/87*   **15–18**

Boxed set available from Time-Life by mail-order.

Elvis contents:
Side 2
  Blue Christmas (Track 4)

This and the second album in the set contain all the classics from the popular Christmas repertoire.

25 GOLDEN YEARS IN LOWERY COUNTRY (2 LP)

Lowery Group (SP) LG-1 . . *80*   **40–60**
Promotional issue only.

Elvis contents:
Side 3
   Walk a Mile in My Shoes (Track 5)

WE'RE PLAYING YOUR SONG (2 LP)

Pickwick (S) 1 . . . . *80*   **25–35**
A various-artists collection, including three Elvis tracks. Promotional issue only.

WHITE CHRISTMAS, VOLUME 1

Scana (SP) 27022 . . . . . *11/86*   **10–15**
A German import that was widely distributed throughout the United States.

Elvis contents:
Side B
   Santa Bring My Baby Back to Me (Track 5)

WHITE CHRISTMAS, VOLUME 2

Scana (SP) 27023 . . . . . *11/86*   **10–15**
A German import that was widely distributed throughout the United States.

Elvis contents:
Side A
   Santa Claus Is Back in Town (Track 5)

WORLD IN SOUND—1977, THE

Associated Press (M) AP-1977
. . . . *1/78*   **80–100**
Associated Press's recap of 1977's top news stories. Contains an excerpt of "Hound Dog," from *Elvis In Concert.*

PART 2
THE BEATLES

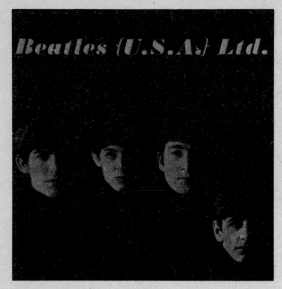

1964 Beatles souvenir tour program.

The Beatles, 1958–1970

John Lennon, 1940–1980
Paul McCartney, 1942–
George Harrison, 1943–
Ringo Starr, 1940–
Pete Best, 1941–

There have been many attempts to account for the Beatles' success in the United States. Amid the first wave of Beatlemania in the first months of 1964, sociologists were brought in by the press to explain the "phenomenon." The *New York Times* devoted three front-page articles to the merchandising of the group. Hormones and hard cash were the initial conclusions. Later, as rock music developed an expanded social view—thanks in no small part to Lennon's comments in 1966 on Christianity—the meteoric rise of the Beatles was explained in terms of America's pain following the assassination of President Kennedy. The Beatles were viewed as a kind of communal "happening," with the various parts contributing to a greater whole.

Cynics just pointed to all of the hype.

No doubt there is some truth in each of these ideas and opinions. Capitol Records had invested a huge amount of money and effort to promote the group in 1964—perhaps to compensate for the shortsightedness manifested in their rejection of the group a year earlier. America had been bewildered by the murder of her president, and the arrival of the Beatles provided a much-needed balm, a kind of joyous distraction for the anguished national psyche. American popular music had also reached a hiatus—there hadn't been a "phenom" since Elvis had blasted on the scene back in 1956—and the sounds of the time really didn't have much energy.

Looking back, so few of the experts actually talked about the music. After all, it was "pop," and music critics at that time dealt only with classical and jazz. When the London *Times* critic compared Lennon's and McCartney's work favorably with the song settings of Beethoven and Schubert, the *New York Times* lashed back with a scathing parody of the critique in February 1964. In fact, it wasn't for their music at all but for a *film* that the Beatles received their first critical accolades from Americans. The concert reviews, such as they were, had focused on all those screaming fans.

But history shows that the quality of the music justified the hype, and barring a few slips here and there, all of the promotion in the world could never prepare us for what the Beatles would accomplish in the six short years they were an active ingredient in the American scene.

A point could be made showing that the Beatles had a lot more in common with Elvis besides a big name. If Tupelo, Mississippi, was a melting pot of black and white American musical traditions, Liverpool, a Lancashire port city on the Irish Sea, was a musical smorgasbord with all the trimmings, a place where people came from all over the world, refugees from a crumbling empire. There one could find a crazy quilt of Irish and West Indian, African, Hindu, and Pakistani all jammed together with an already feisty native culture. And then there were the sailors, sailing away or coming home on leave, bringing with them records from their many ports of call.

Down one street one might hear a steel band; down another, a country and western group. Rock 'n' roll was everywhere. It's important to understand this because, like Elvis, the Beatles were great consolidators, capable of performing in a wide variety of musical styles. To make the grade in such a city they had to appeal to an extremely diverse audience. And given the constant exposure to foreign styles they experienced from America and elsewhere, they had a great deal to choose from in creating their own style.

In the late 1950s, Liverpoolians were under the spell of two styles. On one side there was the ubiquitous rock 'n' roll. Bill Haley and the Comets had them ripping the seats out of the movie houses at screenings of *Rock Around the Clock;* but the hipper crowd was eyeing the harder-to-come-by work of black rhythm 'n' blues performers produced by the small independent labels in America. On the other hand, young musicians had fallen for skiffle—an acoustic style based loosely on jug band music. For one thing, it was cheap to do. You didn't have to have an amplifier, and the bass (occasionally made with washtubs stateside) could be had through an ingenious use of tea chests made of plywood and tin.

One of the many skiffle groups knocking about Liverpool and its suburbs was the Quarrymen, who included among their members John Lennon and Paul McCartney (George Harrison joined them in 1958). Church fetes, talent shows at the union halls—these were the kinds of gigs where the group played their ragtag repertoire of pop standards, folk songs, and rock 'n' roll favorites.

With the advent of drummer Pete Best and the subsequent change of name (from the Quarrymen to the Silver Beatles), the group was invited to perform in Hamburg, Germany, another port town but a rougher, wilder place than even Liverpool. And a different kind of gig, too. Rock 'n' roll clubs then often doubled as strip joints. Nights of playing eight to twelve hours, day after day—people may speak of "playing" instruments, but this was *work*.

But it was a real apprenticeship as well, and in the seasons the Beatles spent in Hamburg they developed their own sound as a group. Lennon, McCartney, and Best (who was replaced by Ringo after the Parlophone audition) provided a solid rhythm section while Harrison became more adept as a lead guitarist. More important, Lennon, McCartney and Harrison developed their style as singers and their unusual vocal blend.

It was during their first "tour of duty" in Germany that the Beatles, backing up Tony Sheridan, made their first recordings. Rocked-out versions of "My Bonnie" and "The Saints" made it onto a German Polydor release in June 1961. These sessions must count among the most reissued material in the Beatle catalog in the United States, appearing on no less than four different labels in the course of some fifteen years.

Nothing of immediate note came of these recordings—the single entered no national charts—but it was through the hometown support garnered by the Beatles that the record got the attention of Brian Epstein. Fans in Liverpool were constantly ordering and reordering the record at the NEMS store, and the record department's manager was intrigued. Because George Harrison had not reached his majority and was playing in a bar, he was deported in the fall of 1961. The rest of the group followed, returning home rebellious, dazed yet triumphant. Soon thereafter, in December 1961, Epstein became their manager.

Within weeks—New Year's Day, in fact—Epstein had the group auditioning for Decca Records in London. The audition was taped live, no overdubs, and the group was almost immediately rejected. From then until their second record company audition the following June, Epstein undertook formulating the group's image. The leather jackets and pants were replaced with matching suits and ties. The Tony Curtis style haircuts were washed out for a more "natural" look. In June 1962 the musicians performed for George Martin of Parlophone/EMI, a producer and A&R ("Artists and Repertoire") man who had specialized in recording comedy albums by such notables as Peter Sellers, Peter Ustinov, and the Goons. He signed the group the following month.

In August, Pete Best was fired from the group, undoubtedly the result of a personality conflict with Epstein and Martin's dissatisfaction with his style, and was replaced by Ringo Starr, a drummer who had worked the Liverpool scene and had been in Hamburg with Rory Storme and the Hurricanes at the same time as the Beatles.

On September 11, 1962, the Beatles recorded "Love Me Do" and "P.S. I Love You," and on October 5, Parlophone released the two tracks as a single. Hometown support played its part again, and the single emerged on the national charts at number 17 before it fell away. The best was yet to come.

On February 16, 1963, "Please Please Me," backed with "Ask Me Why," reached number 1 in England. Over the next four years every Beatle single would hit the top of the English charts. In fact, the only Beatle single not to make number 1 was "Strawberry Fields/Penny Lane" in 1967.

Meanwhile, Epstein was working hard to get the group to America. Capitol, EMI's major label in the United States, passed on the fourteen songs that made up the *Please Please Me* album, and Epstein finally landed a deal with Vee Jay Records. Not a significant event in the group's history, as it turns out, but one that was to have tremendous importance to record collectors (please see the section "The Beatles on Vee Jay" following the Memorabilia section). On February 25, 1963, Vee Jay released "Please Please Me/Ask Me Why." There was practically no response.

In Britain, however, the group was provoking a measure of hysteria quite unlike anything else the island empire had ever seen. On May 4, the *Please Please Me* album reached number 1 on the LP charts, a position it would relinquish only to the Beatles' second British release, *With the Beatles,* some 30 weeks later. Somewhere between the two dates Beatlemania began, and by the end of August it had become front-page news in the press, a regular nightly report on the television, a standard feature in the newsreels. Late in October, in small back-page articles in papers like the *Washington Post* and the *New York Times,* word of Beatlemania reached America.

For the general public in America the story begins with the promotion surrounding the Capitol release of "I Want to Hold Your Hand/I Saw Her Standing There" on January 13, 1964, and the Beatles' first appearance on the "Ed Sullivan Show." Radio stations began "Beatlewatches" and "Beatle Countdowns." Roving reporters at Idlewild Airport and the Warwick Hotel in midtown Manhattan were preparing to describe the events as they happened. When the group finally arrived, on February 7, they gave their first press conference and established the tone that was to become the rule for the next two years—charming but cheeky, honest (to a point) but fun. In sum, a pleasant departure for journalists normally cursed with the job of dealing with the popular performer's cliches. The Beatles were in town, and *everybody* was having a good time.

Newspaper articles following the group's departure at the end of the month highlighted what the group had accomplished. There were the usual descriptions of the throngs, the press conferences, even some talk of the music. There were also the business reports on how much the group was going to make, not only from their tour the following summer but from the licensing of their names and images for use in the manufacture of certain specialty products. Two weeks in America and the group was already making millions of dollars.

Unlike Elvis' commemoratives, the merchandising of the Beatles occurred over the course of a number of years, provoked by the increasingly spectacular nature of their celebrity. *A Hard Day's Night* was a highbrow critical success as well as a box-office smash. The Shea Stadium concert set the standard for the scale of celebration in August 1965. *In His Own Write* proved to be a best-seller in the bookstores. Almost everything the Beatles touched or that touched the Beatles turned to gold.

Much of the memorabilia concocted around the Beatles was an update of the material that had evolved around Elvis—the bubble gum cards, the jewelry, the clothing, the toy instruments, the ceramics. All were intended for the teenage market, both boys and girls, and aimed vaguely at soothing the hormonal distress of early adolescence. The prime target remained girls—the jewelry, the talcum powder, the nylons. For the boys, there were the cuff links and the ties, the metal lunch boxes.

The Beatles products served much the same purpose as the Elvis material. Somehow, the necklace, properly licensed and authorized, would bring the girl closer to the objects of her adoration, as if to wear their necklace was to wear a gift from *them*—never mind that someone had to go to the store to get it. For the boys it was a matter of seeming more Beatle-like. Who can't remember the guys trying to talk with something that vaguely resembled an English accent?

And who can't remember what happened with the *hair?* Until the bangs grew out there was always the Beatle wig—for those quiet times.

In retrospect, 1966 was the turning point. A spring article in the *New York Times Sunday Magazine* by Maureen Cleave portrayed the group waiting—almost happily—for their fall from the top. Then a series of social debacles in the Philippines on the first leg of their Far Eastern tour led to harassment from Mrs. Marcos's henchmen. A crowd in India came close to rioting. Only the appearance at the Budokan in Tokyo that June seemed to fit the bill. But it was on the eve of their American tour in August that the sparks really flew. In another article written by Maureen Cleave for the London *Evening Standard* the previous February, John Lennon was quoted as saying rock was bigger than Christianity. There was no public outcry then, but when the piece was reprinted in *Datebook* that summer, a broad cross-section of Americans took profound exception. Even the Vatican issued a statement abhorring "Mr. Lennon's remarks." Bowed yet unbeaten, the Beatles then spoke out against the war in Vietnam. And just in case their point hadn't been gotten, there was the celebrated yet infamous butcher cover for *Yesterday and Today,* pulled at the last minute from general release by an embarrassed Capitol Records. It was clear that they were no longer in it just for the fun. They were tired of the road, disenchanted with the glory, interested only in making records. On August 29, 1966, the Beatles gave their final live concert at San Francisco's Candlestick Park.

The Beatles had leaped into the recording age.

The Beatles sought in 1966 to be taken seriously as artists, and in their efforts to cast off the "beloved moptop" image they helped to transform rock from a means by which to say "I love you" 999 different ways to a vehicle for social commentary and personal expression. "Strawberry Fields Forever/ Penny Lane" was the harbinger for *Sgt. Pepper's Lonely Hearts Club Band,* and "Magical Mystery Tour"—a self-produced and self-written television show—was a sign of the chaos of what was to come on the business front. (See "Collecting Apple Memorabilia" in the next chapter.)

But all in all, as they came of age and tried to come to grips with what they had wrought, they attempted to bring us along with them. With the memorabilia and recordings from 1962 to 1966 we can recall the sparkle they brought to our lives, and with the later work we see how they touched us all so deeply. With their ever-changing sound—each album, every single seems still to leap at us afresh—the Beatles, like great pioneers, provided us with maps of the uncharted world of what was to come.

Collecting Beatles Memorabilia

Technically, any product pertaining to The Beatles is Beatles memorabilia. From records to toys, from promotional items and record industry by-products to personal objects owned by any of The Beatles—all of these fall into the realm of memorabilia. Every one of these objects can, in its own way, be a source of fascinating information. The problem is that there would be *so much* to include in the guide that it would be ridiculously cluttered.

How to make sense of it all? We decided to concentrate on the mass-produced objects that were officially licensed by the various Beatles organizations (NEMS, Seltaeb, and so on) during the lifetime of the group. These are the objects that have, in fact, generated the greatest collecting activity through the years. Moreover, these objects required the same standards of documentation and verification that we applied to the official recordings.

So what didn't we include? Both during and after the lifetime of the group, hundreds, perhaps thousands, of unauthorized products and reproductions were made both here in the United States and elsewhere. Some of them are, as one might expect, appalling and shoddy work; some are quite fine. But for the purposes of collectibility they are all little more than curios, because it is impossible to detail any aspect of their manufacture. It is impossible to know how many were made or by whom. The only sure thing about them is that they were illegal. As you go through the following pages, then, you might very well find that you have a particular item that is not listed here. If that is the case, the chances are that it's either non-original or that it hasn't generated any real collector appreciation. Or else it's one of a kind. Consider, for example, cels from *Yellow Submarine*—the hand-painted illustrations that were then photographed onto film. These are one-of-a-kind items, not mass-produced, so they are not included here, but they are highly collectible and are beginning to appear in the major auction houses. But then there are the cels from the Beatles cartoon show. Many more of those are available, but there simply isn't any interest in them—at least, none to date. Perhaps because the portrayals of the group didn't really look like any of them; perhaps because the artwork as a whole just wasn't that good.

Or take the example of a relatively recent edition of a book on the Beatles— *The Love You Make* by Peter Brown and Steven Gaines. As of yet, there has been no value establishment above the original retail price. The reason is simple; it was published too recently and it sold in excess of a million copies. Obviously, the supply has met the demand and has generated very little, if any, collector value. Now if there were twenty million people trying to obtain copies when only a million were printed, then we would have the onset of real demand, which in its turn would translate itself into some kind of market value. Of course a copy autographed by the authors is somewhat more significant, but even that has to wait some years before it has any appreciable value beyond the cover price.

Perhaps you have an extremely valuable item that is not mentioned in the guide. In that case it's probably an item that was either produced from the mid-1970s to present (beyond the scope of this guide) or a one-of-a-kind piece that depends strictly on how much the buyer is willing to pay. A good example of this type of memorabilia is the psychedelic Rolls-Royce that belonged to John Lennon. This car was auctioned for $2.9 *million* a few years ago. You can be sure that this kind of thing is not going to pop up on somebody's table at the next Beatle convention.

Another significant area of memorabilia would be personalized items such as originals of official documents—birth certificates, marriage licenses, school report cards, and the like. Other examples include original musical instruments actually owned by group members. Even the experts who determine the value of such items at the major auction houses have trouble with one-of-a-kind Beatle memorabilia. A Japanese guitar owned by John Lennon, estimated value $1,500 to $2,000, actually sold for $19,800. Not only would it be impossible for us to list all of these items, but to "guesstimate" their value would put more weight on guessing than on knowing.

What *is* included in our listings are items that were legitimately produced in quantity, the kind of thing you might have gotten at the five-and-dime, the kind of thing you might have stored away in your attic or display proudly on your mantelpiece. In short, the kind of material that is always coming up at the Beatle shows and conventions.

We welcome your comments or suggestions concerning the contents of this section. Please write to *Cox-Lindsay, P.O. Box 82278, Phoenix, AZ 85071-2278.*

COLLECTING APPLE MEMORABILIA
(A brief look into a few significant items that were produced in connection with The Beatles' own music and production company)

In 1967, The Beatles established their own company to manage their business affairs as well as to finance new talent in the entertainment industry. This enterprise was officially titled "Apple Corps LTD.," and it included five distinct divisions: records, films, electronics, retailing, and publishing.

The record division was a tremendous success in the early years, presenting performers who in subsequent years proved the strength of the Beatles' musical instincts—James Taylor, Badfinger, and producer Peter Asher. But the remaining Apple ventures failed miserably due to extreme mismanagement. By late 1970, all divisions were closed except for a small record division office maintained until 1976.

In Apple's brief but flamboyant history several products and promotional items were manufactured. However esoteric in nature, demand for these items by collectors has increased significantly enough that we felt it necessary to address the subject appropriately. Expansion on the subject is a very real possibility in future editions.

The following are some examples of Apple promotional items:

Apple dartboard—very rare item given by Apple to various personnel and friends. In nice shape, this item can bring as much as $1000.

Key ring—green and red insert with clear plastic housing. A nice example of this will usually yield around $75.

Matches—black book with green apple on the front cover. Individual books are valued at about $40 (with all matches intact). A sealed package of four books will fetch up to $200.

Stationery—official letterhead paper (8½" × 11") with Apple logo on the top, valued at $5 to $10 for each sheet. Envelopes bring about the same.

Wristwatch—extremely rare item featuring an apple on the face. This is worth about $1200.

The Beatles: Memorabilia

Compiled by Joe Lindsay, Perry Cox, and Rick Rann

This section deals entirely with nonrecord products that were legitimately manufactured by licensed, authorized companies from 1964 to the mid-1970s. Only "original" items are listed, excluding any and all reproductions. For the most part, this section mainly deals with U.S.-manufactured items; however, in some cases certain items were imported from other countries for distribution in the United States. We have identified these items in their respective listings.

There are many areas to cover in the diverse world of collecting these "tokens of Beatle history," collectively known as Beatles memorabilia.

Putting such a wide variety of items into order is rather arbitrary. All published materials—hardcover and paperback books, magazines, comics, and so on—make up the first section of this collection of Beatles memorabilia. Subsequent parts are devoted to movie memorabilia, bubble gum cards, fan club items, Yellow Submarine-related products, and general miscellany. The price ranges depend on the nature of the items discussed, so each part has its own introductory material.

If you have any questions or comments about any area of Beatles memorabilia, please write to: *Rick Rann, P.O. Box 877, Oak Park, IL 60303.*

One important point to remember: The price range shown in this guide, for both records and nonrecorded memorabilia, is for *near-mint* condition. You must adjust values downward for items in lesser condition.

PUBLICATIONS

Values given are for the first printing of each publication in near-mint condition. Later printings are generally about half the listed value on copies dated through the 1960s and early 1970s. Subsequent printings are usually valued at little more than than current or recent retail value. The printing information is usually located on the first few pages of any book. Few books published in the mid- to late 1970s have any real collector value, with the exception of a few very limited edition hardcover books such as Harrison's autobiography.

Brief writing, such as a name written neatly on the inside front or back of the cover, will reduce the value of the item by $1 to $3. The value of any of these publications autographed by the author of the book will be enhanced to some extent, depending on the author's stature. Any of these books autographed by any or all of the Beatles will, of course, be worth a great deal more. (See "Collecting Autographs" section for further information.)

Hardcover Books

[Title, year of release, author (when applicable) and publisher]

Beatles Authorized Biography, The (1968), by Hunter Davies
    (McGraw-Hill)

With dust jacket	**25–35**
Without dust jacket	**15–20**

Beatles Authorized Biography, The (1968), by Hunter Davies (McGraw-Hill).

Beatles Book, The (1968), by E. E. Davis (Cowles)
With dust jacket	**55–65**
Without dust jacket	**35–35**

Beatles Illustrated Lyrics Vol. 1, The (1969), by Alan Aldridge
    (Delacorte)
With dust jacket	**15–25**
Without dust jacket	**8–12**

Beatles Illustrated Lyrics Vol. 2, The (1971), by Alan Aldridge
    (Delacorte)
With dust jacket	**15–25**
Without dust jacket	**8–12**

Beatles, The Real Story (1968), by Julius Fast (Putnam) . . . . | **15–20** |

Cellarful of Noise, A (1965), by Brian Epstein (Doubleday)
With dust jacket	**35–45**
Without dust jacket	**15–25**

Dear Beatles (1966), by Bill Adler (Grosset & Dunlap) . . . . | **10–15** |

Help! (Random House souvenir movie book) (1965) . . . . . . | **35–45** |

In His Own Write (1964), by John Lennon (Simon & Schuster)
1st printing	**75–85**
2nd–15th printing	**25–40**

Help! (Random House) (1965).

Lennon Factor, The (1972), by Paul Young (Stein & Day) . . .   **30–40**

Lennon Play, The (1968), by John Lennon, Adrienne Kennedy,
and Victor Spinetti (Simon & Schuster) **25–35**

Lennon Remembers (1972), interviews of John Lennon & Yoko
Ono by Jann Wenner (Straight Arrow)

With dust jacket **15–20**
Without dust jacket **10–15**

Love Letters to the Beatles (1964), by Bill Adler (Putnam) . . .   **8–12**

Spaniard in the Works, A (1965), by John Lennon (Simon &
Schuster)

1st printing **45–55**
2nd or 3rd printing **25–30**

Yellow Submarine (1968), by Max Wilk (Signet) **30–40**

Yellow Submarine Gift Book, The (1968) (World Distributors)   **25–35**

Softcover Books

[Title, year of release, author (when applicable) and publisher]

All About the Beatles (1964), by Edward DeBlasio (McFadden/
Bartell) **8–10**

Beatle Book, The (1964) (Lancer Books) **8–10**

Beatles, The—A Study in Drugs, Sex, and Revolution (1969), by
David Noebel (Christian Crusade) **25–35**

Beatles Authorized Biography, The (1968), by Hunter Davies
(Dell) **8–10**

Various Beatles paperbacks.

The first news of the Beatles was not about the group itself but the wild enthusiasm of their fans. It was only a matter of time until a book about them came out.

Magazines Exclusively Featuring the Beatles

Any copies that are missing pages (cover included) or have any free or loose pages are valued at 50% the VG price. Copies with a few clean cut photos or coupons clipped out would reduce the VG price by $3 to $5.

From the "complete-est fax ever" to the "complete story from birth to now" (1965), the teen mags, above all else, provided endless pix with which to paper the walls of one's room—which explains why the issues that survived youthful scissors are worth so much today.

Beatles Complete Life Stories, The—By Teen Screen (1964) . . .   **15–20**
Beatles Complete Story from Birth till Now, The (1965) **15–20**
Beatlemania Collector's Item (1964) **20–25**
Beatles Film, The (1964) **10–15**
Beatles from the Beginning, The (1970) **10–15**
Beatles Fun Kit (1964) **45–50**

> Note: Many items in this magazine were designed to be easily removed. The values given are for the magazine complete. Missing items reduce the value by 5% per missing item.

Beatles in America, The (1964) **15–20**
Beatles Make a Movie, The (1964) **15–20**
Beatles Meet The Dave Clark Five, The (1964) **15–20**
Beatles Movie (1964) **10–15**
Beatles on Broadway, The (1964) **10–15**
Beatles Personality Annual, The (1964) **10–15**
Beatles 'Round the World (1964)
    #1. 10″ × 13″ with pullout poster intact **25–30**
    #2. 10″ × 13″ without pullout poster **15–20**
    #3. *Elvis vs. The Beatles* **45–50**
Beatles Starring in "A Hard Day's Night," The (1964) **15–20**
Beatles Talk, The (1964) **15–20**
Beatles Whole True Story by Sixteen, The (1966) **15–20**
Best of the Beatles **10–15**
Best of the Beatles from Fabulous (1964) 10″ × 13″ **20–25**
Complete Coverage of Their New York Appearance—The Beatles
    (1964) **10–15**
Dave Clark Five, The Beatles Meet the (1964) **15–20**
Dave Clark Five Vs. the Beatles, The (1964) **15–20**
Hairdos, Beatle (1964) **10–15**
Meet the Beatles (1963) **20–25**
New Beatles, The (1964) **15–20**
Original Beatles Book, The (1964) **15–20**
Original Beatles Book Two, The (1964) **15–20**
Paul McCartney Dead, The Great Hoax (1969) **20–25**
Pictures for Framing, The Beatles (1964) **15–20**
Pop Pics Super (1964) (one complete issue dedicated to each member of the group, George, John, Paul and Ringo; values are
    equal) **10–15**
Real True Beatles, The (1964) **20–25**
Ringo's Photo Album (1964) **15–20**
Sixteen's Help! (1965) **15–20**
Sixteen's Uncut Official Version—A Hard Day's Night (1964) .   **15–20**

Imagine this: the special issue above had *seven* gigantic color pin-ups. Amazing.

Star Time Presents The Beatles	**15–20**
Talking Pictures #1, The Beatles (1964)	**10–15**
Teen Pix Album (1964)	**20–25**
Teen Screen Life Story (1964) (one issue dedicated to each member of the group, George, John, Paul, and Ringo; values are equal)	**20–25**
Teen Talk (1964)	**20–25**
Who Will Beat The Beatles (1964)	**10–15**
Yellow Submarine (1968)	**20–25**
Note: There were two different issues of this title, both of equal value. One is a 48-page issue; the other is a 64-page issue.	**20–25**

Teen Magazines

There were thousands of magazines issued in the United States between 1963 and 1970 that had feature articles and/or covers on the Beatles. Values given are for the magazines in their complete form; clippings and partial issues have little or no value.

Generally, the value placed on an item is in direct relationship to the amount of Beatles material included or the importance of the article it contains. This is particularly true of the August 1966 issue of *Datebook,* in which

By 1968, when *Yellow Submarine* came out, the Beatles had lost their frivolous edge. Gone indeed were the days of the super-hot pix.

Lennon made his celebrated remarks about rock and Christianity—no matter that the story had originally appeared in the London *Evening Standard* six months before with little or no outcry from the English reader. In the main, however, the values are fairly constant from one magazine to another. The question is whether the cover features the Beatles ($10 to $15) or whether the magazine contains one or more features on the group ($8 to $10). The major teen publications from 1963 to 1970 were:

Datebook	*Teen Life*
Dig	*Teen Pinups*
Flip Teen	*Teen Scoops*
For Teens Only	*Teen Scrapbook*
Hit Parader	*Teen Screen*
Hullabaloo	*Teen Set*
Rolling Stone	*Teen Stars*
Sixteen	*Teen Trends*
Startime	*Teen World*
Teen	*Tiger Beat*
Teen Album	*Today's Teens*
Teen Circle	*Top Ten*

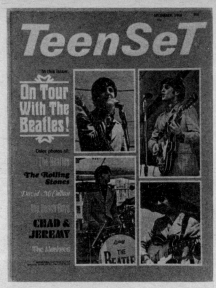

Teen Set was merely one of dozens of teen magazines that were very much a product of the '50s and '60s. From *Dig* to *Tiger Beat,* boys and girls alike bought them to keep abreast with their constellations of stars.

News/Mainstream Magazines

Cosmopolitan (12/64), Lennon on cover **15–20**

Life (8/28/64), Beatles on cover **25–30**

  (9/13/68), Beatles on cover **15–20**

  (9/20/68), Part 2 of article **8–12**

  (11/7/69), Paul on cover **10–15**

  (4/16/71), Paul on cover **10–15**

Look (12/13/66), Lennon on cover **10–15**

  (3/18/69), Lennon on cover **10–15**

  (1/9/68), Lennon on cover (price includes tabloid with poster; deduct

    25% if poster is missing.) **25–30**

Newsweek (2/24/64), Beatles on cover **30–35**

Playboy (2/65), seven-page candid interview with the Beatles .   **10–15**

Post (3/21/64), Beatles on cover **25–30**

  (8/8/64), Beatles on cover **25–30**

  (8/27/66), Beatles on cover **15–20**

Time (9/22/67), Beatles on cover **30–35**

TV Junior (9/64), Beatles on cover **15–20**

By 1967, in the midst of the Love Generation, the Beatles were taken seriously as the voice of a generation that was becoming increasingly disenchanted with the world their parents had created.

Comic Books

Batman, DC Comics, #222 (6/70), Paul death hoax takeoff .   **8–12**

Beatles Complete Life Stories, The, Dell Comics (1964)
   Note: Comic book collectors are largely responsible for the higher
     value placed on this item. **70–80**

Jimmy Olson, DC Comics, #79 (1964), contains Beatles
   satires **15–20**

My Little Margie, Charlton Comics, #54 (11/64), Beatles on
   cover **15–20**

Strange Tales, Marvel Comics, #130 (3/65), "The Thing Meets
   the Beatles" **8–12**

Summer Love, Charlton Comics, #46 (1966), Beatles on cover   **10–15**

Z2Summer Love, Charlton Comics, #47 (1966), Beatles on
   cover **10–15**

Yellow Submarine Comic Book, Gold Key Comics (1968)
   With poster **40–45**
   Without poster **20–25**

From teen mags to news magazines to books, the Beatles were omnipresent on the scene. They even made it into comics.

By the middle '60s, every guy with an eye for the gals was strumming a guitar, and sheet music sales were better than they had been in many years. Unfortunately for the budding young guitarists, the transcriptions were often done in unthinkable keys by jazz musicians who couldn't know any better.

Sheet Music/Songbooks

Authorized, licensed sheet music was issued for most Beatles singles and songbooks were issued for most of The Beatles albums. Values given are for the original sixties and early seventies items. Since all values on these items are relatively equal, we have an average value listed that applies to all items.

Sheet music (all titles) **8–10**
Songbooks (all titles) **10–12**

MOVIE MEMORABILIA

Most movie memorabilia is in some form of paper product. These were items such as posters, lobby cards, press books, programs, and so on. When grading these items, one must consider their intended use within the movie industry. Although any deviation from perfection will certainly devalue an item, some handling procedures that were administered within the movie industry do not greatly affect the value. For example, most large movie posters (27″ × 42″) came folded straight from the factory. This item would still be considered near-mint if it was in fact near-mint in all other areas of grading.

Another example would be lobby cards. For display purposes, most lobby cards were either taped, stapled, or tacked in the theater showcases. Detractions such as these would drop the value only slightly compared to the same items without such detractions. Of course, perfect copies would still command a premium. Any of the above discrepancies in excess would also markedly devalue an item.

Lobby Cards

Note: All lobby cards came in sets of eight. Values given are for each card individually. Add 10% to the total sum of listed values for a complete set.

Hard Day's Night, A **25–30**
  Note: Reproductions of this item exist and are easily identified in that
    the fakes were direct copies of originals that had tack holes in the
    corners; the tack holes are black dots on the fakes.
Help! **25–30**
Let It Be **30–35**
Yellow Submarine **15–20**

Posters (single sheet, 27″ × 42″, commonly referred to as one-sheets)

Two lobby cards—one from the Beatles' most joyous film, the other from their saddest.

Hard Day's Night, A	**125–150**
Help!	**150–175**
Let It Be	**150–175**
Yellow Submarine	**100–125**

Pressbooks

Hard Day's Night, A (13″ × 18″)	**40–45**
Help! (13″ × 18″)	**40–45**
Let It Be (13″ × 18″)	**35–40**
Yellow Submarine (11″ × 17″)	**20–25**

Preview Tickets

Hard Day's Night, A (8/64)

Unused (not torn at perforation)	**15–20**
Used (torn at perforation)	**10–15**
Unused book of 4 tickets (intact with backing card)	**125–150**

Movie Programs (sold at theaters)

Hard Day's Night, A	**30–35**
Help! (hardcover)	**40–45**
In the Yellow Sub	**35–40**

Movie Still Photos (original theater issue with movie title and credits featured at the bottom of the photo, 8″ × 10″)

Hard Day's Night, A (black & white) **5–8**
Help! (black & white) **5–8**
Let It Be
    black & white **4–6**
    color **10–15**
Yellow Submarine (black & white) **5–8**
Souvenir badge, *A Hard Day's Night* (3″ diameter, round card-
    board, reads "I've Got My Ticket") **8–12**

BUBBLE GUM CARDS

Grading: Near mint—card must be very nearly perfect with absolutely no writing, tears, tape, stains, or creases; card should be clean and crisp. Very good—minor wear acceptable, such as small creases and slight wear at the corners. No writing, tears, tape, or very large creases or folds allowable.

Individual Cards (Cards are marked and easily identifiable.)

1st series (black & white), each . . . .   **.75–1**
2nd series (black & white), each . . . .   **.75–1**

Samples from the various series of Beatles bubble gum cards.

3rd series (black & white), each 75–1
Color cards, each 75–1
Diary cards, each 75–1
A Hard Day's Night, each 75–1

Complete Sets

1st series (black & white), #1–#60 (60 cards in set) **50–60**
2nd series (black & white), #61–#115 (55 cards in set) **40–45**
3rd series (black & white), #116–#165 (50 cards in set) . . .   **35–40**
Color cards, #1–#64 (64 cards in set) **45–50**
Diary cards, #1a–#60a (60 cards in set) **45–50**
A Hard Day's Night, #1–#55 (55 cards in set) **40–45**
Note: Black & white series 4, 5, and 6 were manufactured in the 1980s and
are not valued in this guide.

Sealed packs of cards

One of the six 1960s series with cards, wrapper, and gum . . .   **25–30**
Rack pack (3 pack—no gum) with header card **50–60**

Wrappers only

All 1960s series except *A Hard Day's Night* **15–20**
A Hard Day's Night **15–20**

Display boxes (24-count)

Any of the six 1960s series **80–90**

FAN CLUB ITEMS

All the following items were issued by Beatles USA Ltd., except for the tour
programs. All other items in this section were issued only to Beatles fan club
members.

Bulletins
    August 1964 (*A Hard Day's Night* script) **25–30**
    May 1965 . . . .   **20–25**
    April 1966 . . . .   **25–30**

Bulletin/poster

Summer 1967	**20–25**
Summer 1968	**15–20**
Summer 1969	**15–20**
Summer 1970	**15–20**

Cube (in original mailing envelope, 1970)

Unassembled	**25–30**
Assembled	**15–20**

Magazines (eight pages each)

George Harrison Photo Album	**15–20**
Paul McCartney Photo Album	**15–20**
John Lennon Photo Album	**15–20**
Ringo Starr Photo Album	**15–20**
1969	**15–20**
1970	**10–15**
1971	**10–15**

Membership cards (1964–1971), each **8–12**

Photos (black & white, 3¼″ × 5½″, one of each Beatle), each ... **2–3**

Posters (life size, 1964, black & white, 6′ × 2′, one of each Beatle), each **25–30**

Tour programs (sold at concerts, 12″ × 12″)

1964	**15–20**
1965	**15–20**
1966	**25–30**

GENERAL MEMORABILIA

The following items represent a large portion of items made in the 1960s. Though this list is not all-inclusive, it does contain items that we could authenticate as far as licensing goes. Many illegal products were made and distributed, but for reasons noted in the introduction, we have chosen not to include them here.

"Air Flite" carrying case (round vinyl with flat bottom, with zipper and handle, available in red and black, 1964, NEMS) **225–250**

"Air Flite" carrying case (rectangular vinyl-covered carrying case available in various colors, 1964, NEMS) **225–250**

Arcade cards (3″ × 5″ set of five cards, 1964, black & white with bios) **10–15**

Avedon posters (1968) (photos by Richard Avedon, the colors altered; printed on high-quality poster stock and distributed via mail order by *Look* magazine)

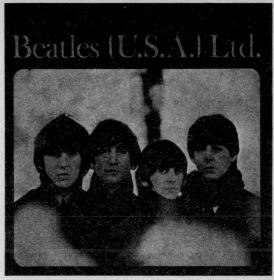

The souvenir program cover from the group's 1965 U.S. tour.

John (22″ × 30″) **30–35**
Paul (22″ × 30″) **30–35**
George (22″ × 30″) **30–35**
Ringo (22″ × 30″) **30–35**
Beatles (black & white) (15″ × 40″) **30–35**
Bag: see Bootie bag
Balloons (various colors)
Sealed in package **50–60**
Opened package with contents **30–35**
Banjo (plastic; rare item produced by NEMS) **300–325**
Bamboo tray (made in Taiwan, 1964)
6″ diameter **50–60**
11″ diameter **60–70**
12″ diameter **70–80**
Bandaid: see Help! bandaid
Beach hat (various colors with black & white group photo image) **70–80**
Beach towel (NEMS, reads "Yeh Yeh Yeh" at lower section, with
Beatles in old-fashioned swim suits with tops, approxi-
mately 30″ × 60″, 1965) **150–175**

Beatle Buddies (set of four color oil portraits, 9″ × 12″, with
    membership card, header cards, 1964)
  Sealed set **25–30**
Bedding sheet piece (packaged piece of bedsheet that a Beatle slept
    in while in a hotel in Detroit or Kansas City in 1964; also
    includes a note of authenticity) **20–25**
Bedspread blanket (54″ × 72″, cotton blanket with silkscreen
    pictures and instruments; UK, 1964) **200–225**
Binder: see Three-ring binder
Birth certificates (1964, sold through mail order, 6″ × 12″ each)
  Set **60–70**
  Each **10–15**
Birth certificates (1968, booklets, set of four)
  Set **8–12**
  Each **2–3**
Bobbing-head dolls: see Dolls
Bolo tie: see Lariat tie
Bongos (NEMS, 1964)
  With original package **400–425**
  Without original package **300–325**
Book covers (10″ × 13″ folded, 1964)
  Sealed package of seven **35–40**
  Individually **4–6**
Booklet: see Dell 20 wallet photo booklet
Booty bag (heavy plastic see-through bag with cartoon picture of
    Beatles with instruments, has drawstring) **50–60**
Bow tie (packaged on card, 1964, issued in various colors) . .   **125–150**
Bracelet: see Charm bracelet
Brooch: see Guitar brooch
Brooch pin (2″ diameter, black & white photo with autographs on
    back in gold-color metal) **40–45**
Bubble bath (Soakies, 12″ high, none made of John or George)
  Ringo **70–80**
  Paul **70–80**
Buttons: see Pins
Cake decorations (small 2″ facsimiles of Beatles, in original pack-
    age, available in blue or gray)
  Each **2–3**
  Set **10–15**
  Heart-shape stickpin **10–15**
Calendar (pocket calendar, playing-card size, has picture of Bea-
    tles) **10–15**

Calendar (pocket calendars, playing-card size, set of four calendars each featuring a Beatle)

Set **40–45**
Each **10–15**

Candy cigarette boxes (with cartoon Beatle on the front; four different boxes made, one of each Beatle) **50–60**

Cap (1964, green or brown corduroy, titled "Ringo Cap" on inside tag) **70–80**

Cards: see Arcade cards

Carrying case: see Air Flite

Cartoon kit: color forms (1966)

Complete in box with instructions **250–275**

Change purse (with zipper, picture looks like Beatles but does not say Beatles)

One of each Beatle, each **20–25**

Charm bracelet (includes four 1″-diameter photos of each Beatle with autograph in metal on reverse; charms hang from metal 7″ chain) **60–70**

Charm bracelet (possibly unauthorized item: includes four Beatle-like heads wearing bow ties, hair colored in; charms hang from metal chain) **10–15**

Charm bracelet (NEMS, by Randall, features group photo, reverse reads "Yeh Yeh Yeh Nems Enterprises Ltd") **40–45**

Christmas seals (4″ × 7″ package of 100 seals) **30–35**

Cigarette box: see Candy cigarette boxes

Coin (commemorative coin of 1964 tour) **8–12**

Color photos: see Photos

Coloring book

Colored in **25–30**
Not colored in **40–45**

Comb (12″ long, NEMS, 1964) **125–150**

When Seltaeb or NEMS sold the license for the use of the Beatles' faces, they also gave the producer the right to use the Beatles' name. There is no Beatle name here, the only hint of the Fab Four coming in the length and coloring of the hair.

Computer slide (promotional slide chart made by Capitol, 1970, lists Beatles LPs and singles plus important dates and events) **20–25**

Cuff links (pair on original card, NEMS, 1964) **100–125**

Cup: see Mug

Decorations: see Cake decorations

Dell poster (1964, 18″ × 52″)

#1 (#1 is not printed on poster) **25–30**

#2 (#2 is printed on poster) **25–30**

Dell 20 wallet photo booklet (5″ × 3¾″) **8–12**

Diary (by Langman & Co., Glasgow, Scotland, 1965, 3″ × 4″, color cover, includes Beatle bios, calendar and photos)

In original box **50–60**

Without box **15–20**

Disk-Go-Case (a round 45rpm record-carrying case, 1966, available in various colors, by Charter Industries, NEMS; originally came with ID card on string) **70–80**

Doll decorations: see Cake decorations

It looks like an angelfood cake mold, but it was actually a handy way to take your favorite 45s from here to there.

Dolls (REMCO, 1964, rooted hair in each, black suits, each with
  instrument strapped around neck, 5″ tall)

John or George with instrument	**70–80**
Paul or Ringo with instrument	**50–60**
John or George without instrument	**35–40**
Paul or Ringo without instrument	**25–30**
Complete set of 4 in boxes with instruments	**500–525**

Dolls ("The Swinger's Music Set" titled on box, does not say
  Beatles on box, only "Yeh Yeh Yeh" and Beatle-like faces,
  each doll is approx. 3″ high)

Dolls complete with box	**35–40**
Set of dolls only	**25–30**
Each	**4–6**

Dolls (inflatable cartoon dolls, 15″, by NEMS/King Features
  Syndicate, made in Hong Kong, 1966)

Set of four	**60–70**
Individually	**15–20**

Dolls, nodder (4″ high dolls, bobbing heads)

Set of four	**40–45**

Dolls, nodder (ceramic 8″ tall, by Carmascot, 1964, with bobbing
  heads, packaged in box with a cellophane window)

Set of four	**300–325**
Set with box and instructions	**400–425**

Drinking glass (6″ tall, available in various designs, made of glass,
  1964)

Ringo	**80–90**
John	**80–90**
George	**80–90**

These not-very-lifelike dolls rank among the most collectible of the Beatles
memorabilia.

Paul **80–90**

Beatles as group **80–90**

Flasher key rings: see Key rings

Flasher rings (3-D effect with each Beatle's face on plastic ring, and each reads "I'm Ringo/Beatles" or "I'm Paul/Beatles," etc., made with silver or gold color plastic)

Complete set **30–35**

Each **4–6**

Flip Your Wig game (1964, Milton Bradley; complete game consists of box, instructions, board, four player pieces, 48 cards, and 1 die) **100–125**

Girl's vinyl lunch pail (soft oval with top zipper, 1965, originally packaged with same style of thermos as the metal 1965 lunch box)

With thermos (with cup and vacuum cap) **225–250**

Without thermos **175–200**

Glass: see Drinking glass

Greeting card (American Greetings, folds out into a 20" × 28" color poster) **40–45**

It's not easy to remember what the Beatles did to our sense of style until you see something like this—a board game based solely on the length of their hair.

Guitar (Mastro 5″ tall) **70–80**
Guitar (plastic, 20″ long, titled "Four Pop Guitar," Mastro Indus-
    tries, NEMS; includes instructions and a pick) **300–325**
Guitar, Jr. (Mastro, 15″ tall, called "Guitar Jr.") **250–275**
Guitar brooch (black plastic with color photo under plastic win-
    dow, NEMS, made in UK, 1964; seven different brooches
    were made including two of Ringo, two group shots, one
    each of Paul, George, and John)
   Each on card **20–25**
   Each with no card **10–15**
Guitar pin (brass pin with four heads around body of guitar, 1½″
    long, 1964, NEMS, on original card) **20–25**
Gumball machine charms (¾″ diameter "record" with Beatle
    photo on one side and Capitol Records' logo with song title
    on other side) **5–8**

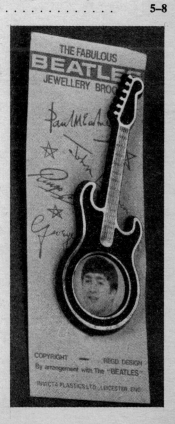

Guitar "jewellery brooch" [sic!] featuring a
youthful Lennon.

Gumball machine figures (rubber, rolled up in a plastic capsule, one of each Beatle, various colors)   5–8
Gumball machine sticker (in gumball machine capsule)   5–8
Hairbrush (made in red, white and blue plastic colors, 1964)
 Each   10–15
Hair spray (by NEMS, 16-oz. can, made by Bronson)   400–425
Halloween costumes (Ben Cooper Costume Co., complete in box, one each of George, John, Paul, and Ringo)
 Each   250–275
Handbag: see Purse
Hangers (by Saunders Ent.)
 Each   30–35
Harmonica box (Hohner, 1964, NEMS; the harmonica itself has no Beatle markings, 4″ × 1¼″)
 Empty box   45–50
 Harmonica in box   60–70

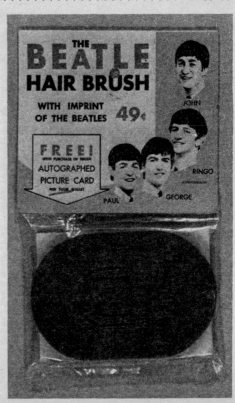

Hairbrush with an imprint of
the Beatles and an
autographed picture card (free!
with purchase of brush).

Hat: see Beach hat, Cap

Headband (1964, stretch nylon)

With original package **50–60**
Without package **20–25**

Help! Band-Aid (sealed in wrapper, 1965; a Band-Aid dispenser
was never made in the 1960s; in the 1970s/80s a dispenser
was fabricated) **25–30**

Hummer (blue plastic, NEMS) **50–60**

Ice cream bar wrapper (Beatle Krunch Bar) **40–45**

Inflatable dolls: see Dolls

Irish linen (1964, 18″ × 28″, made in Ireland) **150–175**

Jr. Guitar: see Guitar, Jr.

Kaboodle Kit (NEMS, 1964, available in various colors, square
vinyl case, 4″ by 7″, complete) **225–250**

Key chain (approximately 1¼″ diameter, round gold color,
resembles a record, has Beatles' names and raised faces on
front and "Beatles MCMLXIV" on back, has gold 1″ chain
attached to metal ring. Also referred to as a medallion and
is commonly found without the chain attached.) **30–35**

Lariat tie (black rope with laminated "brass" logo piece, Bolo Tie,
NEMS) **70–80**

Licorice record and cover (candy with picture inserts, one of each
Beatle and a group photo, 1964, NEMS)

Complete with candy record **100–125**
Wrapper with inserts **80–90**
Wrapper with no inserts **50–60**

Linen: see Irish linen

Locket: see Charm locket

Lunch box (blue metal, 1965, has Beatles' faces on one side and
group playing instruments on other side, NEMS)

With thermos, cup and vacuum cap **150–175**
Without thermos **100–125**

Lunch box: see Girl's vinyl lunch pail

Megaphone (white plastic with faces, NEMS, approx. 8″) . . . **125–150**

Model kits (toys by Revell, unassembled in box with instructions,
NEMS)

Paul or Ringo **100–125**
John or George **125–150**
Assembled without box, each **35–40**

Mug (insulated plastic with paper insert, 4″ tall) **60–70**

Necklace (with approx. 1″ × 1″ booklet with 11 fold-out photos
in leatherlike cover, available in various colors) **30–35**

The Beatles lunch box—a rare culinary treat.

From the makers of World War II fighters and battleships—Paul McCartney, in genuine white plastic!

Necklace (1¾" diameter ceramic-like pendant with photo on
　　front and autographs in gold-color metal on reverse side)　　60–70
Nightshirt (similar to sweatshirt, white, with black design on
　　front, 1963, NEMS) . . . .　125–150
Notebook (color cover with lined paper, 1964) . . . .　35–40
Nylons (Carefree, made in England, brown or black, in original
　　package) . . . .　60–70
Oil paint "portrait" set (includes a paint-by-number 11" × 14"
　　canvas, color print, oil colors, cleaner, and two bristle
　　brushes, by Artistic Creations, in original box; one of each
　　Beatle) . . . .　250–275
Panties: see Underwear
Pen (1964, various colors, has faces on clip, NEMS)
　　On original card . . . .　80–90
　　Ink pen only . . . .　50–60
Pencil case (plastic with zipper, with black & white photo, availa-
　　ble in various colors, 1964, by Standard Plastic Products,
　　NEMS, approx. 3½" × 8")
　　Case . . . .　50–60
　　In original package . . . .　70–80
Pennant (with "I Love The Beatles" inscribed) . . . .　20–25
Pennant (triangular shape, shows faces of Beatles with names,
　　available in various colors) . . . .　20–25
Photo album: see *Yellow Submarine* memorabilia below
Photos (sealed package of 6 different 8" × 10" photos, 1964) .　40–45
Photos (set of four photos, 8" × 10", black & white,
　　Seltaeb) . . . .　35–40
Photo booklet: see Dell 20 wallet photo booklet
Pillow (with both tags intact; deduct $20 if tags are missing,
　　NEMS, manufactured by Nordic House)
　　Beatles without instruments, red . . . .　90–100
　　Beatles without instruments, blue . . . .　90–100
　　Beatles with instruments . . . .　90–100
　　Full figures . . . .　125–150
Pin: see Brooch pin
Pin ("I'm An Official Beatles Fan," approx. 3½" diameter, 1964,
　　red, white, and black with group photo) . . . .　15–20
Pins (approx. 3½" or 4" diameter, 1964 to 1965, available with
　　any of the following inscriptions: "I'm 4 Beatles," "Help
　　Stamp Out Beetles," "Oh Bring Back My Beatles To Me,"
　　"Yeh Yeh Yeh," "I Want To Hold Your Hand," "I'm Bugs
　　About The Beatles," "I'm A Beatles Booster," "I Love The

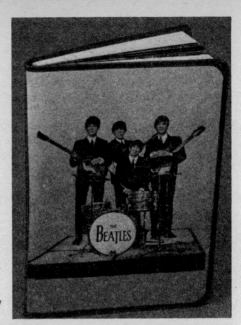

The Fabs pictured at the ready on this notebook cover.

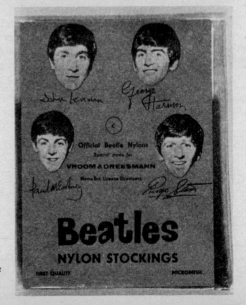

Nylons—in colors appropriate to the English schoolgirl's uniform (brown or black).

Some of the many and sundry pins that represent our true feelings for the Beatles.

Beatles," "I Still Love The Beatles," "In Case Of Emergency, Call John," etc., "Member Beatles Fan Club," "I Love John," "I Love Ringo," etc., "I'm A Beatle Bug," also available with pictures of John, Paul, George and Ringo, as well as a few different group pictures)

Each 4–6

Pin (approx. 3½" or 4" diameter; inscribed "I Hate The Beatles") 8–12

Pins (approx. 2½" diameter, 3-D flasher pins that alternately show a group photo, a solo photo, and the words "The Beatles—I Love John," etc.; four different pins) 4–6

Pins (either ⅞" diameter or 1¼" diameter; "I'm A Beatles Booster," "I Love The Beatles," "John," "George," "Paul," "Ringo," "Member Beatles Fan Club," "I'm A Beatle Bug," or "I'm 4 Beatles," NEMS, 1964, available in gumball machines) 8–12

Pin-up screamers (1964, set of four in original package) 25–30

Portraits: see Beatle Buddies, Oil paint "portrait" set, Punchout portraits

Portraits (by Volpe, 1964, NEMS, 15″ × 18″, package of four,
color with black background; originals have printing in the
lower right-hand corner)

Set of 4	**50–60**
Each	**8–12**

Postcards (1964, set of five color postcards) **10–15**

Postcards (1964, set of four drawings by Gregory Thornton) .   **8–12**

Poster: see Avedon poster, Dell poster, Greeting card, Fan Club
Memorabilia

Poster (billed as the "World's Largest Poster" in *Sixteen* magazine ads, 40″ × 54″, with orange background) **40–45**

Punch-out portraits (by Whitman, 1964)

Unused, intact **50–60**

Purse (10″ × 10″, with metal handle or rope handle) **125–150**

Puzzle: see Pocket puzzle

Record carrying case (45rpm size, square, cardboard with plastic
handle, in red or green) **250–275**

Record carrying case (LP size, square, cardboard with plastic
handle, in red, green, or red and white) **250–275**

Record carrying case: see Disk-Go-Case

Record player (blue phonograph, record player must be in working condition, NEMS, 18″ long × 10″ wide, features full
group photo on the inside of the lift top) **800–825**

Remco dolls: see Dolls

Rings: see Flasher rings

Ring (1″ diameter, ceramic type photo of Beetles, 1964) **45–50**

Scarf (White background with fringe, Beatles pictured with song
titles and records) **35–40**

Scrapbook (Whitman, 1964, color cover with blank pages) . . .   **35–40**

Screamers: see Pin-up screamers

Shirt: see Nightshirt, Sportshirt, Sweatshirt

Sneakers (gym shoes by Wing Ding, manufactured by Hoague-
Sprague)

Slip-on sneakers	**125–150**
In original white box	**200–225**
Lace-up hightops	**250–275**
In original box	**300–325**

Sportshirt (three-button knit, V-neck style, white with black pip-
ing and logo, NEMS, 1964) **80–90**

Stamps (pack of 100 color stamps, 1964, by Hallmark)

Complete package **10–15**

Stockings: see Nylons

Sweatshirt (white with black design, 1963, NEMS) **70–80**

Talcum powder (Margo of Mayfair, NEMS, 16-oz. container, 1964)   **300–325**
Tennis shoes: see Sneakers
Thermos (1965, came with blue lunchbox and girl's vinyl lunch
    pail)
    Thermos with cap and lid **50–60**
Three-ring binder (approx. 10″ × 12″ × 1″ and 10″ × 12″ ×
    1½″, available in various colors, by Standard Plastic Prod-
    ucts and N.Y. Looseleaf, 1964, NEMS)
    White **60–70**
    Other colors **80–90**
Tie: see Bow tie, Lariat tie
Tie tack pins (silver- or gold-toned on individual black & white
    3½″ × 5½″ card, one of each Beatle)
    Each **15–20**
Tie clip (on original card, NEMS, 1964, has name and faces on
    drum) **60–70**
Travel case: see "Air Flite"
Tray (metal, 1964, 13″ × 13″, with "Worcester Ware" or "Metal
    Tray Manufacturing" stickers, new reproductions are
    lighter in weight than originals and do not have sticker)   **45–50**
Tray: see Bamboo tray
Tumbler ("kissing lips" at top, insulated plastic glass with paper
    insert) **60–70**
Underwear panties (made in UK) **50–60**
Wallets (one of each Beatle, shape of cartoon figure on vinyl with
    zipper, in color)
    Each **10–15**
Wallet (plastic, complete with comb, four photos, coin slots, nail
    file and mirror, by Standard Plastic Productions) **80–90**
Wallpaper (1964, made in Canada, sold in rolls, a 21″ × 21″ panel
    shows complete pattern) **25–30**
Wig (in original package, NEMS, 1964) **40–45**
"World's Largest Poster": see Poster

YELLOW SUBMARINE MEMORABILIA

Note: all of these items were issued in 1968.

Alarm clock (Sheffield, color, 4″ high, King Features Syndicate,
    1968)
    Clock **300–325**
    In original box **350–375**

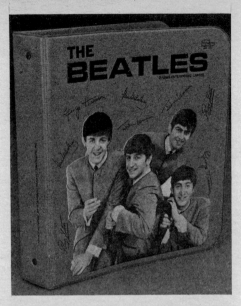

Three-ring binder, available in a variety of colors.

Among the most durable of Beatles memorabilia is this tray (see color insert for full-color display).

Bank (ceramic, Japan, 1968, King Features Syndicate and Pride
    Creations, each Beatle available, hand painted)
    Each **70–80**
    Set **350–375**
Blacklite poster (reads "All You Need Is Love") **20–25**
Binder (King Features Syndicate, by Vernon Royal, 1968, approx.
    10" × 12", originally included a notepad and a notebook,
    all with same cover designs)
    Binder **70–80**
    Notepad **25–30**
    Notebook **40–45**
    All three **150–175**
Books: see Hardcover books, Softcover books
Bulletin boards (7½" × 23", in color, 1968)
    Beatles **30–35**
    Snapping Turk **20–25**
    Blue Meanie **20–25**
    Stamp Out Fun **20–25**
Buttons: see Pins below
Calendar (for 1969, 12" × 12", by Western Publishing) **80–90**
Cards: see Greeting cards below
Coasters: see Party coasters below
Corgi toy submarine (metal with movable parts, 1968, manufac-
    tured in U.K.)
    Submarine only **125–150**
    In box with blue plastic insert **225–250**
Figurines (by Hummel)
    Each **125–150**
Greeting cards (complete set of cards with envelopes in box, by
    Sunshine Art Studios for King Features Syndicate, 1968;
    card set was made in two different styles, one with 14 and
    one with 18 cards per box, also a set of smaller cards made
    with 20 cards per box) **60–70**
Halloween costume (with Blue Meanie face, by Collegeville)
    In original box **125–150**
    Without box **90–100**
Hangers (one of each Beatle, set of four, cardboard, King Features
    Syndicate, by Henderson & Hoggard, 1968)
    Each **40–45**
    Set **150–175**
Key chains (2½" × 6", plastic, with key ring, in color, by King
    Features, 1968)
    Of each Beatle **8–12**
    Of Yellow Submarine **20–25**

Key chain (4″ diameter with key ring, in color, six different key chains: "Mini Meanie," "The Boob," "Robin The Butterfly Stomper," "Jack The Nipper," "Apple Bonkers," and "Blue Meanie")

Each	**20–25**
Set of 6	**125–150**

Lunch box (1968, King Features Syndicate/Suba)

Without thermos	**100–125**
With thermos, plus vacuum and cup caps	**150–175**

Magazine: see Magazines Exclusively Featuring The Beatles

Mobile (complete in original package, 1968, King Features Syndicate, by Sunshine Art Studios, colorful, approx. 8″ × 12″, in package) **50–60**

Model kit of Yellow Submarine (by Model Products or Craftmaster, plastic, 1968, King Features Syndicate; box includes a plastic display of Beatles)

Assembled	**35–40**
Unassembled in box with instructions	**100–125**

Party coasters (set of coasters sealed in package, King Features Syndicate) **50–60**

Photo album (7½″ × 9½″, by King Features/Suba, reads "Beatles Photo Album" in bold green, with cartoon Beatles around a Sgt. Pepper drumhead, 1968) **100–125**

Pins (set of eight different, hand-painted, shaped figures of movie characters, by KFS-SUBA, each backed with stickpin for clothing)

Yellow Submarine, marketed by King Features Syndicate, served as a vehicle for a whole variety of objects, from lightswitch covers to lunch boxes.

Set	**45–50**
Each	**4–6**

Pop-out art decorations (approx. 10″ × 15″, color book of 20 different items, staple-bound) **10–15**

Popstickles (sealed in original package)

Beatles	**15–20**
Yellow Submarine	**10–15**
The Glove	**10–15**

Postcards (1968, King Features Syndicate, set of six, 10″ × 14″)

Each	**4–6**
Set	**40–45**

Postcards (1968, King Features Syndicate, approximately 5″ × 10″)

Set of five	**30–35**
Each	**4–6**

Poster: see Blacklite poster

Poster put-ons (1968, in original box, unused, includes a 15″ × 21″ poster with over 60 put-ons, by Craft Master, King Features/Suba) **50–60**

Like all good animated films, *Yellow Submarine* appealed to both children and adults. These pop-out art decorations were great for either rainy-day activities or boring old staff meetings.

Puzzle (small 5″ × 7″ after assembly, by Bantam) **40–45**

Puzzles (complete in box, six different large puzzles were made; "Sea Monsters," "Beatles In Pepperland," "In The Yellow Sub," "Blue Meanies Attack," "Meanies Invade Pepperland," and "Sgt. Pepper's Band," made by Jaymar, 12″ × 12″ box)

    Medium, over 100 pieces **60–70**

    Large, over 650 pieces, 19″ × 19″ **70–80**

Rub-ons (set of eight, 2½″ × 3½″ sheets; instructions were included, cereal premium)

    Each **10–15**

Spiral notebook: see General Memorabilia

The extraordinary artwork of *Yellow Submarine* was used to advantage in this and other puzzles in the series.

Stationery (sealed box with 20 envelopes and sheets, available in numerous styles, by Unicorn Creations or King Features Syndicate)

The Glove	**20–25**
Snapping Turk	**20–25**
Beatles, and other characters	**35–40**

Submarine toy: see Corgi Toy Submarine

Switchplate covers (each sealed in original package, 6″ × 10½″, by Dal, King Features Syndicate, 1968)

Beatles	**15–20**
Snapping Turk	**10–15**
The Glove	**10–15**
Stamp Out Fun	**10–15**
Meanie	**10–15**

Thermos (with vacuum cap and cup-lid cap; came with Yellow Submarine lunch box)

Thermos	**50–60**

Wall plaque (approx. 9″ × 21″, psychedelic colors with small hole at top for hanging, King Features Syndicate)

Each Beatle	**15–20**
The Glove	**15–20**
Yellow Submarine	**25–30**

Watercolor set (small set has four 6″ × 8″ pictures, colors and brush, made by Craft Master, 1968)

Unused, in original box	**40–45**

Watercolor set (large set has six 8″ × 10″ pictures, paints and brush)

Unused, in original box	**70–80**

Wristwatch (Sheffield, still in original package, original has sharp image of submarine on watch with embossed printing, psychedelic band with Beatles and other characters on yellow background)

With package	**200–225**
Without package	**150–175**

Yellow Submarine Gift Book: see Hardcover books.

The Beatles
on Record

What follows are some highlights of collecting Beatles records, including discussion of some areas of special interest, comprising the various label changes (as opposed to record company changes) their records have gone through over the past twenty-five years, magnetic tape releases, and a list of what are, for the majority of the listening public, the lost songs. We know that they are down on tape somewhere. We just hope that sometime soon a nice reputable company—Capitol EMI, for example—will bring them before the public eye.

MAGNETIC TAPE FORMATS
(Cartridges, Reel-to-Reel Tapes, Cassettes)

For more than three decades, most recorded music has been available in one or more of the different magnetic tape formats. The tape format has always enjoyed a considerable amount of success because of its superior sound quality, mobility, programmability, and compactness.

As with the industry overall, the Beatles' catalog of albums has undergone the evolutionary developments that have occurred in the prerecorded audiotape business.

Reel-to-Reel

The Beatles LPs released in 1964 and 1965 were available only in reel-to-reel format. Reel tapes consisted of the tape in a labeled, fold-open box. The tapes were provided on plastic reels.

Their first Capitol album, *Meet the Beatles,* along with *Yesterday and Today* were the only two titles available on a five-inch reel tape. All other titles were on seven-inch reels. Later tapes of these two LPs were issued in the seven-inch format. *Meet the Beatles* was also one of only two titles that were available in both mono and stereo. The other tape was *A Hard Day's Night,* on the United Artists label.

Three of Capitol's reel tapes were double-album sets consisting of two different titles in one box. The combined titles were *The Early Beatles/Beatles 65, Beatles VI/Something New* and *Rubber Soul/Beatles Second Album.*

Until 1969 Capitol manufactured their own reel tapes, usually packaged with brown boxes. In 1969 Capitol subcontracted the reel tape manufacturing to the Ampex company. Besides having the Ampex logo, the tapes were packaged in blue boxes. Not only did Ampex reissue all previous titles, but they split up all of the double-album sets. The last Beatles LP available in this format was *Let It Be.* The early solo albums through late 1971 were also available on reel tapes.

Prices for reel tapes are generally in the $20 to $40 range, with the *Meet the Beatles* and *Yesterday and Today* five-inch tapes bringing up to $50 (all values stated are for near-mint condition).

The four-track tape cartridge was introduced in 1966. This was a revolutionary format because it allowed listeners an affordable, convenient way to listen to their favorite music in moving vehicles and on portable players. The cartridges were easy to stack and store, and setup was reduced to simply inserting the cartridge into its playback unit.

The Beatles catalog of LPs through *Let It Be* as well as several early solo LPs, were made available in this format. Four-track tapes had a fairly short life span, mainly serving as a stepping stone to the more successful eight-track cartridge. By mid-1970 the eight-track tapes had completely rendered the four-track units obselete. Because of the format's short life span, there were few reissues and label variations.

Most four-track tapes came factory-packaged in cardboard containers that were about the same size as the tape itself. These containers did not list titles or contents, just record company name and format information. The later Apple four-tracks did feature titled boxes.

Values for four-tracks generally fall in the $15 to $20 range.

Eight-Track Tape

Introduced early in 1968, the eight-track cartridge dominated the tape market by year's end. The chief difference between the four-track and eight-track cartridges was programmability. The listener could select from four channels on the eight-track as opposed to two on the four-track. Compared to its predecessor, the eight-track had a long life span, though it eventually gave way to the cassette format that has since been the predominant tape format.

Because of the longevity and popularity of the eight-track, 85 to 90% of the Beatles and solo Beatles catalog was available on this format. The eight-tracks underwent several variations, such as label changes, reissues, promotional issues, plus many different styles of packaging. Capitol also released two cartridges that contained two LPs on one tape. These double sets were *Meet the Beatles/Early Beatles* and *Yesterday and Today/Beatles VI*.

Values for near-mint, eight-track cartridges have generally been in the $8 to $10 range for the single LP tapes and $15 to $20 for the double sets. Remember though, these values can be higher with some obscure tape packages, such as John Lennon's *Two Virgins* LP.

Cassettes

Although the cassette format made its first commercial appearance in 1968, it didn't really acquire a firm stronghold in the market until the mid- to late 1970s. From then to the present, the cassette has dominated the tape market. This dominance was largely due to its convenient small size, its capacity for easy re-recording and sound quality superior to that of the former cartridge formats.

Cassettes were primarily recorded in stereo. Early cassettes featured paper labeling adhered to a plastic housing. These labels were replaced in the early to mid-1970s by tapes that featured the printing on the housing itself.

The protective boxes used to store the cassettes have also undergone developments and changes over the years. Cardboard and various types of plastic boxes were prevalent in the early days. Plastic boxes then featured art slicks adhered to the outside of the box (usually one-piece hinged boxes). Types in which the tape would simply slide out were also used. Like the eight-tracks, cassettes have also experienced such variations as reissues, label changes, promotional issues, and the like.

There have also been a few elaborate cassette packages. These include *The Beatles Deluxe 3-Pak*, a boxed set, twelve inches by twelve inches, of three cassettes or eight-track cartridges, and John Lennon's *Wedding Album*, which was similar to its record counterpart, maintaining its full-sized box and all of the inserts. Special items such as these always command prices higher than that of the standard cassettes. The *Wedding Album* usually goes for around $50 to $60. The *3-Pak* is closer to $100. Generally, the more common cassettes sell in the $8 to $10 range with the more obscure titles commanding higher values.

In 1967 a small New York company, Playtape Inc., marketed in limited national distribution, a small two-track cartridge. These were basically designed for teenagers who could tote their portable players (also manufactured by Playtape Inc.) to the beach, parties, and so on. All Beatles LPs, through the *The Beatles* (the "white album"), were available on this obscure format and were licensed by Capitol Records. Although these tapes carried full LP titles, each cartridge contained only four selections. The two track format did not catch on in this country and within a year or so disappeared from the scene. The two tracks now sell for an easy $25 to $30 each while the players themselves range in value between $35 to $50 depending on the model. However, only eight models were brought out on the market.

At this point the popularity of collecting tapes still takes a back seat to that of collecting records. However, interest in this area seems to steadily be on the increase. If the positive feedback in this area continues, we would certainly consider expanding further on tapes and possibly listing them with the records in future editions. If you would like to encourage us to do so, or would like to contribute any items or information you may have, please write to us at the following address: *Cox-Lindsay, P.O. Box 82278, Phoenix, AZ 85071-2278.*

THE BEATLES ON VEE JAY
(A brief history of a colorful record company's involvement in Beatlemania)

Any long-time Beatle record collector will tell you that the cause of the greatest amount of confusion in the field was the group's involvement with Vee Jay Records, an independent Chicago label. Of course, many major artists have recorded on more than one label. The confusion comes when you realize that Vee Jay produced no less than four differently titled LPs, six singles, and an EP (not to mention dozens of label styles and variations) from *just fourteen tracks.*

Vee Jay Records was formed in 1953 by Vivian *(V)* Carter and James *(J)* Bracken and had been moderately successful through the 1950s and early 1960s with various rhythm and blues artists. They gained solid national attention in September 1962 with the smash hit song "Sherry" by the Four Seasons. This group would go on to have ten Top 40 hits for the label.

In early 1963 the overwhelming British success of the Beatles single "Please Please Me"/"Ask Me Why" prompted Beatles manager Brian Epstein to search frantically for a U.S. record company. After receiving a thumbs-down from all of the major record companies—including Capitol, Columbia, RCA Victor, and others—Brian finally settled for Vee Jay. Though they had enjoyed such success with the Four Seasons, Vee Jay had been unable to make further inroads with any of the other American acts available at the time. So they were willing to sign the new British group and introduce them to the American public.

This was indeed a brave move on their part. English acts had previously had very limited success in the United States. Somehow, English performers had never transcended novelty status. Nevertheless, the Beatles were signed by Vee Jay on January 25, 1963. On February 25, 1963, "Please Please Me"/"Ask Me Why" (VJ-498) was released, and with the exception of some local chart action in Chicago and New York, it was greeted with the same lukewarm reception that most previous British attempts had faced. The single slipped into obscurity soon after its release. This 45, however, was the first true Beatles single to be released in the United States. (The Decca single released in 1962 merely features the Beatles as a backup group.)

While enjoying increasing popularity overseas, the Beatles and their manager were quite discouraged that they were not catching on in America. On May 27, 1963, Vee Jay decided to try again by releasing the group's second single, "From Me to You"/"Thank You Girl" (VJ-522). Although this single did land in the Top 30 in a few areas, such as Los Angeles, it reached only number 116 on the national (*Billboard* magazine) charts. Soon airplay and sales wound down and the record was, in the dubious sense of the word, history.

First U.S. Beatles Album

It was only after much persuasion from Epstein that Vee Jay released the first U.S. Beatles album, *Introducing the Beatles* (VJ LP-1062) on July 22, 1963. After the less-than-captivating sales of the two singles, Vee Jay did very little to distribute and promote the album. The Chicago area and the northeast gave the LP what little success it had.

In the normal scheme of things this would have been the end of yet another industry story. And in a sense it was: Vee Jay passed entirely on the group's next offering, "She Loves You"/"I'll Get You," which ended up on Swan Records, a Philadelphia label. As subsequent events were to prove, though, this was not the normal scheme of things.

Just when the dust was settling on Vee Jay's inventory of Beatles vinyl by the end of 1963, word of Beatlemania from Britain and the Continent was creeping into the American press. Stories about happily screaming crowds were picked up from the wire services and found their way into the papers and onto the radio. Capitol Records, which had rejected the group a year earlier, was urged (if not ordered) by their parent company, EMI, not only to sign the Beatles but to launch the largest promotional campaign ever devised by the music industry. It is only one measure of the success of this venture that we are writing about the Beatles a quarter of a century later.

Vee Jay didn't take long to blow the dust off their Beatles catalog and start cashing in on the sudden success of the group. In January 1964 Vee Jay was shipping all of the remaining inventory of Beatles singles and albums that had languished in the marketplace just months before.

That an independent label was sharing in the enormous success of the Beatles was embarrassing to Capitol—not to mention profit-threatening. Wanting all of the pie for themselves, Capitol wasted no time in putting legal pressure on Vee Jay. Assigning their top legal minds to the case, Capitol dealt their first blow by legally forcing Vee Jay to remove two tracks, "Love Me Do" and "P.S. I Love You," from their *Introducing the Beatles* album. (Apparently, Capitol had gained control of the publishing rights to these two tracks.) With the alacrity that usually comes with the hunt for big money, Vee Jay responded quickly by repackaging the album on January 27, 1964, replacing the two deleted tracks with "Please Please Me" and "Ask Me Why." This explains why, from a collector's standpoint, the first version (which includes "Love Me Do" and "P.S. I Love You") is much rarer and commands a greater value. The second version sold extremely well and is much more common.

Singles

Vee Jay was not about to let the grass grow under its feet in the singles market either. On January 30, 1964, they combined the A sides of their two 1963 discs and released "Please Please Me"/"From Me to You" (VJ-581). Featuring a nice picture sleeve, "Please Please Me" zoomed toward the top of the U.S. charts.

For reasons that are not entirely clear, the people at Vee Jay decided it would be in their best interest to move their headquarters to Santa Monica, California, in February or March 1964. Although the main offices were on the West Coast, most of the record pressing was still handled in Chicago and St. Louis. With the increased demand for Beatles products, Vee Jay was forced to subcontract much of the record production to many various record-pressing plants. That is why there are so many different label, logo, print, and color variations on Vee Jay's 1964 Beatles records (particularly the singles, although the albums had their share as well).

Without any hope of obtaining new Beatles material, which at this point was firmly in the hands of Capitol Records, Vee Jay began to create a small string of album packages intended to entice the ever-hungry public into believing they were purchasing brand-new Beatles albums. The first of these was released on February 26, 1964. With a title like *Jolly What! The Beatles and Frank Ifield on Stage* (VJ 1085), almost anyone would have thought it to be a collection of songs recorded live "onstage." In reality this LP was nothing more than a compilation of four Beatles tracks taken from the *Introducing the Beatles* LP and eight Frank Ifield tracks, also studio recordings.

Even with all of the furor of Beatlemania, most people were smart enough to look at the song listings and realize this was actually a Frank Ifield album with what amounts to two previously released Beatles singles tacked on.

Reluctant to let a bad idea die quickly, Vee Jay tried to stimulate the poor sales and chart action of the album by changing the cover art to make a more appealing package to Beatles buyers. Dropping the original art, which featured an old man with a Beatle haircut, they utilized a full color Beatles portrait in hopes of capturing more unsuspecting buyers. By the time the second covers were released, the public had sensed that a rip-off was afoot, and this version sold even less than the original. (Also due to rarity, this version has greater value; see listings.)

Tollie Label

On March 2, 1964, Vee Jay introduced their new Tollie label, and the next Beatles single, "Twist and Shout"/"There's a Place" (Tollie 9001) was Tollie's debut single. Even though twelve songs were made for only one successful album, those tracks certainly provided several hit singles. Within a short time of its release, "Twist and Shout" was perched near the top of most charts.

Having tasted success with an album and a couple of singles, Vee Jay figured it was time to test the EP (seven-inch extended play record) on the American market. The EP was titled *Souvenir of Their Visit to America* and featured four of the group's milder tracks. Whether because of the format, the selections, or the fact that the public was satisfied by already having these songs on previous releases, this EP received very little attention, and after this failure, Vee Jay didn't try the EP format again. Later promo copies and some of the stock copies carried the song "Ask Me Why" in bolder print than the other three; obviously, Vee Jay figured this track was strong enough to carry the EP to success. The promotional sleeve for the EP carried only "Ask Me Why"/"Anna," and a promotional single was distributed as well. Both items, however, were conceived far too late to save the dying record. (The above-mentioned promo items are now quite rare; see listings.)

While the EP had proved none too successful for Vee Jay, the singles were doing extremely well. "Do You Want to Know a Secret"/"Thank You Girl" (VJ 587) was released on March 23, 1964 (the same day as the EP), and did very well in terms of sales and chart activity.

As Vee Jay was striking gold with one hit after another, Capitol Records was applying heavy legal pressure that would ultimately force Vee Jay to relinquish all rights to its Beatles material. On April 9, 1964, Capitol Records won the court battle that stemmed from the suit originally filed on January 15, 1964. Capitol had successfully proved that Vee Jay breached the original contract by not paying the proper royalties to EMI. An out-of-court settlement had Vee Jay giving up its rights to the fourteen songs, but the actual forfeiture of the material would not take effect until early 1965.

On April 27, 1964, "Love Me Do"/"P.S. I Love You" (Tollie T-9008) was released, and Vee Jay had another monster hit on their hands. In August 1964 Vee Jay deleted their original singles and reissued them on their "Oldies 45" label.

Repackaging

With the sales of *Introducing the Beatles* tapering off and lacking material for new releases, Vee Jay, after sitting through a summer that belonged to Capitol and United Artists (who released the soundtrack to the film *A Hard Day's Night*) decided it was time for another Beatles package (even if it meant disguising *Introducing the Beatles* with a new cover and concept). On October 1, 1964, *The Beatles Vs. the Four Seasons* (VJ-DX 30) was released. This was a double album pairing Vee Jay's *Introducing the Beatles* with *The Golden Hits of the Four Seasons.* Even with the aid of a bonus poster and a colorful jacket—covered with hype of a "battle" and "comparison," musically pitting the Four Seasons against the Beatles—this attempt failed miserably and barely charted at all (thus becoming quite collectible).

Within a couple of weeks after the issue of *The Beatles Vs. the Four Seasons,* Vee Jay released another repackage of *Introducing the Beatles. Songs, Pictures and Stories of the Fabulous Beatles* (VJ 1092) was released on October 12, 1964. This time the concept was that the buyer could learn intimate facts about each of the Beatles, and also obtain even more photographs of their heroes. (The record used in this and the previous repackage contained *Introducing the Beatles* discs with their original title and catalog number.) This album fared somewhat better than the previous attempt and appeared on the Top 100 for a while, but it wasn't long before the public became aware that they were buying the same album for the fourth time.

After 1964 Capitol Records legally took control of the fourteen songs that Vee Jay, in less than two years, had stretched into four albums, six singles, four reissue singles, and one EP.

In early 1965 Capitol released its own version of the Vee Jay material on the LP, *The Early Beatles,* and probably because of the fresh Capitol packaging, the public was willing again to spring for the same songs offered repeatedly in 1964. Also, Capitol transferred Vee Jay's "Oldies" singles to their own "oldies" series label, Starline.

Postscript

After nearly two years of scrambling and hustling in desperation, trying to compete with the big boys, Vee Jay returned to distributing the rhythm and blues, pop, and gospel that had been its lifeblood prior to the Beatles era. Like so many other American independent labels during the British invasion, however, they found trouble at the bottom line. The company closed its doors in May 1966.

In the mid-1970s, Vee Jay surfaced again, mainly as a distributor for reissues of their 1950s and 1960s rhythm and blues material. In 1979 Vee Jay, now called Vee Jay International, released the only Beatles album that Capitol could not obtain control of: *Hear the Beatles Tell All,* a Beatles interview disc originally distributed in 1964, reportedly as a promotional item (although several copies did find their way to the retail record racks). This LP was reissued with a moderate amount of success and as of press time is still available in many retail outlets across the United States.

Vee Jay's involvement with the Beatles' American recording history has certainly added to the appeal of Beatles record collecting. It is the multitude of various records and packages along with the varying label styles, that makes up a major part of what record collecting is all about. Vee Jay has definitely made an interesting and colorful contribution to the hobby, as well as providing some of the most sought-after and valuable Beatles recordings.

LOST SONGS

The following is a list of songs recorded by the Beatles that were never officially released to the public. Some were intended for commercial release but due to better choices of material they fell by the wayside.

Most selections listed here were probably studio "warm-up" songs never intended for release. Not included in these listings are early (or different) versions of songs that were later released. Since studio versions are preferable to "live" radio broadcasts, if the same title was used on radio and in the studio, then it is only listed once below as a studio version.

1962

Demos were made for Brian Epstein to solicit record companies:

"Catwalk"	"The Years Roll Along"
"I Lost My Little Girl"	"Thinking of Linking"
"Keep Looking That Way"	"Winston's Walk"
"Looking Glass"	

Studio out-takes, warm-ups, etc.:

"How Do You Do It"	"Lucille"
"I Forget To Remember To Forget"	

1962 and 1963

BBC radio broadcasts:

"A Shot of Rhythm and Blues"
"A Picture of You"
"Beautiful Dreamer"
"Bound by Love"
"Carol"
"Clarabella"
"Crying, Waiting, Hoping"
"Cry Over You"
"Don't Ever Change"
"Dream Baby"
"Everyone Wants Someone"
"Glad All Over"
"Hippy Hippy Shake"
"I Don't Understand"
"I Forgot to Remember to Forget"
"I Got a Woman"
"I Got to Find My Baby"
"I Just Don't Understand"
"I'll Be on My Way"
"I'm Gonna Sit Right Down and Cry"
"I'm Talking About You"

"Johnny B. Goode"
"Keep Your Hands Off My Baby"
"Lend Me Your Comb"
"Lonesome Tears in My Eyes"
"Lucille"
"Memphis"
"Nothing's Shakin' Like the Leaves on the Tree"
"Oh My Soul"
"Please Don't Ever Change"
"Pop Goes the Pops" (radio show theme)
"Sheila"
"Side by Side"
"So How Come No One Loves Me"
"Some Other Guy"
"Sweet Little Sixteen"
"Sure to Fall"
"That's All Right Mama"
"To Know Her Is to Love Her"
"Too Much Monkey Business"
"Youngblood"

1963

Studio out-takes, warm-ups, etc.:

"Honeymoon Song," also known as "Bound by Love"
"Keep Your Hands Off My Baby"

"One After 909"
"Soldier of Love"
"Tip of My Tongue"

1964

Around the Beatles, a TV Special on the Beatles where they perform medleys of several of their hits plus:

"Shout"

1964

Studio out-takes, warm-ups, etc.:

"Always and Only"   "Leave My Kitten Alone"
"Keep Your Hands Off My Baby"   "You'll Know What To Do"

1965

Studio out-takes, warm-ups, etc.:
"If You Got Troubles"

1966

Studio out-takes, warm-ups, etc.:
"Colliding Circles"   "Pink Litmus Paper Shirt"

1967

Studio out-takes, warm-ups, etc.:

"Annie"   "Peace of Mind"
"Anything"   "Spiritual Regeneration"
"India"   "What's the New Mary Jane"
"Not Unknown"

1968

Studio out-takes, warm-ups, etc.:

"Cottonfields"   "Not Guilty"
"Goodbye"   "Step Inside Love"
"Heather"   "This Is Some Friendly"
"Jubilee," later titled "Junk" "Those Were the Days"

1969

Studio out-takes and warm-ups from the *Get Back/Let It Be* sessions total nearly 100 of "recorded material" on tape from January; the *Abbey Road* sessions were the last time they recorded as a group:

"All Things Must Pass"   "Besame Mucho"
"All Together on the Wireless Ma-   "Come and Get It"
  chine"   "Four Nights in Moscow"
"Back to Commonwealth," later   "Hi Heeled Sneakers"
  "Get Back"   "Hot As Sun"

"House of the Rising Sun"
"I Should Like to Live up a Tree"
"Mailman, Bring Me No More Blues"
"No Pakistanis"
"Save the Last Dance for Me"
"Shakin' in the 60s"

"Shake, Rattle and Roll"
"Suzy Parker"
"Teddy Boy"
"The Walk"
"When I Come to Town"
"What a Shame Mary Jane Had a Pain"

THE CAPITOL–APPLE DISCOGRAPHY

Beginning in early 1964 Capitol Records became the major manufacturer and distributor of American Beatle releases, a role that they continue to hold today. When Apple Records was formed by the Beatles in 1968, Capitol still maintained production and distribution control over Beatle records. When Apple was dissolved in 1975, the entire Beatles catalog, including solo releases, reverted back to Capitol.

The Beatles, collectively and individually, have also appeared on several other labels over the years. However, most of these releases failed to stay in production long enough to experience significant label design changes. The relatively few that did are discussed thoroughly in their respective sections. At this point, however, we feel none of them have undergone enough label changes to warrant a separate label discography.

To date there have been nine standard label changes for the original Beatles catalog of LPs and ten standard label changes on their singles. To our knowledge, this is the greatest number of standard label changes made by any recording artist.

The number of label changes for a particular release depends entirely on its original issue date. For example, *Meet The Beatles* has experienced all nine Capitol label changes since its release in 1964. On the other hand, *Abbey Road* has undergone only six changes since its 1969 release.

It is important to remember, however, that although the record company makes a standard label change at a particular point in time, each individual record will make the transition to the new label when existing stocks (with old labels) are depleted. Subsequently, a few releases with a certain label style have remained in stock after one or more standard label changes have occurred, resulting in some inconsistencies. When applicable, we list exactly which titles are available on each label.

Beatles LPs—Commercial Record Releases Only

1960s black label with rainbow colorband: In use from January 1964 to June 1969, applies to Beatles LPs 2047 through 2835. This label did not apply to the LPs issued on the Beatles' Apple label, starting in late 1968. See explanation under the listing for the Apple label.

1960s black label with rainbow colorband with "subsidiary" print at bottom of label: In use from June 1969 to September 1969, applies to Beatles LPs 2047 through 2835.

Green label: In use from September 1969 to January 1971, applies to Beatles LPs 2047 through 2835.

Apple label and Apple label with Capitol logo at bottom: In use from November 1968 to September 1975 (Capitol logo ceased in June 1971). *Note:* The release of the LP *The Beatles* marked the first Beatles LP on their newly formed, self-owned Apple record company. All new releases from this point were to be pressed with the Apple label.

Since Capitol maintained the manufacturing and distribution of the Apple records released in America, they felt it appropriate to acknowledge the fact by producing many of the Apple labels with their own Capitol logo along with brief information at the bottom of the "sliced" side of the Apple label. The addition of the Capitol logo was apparently not consistent at all three factories in operation at the time because certain quantities of records were pressed without this logo. For example, during the same time period, the LP *The Beatles* was pressed with plain Apple labels at one factory and with Capitol logo labels at another. Both factories, however, made deliveries of this LP to the retail stores at approximately the same time.

Initially, only new-release LPs incorporated the Apple label. The entire catalog did not adopt the Apple label until January 1971, at which time LPs 2047 through 2835 carried the Apple label. As with the earlier pressings, these reissue Apple LPs also experienced inconsistencies in the use of the Apple label versus the Apple label with the Capitol logo.

Apple label: In use from June 1971 to September 1975. During this period all Apple pressings other than custom labels incorporated the standard, plain Apple label.

Apple label with the "all rights" disclaimer: In use from September 1975 to December 1975.

Orange label (Capitol): In use from December 1975 to March 1978.

Purple Label: In use from March 1978 to July 1983.

Green "budget" label: In use from October 1980 to present. Thus far, this label appears on only two Beatles LPs: *Rock 'n' Roll Music Volume 1* and *Rock 'n' Roll Music Volume 2,* as well as on an unreleased version of the *Rarities* LP.

Current black label with rainbow colorband: In use from July 1983 to present. It is very important to learn the differences between this black label and the 1960s black label, to eliminate confusion and to avoid being deceived by someone trying to pass a recent issue off as an original.

The most distinctive difference between the current label and the original 1960s black label is the placement of the fine print around the perimeter. The originals have white print in the black area, whereas the current issues have black print in the colorband area.

Beatles Singles—Commercial Record Releases Only

Orange/yellow swirl label ("version 1" in the listings): In use from December 1963 to July 1968.

Orange/yellow swirl label with extra "subsidiary" print at bottom ("version 2" in the listings): In use from July 1968 to April 1969. This label did not apply to the singles issued on the Apple label, starting in late 1968. See explanation under the listing for the Apple label.

Red/orange target label with the dome style logo: In use from April 1969 to July 1969.

Red/orange target label with the round logo: In use from July 1969 to March 1971. *Note:* a small white dot was added to the center of the logo in January 1971 to enhance logo definition.

Apple label and Apple label with Capitol logo: In use from August 1968 to September 1975. Capitol logo ceased in May 1970. *Note:* The release of "Hey Jude/Revolution" in August 1968 marked the Beatles first product on their Apple label. All material from this point on was to be pressed on the Apple label.

Apple label with a star on the label: In use from March 1971 to July 1971. *Note:* Only singles 5112 thru 2138 can be found with the star.

Apple label: In use from July 1971 to September 1975. *Note:* During this period all Apple pressings other than custom labels incorporated the standard, plain Apple label.

Apple label with the "all rights" disclaimer: In use from September 1975 to December 1975.

Orange label (Capitol): In use from December 1975 to March 1978. *Note:* All of the Beatles catalog of 45s to this point were pressed on this label except for the single "Ballad Of John and Yoko."

Purple label: In use from March 1978 to July 1983. *Note:* This label was used for all singles pressed until November 1981, when record numbers 5112 through 5964 were issued using the blue Capitol "Starline" label along with new number designations (6278 through 6300). The rest of the catalog remained on the purple label until July 1983 (2056 through 2832 plus three new singles: 4274, 4347, and 4612).

Blue Starline label: In use from November 1981 to present. (See preceding note regarding purple labels.)

Current black label with rainbow colorband (and black Starline label): In use from July 1983 to present.

Labels for the Solo Beatles

Capitol's custom black label: Used only on the Paul McCartney catalog of LPs, from *McCartney* through *Band on the Run.* Paul's LPs switched to this label at the same time the others were transferred to Capitol's standard label and remained until Paul signed with Columbia Records in 1979.

There are three minor variations of this label that occurred over the course of its use.

Purple label: In use from March 1978 to July 1983. Titles verified with this label so far are John Lennon's *Live Peace in Toronto, Plastic Ono Band, Mind Games, Imagine, Sometime in New York City, Walls and Bridges, Rock 'n' Roll, Shaved Fish* and George Harrison's *All Things Must Pass* and *The Best of George Harrison.* Ringo Starr had *Sentimental Journey.*

Capitol's green "budget" label: In use from October 1980 to present. LPs found on this label are John Lennon's *Mind Games* and *Rock 'n' Roll.* George Harrison's *Living in the Material World, Dark Horse* and *Extra Texture* and Ringo Starr's *Sentimental Journey, Beaucoups of Blues, Ringo, Goodnight Vienna* and *Blast From Your Past.* (This is Ringo's entire original Apple catalog, all of which are now out of print.)

Capitol's gold Starline label with the round style logo: In use from April 1977 to March 1978. This label was used only on two solo Beatle singles: John Lennon's "Stand by Me"/"Woman Is the Nigger of the World" and George Harrison's "Dark Horse"/"You."

Capitol's gold Starline label with the oval style logo: In use from March 1978 to present. This label applies only to John Lennon's "Stand by Me"/"Woman Is the Nigger of the World" and George Harrison's "Dark Horse"/"You."

Black label with rainbow colorband: In use from July 1983 to present. As of press time, only the following singles have been verified using this label: John Lennon's "Imagine," "Happy Christmas" and "Mind Games," George Harrison's "My Sweet Lord" and "Give Me Love," and Ringo Starr's "It Don't Come Easy," "No No Song," "Photograph," and "You're Sixteen." Which remaining titles will appear on this label, or which will be deleted remains to be seen.

Capitol has now returned, as of July 1988, to the *purple* label. This new, purple label can be distinguished from the older purple label in the following way: Original purple labels read: "MFG. by Capitol." The newer purple label reads: Manufactured by Capitol."

BEATLES OFFICIAL U.S. RELEASES IN CHRONOLOGICAL ORDER

Major Releases Only

(Release date, title, format, label, and number)

4/23/62, My Bonnie/The Saints (45), Decca 31382

2/25/63, Please Please Me/Ask Me Why (45), Vee Jay 498

5/27/63, From Me to You/Thank You Girl (45), Vee Jay 522

7/22/63, *Introducing the Beatles* (LP), Vee Jay 1062

9/16/63, She Loves You/I'll Get You (45), Swan 4152

1/13/64, I Want to Hold Your Hand/I Saw Her Standing There (45), Capitol 5112

1/20/64, *Meet the Beatles* (LP), Capitol (S) T-2047

1/27/64, My Bonnie/The Saints (45), MGM K-13213

1/27/64, *Introducing the Beatles* (LP), Vee Jay 1062

1/30/64, Please Please Me/From Me to You (45), Vee Jay 581

2/3/64, *The Beatles with Tony Sheridan and Guests* (LP), MGM (S) E-4215

2/26/64, *Jolly What! The Beatles and Frank Ifield on Stage* (LP), Vee Jay 1085

3/2/64, Twist and Shout/There's a Place (45), Tollie 9001

3/16/64, Can't Buy Me Love/You Can't Do That (45), Capitol 5150

3/23/64, Do You Want to Know a Secret/Thank You Girl (45), Vee Jay 587

3/23/64, *Souvenir of Their Visit to America* (EP), Vee Jay EP-1-903

3/27/64, Why/Cry for a Shadow (45), MGM K-13227

4/10/64, *The Beatles' Second Album* (LP), Capitol (S) T-2080

4/27/64, Love Me Do/P.S. I Love You (45), Tollie 9008

5/11/64, *Four by the Beatles* (EP), Capitol EAP-1-2121

5/21/64, Sie Liebt Dich/I'll Get You (45), Swan 4182

6/1/64, Sweet Georgia Brown/Take Out Some Insurance on Me Baby (45), Atco 6302

6/26/64, *A Hard Day's Night* (LP), United Artists 6366

7/6/64, Ain't She Sweet/Nobody's Child (45), Atco 6308

7/13/64, A Hard Day's Night/I Should Have Known Better (45), Capitol 5222

7/20/64, I'll Cry Instead/I'm Happy Just to Dance with You (45), Capitol 5234

7/20/64, And I Love Her/If I Fell (45), Capitol 5235

7/20/64, *Something New* (LP), Capitol (S) T-2108

8/10/64, Do You Want to Know a Secret/Thank You Girl (45), Oldies 45 OL-149

8/10/64, Please Please Me/From Me to You (45), Oldies 45 OL-150

8/10/64, Love Me Do/P.S. I Love You (45), Oldies 45 OL-151

8/10/64, Twist and Shout/There's a Place (45) Oldies 45 OL-152

8/24/64, Matchbox/Slow Down (45), Capitol 5255

10/1/64, *Beatles vs. the Four Seasons* (LP), Vee Jay DX (S) 30

10/5/64, *Ain't She Sweet* (LP), Atco 33–169

10/12/64, *Songs, Pictures, and Stories of the Fabulous Beatles* (LP), Vee Jay 1092

11/23/64, I Feel Fine/She's a Woman (45), Capitol 5327

11/23/64, *The Beatles' Story* (LP), Capitol (S) T0BO-2222

12/15/64, *Beatles 65* (LP), Capitol (S) T-2228

2/1/65, *4 by the Beatles* (EP), Capitol R-5365

2/15/65, Eight Days a Week/I Don't Want to Spoil the Party (45), Capitol 5371

3/22/65, *Early Beatles* (LP), Capitol (S) T-2309

4/19/65, Ticket to Ride/Yes It Is (45), Capitol 5407

6/14/65, *Beatles VI* (LP), Capitol (S) T-2358

7/19/65, Help!/I'm Down (45), Capitol 5476

8/13/65, *Help!* (LP), Capitol (S) MAS-2386

9/13/65, Yesterday/Act Naturally (45), Capitol 5498

10/11/65, Twist and Shout/There's a Place (45), Capitol 6061

10/11/65, Love Me Do/P.S. I Love You (45), Capitol 6062

10/11/65, Please Please Me/From Me to You (45), Capitol 6063

10/11/65, Do You Want to Know a Secret/Thank You Girl (45), Capitol 6064

10/11/65, Misery/Roll over Beethoven (45), Capitol 6065

10/11/65, Kansas City/Boys (45), Capitol 6066

12/6/65, *Rubber Soul* (LP), Capitol (S) T-2442

12/6/65, We Can Work It Out/Day Tripper (45), Capitol 5555

2/21/66, Nowhere Man/What Goes On (45), Capitol 5587

5/27/66, Paperback Writer/Rain (45), Capitol 5651

6/15/66, *Yesterday and Today* (LP), Capitol (S) T-2553

8/8/66, Yellow Submarine/Eleanor Rigby (45), Capitol 5715

8/8/66, *Revolver* (LP), Capitol (S) T-2576

8/15/66, *This Is Where It Started* (LP), Metro 563

10/17/66, *Amazing Beatles and Other Great English Group Sounds* (LP), Clarion 601

2/13/67, Penny Lane/Strawberry Fields Forever (45), Capitol 5810

6/2/67, *Sgt. Pepper's Lonely Hearts Club Band* (LP), Capitol (S) MAS-2635

7/20/67, All You Need Is Love/Baby You're a Rich Man (45), Capitol 5964

10/27/67, Hello, Goodbye/I Am the Walrus (45), Capitol 2056

11/27/67, *Magical Mystery Tour* (LP), Capitol (S) MAL-2835

3/18/68, Lady Madonna/Inner Light (45), Capitol 2138

8/26/68, Hey Jude/Revolution (45), Apple 2276

11/25/68, *The Beatles* (LP), Apple SWBO-101

1/13/69, *Yellow Submarine* (LP), Apple SW-153

5/5/69, Get Back/Don't Let Me Down (45), Apple 2490

6/4/69, Ballad of John and Yoko/Old Brown Shoe (45), Apple 2531

10/1/69, *Abbey Road* (LP), Apple SO-383

10/6/69, Something/Come Together (45), Apple 2654

2/26/70, *Hey Jude* (LP), Apple SW-385

3/11/70, Let It Be/You Know My Name (45), Apple 2764

5/4/70, *In the Beginning (circa 1960)* (LP), Polydor 24-4504

5/11/70, Long and Winding Road/For You Blue (45), Apple 2832

5/18/70, *Let It Be* (LP), Apple AR-34001

4/2/73, *The Beatles 1962–1966* (LP), Apple SKBO-3403

4/2/73, *The Beatles 1966–1970* (LP), Apple SKBO-3404

5/31/76, Got to Get You into My Life/Helter Skelter (45), Capitol 4274

6/11/76, *Rock 'n' Roll Music* (LP), Capitol SKBO-11537

11/8/76, Ob-La-Di, Ob-La-Da/Julia (45), Capitol 4347

5/4/77, *The Beatles at the Hollywood Bowl* (LP), Capitol SMAS-11638

6/13/77, *Live at the Star Club in Hamburg, Germany: 1962* (LP), Lingasong
    LS-2-7001

10/21/77, *Love Songs* (LP), Capitol SKBL-11711

8/14/78, Sgt. Pepper's Lonely Hearts Club Band—With a Little Help from
    My Friends/A Day in the Life (45), Capitol 4612

3/24/80, *Rarities* (LP), Capitol SHAL-12060

11/30/81, I Want to Hold Your Hand/I Saw Her Standing There (45),
    Capitol A-6278

11/30/81, Can't Buy Me Love/You Can't Do That (45), Capitol A-6279

11/30/81, A Hard Day's Night/I Should Have Known Better (45), Capitol
    A-6281

11/30/81, I'll Cry Instead/I'm Happy Just to Dance with You (45), Capitol
    A-6282

11/30/81, And I Love Her/If I Fell (45), Capitol A-6283

11/30/81, Matchbox/Slow Down (45), Capitol A-6284

11/30/81, I Feel Fine/She's a Woman, Capitol A-6286

11/30/81, Eight Days a Week/I Don't Want to Spoil the Party (45), Capitol
    A-6287

11/30/81, Ticket to Ride/Yes It Is (45), Capitol A-6288

11/30/81, Help!/I'm Down (45), Capitol A-6290

11/30/81, Yesterday/Act Naturally (45), Capitol A-6291

11/30/81, We Can Work It Out/Day Tripper (45), Capitol A-6293

11/30/81, Nowhere Man/What Goes On (45), Capitol A-6294

11/30/81, Paperback Writer/Rain (45), Capitol A-6298

11/30/81, Yellow Submarine/Eleanor Rigby (45), Capitol A-6291

11/30/81, Penny Lane/Strawberry Fields Forever (45), Capitol A-6299

11/30/81, All You Need Is Love/Baby You're a Rich Man (45), Capitol A-6300

3/22/82, Movie Medley/I'm Happy Just to Dance with You (45), Capitol B-5107

3/22/82, *Reel Music* (LP), Capitol SV-12199

10/15/82, *Twenty Greatest Hits* (LP), Capitol SV-12245

11/19/82, Love Me Do/P.S. I Love You (45), Capitol B-5189

2/10/84, I Want to Hold Your Hand/I Saw Her Standing There (45), Capitol 5112

7/23/86, Twist and Shout/There's a Place (45) Capitol 5624

George Harrison Official U.S. Releases in Chronological Order

(Release date, title, format, label, and number)

12/2/68, *Wonderwall Music* (LP), Apple ST-3350

5/26/69, *Electronic Sound* (LP), Zapple ST-3358

11/23/70, My Sweet Lord/Isn't It a Pity (45), Apple 2995

11/27/70, *All Things Must Pass* (LP), Apple STCH-639

2/15/71, What Is Life/Apple Scruffs (45), Apple 1828

7/28/71, Bangla Desh/Deep Blue (45), Apple 1836

12/20/71, *Concert for Bangla Desh* (LP), Apple SCTX-3385

5/7/73, Give Me Love/Miss O'Dell (45), Apple 1862

5/29/73, *Living in the Material World* (LP), Apple SMAS-3410

11/18/74, Dark Horse/I Don't Care Anymore (45), Apple 1877

12/9/74, *Dark Horse* (LP), Apple SMAS-3418

12/23/74, Ding Dong, Ding Dong/Hari's On Tour (45), Apple 1879

9/15/75, You/World of Stone (45), Apple 1884

9/22/75, *Extra Texture* (LP), Apple SW-3420

12/8/75, This Guitar (Can't Keep from Crying)/Maya Love (45), Apple 1885

11/3/76, This Song/Learning How to Love You (45), Dark Horse DRC-8294

11/8/76, *Best of George Harrison* (LP), Capitol ST-11578

11/19/76, *33 and 1/3* (LP), Dark Horse DH-3005

1/24/77, Crackerbox Palace/Learning How to Love You (45), Dark Horse DRC-8313

4/4/77, Dark Horse/You (45), Capitol 6245

2/9/79, *George Harrison* (LP), Dark Horse DHK-3255

2/14/79, Blow Away/Soft Hearted Hana (45), Dark Horse DRC-8763

5/11/79, Love Comes to Everyone/Soft Touch (45), Dark Horse DRC-8844

5/6/81, All Those Years Ago/Writing on the Wall (45), Dark Horse DRC-49725

5/27/81, *Somewhere in England* (LP), Dark Horse DHK-3492

7/15/81, Teardrops/Save the World (45), Dark Horse DRC-49785

11/4/81, All Those Years Ago/Teardrops (45), Dark Horse GDRC-0410

10/27/82, *Gone Troppo* (LP), Dark Horse 1-23734

10/27/82, Wake Up My Love/Greece (45), Dark Horse 7-29864

2/9/83, I Really Love You/Circles (45), Dark Horse 7-29744

4/23/85, I Don't Want to Do It/Queen of the Hop (45), Columbia 38-04887

10/3/87, Got My Mind Set on You/Lay His Head (45), Dark Horse 7-28178

10/24/87, *Cloud Nine* (LP), Dark Horse 9 25643-1

1/30/88, When We Was Fab/Zig Zag (45), Dark Horse 7-28131

5/10/88, This Is Love/Breath Away From Heaven (45), Dark Horse 7-27913

John Lennon Official U.S. Releases in Chronological Order

(Release date, title, format, label, and number)

11/11/68, *Two Virgins* (LP), Apple T-5001

5/26/69, *Life with the Lions* (LP), Zapple St-3357

7/7/69, Give Peace a Chance/Remember Love (45), Apple 1809

10/20/69, *Wedding Album* (LP), Apple SMAX-3361

10/20/69, Cold Turkey/Don't Worry Kyoko (45), Apple 1813

12/12/69, *Live Peace in Toronto 1969* (LP), Apple SW-3362

2/20/70, Instant Karma/Who Has Seen the Wind (45), Apple 1818

12/11/70, *John Lennon—Plastic Ono Band* (LP), Apple SW-3372

12/28/70, Mother/Why (45), Apple 1827

3/22/71, Power To The People/Touch Me (45), Apple 1830

9/9/71, *Imagine* (LP), Apple SW-3379

10/11/71, Imagine/It's So Hard (45), Apple 1840

12/1/71, Happy Xmas (War Is Over)/Listen, the Snow Is Falling (45), Apple 1842

4/24/72, Woman Is the Nigger of the World/Sisters O Sisters (45), Apple 1848

6/12/72, *Sometime in New York City* (LP), Apple SVBB-3392

10/31/73, Mind Games/Meat City (45), Apple 1868

10/31/73, *Mind Games* (LP), Apple SW-3414

9/23/74, Whatever Gets You Through the Night/Beef Jerky (45), Apple 1874

9/26/74, *Walls and Bridges* (LP), Apple SW-3416

12/16/74, #9 Dream/What You Got (45), Apple 1878

2/17/75, *Rock 'n' Roll* (LP), Apple SK-3419

3/10/75, Stand By Me/Move Over Ms. L (45), Apple 1881

10/24/75, *Shaved Fish* (LP), Apple SW-3421

4/24/77, Stand By Me/Woman Is the Nigger of the World (45), Capitol 6244

10/23/80, (Just Like) Starting Over/Kiss Kiss Kiss (45), Geffen GEF-49604

11/17/80, *Double Fantasy* (LP), Geffen GHS-2001

1/12/81, Woman/Beautiful Boys (45), Geffen 49644

3/13/81, Watching the Wheels/Yes I'm Your Angel (45), Geffen 49695

6/5/81, (Just Like) Starting Over/Woman (45), Geffen GGEF-0408

11/4/81, Watching the Wheels/Beautiful Boy (Darling Boy) (45), Geffen GGEF-0415

11/3/82, *The John Lennon Collection* (LP), Geffen GHSP-2023

11/11/82, Happy Xmas/Beautiful Boy (Darling Boy) (45), Geffen 7-29855

11/9/83, *Heartplay* (LP), Polydor 817-238-1-Y1

12/1/83, Nobody Told Me/O'Sanity (45), Polydor 817-254-7

1/12/84, *Milk and Honey* (LP), Polydor 817-160-1-Y-1

2/14/84, I'm Stepping Out/Sleepless Night (45), Polydor 821-107-7

3/12/84, Borrowed Time/Your Hands (45), Polydor 821-204-7

11/10/84, Every Man Has a Woman Who Loves Him/It's Alright (45), Polydor 881-378-7

2/21/86, *Live in New York City* (LP), Capitol SV-12451

10/30/86, *Menlove Ave.* (LP), Capitol SJ-12533

Paul McCartney Official U.S. Releases in Chronological Order

(Release date, title, format, label, and number)

4/20/70, *McCartney* (LP), Apple STAO-3363

2/22/71, Another Day/Oh Woman Oh Why (45), Apple 1829

5/17/71, *Ram* (LP), Apple SMAS-3375

8/2/71, Uncle Albert—Admiral Halsey/Too Many People (45), Apple 1839

12/7/71, *Wildlife* (LP), Apple SW-3386

2/28/72, Give Ireland Back to the Irish/Give Ireland Back to the Irish (version) (45), Apple 1847

5/29/72, Mary Had a Little Lamb/Little Woman Love (45), Apple 1851

12/4/72, Hi Hi Hi/C Moon (45), Apple 1857

4/9/73, My Love/The Mess (45), Apple 1861

4/30/73, *Red Rose Speedway* (LP), Apple SMAL-3409

6/18/73, Live and Let Die/I Lie Around (45), Apple 1863

11/12/73, Helen Wheels/Country Dreamer (45), Apple 1869

12/5/73, *Band on the Run* (LP), Apple SO-3415

1/28/74, Jet/Mamunia, or Jet/Let Me Roll It (45), Apple 1871

4/8/74, Band on the Run/1985 (45), Apple 1873

11/4/74, Junior's Farm/Sally G (45), Apple 1875

12/2/74, Walking in the Park with Eloise/Bridge over the River Suite *(artist listed as Country Hams)* (45), EMI 3977

5/23/75, Listen to What the Man Said/Love in Song (45), Capitol 4091

5/27/75, *Venus and Mars* (LP), Capitol SMAS-11419

9/29/75, Letting Go/You Gave Me the Answer (45), Capitol 4145

10/27/75, Venus And Mars Rock Show/Magneto & Titanium Man (45), Capitol 4175

3/25/76, *Wings at the Speed of Sound* (LP), Capitol SW-11525

4/1/76, Silly Love Songs/Cook of the House (45), Capitol 4256

6/28/76, Let Em In/Beware My Love (45), Capitol 4293

12/10/76, *Wings over America* (LP), Capitol SWCO-11593

2/7/77, Maybe I'm Amazed/Soily (45), Capitol 4385

5/31/77, Seaside Woman/B-Side To Seaside *(artist listed as Suzy & Red Stripes),* Epic 8-50403

11/14/77, Mull of Kyntyre/Girls School (45), Capitol 4504

3/20/78, With a Little Luck/Backwards Traveler–Cuff Link (45), Capitol 4559

3/31/78, *London Town* (LP), Capitol SW-11777

6/12/78, I've Had Enough/Deliver Your Children (45), Capitol 4594

8/21/78, London Town/I'm Carrying (45), Capitol 4625

11/22/78, *Wings Greatest* (LP), Capitol SOO-11905

3/15/79, Goodnight Tonight/Daytime Nightime Suffering (45), Columbia 3-10939

3/15/79, Goodnight Tonight/Daytime Nightime Suffering (12-inch 45), Columbia 23-10940

5/24/79, *Back to the Egg* (LP), Columbia FC-36057

6/5/79, Getting Closer/Spin It On (45), Columbia 3-11020

8/14/79, Arrow Through Me/Old Siam, Sir (45), Columbia 1-11070

11/20/79, Wonderful Christmastime/Rudolf The Red-Nosed Reggae (45), Columbia 1-11162

4/15/80, Coming Up/Coming Up (live)-Lunch Box Odd Sox (45), Columbia 1-11263

5/21/80, *McCartney II* (LP), Columbia FC-36511

7/22/80, Waterfalls/Check My Machine (45), Columbia 1-11335

12/4/80, *McCartney Interview* (LP), Columbia Pc-36987

12/4/80, Getting Closer/Goodnight Tonight (45), Columbia 13-33405

12/4/80, My Love/Maybe I'm Amazed (45), Columbia 13-33407

12/4/80, Uncle Albert—Admiral Halsey/Jet (45), Columbia 13-33408

12/4/80, Band on the Run/Helen Wheels (45), Columbia 13-33409

4/2/82, Ebony and Ivory/Rainclouds (45), Columbia 18-02860

4/16/82, Ebony and Ivory/Rainclouds–Ebony and Ivory (12-inch 45), Columbia 44-02878

4/26/82, *Tug of War* (LP), Columbia TC-37462

7/10/82, Take It Away/I'll Give You a Ring (45), Columbia 18-03018

7/10/82, Take It Away/I'll Give You a Ring (12-inch 45), Columbia 44-03019

10/2/82, Tug of War/Get It (45), Columbia 38-03235

10/26/82, The Girl Is Mine/Can't Get Outta the Rain (with Michael Jackson) (45), Epic 34-03286

10/4/83, Say Say Say/Ode to a Koala Bear (45), Columbia 38-04168

10/4/83, Say Say Say—Say Say Say (Instrumental)/Ode to a Koala Bear (12-inch 45), Columbia 44-04169

10/26/83, *Pipes of Peace* (LP), Columbia QC-39149

12/13/83, So Bad/Pipes of Peace (45), Columbia 38-04296

10/2/84, No More Lonely Nights/No More Lonely Nights (45), Columbia 38-4581

10/2/84, No More Lonely Nights (Extended Version)/Silly Love Songs—No More Lonely Nights (Ballad) (12-inch 45), Columbia 44-05079

10/16/84, *Give My Regards to Broad Street* (LP), Columbia SC-39613

11/13/85, Spies Like Us/My Carnival (45), Capitol B-5537

11/13/85, Spies Like Us (Party Mix)—Spies Like Us (Alternate Mix)/Spies Like Us (D.J. Version)/My Carnival (12-inch 45), Capitol V-15212

7/16/86, Press/It's Not True (45), Capitol B-5597

7/16/86, Press (Video Soundtrack)—Press (Dub Mix)/It's Not True—Hangtide (12-inch 45), Capitol V-15235

7/30/86, Seaside Woman/B-Side To Seaside (45), Capitol B-5608

7/30/86, Seaside Woman/B-Side To Seaside (12-inch 45), Capitol V-15244

8/21/86, *Press to Play* (LP), Capitol PJAS-12475

10/29/86, Stranglehold/Angry *(Remix)* (45), Capitol B-5636

1/6/87, Only Love Remains/Tough on a Tightrope (45), Capitol B-5672

12/12/87, *All the Best* (LP), Capitol CLW-48287

Ringo Starr Official U.S. Releases in Chronological Order

(Release date, title, format, label, and number)

4/24/70, *Sentimental Journey* (LP), Apple SW-3365

9/28/70, *Beaucoup of Blues* (LP), Apple SMAS-3368

10/5/70, Beaucoup of Blues/Coochy-Coochy (45), Apple 2969

4/16/71, It Don't Come Easy/Early 1970 (45), Apple 1831

3/20/72, Back Off Boogaloo/Blindman (45), Apple 1849

9/24/73, Photograph/Down and Out (45), Apple 1865

10/31/73, *Ringo* (LP), Apple SWAL-3413

12/3/73, You're Sixteen/Devil Woman (45), Apple 1870

2/18/74, Oh My My/Step Lightly (45), Apple 1872

11/11/74, Only You/Call Me (45), Apple 1876

11/18/74, *Goodnight Vienna* (LP), Apple SW-3417

1/27/75, No No Song/Snookeroo (45), Apple 1880

6/2/75, It's All Down to Goodnight Vienna/Oo-Wee (45), Apple 1882

11/20/75, *Blast from Your Past* (LP), Apple SW-3422

9/20/76, A Dose of Rock 'N' Roll/Cryin' (45), Atlantic 3361

9/27/76, *Ringo's Rotogravure* (LP), Atlantic SD-18193

11/22/76, Hey Baby/Lady Gaye (45), Atlantic 3371

8/25/77, Wings/Just a Dream (45), Atlantic 3429

9/26/77, *Ringo the 4th* (LP), Atlantic SD-19108

10/18/77, Drowning in the Sea of Love/Just a Dream (45), Atlantic 3412

4/18/78, Lipstick Traces (on a Cigarette)/Old Time Relovin' (45), Portrait
6-70015

4/21/78, *Bad Boy* (LP), Portrait JR-35378

7/6/78, Heart on My Sleeve/Who Needs a Heart (45), Portrait 6-70018

10/27/81, Wrack My Brain/Drumming Is My Madness (45), Boardwalk
NB7-11-130

10/27/81, *Stop and Smell the Roses* (LP), Boardwalk NB1-33246

1/13/82, Private Property/Stop and Take Time to Smell the Roses (45),
Boardwalk NB7-11-134

Singles

What follows are all the singles, promotional releases, and picture sleeves that have been officially released by the Beatles, both as a group and as solo performers, in the United States. Under each artist's heading, the singles are listed alphabetically by titles. The first and subsequent issues are entered chronologically. The A-sides are in upper case while the B-sides are in upper and lower case. B-sides are also entered separately, cross-referenced to the A-sides.

For an explanation of the various Capitol labels, see the Capitol–Apple Discography, page 303.

Act Naturally: see YESTERDAY.

Ain't Nothing Shaking Like the Leaves on a Tree: see KANSAS CITY.

AIN'T SHE SWEET/Nobody's Child
Atco 6308 . . . . 7/6/64   **10–15**
Yellow and white label.
Counterfeit identification: print on label is blurred and broken up. Wax on counterfeit is pitted.

Atco 6308   **125–150**
Picture sleeve.
Counterfeit identification: graphic and colored areas of counterfeit are rough, while there is a difference in texture between the colored and white areas. The blue print on the counterfeit is noticeably darker than the original, and the B-Side printing is thinner on the fake.

Promotion copy, white label   **100–125**
Counterfeit identification: vinyl has pock marks and pitting. Label printing is not sharp.

AIN'T SHE SWEET/Sweet Georgia Brown
Atlantic OS-13243 83   **2–3**
Gold and black label.

Atlantic OS-13243 86   **2–3**
Red, silver and black label with black print.

ALL MY LOVING/You've Got to Hide Your Love Away
Evatone 420826cs. 7/82   **4–6**
Transparent red vinyl 7¼"-square flexi-disc with white print. The flexi is adhered to a card of the same size with a photo of the group visible through the soundsheet. Giveaways to promote the sale of Beatles LPs at the following retail record chains: Musicland, Discount and Sam Goody record stores. Each sound sheet is individually numbered and marked with the name of the retailer. Value given here is for the red flexi from Musicland. Back of card reads "Musicland."

"Discount"   **8–12**

"Sam Goody"   **15–20**

ALL MY LOVING/This Boy
Capitol 72144 71   **100–125**
Red and orange target label. This single, originally intended for the Canadian market, was mistakenly pressed in small quantities in America. While retaining the Canadian record number, the U.S. issue is identifiable by the title "USA" at the bottom of the disc's label.

ALL YOU NEED IS LOVE/Baby You're a Rich Man
Capitol 5964. . . . . . 7/20/67   **8–12**
Orange and yellow swirl label, version 1.

One of the most frequently repackaged titles in the Beatles catalog.

Capitol 5964   10–15
Orange and yellow swirl label, version 2.

Capitol 5964   10–15
Picture sleeve.
Counterfeit identification: colors and/or photos
are washed out, blurred, or faded.

Capitol P 5964   80–90
Promotion copy, green label.

Capitol 5964. 69   10–15
Red and orange target label.

Apple 5964 71–75   4–6
Apple label.

Capitol 5964. 75–78   2–4
Orange label.

Capitol 5964. 78–83   2–3
Purple label.

Capitol/Starline A/X 6300
. . . . 81–83   2–3
Blue Starline label.
Black Starline label, 83–88.
Purple Starline label, 88 to date.

AND I LOVE HER/If I Fell
Capitol 5235. . . . . . 7/20/64   8–12
Orange and yellow swirl label, version 1.

Capitol 5235   10–15
Orange and yellow swirl label, version 2.

Capitol 5235   35–40
Picture sleeve.

Capitol 5235. 69   10–15
Red and orange target label.

Apple 5235 71–75   4–6
Apple label.

Capitol 5235. 75–78   2–4
Orange label.

Capitol 5235. 78–83   2–3
Purple label.

Capitol/Starline A/X 3283
. . . . 81–83   2–3
Blue Starline label.
Black Starline label, 83–88.
Purple Starline label, 88 to date.

And I Love Her—see also *THIS BOY*.

ASK ME WHY/Anna
Vee Jay Special DJ No. 8 . . 64 **4000–5000**
Promotional copy, white label with blue cross-
bars. Issued to promote the sale of the Vee Jay
EP. See *ASK ME WHY* in the EP section.

Music by the Beatles, suits by
Pierre Cardin.

ASK ME WHY/Twist and Shout
Collectables 1514 . . . . *82*   2–3
Red, white, and blue union jack label. Taken
from the 1962 Hamburg live recordings.

Picture sleeve   2–3

**Ask Me Why: also see *PLEASE
PLEASE ME*.**

**Baby You're a Rich Man—see *ALL
YOU NEED IS LOVE*.**

**BALLAD OF JOHN AND
YOKO/Old Brown Shoe**
Apple 2531 . . . . *6/4/69*   **4–6**
Apple label with Capitol logo.

Apple 2531   **20–25**
Picture sleeve.

Americom M-382 . . . . . . *69*   **450–475**
A 4-inch round "pocket-disc." Flexi-disc was
issued in a red cardboard cover reading "Pocket
Disc," and was available in vending machines in
1969. This is one of four Beatles or Beatles related Flexis made for the "Pocket Disc" series.

Capitol 2531. . . . . . . *78–83*   **2–4**
Purple label.

Capitol 2531. . . . . *83 to date*   **2–3**
Black label with rainbow colorband.

**BE-BOP-A-LULA/Hallelujah, I Love
Her So**
Collectables 1510 . . . . . . *82*   **2–3**
Red, white, and blue union jack label. Taken
from the 1962 Hamburg live recordings.
Picture sleeve.   **2–3**

**Besame Mucho: see *TASTE OF
HONEY*.**

Boys: see *KANSAS CITY*.

**CAN'T BUY ME LOVE/You Can't
Do That**
Capitol 5150. . . . . . *3/16/64*   **8–12**
Orange and yellow swirl label, version 1.

Capitol 5150   **10–15**
Orange and yellow swirl label, version 2.

Capitol 5150   **275–300**
Picture sleeve.
Counterfeit identification: George's head
cropped in group photo. Original "Can't Buy
Me Love" sleeves used only the photo showing
George's full head.

Capitol 5150. . . . . *69*   **10–15**
Red and orange target label.

Apple 5150 . . . . *71–75*   **4–6**
Apple label.

Capitol 5150. . . . . . . *75–78*   **2–4**
Orange label.

Capitol 5150. . . . . . . *78–81*   **2–3**
Purple label.

Capitol/Starline A/X 6279
. . . . *81–83*   **2–3**
Blue Starline label.
Black Starline label, 83–88.
Purple Starline label, 88 to date.

**Can't Help It Blue Angel: see *I SAW
HER STANDING THERE*.**

CHRISTMAS RECORDS (The Fan Club Giveaways)

Christmas records were issued free to all American fan club members from 1964 through 1969. See also *THE BEATLES CHRISTMAS ALBUM* in the LP section.

Seasons Greetings from the Beatles

No label or catalog number . *64* **200–225**
7″ tri-fold soundcard. Inside features include photos and bulletins of the group. The middle section is vinyl coated and contains the recorded message.

The Beatles Third Christmas Record

Lyntone Lyn 948 . . . . . . *65* **125–150**
White label; one-sided 7-inch flexi-disc issued with a picture cover. Although issued to U.S. fan club members, this 1965 package was manufactured entirely in Britain.

Everywhere It's Christmas

No label or catalog number . *66* **125–150**
7″ × 8½″ postcard. Black vinyl with silver print. Soundsheet is adhered to one side of the card. Opposite side features bulletins to fans and two poems most likely written by John and/or Paul. The actual title of this soundcard is only found as the title of one of these poems.

Christmas Time Is Here Again

No label or catalog number . *67* **125–150**
7″ × 8½″ postcard. Vinyl is black with silver print. Soundsheet is adhered to one side of the card. The opposite side features a bulletin to fan club members.

The Beatles 1968 Christmas Record

H 2041. . . . . *68* **70–80**
White print direct on black vinyl; 7-inch flexi-disc issued with a picture cover. Covers used were surplus covers from the 1967 British package. The U.S. fan club decided to update the backs of the surplus covers, and inserted an American-made flexi-disc.

Happy Christmas 1969

H 2565. . . . . *69* **50–60**
One-sided 7-inch flexi-disc issued with a picture cover. Flexi-disc manufactured in the United States. The cover was made in England.

Christmas Sleeve, The Beatles

Vee Jay **40–45**
Picture sleeve. Special sleeve issued with Vee Jay and Tollie Beatle singles during Christmas 1964.

Come Together: see *SOMETHING.*

CRY FOR A SHADOW/Rock and Roll Music

Collectables 1520 **1–3**

Red, white and blue label with black print. Label incorrectly lists "Rock and Roll Music" as by "THE BEATLES." This cut is actually performed by Peter Best.

Cry For a Shadow: see *WHY.*

CRYING, WAITING, HOPING/Take Good Care of My Baby

Backstage BSR-1155 . . . . . *83* **10–15**
7-inch picture disc distributed for promotional purposes only.

Day in the Life: see *SGT. PEPPER'S LONELY HEARTS CLUB BAND.*

Day Tripper: see *WE CAN WORK IT OUT.*

DECADE

Apple MBRF-55551 . . . . . *72* **150–160**
White label with black print; radio advertisements for the Beatles' LPs *1962–1966* and *1967–1970*. One-sided disc. Distributed to radio stations only.

DO YOU WANT TO KNOW A SECRET/Thank You Girl

Vee Jay VJ 587 . . . . . *3/23/64* **15–20**
Black label with rainbow colorband, silver print.

Vee Jay VJ 587 **20–25**
Black label with silver print. Logo style is oval.

Vee Jay VJ 587 **30–35**
Black label with silver print. Logo style is brackets.

Vee Jay VJ 587 **15–20**
Black label with silver print and crossbars.

Vee Jay VJ 587 **35–40**
Yellow label.

Vee Jay VJ 587 **35–40**
Picture sleeve.

Vee Jay VJ 587 **125–150**
White label with blue and black print. For promotional use only.

Oldies 149 . . . . *8/10/64* **8–12**
Red label with black and white print. Counterfeits of this record may be easily identified by their all-black print. "Oldies 45" is printed in white on original copies.

Capitol 6064. . . . . . *10/11/65* **40–45**
Green Starline label.

Don't Let Me Down: see *GET BACK.*

EIGHT DAYS A WEEK/I Don't Want to Spoil the Party

Capitol 5371 . . . . . . *2/15/65* **8–12**
Orange and yellow swirl label, version 1.

Part of Vee Jay's earnest re-issue program when they realized they were on to a *good* thing.

Capitol 5371   **10–15**
Orange and yellow swirl label, version 2.

Capitol 5371   **10–15**
Picture sleeve.

Capitol 5371 . . . . *69*   **10–15**
Red and orange target label.

Apple 5371 . . . . *71–75*   **4–6**
Apple label.

Capitol 5371 . . . . *75–78*   **2–3**
Orange label.

Capitol 5371 . . . . *78–81*   **2–3**
Purple label.

Capitol/Starline A/X 6287
. . . . *81–83*   **2–3**
Blue Starline label.
Black Starline label, 83–88.
Purple Starline label, 88 to date.

Eleanor Rigby: see *YELLOW SUBMARINE.*

Everybody's Trying to Be My Baby: see *TIL THERE WAS YOU.*

Fab 4 On Film: see *MOVIE MEDLEY.*

FALLING IN LOVE AGAIN/Sheila
Collectables 1509 . . . . *82*   **2–3**
Red, white, and blue union jack label.

Collectables 1509   **2–3**
Picture sleeve.

For You Blue: see *LONG AND WINDING ROAD, THE.*

FROM ME TO YOU/Thank You Girl
Vee Jay VJ 522 . . . . . *5/27/63*   **100–125**
Black label with rainbow colorband. Logo style is oval.

Vee Jay VJ 522   **125–150**
Black label with rainbow colorband, silver print. Logo style is brackets.

Vee Jay VJ 522   **175–200**
Black label with silver print and crossbars.

Vee Jay VJ 522   **150–175**
White label. For promotional use only.

From Me to You: see also *PLEASE PLEASE ME.*

GERMAN MEDLEY, THE BEATLES
Evatone 1214825cs *83*   **40–45**
Translucent blue vinyl 7¼"-square flexi-disc with white print. The flexi is adhered to a card of the same size with a photo of the group visible through the soundsheet. Contains the songs "Kohm Gib Mir Deine Hand" and "Sie Liebt Dich," as well as excerpts from the Beatles 1963 Christmas message to the fan club. This flexi was available only through the House of Guitars Inc. music store in New York City as a souvenir for the Beatles 20th anniversary. Back of sheet reads "Not For Sale."

GET BACK/Don't Let Me Down
Apple 2490 . . . . *5/5/69*   **3–5**
Apple label.

Americom M-335 . . . . . . *69*   **450–475**
A 4-inch "pocket" flexi-disc. "Pocket Disc" was available in vending machines in 1969. This is one of four Beatles or Beatles related flexis made for the "Pocket Disc" series.

Capitol 2490 . . . . *75–78*   **2–4**
Orange label.

Capitol 2490 . . . . *78–83*   **2–3**
Purple label.

Capitol 2490 . . . . . *83 to date*   **2–3**
Black label with rainbow colorband.

GIRL/Girl
Capitol P-4506 . . . . *77*   **90–100**
Custom label. Promotion copy. Mono/Stereo. No commercial copies of this disc are known to exist, even though labels were printed.

GIRL/You're Gonna Lose That Girl
Capitol 4506 . . . . *77*   **10–15**
Picture sleeve. Sleeve was produced for cancelled commercial release.

GOT TO GET YOU INTO MY LIFE/Got to Get You into My Life
Capitol P-4274 . . . . *76*   **25–30**
White label with black print. Logo is in olive print. Mono/Stereo. For promotional use only. Label reads "Not For Sale."

GOT TO GET YOU INTO MY LIFE/Helter Skelter
Capitol 4274 . . . . . . *5/31/76*   **2–4**
Orange label.

Capitol 4274   **2–3**
Picture sleeve. "Helter Skelter" is not listed on the sleeve.

Capitol 4274 . . . . *78–83*   **2–4**
Purple label.

Capitol 4274 . . . . . *83 to date*   **2–3**
Black label with rainbow colorband.

Hallelujah, I Love Her So: see BE-BOP-A-LULA.

HARD DAYS NIGHT, A/I Should Have Known Better
Capitol 5222 . . . . . . *7/13/64*   **8–12**
Orange and yellow swirl label, version 1.

Capitol 5222   **10–15**
Orange and yellow swirl label, version 2.

Capitol 5222   **20–25**
Picture sleeve.

Capitol 5222 . . . . *69*   **10–15**
Red and orange target label.

Apple 5222 . . . . *71–75*   **4–6**
Apple label.

Capitol 5222 . . . . *75–78*   **2–4**
Orange label.

Capitol 5222 . . . . *78–81*   **2–3**
Purple label.

Capitol/Starline A/X 6281
. . . . *81–83*   **2–3**
Capitol Blue Starline label.
Black Starline label, 83–88.
Purple Starline label, 88 to date.

United Artists 750 . . . . . . *64*   **200–225**
Picture sleeve. Instrumental versions by George Martin.

HELLO GOODBYE/I Am the Walrus
Capitol 2056 . . . . . *10/27/67*   **8–12**
Orange and yellow swirl label, version 1.

Capitol 2056   **10–15**
Orange and yellow swirl label, version 2.

Capitol 2056   **25–30**
Picture sleeve.

Capitol 2056   **80–90**
Green label. Promotion copy. Label reads "Promotion Record Not For Sale."
Note: Counterfeits have matte-finish labels.

Capitol 2056 . . . . *69*   **10–15**
Red and orange target label.

Apple 2056 . . . . *71–75*   **4–6**
Apple label.

Capitol 2056 . . . . *75–78*   **2–4**
Orange label.

Capitol 2056 . . . . *78–83*   **2–3**
Purple label.

Capitol 2056 . . . . . *83 to date*   **2–3**
Black label with rainbow colorband.

HELP!/I'm Down
Capitol 5476 . . . . . . *7/19/65*   **8–12**
Orange and yellow swirl label, version 1.

Capitol 5476   **10–15**
Orange and yellow swirl label, version 2.

The Official Beatles picture for 1967.

Capitol 5476	**20–25**
Picture sleeve.	
Capitol 5476. . . . . *69*	**10–15**
Red and orange target label.	
Apple 5476 . . . . *71–75*	**4–6**
Apple label.	
Capitol 5476. . . . . . . *75–78*	**2–4**
Orange label.	
Capitol 5476. . . . . . . *78–81*	**2–3**
Purple label.	
Capitol/Starline A/X 6290	
. . . . *81–83*	**2–3**
Blue Starline label.	
Purple Starline label, 88 to date.	

HELTER SKELTER/Helter Skelter

Capitol P-4274 . . . . *76*   **25–30**
White label. Promotion copy. Mono/Stereo. Label reads "NOT FOR SALE."

Helter Skelter: see also GOT TO GET YOU INTO MY LIFE.

Here Comes the Sun: see MAGICAL MYSTERY TOUR.

HEY JUDE/Revolution

Apple 2276 . . . . . . *8/26/68*   **3–5**
Apple label.

Americom M-221. . . . . . *69*   **300–325**
A 4-inch round "pocket" flexi-disc. "Hey Jude" is a 3:25 edited version. Flexi-disc was issued in a red cardboard cover reading "Pocket Disc," and was available in vending machines in 1969. This is one of four Beatles or Beatles-related flexis made for the "Pocket Disc" series.

Capitol 2276. . . . . *75–78*	**2–4**
Orange label.	
Capitol 2276. . . . . *78–83*	**2–3**
Purple label.	
Capitol 2276. . . . . . *83 to date*	**2–3**
Black label with rainbow colorband.	

HIPPY HIPPY SHAKE/Sweet Little Sixteen

Collectables 1502 . . . . *82*   **2–3**
Red, white, and blue union jack label.

Collectables 1502   **2–3**
Picture sleeve.

HOLIDAY INKEEPER, A GIFT FROM YOUR

Capitol/Holiday Inn   **300–325**
Promotional flyer. Yellow paper stock with green print. Special flyer issued in conjunction with Holiday Inn and Capitol Records for promotional purposes. Flyer was either folded around, stapled to, or inserted in plain paper sleeves with stock copies of early 1964 Beatles singles.

I Am the Walrus: see HELLO, GOODBYE.

I Don't Want to Spoil the Party: see EIGHT DAYS A WEEK.

I FEEL FINE/She's a Woman

Capitol 5327. . . . . *11/23/64*   **8–12**
Orange and yellow swirl label, version 1.

Capitol 5327   **10–15**
Orange and yellow swirl label, version 2.

Capitol 5327   **20–25**
Picture sleeve.

Capitol 5327. . . . . *69*   **10–15**
Red and orange target label.

Apple 5327 . . . . *71–75*   **4–6**
Apple label.

Capitol 5327. . . . . . . *75–78*   **2–4**
Orange label.

Capitol 5327. . . . . . . *78–83*   **2–3**
Purple label.

Capitol/Starline A/X 6286
. . . . *83 to date*   **2–3**
Blue Starline label.

**I Remember You: see *LONG TALL
SALLY*.**

**I SAW HER STANDING
THERE/Can't Help It Blue Angel**
Collectables 1515 . . . . . . *82*   **2–3**
Red, white, and blue union jack label.

Collectables 1515   **2–3**
Picture sleeve.

**I Saw Her Standing There: see also *I
WANT TO HOLD YOUR HAND*.**

**I Should Have Known Better: see
HARD DAY'S NIGHT, A.**

**I WANT TO HOLD YOUR HAND/I
Saw Her Standing There**
Capitol 5112. . . . . . *1/13/64*   **8–12**
Orange and yellow swirl label, version 1.

Capitol 5112   **10–15**
Orange and yellow swirl label, version 2.

Capitol 5112   **30–35**
Picture sleeve.

Capitol 5112. . . . . *69*   **10–15**
Red and orange target label.

Apple 5112 . . . . *71–75*   **4–6**
Apple label.

Capitol 5112. . . . . . . *75–78*   **2–4**
Orange label.

Capitol 5112. . . . . . . *78–81*   **2–3**
Purple label.

Capitol/Starline A/X 6278
. . . . *81–83*   **3–5**
Blue Starline label.

Capitol 5112. . . . . . *2/10/84*   **2–3**
Orange and yellow swirl label with black print.
Single was released to celebrate the 20th anni-
versary of the Beatles arrival in the United
States. Nostalgic custom label is similar to the
1964 original, but differs by having rigid wax

and black printing around the label. Original
1964 copies have white printing.

Capitol 5112   **2–3**
Picture sleeve. Same photo as the original 1964
sleeve. Identifiable by a "1984" date printed in
the lower left hand corner.

Capitol P-5112/7-PRO-9076   **10–15**
Promotion copy. Orange and yellow swirl label.
Label reads "Not For Sale."

Capitol 5112. . . . . *85 to date*   **2–3**
Black label with rainbow colorband.
Purple label.

**I WANT TO HOLD YOUR
HAND/WMCA**
Capitol 5112. . . . . *64*   **750–775**
Picture sleeve. Promotion only picture sleeve
distributed in New York by radio station
WMCA. Sleeve has a photo of WMCA disc
jockeys on back. Issued with standard stock
single.

If I Fell: see *AND I LOVE HER*.

**I'LL CRY INSTEAD/I'm Happy Just
to Dance with You**
Capitol 5234. . . . . . *7/20/64*   **8–12**
Orange and yellow swirl label, version 1.

Capitol 5234   **10–15**
Orange and yellow swirl label, version 2.

Capitol 5234   **45–50**
Picture sleeve.

Capitol 5234. . . . . *69*   **10–15**
Red and orange target label.

Apple 5234 . . . . *71–75*   **4–6**
Apple label.

Capitol 5234. . . . . . . *75–78*   **2–4**
Orange label.

Capitol 5234. . . . . . . *78–81*   **2–3**
Purple label.

Capitol/Starline A/X 6282
. . . . *81–83*   **2–3**
Blue Starline label.
Black Starline label, 83–88.
Purple Starline label, 88 to date.

I'LL GET YOU/Blank
Swan 4152. . . . . *9/63*   **225–250**
Glossy white label. Promotion copy. One-sided
record. Has a black label and a silent play
groove on the blank side. The A-side has thin
print and no promotional markings; all Swan
records with white labels and black print are
promotional.

Swan 4152   **200–225**
Flat white label. Promotion copy. One-sided
record. Has a white label and a silent play

The same photo session served the purposes of several record companies. See "She Loves You" (Swan Records) picture sleeve.

groove on the blank side. The A-side has thin print and the words "Promotion Copy" on the label.

Swan 4152   225–250
Flat white label. Promotion copy. One-sided record. Has a white label on the blank side and no silent play groove. The A-side has thick print, two factory "X," and the words "Promotion Copy" on the label.

I'll Get You: see *SHE LOVES YOU* **and** *SIE LIEBT DICH.*

I'm Down: see *HELP!*

I'M GONNA SIT RIGHT DOWN AND CRY/Roll Over Beethoven
Collectables 1501 . . . . . . *82*   2–3
Red, white, and blue union jack label.

Collectables 1501   2–3
Picture sleeve.

I'm Happy Just to Dance with You: see *I'LL CRY INSTEAD* **and** *MOVIE MEDLEY.*

Inner Light: see *LADY MADONNA.*

Julia: see *OB-LA-DI, OB-LA-DA.*

KANSAS CITY/Ain't Nothing Shaking Like the Leaves on a Tree
Collectables 1507 . . . . . . *82*   2–4
Red, white, and blue union jack label.

Collectables 1507   2–4
Picture sleeve.

KANSAS CITY/Boys
Capitol 6066 . . . . . *10/11/65*   30–35
Green Starline label. Issued with blue and white "Starline" sleeve.

Capitol 6066 . . . . *69*   15–20
Red and orange target label.

KFWB: see *YOU CAN'T DO THAT.*

LADY MADONNA/Inner Light
Capitol 2138 . . . . . . *3/18/68*   8–12
Orange and yellow swirl label, version 1.

Capitol 2138   10–15
Orange and yellow swirl label, version 2.

Capitol 2138   20–25
Picture sleeve.

Capitol 2138   15–20
Fan club flyer issued with "Lady Madonna" picture sleeves to promote the Official Beatles Fan Club. This flyer has been counterfeited. The most distinguishable feature of the counterfeit is the low gloss of the paper used.

Capitol 2138   60–70
Green label with black print. Promotion copy. Label reads "Promotion Record Not For Sale." Labels are matte on counterfeits.

Capitol 2138 . . . . *69*   10–15
Red and orange target label.

Apple 2138 . . . . *71–75* **4–6**
Apple label.

Capitol 2138. . . . . *75–78* **2–4**
Orange label.

Capitol 2138. . . . . . . *78–83* **2–4**
Purple label.

Capitol 2138. . . . . . *83 to date* **2–3**
Black label with rainbow colorband.

LEAVE MY KITTEN ALONE/Ob-La-Di, Ob-La-Da
Capitol B-5439 **200–300**
Picture sleeve only. Produced in early 1985. It was to accompany the first single that was to be released from the aborted *Sessions* LP. This picture sleeve was the only product to survive this project.

LEND ME YOUR COMB/Your Feets Too Big
Collectables 1503 . . . . . . *82* **2–3**
Red, white, and blue union jack label.

Collectables 1503 **2–3**
Picture sleeve.

LET IT BE/You Know My Name
Apple 2764 . . . . *3/11/70* **3–5**
Apple label.

Apple 2764 **15–20**
Picture sleeve.

Capitol 2764. . . . . *75–78* **2–4**
Orange label.

Capitol 2764. . . . . . . *78–83* **2–3**
Purple label.

Capitol 2764. . . . . *83 to date* **2–3**
Black label with rainbow colorband.

LET IT BE, DIALOGUE
Beatles Promo 1970 **25–30**
White label. Promotional issue only. One-sided record issued to fan club members in 1970. There are two counterfeits: one is on clear vinyl; the second is on black vinyl but can be distinguished from the original by a target-shaped symbol in the trail-off area of the record. This symbol is stamped on the original and hand-etched on the counterfeit.

LET IT BE
United Artists ULP 42370 **400–425**
White label. Radio spots record. Used to promote the film. 33 1/3 rpm single with small hole. Contains one 60-second, one 30-second, and one 10-second spot.

LET'S DANCE/If You Love Me Baby
Collectables 1521 . . . . . . *87* **1–3**
Red, white, and blue label with black print. B-side performed by "The Beatles with Tony

Sheridan" (B-side also titled "Take Some Insurance Out on Me Baby"). A-side performed by Tony Sheridan only. Label incorrectly lists the performers as the Beatles.

LIKE DREAMERS DO/Love of the Loved
Backstage BSR 1112 . . . . . *82* **8–10**
Red label. Promotion record. Issued by Backstage Records and *Oui* Magazine to promote the *Like Dreamers Do* album. Record number can be found only in the trail-off area.

LIKE DREAMERS DO/Three Cool Cats
Backstage BSR 1122 . . . . . *82* **30–40**
7-inch picture disc distributed for promotional purposes only. Features semi-nude photo of *Penthouse* magazine's "Pet of the Month." Issued in a clear plastic cover. Issued for early airplay and review and was very limited to around 20 copies.

Backstage BSR 1133 . . . . . *83* **10–15**
7-inch picture disc distributed for promotional purposes only. Issued in mylar plastic cover with title sticker. Sticker reads "For Promotional Use Only."

Little Queenie—see *TO KNOW HER IS TO LOVE HER.*

LONG AND WINDING ROAD, THE/For You Blue
Apple 2832 . . . . *5/11/70* **5–8**
Apple label.

Apple 2832 **20–25**
Picture sleeve.

Capitol 2832. . . . . . . *75–78* **2–4**
Orange label.

Capitol 2832. . . . . . . *78–83* **2–3**
Purple label.

Capitol 2832. . . . . *83 to date* **2–3**
Black label with rainbow colorband.

LONG TALL SALLY/I Remember You
Collectables 1513 . . . . . . *82* **2–3**
Red, white, and blue union jack label.

Collectables 1513 **2–3**
Picture sleeve.

LOVE ME DO/Love Me Do
Capitol PB-5189 . . . . . . *82* **10–15**
Orange and yellow swirl label. Promotional release. Identified as a promotion record by the "PB" prefix before the record number. Part of the 20th anniversary celebrating the release of "Love Me Do" in England.

LOVE ME DO/P.S. I Love You

Tollie 9008	*4/27/64*	**15–20**
Yellow label with black print.		
Tollie 9008		**15–20**
Yellow label with green print.		
Tollie 9008		**25–30**
Black label with silver print.		
Tollie 9008		**40–45**
Picture sleeve.		
Tollie 9008		**100–125**
White label, promotion copy.		

Oldies 151	*8/10/64*	**10–15**

Red label with black and white print. Label may have either a glossy or flat finish. Counterfeits of this record are easily identified by their all-black print. "Oldies 45" is printed in white on the originals. Deduct 20% from value for those copies with a cut-out drill hole through the label.

Capitol 6062	*10/11/65*	**40–45**

Green Starline label.

When at first you *do* succeed, why change the formula? Tollie was Vee Jay's re-issue label, and the sleeve was taken from the cover of the justifiably ill-fated *On Stage* album.

Promotional copies of the early Beatles singles are highly prized. This is valued at roughly ten times more than the commercial release.

Capitol B-5189 . . . . *11/19/82*   **2–3**
Orange and yellow swirl label. Issued to celebrate the 20th anniversary of the British release of the single.

Capitol B-5189 . . . . *87*   **2–3**
Black label with colorband.

Capitol B-5189   **2–3**
Picture sleeve.

LOVE OF THE LOVED/Memphis
Backstage BSR-1122 . . . . *83*   **10–15**
7-inch picture disc distributed for promotional purposes only. Issued in mylar plastic cover with title sticker. Sticker reads "For Promotional Use Only."

Love of the Loved: see also *LIKE DREAMERS DO.*

MAGICAL MYSTERY TOUR/Here Comes the Sun
Evatone 420827 CS. *7/82*   **4–6**

MATCHBOX/Slow Down
Capitol 5255 . . . . . . *8/24/64*   **8–12**
Orange and yellow swirl label, version 1.

Capitol 5255   **10–15**
Orange and yellow swirl label, version 2.

Capitol 5255   **40–45**
Picture sleeve.

Capitol 5255. . . . . *69*   **10–15**
Red and orange target label.

Apple 5255 . . . . *71–75*   **4–6**
Apple label.

Capitol 5255. . . . . *75–78*   **2–4**
Orange label.

Capitol 5255. . . . . *78–81*   **2–3**
Purple label.

Capitol/Starline A/X 6284
. . . . *81–83*   **2–3**
Blue Starline label.
Purple Starline label, 88 to date.

Matchbox: see also *RED SAILS IN THE SUNSET.*

Memphis: see *LOVE OF THE LOVED.*

MISERY/Roll Over Beethoven
Capitol 6065. . . . . *10/11/65*   **40–45**
Green Starline label.

Capitol 6065. . . . . *69*   **10–15**
Red and orange target label.

MOVIE MEDLEY/Fab Four On Film
Capitol B 5100   **60–70**
Custom Capitol label. Single was never commercially released due to legal problems involving the B-side interview. Later released featuring the song "I'm Happy Just to Dance with You" on the B-side.

Capitol B 5100   **15–20**
Picture sleeve. Issued only with the promotional single.

Capitol PB 5100   **15–20**
Promotion copy. Custom capitol label. B-side contains a Beatle interview. Label reads "Not For Sale."

CAPITOL SPRO 9758   **45–50**
Custom Capitol label. Promotion copy. 12-inch single issued with a special picture cover. Label reads "Not For Sale."

MOVIE MEDLEY/I'm Happy Just to Dance with You
Capitol B 5107 . . . . . *3/22/82*   **2–3**
Custom Capitol label.

Capitol B 5107   **2–3**
Picture sleeve.

Mr. Moonlight: see *WHERE HAVE YOU BEEN ALL MY LIFE.*

MURRAY THE K AND THE BEATLES: AS IT HAPPENED
BRS-½ *64*   **25–30**
White label with black print. 33⅓rpm, small play hole single featuring a Beatle interview. Record number is only found etched on the trail-off area.
Counterfeit identification: known counterfeit features a blue label and a large play hole.

BRS-½   **75–80**
Picture sleeve. Record number is not printed on the sleeve. Most have staple holes which detract from the value.

IBC Distributing F4 KM-0082/3   **4–6**
Picture sleeve. Black and white photo. No titles on the sleeve.

Music City KFW—Beatles Talking: see *YOU CAN'T DO THAT.*

MY BONNIE/The Saints
Decca 31382 . . . . *4/62* **2800–3000**
Black and white label with color bars and silver and black print. First Beatle record in the United States. Artists' credits listed as "Tony Sheridan and the Beat Brothers."

Decca 31382   **700–750**
Promotion copy. Pink label. No promotional notice on label; however, all pink Decca singles are promotional. Artist listed as "Tony Sheridan and The Beat Brothers." Known counterfeit has "My Bonnie" on both sides of the record.

The 1961 Hamburg sessions have been released at different times by Atco, Polydor (the original label), and Decca, as well as MGM.

MGM K13213 . . . . . *1/27/64*   **10–15**
Black label. Artist listed as "The Beatles with Tony Sheridan."

MGM K13213   **15–20**
Black label. MGM LP number is listed under the artist credits.

MGM K13213   **40–45**
Title sleeve.

MGM K13213   **100–125**
Yellow label. Promotion copy. Reads "Special Disc Jockey Record Not For Sale."

Nobody's Child: see *AIN'T SHE SWEET.*

NOWHERE MAN/What Goes On
Capitol 5587. . . . . . . *2/21/66*   **8–12**
Orange and yellow swirl label, version 1.

Capitol 5587   **10–15**
Orange and yellow swirl label, version 2.

Capitol 5587   **15–20**
Picture sleeve.

Capitol 5587. . . . . *69*   **10–15**
Red and orange target label.

Apple 5587 . . . . *71–75*   **4–6**
Apple label.

Capitol 5587. . . . . *73–78*   **2–4**
Orange label.

Capitol 5587. . . . . *78–81*   **2–3**
Purple label.

Capitol/Starline A/X 6294
. . . . *81–83*   **2–3**
Blue Starline.

Black Starline, 83–88.
Purple Starline, 88 to date.

OB-LA-DI, OB-LA-DA/Julia
Capitol 4347. . . . . . *11/8/76*   **2–4**
Orange label.

Capitol 4347   **2–4**
Title sleeve. Sleeves were individually numbered.

Capitol 4347. . . . . . . *78–83*   **2–4**
Purple label.

Capitol 4347. . . . . *83 to date*   **2–3**
Black label with rainbow colorband.

Capitol P-4347   **25–30**
White label. Promotion copy. Logo is in olive green print. Mono/Stereo. Label reads "Not For Sale."

Old Brown Shoe: see *BALLAD OF JOHN AND YOKO.*

P.S. I Love You: see *LOVE ME DO.*

PAPERBACK WRITER/Rain
Capitol 5651. . . . . . *5/27/66*   **8–12**
Orange and yellow swirl label, version 1.

Capitol 5651   **10–15**
Orange and yellow swirl label, version 2.

Capitol 5651   **15–20**
Picture sleeve.

Capitol 5651. . . . . *69*   **10–15**
Red and orange target label.

Apple 5651 . . . . *71–75*   **4–6**
Apple label.

Capitol 5651. . . . . . . *75–78*   **2–4**
Orange label.

Capitol 5651. . . . . . . *78–83*   **2–3**
Purple label.

Capitol/Starline A/X 6296
. . . . *83 to date*   **2–3**
Blue Starline label.

PENNY LANE/Strawberry Fields Forever

Capitol 5810. . . . . . *2/13/67*   **8–12**
Orange and yellow swirl label, version 1.

Capitol 5810   **10–15**
Orange and yellow swirl label, version 2.

Capitol 5810   **30–35**
Picture sleeve.

Capitol 5810   **100–125**
Promotion copy. Green label. Most copies have a trumpet solo ending which is not found on the commercial copies. Very few have been found without the trumpet ending. Label reads "Promotion Record Not For Sale."
Counterfeit identification: known counterfeit records have a label which lacks the high gloss found on the originals. The star-shaped symbol in the trail-off area is hand etched rather than stamped, as is found on the original.

Capitol 5810. . . . . *69*   **10–15**
Red and orange target label.

Apple 5810 . . . . *71–75*   **4–6**
Apple label.

Capitol 5810. . . . . . . *75–78*   **2–4**
Orange label.

Capitol 5810. . . . . . . *78–81*   **2–3**
Purple label.

Capitol/Starline A/X 6299
. . . . *81–83*   **2–3**
Capitol Starline label.
Black Starline label, 83–88.
Purple Starline label, 88 to date.

PLEASE PLEASE ME/Ask Me Why

Vee Jay 498 . . . . *2/25/63*   **650–750**
Black label with rainbow colorband. Thin print style. Logo style is oval. Artist title is misspelled with two Ts: "Beattles."

Vee Jay VJ 498   **400–425**
Black label with rainbow colorband. Thick print style. Logo style is oval. Artist title is misspelled with two Ts: "Beattles."

Vee Jay VJ 498   **450–475**
Promotion copy. White label with black print. Logo style is oval. Beatles misspelled with two Ts. Label reads "Disc Jockey Advance Sample Not For Sale."

Vee Jay VJ 498   **650–750**
Black label with rainbow colorband, silver print. Logo style is brackets. Beatles misspelled with two Ts: "Beattles."

Vee Jay 498   **675–750**
Black label with rainbow colorband, silver print. Logo style is oval. Beatles misspelled with two Ts. Label has a number symbol (#) before the record number.

Vee Jay VJ 498   **700–775**
Black label with rainbow colorband, silver print. Logo style is oval. "Beatles" spelled correctly. Thin print style. Label has a number (#) symbol before the record number.

Vee Jay VJ 498   **400–425**
Black label with rainbow colorband, silver print. Logo style is oval. "Beatles" spelled correctly. Thin print style.

Vee Jay VJ 498   **500–525**
Black label with rainbow colorband, silver print. Logo style is brackets.

PLEASE PLEASE ME/From Me to You

Vee Jay VJ 581 . . . . . *1/30/64*   **15–20**
Black label with rainbow colorband.

Vee Jay VJ 581   **20–25**
Black label with silver print. Logo style is oval.

Vee Jay VJ 581   **25–30**
Black label with silver print. Logo style is brackets.

Vee Jay VJ 581   **20–25**
Black label with silver print and crossbars. Logo style is brackets.

Vee Jay VJ 581   **40–45**
Yellow label.

Vee Jay VJ 581   **70–80**
White label.

Vee Jay VJ 581   **100–125**
Purple label.

Vee Jay VJ 581   **125–150**
Picture sleeve.

Vee Jay VJ 581   **125–150**
Promotion copy. White label with blue and black print. Logo is a set of blue brackets.

Vee Jay VJ 581   **650–675**
Promotion title sleeve. Sleeve reads "Promotion Copy."

Oldies 150 . . . . *8/10/64*   **10–15**
Red label with black and white print. Label may be glossy or flat. Counterfeits of this record may be easily identified by their all-black print. "Oldies 45" is printed in white on original copies.

When Capitol finally got hold of the fourteen tracks previously licensed to Vee Jay, they re-issued the singles on their Starline label.

Deduct 20% from value for those copies with a cutout drill hole through the label.

Capitol 6063 . . . . .   *10/11/65*   **40–45**
Green Starline label.

Rain: see *PAPERBACK WRITER.*

RED SAILS IN THE SUNSET/Matchbox
Collectables 1511 . . . .   *82*   **2–3**
Red, white, and blue union jack label.

Collectables 1511   **2–3**
Picture sleeve.

Revolution: see *HEY JUDE.*

ROCKY RACCOON/Why Don't We Do It in the Road
Evatone 420828 CS *7/82*   **4–6**
Clear vinyl 7¼-inch square flexi-disc with red print. The flexi is adhered to a card of the same size with a photo of the group visible through the soundsheet. The flexis were issued to promote the sale of Beatles LPs at the three record retail chains with one given away with each album sold. Each sound sheet is individually numbered. Value given here is for the Musicland version. Back card reads "Musicland."

"Discount Records."   **8–12**

"Sam Goody."   **15–20**

ROLL OVER BEETHOVEN
Silhouette Music *86*   **8–12**
6-inch square flexi-disc adhered to photo card. Contains live version from the group's '62 Hamburg shows. Issued with 28-page photo/story booklet. Value includes booklet.

Roll Over Beethoven: see *MISERY* **and** *I'M GONNA SIT RIGHT DOWN.*

RUBY BABY/Ya Ya
Collectables 1523 . . . .   *87*   **1–3**
Red, white, and blue label with black print. This record was performed entirely by Tony Sheridan and the Beat Brothers. Label incorrectly lists the artist's title as "The Beatles." This is not a true Beatles record and is listed only to bring attention to the error.

Saints, The: see *MY BONNIE.*

SGT. PEPPER'S LONELY HEARTS CLUB BAND—WITH A LITTLE HELP FROM MY FRIENDS/A Day in the Life
Capitol 4612 . . . . . .   *8/14/78*   **2–4**
Purple label.

Capitol 4612   **3–5**
Picture sleeve.

Capitol 4612 . . . . .   *83 to date*   **2–3**
Black label with rainbow colorband.

SGT. PEPPER'S LONELY HEARTS CLUB BAND—WITH A LITTLE HELP FROM MY FRIENDS/Sgt. Pepper's Lonely Hearts Club Band—With a Little Help from My Friends
Capitol P-4612   **25–30**
White label with black print. Promotion copy. Mono/Stereo. Label reads "Not For Sale."

SHE LOVES YOU/I'll Get You

Swan 4152. . . . . . . *9/16/63* **175–200**
White label with red print. The words "Don't Drop Out" are not on label. Song titles do not have quotation marks. Label is glossy.
Counterfeit identification: known counterfeits have a trail-off record number which is one-half the size (1/16 inch) of the original. The stamping "Mastering Reco-Art Phila" does not appear on the counterfeit.

Swan 4152 **200–225**
White label with red print. The words "Don't Drop Out" do not appear on label. Song titles have quotation marks. Label is flat (not glossy).

Swan 4152 **225–250**
White label with red print. "Don't Drop Out" is on label.

Swan 4152 **175–200**
White label with blue print. "Don't Drop Out" is on label.

Swan 4152 **15–20**
Black label with silver print. All "She Loves You" singles with black labels are second pressings, issued in 1964. "Don't Drop Out" is not on label.
Counterfeit identification: known counterfeits have a wider B-side trail-off area (3/4 ") than the originals (1/2 "). Also, the record number in the trail-off area is hand etched in the known counterfeit copies, and machine stamped on the originals. The words "Mastering Reco-Art

Phila" are present in the trail-off area of the originals. This is absent in counterfeits.

Swan 4152 **20–25**
Black label. "Don't Drop Out" is present on the label. "Produced by George Martin" is present under "The Beatles."

Swan 4152 **30–35**
Picture sleeve. Accompanied the second pressing black label singles.
Counterfeit identification: known counterfeits' photo lacks the clarity of the original. The counterfeit has larger inside fold (1") than the original (1/2 ").

Swan 4152 **200–225**
Promotion copy. Glossy white label with black print. Has a factory "X" on the A-side, and the words "Promotional Copy Not For Sale" on the label. "Don't Drop Out" is not on the label.

Swan 4152 **150–175**
Promotion copy. Flat white label with black print. Has two factory "x" and the words "Promotion Copy Not For Sale" on the label. "Don't Drop Out" is not on the label.

Slow Down: see *MATCHBOX*.

SOMETHING/Come Together

Apple 2654 . . . . *10/6/69* **10–15**
Apple label with Capitol logo.

Apple 2654 **3–5**
Apple label.

Capitol 2654. . . . . . . *75–78* **2–4**
Orange label.

The Beatles single that even Vee Jay turned down first appeared on the Swan label out of Philadelphia. "She Loves You" had been the Beatles' first million seller in Britain.

Capitol 2654. . . . . . . *78–83*   **2–3**
Purple label.

Capitol 2654. . . . . . *83 to date*   **2–3**
Black label with rainbow colorband.

Strawberry Fields Forever: see *PENNY LANE.*

SWEET GEORGIA BROWN/Take Out Some Insurance on Me Baby
Atco 6302 . . . . *6/1/64*   **40–45**
Yellow and white label with black print.

Atco 45–6302   **125–150**
Promotion copy. White label with black print.

Sweet Georgia Brown: see also *AIN'T SHE SWEET.*

Sweet Little Sixteen: see *HIPPY HIPPY SHAKE.*

Take Good Care of My Baby: see *CRYING, WAITING, HOPING.*

Take Out Some Insurance on Me Baby: see *SWEET GEORGIA BROWN.*

TALKIN' ABOUT YOU/Shimmy Shimmy Shake
Collectables 1512 . . . . *82*   **2–3**
Red, white and blue union jack label.

Collectables 1512   **2–3**
Picture sleeve.

TASTE OF HONEY/Besame Mucho
Collectables 1505 . . . . *82*   **2–3**
Red, white, and blue union jack label.

Collectables 1505   **2–3**
Picture sleeve.

Thank You Girl: see *DO YOU WANT TO KNOW A SECRET* **and** *FROM ME TO YOU.*

There's A Place: see *TWIST AND SHOUT.*

THIS BOY (RINGO'S THEME)/And I Love Her
United Artist 745 . . . . . . *64*   **50–60**
Picture sleeve. Of interest because of photos of the Beatles on both sides of the sleeve. Instrumental versions by George Martin.

This Boy: see also *ALL MY LOVING.*

Three Cool Cats: see *LIKE DREAMERS DO* **and** *TILL THERE WAS YOU.*

TICKET TO RIDE/Yes It Is
Capitol 5407 . . . . . . *4/19/65*   **8–12**
Orange and yellow swirl label, version 1.

Capitol 5407   **10–15**
Orange and yellow swirl label, version 2.

Capitol 5407   **50–60**
Picture sleeve.

Capitol 5407 . . . . *69*   **10–15**
Red and orange target label.

Apple 5407 . . . . *71–75*   **4–6**
Apple label.

Capitol 5407 . . . . *75–78*   **2–4**
Orange label.

Another single from the '61 Hamburg sessions with Tony Sheridan. Things had changed a great deal since the record had been first released by "Tony Sheridan and the Beat Brothers" on Decca.

Capitol 5407. . . . . . .   *78–83*   **2–3**
Purple label.

Capitol/Starline A/X 6288
. . . .   *83 to date*   **2–3**
Blue Starline label.
Black Starline label, 83–88.
Purple Starline label, 88 to date.

TILL THERE WAS YOU/Everybody's Trying To Be My Baby

Collectables 1506 . . . . . .   *82*   **2–3**
Red, white, and blue union jack label.

Collectables 1506   **2–3**
Picture sleeve.

TILL THERE WAS YOU/Three Cool Cats

Evatone 830771-X *3/83*   **4–6**
Promotional flexi-disc. Red vinyl with white print. A bonus to buyers of limited-edition *Complete Beatles U.S. Record Price Guide.* Label reads "For Promotional Purposes Only."

TWIST AND SHOUT/There's a Place

Tollie 9001 . . . .   *3/2/64*   **15–20**
Yellow label with black print.

Tollie 9001   **20–25**
Yellow label with black print. Logo 2.

Tollie 9001   **25–30**
Yellow label with green print. Logo 1.

Tollie 9001   **15–20**
Yellow label with green print. Logo 5.

Tollie 9001   **40–45**
Yellow label with blue print. Logo 4.

Tollie 9001   **35–40**
Yellow label with purple print. Logo 2.

Tollie 9001   **25–30**
Black label with silver print. Logo 3.

Oldies 152 . . . .   *8/10/64*   **10–15**
Red label with black and white print. Deduct 20% from value for those copies with cut-out drill hole through the label.

Capitol 6061. . . . .   *10/11/65*   **25–30**
Green Starline label.

Capitol B-5624 . . . . .   *7/23/86*   **2–3**
Black label.

Capitol P-B-5624   **10–12**
Promotion copy. White label. Label reads "Not For Sale."

Twist and Shout: see also *ASK ME WHY.*

WE CAN WORK IT OUT/Day Tripper

Capitol 5555. . . . . .   *12/6/65*   **8–12**
Orange and yellow swirl label, version 1.

Capitol 5555   **10–15**
Orange and yellow swirl label, version 2.

Capitol 5555   **15–20**
Picture sleeve.

Capitol 5555. . . . .   *69*   **10–15**
Red and orange target label.

Capitol 5555   **600–650**
Red and white Starline label. Only Beatles record issued on this label. This single was released in error in mid-1969.

Apple 5555 . . . .   *71–75*   **4–6**
Apple label.

Capitol 5555. . . . .   *75–78*   **2–4**
Orange label.

Capitol 5555. . . . . . .   *78–81*   **2–3**
Purple label.

Capitol A/X 6293 . . . .   *81–83*   **2–3**
Blue Starline label.

What Goes On: see *NOWHERE MAN.*

WHAT'D I SAY/Sweet Georgia Brown

Collectables 1522 . . . . . .   *87*   **1–3**
Red, white, and blue label with black print. B-Side performed by the Beatles with Tony Sheridan. A-side performed by Tony Sheridan and the Beat Brothers. Labels incorrectly list the artists as "The Beatles."

WHERE HAVE YOU BEEN ALL MY LIFE/Mr. Moonlight

Collectables 1504 . . . . . .   *82*   **2–3**
Red, white and blue union jack label.

Collectables 1504   **2–3**
Picure sleeve.

WHY/Cry for a Shadow

MGM K-13227 . . . . .   *3/27/64*   **20–25**
Black label with silver print. Artists listed as "The Beatles with Tony Sheridan."

MGM K-13227   **100–125**
Title sleeve. Artists listed as "The Beatles with Tony Sheridan."

MGM K-13227   **100–125**
Promotion copy. Label reads "Special Disc Jockey Record Not For Sale."

WHY/I'll Try Anyway

Collectables 1524 . . . . . .   *87*   **1–3**
Red, white, and blue label with black print. Label incorrectly lists artist's title on the B-side as "The Beatles." B-side is actually by Peter Best.

Discounting stock: some record companies use a big saw; others, like Cameo, just pull the trigger. Whatever means they use, the effect is the same—roughly 20% to 25% off the value.

Why Don't We Do It in the Road: see *ROCKY RACCOON.*

WMCA: see *I WANT TO HOLD YOUR HAND.*

YELLOW SUBMARINE/Eleanor Rigby
Capitol 5715. . . . . . . 9/8/66   **8–12**
Orange and yellow swirl label, version 1.

Capitol 5715   **10–15**
Orange and yellow swirl label, version 2.

Capitol 5715   **15–20**
Picture sleeve.

Capitol 5715. 69   **10–15**
Red and orange target label.

Apple 5715 71–75   **4–6**
Apple label.

Capitol 5715. 75–78   **2–4**
Orange label.

Capitol 5715. 78–81   **2–3**
Purple label.

Capitol/Starline A/X 6297
. . . . 81–83   **2–3**
Blue Starline label.
Black Starline label, 83–88.
Purple Starline label, 88 to date.

YESTERDAY/Act Naturally
Capitol 5498. . . . . . 9/13/65   **8–12**
Orange and yellow swirl label, version 1.

Capitol 5498   **10–15**
Orange and yellow swirl label, version 2.

Capitol 5498   **15–20**
Picture sleeve.

Capitol 5498. 69   **10–15**
Red and orange target label.

Apple 5498 71–75   **4–6**
Apple label.

Capitol 5498. 75–78   **2–4**
Orange label.

Capitol 5498. 78–81   **2–3**
Purple label.

Capitol/Starline A/X 6291
. . . . 81–83   **2–3**
Blue Starline label.
Black Starline label, 83–88.
Purple Starline label, 88 to date.

YOU CAN'T DO THAT/Music City KFWBeatles
Capitol Custom RB-2637 . . 64   **250–275**
Promotion copy. Red label with black print. Available in the Los Angeles area briefly in 1964 through KFWB and Music City Record Stores. The B-side of this record features Beatle interviews.
Counterfeit identification: known counterfeit label lacks the Capitol Custom logo present on the original.

Capitol Custom RB-2637   **600–625**
Title sleeve. Yellow envelope with red print.

You Can't Do That: see also *CAN'T BUY ME LOVE.*

You Know My Name: see *LET IT BE.*

Your Feets Too Big: see *LEND ME YOUR COMB.*

You've Got to Hide Your Love Away: **see** *ALL MY LOVING.*

PETER BEST: SINGLES, PROMOS, AND PICTURE SLEEVES

BOYS/Kansas City
Cameo C-391-A/B *66*   **20–25**
Black and red label. Artist listed as "Peter Best (formerly of the Beatles)." Usually found with a punched bb-hole in the label. (Deduct 20% for singles with bb-holes.)

Cameo C-391-A/B   **50–55**
Title sleeve. Deduct 20% for sleeves with bb-holes.

Cameo C-391-A/B   **20–25**
Promotion copy. Black and red label. Label reads "D.J. Copy Not For Sale."

CASTING MY SPELL/I'm Blue
Mr. Maestro 712 . . . . . . *65*   **35–40**
Light blue label.

Mr. Maestro 712   **40–45**
Promotion copy. Blue vinyl.

HOW'D YOU GET TO KNOW HER NAME/If You Can't Get Her
Collectables 1519 . . . . . . *87*   **1–3**
Red, white, and blue label with black print. Although the label incorrectly prints the artists as "The Beatles," the artist is actually Peter Best.

I CAN'T DO WITHOUT YOU/Keys to My Heart
Mr. Maestro 711 . . . . *65*   **35–40**
Light blue label.

Mr. Maestro 711   **40–45**
Promotion copy. Blue vinyl.

IF YOU CAN'T GET HER/Don't Play with Me
Happening 405 . . . . *64*   **40–45**
White label.

IF YOU CAN'T GET HER/The Way I Feel About You
Happening Ha-1117/8 . . . . *66*   **40–50**
Red label with blue print.

I'LL HAVE EVERYTHING TOO/I'm Checking Out Now Baby
Collectables 1518 . . . . *87*   **1–3**
Red, white, and blue label with black print. Although the label incorrectly lists the artists as "The Beatles," the artist is actually Peter Best.

(I'LL TRY) ANYWAY/I Wanna Be There
Beatles BEST-800 A/B. . . . *64*   **40–45**
Black label.

One of those curses of history, ironically set off by the use of the artist's name on this single—"BEST of the BEATLES."

I'LL TRY ANYWAY/I Don't Know Why I Do (I Just Do)
Collectables 1516 . . . . . . *87*   **1–3**
Red, white, and blue label with black print. Although the label incorrectly lists the artists as "The Beatles," the artist is actually Peter Best. Some copies can be found with a sticker reading "PETER BEST of the Beatles" over the incorrect title.

I'LL TRY ANYWAY/Why
Collectables 1524 . . . . . . *87*   **1–3**
Red, white, and blue label with black print. Disc label incorrectly lists the B-side as being by "The Beatles," the artist on the B-side is actually Peter Best. A-side is performed by The Beatles.

ROCK AND ROLL MUSIC/Cry for a Shadow
Collectables 1520 . . . . . . *87*   **1–3**
Red, white, and blue label with black print. Label incorrectly lists the A-side as being by "The Beatles." The artist on the A-side is actually Peter Best. B-side is composed and performed by the Beatles.

SHE'S NOT THE ONLY GIRL IN TOWN/More Than I Need Myself
Collectables 1517 . . . . . . *87*   **1–3**
Red, white, and blue label with black print. Although the label lists the artist's title as "The Beatles," the artist is actually Peter Best.

The following is a list of singles by the Beatles with Peter Best as drummer. Only the titles are given here. Values and descriptions remain in the Beatles singles section:

"Ain't She Sweet"

"Crying, Waiting, Hoping"

"Like Dreamers Do"

"Love of the Loved"

"My Bonnie"

"Sweet Georgia Brown"

"Till There Was You"

"Why"

GEORGE HARRISON: SINGLES, PROMOS, AND PICTURE SLEEVES

ALL THOSE YEARS AGO/All Those Years Ago
Dark Horse DRC-49725   **10–15**
Promotion copy. Tan label. Mono/Stereo. Label reads "Promotion Not For Sale."

Dark Horse PRO-A-949   **25–30**
Promotion 12-inch single. Tan label. Stereo only single. Issued with a title cover. Label reads "Promotion Not For Sale."

ALL THOSE YEARS AGO/Teardrops
Dark Horse GDRC-0410
. . . . *11/4/81*   **2–3**
Tan label.

Dark Horse GDRC-0410 . . *86*   **2–3**
Tan label with "Back to Back Hits" on the label.

ALL THOSE YEARS AGO/Writings on the Wall
Dark Horse DRC-49725 . *5/6/81*   **2–3**
Tan label.

Dark Horse DRC-49725   **2–3**
Picture sleeve.

Apple Scruffs: see *WHAT IS LIFE.*

BANGLA DESH/Deep Blue
Apple 1836 . . . . *7/28/71*   **4–6**
Apple label.

Apple 1836   **10–15**
Picture sleeve.

Capitol 1836. . . . . *75–78*   **4–6**
Orange label.

Capitol 1836. . . . . . . *78–83*   **2–3**
Purple label.

Capitol 1836. . . . . . . *83–86*   **2–3**
Black label with rainbow colorband.

BANGLA DESH, THE CONCERT FOR

Apple/20th Century Fox WLC-
791. . . . . *71*   **350–375**
Radio spots record. White label. One-sided 7-
inch 33 1/3 rpm record, with a small play hole,
containing two 60-second and two 30-second
radio spots.

BLOW AWAY/Blow Away

Dark Horse DRC 8763   **10–15**
Promotional copy. Tan label. Mono/Stereo.
Label reads "Promotion Not For Sale."

BLOW AWAY/Soft Hearted Hana

Dark Horse DRC 8763 *2/24/74*   **2–3**
Tan label.

Dark Horse DRC 8763   **2–4**
Picture sleeve.

Circles: see *I REALLY LOVE YOU.*

CRACKERBOX PALACE/Crackerbox Palace

Dark Horse DRC-8313   **10–15**
Promotion copy. Tan label. Mono/Stereo.
Label reads "Promotion Copy Not For Sale."

CRACKERBOX PALACE/Learning to Love You

Dark Horse DRC-8313 *1/24/77*   **2–3**
Tan label.

DARK HORSE/I Don't Care Anymore

Apple 1877 . . . . . . *11/18/74*   **3–5**
White or blue and white custom photo label.

Apple 1877   **40–45**
Title sleeve.

Apple 1877   **25–30**
Promotion copy. White label. Label reads "Not
For Sale."

DARK HORSE/You

Capitol 6245. . . . '. . . . *4/4/77*   **3–5**
Tan Starline label. Capitol logo.

Capitol 6245. . . . . *78*   **2–3**
Tan Starline label. Capitol logo.

Capitol/Starline X-6245 . . . *87*   **2–3**
Black label with colorband.

Deep Blue: see *BANGLA DESH*

DEVIL'S RADIO [Gossip] (LP Version)/Devil's Radio [Gossip] (LP Version)

Dark Horse PRO-A-2889 . . *87*   **20–25**
Promotional only 12-inch single. Tan label. Is-
sued with picture cover. Label reads "PROMO-
TION COPY. NOT FOR SALE."

DING DONG, DING DONG/Ding Dong, Ding Dong

Apple P-1879   **25–30**
Promotion copy. White label. Mono/Stereo.
Mono version is a different mix than the stock
record. Label reads "Not For Sale."

DING DONG, DING DONG/Hari's On Tour (Express)

Apple 1879 . . . . . . *2/23/74*   **10–15**
Black and white custom photo label.

Apple 1879   **10–15**
Title sleeve.

Capitol 1879. . . . . . . *78–83*   **2–3**
Purple label.

GIVE ME LOVE/Give Me Love

Apple PRO 6676 (P-1862)   **30–35**
Promotion copy. Apple label. Mono/Stereo.
Label reads "Not For Sale."

GIVE ME LOVE/Miss O'Dell

Apple 1862 . . . . *5/7/73*   **3–5**
Apple label.

Capitol 1862. . . . . . . *78–83*   **2–3**
Purple label.

Capitol 1862. . . . . *83 to date*   **2–3**
Black label with rainbow colorband.

GOT MY MIND SET ON YOU/Got My Mind Set On You

Dark Horse 7-28178-A   **10–15**
Promotional issue. Tan label. Label reads "Promotion—not for sale."

Dark Horse PRO-A-2845   **15–20**
Promotional 12-inch single. Tan label. Label
reads "Promotional copy—not for sale." Issued
with picture cover.

GOT MY MIND SET ON YOU/Lay His Head

Dark Horse 7-28178 . . . *10/87*   **2–3**
Tan label.

Dark Horse 7-28178   **2–3**
Picture sleeve.

Greece: see *WAKE UP MY LOVE.*

Hari's On Tour: see *DING DONG, DING DONG.*

I Don't Care Anymore: see *DARK HORSE.*

I DON'T WANT TO DO IT/I Don't Want To Do It
Columbia 38-04887   **10–15**
Promotion copy. White label. Label states "Demonstration—Not For Sale."

Columbia CAS-2085   **15–20**
Promotional 12-inch single. Red label. Label reads "Demonstration—Not For Sale."

I DON'T WANT TO DO IT/Queen of the Hop
Columbia 38-04887. . . *4/23/85*   **2–3**
Orange and yellow label. From the soundtrack LP *Porky's Revenge.* B-side performed by Dave Edmunds.

I REALLY LOVE YOU/Circles
Dark Horse 7-29744 . . . *2/9/83*   **5–8**
Tan label.

LOVE COMES TO EVERYONE/Love Comes To Everyone
Dark Horse DRC 8844   **10–15**
Promotion copy. Tan label. Mono/Stereo. Label reads "Promotion Not For Sale."

LOVE COMES TO EVERYONE/Soft Touch
Dark Horse DRC 8844 *5/11/79*   **2–4**
Tan label.

Dark Horse DRC 8844   **250–275**
Picture sleeve.

Maya Love: see *THIS GUITAR.*

Miss O'Dell: see *GIVE ME LOVE.*

MY SWEET LORD/Isn't It a Pity
Apple 2995 . . . . . . *11/23/70*   **4–6**
Apple label. *All* Apple "My Sweet Lord" variations have unsliced apples on both sides of the records.

Apple 2995   **20–25**
Picture sleeve.

Capitol 2995. . . . . *75–78*   **3–5**
Orange label.

Capitol 2995. . . . . *78–83*   **2–4**
Purple label.

Capitol 2995. . . . . *83–88*   **2–3**
Black label with rainbow colorband. New purple label, 88 to date.

Queen of the Hop (by Dave Edmunds): see *I DON'T WANT TO DO IT.*

Save the World: see *TEARDROPS.*

Soft Hearted Hana: see *BLOW AWAY.*

Soft Touch: see *LOVE COMES TO EVERYONE.*

TEARDROPS/Save the World
Dark Horse DRC49785 *7/15/81*   **3–5**
Tan label.

TEARDROPS/Teardrops
Dark Horse DRC49785   **10–15**
Tan label. Promotional copy.

Teardrops: see also *ALL THOSE YEARS AGO.*

THIS GUITAR/This Guitar
Apple P-1885   **30–35**
Promotion copy. Apple label. Mono/Stereo. Label reads "Not For Sale."

THIS GUITAR/Maya Love
Apple 1885 . . . . *12/8/75*   **4–6**
Apple label.

THIS SONG/Learning How To Love You
Dark Horse DRC 8294 *11/3/76*   **5–8**
Tan label.

THIS SONG/This Song
Dark Horse DRC 8294   **35–40**
Promotional title sleeve.

Dark Horse DRC 8294   **20–25**
Promotional flyer.

WAKE UP MY LOVE/Greece
Dark Horse 7-29864 . *10/27/82*   **3–5**
Tan label.

WAKE UP MY LOVE/Wake Up My Love
Dark Horse 7-29864   **10–15**
Promotion copy. Tan label. Mono/Stereo. Label reads "Promotion Not For Sale."

Dark Horse PRO-A-1075   **25–30**
Promotional 12-inch single. Tan label. Issued with a title cover. Label reads "Promotion—Not For Sale."

WHAT IS LIFE/Apple Scruffs
Apple 1828 . . . . *2/15/71*   **4–6**
Apple label.

Apple 1828   **20–25**
Picture sleeve.

Capitol 1828. . . . . *75–78*   **5–8**
Orange label.

Capitol 1828. . . . . *78–83*   **2–3**
Purple label.

WHEN WE WAS FAB/When We Was Fab
Dark Horse 7-28131-A. . . *1/88*   **10–15**
Promotion copy. Tan label. Contains LP version (3:55). Label reads "PROMOTION NOT FOR SALE."

WHEN WE WAS FAB (LP version)/When We Was Fab (LP version)
Dark Horse PRO-A-2885 . . *87*   **12–15**
Promotional 12-inch single. Tan label. Issued in a plain white cover. Label reads "PROMOTIONAL COPY. NOT FOR SALE."

WHEN WE WAS FAB/Zig Zag
Dark Horse 7-28131 . . . . *1/88*   **2–3**
Tan label.

Dark Horse 7-28131   **2–3**
Picture sleeve.

World of Stone: see *YOU*.

Writing on the Wall: see *ALL THOSE YEARS AGO*.

YOU/World of Stone
Apple 1884 . . . . . . *9/15/75*   **3–5**
Orange and blue custom label.

Apple 1884   **10–15**
Picture sleeve.

YOU/You
Apple P-1884   **30–35**
Promotion copy. Orange and blue custom label. Mono/Stereo. Label reads "Not For Sale."

You: see also *DARK HORSE*.

JOHN LENNON: SINGLES, PROMOS, AND PICTURE SLEEVES

AIN'T THAT A SHAME/Ain't That a Shame
Apple P-1883 . . . . . . *6/2/75*   **100–125**
Promotion copy. Apple label. Mono/Stereo. Record was never commercially released. Label reads "Not For Sale."

Beautiful Boy (Darling Boy): see *HAPPY XMAS* and *WATCHING THE WHEELS*.

Beautiful Boys: see *WOMAN*.

Beef Jerky: see *WHATEVER GETS YOU THROUGH THE NIGHT*.

BORROWED TIME/Your Hands
Polydor 821-204-7 . . . . . . *84*   **2–3**
Red label. B-side by Yoko Ono.

Polydor 821-204-7   **2–3**
Picture sleeve.

Not every record pressed makes it into the stores. "Ain't That a Shame" was going to be the single released in conjunction with Lennon's *Rock 'n' Roll* LP, but it was abandoned in favor of "Stand by Me."

Polydor 821-204-7   **10–15**
Promotion copy. Red label. Label reads "Promotional Copy Not For Sale."

COLD TURKEY/Don't Worry Kyoko

Apple 1813 . . . . . .   *10/20/69*   **3–5**
Apple label. Artists listed as "John Lennon & The Plastic Ono Band." B-side performed by Yoko Ono.

Apple 1813   **70–80**
Picture sleeve.

Come Together: see *IMAGINE.*

Don't Worry Kyoko: see *COLD TURKEY.*

EVERY MAN HAS A WOMAN WHO LOVES HIM/Every Man Has a Woman Who Loves Him

Polydor 881-378-7 DJ *84*   **10–15**
Promotion copy. Red label. Label reads "Promotional Copy Not For Sale."

EVERY MAN HAS A WOMAN WHO LOVES HIM/It's Alright

Polydor 881-378-7 . . . . . . *84*   **2–3**
Red label. B-side performed by Sean Ono Lennon.

Polydor 881-378-7   **2–3**
Picture sleeve.

GIVE PEACE A CHANCE/Remember Love

Apple 1809 . . . . *7/7/69*   **3–5**
Apple label. Artists listed as "Plastic Ono Band." B-side by Yoko Ono.

Apple 1809   **10-15**
Picture sleeve.

Americom M 435 A-B *69*   **450–475**
A 4-inch round "pocket-disc." Flexi-disc was issued in a red cardboard cover reading "Pocket Disc," and was available in vending machines in 1969. This is one of four Beatles or Beatles-related Flexis made for the "Pocket Disc" series.

HAPPY XMAS (WAR IS OVER)/Beautiful Boy (Darling Boy)

Geffen 7-29855 . . . . *11/11/82*   **2–3**
Cream label.

Geffen 7-29855   **2–3**
Picture sleeve.

Geffen PRO A 1079   **25–30**
Promotion 12-inch single. Cream label. Issued in a special title cover. Label and cover read "Promotional Copy Not For Sale."

HAPPY XMAS (WAR IS OVER)/Happy Xmas (War Is Over)

Geffen 7-29855   **10–15**
Promotion copy. Cream label. Mono/Stereo. Label reads "Promotion Not For Sale."

Lennon's second solo single was an auspicious step into the primal mood. The introspection is evidenced by this X-ray photo of his head.

Capitol SPRO-9894. . . . *11/86* **200–225**
Promotion only 12-inch single. Black label with colorband. Very limited issue (2000 copies) specially pressed for a benefit sponsored by the Central Virginia food bank and some local Virginia radio and TV stations. Copies obtained directly at the benefit were issued with special photo/title covers. These covers were sequentially numbered 1 to 2000. Disc label and cover read "NOT FOR SALE." Value separation: cover 75%/disc 25%.

HAPPY XMAS (WAR IS OVER)/Listen, the Snow Is Falling
Apple 1842 . . . . *12/1/71* **8–12**
Custom faces label. Green vinyl. B-side by Yoko Ono.

Apple 1842 **4–6**
Apple label.

Apple 1842 **15–20**
Picture sleeve.

Apple S-45X-47663/4 **200–225**
Promotion copy. White label. Black vinyl. Label reads "Not For Sale—For Radio Station Play Only."

Capitol 1842. . . . . *75–78* **8–12**
Orange label.

Capitol 1842. . . . . . . *78–83* **2–3**
Purple label.

Capitol 1842. . . . . *83 to date* **2–3**
Black label with rainbow colorband.

Capitol SPRO-9929. . . . *12/86* **40–45**
Promotion only 12-inch single. Custom Silver label with red and white print. Issued in clear plastic cover with title sticker. Pressings were limited to 2500 copies. Disc label and title sticker read "Not For Sale."

I'M STEPPING OUT/I'm Stepping Out
Polydor 821-107-7 DJ *84* **10–15**
Promotion copy. Label reads "Promotional Copy Not For Sale."

I'M STEPPING OUT/Sleepless Night
Polydor 821-107-7 . . . . . . *84* **2–3**
Red label. B-side by Yoko Ono.

Polydor 821-107-7 **2–3**
Picture sleeve.

IMAGINE/It's So Hard
Apple 1840 . . . . . *10/11/71* **3–5**
Tan or green Apple label.

Capitol 1840. . . . . *78–83* **2–3**
Purple label.

Capitol 1840. . . . . *83 to date* **2–3**
Black label with rainbow colorband.

IMAGINE/Come Together
Capitol SPRO 9585/6 . . . . *86* **30–35**
Promotional only 12-inch single. New black label with rainbow colorband. Issued in a plain white cover with a title sticker. Label reads "Not For Sale."

INSTANT KARMA/Who Has Seen the Wind
Apple 1818 . . . . *2/20/70* **4–6**
Apple label. B-side by Yoko Ono.

Apple 1818 **10–15**
Picture sleeve.

INSTANT KARMA
Apple 1818 **125–150**
Promotion copy. Apple label with black and green print. One-sided promotional issue. B-side label is all black with no print. No promotional markings on the label.

It's Alright: see *EVERY MAN HAS A WOMAN WHO LOVES HIM.*

It's So Hard: see *IMAGINE.*

JOHN LENNON AND YOKO ONO
Evatone Aspen No. 7 section 11
. . . . *69* **200–225**
Flexi-disc. Black vinyl. Issued with *Aspen 7 3D* magazine. Issued in an 11″ × 11″ × 1½″ box, titled "The British Box—spring and summer issue" with a 3″ × 4″ diary book. A-side features John talking. B-side features John and Yoko reciting poetry.

JOHN LENNON INTERVIEW/In My Life
Orange Peel Pub.—Hoffman Music OR-70078 . . . . . . *81* **15–20**
7-inch picture disc featuring photo of John Lennon and David Peel. Contains interview about Peel by John Lennon backed with the song "In My Life" by David Peel and the Apple Band.

JOHN LENNON ON RONNIE HAWKINS—THE LONG RAP/The Short Rap
Atlantic PRO-104/105 . . . . *70* **50–60**
Promotion copy. White label. Message by John Lennon to promote the Ronnie Hawkins single "Down in the Alley." Label reads "Promo Record."

Cotillion PR-104/105 **30–35**
Promotion copy. White label. Label reads "Promotional Copy Not For Sale."
Counterfeit identification: print on the known counterfeit label is blurred and faded. The registered trademark symbol is absent on the

counterfeit. This symbol is located on the original in the upper right hand corner of the Cotillion logos box. Known counterfeit has the song "Down in the Alley" listed on the label along with "The Short Rap."

Just Like Starting Over: see *(Just Like) STARTING OVER.*

Kiss Kiss Kiss: see *(Just Like) STARTING OVER.*

Listen, the Snow Is Falling: see *HAPPY XMAS (WAR IS OVER).*

Long Rap, The/The Short Rap: see *JOHN LENNON ON RONNIE HAWKINS.*

Meat City: see *MIND GAMES.*

MIND GAMES/Meat City
Apple 1868 . . . . . . *10/31/73*   **3–5**
Apple label.

Apple 1868   **8–12**
Picture sleeve.

Capitol 1868. . . . . *78–83*   **2–3**
Purple label.

Capitol 1868. . . . . . *83 to date*   **2–3**
New black label with colorband.

MIND GAMES/Mind Games
Apple 1868   **30–35**
Promotion copy. Apple label. Mono/Stereo. Label reads "Not For Sale."

MOTHER/Why
Apple 1827 . . . . . . *12/28/70*   **3–5**
Apple label.

Apple 1827   **8–12**
Apple label. The word "Mono" is printed below the A-side song title.

Apple 1827   **80–90**
Picture sleeve.

Move Over Ms. L.: see *STAND BY ME.*

NOBODY TOLD ME/O'Sanity
Polydor 817 254-7 . . . . . *83*   **3–5**
Red label. Bottom of the label reads "Manufactured by Polydor Incorporated/810 Seventh

The first glimmering of Lennon's legacy on tape—a song that did not make it onto *Double Fantasy* but appeared in the posthumous *Milk and Honey* LP.

Avenue/New York, N.Y. 10019." B-side by Yoko Ono.

Polydor 817 254–7   **2–3**
Red label. Bottom of the label reads "Manufactured and Marketed by Polygram Records, Inc. 810 Seventh Avenue New York, N.Y. 10019."

Polydor 817 254–7   **2–3**
Picture sleeve.

Polydor PRO-250-1   **30–35**
Promotion 12-inch single. Red label. Issued in a special picture cover featuring the same photo as the 7-inch picture sleeve. Issued with either black or translucent purple vinyl. Label and cover read "Promotional Copy Not For Sale."

NOBODY TOLD ME/Nobody Told Me

Polydor 817-254–7   **10–15**
Promotion copy. Red label. Issued with either black or translucent purple vinyl. Label reads "Promotional Copy Not For Sale."

#9 DREAM/#9 Dream

Apple P-1878   **30–35**
Promotion copy. Apple label. Mono/Stereo. Label reads "Not For Sale."

#9 DREAM/What You Got

Apple 1878 . . . . . . *12/16/74*   **3–5**
Apple label.

Capitol 1878. . . . . *75–78*   **8–10**
Orange label.

Capitol 1878. . . . . . . *78–83*   **2–3**
Purple label.

O'Sanity: see *NOBODY TOLD ME.*

POWER TO THE PEOPLE/Touch Me

Apple 1830 . . . . *3/22/71*   **3–5**
Apple label. B-side by Yoko Ono.

Apple 1830   **20–25**
Picture sleeve.

Capitol 1830. . . . . . . *78–83*   **2–3**
Purple label.

Capitol 1830. . . . . *83 to date*   **2–3**
Black label with rainbow colorband.

Remember Love: see *GIVE PEACE A CHANCE.*

ROCK 'N' ROLL

Quaye/Trident SK 3419 . . . *75*   **250–275**
Radio spots record. White label. Small hole single containing one 60-second radio spot. Used to promote John's *Rock 'n' Roll* LP.

ROCK AND ROLL PEOPLE/Rock and Roll People

Capitol SPRO 9917. . . . . . *86*   **25–30**
Promotion only 12-inch single. Black label with colorband. Label reads "Not For Sale."

Sisters O Sisters: see *WOMAN IS THE NIGGER OF THE WORLD.*

Sleepless Night: see *I'M STEPPING OUT.*

SLIPPIN' AND SLIDIN'/Slippin' and Slidin'

Apple P-1883 . . . . *6/2/75*   **100–125**
Promotion copy. Apple label. Mono/Stereo. Record was never commercially released. Label reads "Not For Sale."

STAND BY ME/Move Over Ms. L.

Apple 1881 . . . . *3/10/75*   **3–5**
Apple label.

STAND BY ME/Stand by Me

Apple 1881   **30–35**
Promotion copy. Apple label. Mono/Stereo. Label reads "Not For Sale."

STAND BY ME/Woman Is the Nigger of the World

Capitol 6244. . . . . *4/4/77*   **3–5**
Tan Starline label.

Capitol 6244. . . . . *78*   **2–3**
Tan Starline label. Oval Capitol logo.

Capitol 6244. . . . . *86*   **3–5**
Blue Starline label.

Capitol X-6244   **2–3**
Black label with rainbow colorband.

(Just Like) STARTING OVER/Kiss Kiss Kiss

Geffen GEF-49604 . . *10/23/80*   **2–3**
Cream label. B-side by Yoko Ono.

Geffen GEF-49604   **2–3**
Picture sleeve.

Geffen PRO-A-919   **45–50**

(Just Like) STARTING OVER/(Just Like) Starting Over

Geffen GEF-49604   **10–15**
Promotion copy. Cream label. Mono/Stereo. Label reads "Promotion Not For Sale."

(Just Like) STARTING OVER/Woman

Geffen GGEF-0408. . . . *6/5/81*   **2–3**
Cream label.

Geffen GGEF-0408   **2–3**
Black label.

Touch Me: see *POWER TO THE PEOPLE.*

TRIBUTE TO JOHN LENNON, A

Quaker Granola Dips . . *10/86*
5¼" photocard vinyl soundsheet. Contains a narrative/musical tribute to John Lennon. Features excerpts of songs from the *Double Fantasy* and *Milk and Honey* LPs. One of five discs issued in a series titled *Great Moments in Rock and Roll.* One was issued with each specially marked box of Quaker's Granola Dips available from late 1986 thru early 1987. A contest for prizes was determined by an audible "Win" or "Lose" message at the end of the program. The other four discs featured various other artists. "Losing" Lennon discs valued at $10–$15. "Winning" discs valued at $50–$60 (so far we have not verified any "Winning" discs).

WATCHING THE WHEELS/Beautiful Boy (Darling Boy)

Geffen GGEF0415 . . . . *6/5/81*   2–3
Cream label.

Geffen GGEF0415 . . . . . . *86*   2–3
Black label.

WATCHING THE WHEELS/Yes, I'm Your Angel

Geffen GEF-49695 . . . *3/13/81*   2–3
Cream label. B-side is by Yoko Ono.

Geffen GEF-49695   2–3
Picture sleeve.

Geffen GEF-49695   10–15
Promotion copy. Cream label. Label reads "Promotion Not For Sale."

WHAT YOU GOT/What You Got

Apple P-1878 . . . . *74*   40–45
Promotion copy. Apple label. Mono/Stereo. Released commercially as B-side to "#9 Dream." Label reads "Not For Sale."

What You Got: see *#9 DREAM.*

WHATEVER GETS YOU THROUGH THE NIGHT/Beef Jerky

Apple 1874 . . . . . . *7/23/74*   3–5
Apple label.

Capitol 1874. . . . . *78–83*   2–3
Purple label.

Capitol 1874. . . . . *83 to date*   2–3
Black label with rainbow colorband.

WHATEVER GETS YOU THROUGH THE NIGHT/Whatever Gets You Through the Night

Apple P-1874   25–30
Promotion copy. Apple label. Mono/Stereo. Label reads "Not For Sale."

Who Has Seen the Wind: see *INSTANT KARMA.*

Why: see *MOTHER.*

WOMAN/Beautiful Boys

Geffen GEF-49644 . . . *1/12/81*   2–3
Cream label. B-side by Yoko Ono.

Geffen GEF-49644   2–3
Picture sleeve.

Geffen GEF-49644   10–15
Promotion copy. Cream label. Label reads "Promotion Not For Sale."

Woman: see also *(JUST LIKE) STARTING OVER.*

WOMAN IS THE NIGGER OF THE WORLD/Sisters O Sisters

Apple 1848 . . . . *4/24/72*   3–5
Custom Apple faces label. B-side by Yoko Ono.

Apple 1848   15–20
Picture sleeve.

Woman Is the Nigger of the World: see also *STAND BY ME.*

PAUL McCARTNEY: SINGLES, PROMOS, AND PICTURE SLEEVES

ANGRY/Angry

Capitol SPRO-9797. . . . . . *86*   15–20
Promotional 12-inch single. Black label with colorband.

ANOTHER DAY/Oh Woman, Oh Why

Apple 1829 . . . . *2/22/71*   3–5
Apple label.

Apple PRO 6193/4   35–40
Promotion copy. Apple label. Label reads "Promotional Record Not For Sale."

Capitol 1829. . . . . *79*   2–4
Black label.

ARROW THROUGH ME/Old Siam, Sir

Columbia 1-11070 . . . *8/14/79*   2–4
Orange and yellow label.

McCartney did not release a single after leaving the Beatles until this one. In true British Beatle fashion, it did not appear on an LP for another eight years.

Columbia 1-11070   **10–15**
Promotion copy. White label. Label reads "Demonstration Not For Sale."

B-side to Seaside: see *SEASIDE WOMAN.*

Backwards Traveler—Cuff Link: see *WITH A LITTLE LUCK.*

BAND ON THE RUN/Band On The Run
Apple P-1873   **30–35**
Promotion copy. Apple label. Variation one of this promo has a full length stereo version on one side, and an edited mono version on the other. Variation two has edited versions on both the mono and stereo side (short version: 3:50; long version; 5:09). Label reads "Not For Sale." Add 25% more to value for the double edit version.

BAND ON THE RUN/Helen Wheels
Columbia 13-33409 . . . *12/4/80*   **2–3**
Red label. "Hall of Fame" series.

Columbia 13-33409 . . . . . . *85*   **2–3**
Gray label.

BAND ON THE RUN/Nineteen Hundred and Eighty Five
Apple 1873 . . . . *4/8/74*   **3–5**
Apple label.

Capitol 1873. . . . . *79*   **2–4**
Black label.

Beware My Love: see *LET EM IN.*

Bridge on the River Suite: see *WALKING IN THE PARK WITH ELOISE.*

C Moon: see *HI HI HI.*

Can't Get Outta the Rain: see *THE GIRL IS MINE.*

Check My Machine: see *WATERFALLS.*

COMING UP/Coming Up
Columbia 1-11263   **10–15**
Promotion copy. White label with orange and black print. Label reads "Demonstration Not For Sale."

COMING UP/Coming Up (Live at Glasgow)
Columbia AS-775   **50–60**
Promotional 12-inch single. White label with black print. Label reads "Demonstration Not For Sale."

Columbia AS-775   **50–60**
Promotional 12-inch single. Red label. Label reads "Demonstration Not For Sale."

COMING UP/Coming Up (Live at Glasgow), Lunch Box Odd Sox
Columbia 1-11263 . . . *4/15/80*   **2–3**
Orange and yellow label.

Columbia 1-11263   **2–3**
Picture sleeve.
Note: Beware of counterfeit promotional sleeves. No legitimate promotional sleeves exist.

COMING UP (Live at Glasgow)
Columbia AE7-1204   **4–6**
Promotion one-sided copy. White label with orange and black print. Small hole. Label reads "Demonstration Not For Sale." Issued free with early issues of *McCartney II* LP.

Cook of the House: see *SILLY LOVE SONGS.*

COUNTRY DREAMER/Country Dreamer
Apple PRO-6787 . . . . . . *73*   **50–60**
Promotion copy. Apple label. Mono/Stereo. Released commercially as B-side of "Helen Wheels."

Country Dreamer: see *HELEN WHEELS.*

Daytime, Nightime Suffering: see *GOODNIGHT TONIGHT.*

Deliver Your Children: see *I'VE HAD ENOUGH.*

EBONY & IVORY/Ebony & Ivory
Columbia 18-02860 . . . . . *82*   **10–15**
Promotion copy. Orange and yellow label. Early promotion copies have an "&" symbol and no "MPL" logo on the label. Label reads "Demonstration Not For Sale."

Columbia 18-02860   **10–15**
Promotion copy. Orange and yellow label with the word "and" spelled out in the title and the "MPL" logo with the juggling man on the label. Label reads "Demonstration Not For Sale."

EBONY AND IVORY
Columbia 18-02860   **5–8**
Promotion picture sleeve. Reads "Demonstration Not For Sale."

EBONY AND IVORY/Rainclouds
Columbia 18-02860 . . . . *4/2/82*   **2–3**
Orange and yellow label.

Columbia 18-02860   **2–3**
Picture sleeve.

EBONY AND IVORY/Rainclouds, Ebony and Ivory
Columbia 44-02878 . . . . . *4/82*   **10–15**
12-inch single. Red label. Issued with a picture cover. Side 1 features a duet with Stevie Wonder. Side 2 has only McCartney singing.

Get It: see *TUG OF WAR.*

GETTING CLOSER/Getting Closer
Columbia 3-11020 . . . . . . *79*   **10–15**
Promotion copy. White label. Mono/Stereo. Label reads "Demonstration Not For Sale."

GETTING CLOSER/Spin It On
Columbia 3-11020 . . . . *6/5/79*   **2–4**
Orange and yellow label.

Columbia 3-11020   **25–30**
Title sleeve.

Getting Closer: see also *GOODNIGHT TONIGHT.*

Girl School: see *MULL OF KINTYRE.*

GIVE IRELAND BACK TO THE IRISH/Give Ireland Back to the Irish (Version)
Apple 1847 . . . . *2/28/72*   **3–5**
White custom label with green print.

Apple 1847   **15–20**
Title sleeve.

Capitol 1847. . . . . *79*   **2–4**
Black label.

GOODNIGHT TONIGHT/Daytime, Nightime Suffering
Columbia 3-10939 . . . *3/15/79*   **2–4**
Orange and yellow label.

Columbia 23–10940 . . . . . *3/79*   **15–20**
12-inch single. Purple label. Issued with a special photo cover.

Columbia 23-10940 . . . . . *3/79*   **30–35**
12″ single. Purple label. Issued with a white cover with a 4″ × 11″ sticker. Sticker is blue and white, and lists artists and song titles.

GOODNIGHT TONIGHT/Getting Closer
Columbia 13-33405 . . . *12/4/80*   **2–3**
Red label. "Hall of Fame" series.

GOODNIGHT TONIGHT/Goodnight Tonight
Columbia 3-10939   **10–15**
Promotion copy. White label with orange and black print. Mono/Stereo. Label reads "Demonstration Not For Sale."

Columbia 23-10940   **20–25**
Promotional 12-inch single. White label. Label reads "Demonstration Not For Sale."

HELEN WHEELS/Country Dreamer
Apple 1869 . . . . . . *11/12/73*   **3–5**
Apple label.

Capitol 1869. . . . . *79*   **2–4**
Black label.

HELEN WHEELS/Helen Wheels
Apple PRO-6786   **30–35**
Promotion copy. Apple label. Mono/Stereo. Label reads "Not For Sale."

McCartney's first release on Columbia occurred at the height of the disco craze, hence the special 12-inch disco version.

Helen Wheels: see also *BAND ON THE RUN.*

HI HI HI/C Moon
Apple 1857 . . . . . . *12/4/72*   **3–5**
Red custom label.

Capitol 1857. . . . . *79*   **2–4**
Black label.

I Lie Around: see *LIVE AND LET DIE.*

I'll Give You a Ring: see *TAKE IT AWAY.*

I'm Carrying: see *LONDON TOWN.*

I'VE HAD ENOUGH/Deliver Your Children
Capitol 4594. . . . . . *6/12/78*   **2–4**
Blue and gray custom photo label.

I'VE HAD ENOUGH/I've Had Enough
Capitol P-4594   **15–20**
Promotion copy. Blue and gray custom photo label. Mono/Stereo. Some copies came with a special promotional flyer. Add $4 for value of flyer. Label reads "Not For Sale."

JET/Jet
Apple P-1871 . . . . *74*   **30–35**
Promotion copy. Apple label. Mono/Stereo. Artists listed as "Paul McCartney & Wings." Label reads "Not For Sale."

JET/Let Me Roll It
Apple 1871 . . . . *2/74*   **3–5**
Apple label. Artists listed as "Paul McCartney & Wings."
Note: "Let Me Roll It" replaced "Mamunia" as the B-side soon after the initial release.

Capitol 1871. . . . . *79*   **2–4**
Black label.

JET/Mamunia
Apple 1871 . . . . *1/28/74*   **4–6**
Apple label. Artists listed as "Paul McCartney & Wings." B-side was changed to "Let Me Roll It."

JET/Uncle Albert—Admiral Halsey
Columbia 13-33408 . . . *12/4/80*   **2–3**
Red label. "Hall of Fame" series.

Columbia 13-33408 . . . . . . *85*   **2–3**
Gray label.

JUNIORS FARM/Juniors Farm
Apple P-1875 . . . . *11/74*   **30–35**
Promotion copy. Apple label. Mono/Stereo. Label reads "Not For Sale."

JUNIORS FARM/Sally G
Apple 1875 . . . . *11/4/74*   **3–5**
Apple label.

Capitol 1875. . . . . *79*   **2–4**
Black label.

LET EM IN/Beware My Love
Capitol 4293. . . . . . *6/28/76*   **2–4**
Custom Capitol label.

Capitol 4293. . . . . *79*   **2–4**
Black label.

LET EM IN/Let Em In
Capitol P-4293   **15–20**
Promotion copy. White label. Artists listed as "Wings." Mono/Mono. Label reads "Not For Sale."

Capitol P-4293   **15–20**
Promotion copy. White label. Artists listed as "Wings." Stereo/Stereo. One side is the stock 5:08 time length, the other is a 3:43 edit. Label reads "Not For Sale."

LET IT BE/Let It Be (Gospel jam mix)
Profile PRO-5147. . . . . . *6/87*   **2–3**
Black label with silver, red and white print. Artists listed as "Sun Ferry Aid." Issued to benefit Sun's Zeebrugge disaster fund. Performance includes original 1969 version of the Beatles song "Let It Be" with an overdub of Paul and a host of others singing along.

Profile PRO-5147   **2–3**
Picture sleeve.

LET IT BE/Let It Be
Profile PRO-5147. . . . . . *6/87*   **8–10**
Promotional issue. Label reads "Loaned for promotional purposes—Not for sale."

LET IT BE/Let It Be (Megamessage mix)
Profile PRO-7147. . . . . . *6/87*   **4–6**
12-inch single. Silver, red and white print. Issued with a picture cover. Contains extended versions of the song.

Profile PRO-7147   **15–20**
Promotional 12-inch single. White label with black print. Issued with picture cover. Contains extended versions of the songs. Label reads "Loaned for promotional purposes—Not for sale."

Let Me Roll It: see *JET.*

LETTING GO/Letting Go
Capitol PRO-4145   **15–20**
Promotion copy. Black label. Mono/Stereo. Label reads "Not For Sale."

LETTING GO/You Gave Me the Answer
Capitol 4145. . . . . . *9/29/75*   **2–4**
Black label.

LISTEN TO WHAT THE MAN SAID/Love in Song
Capitol 4091. . . . . . *5/23/75*   **2–4**
Black label with silver print and additional label graphics. Artists listed as "Wings."

Capitol 4091   **4–6**
Picture sleeve.

Capitol PRO-8138   **15–20**
Promotion copy. Black label. Artists listed as "Wings." Mono/Stereo. Label reads "Not For Sale."

Little Woman Love: see *MARY HAD A LITTLE LAMB.*

LIVE AND LET DIE/I Lie Around
Apple 1863 . . . . *6/18/73*   **3–5**
Apple label.
Note: "Live and Let Die" marked the first time Paul worked with George Martin after the Beatles broke up.

Capitol 1863. . . . . *79*   **2–4**
Black label.

LONDON TOWN/I'm Carrying
Capitol 4625. . . . . . *8/21/78*   **2–4**
Blue and gray custom label.

LONDON TOWN/London Town
Capitol P-4625   **15–20**
Promotional copy. Blue and gray custom label. Mono/Stereo. Label reads "Not For Sale."

Love in Song: see *LISTEN TO WHAT THE MAN SAID.*

Magneto & Titanium Man: see *VENUS AND MARS ROCK SHOW.*

Mamunia: see *JET.*

MARY HAD A LITTLE LAMB/Little Woman Love
Apple 1851 . . . . *5/29/72*   **3–5**
Custom Apple label.

Apple 1851   **10–15**
Picture sleeve. Does not list "Little Woman Love" on the back of the sleeve.

Apple 1851   **25–30**
Picture sleeve. "Little Woman Love" printed on back side of the sleeve.

Apple 1851   **50–60**
Promotion copy. White label. Label reads "Promotional Record Not For Sale."

Capitol 1851. . . . . *79* **2–4**
Black label.

MAYBE I'M AMAZED/Maybe I'm Amazed
Capitol PRO-8570/1 **15–20**
Promotion copy. Black label. Mono/Stereo. Label reads "Not For Sale."
Note: This was a live version of the song, taken from the *Wings Over America* LP.

Capitol (S) PRO-8574 **50–60**
Promotional 12-inch single. Issued with a custom title cover. Label reads "Not For Sale."

MAYBE I'M AMAZED/Soily
Capitol 4385. . . . . . . *2/7/77* **2–4**
Custom Capitol label. Taken from the *Wings Over America* LP.

Capitol 4385. . . . . *79* **8–12**
Black label. Artists listed as "Wings."

Maybe I'm Amazed: see also *MY LOVE.*

MULL OF KINTYRE/Girl School
Capitol 4504. . . . . *11/14/77* **2–4**
Black label.

Capitol 4504 **8–12**
Picture sleeve.

Capitol SPRO-8746/7 **15–20**
Promotion copy. Black label. Label reads "Not For Sale."

My Carnival: see *SPIES LIKE US.*

MY LOVE/Maybe I'm Amazed
Columbia 13-33407 . . . *12/4/80* **2–3**
Red label. "Hall of Fame" series.

Columbia 13-33407 . . . . . *85* **2–3**
Gray label.

MY LOVE/The Mess
Apple 1861 . . . . *4/9/73* **3–5**
Custom Apple label. Artists listed as "Paul McCartney & Wings."

Apple 1861 **60–70**
Promotion copy. White label. No promotional writing on the label.

Capitol 1861. . . . . *79* **2–4**
Black label.

Nineteen Hundred and Eighty Five: see *BAND ON THE RUN.*

NO MORE LONELY NIGHTS (Ballad)/No More Lonely Nights (Playout version)
Columbia 38-04581 . . . *10/2/84* **2–3**
Orange and yellow label.

Columbia 38-04581 **2–3**
Picture sleeve.

NO MORE LONELY NIGHTS (Ballad)/No More Lonely Nights (Ballad)
Columbia 38-04581 **8–12**
Promotion copy. White label. Label reads "Demonstration Not For Sale."

Columbia 38-04581 **5–8**
Promotion picture sleeve. Reads "Demonstration Not For Sale."

Columbia AS-1940 **15–20**
Promotional 12-inch single. Red label. Issued in a plain black cover with a red and white title sticker. Label reads "Demonstration Not For Sale."

NO MORE LONELY NIGHTS (Ballad)/No More Lonely Nights (Special dance mix)
Columbia 38-04581 **2–3**
Orange and yellow label.

NO MORE LONELY NIGHTS (Special dance mix)/No More Lonely Nights (Special dance mix)
Columbia AS-1990 **10–15**
Promotional 12-inch single. Red label. Issued in a plain black cover with a pink title sticker. Sticker reads "special dance mix." Label reads "Demonstration Not For Sale."

Ode to a Koala Bear: see *SAY SAY SAY.*

Oh Woman, Oh Why: see *ANOTHER DAY.*

Old Siam Sir: see *ARROW THROUGH ME.*

ONLY LOVE REMAINS/Only Love Remains
Capitol P-B-5672 . . . . *87* **8–12**
Promotion copy. White label with black print. Label reads "NOT FOR SALE."

ONLY LOVE REMAINS/Tough on a Tightrope
Capitol B-5672 . . . . *1/87* **2–3**
Black label with colorband.

Capitol B-5672 **2–3**
Picture sleeve.

PAUL McCARTNEY AND WINGS ROCK SHOW
Miramax CPS-4202. . . . . . *75* **175–200**
Radio spots record. White label. One-sided 7-inch record with two 60-second and one 30-second radio spots.

Pipes of Peace: see *SO BAD.*

PRESS/It's Not True
Capitol B-5597 . . . . . 7/16/86   2–3
Black label with colorband.

Capitol B-5597   2–3
Picture sleeve.

PRESS (video soundtrack) IT'S NOT TRUE/Hanglide—Press (dub mix)
Capitol V-15235 86   2–3
12-inch single. Black label with colorband. Issued with picture sleeve.

PRESS/Press
Capitol P-B-5597   8–12
Promotion copy. White label with black print. Label reads "Not For Sale."

Capitol SPRO-9763   15–20
12-inch promotional copy. Black label with colorband. Label reads "Not For Sale."

PRETTY LITTLE HEAD/Pretty Little Head
Capitol SPRO 9928. . . . 12/86   20–25
Promotion only 12-inch single. Black label with colorband.

Rainclouds: see *EBONY AND IVORY.*

Rudolf the Red Nosed Reggae: see *WONDERFUL CHRISTMASTIME.*

SALLY G/Sally G
Apple P-1875 74   35–40
Promotion copy. Apple label. Mono/Stereo.

Sally G: see *JUNIORS FARM.*

SAY SAY SAY/Ode to a Koala Bear
Columbia 38-04168 . . . 10/4/83   2–3
Orange and yellow label. A-side co-written and performed with Michael Jackson.

Columbia 38-04168   2–3
Picture sleeve.

SAY SAY SAY/Say Say Say
Columbia 38-04168   8–12
Promotion copy. White label. Stereo only. Label reads "Demonstration Not For Sale."

Columbia 38-04168   5–8
Promotion picture sleeve. Identical to commercial issue, except excludes B-side and reads "Demonstration Not For Sale."

Columbia AS-1758   10–15
Promotional 12-inch single. Red label. Issued in a plain black cover with a promo stamp. Label reads "Demonstration Not For Sale."

SAY SAY SAY/Say Say Say (instrumental)—Ode to a Koala Bear
Columbia 44-04169 83   5–8
12-inch single. Red label. Issued with a special picture cover.

Columbia 44-04169
Promotional 12-inch single. Red label. Issued with a special picture cover with gold embossed promo stamp. Label reads "Demonstration Not For Sale."

SEASIDE WOMAN/B-side to Seaside
Epic 8-50403 . . . . . . 5/31/77   4–6
Orange label. Artists listed as "Suzy & The Red Stripes" (actually Linda McCartney and Wings).

Capitol B-5608 86   2–3
Black label with colorband. Artist shown as "Suzy And The Red Stripes." Remixed version of 1977 single by Linda McCartney & Wings.

Capitol V-15244 86   2–3
12-inch single. Black label with colorband. Artist shown as "Suzy and The Red Stripes." Features extended versions of both cuts. Issued in stock Capitol cover with title sticker.

SEASIDE WOMAN/Seaside Woman
Epic 8-50403   30–35
Advance promotion copy. White label. Black vinyl. Mono/Stereo. label reads "Advance Promotion" and "Demonstration Not For Sale."

Epic 8-50403   15–20
Promotion copy. Mono/Stereo. Mono label is orange with white and black print, stereo label is white with orange and black print. Issued on red vinyl. Label reads "Demonstration Not For Sale."

Epic 8-50403   30–35
Promotion copy. Mono/Stereo. Mono label is orange with white and black print, stereo label is white with orange and black print. Black vinyl. Label reads "Demonstration Not For Sale."

Epic ASF-361   25–30
Promotion 12-inch single. White label. Artists listed as "Suzy & The Red Stripes." Label reads "Demonstration Not For Sale."

SEASIDE WOMAN/Seaside Woman (remixed version)
Capitol P-B-5608 86   8–12
Promotional copy. White label with black print. Artist shown as "Suzy And The Red Stripes." Label reads "Not For Sale."

SILLY LOVE SONGS/Cook of the House

Capitol 4256. . . . . . . *4/1/76*   2–4
Custom Capitol label.

Capitol 4256   2–4
Black label.

Columbia 18-02171. . . . . . *80*   2–3
Orange and yellow label.

SILLY LOVE SONGS/Silly Love Songs

Capitol P-4256   15–20
Promotion copy. White label. Contains a full length and an edited version. Label reads "Not For Sale."

SO BAD/Pipes of Peace

Columbia 38-04296 . . *12/13/83*   2–3
Orange and yellow label.

Columbia 38-04296   2–3
Picture sleeve.

SO BAD/So Bad

Columbia 38-04296   8–12
Promotion copy. White label. Label reads "Demonstration Not For Sale."

Columbia 38-04296   5–8
Promotion picture sleeve. Identical to commercial issue, except excludes B-side and reads "Demonstration Not For Sale."

Soily: see *MAYBE I'M AMAZED.*

Spin It On: see *GETTING CLOSER.*

SPIES LIKE US/My Carnival

Capitol B-5537 . . . . *11/13/85*   2–3
Black label with rainbow colorband.

Capitol B-5537   2–3
Picture sleeve.

SPIES LIKE US/Spies Like Us

Capitol 7PRO-9552/3   8–12
Promotion copy. Custom white label. Contains two edited versions with time lengths of 4:40 and 3:46.

SPIES LIKE US (Party Mix)—SPIES LIKE US (Alternate mix)/Spies Like Us (DJ version)—My Carnival

Capitol V-15212 . . . . . *11/85*   5–8
12-inch single. Black label with rainbow colorband. Issued in a special picture cover.

SPIES LIKE US/Spies Like Us

Capitol SPRO-9556   25–30
Promotional 12-inch single. Custom white label. Issued in a plain black cover.

STRANGLEHOLD/Angry (Remix)

Capitol B-5636 . . . . *10/29/86*   2–3
Black label with colorband.

Capitol B-5636   2–3
Picture sleeve.

Capitol SPRO 9861. . . . *11/86*   25–30
Promotional 12-inch single. Gray label. Label reads "Promotional Copy—Not for Sale."

STRANGLEHOLD/Stranglehold

Capitol P-B-5636   8–12
Promotion copy. White label. Label reads "Not For Sale."

TAKE IT AWAY/I'll Give You a Ring

Columbia 18-03018 . . . . *7/3/82*   2–3
Orange and yellow label.

Columbia 18-03018   2–3
Picture sleeve.

TAKE IT AWAY/Take It Away

Columbia 18-03018   5–8
Promotion copy. White label. Label reads "Demonstration Not For Sale."

Columbia 18-03018   3–5
Promotion picture sleeve. Identical to commercial issue, except B-side and reads "Demonstration Not For Sale."

THE GIRL IS MINE

Epic ENA-03372 . . . . *82*   8–10
Blue label. One-sided commercially released single.

THE GIRL IS MINE/Can't Get Outta the Rain

Epic 34-03288. . . . . *10/26/82*   2–4
Blue label. A-side written by and performed with Michael Jackson.

Epic 34-03288   2–4
Picture sleeve.

Epic 55-03288. . . . . *84*   2–3
Gold label. "Instant Classics" series.

THE GIRL IS MINE/The Girl Is Mine

Epic 34-03288   8–12
Promotion copy. White label. Stereo only. Label reads "Demonstration Not For Sale."

Epic 34-03288   5–8
Promotion picture sleeve. Identical to the commercial issue, except the words "Demonstration Not For Sale" are added to the sleeve. Issued with the non-edited promotional singles only.

Epic 34-03288   15–20
Promotion copy. White label. Stereo only. Label reads "New Edited Version Demonstration Not For Sale." No sleeve was issued with this promo.

The Mess: see *MY LOVE.*

Too Many People: see *UNCLE ALBERT—ADMIRAL HALSEY.*

TUG OF WAR/Get It
Columbia 38-03235. . .   *9/26/82*   2–3
Orange and yellow label. Counterfeit picture sleeves exist for this single; legitimate sleeves were never produced.

TUG OF WAR/Tug of War
Columbia 38-03235   10–15
Promotion copy. White label. Label reads "Demonstration Not For Sale." No legitimate promo picture sleeves were produced for this single; counterfeits do exist.

UNCLE ALBERT—ADMIRAL HALSEY/Too Many People
Apple 1837 . . . . *8/2/71*   3–5
Apple label.

Apple 1837   8-12
Apple label. Label has an unsliced apple on the B-side.

Apple P-1837   40–45
Promotion copy. Apple label. Artist listed as "Paul & Linda McCartney." Label reads "Promotional Record Not For Sale."

Capitol 1837. . . . . *79*   2–4
Black label.

Uncle Albert—Admiral Halsey: see *JET.*

VENUS AND MARS ROCK SHOW/Magneto & Titanium Man
Capitol 4175. . . . .   *10/27/75*   2–4
Black label.

VENUS AND MARS ROCK SHOW/Venus and Mars Rock Show
Capitol P-4175   15–20
Promotion copy. Mono/Stereo. Label reads "Not For Sale."

WALKING IN THE PARK WITH ELOISE/Bridge on the River Suite
EMI 3977 . . . . *12/2/74*   15–20
Brown label. Artists listed as "The Country Hams."

EMI 3977   50–60
Picture sleeve.

WALKING IN THE PARK WITH ELOISE/Walking in the Park with Eloise
EMI P-3977   25–30
Promotion copy. Brown label. Artists listed as "The Country Hams." Mono/Stereo. Label reads "Not For Sale."

WATERFALLS/Check My Machine
Columbia 1-11335 . . . *7/22/80*   2–4
Orange and yellow label.

Columbia 1-11335   15–20
Picture sleeve.

WATERFALLS/Waterfalls
Columbia 1-11335   10–15

McCartney was travelling incognito on this one, going under his christened name on the writing credits and publishing it through Kidney Punch Music, previously heard from only with "Give Ireland Back to the Irish."

Promotion copy. White label. Label reads "Demonstration Not For Sale."

WITH A LITTLE LUCK/Backwards Traveler—Cuff Link
Capitol 4559. . . . . . *3/20/78*   **2–4**
Blue and gray custom photo label.

WITH A LITTLE LUCK/With a Little Luck
Capitol PRO-8812   **15–20**
Promotion copy. Blue and gray custom photo label. Mono/Stereo. Label reads "Not For Sale."

WONDERFUL CHRISTMASTIME/Rudolf the Red Nosed Reggae
Columbia 1-11162 . . *11/20/79*   **2–4**
Orange and yellow label.

Columbia 1-11162   **4–6**
Picture sleeve.

Columbia 38-04127. . . . . *1983*   **2–4**
Orange and yellow label. B-side on this version is issued in stereo. Original B-side is mono.

WONDERFUL CHRISTMASTIME/Wonderful Christmastime
Columbia 1-11162   **10–15**
Promotion copy. White label. Label reads "Not For Sale."

You Gave Me the Answer: see *LETTING GO*.

RINGO STARR: SINGLES, PROMOS, AND PICTURE SLEEVES

BACK OFF BOOGALOO/Blindman
Apple 1849 . . . . . . *3/20/72*   **15–20**
Blue custom apple label.

Apple 1849   **3–5**
Green apple label.

Pictured here is a nod of the head to Ringo's on-again, off-again film with Harry Nilsson, *Son of Dracula*.

Apple 1849   **10–15**
Picture sleeve.

Apple 1849   **45–50**
Promotion copy. White label.

Capitol 1849. . . . . *75–78*   **8–12**
Orange label.

Capitol 1849. . . . . *78*   **2–3**
Purple label.

BEAUCOUPS OF BLUES/Coochy Coochy

Apple 2969 . . . . *10/5/70*   **4–6**
Apple label.

Apple 2969   **25–30**
Picture sleeve. Incorrect record number #1826
is printed on the sleeve.

Apple 2969   **15–20**
Picture sleeve.

Capitol 2969. . . . . *75*   **8–12**
Orange label.

Blindman: see *BACK OFF BOOGALOO.*

Call Me: see *ONLY YOU.*

Coochy Coochy: see *BEAUCOUPS OF BLUES.*

Cryin': see *DOSE OF ROCK 'N' ROLL.*

Devil Woman: see *YOU'RE SIXTEEN.*

DOSE OF ROCK 'N' ROLL/Cryin'

Atlantic 45-3361 . . . . *9/20/76*   **8–12**
Orange and brown label.

DOSE OF ROCK 'N' ROLL/Dose of Rock 'N' Roll

Atlantic 45-3361   **25–30**
Advance promotion copy. White label.

Atlantic 45-3361   **10–15**
Promotion copy. Blue label. One side contains
an intro, the other does not. Label reads "Promotion Copy Not For Sale."

Down and Out: see *PHOTOGRAPH.*

DROWNING IN THE SEA OF LOVE/Drowning in the Sea of Love

Atlantic 3412 . . . . *77*   **10–15**
Promotion copy. Blue label. Contains a long,
and short, stereo version of this song. Label
reads "Promotion Copy Not For Sale."

Atlantic DS KO-93   **25–30**
Promotion 12-inch single. Yellow label.

DROWNING IN THE SEA OF LOVE/Just a Dream

Atlantic 3412 . . . . . *10/18/77*   **20–25**
Orange and brown label.

Drumming Is My Madness: see *WRACK MY BRAIN.*

Early 1970: see *IT DON'T COME EASY.*

HEART ON MY SLEEVE/Heart on My Sleeve

Portrait 6-70018   **10–15**
Promotion copy. White label. Mono/Stereo.
Label reads "Demonstration Not For Sale."

HEART ON MY SLEEVE/Who Needs a Heart

Portrait 6-70018 . . . . . *7/6/78*   **8–12**
Gray label.

HEY BABY

Atlantic 45-3371   **30–35**
One-sided promotional issue. Blue label. Reads
"Promotion copy—Not for sale."

HEY BABY/Hey Baby

Atlantic 45-3371   **25–30**
Advance promotion copy. White label.

Atlantic 45-3371   **25–30**
Promotion copy. Label on mono side is red and
white, stereo label is blue. Mono/Stereo. Label
reads "Promotion Copy Not For Sale."

HEY BABY/Lady Gaye

Atlantic 45-3371 . . . *11/22/76*   **10–15**
Orange and brown label.

IT DON'T COME EASY/Early 1970

Apple 1831 . . . . *4/16/71*   **4–6**
Apple label.

Apple 1831   **10–15**
Picture sleeve.

Capitol 1831. . . . . . . *75–78*   **3–5**
Orange label.

Capitol 1831. . . . . . . *78–83*   **2–4**
Purple label.

Capitol 1831. . . . . *83 to date*   **2–3**
Black label with rainbow colorband.

IT'S ALL DOWN TO GOODNIGHT VIENNA/Oo-Wee

Apple 1882 . . . . *6/2/75*   **3–5**
Custom nebula label. Contains a longer version
(2:58) of the song "Goodnight Vienna" than the
LP.

Apple 1882   **8–12**
Picture sleeve.

TITLE:
HEY BABY

ST-A-32632 SP
STEREO

45-3371
Publisher,
Unart Music Corp.,
Le Belle Music
Inc., BMI
Time: 3:10

ARTIST:
RINGO STARR

A promotional copy of Ringo's first release after the demise of Apple Records.

Capitol 1882. . . . . *78*   **2–3**
Purple label.

IT'S ALL DOWN TO GOODNIGHT VIENNA/It's All Down to Goodnight Vienna
Apple 1882   **25–30**
Promotion copy. Apple label. Mono/Stereo. Label reads "Not For Sale."

Just a Dream: see *DROWNING IN THE SEA OF LOVE* **and** *WINGS.*

Lady Gaye: see *HEY BABE.*

LIPSTICK TRACES/Lipstick Traces
Portrait 6-70015   **10–15**
Promotion copy. White label. Mono/Stereo. Mono version contains a different mix. Label reads "Demonstration Not For Sale."

LIPSTICK TRACES/Old Time Relovin'
Portrait 6-70015 . . . . *4/18/78*   **8–12**
Gray label.

NO NO SONG/Snookeroo
Apple 1880 . . . . . . *1/27-75*   **3–5**
Custom nebula label.

Apple P-1880   **25–30**
Promotion copy. White label. Contains "mono" versions of these two songs. Label reads "Not For Sale."

Apple P-1880   **25–30**
Promotion copy. White label. Record contains "stereo" versions of these two songs. Label reads "Not For Sale."   **25–30**

Capitol 1880. . . . . . . *78–83*   **2–4**
Purple label.

Capitol 1880. . . . . . *83 to date*   **2–3**
Black label with rainbow colorband.

OH MY MY/Oh My My
Apple P-1872   **25–30**
Promotion copy. Apple label. Short mono version and long stereo version. Label reads "Not For Sale."

OH MY MY/Step Lightly
Apple 1872 . . . . *2/18/74*   **3–5**
Custom star label.

Apple 1872   **4–6**
Apple label.

Old Time Relovin': see *LIPSTICK TRACES.*

ONLY YOU/Call Me
Apple 1876 . . . . . . *11/11/74*   **3–5**
Custom nebula label.

Apple 1876   **5–8**
Apple label.

Apple 1876   **8–12**
Picture sleeve.

Capitol 1876. . . . . *78*   **2–3**
Purple label.

ONLY YOU/Only You
Apple P-1876   **25–30**
Promotion copy. Apple label. Mono/Stereo.
Label reads "Not For Sale."

OO-WEE/Oo-Wee
Apple P-1882   **30–35**
Promotion copy. Apple label. Mono/Stereo.
Label reads "Not For Sale."

Oo-Wee: see *IT'S ALL DOWN TO GOODNIGHT VIENNA.*

PHOTOGRAPH/Down and Out
Apple 1865 . . . . *9/24/73*   **3–5**
Custom star label.

Apple 1865   **8–12**
Picture sleeve.

Capitol 1865. . . . . . . *78–83*   **2–4**
Purple label.

Capitol 1865. . . . . *83 to date*   **2–3**
Black label with rainbow colorband.

PHOTOGRAPH/Photograph
Apple P-1865   **25–30**
Promotion copy. Custom star label. Mono/
Stereo. Label reads "Not For Sale."

PRIVATE PROPERTY/Private Property
Boardwalk NB7-11-134 DJ   **10–15**
Promotion copy. Blue and white skyline label.
Label reads "Promotional Copy Not For Sale."

PRIVATE PROPERTY/Stop and Take the Time to Smell the Roses
Boardwalk NB7-11-134 *1/13/82*   **2–4**
Blue and white skyline label.

Snookeroo: see *NO NO SONG.*

Step Lightly: see *OH MY MY.*

Stop and Take Time to Smell the Roses: see *PRIVATE PROPERTY.*

Who Needs a Heart: see *HEART ON MY SLEEVE.*

WINGS/Just a Dream
Atlantic 3429 . . . . . *8/25/77*   **10–15**
Orange and brown label.

WINGS/Wings
Atlantic 3429   **25–30**
Advance promotion copy. White label.

Atlantic 3429   **10–15**
Promotion copy. Mono/stereo. Label on mono
side is red and white; label on stereo side is blue.
Label reads "Promotion Copy Not For Sale."

WRACK MY BRAIN/Drumming Is My Madness
Boardwalk NB7-11-130 *10/27/81*   **2–4**
Blue and white skyline label.

Boardwalk NB7-11-130   **2–4**
Picture sleeve.

WRACK MY BRAIN/Wrack My Brain
Boardwalk NB7-11-130 DJ   **10–15**
Promotion copy. Blue and white skyline label.
Can be found with the words "D.J. Copy Not
For Sale" or "Promotional Copy Not For Sale"
on the label. Mono/Stereo.

YOU'RE SIXTEEN/Devil Woman
Apple 1870 . . . . *12/3/73*   **3–5**
Custom star label.

Apple 1870   **8–12**
Apple label.

Apple 1870   **8–12**
Picture sleeve.

Capitol 1870. . . . . . . *75–78*   **8–10**
Orange label.

Capitol 1870. . . . . . . *78–83*   **2–4**
Purple label.

Capitol 1870. . . . . *83 to date*   **2–3**
Black label with rainbow colorband.

YOU'RE SIXTEEN/You're Sixteen
Apple P-1870   **25–30**
Promotion copy. Apple label. Mono/Stereo.
Label reads "Not For Sale."

A mono/stereo promo version of a song from Ringo's most successful solo album, *Ringo*.

Beatles (Together and Solo): EPs

The EP—be it a 7-inch 45rpm or a 12-inch—has never been a mainstream format in the American record industry, which explains the scarcity of Beatle EP releases even from the early years. The format has demonstrated a curious resilience over the years, however, making resurgences here and there, particularly in the late '70s and early '80s—witness the McCartney EPs (often miscalled "maxi-singles" by record companies) from *Tug of War* and *Give My Regards to Broad Street*. In the present day, it has become a kind of dumping for alternate mixes, whether it is to be found in the "Spies Like Us" "party mix" or the "playout" version of "No More Lonely Nights."

EPs featuring various artists are listed here, with cross-references to the "Various-Artists Compilations" section that will be found at the end of the LP section.

BEATLES INTRODUCE NEW SONGS, THE: see Various-Artists Compilations section.

BEATLES, BEACH BOYS, AND THE KINGSTON TRIO: see Various-Artists Compilations section.

BEATLES SECOND OPEN-END INTERVIEW, THE
Capitol Compact 33 PRO-2598/9
. . . . *4/64*   **175-200**
Black label with colorband. 33 1/3 rpm. Promotional 7-inch EP issued to promote *The Beatles Second Album.* Contains an open-end interview with the group and a few tracks from the LP. Issued with script/picture sleeve. Label reads "Especially Prepared for Radio and TV Programming—Not For Sale."

Capitol PRO-2598/9   **350–375**
Script/picture sleeve. Contains the script for the Beatles open-end interview.

CAPITOL SOUVENIR RECORD, THE: see Various-Artists Compilations section.

EBONY AND IVORY/Ballroom Dancing, The Pound Is Sinking (titled "McCartney—a Sample from *Tug of War*") (Paul McCartney)
Columbia AS-1444   **25–30**
12-inch promotional EP. Black label. White vinyl. Issued with a black and white picture cover. Label reads "Demonstration Not For Sale."

EVERYNIGHT: see Various-Artists Compilations section.

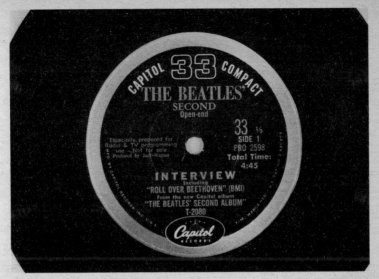

An open-ended interview EP featuring material from the Beatles' second Capitol album. The sleeve provided the dee jay with a script so he could keep up his half of the conversation.

FOUR BY THE BEATLES

Capitol EAP 1-2121 . . *5/11/64*   **150–175**

Available with two different label styles, version one features a blue label with silver print. Version two features a green label with silver print.

Side 1
Roll Over Beethoven
All My Loving
Side 2
This Boy
Please Mr. Postman

4-BY THE BEATLES

Capitol R-5365 . . . . . *2/11/65*   **100–125**

Orange and yellow swirl label with black print.

Side 1
Honey Don't
I'm a Loser
Side 2
Mr. Moonlight
Everybody's Trying to Be My Baby

MEET THE BEATLES

Capitol Compact 33 SXA-2047

. . . . *1/64*   **375–450**

Black label with colorband. 33 1/3rpm. Stereo only. Issued for jukeboxes. Issued with three 1¾"-square cover miniatures and five title strips.

Side 1
It Won't Be Long
This Boy
All My Loving
Side 2
Don't Bother Me
All I've Got to Do
I Wanna Be Your Man

NO MORE LONELY NIGHTS
(Ballad and extended versions)/Silly
Love Songs (Paul McCartney)

Columbia 8 C8-39927-S1   **10–15**

12-inch picture disc. Issued in a clear plastic cover. Cover has a blue title sticker.

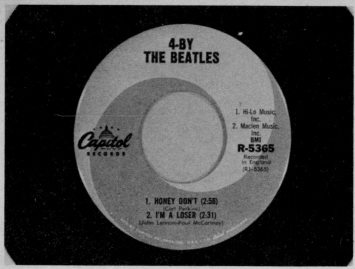

Capitol released only two Beatles EPs in the United States commercially. *4-By the Beatles* was the second of these releases, in February 1965.

NO MORE LONELY NIGHTS
(Ballad and extended versions)/Silly
Love Songs—No More Lonely Nights
(Ballad) (Paul McCartney)
Columbia 44-05077.... *11/84*   **5–8**
12-inch single. Red label. Issued with a special picture cover.

NO MORE LONELY NIGHTS
(Special dance mix)/Silly Love
Songs—No More Lonely Nights
(Ballad) (Paul McCartney)
Columbia 44-05077   **15–20**
12-inch disc. Red label. Issued with the same picture cover, but with a pink title sticker denoting "special dance mix." This release superseded the original "playout" version.

OPEN END INTERVIEW WITH
THE BEATLES
Capitol Compact 33 PRO-2548/9
. . . . *2/64*   **500–600**
Black label with colorband. 33 1/3 rpm. 7-inch promotional EP issued to publicize the *Meet the Beatles* LP. Contains an open-end interview with the group and a few tracks from the LP.

Issued with script/picture sleeve. Label reads "Especially Prepared for Radio and TV Programming—Not for Sale."
Counterfeit identification: the known fake lacks the colorband on the disc label that is found on the original.
Capitol Compact 33 PRO-2548/9   **500–600**
Script/picture sleeve. Contains the script for the Beatles interview.

SECOND ALBUM, THE BEATLES
Capitol Compact 33 SXA-2080
. . . . *4/64*   **375–450**
Black label with colorband. 33 1/3 rpm. Stereo only. Issued for jukeboxes. Issued with three 1¾"-square cover miniatures and five title strips.

Side 1
   Thank You Girl
   Devil in Her Heart
   Money
Side 2
   Long Tall Sally (spelled "Salley")
   I Call Your Name
   Please Mr. Postman

SOMETHING NEW
Capitol Compact 33 SXA-2108
. . . . *4/64* **375–450**
Black label with colorband. 33⅓rpm. Stereo
only. Issued for jukeboxes. Issued with three
1¾"-square cover miniatures and five title
strips.

Side 1
  I'll Cry Instead
  And I Love Her
  Slow Down
Side 2
  If I Fell
  Tell Me Why
  Matchbox

SOUVENIR OF THEIR VISIT TO AMERICA
Vee Jay EP 1-903. . . . *3/23/64* **45–50**
Black label with colorband. Issued with picture
cover. Logo 1.

Vee Jay EP 1-903 **45–50**
Black label with colorband. Logo 2.

Vee Jay EP 1-903 **60–70**
Black label with colorband. The track "Ask Me
Why" is in much bolder print than the other
tracks. Logo 2.

Vee Jay EP 1-903 **70–80**
All-black label with silver print. Logo 1.

Vee Jay EP 1-903 **90–100**
All-black label with silver print. Two horizontal
silver bars on label. Logo 2.

Vee Jay EP 1-903 **70–80**
All-black label with silver print. Issued with
hard picture cover. Value separation: cover
30%/disc 70%. Logo 3.

Vee Jay EP 1–903 **125–150**
Promotional copy. Blue and white label with
black and blue print. Label reads "Promotional
Copy." Value given is for the disc only as these
were most often issued without covers.

Vee Jay EP 1–903 **3000–4000**
Promotional sleeve. Actually titled *Ask ME
Why—The Beatles*, it maintains the same rec-
ord number and has references to the EP.

Side 1
  Misery
  A Taste of Honey
Side 2
  Ask Me Why
  Anna

TAKE IT AWAY/I'll Give You a Ring—Dress Me Up As a Robber
Columbia 44-03019 . . . . . *7/82* **10–15**
12-inch single. Red label. Issued with a special
picture cover.

Tug of War, A Sample from: see
EBONY AND IVORY.

Beatles: LPs

What follows are all the LPs and promotional releases that have been officially released by the Beatles, both as a group and as solo performers, in the United States. Under each artist's heading, the albums are listed alphabetically by titles. The first and subsequent issues are entered chronologically.

For an explanation of the various Capitol labels, see the Capitol–Apple Discography, page 303.

In 1983, Capitol introduced a label that was very similar in design to their original '60s label. The way to distinguish the new colorband label from the old is that the small printing is black in the colorband of the new label, while on the originals, this print is in white.

ABBEY ROAD

Apple SO-383 . . . . . . *10/1/69*   **15–20**
Apple label with Capitol logo.

Apple SO-383   **10–15**
Apple label.

Capitol SO-383 . . . . . . *75–78*   **8–12**
Orange label.

Capitol SO-383 . . . . . . *78–83*   **8–10**
Purple label.

Capitol SJ-383 . . . . *83 to date*   **5–8**
Black label with colorband.

Capitol SEAX-11900 . . . . . *78*   **30–35**
Picture disc.

Mobile Fidelity Sound Lab MFSL-
1-023. . . . . *79*   **25–30**
Half-speed mastered. High quality vinyl pressing.

Side 1
  Come Together
  Something
  Maxwell's Silver Hammer
  Oh! Darling
  Octopus's Garden
  I Want You (She's So Heavy)

Side 2
  Here Comes the Sun
  You Never Give Me Your Money
  Sun King
  Mean Mr. Mustard
  Polythene Pam
  She Came in Through the Bathroom Window
  Golden Slumbers
  Carry That Weight
  The End
  Her Majesty

AIN'T SHE SWEET

Atco 33-169 . . . . . . *10/5/64*   **80–90**
Monaural. Blue and gold label.

Atco SD 33-169 . . . . *10/5/64*   **100–125**
Stereo. Tan and lavender label.

Atco 33-169 . . . . *10/64*   **350–375**
Promotional copy. White label.

Atco SD 33-169 . . . . *69*   **150–175**
Stereo. Yellow label.
Songs include:
Ain't She Sweet/Sweet Georgia Brown/Take Out Some Insurance on Me Baby/Nobody's Child *(plus eight songs by the Swallows)*

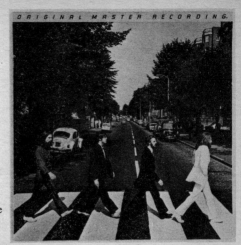

A state-of-the-art audiophile edition of *Abbey Road* by Mobile Fidelity Sound Lab. Their releases of the previous Beatles LPs were based on the British and not the American albums.

Atco was one of several labels to get their hands on the '61 Hamburg sessions with Tony Sheridan. The Swallows were a sound-alike band who profited from the fact that there wasn't enough original material to fill up an album.

ALL OUR LOVING

Cicadelic LP-1963 . . . . . . *86* **5–8**
Silver label. Contains interviews circa 1964 and 1965.

AMAZING BEATLES AND OTHER GREAT ENGLISH GROUP SOUNDS, THE

Clarion 601 . . . . . . *10/17/66* **50–60**
Monaural. Red, white and blue label. Re-issue of Atco's *Ain't She Sweet* LP. Back cover features LP song listing plus 21 miniature LP photo ads.

Clarion 601 **70–80**
Monaural. This version does not list the song titles on the back of the cover.

Clarion 601 **70–80**
Stereo. Orange, white and green label. Back cover features LP song listings plus 21 miniature LP photo ads.

Clarion 601 **100–125**
Stereo. This version does not list the song titles on the back of the cover.
Songs include:
Ain't She Sweet/Take Out Some Insurance on Me Baby/Nobody's Child/Sweet Georgia Brown *(plus six songs by the Swallows)*

AMERICAN TOUR WITH ED RUDY #2, THE

Radio Pulsebeat News . . *6/9/64* **50–60**
Yellow label. Contains interviews with the Beatles in 1964. Many early copies were issued with a special picture-packed Beatles edition of *Teen Talk* magazine, valued at $35, and a 3" × 5" card valued at $5.

I.N.S. Radio News *80* **15–20**
Blue label. This re-issue features a portrait cover drawing of the Beatles on the front.

AMERICAN TOUR WITH ED RUDY #3, THE

Radio Pulsebeat News *65* **70–80**
(Actually titled *1965 Talk Album, Ed Rudy with New U.S. Tour;* however, it is placed here to remain with its counterparts.) Orange label. Many original copies were issued with two flyers advertising other Ed Rudy albums. The value of each flyer is $5.

Audio Guide to the Alan Parsons Project: **see Various-Artists Compilations section.**

BEATLE TALK

Great Northwest Music Co.
GNW-4007 . . . . *78* **8–12**
Red label. Contains interview from the 1964 press conference with Red Robinson. Deduct 25% from the value if LP has a "cut-out" marking on the cover.

Music International M-4007 **8–12**
White label with black print. All white cover with raised embossed title and graphics. 1985 re-issue.

BEATLEMANIA TOUR COVERAGE

I.N.S. Radio News—DOC 1. *64* **200–225**
Open end interview disc distributed by Ed Rudy Productions. Issued in a plain white cover with a questionnaire script. For promotional use only.

BEATLES, THE *("The White Album")*

Apple SWBO-101. . . *11/25/68* **40–45**
Apple label with Capitol logo. Double LP title *The Beatles* is embossed on the front. Each LP is sequentially numbered on the lower right of the front cover. Issued with a large poster and four photos.

Apple SWBO-101 **20–25**
Apple label. Title *The Beatles* is embossed on the front. These and subsequent issues were not numbered. Includes a poster and four photos.

Capitol SWBO-101 . . . . *75–78* **12–15**
Orange label. Includes poster and four photos.

Capitol SWBO-101 . . . . *75–78* **12–15**
Purple label. Includes poster and four photos.

Capitol SEBX-11841 . . . . . *78* **20–25**
White vinyl. Purple label. Includes poster and four photos.

Capitol SEBX-11841 . . . . . *78* **100–125**
Gray vinyl. Only the disc with side one and two was produced. LP cover and inserts do not accompany this LP.

Mobile Fidelity Sound Lab MFSL-2-072. . . . . *82* **10–15**
Half-speed mastered pressing. White label. The poster and photos were not included in this package.

Capitol SWBO-101 . . *83 to date* **10–12**
Black label with colorband. Includes poster and four photos.

Side 1
  Back in the U.S.S.R.
  Dear Prudence
  Glass Onion
  Ob La Di Ob La Da
  Wild Honey Pie

The '61 Hamburg sessions yet
again. Note the absence of
faces on a cover strikingly
reminiscent of the '64 Capitol
picture sleeves on this '66
release.

American dee jays often vied
for the title of "Fifth Beatle."
Ed Rudy did better than most,
culling three interview/talk
albums from the effort.

The Continuing Story of Bungalow Bill
While My Guitar Gently Weeps
Happiness Is a Warm Gun
Side 2
　Martha My Dear
　I'm So Tired
　Black Bird
　Piggies
　Rocky Raccoon
　Don't Pass Me By
　Why Don't We Do It in the Road
　I Will
　Julia
Side 3
　Birthday
　Yer Blues
　Mother Nature's Son
　Everybody's Got Something to Hide Except
　　for Me and My Monkey
　Sexy Sadie
　Helter Skelter
　Long, Long, Long
Side 4
　Revolution
　Honey Pie
　Savoy Truffle
　Cry Baby Cry
　Revolution #9
　Goodnight

Beatles Again, The: see *HEY JUDE.*

BEATLES AND FRANK IFIELD ON STAGE—JOLLY WHAT!, THE
Vee Jay LP-1085 . . . . *2/26/64*　**70–80**
Monaural. Drawing of an old man with a Beatle haircut on the cover. Referred to as the "Jolly What" cover. Black label with colorband.

Counterfeit identification: counterfeit cover has no spine printing. So far, we have only verified the counterfeit with the "all-black" label.

Vee Jay LPS-1085　**175–200**
Stereo. Drawing of an old man with a Beatle haircut on the cover. Referred to as the "Jolly What" cover. Black label with rainbow colorband.

Counterfeit identification: counterfeit cover has no spine printing. We have only verified the counterfeit with the "all-black" label.

Vee Jay LP-1085 . . . . . . *64*　**750–800**
Monaural. Portrait painting of the group on the cover. Referred to as the "Portrait Cover." Black label with colorband.

Vee Jay LPS 1085 . . . . . . *64*　**1750–2000**
Stereo. Portrait painting of the group on the cover. Referred to as the "Portrait Cover."

Black label with colorband. Produced for a very short time in 1964 as a re-issue.

Songs include:
Please Please Me/From Me to You/Thank You Girl/Ask Me Why *(plus songs by 'Frank Ifield')*

BEATLES COLLECTION, THE
Capitol-EMI BC-13. . . . . *78*　**300–325**
14-LP boxed set packaged by Capitol. Boxed set consists of the first 13 British LPs and an unreleased American pressing of *Rarities.* Box is blue with gold print and each one is sequentially numbered 0001 to 3000. This U.S.-packaged box set can be distinctly identified by the EMI logo and the number BC-13 located on the side of the box.

Mobile Fidelity Sound Lab　*9/82*　**400–425**
13-LP boxed set of half-speed mastered recordings on high-quality Japanese vinyl. The LPs are the 13 British titles. Black box with gold print. Numbered sequentially inside the 38-page booklet that is included with the set.

Please Please Me
Side 1
　I Saw Her Standing There
　Misery
　Anna (Go to Him)
　Chains
　Secret
　Boys
　Ask Me Why
　Please Please Me
Side 2
　Love Me Do
　P.S. I Love You
　Baby It's You
　Do You Want to Know a Secret
　A Taste of Honey
　There's a Place
　Twist and Shout

With the Beatles
Side 1
　It Won't Be Long
　All I've Got to Do
　All My Loving
　Don't Bother Me
　Little Child
　Till There Was You
　Please Mister Postman
Side 2
　Roll Over Beethoven
　Hold Me Tight
　You Really Got a Hold on Me
　I Wanna Be Your Man
　Devil in Her Heart

Not a Second Time
Money

A Hard Day's Night
Side 1
  A Hard Day's Night
  I Should Have Known Better
  If I Fell
  I'm Happy Just to Dance with You
  And I Love Her
  Tell Me Why
  Can't Buy Me Love
Side 2
  Any Time At All
  I'll Cry Instead
  Things We Said Today
  When I Get Home
  You Can't Do That
  I'll Be Back

Beatles For Sale
Side 1
  No Reply
  I'm a Loser
  Baby's in Black
  Rock and Roll Music
  I'll Follow the Sun
  Mr. Moonlight
  Kansas City
Side 2
  Eight Days a Week
  Words of Love
  Honey Don't
  Every Little Thing
  I Don't Want to Spoil the Party
  What You're Doing
  Everybody's Trying to Be My Baby

Help!
Side 1
  Help!
  The Night Before
  You've Got to Hide Your Love Away
  I Need You
  Another Girl
  You're Going to Lose That Girl
  Ticket to Ride
Side 2
  Act Naturally
  It's Only Love
  You Like Me Too Much
  Tell Me What You See
  I've Just Seen a Face
  Yesterday
  Dizzy Miss Lizzy

Rubber Soul
Side 1
  Drive My Car
  Norwegian Wood

You Won't See Me
Nowhere Man
Think for Yourself
The Word
Michelle
Side 2
  What Goes On
  Girl
  I'm Looking Through You
  In My Life
  Wait
  If I Needed Someone
  Run for Your Life

Revolver
Side 1
  Taxman
  Eleanor Rigby
  I'm Only Sleeping
  Love You To
  Here, There and Everywhere
  Yellow Submarine
  She Said She Said
Side 2
  Good Day Sunshine
  And Your Bird Can Sing
  For No One
  Dr. Robert
  I Want to Tell You
  Got to Get You into My Life
  Tomorrow Never Knows

Sgt. Pepper's Lonely Hearts Club Band
Side 1
  Sgt. Pepper's Lonely Hearts Club Band
  With a Little Help from My Friends
  Lucy in the Sky with Diamonds
  Getting Better
  Fixing a Hole
  She's Leaving Home
  Being for the Benefit of Mr. Kite
Side 2
  Within You Without You
  When I'm Sixty Four
  Lovely Rita
  Good Morning Good Morning
  Sgt. Pepper's Lonely Hearts Club Band (re-
    prise)
  A Day in the Life (repeating groove)

Magical Mystery Tour
Side 1
  Magical Mystery Tour
  The Fool on the Hill
  Flying
  Blue Jay Way
  Your Mother Should Know
  I Am the Walrus

Side 2
   Hello Goodbye
   Strawberry Fields Forever
   Penny Lane
   Baby, You're a Rich Man
   All You Need Is Love

The Beatles
Side 1
   Back in the U.S.S.R.
   Dear Prudence
   Glass Onion
   Ob La Di Ob La Da
   Wild Honey Pie
   The Continuing Story of Bungalow Bill
   While My Guitar Gently Weeps
   Happiness Is a Warm Gun
Side 2
   Martha My Dear
   I'm So Tired
   Black Bird
   Piggies
   Rocky Raccoon
   Don't Pass Me By
   Why Don't We Do It in the Road
   I Will
   Julia
Side 3
   Birthday
   Yer Blues
   Mother Nature's Son
   Everybody's Got Something to Hide Except
      for Me and My Monkey
   Sexy Sadie
   Helter Skelter
   Long, Long, Long
Side 4
   Revolution
   Honey Pie
   Savoy Truffle
   Cry Baby Cry
   Revolution #9
   Goodnight

Yellow Submarine
Side 1
   Yellow Submarine
   Only a Northern Song
   All Together Now
   Hey Bulldog
   It's All Too Much
   All You Need Is Love
Side 2
   Instrumentals by George Martin

Hey Jude
Side 1
   Can't Buy Me Love
   I Should Have Known Better

   Paperback Writer
   Rain
   Lady Madonna
   Revolution
Side 2
   Hey Jude
   Old Brown Shoe
   Don't Let Me Down
   The Ballad of John and Yoko

Abbey Road
Side 1
   Come Together
   Something
   Maxwell's Silver Hammer
   Oh! Darling
   Octopus's Garden
   I Want You (She's So Heavy)
Side 2
   Here Comes the Sun
   You Never Give Me Your Money
   Sun King
   Mean Mr. Mustard
   Polythene Pam
   She Came in Through the Bathroom Win-
      dow
   Golden Slumbers
   Carry That Weight
   The End

Let It Be
Side 1
   Two of Us
   I Dig a Pony
   Across the Universe
   I, Me, Mine
   Dig It
   Let It Be
   Maggie May
Side 2
   I've Got a Feeling
   One After 909
   The Long and Winding Road
   For You Blue
   Get Back

Rarities (included in the BC-13 set; not available in the Mobile Fidelity package)

Side 1
   Across the Universe
   Yes It Is
   This Boy
   The Inner Light
   I'll Get You
   Thank You Girl
   Komm, Gib Mir Deine Hand
   You Know My Name
   Sie Liebt Dich

Side 2
   Rain
   She's a Woman
   Matchbox
   I Call Your Name
   Bad Boy
   Slow Down
   I'm Down
   Long Tall Sally

BEATLES COLLECTION, THE PLATINUM SERIES

Capitol. *84*   **500–525**
18-LP boxed set to promote the introduction of Capitol's commercial line of computer software. Box is silver with black print and reads "Compliments of Capitol Records Inc." The sealed LPs in the boxed set are most likely on Capitol's purple label.

BEATLES FOR SALE

Mobile Fidelity Sound Lab MFSL
1-104. . . . . *87*   **5–8**
White label with black and tan print. Half-speed mastered recording on high quality vinyl.

Side 1
   No Reply
   I'm a Loser
   Baby's in Black
   Rock and Roll Music
   I'll Follow the Sun
   Mr. Moonlight
   Kansas City
Side 2
   Eight Days a Week
   Words of Love
   Honey Don't
   Every Little Thing
   I Don't Want to Spoil the Party
   What You're Doing
   Everybody's Trying to Be My Baby

Beatles VI: **see** *VI, BEATLES.*

Beatles 65: **see** *65, BEATLES.*

Beatles Story, The: **see** *STORY, THE BEATLES.*

BEATLES TAPES: **see** *WIGG, DAVID INTERVIEWS.*

Beatles vs. the Four Seasons: **see** *FOUR SEASONS . . .*

BEATLES WITH TONY SHERIDAN AND GUESTS, THE

MGM E-4215. . . . . . *2/3/64*   **50–60**
Monaural. Black label. Contains four tracks by the Beatles with Tony Sheridan, two tracks by Tony Sheridan, and six tracks by the Titans.

This is a compilation LP; it is kept here due to the capitalizing of the Beatles' name on the cover.
MGM SE-4215   **100–125**
Stereo. Black label.

Big Hits from Britain and the U.S.A.: **see Various-Artists Compilations section.**

BRITISH ARE COMING, THE

Silhouette SM-10013 . . . *11/84*   **5–8**
Orange label. Contains interviews with the Beatles circa '64 through '67. LP cover features 3-D photos of the group. Issued with a 3-D viewer. Each LP is sequentially numbered.

British Gold: **see Various-Artists Compilations section.**

British Rock Classics: **see Various-Artists Compilations section.**

British Sterling: **see Various-Artists Compilations section.**

Capitol Hits through the Years: **see Various-Artists Compilations section.**

Capitol In-Store Sampler: **see Various-Artists Compilations section.**

Chart Busters: **see Various-Artists Compilations section.**

CHRISTMAS ALBUM, THE BEATLES

Apple SBC-100 . . . . *70*   **100–125**
Apple label. LP is a compilation of the Beatles fan club Christmas messages issued as singles from 1963 through 1969. Distributed exclusively to the "Beatles USA, LTD" fan club members. Back of cover and disc label read "Not For Sale."

Counterfeit identification: All colored vinyl copies are fake. The title on the label of the fake is approximately 2½″ long, the original is 2¼″. All copies of this LP with posterboard construction are fakes.

CHRISTMAS REFLECTIONS

Desert Vibration Heritage Series
HSRD-SP1 . . . . *12/82*   **10–15**
White label. Contains the Beatles Christmas messages from 1963 through 1966.

Collier's Encyclopedia 1965 Edition of Year of Sound: **see Various-Artists Compilations section.**

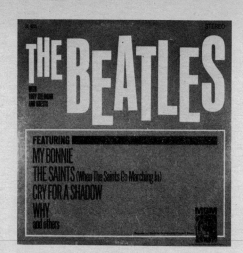

Just when you think you have them all, up pops *another* release of the '61 Hamburg sessions. On this '64 LP, the special guests are the Titans.

Seven years of British and American Fan Club Christmas messages that chart the rise and fall of the Beatles in an unusual way.

COMPLETE SILVER BEATLES, THE

Audio Rarities AR-2452 . . . *82*   **8–12**
Silver label. Contains 12 tracks from the Decca audition sessions in 1962.

Custom Fidelity Sound Promotions: see Various-Artists Compilations section.

DAWN OF THE SILVER BEATLES

Pac UDL-2333 . . . . . *4/2/81*   **15–20**
Silver label. Contains 10 tracks from the 1962 audition sessions for Decca. The first 750 copies of this LP were sequentially numbered (00251 through 01000). These first 750 pressings also came with a letter of authenticity from the company. Each LP was numbered on the disc label and the back of the cover. All later pressings were numbered on a registration card that was issued with the later copies. These were started at 001999 and supposed to run through 153,000; however, the actual figure ended up a reported 2500. Value given is for the later, more common pressing; add 50% to value for the early hand-numbered copies with the letter.

Discotheque in Astrosound: see Various-Artists Compilations section.

Do It Now: see Various-Artists Compilations section.

EARLY BEATLES, THE

Capitol T-2309 . . . . . *3/22/65*   **40–45**
Monaural. Black label with colorband.

Capitol ST-2309   **30–35**
Stereo. Black label with colorband.

Capitol ST-2309. . . . . *69–71*   **20–25**
Stereo. Green label.

Apple ST-2309 . . . . *1/71–6/71*   **15–20**
Stereo. Apple label with Capitol logo.

Apple ST-2309 . . . . . . *71–75*   **15–20**
Stereo. Plain Apple label.

Capitol ST-2309. . . . . *75–78*   **8–12**
Stereo. Orange label.

Capitol ST-2309. . . . . *78–83*   **8–10**
Stereo. Purple label.

Capitol ST-2309. . . *83 to date*   **5–8**
Stereo. Black label with colorband.
Note: All of the songs on *The Early Beatles* LP were originally released in the United States by Vee Jay on the *Introducing the Beatles* album (see *Introducing the Beatles*).

Side 1
  Love Me Do
  Twist and Shout
  Anna
  Chains
  Boys
  Ask Me Why
Side 2
  Please Please Me
  P.S. I Love You
  Baby It's You
  A Taste of Honey
  Do You Want to Know a Secret

EAST COAST INVASION

Cicadelic CICLP-1964 . . . . *85*   **5–8**
Red label. Contains various interviews circa 1964.

1ST LIVE RECORDINGS, VOL. I, THE BEATLES

Pickwick SPC-3661   **8–12**
Black label. Deduct 30% if cover has a cut-out marking.

1ST LIVE RECORDINGS, VOL. II, THE BEATLES

Pickwick SPC-3662   **8–12**
Black label. Deduct 30% if cover has a cut-out marking.

FIRST MOVEMENT, BEATLES

Audio Fidelity (Phoenix 10) PHX-339 . . . . *82*   **8–12**
White label. Contains eight tracks by the Beatles with Tony Sheridan. Deduct 20% if cover has cut-out marking.

Audio Fidelity PD-339   **10–15**
Picture disc.

  Ain't She Sweet
  Sweet Georgia Brown
  Take Out Some Insurance On Me, Baby
  Ruby Baby
  Ya Ya
  Why (Can't You Love Me Again)
  Nobody's Child
  Cry for a Shadow

First Vibration: see Various-Artists Compilations section.

Flashback: see Various-Artists Compilations section.

FOUR SEASONS, THE BEATLES VS. THE

Vee Jay DX-30 . . . . . *10/1/64*   **275–300**
Monaural. Double LP with gatefold cover. An 11½″ × 23″ color poster was issued with each album. Value for the poster is $100, which is separate from the list value of the LP.

Vee Jay DXS-30   **500–525**
Stereo.
Note: Repackage set combining two previously released albums: *Introducing the Beatles* and

The Golden Hits of the Four Seasons (Vee Jay LP 1065). An 11½" × 23" color poster was issued with each album. Value for the poster is $100, which is separate from the list value of the LP.

Side 1
    I Saw Her Standing There
    Misery
    Anna
    Chains
    Boys
    Ask Me Why
Side 2
    Please Please Me
    Baby It's You
    Do You Want to Know a Secret
    A Taste of Honey
    There's a Place
    Twist and Shout

FROM BRITAIN WITH A BEAT
Cicadelic 1967 . . . . *7/87*   **5–8**
Silver label with black label graphics. Contains interviews with the group circa 1964–65.

GOLDEN BEATLES, THE
Silhouette SM-10015 . . . . *6/85*   **5–8**
Gold label with black print. Contains interviews circa 1965 and 1968. Also features a few novelty songs performed by other artists.

Golden Days of British Rock: **see Various-Artists Compilations section.**

Grammy Award Winners: **see Various-Artists Compilations section.**

GREAT AMERICAN TOUR, 1965 LIVE BEATLEMANIA CONCERT
Lloyds ER MC LTD. *65*   **200–225**
The third and last LP by Ed Rudy covering the Beatles. Contains actual "live" tracks by the Beatles.

Great New Releases: **see Various-Artists Compilations section.**

Greatest Music Ever Sold: **see Various-Artists Compilations section.**

HAPPY MICHAELMAS
Adirondack Group AG-8146
. . . . *81*   **10–15**
Blue label with black print. Contains Christmas messages from 1967 through 1969.

HARD DAY'S NIGHT, A
United Artists UAL-3366
. . . . *6/26/64*   **40–45**
Monaural. Black label.

United Artists UAL-3366 . *7/64*   **350–375**
Promotion copy. Monaural only. White label. Label reads "Not For Sale."

United Artists T-90828   **100–125**
Monaural record club issue. Black label with silver print. Issued by the Capitol Record Club. This is the only known 'mono' Beatles or Beatles-related record club issue.

United Artists ST-90828   **50–60**
Record club issue. Black label. Available through the Capitol Record Club.

United Artists UAS-6366   **40–45**
Stereo. Black label.

United Artists UAS-6366 . . *68*   **20–25**
Stereo. Pink and orange label.

United Artists UAS-6366 . . *70*   **20–25**
Stereo. Black and orange label.

United Artists UAS-6366 . . *71*   **10–15**
Stereo. Tan label.

United Artists UAS-6366 . . *77*   **10–12**
Stereo. Orange and yellow sunrise label.

Capitol SW-11921 . . . . *80–83*   **8–12**
Stereo. Purple label.

Capitol SW-11921 . . . . . . *84*   **5–8**
Stereo. New black label with colorband.

Side 1
    Hard Day's Night
    I'll Cry Instead
    Tell Me Why
    I'm Happy Just to Dance with You
        (plus four George Martin instrumentals)
Side 2
    If I Fell
    I Should Have Known Better
    And I Love Her
    Can't Buy Me Love

HARD DAY'S NIGHT, A
Mobile Fidelity Sound Lab MFSL
1-103. . . . . *87*   **5–8**
White label. Half-speed master recording on high quality vinyl. Taken from the British release.

Side 1
    A Hard Day's Night
    I Should Have Known Better
    If I Fell
    I'm Happy Just to Dance with You
    And I Love Her
    Tell Me Why
    Can't Buy Me Love
Side 2
    Any Time At All
    I'll Cry Instead
    Things We Said Today

This was the only non-Capitol release of new Beatles material in the United States. United Artists relinquished the rights in 1979.

When I Get Home
You Can't Do That
I'll Be Back

HARD DAY'S NIGHT, A—UNITED ARTISTS PRESENTS
United Artists SP-2362/3 . 7/64 **450–475**
Radio spots. Red label. Promotional only LP containing radio spot announcements for the movie.
United Artists SP-2359/60. . 64 **550–575**
Open-end interview. Red label. Promotional only LP containing an open-end interview with the Beatles to promote the movie. Issued with a 12-page script on United Artists letterhead.

HEAR THE BEATLES TELL ALL
Vee Jay VJLP-PRO-202 . . . 64 **60–70**
Monaural. Black label with rainbow colorband. "Brackets" logo only. Contains interviews with the group circa 1964.

Counterfeit identification: counterfeit cover has no spine printing. The counterfeit discs we examined had an all-black label, originals have the black label with colorband.
Vee Jay VJLP-PRO-202 . . . 79 **5–8**
Cover reads "Stereo." Black label with colorband.
Vee Jay PRO 202. . . . . . 8/87 **8–10**
Shaped picture disc. Issued in clear plastic cover with title sticker.

HELP!
Capitol MAS-2386 . . . 8/13/65 **40–45**
Monaural. Black label with colorband. Single LP with gatefold cover.

Capitol SMAS-2386 **30–35**
Stereo. Black label with colorband.

Capitol SMAS-8-2386 **30–35**
Record Club issue. Available on original black or green label. The "8" in the record number identifies the record as being a record club issue.

Capitol SMAS-2386 . . . 69–71 **20–25**
Stereo. Green label.

Apple SMAS-2386 . . 1/71–6/71 **10–15**
Stereo. Apple label with Capitol logo.

Apple SMAS-2386 . . . 6/71–75 **10–15**
Stereo. Plain Apple label.

Capitol SMAS-2386 . . . 75–78 **8–12**
Stereo. Orange label.

Capitol SMAS-2386 . . . 78–83 **8–10**
Stereo. Purple label.

Capitol SMAS-2386 . 83 to date **8–12**
Stereo. New black label with colorband.

Side 1
  Help!
  The Night Before
  You've Got to Hide Your Love Away
  I Need You
    (plus George Martin instrumentals)
Side 2
  Another Girl
  Ticket to Ride
  You're Gonna Lose That Girl
Mobile Fidelity Sound Lab MFSL-
1-105. . . . . 85 **5–8**

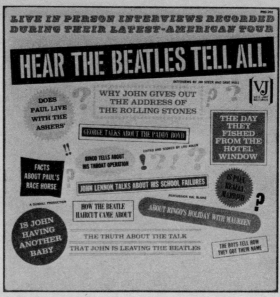

This is the only material Vee Jay held onto after they lost the rights to the Beatles' first fourteen tracks. Originally issued in 1964, Vee Jay re-issued the record in 1979.

White label. Half-speed mastered recording on high quality vinyl. Song sequence from British release.

Side 1
Help!
The Night Before
You've Got to Hide Your Love Away
I Need You
Another Girl
You're Going to Lose That Girl
Ticket to Ride

Side 2
Act Naturally
It's Only Love
You Like Me Too Much
Tell Me What You See
I've Just Seen a Face
Yesterday
Dizzy Miss Lizzy

HELP!, UNITED ARTISTS PRESENTS
United Artists UA-HELP-A/B
. . . . 65   **450–500**

Radio spots. Red label. Promotional LP containing radio spot announcements for the movie.

United Artists UA-HELP-INT
. . . . 65   **550–600**
Open-end interview. Red label. Promotional LP containing an open-end interview with the group and others about the movie. Issued with a script.

HELP! 65   **650–675**
Open-end interview. Blue label. Features 29:50 interview with the Beatles. Issued with script.

HEY JUDE ("The Beatles Again")
Apple SW (SO)-385 . . *2/26/70*   **15–20**
Plain Apple label. Disc label is titled "The Beatles Again." These early albums were all released with *Hey Jude*-titled covers.

Apple SW-385   **25–30**
Apple label with Capitol logo. The title *Hey Jude* is printed on this and all subsequent issues.

Apple SW-385		**25–30**

Plain Apple label.

Capitol SW-385	*75–78*	**8–12**

Orange label.

Capitol SW-385	*78–83*	**8–10**

Purple label.

Capitol SW-385	*83 to date*	**5–10**

Black label with colorband.

Side 1

Can't Buy Me Love
I Should Have Known Better
Paperback Writer
Rain
Lady Madonna
Revolution

Side 2

Hey Jude
Old Brown Shoe
Don't Let Me Down
The Ballad of John and Yoko

HISTORIC FIRST LIVE RECORDINGS, THE

Pickwick PTP-2098	**10–15**

Black label. Double LP with gatefold cover. Deduct 25% if cover has a cut-out marking.

Side 1

I'm Gonna Sit Right Down and Cry
Roll Over Beethoven
Hippy Hippy Shake
Sweet Little Sixteen
Lend Me Your Comb
Your Feets Too Big

Side 2

Where Have You Been All My Life
Mr. Moonlight
A Taste of Honey
Besame Mucho
Til There Was You
Kansas City

Side 3

Ain't Nothing' Shakin' Like the Leaves on a Tree
To Know Her Is to Love Her
Little Queenie
Falling in Love Again
Sheila
Be-Bop-a-Lula
Hallelujah I Love Her So

Side 4

Red Sails in the Sunset
Everybody's Trying to Be My Baby
Matchbox
I'm Talking About You
Shimmy Shake

Long Tall Sally
I Remember You

History of British Rock: see
Various-Artists Compilations section.

HOLLYWOOD BOWL, THE BEATLES AT THE

Capitol SMAS-11638 . . .	*5/4/77*	**8–12**

Custom label. Single LP with gatefold cover. "LP Title" and "Ticket" graphics on cover are embossed.

Capitol SMAS-11638	**125–150**

Advance promotional issue. Light tan label. Plain white cover with the stamped printing "Advance Pressing, The Beatles At The Hollywood Bowl." Issued with programming insert.

Capitol SMAS-11638	*5/77*	**5–8**

This and subsequent re-issues no longer have the embossed cover.

Side 1

Twist and Shout
She's a Woman
Dizzy Miss Lizzy
Ticket to Ride
Can't Buy Me Love
Things We Said Today
Roll Over Beethoven

Side 2

Boys
A Hard Day's Night
Help!
All My Loving
She Loves You
Long Tall Sally

I APOLOGIZE

Sterling Productions 8895-6481

. . . .	*66*	**100–125**

Yellow label. One-sided LP featuring interviews with the Beatles during a 1966 press conference in which Lennon's remarks on Christianity are addressed. Available through a mail-order ad that was featured in a prominent Chicago, Illinois, newspaper. Issued with an 8″ × 10″ glossy black and white photo of the group.

I Can Hear It Now: see **Various-Artists Compilations section.**

IN THE BEGINNING (CIRCA 1960)

Polydor 24-4504	*5/4/70*	**15–20**

Red label. Single LP with gatefold cover. Features material recorded by the Beatles with Tony Sheridan in 1961 (cover incorrectly states "1960").

Polydor SKAO-93199   **15–20**
Record Club issue. Red label. Available through the Capitol Record Club in the early seventies.

Polydor 24-4504 . . . . *81*   **8–10**
Red label. Bottom of label reads "Manufactured by Polydor Incorporated/810 Seventh Avenue/New York, N.Y. 10019." Single-sleeve jacket.

Polydor-Polygram 24-4504. . *84*   **5–8**
Red label. Bottom of the label reads "Manufactured and Marketed by Polygram Records."

Side 1
  Ain't She Sweet
  Cry for a Shadow
  My Bonnie
  Take Out Some Insurance on Me Baby
    (plus songs by "Tony Sheridan & The Beat
    Brothers")
Side 2
  Sweet Georgia Brown
  The Saints
  Why
  Nobody's Child

In the Beginning: see **Various-Artists Compilations section.**

Just Let Me Hear Some of That Rock 'n' Roll Music: see **Various-Artists Compilations section.**

**INTRODUCING THE BEATLES
(Version 1)**
Vee Jay LP-1062 . . . . *7/22/63* 350–375
Monaural. Black label with colorband. Logo 1, and includes "Love Me Do" and "P.S. I Love You." Back cover displays 25 LP ad miniatures (in color).
Note: The words "PRINTED IN U.S.A." in the lower left of the front in small black print—this distinguishes the original issue from subsequent re-issues.

Vee Jay SR-1062   **750–775**
Stereo. Black label with colorband. Logo 1 with the songs "Love Me Do" and "P.S. I Love You." Logo style is oval. Back cover displays 25 LP ad miniatures (in color). Front cover has white banner across the top with gray print which reads "STEREOPHONIC."
Note: All original covers have the words "PRINTED IN U.S.A." in the lower left of the front in small black print.

Vee Jay LP-1062 . . . . . . *1/64* **300–325**
Blank label (Promotional) issue. Monaural. Black label with colorband. Logo 1. Back cover is glossy white and blank.

Vee Jay SR-1062   **650–675**
Black label with colorband. Logo 1, contains the songs "Love Me Do" and "P.S. I Love You." Description as above, but the front cover has a white banner across the top with gray print which reads "STEREOPHONIC."

Vee Jay LP-1062   **70–80**
Monaural. Black label with colorband. Logo 1, with the songs "Love Me Do" and "P.S. I Love You." Back cover lists the song titles in two large columns.

Vee Jay LP-1062   **100–125**
Monaural. Black label with colorband. Logo 2, with the songs "Love Me Do" and "P.S. I Love You." Back cover lists the song titles in two large columns.

Side 1
  I Saw Her Standing There
  Misery
  Anna
  Chains
  Boys
  Love Me Do
Side 2
  P.S. I Love You
  Baby It's You
  Do You Want to Know a Secret
  A Taste of Honey
  There's a Place
  Twist and Shout

**INTRODUCING THE BEATLES
(Version 2)**
Vee Jay LP-1062 . . . . *1/27/64* **70–80**
Monaural. Black label with colorband. Logo 1.

Vee Jay SR-1062 . . . . *1/27/64* **250–275**
Stereo. Black label with colorband. Logo 1, with the songs "Please Please Me" and "Ask Me Why." Covers exist in three distinct variations. The most common version features the word "STEREOPHONIC" in gray print on a white banner across the top of the front. Others include the word in black print on a white sticker adhered to a mono cover, or the word embossed in black print on a mono cover. Value given is for the banner version; add $50 for the sticker version and $75 for the embossed version. It was common for Vee Jay to print stereo markings on mono covers.

Vee Jay LP-1062   **40–45**
Monaural. Black label with colorband. Logo 2, with the songs "Please Please Me" and "Ask Me Why."

Vee Jay SR-1062   **175–200**
Stereo. Black label with colorband. Logo 2.

Vee Jay LP-1062   **40–45**
Monaural. Black label with silver print. Logo 3.

Vee Jay SR-1062   **200–225**
Stereo. Black label with silver print. Logo 3.

Vee Jay LP-1062   **90–100**
Monaural. Black label with silver print. Logo 1.

Vee Jay LP-1062   **100–125**
Monaural. Black label with silver print. Logo 2.

Side 1
  I Saw Her Standing There
  Misery
  Anna
  Chains
  Boys
  Ask Me Why
Side 2
  Please Please Me
  Baby It's You
  Do You Want to Know a Secret
  A Taste of Honey
  There's a Place
  Twist and Shout

First released in July 1963, *Introducing the Beatles* originally fell with a quiet thud in the American marketplace. Within 18 months, however, Vee Jay would find no less than eleven ways to get these tracks into stores.

Special Note: **Notes About Counterfeit Identification**

Because of the seemingly limitless variations presented in genuine issues of *Introducing the Beatles,* it is easy to understand why this ranks as the most counterfeited album in all of Beatles collecting. What follows is a precise description of the original covers to aid the reader in his or her search for this highly prized (and much misunderstood) record.

From 1963 to late 1964 Vee Jay manufactured this LP at their plants in Chicago and St. Louis. The front and back of the covers produced at these plants had a glossy (though not a high-gloss) finish—any copies that have a flat finish *on either side* are fakes. Although color shades and tint can vary even among originals, the print is almost always sharp and the image clear. A copy featuring *broken print* and/or a poor quality cover photo is most likely to be counterfeit.

As far as cover construction is concerned, all of the copies we have seen from the Chicago plant had a characteristic ¼″ flap of cardboard that was folded over at the top and bottom of the inside cover. Many fakes have fold flaps either larger than the ¼″ or that are not there at all.

Cover construction: All original covers were made of either gray or tan cardboard or varied shades of both. In early 1964 Vee Jay moved to Santa Monica; however, their pressing facilities remained in Chicago and St. Louis. Only a few pieces were subcontracted in California. The covers constructed in California were identical to the above descriptions except for the following: back slicks were somewhat less glossy, and the ¼″ fold flap discussed above was not present. The albums pressed in California were not nearly as widely distributed as the Chicago copies and are somewhat rare in comparison.

It should be noted that some counterfeits have 95% cover photo clarity; however, even those copies fall short in the areas of cover construction and/or disc reproduction.

Original disc identification: Most, but not all, counterfeit discs use the version I song selection ("P.S. I Love You" and "Love Me Do") on the disc label printing. A good many of the fakes will actually play the version II selections ("Please Please Me" and "Ask Me Why"). Any copies that list version I and play version II are most likely counterfeits. Some factory errors have been verified involving similar mislabeling; however, these are quite rare and check out well in every other area of testing.

All original disc labels print the artist and LP title together above the play hole; any copies that separate the two titles by the play holes are fakes. The largest trail-off area we have ever seen on an original disc is 1″ (most are ⅞″). Any copies with trail-off areas larger than this are most likely fakes. Most of all the discs that were pressed out of Chicago had some sort of machine stamping in the trail-off areas. Symbols like "Audio Matrix," a circled "MR," and "ARP" or any combination of these are quite common on these pressings. Copies pressed later at the California location have very seldom been found with these trail-off stampings.

So far, we have not verified any counterfeits with trail-off stampings, and disc labels on the fakes usually lack color, print sharpness, and/or clarity. We have found also no fake copies with the word "Stereo" printed on the label.

Remember, that any given item must conform in *every* area of originality to merit serious consideration as a buy or a sale. If the item fares reasonably well in one aspect and fails in another, it is probably a counterfeit.

JERRY G., THE BEATLES TALK WITH
Backstage BSR-1165 . . . . . *82*   **10–12**
Picture disc. Contains interviews with the group from their 1965 and 1966 U.S. tours. Each copy was sequentially numbered.

JERRY G., VOL. 2, THE BEATLES TALK WITH
Backstage BSR-1175 . . . . . *83*   **8–12**
Picture disc. Contains interviews with the group from their 1965 and 1966 U.S. tours.

LET IT BE
Apple AR-34001 . . . . *5/18/70*   **10–15**
Red Apple label. Single LP with gatefold cover. *Note:* This LP was originally distributed by United Artists, which explains the change in the color of the label.

Capitol SW-11922 . . . . *78–83*   **8–12**
Purple label. Issued with a full color poster.

Capitol SW-11922 . . *83 to date*   **5–8**
Black label with colorband. Issued with a full color poster.

Mobile Fidelity Sound Lab MFSL
1-109. . . . . *8/87*   **5–8**
Half-speed mastered pressing on high quality Japanese vinyl. White label with black and tan print. Issued in limited quantities.

Side 1
  Two of Us
  I Dig a Pony
  Across the Universe
  I, Me, Mine
  Dig It
  Let It Be
  Maggie May
Side 2
  I've Got a Feeling
  One After 909
  The Long and Winding Road
  For You Blue
  Get Back

LIGHTNING STRIKES TWICE
United Distributors Lyrics LTD.
UDL-2382. . . . . *81*   **25–30**
White label. Side 1 contains five tracks by the Beatles from their 1962 audition sessions for Decca. Side 2 features Elvis.

Side 1
  September in the Rain
  Besame Mucho
  Shiek of Araby
  To Know You
  Hello Little Girl

LIKE DREAMERS DO
Backstage BSR-1111 . . . . . *82*   **25–30**
Three-LP set with gatefold cover containing two picture discs and one white vinyl LP. The white vinyl LP is a bonus copy and features identical material to the 10-song picture disc. The 10 tracks are from the Beatles '62 Decca audition sessions. The set also includes interviews with the Beatles circa 1964 and 1965 as well as a 1982 interview with Pete Best (former Beatle drummer). The artists are listed as THE SILVER BEATLES.

Backstage BSR-1111 . . . . . *82*   **40–45**
Identical to above, except the colored vinyl LP is gray.

Backstage BSR-1111   **30–35**
Promotional copy. Silver label. Single LP with plain white cover. Available in either white or gray vinyl. Label reads "Promotional Copy Not For Sale."

Backstage BSR-1111   **35–40**
Identical to above, except one side of one of the picture discs features the logo of Rockaway Records.

Backstage BSR-1111   **35–40**
Identical to above, except one side of one of the picture discs features the logo from Ticket to Ryde Ltd.

Backstage BSR-1111   **35–40**
Identical to above, except one side of one of the picture discs features the logo from KEZE-Strawberry Jams.

Backstage BSR-1111   **35–40**
Identical to above, except one side of one of the picture discs features the logo from the publication *Hot Wacks Quarterly.*

Backstage BSR 1111 . . . . . *82*   **30–40**
Promotional issue. White label with black print. White or gray colored vinyl. Contains 10 tracks from the Beatles 1962 Decca audition sessions. Label reads "Promotional Copy—Not For Sale."

Backstage BSR-2-201   **15–20**
Contains one picture disc and one white vinyl disc. Each LP was sequentially numbered on an INFO sticker adhered to the front.

Backstage BSR-2-201   **25–30**
Identical to above, except one side of one of the picture discs features the logo from Ticket to Ryde Ltd.

Backstage BSR-2-201   **15–20**
Identical to above, except this version is not numbered and does not have a gatefold cover (as do all other issues).

LIVE AT THE STAR CLUB IN HAMBURG, GERMANY; 1962, THE BEATLES

Lingasong LS-2-7001 . . *6/13/77*   **10–15**
Multi-colored label. Double LP with gatefold cover. Deduct 25% from value for LP covers with a cut-out marking.

Lingasong LS-2-7001   **100–125**
Promotional copy. Multi-colored label. Promotional pressings on red or blue vinyl. Label reads "DJ Copy Not For Sale." Add 25% to price for blue vinyl version.

Lingasong LS-2-7001   **35–40**
Promotional copy. Multi-colored label, black vinyl. Label reads "DJ Copy Not For Sale."

LIVE—1962—HAMBURG, GERMANY, THE BEATLES

Hall of Music HM-1-2200 . . *81*   **20–25**
Double LP.

LOVE SONGS, THE BEATLES

Capitol SKBL-11711 . *10/21/77*   **12–15**
Gold and brown label with gold embossed print. Double LP with gatefold cover. Issued with 28-page booklet.

Capitol SKBL-11711   **10–12**
Double LP with gatefold cover. Custom labels. LP cover no longer features gold embossed print or textured features.

Side 1
  Yesterday
  I'll Follow the Sun
  I Need You
  Girl
  In My Life
  Words of Love
  Here, There, and Everywhere
Side 2
  Something
  And I Love Her
  If I Fell
  I'll Be Back
  Tell Me What You See
  Yes It Is
Side 3
  Michelle
  It's Only Love
  You're Gonna Lose That Girl
  Every Little Thing
  For No One
  She's Leaving Home
Side 4
  The Long and Winding Road
  This Boy
  Norwegian Wood (This Bird Has Flown)
  You've Got to Hide Your Love Away
  I Will
  P.S. I Love You

LOWERY GROUP: see
Various-Artists Compilations section.

MAGICAL MYSTERY TOUR

Capitol MAL-2835 . . *11/27/67*   **45–50**
Monaural. Black label with colorband. Issued with 24-page booklet adhered to the inside of gatefold cover.

Capitol SMAL-2835   **20–25**
Stereo. Black label with colorband.

Capitol SMAL-2835 . . . . . *69*   **20–25**
Stereo. Green label.

Apple SMAL-2835 . . *1/71–6/71*   **15–20**
Stereo. Apple label with the Capitol logo.

Apple SMAL-2835 . . . *6/71–75*   **10–15**
Stereo. Plain Apple label.

Capitol SMAL-2835 . . . *75–78*   **8–12**
Stereo. Orange label.

Capitol SMAL-2835 . . . *78–83*   **8–10**
Purple label.

Capitol SMAL-2835 . *83 to date*   **5–8**
Stereo. Black label with colorband.

Mobile Fidelity Sound Lab MFSL-
1-047. . . . . *81*   **20–25**
Half-speed mastered pressing on high quality
Japanese vinyl. White label:

Side 1
 Magical Mystery Tour
 The Fool on the Hill
 Flying
 Blue Jay Way
 Your Mother Should Know
 I Am the Walrus
Side 2
 Hello Goodbye
 Strawberry Fields Forever
 Penny Lane
 Baby, You're a Rich Man
 All You Need Is Love
Note: "I Am the Walrus" exists in two forms.
The English version has two more measures in
the introduction, while the American has two
more measures than the English in the transi-
tion to the bridge.

MEET THE BEATLES

Capitol T-2047 . . . . . *1/20/64*   **20–25**
Monaural. Black label with colorband.

Capitol ST-2047   **30–35**
Stereo.

Capitol ST-82047   **30–35**
Stereo. Record Club issue. Available on Capitol's original black or green label.

Capitol ST-2047. . . . . . . *69*   **20–25**
Stereo. Green label.

Apple ST-2047 . . . . *1/71–6/71*   **15–20**
Stereo. Apple label with the Capitol logo.

Apple ST-2047 . . . . . *6/71–75*   **10–15**
Stereo. Plain Apple label.

Capitol ST-2047. . . . . . *75–78*   **8–12**
Stereo. Orange label.

Capitol ST-2047. . . . . . *78–83*   **8–10**
Purple label.

Capitol ST-2047. . . . *83 to date*   **5–8**
Stereo. Black label with colorband.

Side 1
 I Want to Hold Your Hand
 This Boy
 I Saw Her Standing There
 It Won't Be Long
 All I've Got to Do
 All My Loving
Side 2
 Little Child
 Don't Bother Me
 Till There Was You

 Hold Me Tight
 Not a Second Time
 I Wanna Be Your Man

More Solid Gold Programming from
Screen Gems: **see Various-Artists**
Compilations section.

MOVIEMANIA

Cicadelic LP 1960 . . . . . . *87*   **5–8**
Silver label with black print graphics. Contains
rare interviews about the Beatles movies *A*
Hard Day's Night and *Help!*.

1962–1966, THE BEATLES

Apple SKBO-3403 . . . . *4/2/73*   **15–20**
Custom Apple label. Double LP with gatefold
cover.

Capitol SKBO-3403 . . . . . *75*   **10–12**
Custom red label. Double LP with gatefold
cover.

Capitol SEBX-11842 . . . . . *78*   **20–25**
Custom Capitol red label. Red vinyl.

Side 1
 Love Me Do
 Please Please Me
 From Me to You
 She Loves You
 I Want to Hold Your Hand
 All My Loving
 Can't Buy Me Love
Side 2
 A Hard Day's Night
 And I Love Her
 Eight Days a Week
 I Feel Fine
 Ticket to Ride
 Yesterday
Side 3
 Help!
 You've Got to Hide Your Love Away
 We Can Work It Out
 Day Tripper
 Drive My Car
 Norwegian Wood (This Bird Has Flown)
Side 4
 Nowhere Man
 Michelle
 In My Life
 Girl
 Paperback Writer
 Eleanor Rigby
 Yellow Submarine

1967–1970, THE BEATLES

Apple SKBO-3404 . . . . *4/2/73*   **15–20**
Custom Apple label. Double LP with gatefold
cover.

Capitol SKBO-3404 . . . . . *75*   **10–12**
Custom Capitol blue label. Double LP with
gatefold cover.

Capitol SEBX-11843 . . . . . *78*   **20–25**
Custom Capitol blue label. Blue vinyl.

Side 1
    Strawberry Fields Forever
    Penny Lane
    Sgt. Pepper's Lonely Hearts Club Band
    With a Little Help from My Friends
    Lucy in the Sky with Diamonds
    A Day in the Life
    All You Need Is Love
Side 2
    I Am the Walrus
    Hello Goodbye
    The Fool on the Hill
    Magical Mystery Tour
    Lady Madonna
    Hey Jude
    Revolution
Side 3
    Back in the U.S.S.R.
    While My Guitar Gently Weeps
    Ob La Di Ob La Da
    Get Back
    Don't Let Me Down
    Ballad of John and Yoko
    Old Brown Shoe
Side 4
    Here Comes the Sun
    Come Together
    Something
    Octopus's Garden
    Let It Be
    Across the Universe
    The Long and Winding Road

NOT A SECOND TIME
Cicadelic CICLP-1961 . . . . *86*   **5–8**
Silver label.

Playboy Music Hall of Fame: see
Various-Artists Compilations section.

PLEASE PLEASE ME
Mobile Fidelity Sound Lab MFSL-
1-101. . . . . *86*   **5–8**
White label. Half-speed master recording on
high quality vinyl.

Side 1
    I Saw Her Standing There
    Misery
    Anna (Go to Him)
    Chains
    Boys

Ask Me Why
Please Please Me
Side 2
    Love Me Do
    P.S. I Love You
    Baby It's You
    Do You Want to Know a Secret
    A Taste of Honey
    There's a Place
    Twist and Shout

Radio's Million Performance Songs: see
Various-Artists Compilations section.

RARITIES, THE BEATLES
Capitol SHAL-12060. . *3/24/80*   **10–15**
Black label with colorband and white print
(nostalgic re-issue label, not to be confused with
Capitol's black standard label which uses silver
print). Front photo is embossed.

Capitol SHAL-12060   **5–8**
Identical to above, except cover is not embossed.

Side 1
    Love Me Do
    Misery
    There's a Place
    Sie Liebt Dich
    And I Love Her
    Help!
    I'm Only Sleeping
    I Am the Walrus
Side 2
    Penny Lane
    Helter Skelter
    Don't Pass Me By
    The Inner Light
    Across The Universe
    You Know My Name
    Sgt. Pepper Inner Groove

RARITIES, THE BEATLES (British Version)
Capitol SPRO-8969. . . . . . *78*   **35–40**
Purple label. Issued as a bonus record in *The
Beatles Collection.* Issued with a blue paper title
sleeve.

Capitol SN-12009   **60–70**
Green label.

Side 1
    Across the Universe
    Yes It Is
    This Boy
    The Inner Light
    I'll Get You
    Thank You Girl
    Komm, Gib Mir Deine Hand

You Know My Name
Sie Liebt Dich
Side 2
  Rain
  She's a Woman
  Matchbox
  I Call Your Name
  Bad Boy
  Slow Down
  I'm Down
  Long Tall Sally

RECORDED LIVE IN HAMBURG—1962, VOL. I, THE BEATLES

Pickwick BAN-90051 . . . . *78* **10–15**
White label. Deduct 30% if cover has a cut-out marking.

RECORDED LIVE IN HAMBURG—1962, VOL. II, THE BEATLES

Pickwick BAN-90061 . . . . *78* **10–15**
White label. Deduct 30% if cover has a cut-out marking.

RECORDED LIVE IN HAMBURG—1962, VOL. III, THE BEATLES

Pickwick BAN-90071 . . . . *78* **20–25**
White label. Deduct 30% if the cover has a cut-out marking.

REEL MUSIC

Capitol SV-12199 . . . . *3/22/82* **5–8**
Custom Capitol label. Issued with "photo inner sleeve" and a 12-page souvenir program.

Capitol SV-12199 **50–60**
Promotional copy. Gold vinyl. Top right corner of back cover is numbered sequentially. Back cover reads "Not For Sale."

Side 1
  A Hard Day's Night
  I Should Have Known Better
  Can't Buy Me Love
  And I Love Her
  Help!
  You've Got to Hide Your Love Away
  Ticket to Ride
  Magical Mystery Tour
Side 2
  I Am the Walrus
  Yellow Submarine
  All You Need Is Love
  Let It Be
  Get Back
  The Long and Winding Road

REVOLVER

Capitol T-2576 . . . . . . *8/8/66* **30–40**
Monaural. Black label with colorband.

Capitol ST-2576 **25–35**
Stereo. Black label with colorband.

Capitol ST-8-2576 **30–35**
Stereo. Record Club issue. Available on Capitol's original black label or green label.

Capitol ST-2576. . . . . . . *69* **20–25**
Stereo. Green label.

Apple ST-2576 . . . . *1/71–6/71* **15–20**
Stereo. Apple label with Capitol logo.

Apple ST-2576 . . . . . *6/71–75* **10–15**
Stereo. Plain Apple label.

Capitol SW-2576 . . . . . *75–78* **8–12**
Stereo. Orange label.

Capitol SW-2576 . . . . . *78–83* **8–10**
Stereo. Purple label.

Capitol SW-2576 . . . *83 to date* **5–8**
Black label with colorband.

Side 1
  Tax Man
  Eleanor Rigby
  Yellow Submarine
  Here, There, and Everywhere
  Love You To
  She Said She Said
Side 2
  For No One
  Good Day Sunshine
  I Want to Tell You
  Got to Get You into My Life
  Tomorrow Never Knows

Mobile Fidelity Sound Lab MFSL
1-107. . . . . *86* **5–8**
White label. Half-speed master recording on high quality vinyl.

Side 1
  Taxman
  Eleanor Rigby
  I'm Only Sleeping
  Love You To
  Here, There and Everywhere
  Yellow Submarine
  She Said She Said
Side 2
  Good Day Sunshine
  And Your Bird Can Sing
  For No One
  Dr. Robert

I Want To Tell You
Got To Get You into My Life
Tomorrow Never Knows

ROCK 'N' ROLL MUSIC

Capitol SKBO-11537. . *6/11/76* **15–20**
Custom Capitol labels. Double LP with gatefold cover.

Side 1
Twist and Shout
I Saw Her Standing There
You Can't Do That
I Wanna Be Your Man
I Call Your Name
Boys
Long Tall Sally
Side 2
Rock 'n' Roll Music
Slow Down
Kansas City
Money
Bad Boy
Matchbox
Roll Over Beethoven
Side 3
Dizzy Miss Lizzy
Anytime at All
Drive My Car
Everybody's Trying to Be My Baby
The Night Before
I'm Down
Revolution
Side 4
Back in the U.S.S.R.
Helter Skelter
Tax Man
Got to Get You into My Life
Hey Bulldog
Birthday
Get Back

ROCK 'N' ROLL MUSIC, VOL. I

Capitol SN-16020 **5–8**
Green budget series label. Single LP.

Side 1
Twist and Shout
I Saw Her Standing There
You Can't Do That
I Wanna Be Your Man
I Call Your Name
Boys
Long Tall Sally
Side 2
Rock 'n' Roll Music
Slow Down
Kansas City
Money

Bad Boy
Matchbox
Roll Over Beethoven

ROCK 'N' ROLL MUSIC, VOL. II

Capitol SN-16021 **5–8**
Green budget series label. Single LP.

Side 1
Dizzy Miss Lizzy
Anytime at All
Drive My Car
Everybody's Trying to Be My Baby
The Night Before
I'm Down
Revolution
Side 2
Back in the U.S.S.R.
Helter Skelter
Tax Man
Got to Get You into My Life
Hey Bulldog
Birthday
Get Back

'ROUND THE WORLD

Cicadelic CICLP-1965 . . . . *86* **5–8**
Silver label. LP containing various interviews
circa 1963 thru 1965.

RUBBER SOUL

Capitol T-2442 . . . . . *12/6/65* **30–40**
Monaural. Black label with colorband.

Capitol ST-2442 **25–35**
Stereo. Black label with colorband.

Capitol ST-8-2442 **30–35**
Stereo. Record Club issue. Available on Capitol's original black label or green label. The "8"
in the record number on the cover and the disc
label identifies the record as being a record club
issue.

Capitol ST-2442. . . . . . . *69* **20–25**
Stereo. Green label.

Apple ST-2442 . . . . *1/71–6/71* **15–20**
Stereo. Apple label with the Capitol label.

Apple ST-2442 . . . . . *6/71–75* **10–15**
Stereo. Plain Apple label.

Capitol SW-2442 . . . . . *75–78* **8–12**
Stereo. Orange label.

Capitol SW-2442 . . . . . *78–83* **8–10**
Stereo. Purple label.

Capitol SW-2442 . . . *83 to date* **5–8**
Stereo. New black label with colorband.

Side 1
I've Just Seen a Face
You Won't See Me

Norwegian Wood (This Bird Has Flown)
Think for Yourself
The Word
Michelle
Side 2
It's Only Love
Girl
I'm Looking Through You
In My Life
Wait
Run for Your Life

Note: When Capitol released the CD editions of the Beatles albums, they decide to follow the British releases and song sequences. As with *Revolver, A Hard Day's Night,* and *Help!,* the British version of *Rubber Soul* is vastly different from the American release.

Side 1
Drive My Car
Norwegian Wood
You Won't See Me
Nowhere Man
Think for Yourself
The Word
Michelle
Side 2
What Goes On
Girl
I'm Looking Through You
In My Life
Wait
If I Needed Someone
Run for Your Life

SAVAGE YOUNG BEATLES, THIS IS THE

Savage BM-69. . . . . *64*   **60–70**
Monaural only. Orange label with black print. Yellow front cover. Contains four tracks by the Beatles with Tony Sheridan.
Counterfeit identification: the known counterfeit has the LP number in red print on the front of the cover and the word "Stereo." The record number on the original is in black and the record was only available in mono.

Savage BM-69. . . . . *64*   **125–150**
Monaural. This version has a yellow label and a glossy orange front cover. Back cover on this version features the address of Savage Records.

SECOND ALBUM, THE BEATLES

Capitol T-2080 . . . . . *4/10/64*   **30–40**
Monaural. Black label with color band.

Capitol ST-2080   **25–35**
Stereo. Black label with colorband.

Capitol ST-8-2080   **30–35**
Stereo. Record club issue. Available on Capitol's original black label or green label. The "8" in the record number identifies the record as being a record club issue.

Capitol ST-2080. . . . . . . *69*   **20–25**
Stereo. Green label.

Apple ST-2080 . . . . *1/71–6/71*   **15–20**
Stereo. Apple label with the Capitol logo.

Apple ST-2080 . . . . . *6/71–75*   **10–15**
Stereo. Plain Apple label.

Capitol ST-2080. . . . . *75–78*   **8–12**
Stereo. Orange label.

Capitol St-2080 . . . . . . *78–83*   **8–10**
Stereo. Purple label.

Capitol ST-2080. . . . *83 to date*   **5–8**
Stereo. New black label with colorband.

Side 1
Thank You Girl
Roll Over Beethoven
You Really Got a Hold on Me
Devil in Her Heart
Money
You Can't Do That
Side 2
Long Tall Sally
I Call Your Name
Please Mr. Postman
She Loves You
I'll Get You

SGT. PEPPERS LONELY HEARTS CLUB BAND

Capitol MAS-2653 . . . . *6/2/67*   **35–45**
Monaural. Black label with colorband. Issued with an insert of St. Pepper cut-outs.

Capitol SMAS-2653   **25–35**
Stereo copy. Black label with colorband. Issued with an insert of St. Pepper cut-outs.

Capitol SMAS-2653 . . . . . *69*   **20–25**
Stereo. Green label.

Apple SMAS-2653 . . *1/71–6/71*   **15–20**
Stereo. Apple label with the Capitol logo.

Apple SMAS-2653 . . . *6/71–75*   **10–15**
Stereo. Plain Apple label.

Capitol SMAS-2653 . . . *75–78*   **8–12**
Stereo. Orange label.

Capitol SEAX-11840 . . . . *78*   **15–20**
Picture disc. Issued with special die-cut cover. Deduct 20% if cover has a cut-out marking.

Capitol SMAS-2653 . . . *78–83*   **8–10**
Stereo. Purple label.

The Sgt. Pepper's picture disc.
Released at the same time as
the ill-fated *Sgt. Pepper*
soundtrack (1978).

Capitol SMAS-2653 . *83 to date*   **5–10**
Stereo. New black label with colorband.

Side 1
  Sgt. Pepper's Lonely Hearts Club Band
  With a Little Help from My Friends
  Lucy in the Sky with Diamonds
  Getting Better
  Fixing a Hole
  She's Leaving Home
  Being for the Benefit Of Mr. Kite
Side 2
  Within You Without You
  When I'm Sixty Four
  Lovely Rita
  Good Morning Good Morning
  Sgt. Pepper's Lonely Hearts Club Band (re-
    prise)
  A Day in the Life
Note: The British edition of this LP featured a
repeating inner groove. See the American edi-
tion for *Rarities* for details.

SGT. PEPPERS LONELY HEARTS CLUB BAND

Mobile Fidelity Sound Lab
UHQR-1-100 . . . . *9/82*   **150–175**
Half-speed mastered pressing on high quality
Japanese vinyl. Nicely boxed. Issued with se-
quentially numbered authenticity card and
technical data sheets.

Mobile Fidelity Sound Lab MFSL-
1-100. . . . . *85*   **5–8**
Half-speed mastered pressing on high quality
Japanese vinyl. White label.

Note: This edition, based like the rest of the
Mobile Fidelity releases on the British versions,
features the same title sequence as above as well
as the repeating inner groove.

SILVER BEATLES

(Ultra Sound Co.) Audio Rarities
AR-30003 . . . . *82*   **20–25**
Picture disc. Price is for the U.S. pressing (not
to be confused with the common import version).

SILVER BEATLES, THE

Orange Records ORC-12880
. . . . *85*   **50–60**
White label (test pressing). Half-speed mastered
recording on Teldec virgin vinyl. Contains all
15 songs from the 1962 Decca audition sessions.
Although the disc is a test pressing, it's included
here because the cover proofs were made and
the album was packaged and sold briefly via
mail-order in early 1985.

SILVER BEATLES, VOL. I, THE

Phoenix 10 PHX-352. . . . . *82*   **8–12**
Silver label. Contains seven tracks from the
Beatles '62 Decca audition sessions.

SILVER BEATLES, VOL. II, THE

Phoenix 10 PHX-353. . . . . *82*   **8–12**
Silver label. Contains seven tracks from the
Beatles '62 Decca audition sessions.

Silver Years: **see Various-Artists
Compilations section.**

VI, BEATLES

Capitol T-2358 . . . . . *6/14/65* **25–35**
Monaural. Black label with colorband.

Capitol ST-2358 **30–35**
Stereo. Black label with colorband.

Capitol ST-8-2358 **30–40**
Record club issue. Available on Capitol's original black or Capitol's green labels.

Capitol ST-2358. . . . . . . *69* **20–25**
Stereo. Green label.

Apple ST-2358 . . . . *1/71–6/71* **15–20**
Stereo. Apple label with the Capitol logo.

Apple ST-2358 . . . . . *6/71–75* **10–15**
Stereo. Plain Apple label.

Capitol ST-2358. . . . . *75–78* **8–12**
Stereo. Orange label.

Capitol ST-2358. . . . . *78–83* **8–10**
Stereo. Purple label.

Capitol ST-2358. . . . *83 to date* **5–8**
Stereo. Black label with colorband.

Side 1
Kansas City
Eight Days a Week
You Like Me Too Much
Bad Boy
I Don't Want to Spoil the Party
Words of Love
Side 2
What You're Doing
Yes It Is
Dizzy Miss Lizzy
Tell Me What You See
Every Little Thing

65, BEATLES

Capitol T-2228 . . . . *12/15/64* **30–40**
Monaural. Black label with colorband.

Capitol ST-2228 **25–35**
Stereo. Black label with colorband.

Capitol ST-2228. . . . . . . *69* **20–25**
Stereo. Green label.

Apple ST-2228 . . . . *1/71–6/71* **15–20**
Stereo. Apple label with Capitol logo.

Apple ST-2228 . . . . . *6/71–75* **10–15**
Stereo. Plain Apple label.

Capitol ST-2228. . . . . *75–78* **8–12**
Stereo. Orange label.

Capitol ST-2228. . . . . *78–83* **8–10**
Stereo. Purple label.

Capitol ST-2228. . . . *83 to date* **5–8**
Stereo. Black label with colorband.

Side 1
No Reply
I'm a Loser
Baby's in Black
Rock and Roll Music
I'll Follow the Sun
Mr. Moonlight
Side 2
Honey Don't
I'll Be Back
She's a Woman
I Feel Fine
Everybody's Trying to Be My Baby

Solid Gold: Gerry Goffin and Carole King: **see Various-Artists Compilations section.**

SOMETHING NEW

Capitol T-2108 . . . . . *7/20/64* **30–40**
Monaural. Black label with colorband.

Capitol ST-2108 **25–35**
Stereo. Black label with colorband.

Capitol ST-8-2108 **30–35**
Stereo. Record Club issue.

Capitol ST-2108. . . . . . . *69* **20–25**
Stereo. Green label.

Apple ST-2108 . . . . *1/71–6/71* **15–20**
Stereo. Apple label with the Capitol logo.

Apple ST-2108 . . . . . *6/71–75* **10–15**
Stereo. Plain Apple label.

Capitol ST-2108. . . . . *75–78* **8–12**
Stereo. Orange label.

Capitol ST-2108. . . . . *78–83* **8–10**
Stereo. Purple label.

Capitol ST-2108. . . . *83 to date* **5–8**
Stereo. Black label with colorband.

Side 1
Things We Said Today
I'll Cry Instead
When I Get Home
Any Time at All
Slow Down
Match Box
Side 2
And I Love Her
If I Fell
I'm Happy Just to Dance with You
Komm, Gib Mir Diene Hand
Tell Me Why

SONGS, PICTURES, AND STORIES OF THE FABULOUS BEATLES

Vee Jay VJ-1092 . . . *10/12/64* **70–80**
Monaural. Single LP with gatefold cover. Front flap is two-thirds of full length. Disc used in this

Vee Jay going to the well one
more time.

package is *Introducing the Beatles* (version 2;
see *Introducing the Beatles*). Some covers can
be found with a sticker/banner from any of the
group's '64 U.S. concerts. Add $35 to the value
for copies with the banner. Price is for black
label with colorband. Logo 2.

Vee Jay VJS-1092	**250–275**

Stereo. Logo 2.

Side 1
  I Saw Her Standing There
  Misery
  Anna
  Chains
  Boys
  Ask Me Why
Side 2
  Please Please Me
  Baby It's You
  Do You Want to Know a Secret
  A Taste of Honey
  There's a Place
  Twist and Shout

Sounds of Solid Gold: see
Various-Artists Compilations section

STORY, THE BEATLES'

Capitol TBO-2222 . . *11/23/64* **35–45**
Monaural. Black label with colorband. Double
LP with gatefold cover.

Capitol STBO-2222 **25–35**
Stereo. Black label with colorband.

Capitol STBO-2222 . . . . . *69* **25–30**
Stereo. Green label.

Apple STBO-2222 . . *1/71–6/71* **20–25**
Stereo. Apple label with the Capitol logo.

Apple STBO-2222 . . . *6/71–75* **15–20**
Stereo. Plain Apple label.

Capitol STBO-2222. . . . *75–78* **12–15**
Stereo. Orange label.

Capitol STBO-2222. . . . *78–83* **10–15**
Stereo. Purple label.

Capitol STBO-2222. . *83 to date* **10–12**
Stereo. New black label with colorband.

TALK DOWN UNDER, THE BEATLES

Raven PVC-8911 . . . . *81* **8–12**
Blue and yellow label. Contains interviews from
their '64 Australian tour.

Raven PVC-RO **25–30**
Promotional copy. Blue and yellow label. Issued in white cover with title sticker which
reads "Promotional Copy—Not For Sale."
Disc label reads "For Radio Play Only."

THINGS WE SAID TODAY

Cicadelic CICLP-1962 . . . . *86* **5–8**
Silver label. Contains interviews with the group
circa 1964 and 1965.

THIS IS WHERE IT STARTED

Metro M-563 . . . . . . *8/15/66* **40–45**
Monaural. Black label with silver print. Re-
package of "The Beatles with Tony Sheridan &
Guests" with two fewer Titans tracks.

Metro MS-563 **60–70**
Stereo. Black label with silver print.

This may be where it started, but the saga of the '61 Hamburg sessions still hasn't finished by 1966. By 1969, it will have gone back to Polydor by way of Atco.

Beatles' songs include:
My Bonnie/Cry for a Shadow/The Saints/Why (plus songs by Tony Sheridan and by The Titans)

TIMELESS
Silhouette SM-10004 . . . . . *81* **10–15**
Picture disc. Contains interviews with the Beatles in Vancouver and John Lennon in Chicago, 1964. Some copies have cover versions of "Imagine" and "Let It Be." Add 25% for these.

Silhouette SM-10004 . . . . . *83* **10–15**
Picture disc. Same as above, except "Imagine" and "Let It Be" have been deleted.

TIMELESS II
Silhouette SM-10010 . . . . . *82* **8–12**
Picture disc. Interviews with the Beatles circa 1964 and 1966, plus a novelty tune.

TWENTY GREATEST HITS
Capitol SV-12245 . . . *10/15/82* **10–15**
Purple label.

Capitol SV-12245 . . . *83 to date* **5–8**
Black label with colorband.

Side 1
  She Loves You
  Love Me Do
  I Want to Hold Your Hand
  Can't Buy Me Love
  A Hard Day's Night
  I Feel Fine
  Eight Days a Week
  Ticket to Ride

  Help
  Yesterday
  We Can Work It Out
  Paperback Writer
Side 2
  Penny Lane
  All You Need Is Love
  Hello, Goodbye
  Hey Jude
  Get Back
  Come Together
  Let It Be
  The Long and Winding Road

20 HITS, THE BEATLES
Phoenix 20 P20–623 . . . . . *83* **8–12**
Tan label. Contains 12 tracks from the Beatles 1962 Decca audition sessions, plus four tracks from the 61 Polydor sessions with Tony Sheridan.

Phoenix 20 P20–629 . . . . . *83* **8–12**
Tan label. Contains material from the 1962 Hamburg, Germany, shows.

Ultimate Radio Bootleg: **see**
Various-Artists Compilations section.

WEST COAST INVASION, THE BEATLES
Cicadelic CICLP-1966 . . *10/85* **5–8**
Red label. Contains various interviews with the group circa 1964 and 1966.

WIGG, DAVID INTERVIEWS (THE BEATLES TAPES)

PBR International-7005/6 . .   *78*   **30–35**
Silver label. Blue vinyl. Issued with an eight page photo booklet. Also issued with a white label and on black vinyl.

WITH THE BEATLES

Mobile Fidelity Sound Lab MFSL-
1-102. . . . .   *86*   **30–40**
White label. Half-speed master recording on high quality vinyl.

Side 1
   It Won't Be Long
   All I've Got to Do
   All My Loving
   Don't Bother Me
   Little Child
   Till There Was You
   Please Mister Postman
Side 2
   Roll Over Beethoven
   Hold Me Tight
   You Really Got a Hold on Me
   I Wanna Be Your Man
   Devil in Her Heart
   Not a Second Time
   Money

Withnail and I: see Various-Artists Compilations section.

YELLOW SUBMARINE

Apple SW-153 . . . . .   *1/13/69*   **15–20**
Apple label with the Capitol logo.

Apple SW-153 . . . . .   *6/71–75*   **10–15**
Plain Apple label.

Capitol SW-153 . . . . . .   *75–78*   **8–12**
Orange label.

Capitol SW-153 . . . . . .   *78–83*   **8–10**
Purple label.

Capitol SW-153 . . . .   *83 to date*   **5–8**
Black label with colorband.

Side 1
   Yellow Submarine
   Only a Northern Song
   All Together Now
   Hey Bulldog
   It's All Too Much
   All You Need Is Love
Side 2
   Instrumentals by George Martin

YELLOW SUBMARINE, APPLE FILMS PRESENTS

KAL-004 . . . .   *69*   **500–525**
Radio spots. Yellow label. One-sided 12-inch disc containing radio spot announcements for the animated film.

Yesterday and Today: A Conflict Between Taste and Commentary

In 1966, the Beatles threw themselves off the cloud of Beatlemania. Laughable, frolicsome, beloved moptops no more, they managed in the space of four months to antagonize a nation's First Lady—Mrs. Marcos—enrage the American fundamentalist right, and still find time to take a swing at both their record company and the American "police action" in Vietnam.

The weapon, as far as Capitol-EMI and the United States Government were concerned, was the much maligned and justly celebrated butcher cover (see photo in the color insert). Bloodied Beatles in butcher smocks holding broken dolls and cuts of raw meat leering at the camera—that was the statement. Its meaning as far as President Johnson went was clear, but in terms of Capitol-EMI, the butcher cover was an artistic assault on the curious way in which Capitol had managed to create eleven albums from material that had been recorded for only six records. Chopping up babies indeed!

Because of the public outrage, Capitol withdrew the cover from the market, either destroying the stock or pasting it over with the subdued "trunk" cover. Estimates vary—anywhere between 6,000 and 60,000 survived. But such problems are the essence of collecting, and of all the Beatles records,

Yesterday and Today represents one of the most highly prized items. It has been often counterfeited; some of the paste-over trunk covers have been removed. The result of all this has been a remarkably detailed analysis of the different types of covers for this album. What follows is a key for the shorthand we use in the entries:

First State Butcher: Cover features a photo of the group dressed in white butcher smocks adorned with cuts of raw meat and toy doll parts. Has uniform texture on the front slick. Any discrepancy, such as glue residue, stains or excessive roughness (due to removal of replacement slick) will denote that the cover has been peeled and is not a first state cover.

Identification: The glue used to bond the replacement over the butcher slick was a water-based latex adhesive. To determine if the cover was peeled, lightly moisten a piece of tissue paper, press paper lightly on any area of the front slick, then allow to dry. If the cover is a true first state, the paper will brush or blow off easily. If the paper sticks, it is most probably not a first state cover. (If paper does stick to the cover, lightly moisten to remove.)

Counterfeit Identification: Fake butcher slicks have been found pasted on original non-butcher copies of *Yesterday and Today.* Fake slicks feature high glossiness, originals are very low gloss, almost flat. Counterfeits are lacking in photo quality and clarity.

Second State or *Paste-Over:* The original butcher front slick covered with the "trunk" cover. Named because of the group being photographed around an empty luggage trunk. *The trunk cover must be unaltered with the butcher cover underneath.* In good light, the butcher cover can be detected underneath the slightly larger trunk slick. The most notable area that shows through is the back of Ringo's turtleneck sweater, which is V-shaped beneath the neck line of his white smock. Other areas of the butcher cover are visible as well through the white areas of the trunk slick.

Peeled: The replacement trunk cover has been removed. Note that near perfect removal of the pasted-over slick is quite difficult. The cleaner the peel job, the higher the value will be. Any tears, stains, or otherwise unattractive results from the peeling attempt detracts from the value. See the tests described above for identifying the cover.

YESTERDAY AND TODAY

Capitol T-2553 . . . . . *6/15/66* **1200–1600**
Monaural. Black label with colorband. First state butcher cover.

Capitol ST-2553 **3000–4000**
Stereo. The words "New Improved Full Dimensional Stereo" appear in a gray banner at the top of the front cover. First state butcher cover.

Capitol T-2553 **350–400**
Monaural. Black label with colorband. Second state or paste-over cover.

Capitol ST-2553 **650–750**
Stereo. Paste or second state. The words "New Improved Full Dimensional Stereo" appear at

the top of the front cover. Disc value $15–$20 in near-mint condition.

Capitol T-2553   **400–425**
Monaural. Black label with colorband. Peeled cover. Value varies greatly, depending on the quality of the peeling job. The above price range represents the value of a good peeling job, with little glue residue or damage to the rest of the cover.

Capitol ST-2553   **650–675**
Stereo. Peeled butcher cover. The words "New Improved Full Dimensional Stereo" appear in a gray banner at the top of the front cover. Value varies greatly, depending on the quality of the peeling job. The above price range represents the value of a good peeling job, with little glue residue or damage to the rest of the cover.

Capitol T-2553   **30–40**
Monaural. Black label with colorband. Trunk cover.

Capitol ST-2553   **25–35**
Stereo copy. Black label with colorband. Trunk cover.
Note: All subsequent issues features the trunk cover.

Capitol ST-8-2553   **30–35**
Stereo. Record club issue. Available on black label or green label.

Capitol ST-2553. . . . . . . *69*   **20–25**
Stereo. Green label.

Apple ST-2553 . . . . *1/71–6/71*   **15–20**
Stereo. Apple label with Capitol logo.

Apple ST-2553 . . . . . *6/71–75*   **10–15**
Stereo. Apple label.

Capitol ST-2553. . . . . . *75–78*   **8–12**
Stereo. Orange label.

Capitol ST-2553. . . . . . *78–83*   **8–10**
Stereo. Purple label.

Capitol ST-2553. . . . *83 to date*   **5–8**
Stereo. Black label with colorband.

Capitol ST-8-2553   **30–35**
Stereo. Record club issue. Available on black label or green label.

Side 1
  Drive My Car
  I'm Only Sleeping
  Nowhere Man
  Dr. Robert
  Yesterday
Side 2
  And Your Bird Can Sing
  If I Needed Someone
  We Can Work It Out
  What Goes On
  Day Tripper

PETER BEST: LPs (BEATLES DRUMMER, 1960–1962)

BEATLE THAT TIME FORGOT, THE
Phoenix 10 (Audio Fidelity) PHX-
340. . . . . *82*   **10–15**
Orange label. Deduct 20% for copies with a cut-out marking on the cover. Can also be found with white labels.

BEST OF THE BEATLES
Savage BM-71. . . . . *66*   **70–80**
Orange label. LP cover features early photo of the group which includes Pete Best and Stu

Sutcliffe. Although the LP did not feature any Beatles tracks, the cover was designed to mislead the buyer into thinking this was an actual 'greatest hits" package.

Counterfeit identification: known counterfeit features a red disc label, original labels are orange. Counterfeit LP cover features a blue circle around Pete's head, circles on originals are white. The oval in the Savage logo is yellow on the counterfeit; it is white on the original.

    The following LPs all featured the Beatles with Pete Best as drummer. Although recorded in 1961 and 1962, all were released in 1964 and thereafter. Below are the titles of these discs. Descriptions and values are listed in the Beatles LP section.

Ain't She Sweet

Amazing Beatles

Beatles with Tony Sheridan and
   Their Guests, The

Complete Silver Beatles, The

Dawn of the Silver Beatles

First Movement

In the Beginning (circa 1960)

Like Dreamers Do

Savage Young Beatles, The

Silver Beatles, Volumes I and II

Silver Beatles (picture disc)

Silver Beatles, The

This Is Where It Started

20 Hits

The following are compilation (various artists) LPs that feature the Beatles with Pete Best as drummer. Descriptions and values of these discs are listed in the Various-Artists Compilations section.

British Gold

British Rock Classics

British Sterling

Discotheque in Astrosound

Flashback Greats of the 60's

Golden Days of British Rock

History of British Rock

History of British Rock, Vol. II

History of British Rock, Vol. III

GEORGE HARRISON: LPs

ALL THINGS MUST PASS
Apple STCH-639 . . . *11/20/70*   **15–20**
Three-LP box set. Two LPs have orange Apple labels, one has custom label. Issued with lyric liner sleeves and 24″ × 36″ poster.

Capitol STCH-639 . . . . *75–78*   **15–20**
Orange label.

Capitol STCH-639 . . . . *78–83*   **12–15**
Purple label.

Capitol STCH-639 . . *83 to date*   **10–12**
Black label with colorband.

Side 1
  I'd Have You Anytime
  My Sweet Lord
  Wah Wah
  Isn't It a Pity
Side 2
  What Is Life
  If Not for You
  Behind That Locked Door
  Let It Down
  Run of the Mill

Side 3
  Beware of Darkness
  Apple Scruffs
  Ballad of Sir Frankie Crisp
  Awaiting on You All
  All Things Must Pass
Side 4
  I Dig Love
  Art of Dying
  Isn't It a Pity
Side 5
  Out of the Blue
  It's Johnny's Birthday
  Plus Me In
Side 6
  I Remember Jeep
  Thanks for the Pepperoni

BEST OF GEORGE HARRISON
Capitol ST-11578 . . . . *11/8/76*   **8–12**
Custom photo label. Side one features tracks by George with the Beatles, side two features George on his own recordings.

Capitol ST-11578 . . . . . *78–83*   **5–8**
Purple label.

Capitol ST-11578 . . . *83 to date*   **5–8**
Black label with rainbow colorband.

Side 1
Something
If I Needed Someone
Here Comes the Sun
Taxman
Think for Yourself
For You Blue
While My Guitar Gently Weeps
Side 2
My Sweet Lord
Give Me Love (Give Me Peace On Earth)
You
Bangla Desh
Dark Horse
What Is Life

CLOUD NINE

Dark Horse 9 25643–1 . . *11/87*   **5–8**
Tan label. Issued with custom photo liner
sleeve.

Side 1
Cloud Nine
That's What It Takes
Fish on the Sand
Just for Today
This Is Love
When We Was Fab
Side 2
Devil's Radio
Someplace Else
Wreck of the Hesperus
Breath Away from Heaven
Got My Mind Set on You

Concert for Bangla Desh: **see**
Various-Artists Compilations section.

DARK HORSE

Apple SMAS-3418 . . . *12/9/74*   **10–15**
Custom Apple label. Single LP with gatefold
cover. Issued with graphics liner sleeve.

Capitol SN-16055   **5–8**
Green Budget Series label. LP cover now features the original back cover on the front.

Side 1
Hari's On Tour (Express)
Simply Shady
So Bad
Bye Bye Love
Maya Love
Side 2
Ding Dong, Ding Dong
Dark Horse

Far East Man
Is It He (Jai Sri Krishna)

DARK HORSE RADIO SPECIAL

Dark Horse *74*   **125–150**
Promotional only issue. Tan label. Special LP in
which George introduces his new record company. Features introductions and excerpts to
several Dark Horse artists and projects. Issued
with script sheet. Label reads "Promotional
Copy."

ELECTRONIC SOUND

Zapple ST-3358 . . . . . *4/26/69*   **20–25**
Apple label with Zapple logo.

Side 1
Under the Mersey Wall
Side 2
No Time for Space

EXTRA TEXTURE

Apple SW-3420 . . . . *10/22/75*   **10–15**
Custom Apple label. LP title is die cut on the
front cover exposing the photo on the liner
sleeve.

Capitol SN-16217   **8–12**
Green Budget Series label. LP title is printed on
the front cover.

Side 1
You
The Answer's at the End
This Guitar (Can't Keep From Crying)
Ooh Baby (You Know That I Love You)
World of Stone
Side 2
A Bit More of You
Can't Stop Thinking About You
Tired of Midnight Blue
Grey Cloudy Lies
His Name Is Legs (Ladies and Gentlemen)

GEORGE HARRISON

Dark Horse DHK-3255 . *2/9/79*   **8–12**
Tan label. Deduct 25% if LP has a cut-out
marking.

Side 1
Love Comes to Everyone
Not Guilty
Here Comes the Moon
Soft Hearted Hana
Blow Away
Side 2
Faster
Dark Sweet Lady
Your Love Is Forever
Soft Touch
If You Believe

One of only two records
released on Apple's
experimental Zapple label. The
other was John and Yoko's
Life with the Lions.

GONE TROPPO
Dark Horse 1-23734 . *10/27/82* **8–12**
Tan label. Deduct 25% if LP cover has a cut-
out marking.

Dark Horse 1-23734 **20–25**
Promotional copy. Tan label. Issued on high
quality Quiex II vinyl. This LP is identified by
the additional number 40967 which is located in
the trail-off area of the disc, and a Quiex II
sticker which is adhered to the front cover. A
gold embossed promotional stamping is located
on the back cover.

Side 1
  Wake Up My Love
  That's the Way It Goes
  I Really Love You
  Greece
  Gone Troppo
Side 2
  Mystical One
  Unknown Delight
  Baby Don't Run Away
  Dream Away
  Circles

Greenpeace: **see Various-Artists
Compilations section.**

LIVING IN THE MATERIAL
WORLD
Apple SMAS-3410 . . . *5/29/73* **10–15**
Custom Apple label. Single LP with gatefold
cover. Issued with an 11¾" × 23½" art/lyric
insert.

Capitol SN-16216 **5–8**
Green Budget Series label. No longer issued
with gatefold cover or insert.

Side 1
  Give Me Love (Give Me Peace on Earth)
  Sue Me, Sue You Blues
  The Light That Has Lighted the World
  Don't Let Me Wait Too Long
  Who Can See It
  Living in the Material World
Side 2
  The Lord Loves the One (That Loves the
    Lord)
  Be Here Now
  Try Some, Buy Some
  The Day the World Gets 'Round
  That Is All

SOMEWHERE IN ENGLAND
Dark Horse DHK-3492 *5/27/81* **5–8**
Tan label. Deduct 25% if LP cover has a cut-
out marking.

Side 1
  Blood from a Clone
  Unconsciousness Rules
  Life Itself
  All Those Years Ago
  Baltimore Oriole
Side 2
  Teardrops
  That Which I Have Lost
  Writings on the Wall
  Hong Kong Blues
  Save the World

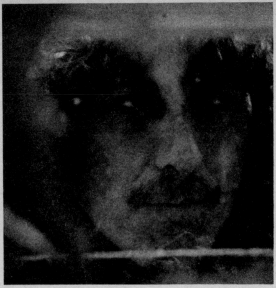

This LP marked the first former Beatle's musical response to Lennon's murder with the song, "All Those Years Ago."

Monsters: see Various-Artists Compilations section.

THIRTY THREE AND ⅓

Dark Horse DH-3005 *11/19/76* **8–12**

Tan label. Single LP with gatefold cover. Deduct 35% if LP cover has a cut-out marking.

Side 1
Woman Don't You Cry for Me
Dear One
Beautiful Girl
This Song
See Yourself
Side 2
It's What You Value
True Love
Pure Smokey
Crackerbox Palace
Learning How to Love You

33⅓, PERSONAL MUSIC DIALOGUE AT

Dark Horse PRO-649 **35–40**

Promotional issue only. Tan label. Issued with special title/program script cover. Disc label and LP cover read "This Is A Promotional Item—Not For Sale."

Porky's Revenge: see Various-Artists Compilations section.

WONDERWALL MUSIC

Apple ST-3350 . . . . . *12/2/68* **20–25**

Plain Apple label. Issued with a 10" × 10" glossy photo.

Side 1
Microbes
Red Lady Too
Tabla and Paka Vaj
In the Park
Drilling a Home
Guru Vandana
Greasy Legs
Ski-ing and Gat Kirwani
Dream Scene
Side 2
Party Seacombe
Love Scene
Crying
Cowboy Museum

Fantasy Sequins
Glass Box
On the Bed

Wonderwall To Be Here
Singing Om

Yulesville: **See Various-Artists Compilations section.**

JOHN LENNON: LPs

COLLECTION, THE JOHN LENNON

Geffen GHSP-2023 . . *11/23/82* **8–10**
Cream color label. Issued with lyric/photo liner sleeve. Deduct 25% if LP cover has a cut-out marking.

Geffen GHSP-2023 **25–30**
Promotional copy. Cream color label. Issued on high quality Quiex II vinyl. This LP is identified by the additional numbers 40945 which are located on the trail-off area of the disc, and a Quiex II sticker which is adhered to the front cover.

Side 1
Give Peace a Chance
Instant Karma
Power to the People
Whatever Gets You Through the Night
#9 Dream
Mind Games
Love
Side 2
Imagine
Jealous Guy
(Just Like) Starting Over

Woman
I'm Losing You
Beautiful Boy (Darling Boy)
Dear Yoko
Watching the Wheels

DOUBLE FANTASY

Geffen GHS-2001 . . . *11/17/80* **8–10**
Cream color label. Label has thin print logo and perimeter printing. Issued with lyric/photo liner sleeve. First pressings had song selections out of playing order on the back cover. This was corrected on later pressings.

Geffen GHS-2001 **5–8**
Cream color label. Label features thick print logo and lacks the perimeter printing.

Geffen GHS-2001 **10–15**
Record club issue. Cream color label. Back cover reads "Manufactured by Columbia House."

Geffen GHS-2000 . . . . . . *86* **5–8**
Black label with silver print.

Nautilus NR-47 . . . . *82* **20–25**
Half-speed mastered recording on high quality vinyl. Cream color label. Issued with poster.

The first posthumous release of Lennon's work, this is noteworthy in that it contains all but one of the Lennon songs from *Double Fantasy*. This was a promotional copy.

Geffen GHS-2001/R-104689   **15–20**
Record club issue. Cream color label. The additional record number is located on the cover and the disc label.

Side 1
   (Just Like) Starting Over
   Kiss Kiss Kiss
   Clean Up Time
   Give Me Something
   I'm Losing You
   I'm Moving On
   Beautiful Boy (Darling Boy)
Side 2
   Watching the Wheels
   I'm Your Angel
   Woman
   Beautiful Boys
   Dear Yoko
   Every Man Has a Woman Who
     Loves Him
   Hard Times Are Over

Every Man Has a Woman: see
Various-Artists Compilations section.

Greatest Music Ever Sold: See
Various-Artists Compilations section.

HEARTPLAY (Unfinished Dialogue)
Polydor 817-238-1-Y1 . . *11/83*   **5–8**
Red label. Contains interviews with John and Yoko circa the late seventies and 1980. Issued with small letter from Yoko.
Polydor 817-238-1-Y1   **20–25**
Promotional copy. Red label. Issued with program sheet and letter from Yoko. Back cover has gold embossed promotional stamping. Issued in 1983.

IMAGINE
Apple SW-3379 . . . . . *9/9/71*   **15–20**
Custom Apple photo label. Bottom of label reads "MFG. By Apple Records Inc." Issued with a 22" × 33" poster. Some copies were issued with either one of two 4" × 6" photo cards. The pig card is more common and valued separately from the LP at $2.50, the John and Yoko card is $5.00.

Apple SW-3379   **10–15**
Custom Apple photo label. Bottom of label reads "MFG. By Apple Records Inc. All Rights Reserved. Unauthorized duplication is a violation of Applicable laws."

Capitol SW-3379 . . . . . *78–82*   **5–8**
Purple label. Issued with poster.

Capitol SW-3379 . . . . . *83–86*   **8–12**
New black label with colorband.

Capitol SW-3379 . . . *86 to date*   **5–8**
New black label with colorband. Top of LP cover and disc label read "Digitally Remastered."

Mobile Fidelity Sound Lab MFSL
1–153 . . . . *84*   **10–15**
White label. Half-speed mastered recording on high quality vinyl.

Side 1
   Imagine
   Crippled Inside
   Jealous Guy
   It's So Hard
   I Don't Want to Be A Soldier
Side 2
   Give Me Some Truth
   Oh My Love
   How Do You Sleep
   How
   Oh Yoko

JOHN LENNON SINGS THE GREAT ROCK & ROLL HITS (ROOTS)
Adam VIII LTD-8018 . . . . *75*   **200–225**
Orange label.
Note: Available briefly until production ceased due to legal action brought against Adam VIII LTD by Apple Records and John Lennon. There have been a few counterfeit versions of this LP over the years. All copies that print the word "Greatest" in the title on the spine of the cover are fakes (some later fakes corrected this). All copies with covers constructed of slicks pasted on cardboard are fakes, originals are made of posterboard. The song titles on both ads and LP photo miniatures are too blurry to read (particularly the *20 Solid Gold Hits* ad). The number A-8018-A is found lightly hand etched on the disc label of all originals. The Adam VIII logo on the upper left of back cover is distinctly sharp and clear on the original, while the fake copies all have blurring in this logo. Any copies with unusually large disc labels are fakes. Features all titles from Lennon's *Rock 'n' Roll* LP plus "Be My Baby" and "Angel Baby."

LIFE WITH THE LIONS (UNFINISHED MUSIC No. 2)
Zapple ST-3357 . . . . . *5/26/69*   **20–25**
Apple label with the Zapple logo. Artist listed as "John Lennon and Yoko Ono."

Side 1
   Cambridge 1969

Legally suppressed shortly after its release, this Adam VIII LP was available by mail order. Lennon himself supplanted it with the *Rock 'n' Roll* LP.

Side 2
  No Bed for Beatle John
  Baby's Heartbeat
  Two Minutes Silence
  Radio Play

LIVE IN NEW YORK CITY
Capitol SV-12451/R-144497   **5–8**
Record club issue. Black label with colorband. Available through the RCA Record Club. Cover does *not* feature the embossed print found on commercial issues. Disc, label and cover read "Manufactured by RCA Music Service," etc.

LIVE IN NEW YORK CITY, JOHN LENNON
Capitol SV-12451 . . . . *2/21/86*   **5–8**
Black label with colorband. Contains live material from the "One to One" concert. Recorded 8/30/72.

Capitol SV-512451 . . . . . . *86*   **15–20**
Record club issue. New black label with colorband. Available through the Columbia Record Club. Disc label and cover read "Manufactured by Columbia House," etc.

Side 1
  New York City
  It's So Hard
  Woman Is the Nigger of the World
  Well, Well, Well
  Instant Karma (We All Shine On)
Side 2
  Mother
  Come Together
  Imagine
  Cold Turkey
  Hound Dog
  Give Peace a Chance

LIVE PEACE IN TORONTO
Apple SW-3362 . . . . *12/12/69*   **10–15**
Apple label. Live album material taken from the 1969 concert in Toronto, Canada. Early copies of this LP were issued with a 16-page 1970 photo/poetry calendar. These calendars can be found with binders made from either plastic or metal. The calendar is valued separately from the LP at $12. Some copies issued without the calendar contained a 3" × 5" postcard entitling the holder to send in for the calendar from either one of three Capitol-

Apple factories. The value of these are $6 each.

Apple SW-3362   20–25
Apple label with the Capitol logo.

Capitol ST-12239 . . . . *78*   5–8
Purple label.

Side 1
 Blue Suede Shoes
 Money
 Dizzy Miss Lizzy
 Yer Blues
 Cold Turkey
 Give Peace a Chance
Side 2
 Don't Worry Kyoko
 John, John (Let's Hope for Peace)

MENLOVE AVE.
Capitol SJ-12533 . . . *10/30/86*   5–8
Black label with colorband. Features out-takes and rough versions from various Lennon sessions. Also includes two songs recorded for but not included in the *Rock 'n' Roll* LP.

Capitol SV-12533/R-46219 . *87*   15–20
Record club issue. New black label with colorband. Available through the RCA Record Club. Disc and cover read "Manufactured by RCA Music Service," etc.

MILK AND HONEY
Polydor 817-160-1-Y-1 . . . *1/84*   5–8
Red label. Single LP with gatefold cover. Contains material from both John Lennon and Yoko Ono.

Side 1
 I'm Stepping Out
 Sleepless Night
 I Don't Want to Face It
 Don't Be Scared
 Nobody Told Me
 O'Sanity
Side 2
 Borrowed Time
 Your Hands
 (Forgive Me) My Little Flower Princess
 Let Me Count the Ways
 Grow Old with Me
 You're the One

MIND GAMES
Apple SW-3414 . . . . *10/31/73*   10–15
Apple label.

Capitol SN-16068   5–8
Green Budget Series label.

Capitol SW-3414 . . . . *78*   25–30
Purple label.

Side 1
 Mind Games
 Tight A$
 Aisumasen (I'm Sorry)
 One Day at a Time
 Bring on the Lucy (Freeda Peeple)
 Nutopian International Anthem
Side 2
 Intuition
 Out of the Blue
 Only People
 I Know (I Know)
 You Are Here
 Meat City

PLASTIC ONO BAND/JOHN LENNON
Apple SW-3372 . . . . *12/11/70*   15–20
White Apple label.

Capitol SW-3372 . . . . . *78–83*   5–8
Purple label.

Capitol SW-3372 . . . *83 to date*   5–8
New black label with colorband.

Side 1
 Mother
 Hold On
 I Found Out
 Working Class Hero
 Isolation
Side 2
 Remember
 Love
 Well Well Well
 Look at Me
 God
 My Mummy's Dead

REFLECTIONS AND POETRY
Silhouette SM-10014 . . . . . *84*   10–15
Photo label. Double LP with gatefold cover. Contains interviews and poetry by John and Yoko circa 1980. Each LP is sequentially numbered and reportedly only 10,000 copies were pressed. Issued with poster.

Silhouette SM-10014   50–60
Promotional issue. White label with black print. Double LP with gatefold cover. Label reads "Promotional Issue—Not For Sale."

ROCK 'N' ROLL
Apple SK-3419 . . . . *2/17/75*   10–15
Apple label. This LP was rush-released to offset sales of legally restrained release *John Lennon Sings the Great Rock 'n' Roll Hits (Roots)*. Original issue.

Capitol SK-3419   10–15
Purple label.

Capitol SN-16069   **5–8**
Green Budget Series label.

Side 1
Be-Bop-a-Lula
Stand by Me
Ready Teddy
Rip It Up
You Can't Catch Me
Ain't That a Shame
Do You Want to Dance
Sweet Little Sixteen

Side 2
Slippin' and Slidin'
Peggy Sue
Bring It on Home to Me
Send Me Some Lovin'
Bony Maronie
Ya Ya
Just Because

SHAVED FISH

Apple SW-3421 . . . .   *10/24/75*   **10–15**
Apple label.

Capitol SW-3421 . . . . .   *78–83*   **5–8**
Purple label.

Capitol SW-3421 . . . *83 to date*   **5–8**
Black label with rainbow colorband.

Side 1
Give Peace a Chance
Cold Turkey
Instant Karma
Power to the People
Mother
Woman Is the Nigger of the World

Side 2
Mind Games
#9 Dream
Happy Christmas (War Is Over)
Give Peace a Chance
Imagine
Whatever Gets You Through the Night

SOMETIME IN NEW YORK CITY

Apple SVBB-3392 . . . *6/12/72*   **20–25**
Custom Apple photo label. Double LP with
gatefold cover. Issued with a 3½″ × 5″ photocard and an 8″ × 11″ petition (to keep Lennon
in the United States). The value of each is $3.

Apple SVBB-3392   **300–325**
Promotion copy. White label. Double LP with
gatefold cover.

Capitol SVBB-3392 . . . . . .   *78*   **5–8**
Purple label.

Side 1
Woman Is the Nigger of the World
Sisters O Sisters

Attica State
Born in a Prison
New York City

Side 2
Sunday Bloody Sunday
The Luck of the Irish
John Sinclair
Angela
We're All Water

Side 3
Cold Turkey
Don't Worry Kyoko

Side 4
Well Baby Please Don't Go
Jamrag
Scum Bag
Au

TWO VIRGINS—UNFINISHED MUSIC NO. 1

Apple T-5001 . . . . .   *11/11/68*   **100–125**
Apple label. Artists listed as "John Lennon and
Yoko Ono." Due to its controversial nature,
Capitol-EMI would not distribute this LP and
thus the Tetragrammaton Record Company
was hired for the task. Issued with brown paper
outer sleeve. Deduct $30 if sleeve is missing.
Counterfeit identification: Counterfeit covers
tend to be taller (from top to bottom) than originals, at about 12⅜″. Originals are just under
12¼″. Originals have a machine stamped
"MR" in the trail-off area, while counterfeit
copies may or may not have this symbol hand
etched in the trail-off. All originals have high
gloss labels. Outer sleeves on the counterfeits
tend to be of greenish-gold tint, while originals
are golden brown. Most originals had the outer
sleeve sealed with a 2-inch white round sticker
which had to be cut or removed to withdraw the
contents. All color vinyl copies of this LP are
counterfeits.

Apple/Tetragrammaton T-5001
. . . .   *85*   **4–6**
Apple label. Reportedly a legitimate re-issue by
the company who bought the rights to all Tetragrammaton material. Cover photos are of equal
quality to the original. Brown paper sleeves also
feature comparable quality to the original; however, they are cut ¾ inch short of the length of
the cover. Disc labels are flat but of nice clarity
and sharpness (originals are glossy).

Side 1
Two Virgins No. 1
Together
Two Virgins No. 2
Two Virgins No. 3
Two Virgins No. 4

Two Virgins No. 5
Two Virgins No. 6
Side 2
 Hushabye Hushabye
 Two Virgins No. 7
 Two Virgins No. 8
 Two Virgins No. 9
 Two Virgins No. 10

WALLS AND BRIDGES

Apple SW-3416 . . . . . *9/20/74*   **10–15**
Apple label. Custom gatefold cover with two
front sections measuring 4″ × 12″ that open
separately. Issued with an 8-page photo/lyric
booklet.

Capitol SW-3416 . . . . . . *79*   **5–8**
Purple label.

Side 1
 Going Down on Love
 Whatever Gets You Through the Night
 Old Dirt Road
 What You Got
 Bless You
 Scared
Side 2
 #9 Dream
 Surprise, Surprise (Sweet Bird of Paradox)
 Steel and Glass
 Beef Jerky

PAUL McCARTNEY: LPs

ALL THE BEST

Capitol CLW-48287 . . . *12/87*   **10–12**
Custom black label. Double LP with gatefold
cover. Greatest hits package. Issued with
printed lyric liner sleeves.

Side 1
 Band on the Run
 Jet
 Ebony and Ivory
 Listen to What the Man Said
Side 2
 No More Lonely Nights
 Silly Love Songs
 Let 'Em In
 Say Say Say

Side 3
 Live and Let Die
 Another Day
 C Moon
 Junior's Farm
 Uncle Albert/Admiral Halsey
Side 4
 Coming Up
 Goodnight Tonight

Nobody Loves You (When You're Down and
 Out)
Ya Ya

WEDDING ALBUM

Apple SMAX-3361 . . *10/20/69*   **80–90**
Apple label. Artists listed as "John Ono Lennon
and Yoko Ono Lennon." Boxed set consisting
of a single LP and the following various inserts:
A. 1½″ × 6″ photo strip
B. a 3½″ × 5½″ postcard
C. 24″ × 36″ poster of the wedding photos
D. 12″ × 36″ poster of John and Yoko litho-
 graphs
E. a 12″ × 12″ white mylar bag with the word
 "Bagism" printed on it
F. a 17-page booklet of wedding photos and
 clippings.
Note: The value of this LP includes all of the
inserts; value is negotiable at an average price of
$8 per item. A copy of John and Yoko's mar-
riage certificate is adhered to the inside of the
box top. Single LP issued in the boxed set features a gatefold cover, and is valued separately
at $35.

Side 1
 John and Yoko
Side 2
 Amsterdam

With a Little Luck
My Love

BACK TO THE EGG

Columbia FC-36057 . . *5/24/79*   **8–12**
Custom photo label.

Columbia FC-36057   **30–35**
Promotion copy. Custom photo label. Label
reads "Demonstration—Not For Sale."

Columbia PC-36057   **5–8**
Red label.

Side 1
 Reception
 Getting Closer
 We're Open Tonight
 Spin It On
 Again and Again and Again
 Old Siam, Sir
 Arrow Through Me
Side 2
 Rockestra Theme
 To You
 After the Ball
 Million Miles
 Winter Rose

Love Awake
The Broadcast
So Glad to See You Here
Baby's Request

BAND ON THE RUN
Apple SO-3415 . . . . . *12/3/73* **10–15**
Custom Apple photo label. Artists listed as "Paul McCartney and Wings." Issued with photo/lyric liner sleeve and a 20″ × 27″ poster.

Capitol SO-3415 **10–15**
Black label.

Capitol MPL SO-3415 **10–15**
Custom photo label. Disc features the MPL logo only and reads "Mfg. by MPL Communications."

Capitol SEAX-11901 . . . *12/78* **30–35**
Picture disc. Issued with special die cut cover to expose disc. Deduct 30% if LP cover has a cut-out marking.

Columbia JC-36482 **8–12**
Custom photo label.

Columbia PC-36482 **5–8**
Red label.

Columbia HC-36482 . . . . . *81* **20–25**
Half-speed mastered recording on high quality vinyl. Red label. Issued with photo/lyric insert and 20″ × 27″ poster.

Side 1
  Band on the Run
  Jet
  Bluebird
  Mrs. Vanderbilt
  Let Me Roll It
Side 2
  Mamunia
  No Words
  Helen Wheels
  Picasso's Last Words (Drink to Me)
  1985

BAND ON THE RUN—RADIO INTERVIEW SPECIAL WITH PAUL AND LINDA McCARTNEY
Capitol/National Features Corp.
PRO-2955/6. . . . . *1973* **250–275**
Promotion only issue. White label. Issued in plain white cover with script and two glossy promo photos.

Counterfeit identification: known counterfeit has a yellow disc label with entirely incorrect type.

BRUNG TO EWE BY
Apple SPRO-6210 . . . . . *71* **200–225**
Promotion issue only. White label. Special promo LP containing introduction spots to the song selections on Paul's *Ram* LP. Issued with two introductory letters from Paul McCartney Productions.

Counterfeit identification: known counterfeit disc has uneven spacing between the banding; original spacing is even. Most counterfeits we have examined featured the above mentioned letter information in black type printed on a white cover.

Columbia's 21 Top 20: see **Various-Artists Compilations section.**

Columbia's 24 Hits in the Top 20 for 1982: see **Various-Artists Compilations section.**

Concerts for the People of Kampuchea: see **Various-Artists Compilations section.**

FAMILY WAY, THE
London M-76007 . . . . *6/12/67* **56–60**
Monaural. Black label. Soundtrack LP with music composed by Paul McCartney. Although not a true McCartney LP, this album has gained much significance because it was the first solo record project by Paul or any of the Beatles.

Counterfeit identification: known counterfeit features thin posterboard cover construction. Originals used slicks pasted-on tan fiberboard. Disc labels are glossy on the counterfeits, and flat on the originals.

London MS-82007 **70–80**
Stereo copy. Black label.

GIVE MY REGARDS TO BROADSTREET
Columbia SC-39613 . . . *10/84* **5–8**
Custom photo label. Single LP with gatefold cover. Issued with photo/lyric liner sleeve.

Side 1
  No More Lonely Nights
  Good Day Sunshine
  Corridor Music
  Yesterday
  Here, There and Everywhere
  Wanderlust
  Ballroom Dancing
  Silly Love Songs
Side 2
  Silly Love Songs (Reprise)
  Not Such a Bad Boy
  No Values

No More Lonely Nights (Ballad Reprise)
For No One
Eleanor Rigby/Eleanor's Dream
The Long and Winding Road (Playout version)

Gold and Platinum: see **Various-Artists Compilations** section.

Hit Line 80: see **Various-Artists Compilations** section.

Hot Tracks: see **Various-Artists Compilations** section.

James Bond: see **Various-Artists Compilations** section.

Live and Let Die: see **Various-Artists Compilations** section.

LONDON TOWN
Capitol SW-11777 . . . *3/31/78*   **8–12**
Custom photo label. Artists listed as "Wings."
Issued with lyric liner sleeve and a 23″ × 34″
poster.

Side 1
  London Town
  Cafe on the Left Bank
  I'm Carrying
  Backwards Traveler
  Cuff Link
  Children Children
  Girlfriend
  I've Had Enough
Side 2
  With a Little Luck
  Famous Groupies
  Deliver Your Children
  Name and Address
  Don't Let It Bring You Down
  Morse Moose and the Grey Goose

McCARTNEY
Apple STAO-3363 . . . *4/20/70*   **15–20**
Apple label. Single LP with gatefold cover with
the name "Paul McCartney" under the title on
the label (later issues featured only the LP title).

Apple STAO-3363   **20–25**
Apple label with Capitol logo.

Apple STAO-3363   **15–20**
Apple label. Single LP with gatefold cover.
Label features the album title only. Later disc
labels featured the letters "SMAS" as the prefix
to the record number (add $3 to this version in
"NM" condition).

Capitol SMAS-3363 . . . . *78*   **15–20**
Black label. Top of the label reads "Manufactured by McCartney Music Inc."

Capitol SMAS-3363   **10–15**
Black label. Top of the label reads "Manufactured by MPL Communications Inc."

Columbia JC-36478   **8–12**
Red label.

Columbia PC-36478   **5–8**
Red label.

Side 1
  The Lovely Linda
  That Would Be Something
  Valentine Day
  Every Night
  Hot As Sun
  Glasses
  Junk
  Man We Was Lonely
Side 2
  Oo You
  Momma Miss America
  Teddy Boy
  Singalong Junk
  Maybe I'm Amazed
  Kreen-Akrore

McCARTNEY INTERVIEW, THE
Columbia PC-36987 . . *12/4/80*   **8–12**
Red label. LP containing May 1980 interview of
Paul by Vic Garbarini of *Musician* magazine.

Columbia A2S-821 . . . . *12/80*   **25–30**
Promotion copy. White label. Double LP with
single sleeve cover. One LP identical to the
commercial copy, the other is banded to allow
time between Paul's responses for the DJ to use
the enclosed script to ask the questions. This is
referred to as an open-end interview. The enclosed script with this set is an actual copy of
the 5/80 issue of *Musician* magazine (add $20
to value for copies with the magazine). Also
issued with a letter from Columbia (separately
valued at $8).

Counterfeit identification: known counterfeit
lacks gloss on the LP cover, originals are glossy.
Counterfeit discs feature blank labels with no
printing.

McCARTNEY II
Columbia FC-36511 . . *5/21/80*   **8–12**
Red label. Many copies of this LP were issued
with a one-sided 7-inch promo copy of the live
version of "Coming Up." Add $5 to value for
copies with this record. Original issue.

Columbia FC-36511   **20–25**
Promotion copy. White label. "Demonstration—Not For Sale."

Columbia PC-36511   **5–8**
Red label.

Side 1
Coming Up
Temporary Secretary
On the Way
Waterfalls
Nobody Knows
Side 2
Front Parlour
Summer Day Song
Frozen Jap
Bogey Music
Darkroom
One of These Days

PIPES OF PEACE
Columbia QC-39149 .   *10/26/83*   **5–8**
Custom label. Gatefold cover. Issued with lyric inner sleeve.

PRESS TO PLAY
Capitol PJAS-12475 . . *8/21/86*   **5–8**
Custom label.

Side 1
Stranglehold
Good Times Coming/Feel The Sun
Talk More Talk
Footprints
Only Love Remains
Side 2
Press
Pretty Little Head
Move Over Busker
Angry
However Absurd

Prince's Trust: see **Various-Artists Compilations section.**

Programmer's Digest: see **Various-Artists Compilations section.**

RAM
Apple SMAS-3375 . . . *5/17/71*   **15–20**
Apple label. Artists listed as "Paul and Linda McCartney."

Apple SMAS-3375   **20–25**
Apple label with Capitol logo.

Apple MAS-3375   **300–325**
Monaural. Mono copies. Issued for promotional purposes. Standard stereo covers were issued with these LPs.

Capitol SMAS-3375   **15–20**
Black label. Top of label reads "Manufactured by McCartney Music Inc."

Capitol SMAS-3375   **15–20**
Black label. Top of the label reads "Manufactured by MPL Communications Inc."

Columbia JC-36479   **8–12**
Red label.

Columbia PC-36479
Red label.

Side 1
Too Many People
3 Legs
Ram On
Dear Boy
Uncle Albert—Admiral Halsey
Smile Away
Side 2
Heart of the Country
Monkberry Moon Delight
Eat at Home
Long Haired Lady
Ram On
The Back Seat of My Car

RED ROSE SPEEDWAY
Apple SMAL-3409 . . . *4/30/73*   **10–15**
Custom Apple label. Single LP with gatefold cover. Issued with 12-page photo/lyric booklet adhered to the inside of the cover. Braille print on the back cover reads "we love you baby," a message to Stevie Wonder.

Capitol SMAL-3409   **15–20**
Black label. Top of label reads "Manufactured by McCartney Music Inc."

Capitol SMAL-3409   **10–15**
Black label. Version II: top of label reads "Manufactured by MPL Communications Inc."

Columbia JC-36481   **8–12**
Red label. Issued with a 12-page photo/lyric booklet.

Columbia PC-36481   **5–8**
Red label. 12-page booklet has been deleted.

Side 1
Big Barn Red
My Love
Get on the Right Thing
One More Kiss
Little Lamb Dragonfly
Side 2
Single Pigeon
When the Night
Loup (First Indian on the Moon)
Medley; Hold Me Tight
Lazy Dynamite

Hands of Love
Power Cut

Rock for Amnesty: **see Various-Artists Compilations section.**

THRILLINGTON

Capitol ST-11642 . . . . . . *77*   **30–35**
Purple label. Orchestral arrangement and performance of Paul's *Ram* LP. Reportedly packaged to satisfy Paul's contractual obligation to Capitol Records prior to his transition to the Columbia label. Artists listed as "Percy Thrills Thrillington."

TUG OF WAR

Columbia TC-37462 . . *4/26/82*   **8–12**
Custom label. Original issue.

Columbia PC-37462   **5–8**
Red label.

Side 1
Tug of War
Take It Away
Somebody Who Cares
What's That You're Doing?
Here Today
Side 2
Ballroom Dancing
The Pound Is Sinking
Wanderlust
Get It
Be What You See
Dress Me Up As a Robber
Ebony and Ivory

VENUS AND MARS

Capitol SMAS-11419 . . *5/27/75*   **10–15**
Custom label. Single LP with gatefold cover. Artists listed as "Wings." Issued with two 20" × 30" posters, one 1½" × 12" sticker and one 4" round sticker. Value given includes all inserts.

Columbia JC-36801   **5–8**
Red label. Issued with two posters. The two stickers which were inserts in the original Capitol issue are adhered to the inside of this cover.

Columbia PC-36801   **5–8**
Red label. All inserts have been deleted.

Side 1
Venus and Mars
Rock Show
Love in Song
You Gave Me the Answer
Magneto and Titanium Man
Letting Go
Side 2
Venus and Mars (reprise)
Spirits of Ancient Egypt

Medicine Jar
Call Me

WILDLIFE, WINGS

Apple SW-3386 . . . . . *12/7/71*   **15–20**
Custom Apple photo label. Artists listed as "Wings."

Capitol SW-3386   **15–20**
Black label. Version I: top of label reads "Manufactured by McCartney Music Inc."

Capitol SW-3386   **10–15**
Black label. Version II: top of label reads "Manufactured by MPL Communications Inc."

Columbia JC-36480   **8–12**
Red label.

Columbia PC-36480   **5–8**
Red label.

Side 1
Mumbo
Big Bop
Love Is Strange
Wildlife
Side 2
Some People
Never Know
I Am Your Singer
Tomorrow
Dear Friend

WINGS AT THE SPEED OF SOUND

Capitol SW-11525 . . . *3/25/76*   **10–15**
Custom photo label. Artists listed as "Wings."

Capitol SW-11525   **80–90**
Advance promotional copy. White label. Issued in plain white cover or a stock cover with a promo punch hole in the upper corner.

Columbia FC-37409   **8–12**
Custom photo label.

Columbia PC-36801   **5–8**
Red label.

Side 1
Let Em In
The Note You Never Wrote
She's My Baby
Beware My Love
Wino Junko
Side 2
Silly Love Songs
Cook of the House
Time to Hide
Must Do Something About It
San Ferry Anne
Warm and Beautiful

WINGS GREATEST HITS
Capitol SOO-11905. . *11/22/78* **10–15**
Custom label. Issued with 20″ × 30″ poster.

Side 1
  Another Day
  Silly Love Songs
  Live and Let Die
  Juniors Farm
  With a Little Luck
  Band on the Run
Side 2
  Uncle Albert—Admiral Halsey
  Hi Hi Hi
  Let Em In
  My Love
  Jet
  Mull of Kintyre

WINGS OVER AMERICA
Capitol SWCO-11593. *12/10/76* **15–20**
Custom label. Artists listed as "Wings." Three-LP set issued with 20″ × 30″ poster.

Columbia C3X-37990 **10–15**
Red label. Three-LP set. Poster has been deleted.

Side 1
  Venus and Mars
  Rock Show
  Jet
  Let Me Roll It

  Spirits of Ancient Egypt
  Medicine Jar
Side 2
  Maybe I'm Amazed
  Call Me Back Again
  Lady Madonna
  The Long and Winding Road
  Live and Let Die
Side 3
  Picasso's Last Words
  Richard Corey
  Bluebird
  I've Just Seen a Face
  Black Bird
  Yesterday
Side 4
  Letting Go
  Band on the Run
  Hi Hi Hi
  Soily
Side 5
  You Gave Me the Answer
  Magneto and Titanium Man
  Go Now
  My Love
Side 6
  Listen to What the Man Said
  Let 'Em In
  Time to Hide
  Silly Love Songs
  Beware My Love

RINGO STARR: LPs

BAD BOY
Portrait JR-35378. . . . *4/21/78* **10–15**
Gray label. Deduct 40% from value if LP cover has a cut-out marking.

Portrait JR-35378 **30–35**
Advance promotion copy. White label. Issued in plain white cover. Label reads "Advance Promotion."

Portrait JR-35378 **20–25**
Promotion copy. White label. Issued in stock cover with gold embossed promotional stamping. Label reads "Demonstration—Not For Sale."

Side 1
  Who Needs a Heart
  Bad Boy
  Lipstick Traces
  Heart on My Sleeve
  Where Did Our Love Go

Side 2
  Hard Times
  Tonight
  Monkey See Monkey Do
  Old Time Relovin'
  A Man Like Me

BEAUCOUPS OF BLUES
Apple SMAS-3368 . . . *9/28/70* **15–20**
Apple label. Single LP with gatefold cover.

Capitol SN-16235 **8–12**
Green Budget Series label.

Side 1
  Beaucoups of Blues
  Love Don't Last Long
  Fastest Growing Heartache in the West
  Without Her
  Woman of the Night
  I'd Be Talking All the Time

Side 2
$15 Draw
Wine, Women and Loud Happy Songs
I Wouldn't Have You Any Other Way
Loser's Lounge
Waiting
Silent Home Coming

BLAST FROM YOUR PAST
Apple SW-3422 . . . .   *11/20/75*   **10–15**
Red Apple label.

Capitol SN-16236   **5–8**
Green Budget Series label.

Side 1
You're Sixteen
No No Song
It Don't Come Easy
Photograph
Back Off Boogaloo
Side 2
Only You
Beaucoups of Blues
Oh My My
Early 1970
I'm the Greatest

GOODNIGHT VIENNA
Apple SW-3417 . . . . .   *4/18/74*   **10–15**
Custom Apple label.

Capitol SN-16218   **8–12**
Green Budget Series label.

Side 1
Goodnight Vienna
Occapella
Oo-Wee
Husbands and Wives
Snookeroo
Side 2
All By Myself
Call Me
No No Song
Only You
Easy for Me
Goodnight Vienna (reprise)

RINGO
Apple SWAL-3413 . .   *10/31/73*   **15–20**
Custom Apple photo label. Single LP with gate-fold cover. Issued with 20-page lyric booklet.

Apple SWAL-3413   **100–125**
Custom Apple photo label. This pressing features the long version of the song "Six O'-Clock." Only early copies which had a promotional punch hole out of the top corner have been verified with the long version (some test pressings have the long version as well). These were entirely stock albums with the exception of the promo hole. Although all Apple copies of

this LP list the song at 5:26, the song was actually edited to 4:05 on copies released to the public. Copies that were specifically designed for in-store promotion included a 12½″ × 34½″ poster which is separately valued at $25. Value given is for the LP with the long version (5:26) of "Six O'Clock." Copies with the long version are easily identifiable: on Side 2 the song "Six O'Clock" is the widest band on the side. It is the second to the smallest on the common short version. Remember that not all copies with promo hole covers contain the long version.

Capitol SN-16114   **5–8**
Green Budget Series label.

Side 1
I'm the Greatest
Have You Seen My Baby
Photograph
Sunshine Life for Me (Sail Away Raymond)
You're Sixteen
Side 2
Oh My My
Step Lightly
Six O'Clock
Devil Woman
You and Me (Babe)

RINGO THE 4TH
Atlantic SD-19108 . . .   *9/26/77*   **10–15**
Green and orange label. Deduct 50% if LP cover has a cut-out marking.

Side 1
Drowning in the Sea of Love
Tango All Night
Wings
Gave It All Up
Out on the Streets
Side 2
She Can Do It Like She Dances
Sneaking Sally Through the Alley
It's No Secret
Gypsies in Flight
Simple Love Songs

ROTOGRAVURE, RINGO'S
Atlantic SD-18193 . . .   *9/27/76*   **10–15**
Green and orange label. Deduct 60% if the LP cover has a cut-out marking.

Side 1
A Dose of Rock 'N' Roll
Hey Baby
Pure Gold
Cryin'
You Don't Know Me At All

Side 2
  Cookin' (in the Kitchen of Love)
  I'll Still Love You
  This Be Called a Song
  Las Brisas
  Lady Gaye
  Spooky Weirdness

Season's Best, The: see Various-Artists
Compilations section.

SENTIMENTAL JOURNEY

Apple SW-3365 . . . . . *4/24/70*	**15–20**	
Apple label.		
Capitol SW-3365 . . . . *78*	**15–20**	
Purple label.		
Capitol SN-16218	**8–12**	
Green "Budget Series" label.		

Side 1
  Sentimental Journey
  Night and Day
  Whispering Grass (Don't Tell the Trees)
  Bye Bye Blackbird
  I'm a Fool to Care
  Stardust
Side 2
  Blue, Turning Grey Over You
  Love Is a Many Splendored Thing

Dream
You Always Hurt the One You Love
Have I Told You Lately That I Love You
Let the Rest of the World Go By

Songs of Randy Newman: see
Various-Artists Compilations section.

STOP AND SMELL THE ROSES
Boardwalk NB1-33246 *10/27/81*   **8–12**
Blue and white skyline label. Deduct 30% from
value for copies with a cut-out marking on the
cover.

Side 1
  Private Property
  Wrack My Brain
  Drumming Is My Madness
  Attention
  Stop and Take Time to Smell the Roses
Side 2
  Dead Giveaway
  You Belong to Me
  Sure to Fall
  Nice Way
  Back Off Boogaloo

Tommy: see Various-Artists
Compilations section.

Various Artists Compilations

EPs

BEATLES, BEACH BOYS, AND THE KINGSTON TRIO (a Surprise Gift from the . . .)

Evatone 8464   350–375

A 7-inch tri-fold square card featuring various LP ads, and a nice photo of the Beatles. The middle section is vinyl coated and features the song selections "Roll Over Beethoven" by the Beatles, "Little Deuce Coupe" by the Beach Boys, and "The Saints" by the Kingston Trio. This 33 1/3 rpm promotional soundsheet was inserted and distributed in 1964 in several large publications throughout the United States.

Evatone 8464   250–275

This version is a 5-inch flexi-disc with black vinyl and white print.

BEATLES INTRODUCE NEW SONGS, THE

Capitol PRO-2720/1 64   800–825

Promotion copy. Burgundy label. Promotional only single featuring John and Paul introducing new artists (Cilla Black and Peter and Gordon) performing Lennon-McCartney compositions.

Counterfeit identification: two known counterfeits. The first is a fairly good reproduction of the original; however, the trail-off area features no stampings of any kind. The second is a poorer attempt that features a red label and poor print clarity.

CAPITOL SOUVENIR RECORD, THE

Capitol Compact 33 SPRO-2905

. . . . 65   80–90

Black label with colorband. Promotional only EP containing the Beatles' "I Want to Hold Your Hand." Issued to celebrate the grand opening of Capitol's Jacksonville, Illinois, pressing plant. Issued with picture sleeve.

Capitol Compact 33 SPRO-2905   70–80

Picture sleeve.

EVERYNIGHT

Atlantic PR 388   80–85

Promotional 12-inch EP. Green and red label promotional EP to promote the LP *Concerts for the People of Kampuchea.* Additional songs by the Who, Rockpile and Rockestra. Artist listed as "Paul McCartney & Wings." Label reads "Promotional Copy Not For Sale."

I DON'T WANT TO DO IT

Columbia CAS-2085   15–20

Promotional 12-inch EP. Red label. Features selections from the soundtrack LP PORKY'S REVENGE (also features songs by Jeff Beck and Dave Edmunds). Includes George Harrison's "I Don't Want to Do It." Label reads "Demonstration Not For Sale."

LPs

AMERICAN CHRISTMAS, AN (12 LP)

Otis Connor Productions SP

. . . . 12/84   150–200

Boxed set from the archives of *The Saturday Evening Post.* Issued only to radio stations. Includes 14 pages of script and cue sheets. Includes John and Yoko on:

Hour 2, Side 1, Segment 2:
Happy Christmas and Paul McCartney on:
Hour 7, Side 1, Segment 3:
Wonderful Christmas Time

AMERICAN TOP 40

Any of the *American Top 40* boxed
sets containing a Beatles track
should fall into a $30–60 range.

AUDIO GUIDE TO THE ALAN PARSONS PROJECT

Artista SP-68 . . . . *79*   **25–30**
Promotional issue only. Blue and tan label.
Double LP issued with a boxed set of Alan
Parsons albums. Has songs that Parsons was
involved with prior to forming his group. Has
three Beatles tracks: "Get Back," "Maxwell's
Silver Hammer," and "A Day in the Life" as
well as three McCartney tunes: "Hi Hi Hi,"
"I'm Your Singer," and "Maybe I'm Amazed."
Disc label reads "For Promotion Only—Not
For Sale." Value is for the double LP only.
Price for entire boxed set is $50.

BIG HITS FROM ENGLAND AND THE U.S.A., THE

Capitol T-2125 . . . . *64*   **30–35**
Monaural. Black label with colorband. Con-
tains two tracks by the Beatles: "Can't Buy Me
Love" and "You Can't Do That."

Capitol DT-2125 . . . . . . *64*   **40–45**
Duophonic (Simulated Stereo). Black label with
colorband.

BRITISH GOLD

Sire R-224095 . . . . *78*   **15–20**
Yellow label with black print. Double LP. Con-
tains one track by the Beatles: "Ain't She
Sweet."
RCA Record Club issue.

BRITISH ROCK CLASSICS

Sire R-234021 . . . . *79*   **15–20**
Yellow label. Double LP. Contains one track by
the Beatles with Tony Sheridan: "My Bonnie."
RCA Record Club issue.

Available in splendid "duophonic" (simulated stereo) sound, this various artists
package featured two British acts closely affiliated with the Beatles.

BRITISH STERLING
Lakeshore Music LSM-811 . *81*   20–25
Tan label. Double LP. Contains one track by the Beatles with Tony Sheridan: "My Bonnie."

CAPITOL HITS THROUGH THE YEARS
Capitol PRO-4724 . . . . . . *69*   40–45
Promotional issue only. Black label with rainbow colorband. Contains brief segments of the songs "I Want to Hold Your Hand," "Can't Buy Me Love," "Yesterday," "Paperback Writer," "Yellow Submarine," "All You Need Is Love," "Eleanor Rigby," "Strawberry Fields Forever," and "Hey Jude."

Capitol PRO-4724 . . . . . . *84*   25–30
Purple label. Re-issue.

CAPITOL IN-STORE SAMPLER
Capitol SPRO-9867. . . . . . *82*   15–20
Promotional issue only. Purple label. Contains one track by the Beatles: "Love Me Do." Plain white cover with title sticker. Title sticker reads "Not For Sale."

CHARTBUSTERS VOLUME 4
Capitol T-2094 . . . . *64*   35–40
Monaural. Black label with colorband. Contains two tracks by the Beatles: "I Want to Hold Your Hand" and "I Saw Her Standing There."

Capitol ST-2094. . . . . *64*   45–50
Stereo. Black label with colorband.

COLLIERS ENCYCLOPEDIA 1965 EDITION OF YEAR IN SOUND
Radio Press International . . *65*   20–25
Black, blue and white label. LP covering the historic events of 1964. Contains brief interviews with John and Paul.

COLUMBIA'S 21 TOP 20
Columbia A2S-700 . . . . . . *79*   20–25
Promotional issue only. White label. Double LP with gatefold cover. Contains two tracks by Paul, "Goodnight Tonight" and "Getting Closer."

COLUMBIA'S 24 HITS IN THE TOP 20 FOR 1982
Columbia A2S-1558 . . . . . *82*   15–20
Promotional issue only. Red label. Double LP. Contains two tracks by Paul, "Ebony and Ivory" and "Take It Away."

COMPLETE AUDIO GUIDE TO THE ALAN PARSONS PROJECT
Arista SP 140   25–30
1982 re-issue. This version features a brown cover. Disc labels and cover read "Loaned for promotion only—Not for sale." Value for entire boxed set is $50.

CONCERT FOR BANGLA DESH, THE
Apple STCX-3385 . . *12/20/71*   15–20
Custom Apple label. Three-LP boxed set. Live LP featuring performances by George, Ringo, Bob Dylan, Leon Russell, Ravi Shankar, Eric Clapton and others. Issued with 64-page photo booklet. Original issue.

Wah Wah/My Sweet Lord/Awaiting on You All/Beware of Darkness/While My Guitar Gently Weeps/Here Comes the Sun/Something/Bangla Desh/It Don't Come Easy (Ringo) (plus performances by other artists)

CONCERTS FOR THE PEOPLE OF KAMPUCHEA
Atlantic SD-2-7005. . . . . . *81*   10–15
Green and red label. Double LP with gatefold cover. Live benefit concert LP with Paul McCartney and Wings performing "Coming Up," "Every Night," and "Got to Get You into My Life."

Note: Paul and Wings also perform on three additional cuts by the group "Rockestra."

Atlantic PR-388
Promotional only compilation 12-inch EP.

CUSTOM FIDELITY RECORD PROMOTIONS
Custom Fidelity Special Products
CFS 3281   20–30
Gold label with black print. Contains excerpt of "I Saw Her Standing There."

DISCOTEQUE IN ASTROSOUND
Clarion 609 . . . . *66*   40–45
Monaural. Red, white and blue label. Contains one track by the Beatles with Tony Sheridan, "Take Out Some Insurance on Me Baby."

Clarion 609 . . . . *66*   50–60
Stereo. Green, orange and white label.

DO IT NOW—20 GIANT HITS
Ronco LP-1001 . . . . *70*   10–15
Green label. Contains one track by the Beatles: "Nowhere Man."

EPIC OF THE 70s (6 LP)
Century 21 Productions (SP) 1A-6B   150–200
A six-hour program, highlighting the songs of the 70s, along with interviews with most of the artists featured.

Note: The set was issued to radio stations only. In all probability, a script and programming information was issued with the set.

The concert that planted the seeds for the likes of *Live Aid*. Alleged mismanagement by Allen Klein delayed the disbursement of millions of dollars to the refugees.

Side 3A:
John Lennon Interview
Whatever Gets You Through the Night
Side 5A:
Paul McCartney Interview
Let It Be (the Beatles)

EVERY MAN HAS A WOMAN
Polydor 823-490-1Y-1 . . . . *84*   **8–10**
Red label. LP of material composed by Yoko Ono and performed by other artists. Contains "Every Man Has a Woman Who Loves Him" by John Lennon. Also contains a cut by Sean Lennon. Deduct 30% for copies with cut-out markings on the cover.

FIRST VIBRATION
Do It Now Foundation LP-5000
. . . . *69*   **20–25**
Red label. Contains one track by the Beatles: "Nowhere Man."

FLASHBACK GREATS OF THE 60'S
K-Tel TU-229. . . . . *73*   **10–15**
Contains one track by the Beatles with Tony Sheridan: "My Bonnie."

GOLD & PLATINUM
Realm Records IP-7679 . . . *84*   **8–12**
Green label. Contains "Say Say Say" by Paul and Michael Jackson. Available through the Columbia Record Club.

Realm Records R-172499-IP-7679
. . . . *84*   **10–15**
Blue label. Contains "Say Say Say" by Paul and Michael Jackson. Available through RCA Record Club.

GOLDEN DAYS OF BRITISH ROCK
Sire 4V-8046 . . . . *76*   **30–35**
Yellow label. Four-LP box set. Contains one song by the Beatles: "Ain't She Sweet."

GRAMMY AWARD WINNERS, 1966
XTV-123942 . . . . *67*   **50–60**
Promotional issue only. White label. Contains "Eleanor Rigby" by the Beatles. Label reads "Not For Sale."

GREAT NEW RELEASES FROM THE SOUND CAPITOL OF THE WORLD
Capitol PRO-2538 . . . . . *2/64*   **70–80**
Promotional issue only. Black label with color-band. Contains two tracks by the Beatles: "It Won't Be Long" and "This Boy." Label reads "For Promotional Use Only—Not For Sale."

GREATEST MUSIC EVER SOLD, THE
Capitol SPRO-8511/2 . . . . *76*   **35–40**
Promotional issue only. Custom purple label. Contains three tracks by the Beatles: "Eleanor Rigby," "Got to Get You into My Life," and "Ob La Di, Ob La Da." Also contains

"Imagine" by John Lennon and "You're Six-teen" by Ringo Starr. Label reads "Not For Sale."

GREENPEACE
A&M SP-5091 . . . . . . *8/85*   **8–12**
Silver label. Contains "Save the World" by George Harrison. Issued with flyer.

HISTORY OF BRITISH ROCK
Sire 2P-6547. . . . . *76*   **15–20**
Yellow label. Double LP. Contains one track by the Beatles: "Ain't She Sweet." Available through the Columbia Record Club.

HISTORY OF BRITISH ROCK VOLUME II
Sire SASH-3705-2 . . . . . . *74*   **15–20**
Yellow label. Double LP. Contains one track by the Beatles: "Ain't She Sweet."

Sire SASH-3705-2   **15–20**
Promotional copy. White label. Label reads "Promotional Copy—t For Sale."

HISTORY OF BRITISH ROCK VOLUME III
Sire SASH-3712-2 . . . . . . *75*   **15–20**
Yellow label. Double LP with gatefold cover. Contains one track by the Beatles with Tony Sheridan: "My Bonnie."

Sire SASH-3712-2   **20–30**
Promotion copy. White label. Label reads "Promotional copy—Not for sale."

HISTORY OF SYRACUSE MUSIC, VOLS. VIII & IX
ECEIP 1015, 16, 17, 18   **25–30**
Red and yellow label with black print. Double LP with gatefold cover. Contains 10/8/71 press conference with John and Yoko. LP cover features photo of John and Yoko. Also includes interview with Joe English of Wings, and a cover photo of that group. Issued in 1976 and available largely on the east coast.

HISTORY OF SYRACUSE MUSIC VOLS. X & XI
ECEIP 1019, 20, 21, 22 . . . *80*   **25–30**
Red and yellow label with black print. Double LP with gatefold cover. Contains 10/8/71 press conference with John and Yoko (different segment than above). LP cover features a satirical takeoff of the Beatles' *Sgt. Pepper* LP.

HIT LINE 80
Columbia A2S-890 . . . . . . *80*   **20–25**
Promotional issue only. White label. Double LP with gatefold cover. Contains "Coming Up" by Paul McCartney and Wings.

HITS ON BOARD
Capitol SPRO-9864. . . . . *86*   **15–20**
White label. Promotion only 12-inch sampler. Contains "Twist and Shout" by the Beatles and "Press" by Paul McCartney. Features white cover with title sticker. Label and cover read "Promotional Copy—Not For Sale."

HOT TRACKS
Hot Tracks SA-3-8 . . . . . *84*   **70–80**
Purple label. Promotional only 12-inch disc containing four tracks. Includes "No More Lonely Nights" by Paul. This version was mixed by Warren Sanford and is only available on this record.

I CAN HEAR IT NOW, THE SIXTIES
Columbia M3X-30353 . . . . *70*   **15–20**
Gray label. Three-LP box set. Narration by Walter Cronkite. Contains excerpt of the Beatles' "I Want to Hold Your Hand."

Columbia AS-13   **20–25**
White label. Promotional LP containing excerpts from M3X-30353. Label reads "Demonstration—Not For Sale."

IN THE BEGINNING
ATV Music Group ATV-VMI
. . . . *80*   **20–25**
Promotional issue only. White label. Contains two tracks by the Beatles: "Bad Boy" and "Dizzy Miss Lizzy." Disc label and cover read "For Broadcast Use Only—Not For Sale."

JAMES BOND 007—13 ORIGINAL THEMES
Liberty LO-51138. . . . . . *83*   **5–8**
Gray label. Contains the track "Live and Let Die" by Paul.

JAMES BOND 13 ORIGINAL THEMES
Liberty LO-551138   **10–15**
Record club issue. Gray label with black print. Issued by the Columbia Record Club. Disc and cover read "Manufactured by Columbia House," etc. Contains "Live and Let Die" by Paul.

JOY OF CHRISTMAS, THE (18 LP)
Creative Radio (SP) *no number given*   **150–200**
This edition programmed for adult contemporary formats. Price includes 18 pages of programming instructions and cues. Deduct $15–$25 if these pages are missing. Issued to radio stations only.

Beatles tracks include:
Hour 1:
  Wonderful Christmas Time (Paul McCartney)
Hour 5:
  Happy Christmas (John and Yoko)
Hour 7:
  Wonderful Christmas Time (Paul McCartney)
Hour 10:
  Happy Christmas (John and Yoko)

JUST LET ME HEAR SOME OF THAT ROCK 'N' ROLL MUSIC

Goodman GG PRO-1   30–40
A two-record set containing excerpts of 100 songs. Promotional issue only.
Beatles tracks include:
Record 2, Side B:
  Thank You Girl (track 3)

LET'S BEAT IT

K-tel TV-2200 . . . . *84*   8–12
Tan and red label. Contains the track "Say Say Say" by Paul and Michael Jackson.

LISTEN IN GOOD HEALTH

Capitol SPRO-5003/4 . . . *4/70*   30–35
Promotional only issue. White label. Contains one track by the Beatles: "Here Comes the Sun." Label reads "Promotional Record—Not For Sale."

LIVE AND LET DIE

United Artists Ua-La-100-G
. . . . *7/2/73*   20–25
Tan label. Soundtrack LP with the title track composed and performed by Paul McCartney and Wings. Single LP with gatefold cover. Original issue. Deduct 25% if LP cover has a cutout marking.

United Artists Ua-La-100-G   10–15
Orange and yellow sunrise label. Soundtrack LP with the title track by Paul and Wings.

Liberty LMAS-100   10–15
Gray label.

Liberty LT-50100   8–10
Gray label.

United Artists SWAO-95120   25–30
Record club issue. Issued by the Capitol Record Club in the mid-seventies.

LOWERY GROUP, THE—25 GOLDEN YEARS

Lowery Group *71*   25–30
Promotional issue only. White label. Double LP with gatefold cover. Contains one track by the Beatles: "Mr. Moonlight." Label and cover read "For Radio and TV Broadcasting Only— Not For Sale."

MCA MUSIC

MCA Music   40–60
Gold label with black print. Four-LP set with gatefold cover. Promotional issue only. Includes excerpt of "I Want to Hold Your Hand."

MISCELLANEOUS SYNDICATED RADIO SHOWS

There have been quite a number of syndicated radio shows, such as "Wolfman Jack," "Robert W. Morgan," "Ralph Emery," and others, that were issued to subscribing stations on disc. Some of these feature Beatles' recordings and may be of interest to their fans. Generally speaking, these types of LP would fall into the $10–$20 range for near-mint copies.

MONSTERS

Warner Bros. PRO-A-796   20–25
White label. Double LP with gatefold cover. Contains "Not Guilty" by George Harrison. Available through mail-order in 1982.

MORE SOLID GOLD PROGRAMMING FROM SCREEN GEMS

EMI-717   30–35
Promotional issue only. White label. Double LP with gatefold cover. Contains three tracks by the Beatles: "Love Me Do," "P.S. I Love You," and "Chains." Label and cover read "For Broadcasting Use Only."

NATIONAL LAMPOON ALBUM OF THE MONTH

N.L. Jan-76 A/B *1/76*   20–25
Pink label. Contains "Imagine" by John Lennon. Issued for in-store air play only.

OFFICIAL GRAMMY AWARDS ARCHIVE COLLECTION, THE

Franklin Mint
Red vinyl. 100-album set available via mail-order featuring Grammy award winning music from 1958 to 1983. Retail value of the entire set was $1170. Record #GRAM #2 contains "I Want to Hold Your Hand," by the Beatles. Record #GRAM #5 contains "My Sweet Lord" by George Harrison. A cut by Paul McCartney and Wings was slated as well but as of press time, it has not been issued. The entire set was to be issued over a four-year period. Value of each disc containing a Beatle-related track is $75. Released beginning 1983.

PLAYBOY MUSIC HALL OF FAME WINNERS, THE
Playboy PB-7473 . . . . . . *78*   **35–50**
Silver and white label. Contains one track by the Beatles: "A Hard Day's Night." Back cover reads "Not For Sale."

PORKY'S REVENGE
Columbia JS-39983 . . . . . *3/85*   **8–12**
Red label. Soundtrack LP containing one track by George Harrison: "I Don't Want to Do It."

PRINCE'S TRUST 10TH ANNIVERSARY BIRTHDAY PARTY
A&M SP-3906 . . . . *5/87*   **5–8**
Black label with silver print. LP issued to benefit the "Prince's Trust" charity fund. Contains live version of Paul performing "Get Back."

PROGRAMMERS DIGEST (APRIL 74)
Audio Video Corp AV-14-1033   **35–40**
Blue and yellow label. Double LP. Contains telephone interview with Paul and Wings.

RADIO'S MILLION PERFORMANCE SONGS
CBS Songs SNGS-101 . . . . *84*   **20–40**
Promotional issue only. Back of cover reads "Not For Sale."

Beatles songs include:
Side 2:
   Hard Days Night (the Beatles)

ROCK FOR AMNESTY
Mercury 830-617-1M-1 . . . . *86*   **5–8**
Black label with silver print. LP issued to celebrate Amnesty International's 25th anniversary. Contains "Pipes of Peace" by Paul McCartney.

Mercury 830-617-1M-1   **10–15**
Promotional issue. Black label with silver print. Disc label reads "PROMOTIONAL—NOT FOR SALE"; cover has promotional stamping.

ROCK, ROLL & REMEMBER (6 LP)
Dick Clark Productions (SP) DPE-402 . . . . *77*   **225–250**

Beatles tracks include:
Side 4B:
   She Loves You

SEASON'S BEST, THE
Warner-Elektra-Atlantic   WEA-SMP-2-10-76 . . . . *10/76*   **15–20**
Promotional issue only. White label. Double LP. Contains "A Dose of Rock 'n' Roll" by Ringo. Label reads "For In-Store Play Only—Not For Sale."

SILVER PLATTER SERVICE
Capitol PRO-3143/4 . . . . *3/65*   **175–200**
Promotional issue only. Gray label with black print. Label reads "Especially prepared for radio programming use—NOT FOR SALE."

SILVER YEARS—25—THE (CAPITOL'S 25TH ANNIVERSARY CELEBRATION)
Capitol PRO-4411/2 . . . . . *67*   **30–35**
Promotional issue only. Black label with colorband. Contains brief message about, and segment of, "I Want to Hold Your Hand."

SOLID GOLD, GERRY GOFFIN AND CAROLE KING
Screen Gems—Columbia Music
. . . . *70*   **25–30**
Promotional issue only. White label with black print. Contains one track by the Beatles: "Chains."

SONGS OF RANDY NEWMAN, THE
Interworld Music Group IMG-1000
   15–20
Promotional issue only. White label. Contains edited version of "Have You Seen My Baby" by Ringo. Label reads "Not For Sale—Demonstration Record."

SOUNDS OF SOLID GOLD VOLUME 2
U.S. Marine Corps Public Service Program   **20–25**
Six-LP box set. Contains one track by the Beatles: "Do You Want to Know a Secret."

TOMMY
Ode Records SP-9901 *11/27/72*   **20–25**
Double-LP boxed set. Silver label. Soundtrack LP. Contains two tracks by Ringo: "Fiddle About" and "Tommy's Holiday Camp." Issued with 28-page lyric booklet.

212 HITS
Screen Gems-Colgems-EMI-212
. . . . *84*   **25–30**
White label. Double LP. Contains brief segments of the songs "Love Me Do," "P.S. I Love You," and "Twist and Shout."

ULTIMATE RADIO BOOTLEG
Mercury MK-2-121 . . . . . . *79*   **25–30**
Photo label. Promotional only double LP set with gatefold cover. Contains six-minute interview with the group via telephone in 1964.

WHEREHOUSE SINGLES OF THE WEEK
Integrity LP 6/13/79. . . . *6/79* **30–35**
Promotion only LP. White label with black print. Issued in plain white cover. Contains "Getting Closer" by Wings.

WITHNAIL AND I
DRG SBL-12590 . . . . . . *8/87* **5–8**
Purple label with black print. Motion picture soundtrack. Contains "While My Guitar Gently Weeps."

YULESVILLE
Warner Bros. PRO-A-2896 . *87* **10–15**
Promotional only comp. LP. Gold label. Special Christmas LP containing tunes and brief messages from various artists. Contains message by George Harrison. Issued in red vinyl. LP cover and disc label read "PROMOTIONAL COPY NOT FOR SALE."

PART 3
APPENDIXES

Elvis and The Beatles on Compact Disc: A Brief Look into the Future of Music Collecting

Collecting CDs by Elvis and the Beatles (group or solo) has, due to the youth of the format, been experienced in relatively small numbers when compared to their vinyl forefathers. However, this whole new area is one of great interest and enthusiasm.

When Capitol issued the first four Beatles CDs in early 1987, many were produced in Germany, Japan, and the U.K. to keep up with the expected demand of brisk sales. Copies manufactured outside the United States—as of the time of writing, there are only seven American CD plants—are identified with a sticker adhered to the back of the box under the shrinkwrap that reads "made in Germany," "made in Japan" or "made in the U.K." So far, these "stickered" CD boxes have not gained much notoriety. Variations of many other Beatles' record items have indeed increased in value, sometimes a hundredfold, over the years. These CD variations will likely be slow to command a more significant amount, but they will undoubtedly find their place in the collecting arena.

The stand-out among collectible CDs, however, must be the Japanese EMI-Odeon release of "Abbey Road." A few found their way into the American market around the end of 1984, but were quickly suppressed when they interfered with Capitol's CD release program. One copy even turned up at Christie's auction house in London in 1987, valued at $180 to $360.

Thus far, only a handful of "solo" CDs are of collector interest. Among these are three promotional single CDs and the promotional picture CD (LP) for "Cloud Nine" by George Harrison. His three Dark Horse single CDs are "Got My Mind Set On You," "Cloud Nine," and "That's What It Takes." These sell for $25 to $35 each. His LP picture CD, which features a silk screen silhouette of George, goes for about $90. The values of Harrison's three promo CDs may well serve as a guide in establishing some dollar amount to any future, "DJ only" CDs by other ex-Beatles.

Among other items of definite interest are the few short-lived Columbia CDs by McCartney before Capitol reissued them in early 1988. These CDs include "Venus and Mars" (this one has yet to be reissued by Capitol), "Wings Over America," "Band On the Run" and "Tug of War." These four releases have not yet found a stable value among collectors. Each should be worth picking up now at twice the original "retail" price.

Finally, a few radio samplers with John Lennon and George Harrison tracks included on them. One is called "Album Network, CD Tune Up Christmas '87." Among the 19 songs included on this $35 promotional CD are Lennon's "Happy Xmas" and Elvis Presley's "Santa Bring My Baby Back." The other various artists sampler is titled "Making History." This Warner Brother's issue is a set of four CDs (each in their own individual jewel box that includes a booklet) and 74 song selections, among which John Lennon's "Just Like Starting Over" is featured. Issued in 1986, these four CDs are worth about $250 as a set. The Lennon CD is valued at $75 separately. The Harrison CD sampler is titled "The Hard Report" and contains "Devil's Radio" by George. You can expect to pay up to $30 for this one.

LPs will always have the distinction of being the original format for Elvis and the Beatles' work. There's something wonderful about sifting through records that feature the cover art as it was intended to be seen. The CDs have their many technical advantages, but the pleasure of handling the substance of the LP is lacking. Gone will be the gatefold covers, the imaginative use of the liner sleeve. But you can be sure that as designers come to think in terms of the CD format, they will come up with that extra something that will capture the imagination.

Some people are of the opinion that CDs have diminished the value of collectible records and have been responsible for decreased demand for many a record title. The answer is definitely "yes" and "no." Yes, we believe that any title that is valued strictly for its musical content may decrease in value as CDs dominate the market more and more. For instance, how much would you pay for "Johnny Mathis' Greatest Hits" in the 4-track tape format? Not much, right? A Johnny Mathis collector might pay a certain amount, but there are not enough Mathis collectors to create a serious demand for a popular title on a dead format. This will probably hold true for any LP title or artist valued strictly for the musical content.

On the other hand, collectible artists such as The Beatles, Elvis, The Rolling Stones, and the like are valued as much for their historical contributions as they are for their music. Giants such as these generate large followings, which translates into varying degrees of heavy demand for virtually every product released pertaining to them. For example, a 78rpm record by Ray Coniff and His Orchestra probably has very little collector value, and possibly a musical value of maybe $1 to $3. Yet, an Elvis 78 on the Sun label can bring as much as $400. Not because of the value of the music, but because it is a rare item by the "King of Rock 'n' Roll" and is a representative of a major musical influence. In some cases, the very fact that the format has become obsolete is the reason that the item is so desirable. These age-old principles of collecting and collectibility will have the same kind of impact that occurred with the passing of other reproduction formats. In a nutshell: If it's a collectible record by a collectible artist, it will always be desirable.

Even so, apart from the great thirst of Elvis and Beatles collectors to acquire CDs of special interest, there is also a new wave of collectors who hunt only for CDs. This new generation of collectors seems to have been waiting for a new area in the hobby that they can call their own. A unique aspect of the CD market is that it is truly international in origin. There is great interest and demand to acquire CDs from all over the world by collectors from all around the globe. Combined with the quality of an audiophile performance, the ease to keep the item in mint condition, and its rarity, CD collecting is a hobby whose time has come.

ELVIS PRESLEY CD DISCOGRAPHY

When CBS/Sony introduced the first 16 compact discs, in early 1983, lovers of Elvis' music were immediately intrigued by the prospects of hearing his many great tunes on CD, in studio-quality sound. Even though there were no Elvis CDs among the first sixteen (twelve of which were classical and jazz), it wasn't long before *Elvis' Golden Records* appeared on CD (PCD1-1707). Months of anticipation by Elvis fans went up in smoke the minute they read the following cursed statement on the first Elvis CD: "Stereo effect reprocessed from monophonic." Unbelievable was the only way to describe our reaction. Imagine the contradiction of using crystal-clear sonic CD capabilities to reproduce the most heinous audio crime in Elvis-RCA history. Fortunately, the insanity of such a maneuver was not overlooked by RCA. *Elvis' Golden Records* was remastered in 1985, from original monaural masters. Pathetically, RCA repeated the mistake in 1987, destroying the original Sun sound on *The Complete Sun Sessions.* From a collector's viewpoint, deletion from the catalog has given this muddled CD (PCD1-1707) value in excess of many other Elvis CDs: about $20 to $40. Promotional issues (with designate promotional "Demonstration—Not For Sale" stamp on box) sell for a bit more: $30 to $50.

Note: No price ranges are provided in this list because Elvis CDs are readily available in record stores at the prevailing rates—between $10.00 and $18.00. In future editions, as the CD collecting market develops and participants become aware of scarce items in the realm of Elvis CDs, then Elvis collectors will establish a market base akin to that already prevailing for the Beatles' works on CD.

ALWAYS ON MY MIND (6/85) . . . . . . RCA Victor PCD1-5430

BLUE HAWAII (4/88) . . . . RCA Victor 3683-2

BURNING LOVE (AND HITS FROM HIS
      MOVIES, VOL. 2) (12/87) . . . . . . RCA/Camden CAD1-2595

COMPLETE SUN SESSIONS, The (7/87) . RCA Victor 6414-2

DOUBLE DYNAMITE (1987) . . . . Pair PDC2-1010

ELVIS (11/84) . . . . RCA Victor PCD1-5199

ELVIS ARON PRESLEY FOREVER (3/88) Pair PDC2-1185

ELVIS' CHRISTMAS ALBUM (8/85) . . . . RCA Victor PCD1-5486

ELVIS' CHRISTMAS ALBUM (10/87) . . . RCA/Camden CAD1-2428

ELVIS COUNTRY (3/88) . . . . RCA Victor 6330-2

ELVIS' GOLDEN RECORDS (5/84) . . . . RCA Victor PCD1-1707

ELVIS' GOLDEN RECORDS (11/84) . . . . RCA Victor PCD1-5196

ELVIS' GOLD RECORDS, VOLUME 2
      (11/84) . . . . RCA Victor PCD1-5197

ELVIS' GOLD RECORDS, VOLUME 5
      (11/84) . . . . RCA Victor PCD1-4941

ELVIS PRESLEY (11/84) . . . . RCA Victor PCD1-5198

ESSENTIAL ELVIS (1/88) . . . . RCA Victor 6738-2-R

G.I. BLUES (4/88) . . . . RCA Victor 3735-2

KING CREOLE (4/88) . . . . RCA Victor 3733-2

LOVING YOU (4/88) . . . . RCA Victor 1515-2

MEMPHIS RECORD, The (7/87) . . . . . . RCA Victor 6221-2

MEMORIES OF CHRISTMAS (11/87) . . . RCA Victor 4395-2

MERRY CHRISTMAS (12/84) . . . . RCA Victor PCD1-5301

NUMBER ONE HITS, The (7/87) . . . . . RCA Victor 6382-2

POT LUCK (4/88) . . . . RCA Victor 2523-2

RECONSIDER BABY (4/85) . . . . RCA Victor PCD1-5418
REMEMBERING ELVIS (3/88) . . . . . . Pair PDC2-1037
RETURN OF THE ROCKER (4/86) . . . . RCA Victor 5600-2-R
ROCKER (11/84) . . . . RCA Victor PCD1-5182
TOP TEN HITS, The (7/87) . . . . RCA Victor 6383-2
VALENTINE GIFT FOR YOU, A (2/85) . RCA Victor PCD1-5353
YOU'LL NEVER WALK ALONE (11/87) . RCA/Camden CAD1-2472

THE BEATLES CD DISCOGRAPHY
(Including solo titles by George, John, Paul, and Ringo, with valuations on appropriate titles.)

Note: Each CD package issued with photo/information booklet and/or outer title/photo box.

The Beatles

ABBEY ROAD
Capitol CDP 7 46446 2 . *10/87* **14–18**
Outer box has "CCT" prefix to the catalog number.

BEATLES, THE
Capitol CDP 7 46444 2 . . *8/87* **25–30**
Double CD set—Outer box has "CCP" prefix to the catalog number. Early sets were sequentially numbered on the inner booklet of disc 1.

BEATLES FOR SALE
Capitol CDP 7 46438 2 . . *2/87* **14–18**
Monaural recording.

EARLY TAPES, THE–THE BEATLES
Polydor/Polygram 823 701-2 *7/87* **14–18**

HARD DAY'S NIGHT, A
Capitol CDP 7 46437 2 . . *2/87* **14–18**
Monaural recording.

HELP
Capitol CDP 7 46439 2 . . *4/87* **14–18**

LIVE IN HAMBURG 62, THE BEATLES
K-tel CD 1473 . . . . . . *2/87* **14–18**

MAGICAL MYSTERY TOUR
Capitol CDP 7 48062 2 . . *9/87* **14–18**
Outer box has "CCT" prefix to the catalog number.

PAST MASTERS—VOLUME ONE
Capitol CDP 7 90043 2 . . *3/88* **14–18**
Outer box has "C2" prefix to the catalog number.

PAST MASTERS—VOLUME TWO
Capitol CDP 7 90044 2 . . *3/88* **14–18**
Outer box has "C2" prefix to the catalog number.

PLEASE PLEASE ME
Capitol CDP 7 46435 2 . . *2/87* **14–18**
Monaural recording.

REVOLVER
Capitol CDP 7 46441 2 . . *4/87* **14–18**

RUBBER SOUL
Capitol CDP 7 46440 2 . . *4/87* **14–18**

SGT. PEPPER'S LONELY HEARTS CLUB BAND
Capitol CDP 7 46442 2 . . *6/87* **14–18**

WITH THE BEATLES
Capitol CDP 7 46436 2 . . *2/87* **14–18**
Monaural recording.

YELLOW SUBMARINE
Capitol CDP 7 46445 2 . . *8/87* **14–18**
Outer box has "CCT" prefix to the catalog number.

George Harrison

ALL THINGS MUST PASS
Capitol CDP 7 46688 2 . . *3/88* **25–30**
Double CD set—Outer box has a "C2" prefix to the catalog number.

BEST OF GEORGE HARRISON
Capitol CDP 7 46682 2 . . *3/88* **14–18**
Outer box has a "CCT" prefix to the catalog number.

CLOUD NINE
Warner Bros. 9 25643–2 . *10/87* **14–18**

Promotional issue **60–75**
Silk-screened image of George on the print side of disc—The print "FOR PROMOTIONAL USE ONLY NOT FOR SALE" is located on the "inner play hub."

CLOUD NINE
Warner Bros. PRO-CD-2924
. . . . *2/88* **25–35**
Promotional single. Label reads "PROMOTIONAL COPY. NOT FOR SALE."

GOT MY MIND SET ON YOU
Warner Bros. PRO-CD-2846
. . . . *10/87* **25–35**
Promotional single. Label reads "PROMOTIONAL COPY. NOT FOR SALE."

THIS IS LOVE
Warner Bros. PRO-CD-3068
. . . . *4/88* **25–35**
Promotional single. Label reads "PROMOTIONAL COPY. NOT FOR SALE."

John Lennon

DOUBLE FANTASY
Geffen 2001-2 . . . . *85* **14–18**

IMAGINE
Capitol CDP 7 46641 2 . . *3/88* **14–18**
Outer box has a "C2" to the catalog number.

LIVE IN NEW YORK CITY
Capitol CDP 7 46196 2 . . *2/86* **14–18**

MENLOVE AVE.
Capitol CDP 7 46576 2 . *10/86* **14–18**

MILK AND HONEY
Polydor/Polygram 817-160-2 *1985* **18–22**
First issue

Budget re-issue **12–14**

MIND GAMES
Capitol CDP 7 46057 2 . . *3/88* **14–18**
Outer box has a "CCT" prefix to the catalog number.

PLASTIC ONO BAND—JOHN LENNON
Capitol CDP 7 46770 2 . . *4/88* **14–18**
Outer box has "C2" prefix to the catalog number.

ROCK 'N' ROLL
Capitol CDP 7 46707 2 . . *4/88* **14–18**
Outer box has a "CCT" prefix to the catalog number.

WALLS AND BRIDGES
Capitol CDP 7 46768 2 . . *4/88* **14–18**
Outer box has a "CCT" prefix to the catalog number.

Paul McCartney

ALL THE BEST
Capitol CDP 7 48287 2 . *11/87* **14–18**
Double LP issued on one CD. Outer box has a "CCT" to the catalog number.

BAND ON THE RUN
Columbia CK 36482 . . . . . *84* **35–45**

Capitol CDP 7 46055 2 . *11/86* **14–18**
Early copies do not contain the track "HELEN WHEELS"; this was added to later issues and

was noted by a sticker adhered to the front of the outer box.

GIVE MY REGARDS TO BROADSTREET
Columbia CK 39613 . . . . . *84* **14–18**

McCARTNEY
Capitol CDP 7 46611 2 . . *2/88* **14–18**
Outer box has a "C2" prefix to the catalog number.

PIPES OF PEACE
Columbia CK 39149 . . . . . *84*   **14–18**

PRESS TO PLAY
Capitol CDP 7 46269 2 . . *8/86*   **14–18**

RAM
Capitol CDP 7 46612 2 . . *3/88*   **14–18**
Outer box has "CCT" prefix to catalog number.

TUG OF WAR
Columbia CK 37462 . . . . . *84*   **23–27**

Capitol CDP 7 46057 2 . . *3/88*   **14–18**
Outer box has a "C2" prefix to the record number.

VENUS AND MARS
Columbia CK 36801 . . . . . *84*   **35–45**

WINGS GREATEST HITS
Capitol CDP 7 46056 2 . *12/86*   **14–18**

WINGS OVER AMERICA
Columbia CK 37990 . . . . . *84*   **65–75**
Double CD set.
Capitol CDP 7 46715 2 . . *2/88*   **25–30**
Double CD set.

Ringo Starr

BLAST FROM YOUR PAST
Capitol CDP 7 46663 2 . . *4/88*   **14–18**
Outer box has a "C2" prefix to the record number.

Elvis and The Beatles on Video

In a brief but important departure from the records and memorabilia we lovingly refer to as collectors' items, this chapter provides a complete listing of films and documentaries now available on video cassette. They may not be collectible yet, but who's to know what the future will bring?

Source: *Music Video: The Consumers Guide,* by Michael Shore (Sarah Lazin, Ballantine Books)

ELVIS PRESLEY

ALOHA FROM HAWAII (Media, 1973)
BLUE HAWAII (CBS/Fox, 1961)
DOUBLE TROUBLE (MGM/UA, 1966)
EARLY ELVIS (Video Yesteryear, 1981)
ELVIS! '68 COMEBACK SPECIAL (Media, 1981)
ELVIS ON TOUR (MGM/UA, 1973)
FLAMING STAR (CBS/Fox, 1960)
FUN IN ACAPULCO (CBS/Fox, 1963)
G. I. BLUES (CBS/Fox, 1960)
GIRLS! GIRLS! GIRLS! (CBS/Fox, 1962)
HARUM SCARUM (MGM/UA, 1965)
IT HAPPENED AT THE WORLD'S FAIR (MGM/UA, 1963)
JAILHOUSE ROCK (MGM/UA, 1957)
KING CREOLE (CBS/Fox, 1958)
LOVE ME TENDER (CBS/Fox, 1956)
LOVING YOU (Warner Home Video, 1957)
ONE NIGHT WITH YOU (Media, 1985)
PARADISE HAWAIIAN STYLE (CBS/Fox, 1966)
ROUSTABOUT (CBS/Fox, 1964)

SPEEDWAY (MGM/UA, 1968)
THIS IS ELVIS (Warner Home Video, 1981)
TICKLE ME (CBS/Fox, 1965)
VIVA LAS VEGAS (MGM/UA, 1964)
WILD IN THE COUNTRY (CBS/Fox, 1961)

THE BEATLES

BEATLES BUDOKAN CONCERT, The (VAP Import, Apple Corps Ltd.)
BEATLES VIDEO SCRAPBOOK, The (Encore Entertainment, import)
COMPLEAT BEATLES, The (MGM/UA, 1982)
HARD DAY'S NIGHT, A (MPI, 1983)
HELP! (MPI, 1986)
LET IT BE (Magnetic, 1970, 1981)
MAGICAL MYSTERY TOUR (Media, 1982)
READY STEADY GO! SPECIAL EDITION: BEATLES LIVE (Sony, 1985)

George Harrison

CONCERT FOR BANGLADESH (with others) (HBO/Cannon, 1981)

John Lennon

IMAGINE (with Yoko Ono) (Sony, 1986)
INTERVIEW WITH A LEGEND (Karl-Lorimar, 1981)
LIVE IN NEW YORK CITY (Sony, 1986)

Paul McCartney

GIVE MY REGARDS TO BROADSTREET (CBS/Fox, 1984)
ROCKSHOW (with Wings) (HBO/Cannon, 1981)

Ringo Starr

POINT, The (Vestron, 1986)
  (Harry Nilsson with Ringo Starr)

Buyers–Sellers Directory

After you have learned the current value of your records, you may wish to offer them for sale. Just as likely, you may decide you would like to purchase out-of-print records for your collection. Either way, the authors recommend you do two things: First, request a sample issue of *DISCoveries,* the record collector's publication where buyers and sellers get together each month. From the pages of *DISCoveries* you'll get an idea of what's being traded and the prices being asked for music collectibles of all types, including Elvis and the Beatles.

DISCoveries
P.O. Box 255
Port Townsend, WA 98368

Second, here is a random sampling of well-known buyers and sellers of Elvis and Beatles memorabilia, any of whom may be the right one to assist you.

ARC PROMOTIONS
(317) 646-5305
Information about upcoming
   record conventions

ALWAYS ELVIS
P.O. 528, Dearborn Hts., MI
   48127

B'S WAX
P.O. Box 1803,
Greenville, NC 27835

BEATLEFAN
P.O. Box 33515, Decatur, GA
   30033

DAVE BUSHEY
103 Arkansas–Box 473, Hoffman,
   MN 56339
(612) 986-2629

COLLECTORS RECORDS
2631 E. Platte Ave., Colorado
   Springs, CO 80909
(303) 577-4653

COLLEEN'S COLLECTABLES
1482 Oakland Park, Columbus,
   OH 43224
(614) 261-1585

LLOYD DAVIS
P.O. Box 1305, Ashland, OR
  97520
(503) 488-0268

ELVIS INTERNATIONAL
  FORUM
P.O. Box 11203, Burbank, CA
  91510

ELVIS SPECIALTIES
P.O. Box 504, Pasadena, MD
  21122
(301) 437-2278

ELVIS WORLD
Box 16792, Memphis, TN 38186
(901) 327-1128

GOOD DAY SUNSHINE
397 Edgewood Ave., New Haven,
  CT 06511
(203) 865-8131

GRACELAND
P.O. Box 16508,
Memphis, TN 38116
(901) 332-3322
Elvis' Memphis home. Tour
  information available.

JELLYROLL PRODUCTIONS
P.O. Box 255, Port Townsend, WA
  98363
(206) 385-3029
Distributor of Elvis and Beatles
  books

JUST KIDS NOSTALGIA
5 Green St., Huntington, NY
  11743
(516) 423-8449

BOB LIVINGSTON
P.O. Box 140, Vergennes, VT
  05491
(802) 862-5820

MEMORY LANE
  OUT-OF-PRINT
  RECORDS
1940 E. University Dr.,
Tempe, AZ 85281
(602) 968-1512

MIDNIGHT RECORDS
P.O. Box 390,
New York, NY 10011
(212) 675-2768

MIGHTY JOHN'S
9 Birchwood Blvd., Brewer, ME
  04412
(207) 989-3635

PINK FLAMINGO RECORDS
P.O. Box 3663, Rubidoux, CA
  92519
(714) 682-9241

POSITIVELY 4TH STREET
208 W. 4th Ave., Olympia, WA
  98501
(206) SUN-TAPE

PRINCETON RECORD
  EXCHANGE
20 S. Tulane St., Princeton, NJ
  08542
(609) 921-0881

RICK RANN BEATLELIST
P.O. Box 877, Oak Park, IL 60303
(312) 442-7907

HELMUT RAUCH
1702 W. Belle Plaine, Chicago, IL
  60613
(312) 348-4425

RECORD EXCHANGE
5840 Hampton, St. Louis, MO
  63109
(314) 832-2249

ROCKIN' ROBIN
1657 S. Wooster St., Los Angeles,
  CA 90035
(213) 275-0808

ROCK ISLAND
3331 Foxridge Cr., Tampa, FL
  33618
(813) 969-2299

ROWE'S RARE RECORDS
54 W. Santa Clara St., San Jose,
  CA 95113
(408) 294-7200

LYNN RUSSWURM
Box 63, Elmira, Ontario, Canada
  N3B 2Z5
(519) 669-2386

SALTY'S RECORD ATTIC
1326 9th St., Modesto, CA 95354
(209) 527-4010

DAVE SLOBODIAN
4533 Napier St., Burnaby, B.C.,
  Canada V5C 3H4
(604) 299-7902

SOCIAL INSECT RECORDS
923 Baldwin, Danville, IL 61832
(217) 443-3321

TICKET TO RYDE, LTD
P.O. Box 3393, Lacey, WA 98503
(206) 491-7343

TIMES SQUARE RECORDS
P.O. Box 391, Knigsbridge Sta.,
  Bronx, NY 10463
(212) 549-7497

TRACKS IN WAX RECORDS
4741 N. Central Ave., Phoenix,
  AZ 85012
(602) 274-2660

USED (BUT NOT ABUSED)
  RECORDS
P.O. Box 2456, Russellville, AR
  72801

VERY ENGLISH & ROLLING
  STONE
P.O. Box 7061, Lancaster, PA
  17604
(717) 627-2081

VINYL VENDORS
1800 S. Robertson Blvd. #279,
  Los Angeles, CA 90035
(213) 935-6553

☐ Please send me the following price guides—
☐ ... me the most current edition of the books listed below.

☐ ☐ OFFICIAL PRICE GUIDES TO:

☐ 753-3	American Folk Art (ID) 1st Ed.	$14.95
☐ 199-3	American Silver & Silver Plate 5th Ed.	11.95
☐ 513-1	Antique Clocks 3rd Ed.	10.95
☐ 283-3	Antique & Modern Dolls 3rd Ed.	10.95
☐ 287-6	Antique & Modern Firearms 6th Ed.	11.95
☐ 755-X	Antiques & Collectibles 9th Ed.	11.95
☐ 289-2	Antique Jewelry 5th Ed.	11.95
☐ 362-7	Art Deco (ID) 1st Ed.	14.95
☐ 447-X	Arts and Crafts: American Decorative Arts, 1894–1923 (ID) 1st Ed.	12.95
☐ 539-5	Beer Cans & Collectibles 4th Ed.	7.95
☐ 521-2	Bottles Old & New 10th Ed.	10.95
☐ 532-8	Carnival Glass 2nd Ed.	10.95
☐ 295-7	Collectible Cameras 2nd Ed.	10.95
☐ 548-4	Collectibles of the '50s & '60s 1st Ed.	9.95
☐ 740-1	Collectible Toys 4th Ed.	10.95
☐ 531-X	Collector Cars 7th Ed.	12.95
☐ 538-7	Collector Handguns 4th Ed.	14.95
☐ 748-7	Collector Knives 9th Ed.	12.95
☐ 361-9	Collector Plates 5th Ed.	11.95
☐ 296-5	Collector Prints 7th Ed.	12.95
☐ 001-6	Depression Glass 2nd Ed.	9.95
☐ 589-1	Fine Art 1st Ed.	19.95
☐ 311-2	Glassware 3rd Ed.	10.95
☐ 243-4	Hummel Figurines & Plates 6th Ed.	10.95
☐ 523-9	Kitchen Collectibles 2nd Ed.	10.95
☐ 080-6	Memorabilia of Elvis Presley and The Beatles 1st Ed.	10.95
☐ 291-4	Military Collectibles 5th Ed.	11.95
☐ 525-5	Music Collectibles 6th Ed.	11.95
☐ 313-9	Old Books & Autographs 7th Ed.	11.95
☐ 298-1	Oriental Collectibles 3rd Ed.	11.95
☐ 761-4	Overstreet Comic Book 18th Ed.	12.95
☐ 522-0	Paperbacks & Magazines 1st Ed.	10.95
☐ 297-3	Paper Collectibles 5th Ed.	10.95
☐ 744-4	Political Memorabilia 1st Ed.	10.95
☐ 529-8	Pottery & Porcelain 6th Ed.	11.95
☐ 524-7	Radio, TV & Movie Memorabilia 3rd Ed.	11.95
☐ 081-4	Records 8th Ed.	16.95
☐ 763-0	Royal Doulton 6th Ed.	12.95
☐ 280-9	Science Fiction & Fantasy Collectibles 2nd Ed.	10.95
☐ 747-9	Sewing Collectibles 1st Ed.	8.95
☐ 358-9	Star Trek/Star Wars Collectibles 2nd Ed.	8.95
☐ 086-5	Watches 8th Ed.	12.95
☐ 248-5	Wicker 3rd Ed.	10.95

THE OFFICIAL:

☐ 760-6	Directory to U.S. Flea Markets 2nd Ed.	5.95
☐ 365-1	Encyclopedia of Antiques 1st Ed.	9.95
☐ 369-4	Guide to Buying and Selling Antiques 1st Ed.	9.95
☐ 414-3	Identification Guide to Early American Furniture 1st Ed.	9.95
☐ 413-5	Identification Guide to Glassware 1st Ed.	9.95

☐ 412-7	Identification Guide to Pottery & Porcelain 1st Ed.	$9.95
☐ 415-1	Identification Guide to Victorian Furniture 1st Ed.	9.95

THE OFFICIAL (SMALL SIZE) PRICE GUIDES TO:

☐ 309-0	Antiques & Flea Markets 4th Ed.	4.95
☐ 269-8	Antique Jewelry 3rd Ed.	4.95
☐ 085-7	Baseball Cards 8th Ed.	4.95
☐ 647-2	Bottles 3rd Ed.	4.95
☐ 544-1	Cars & Trucks 3rd Ed.	5.95
☐ 519-0	Collectible Americana 2nd Ed.	4.95
☐ 294-9	Collectible Records 3rd Ed.	4.95
☐ 306-6	Dolls 4th Ed.	4.95
☐ 762-2	Football Cards 8th Ed.	4.95
☐ 540-9	Glassware 3rd Ed.	4.95
☐ 526-3	Hummels 3rd Ed.	4.95
☐ 279-5	Military Collectibles 3rd Ed.	4.95
☐ 764-9	Overstreet Comic Book Companion 2nd Ed.	4.95
☐ 278-7	Pocket Knives 3rd Ed.	4.95
☐ 527-1	Scouting Collectibles 4th Ed.	4.95
☐ 494-1	Star Trek/Star Wars Collectibles 3rd Ed.	3.95
☐ 088-1	Toys 5th Ed.	4.95

THE OFFICIAL BLACKBOOK PRICE GUIDES OF:

☐ 092-X	U.S. Coins 27th Ed.	4.95
☐ 095-4	U.S. Paper Money 21st Ed.	4.95
☐ 098-9	U.S. Postage Stamps 11th Ed.	4.95

THE OFFICIAL INVESTORS GUIDE TO BUYING & SELLING:

☐ 534-4	Gold, Silver & Diamonds 2nd Ed.	12.95
☐ 535-2	Gold Coins 2nd Ed.	12.95
☐ 536-0	Silver Coins 2nd Ed.	12.95
☐ 537-9	Silver Dollars 2nd Ed.	12.95

THE OFFICIAL NUMISMATIC GUIDE SERIES:

☐ 254-X	The Official Guide to Detecting Counterfeit Money 2nd Ed.	7.95
☐ 257-4	The Official Guide to Mint Errors 4th Ed.	7.95

SPECIAL INTEREST SERIES:

☐ 506-9	From Hearth to Cookstove 3rd Ed.	17.95
☐ 504-2	On Method Acting 8th Printing	6.95

TOTAL	

SEE REVERSE SIDE FOR ORDERING INSTRUCTIONS